LIBRARY OF HEBREW BIBLE/ OLD TESTAMENT STUDIES

456

Formerly Journal for the Study of the Old Testament Supplement Series

MESSIANISM WITHIN THE
SCRIPTURAL SCROLL OF ISAIAH

Randall Heskett

t&t clark

NEW YORK • LONDON

Copyright © 2007 by Randall Heskett

T & T Clark International, 80 Maiden Lane, New York, NY 10038

T & T Clark International, The Tower Building, 11 York Road, London SE1 7NX

T & T Clark International is a Continuum imprint.

Library of Congress Cataloging-in-Publication Data
Heskett, Randall.
  Messianism within the scriptural scroll of Isaiah / Randall Heskett.
    p. cm. -- (Library of Hebrew Bible/Old Testament studies ; 456)
  Includes bibliographical references and index.
  ISBN-13: 978-0-567-02922-5 (hardcover : alk. paper)
  ISBN-10: 0-567-02922-0 (hardcover : alk. paper)
  1. Bible. O.T. Isaiah--Canonical criticism. 2. Messiah. I. Title. II. Series.

  BS1515.6.M44H47 2007
  224'.106--dc22

                                        2006038532

  06 07 08 09 10   10 9 8 7 6 5 4 3 2 1

To the love of my life,
my wife,
Kim

CONTENTS

ACKNOWLEDGMENTS

I want to acknowledge three of my early teachers at Bethany College, the late James Rider who offered an exceptional undergraduate background in Greek and a start in Hebrew, Rick Howard who served as an early mentor and Truett Edsel Bobo who grounded me in Systematic Theology.

I am also appreciative of my professors at Central Baptist Theological Seminary: Gam Shae, who encouraged my work and asked me to teach Greek after my first semester as a seminarian; Fred Young, who taught me several semesters of Ugaritic, Sumerian, Egyptian hieroglyphics, Coptic and Syriac; and the late Kenneth Wolf, who brutally instilled in me an understanding of comparative Semitics while teaching Arabic and Aramaic. I am pleased that President William Kuetcher allowed me to replace a pastoral theology course with Ugaritic and his successor John Landgraf for helping me to get my start as a pastoral counselor and for creating many possibilities for further study. I thank those at Nazarene Seminary who allowed me to cross-register during seminary years, Harvey Findley in advanced Hebrew and Al Truesdale in Philosophy. I acknowledge my friend and former professor at Central David Wheeler for challenging me to look beyond my narrow theological box in theology and philosophy of religion. I particularly thank Henry Moeller, who encouraged me by teaching me biblical languages, intertestamental literature, patristics and asking me to be his only teaching assistant during his thirty-five year tenure.

I am also grateful to all of my professors at Yale, who gave me my start in critical methods and helped me to advance in philological pursuits. I thank Ben Foster and William Hallo for their teaching of basic and advanced Akkadian, Michael Holquist for providing the most excellent series of hermeneutical lectures I have ever heard in his class on literary theory, Bob Wilson for providing superb teaching of Hebrew and critical methods and Chris Seitz for sparking my interest in Isaiah studies. I credit Peter Schäfer for not only teaching a solid course on Messianism in Ancient Judaism when he was a visiting professor at Yale, but also for sitting on my doctoral defense and offering great encouragement. I am most appreciative of Brevard Childs who most skillfully taught me historical-critical methods, their application and the history of interpretation. I also thank him for the huge encouragement that he has offered through the years.

I thank some of my professors at University of Toronto, who modeled wonderful scholarship through my doctoral journey. Albert Pietersma provided effortless energy in uniquely teaching me Septuagint for three years in a most sophisticated fashion. I owe a great deal of gratitude to the late George Schner, who encouraged me in my work and allowed me to audit several courses he taught in theology, philosophical theology and hermeneutics. David Demson has been a great mentor in helping in helping me to think theologically. I am grateful to Brian Peckham who has been a mentor, encourager and a very good friend. Brian reviewed every chapter of Messianism within the Scriptural Scroll of Isaiah and offered wonderful feedback. I am grateful to my friend and colleague, Michael Dempsey, who has helped me to understand Aquinas and Barth in a manner that illumines the history of interpretation in the book of Isaiah. I want to thank Duncan Burns for all of his fine editorial work. His sound scholarship in Hebrew and Old Testament enables him to be such a great copy editor. His patience and humor have been wonderful.

I am most indebted to my brilliant mentor and friend, the late Gerald Sheppard, whose love and scholarship has forever impacted me. Gerry was not only my Chief mentor, cheer leader and friend, but he was like an older brother to me. Gerry died a few years ago and ever since I helped carry his casket to usher his soul into eternity, I knew that his life and teachings would touch me forever.

I am grateful for my beautiful, lovely and brilliant daughter Hannah, who loves me unconditionally, helps me to find the balance between work and play, and who, in faithfully tolerating my silly and serious ravings about "the Messiah," has become the leading messianic scholar of her seventh-grade class. I thank my step-daughter Allison for sharing her mother with me and being like a daughter to me. Finally, I am most grateful for my wife and lover, Kim, who has given me a new start to life, who has given me more joy than any person I have ever known and who has encouraged me to write, live and take chances. It is to Kim that I dedicate this book.

ABBREVIATIONS

AB	Anchor Bible
ABD	*The Anchor Bible Dictionary*. Edited by David Noel Freedman. 6 vols. New York: Doubleday, 1992
ABRL	Anchor Bible Reference Library
AcOr	*Acta Orientalia*
AJSL	*American Journal of Semitic Languages and Literatures*
AJTh	*American Journal of Theology*
ALBO	Analecta Lovaniensia Biblica et Orientalia
AnBib	Analecta biblica
ANET	*Ancient Near Eastern Texts Relating to the Old Testament*. Edited by James B. Pritchard. 3d ed. Princeton, N.J.: Princeton University Press, 1969
AnOr	*Analecta Orientalia*
AS	Assyriological studies
BASOR	*Bulletin of the American Schools of Oriental Research*
BAT	Die Botschaft Des Alten Testament
BDB	Brown, F., S. R. Driver and C. A. Briggs. *A Hebrew and English Lexicon of the Old Testament*. Oxford: Clarendon, 1907
BETL	Bibliotheca ephemeridum theologicarum lovaniensium
BEvT	Beiträge zur evangelischen Theologie
BHT	Beiträge zur historischen Theologie
Bib	*Biblica*
BibS(N)	Biblische Studien (Neukirchen, 1951–)
BJRL	*Bulletin of the John Rylands University Library of Manchester*
BT	*Bible Translator*
BWANT	Beiträge zur Wissenschaft vom Alten und Neuen Testament
BZ	*Biblische Zeitschrift*
BZAW	Beihefte zur Zeitschrift für die alttestamentliche Wissenschaft
CBC	Cambridge Bible Commentary
CBQ	*Catholic Biblical Quarterly*
CBQMS	Catholic Biblical Quarterly Monograph Series
ConBOT	Coniectanea Biblica, Old Testament Series
EBib	Etudes bibliques
EdF	Erträge der Forschung
ErIsr	*Eretz-Israel*
ETL	*Ephemerides Theologicae Lovanienses*
EvQ	*Evangelical Quarterly*
EvTh	*Evangelische Theologie*
ExpTim	*Expository Times*
FB	Forschung zur Bibel
FOTL	The Forms of the Old Testament Literature
FRLANT	Forschungen zur Religion und Literatur des Alten und Neuen Testaments

FZPhTh	*Freiburger Zeitschrift für Philosophie und Theologie*
HCOT	Historical Commentary on the Old Testament
HKAT	Handkommentar zum Alten Testament
HSM	Harvard Semitic Monographs
HTR	*Harvard Theological Review*
HUCA	*Hebrew Union College Annual*
HUCM	Monographs of the Hebrew Union College
IKZ	*Internationale kirchliche Zeitschrift*
Int	*Interpretation*
ITC	International Theological Commentary
JAOS	*Journal of the American Oriental Society*
JBL	*Journal of Biblical Literature*
JCS	*Journal of Cuneiform Studies*
JETS	*Journal of the Evangelical Theological Society*
JJS	*Journal of Jewish Studies*
JNSL	*Journal of Northwest Semitic Languages*
JSJ	*Journal for the Study of Judaism in the Persian, Hellenistic and Roman Period*
JSNTSup	Journal for the Study of the New Testament: Supplement Series
JSOT	*Journal for the Study of the Old Testament*
JSOTSup	Journal for the Study of the Old Testament: Supplement Series
JSPSup	Journal for the Study of the Pseudepigrapha: Supplement Series
JSS	*Journal of Semitic Studies*
JTS	*Journal of Theological Studies*
KAT	Kommentar zum Alten Testament
KB	Koehler, L., and W. Baumgartner. *Lexicon in Veteris Testamenti libros.* 2d ed. Leiden: Brill, 1958
KHC	Kurzer Hand-Kommentar Zum Alten Testament
LD	Lectio Divina
LQ	*Lutheran Quarterly*
LSUr	Lament of Sumer and Ur
LXX	Septuagint
MT	Masoretic Text
NedTT	*Nederlands theologisch tijdschrift*
NICOT	New International Commentary on the Old Testament
NTS	*New Testament Studies*
OBT	Overatures to Biblical Theology
OTL	Old Testament Library
OTM	Old Testament Message
OTP	*Old Testament Pseudepigrapha.* Edited by J. H. Charlesworth. 2 vols. New York: Doubleday, 1983
OtSt	*Oudtestamentische Studiën*
QD	Questiones disputatae
RB	*Revue biblique*
RechBib	Recherches bibliques
RevExp	*Review and Expositor*
RevQ	*Revue de Qumran*
RocTKan	*Roczniki Teologiczno-Kanoniczne*
RSR	*Recherches de Science Religieuse*
RTR	*Reformed Theological Review*
SBLCP	Society of Biblical Literature Centennial Publications

SBLDS	Society of Biblical Literature Dissertation Series
SBLEJL	Society of Biblical Literature Early Judaism and Its Literature
SBLMS	Society of Biblical Literature Monograph Series
SBLSP	Society of Biblical Literature Seminar Papers
SBS	Stuttgarter Bibelstudien
SBT	Studies in Biblical Theology
Sem	*Semitica*
SP	*Sacra Pagina*
ST	*Studia Theologica*
STDJ	Studies on the Texts of the Desert of Judah
TBC	Torch Bible Commentaries
TDNT	*Theological Dictionary of the New Testament.* Edited by G. Kittel and G. Friedrich. Translated by Geoffrey W. Bromiley. 10 vols. Grand Rapids: Eerdmans, 1964–1976
TDOT	*Theological Dictionary of the Old Testament.* Edited by G. J. Botterweck and H. Ringgren. Translated by J. T. Willis, G. W. Bromiley and D. E. Green. 8 vols. Grand Rapids: Eerdmans, 1974–
ThSt	Theologische Studien
ThViat	*Theologia viatorum*
TLOT	*Theological Lexicon of the Old Testament.* Edited by E. Jenni, with assistance from C. Westermann. Translated by M. E. Biddle. 3 vols. Peabody, Mass.: Hendrickson, 1997
TJT	*Toronto Journal of Theology*
TTZ	*Trierer theologische Zeitschrift*
TWOT	*Theological Wordbook of the Old Testament.* Edited by R. L. Harris, G. L. Archer Jr. and B. K. Waltke. 2 vols. Chicago: Moody, 1980
TynBul	*Tyndale Bulletin*
WBC	Word Biblical Commentary
WTJ	*Westminster Theological Journal*
WUNT	Wissenschaftliche Untersuchungen zum Neuen Testament
VT	*Vetus Testamentum*
VTSup	Supplements to Vetus Testamentum
YNER	Yale Near Eastern researches
ZAW	*Zeitschrift für die alttestamentliche Wissenschaft*
ZDPV	*Zeitschrift des deutschen Palästina-Vereins*
ZNW	*Zeitschrift für die neutestamentliche Wissenschaft*
ZThK	*Zeitschrift für Theologie und Kirche*

Chapter 1

INTRODUCTION: MESSIANISM WITHIN THE BOOK OF ISAIAH AS A WHOLE

Jews and Christians traditionally interpreted many passages in the book of Isaiah as containing messianic promise more than any other books. Later rabbinic Jews and Christians sometimes agreed that a passage from Isaiah was messianic. Other passages important for Christian messianic interpretation played no such role in Jewish interpretation. With the rise of eighteenth-century historical criticisms, scholars tended to focus on the "original" sources in terms of First, Second and Third Isaiah. Most scholars could easily discredit the idea that the eighth-century prophet expressed messianic hope. These same scholars usually called the traditions that they reconstructed from the Bible, "biblical traditions," although in most cases, these original traditions were pre-biblical. Isaiah in the eighth century did not intend to write scripture anymore than did the apostle Paul when he penned letters which later came to belong to the New Testament.

In more recent studies, some scholars have begun to examine how later levels of editing within the book of Isaiah began to present non-messianic traditions as messianic promises when the book was edited into a scriptural scroll. These efforts to redescribe the form and function of passages within this biblical book have already been fruitful in treating certain passages. However, no scholar has systematically attempted a thorough examination of how such originally pre-scriptural passages gained a new scriptural function through the later redaction of the book as a whole. That effort is the aim of this investigation. At the outset, two problems will be briefly addressed: the definition of messianism and the strategy employed in this study of that subject as it pertains to the biblical book of Isaiah.

I. *Definition of Messianism*

Studies by such individuals as Peter Schäfer, Jacob Neusner and James Charlesworth have reminded us that the view of messianism that one brings to the text will influence what will seem to be messianic.[1] So, part of the problem in my own study of messianic interpretation in Isaiah depends on how one interprets the term "Messiah" and selects texts that reflect that understanding. How narrowly one defines messianism will determine what sorts of data one will rule out. The problem any reader faces is declaring what kind of messianism to look for in scripture.

Therefore, we must operate within a restricted set of descriptions that takes seriously the problems in defining messianism and what in each Isaianic text lends itself to a messianic reading. There are many definitions of messianism. For example, Oegema's definition of the Messiah as "a priestly, royal or otherwise characterized figure, who will play a liberating role at the end of time" provides a broad description to account for the messianisms that existed from the time of Maccabees to Bar Kochba but does not supply the nuances that are central to the book of Isaiah.[2] Others reduce the meaning of messianism to mirror the use of the word משיח in a pre-exilic setting when the word spoke merely of an Israelite or Judean king before the monarchy was terminated and messianism had later developed into an eschatological concept.[3] However, this

---

1. Peter Schäfer rightly states that "Die messianischen Vorstellungen des rabbinischen Judentums sind sehr vielfältig und komplex." See his "Die messianischen Hoffnungen des rabbinischen Judentums zwischen Naherwartung und religiösem Pragmatismus," *Zukunft in der Gegenwart: Wegweisungen in Judentum und Christentum* (Bern: Herbert Lang, 1976), 96. James H. Charlesworth also asserts that no one can pinpoint "a common Jewish Messianic hope" by the time of Christ. See his "Introduction," in *The Messiah: Developments in Earliest Judaism and Christianity* (ed. James H. Charlesworth; Minneapolis: Fortress, 1992), 5. See also Jacob Neusner, *Messiah in Context* (Philadelphia: Fortress, 1984); idem, *Judaisms and Their Messiahs at the Turn of the Christian Era* (ed. Jacob Neusner, William Scott Green and Ernest S. Frerichs; Cambridge: Cambridge University Press, 1987).

2. Gerbern S. Oegema, *The Anointed and His People: Messianic Expectations from Maccabees to Bar Kochba* (JSPSup 27; Sheffield: Sheffield Academic Press, 1998), 26.

3. For example, John Watts considers any passage that depicts a threat to the Davidic throne to be messianic, and R. B. Y. Scott regards the next anointed king to be "the Messiah." At one level this may be true, but this minimalist definition fails to account for the meaning of משיח and messianism within the post-exilic book of Isaiah. See, John D. W. Watts, *Isaiah 1–33* (ed. David Hubbard and Glenn W. Barker; WBC 24; Waco, Tex.: Word, 1985), 102, 137–38, 174–76; R. B. Y. Scott, *The Book of Isaiah: Introduction and Exegesis, Chapters 1–39*, in *The Interpreter's Bible*, vol. 5 (ed. George Arthur Buttrick; Nashville: Abingdon, 1956), 231–32, 247.

definition of messianism fails to account for the semantic change in the meaning and use of the word מָשִׁיחַ in the post-exilic era. Similarly, Paul Wegner, who claims that the editors have reinterpreted Isa. 7:14; 8:23–9:6 and 11:1–5 to be nuanced messianically at the latest levels of Isa 7–11 (701 B.C.E.), argues for pre-exilic messianism:

> In several early studies, such as S. Mowinckel (1956) and J. Becker (1980), it has been argued that the completed concept of the Messiah arose during the post-exilic period which may indeed be very correct, but very little attention has been paid to the background and development of this concept. We intend to demonstrate that the actual development of the concept is much more complicated and the basic elements of constituting this concept existed much earlier than the post-exilic period.[4]

Wegner's claim for an early dating of the origins and editing around Isa. 7:14; 9:1–6 and 11:1–9 fails to examine why there would be a need for messianic expectation when a king still sat on the throne.[5]

Our working definition of messianism exceeds a mere threat to the Davidic throne or someone who is merely anointed or blessed. Our definition also distinguishes between an ideal king and the Messiah because idealism about the king only fits a very broad definition and cannot provide a rationale for messianism.[6] Since the hope of an ideal king uses exaggerated language, David, Hezekiah and Josiah only approximate an ideal king but not a Messiah. Hope of an ideal kingship cannot necessarily be construed as messianic since our definition requires an eschatological event that fulfills the promises of 2 Sam 7 especially after the monarchy has ceased to exist. Therefore, any text functioning at a pre-exilic level of tradition history does not meet our criteria for messianic interpretation. Our definition of a Messiah requires that a person or persons offer a solution in an extraordinary way to activate and restore within this world the promises made to David after the monarchy has ended. Modern scholars have generally agreed that part of the definition of messianism involves the hope for a glorious future through the agency of a Davidic kingly figure who will establish his throne forever, bring redemption and salvation, restore the land and offer an era of happiness.[7]

---

4. Paul Wegner, *An Examination of Kingship and Messianic Expectation in Isaiah 1–35* (Lewiston, N.Y.: Edwin Mellen, 1992), 2.

5. Ibid., 131–35, 136, 211, 212, 268.

6. Note that R. B. Y. Scott argues that the king is "messianic" only from the perspective that "every monarch of the Davidic dynasty was then an anointed representative of Yahweh, and a sacred, even semi-divine, person"; see Scott, *The Book of Isaiah, 1–39*, 247. Similarly, see Watts, *Isaiah 1–33*, 102, 137–38, 174–76.

7. See, most specifically, Sigmund Mowinckel, *He That Cometh* (trans. G. W. Anderson; Oxford: Blackwell, 1956), 3–9; John Barton, *Isaiah 1–39* (OTG;

This provides hope for the community's understanding of God's divine intervention into history in Second Temple Judaism that restores and sustains a promise of a king who will rule forever after Davidic monarchy has already been cut off by the events of 587 B.C.E. This view represents a proximate consensus.

When we speak of the end of the Davidic monarchy, we recognize that after the king went into exile in 597, his uncle Zedekiah served as a puppet king for nine years. By the encouragement of Egypt, Zedekiah revolted against Babylon in 589 along with Tyre and Ammon. When Nebuchadnezzar advanced on Jerusalem a second time with a large army, the city did not yet surrender (589). After the city was kept under tight siege for two years, Nebuchadnezzar's army breached the northern wall of the city with battering rams. Subsequently, Gedaliah was established as governor and was murdered (2 Kgs 24–25). These events mark the termination of the monarchy along with the events of 587. Although many Judeans in exile may have hoped that he would return to Jerusalem and re-establish the throne, Jehoiachin was never reinstated as king but was released from prison and given a place at the king's table. There must have been many hopes during the exilic and post-exilic era that the kingship would be restored. For example, Haggai refers to Zerubbabel as a possible candidate for the revitalization of the kingship (Hag 2:12–23) but he seems to have disappeared and his end is unknown. Such pretenders to the Davidic throne ceased to exist after 520 B.C.E. They only represented a hopeful imagination to restore the monarchy ("the anointed one"). Yet they never functioned as the true kings who reigned before 587 B.C.E.[8] Therefore, the termination of the monarchy provides a climate for the inception of messianic hope for a Davidic king to bring salvation and restore the promises to David in a supernatural way. This

Sheffield: Sheffield Academic Press, 1995), 115–17; Walter C. Kaiser, *The Messiah in the Old Testament* (Studies in Old Testament Theology; Grand Rapids: Zondervan, 1995), 14–18.

8. David Petersen uses these pretender kings as evidence that the monarchy functioned until 520 B.C.E. to claim that prophecy and the monarchy are co-terminus; see David L. Petersen, *Late Israelite Prophecy: Studies in Deutero-Prophetic Literature and in Chronicles* (SBLMS 23; Missoula, Mont.: Scholars Press, 1977), 6, 29. However, such prophets as Haggai, Zechariah, Malachi and possibly Obadiah and Joel extended beyond the time period that Petersen estimates and, more importantly, these claimants to the throne do not constitute Israelite or Judean kings. See Gerard Sheppard, "True and False Prophecy Within Scriptures," in *Canon, Theology, and Old Testament Interpretation: Essays in Honor of Brevard S. Childs* (ed. Gene M. Tucker, David L. Petersen and Robert R. Wilson; Philadelphia: Fortress, 1988), 274–75.

salvation takes on eschatological dimensions as opposed to a military deliverance.

This definition has been chosen with full awareness that key features of messianism have varied greatly within the history of Judaism. For example, during the Maccabean period, the notion of a kingly Messiah became eclipsed by the priestly type (e.g. Judah Moon and Levi Sun) among some Levitical priests.[9] Others expected a prophetic Messiah.[10] The Qumran community foresaw two Messiahs.[11] Likewise, Jews and Christians have disagreed among themselves concerning what texts should be regarded as messianic. Later Christians even found some messianic interpretations by New Testament writers less compelling than our own messianic interpretations of other Old Testament texts.[12] Since my study will concentrate primarily on classical Jewish and Christian interpretation in my working definition of a Messiah, I will need to allow room for some later definitions of messianism along these lines.

While the term המשיח never appears in the Old Testament, משיח appears thirty-nine times in the Old Testament for kings (30×), for Cyrus (1×), for high priests (6×) and for patriarchs (2×). In fact, some scholars even assert that "not one of the thirty-nine occurrences of מָשִׁיחַ in the Hebrew canon refer to an expected figure of the future whose coming will coincide with the inauguration of an era of salvation."[13] Certainly, a

9. Sirach also envisaged a Messiah that would be a priest who was not an offspring of David (ch. 50).

10. Geza Vermes, *Jesus the Jew: A Historian's Reading of the Gospels* (London: William Collins Sons, 1973), 135, 137.

11. 1QS 9:5–19 states, "…there shall come the Prophet and the Messiahs of Aaron and Israel. 1QSa. 2:11–20 declares that the Messiah would be a priest and a king. According to the pesher of Isa. 11:1–5, the Messiah would have to do what the priests ordered. The *Psalms of Solomon* 17 anticipates either a Zadokian priest or a Davidic king. Enoch expects either a priest or a king (cf. George Nickelsburg, "Salvation Without or With a Messiah: Developing Beliefs in Writings Ascribed to Enoch," in Neusner, Green, and Frerichs, eds., *Judaisms and Their Messiahs*, 49–68).

12. For example, G. Sheppard shows that while Henry Ainsworth recalled that New Testament writers cited some Psalms christologically, he did not necessarily use this as a warrant for interpretation because in his mind the writers had special dispensation to make such interpretational decisions under the influence of the Holy Spirit. Hence, Ainsworth did not use this as a warrant for his own messianic exegesis or consider it a precedent for interpretation. See Gerald T. Sheppard, "Pre-modern Criticism in the English Protestant Translations of the Psalms During the 17th Century," in *SBL Seminar Papers, 1994* (ed. Eugene H. Lovering, Jr.; SBLSP 33; Atlanta: Scholars Press, 1994), 346–76.

13. J. J. M. Roberts, "The Old Testament's Contribution to Messianic Expectations," in Charlesworth, ed., *The Messiah*, 39. See also, in the same volume, Talmon, "The Concept of Mashiah and Messianism in Early Judaism," 80–83.

passage does not need to use the word מָשִׁיחַ to be classified as messianic. Most biblical texts interpreted as messianic by later Jews and Christians lack the term מָשִׁיחַ while containing other pertinent ideas that describe a Messiah without naming him as one. Only one text in the book of Isaiah uses the noun מָשִׁיחַ (45:1) and only one uses the verb √משׁח (61:1). Therefore, we will examined how other titles, images and portraits of deliverers within the book of Isaiah evoke either messianic or non-messianic interpretation.

II. *Strategy for this Investigation*

Since the 1970s, a variety of new strategies have arisen and, as a result, biblical scholarship has raised a new set of questions that are informed by both historical-critical methods and attention to the later formation and context of the biblical book.[14] During the SBL Isaiah Seminar in the 1990s, scholars from differing perspectives tried to reassess various parts of the book of Isaiah in light of the whole. While some took a literary synchronic approach (Edgar Conrad, Chris Franke), others employed historical-critical approaches (Marvin Sweeney, Christopher Seitz, Roy Melugin, Ronald Clements, Benjamin Sommer, Gerald Sheppard and Rolf Rendtorff). When talking about the scriptural scroll of Isaiah, I make no claim whatsoever to be reading it "synchronically" as if one could choose between synchronic or diachronic in attempting to describe this biblical book. Since I am interested in the diachronic dimensions of scripture, I will describe the changes in smaller units of tradition when they are woven into the tapestry of the scroll of Isaiah as a whole. Moreover, I aim to examine the context within which these older traditions now function and the significance which they have attained in the latter formation of the whole scroll of Isaiah.

Recently, Paul Wegner and Gerald Sheppard have independently argued for warrants within the edited book of Isaiah that invite messianic interpretation, especially in Isa 7–11.[15] Under the direction of Clements, Wegner argues in his published dissertation that, if one takes seriously the juxtaposition that exists in the tension between the original context

14. Such as: *relecture* (J. Vermeylen), canonical criticism (James Sanders) and a concern for the Bible as scripture by making a new effort to understand the form and function of the biblical material as Jewish and Christian scripture (Brevard Childs, Rolf Rendtorff, Gerald Sheppard).

15. Wegner, *An Examination of Kingship*. This is also the view of Sheppard. See his work on Isaiah in the *HarperCollins Bible Commentary* (rev. ed.; San Francisco: Harper Collins, 2000), 489–537.

and later editing, we begin to see how older traditions have at times been overtly reinterpreted messianically. In other words, Wegner asks, "Does the final form contain any message of its own or is it merely an anthology of various writers inspired by Isaiah Ben Amoz?"[16] This question finds its answer when later editors "reread" the original texts in light of the promise of a Davidic king. Wegner is the only person who has looked at how redactional features have affected several selected messianic passages in Isa 1–39.[17] His approach to Isaiah moves in the same direction as recent studies on messianism in the biblical book of Psalms.[18]

However, Wegner's claim that *pre-exilic editors* have reinterpreted originally non-messianic oracles of Isaiah as messianic does not meet our definition of messianism because at this level of tradition history the monarchy still exists.[19] He also disregards how post-exilic layers in chs. 1–39 may have reshaped earlier traditions to be heard as messianic. Hence, Wegner has overlooked the effect that the final text of Isaiah has had on the interpretation of each passage. Moreover, his attempts to find a maximal amount of original Isaianic material does not help to explain how earlier traditions came to be understood as messianic within the "final form" of the later book of Isaiah.[20]

Another weakness of Wegner's position is that Wegner confuses Child's "canonical approach" with Sander's "canonical criticism."[21] Similar to Sanders, Wegner seeks to establish a "canonical hermeneutic" which aims to identify a consistent factor in the process of tradition history. In this way, he hopes to explain how the same normative tradition might properly lead to vastly different interpretations in different times and circumstances.[22] Wegner endeavors to find this pattern behind

---

16. Wegner, *An Examination of Kingship*, 15.

17. Ibid., 134.

18. James Luther Mays, "The Place of the Torah Psalms in the Psalter," *JBL* 106 (1987): 3–12; Gerald T. Sheppard, *Wisdom as a Hermeneutical Construct: A Study in the Sapientializing of the Old Testament* (BZAW 151; Berlin: de Gruyter, 1980); idem, *The Future of the Bible: Beyond Liberalism and Literalism* (Toronto: The United Church of Canada Publishing House, 1990).

19. See Wegner, *An Examination of Kingship*, 131–35, 136, 211, 212, 268.

20. Wegner accuses his opponents for failing to acknowledge certain material as Isaianic. Cf. Hermann Barth, "Israel und das Assyrerreich in den nichtjesajanischen Texten des Protojesajabuches: Eine Untersuchung zur produktiven Neuinterpretation der Jesajauberlieferung" (Ph.D. diss., University of Hamburg).

21. Wegner, *An Examination of Kingship*, 14.

22. This theory of redaction harmonizes differences in redactional layers that stand worlds apart from one another. J. A. Sanders called this factor "the canonical hermeneutic," while acknowledging that not every interpretation found in scripture

every redactional reinterpretation of preceding tradition.[23] Like Kaiser, Becker, Barth, Vermeylen, Clements and Sweeney, Wegner focuses on independent levels of editing without viewing the scriptural context of Isaiah as a whole. Each scholar has only concentrated on independent redactional layers without considering adequately the role of these traditions within the later formation of the scroll of Isaiah.

Sheppard's contribution more accurately represents an approach that takes seriously the scriptural function of such texts and their diachronic prehistory, but he does not thoroughly explore the implications of these and other related messianic texts within the book. My aim is to conduct a detailed investigation of the role of messianic texts in the entire book of Isaiah.

On the one hand, what I am doing is not entirely new because a number of scholars have attempted to describe the later levels of editing in the formation of biblical books as scripture.[24]

---

itself met that standard. See his *Canon and Community: A Guide to Canonical Criticism* (Old Testament Series; Philadelphia: Fortress, 1984), and *From Sacred Story to Sacred Text: Canon as Paradigm* (Philadelphia: Fortress, 1987).

23. One main problem with Wegner's use of *relecture* is that he aims to show how all texts became reinterpreted using the same method at every stage. *Relecture* solves a problem in the environment of change of tradition history by finding a solution within the mind of the redactor at each level of change. The formation of scripture is merely one incidental phase. Every moment of reinterpretation speaks of a canonical hermeneutic. I find this unconvincing that every single moment in tradition history represents the same kind of theological rereading. This line of criticism appears to be a pious accounting or over-theologizing of all the changes in tradition history. The things that give rise to changes in the text are not so predictable but are tremendously diverse.

24. Brevard S. Childs, *Introduction to the Old Testament as Scripture* (Philadelphia: Fortress, 1979); Rolf Rendtorff, *The Old Testament: An Introduction* (trans. John Bowden; London: SCM Press, 1985); idem, *Canon and Theology* (trans. Margaret Kohl; OBT; Minneapolis: Fortress, 1993); Sheppard, *Wisdom as a Hermeneutical Construct.* For later editing in the Psalms, see Mays "The Place of the Torah Psalms in the Psalter"; idem, "The Question of Context in Psalm Interpretation," in *Shape and Shaping of the Psalter* (ed. J. C. McCann; JSOTSup 159; Sheffield: JSOT Press, 1993), 14–20; Sheppard, *The Future of the Bible*, 49–95; Matthias Millard, *Die Komposition des Psalters: Ein formgeschichtlicher Ansatz* (Tübingen: J. C. B. Mohr, 1994). For the same topic in the New Testament, see David Trobisch, *Die Entstehung der Paulusbriefsammlung* (NTOA 10; Freiburg, Schweiz: Universitätsverlag; Göttingen: Vandenhoeck & Ruprecht, 1989); idem, *Die Endredaktion des Neuen Testaments: Eine Untersuchung zur Entstehung der christlichen Bibel* (Freiburg, Schweiz: Universitätsverlag; Göttingen: Vandenhoeck & Ruprecht, 1996). For the most extensive work in this area, see Gerald T. Sheppard, "The Anti-Assyrian Redaction and the Canonical Context of Isaiah 1–39," *JBL* 104, no. 2 (1985): 193–

On the other hand, no one has gone through the whole book of Isaiah to establish a context for understanding messianic interpretation within the various parts of this book and how messianic texts in Isa 1–39 must clarify similar traditions in chs. 40–66 and vice versa. Even though some have tried to discuss all the messianic texts in this book, they have not adequately described the significance of the texts within the scriptural form of Isaiah. Most modern efforts have failed fully to recognize the semantic alterations that occur when pre-biblical traditions become part of the biblical testimony.[25] No one has focused on the problem of messianism as it relates to the formation of Jewish and Christian scripture.

My approach is wedded with what has been called "a canonical approach" (Childs), "composition history" (Rendtorff) or "a scriptural approach" (Sheppard). In the work of Childs, Rendtorff and Sheppard, the aim has not been to create a whole new methodology but to seek a more illuminating way to redescribe the form and function of scriptural books. Hence, I make *no* claim to be applying "canonical criticism" as if we can pile up "one more methodology on top of an already unstackable accumulation of modern methods."[26] In order to describe messianism as it relates to the formation of scriptural books, I will take seriously the role of historical criticisms in that effort to redescribe selected texts within the book of Isaiah as a whole. My efforts to respond to these questions about messianism do not advocate new methodologies, but I will use a variety of historical criticisms to redescribe selected texts within the book of Isaiah as a whole. A similar set of concerns lies behind Wilfred

216; idem, "Isaiah 1–39," in *Harper's Bible Commentary* (ed. James L. Mays; San Francisco: Harper & Row, 1988), 542–70; idem, "The Role of the Canonical Context in the Interpretation of the Solomonic Books," in *William Perkins' A Commentary on Galatians (1617), with Introductory Essays* (ed. G. T. Sheppard; Cleveland, Ohio: Pilgrim, 1989), 67–107; idem, *The Future of the Bible*; idem, "The Book of Isaiah: Competing Structures According to a Late Modern Description of Its Shape and Scope," in *SBL Seminar Papers, 1992* (ed. Eugene H. Lovering, Jr.; SBLSP 31; Atlanta: Scholars Press, 1992), 549–81; idem, "The Book of Isaiah as a Human Witness to Revelation Within the Religions of Judaism and Christianity," in *SBL Seminar Papers, 1993* (ed. Eugene H. Lovering, Jr.; SBLSP 32; Atlanta: Scholars Press, 1993), 274–80; idem, "Two Turbulent Decades of Isaiah Research," *TST* 9, no. 1 (1993): 107–16; idem, "The Scope of Isaiah as a Book of Jewish and Christian Scriptures," in *New Visions of Isaiah* (ed. R Melugin and M. Sweeney; JSOTSup 214; Sheffield: Sheffield Academic Press, 1996), 257–81.

25. Gerald T. Sheppard, "Canon Criticism," *ABD* 1:861–66.

26. G. T. Sheppard ("Biblical Wisdom Literature at the End of the Modern Age," in *Congress Volume, Oslo 1998* [ed. A. Lemaire and M. Sæbø; Leiden: Brill, 2000], 369) clarifies that we do not claim to apply "canonical criticism" as a methodology that stands on its own.

Cantwell Smith's book, *What is Scripture? A Comparative Approach.*[27] Therefore, I will illustrate how Isaiah functions as a scriptural book among other biblical books and how this feature illumines messianic interpretation within the context of scripture.

In order to focus on the book of Isaiah as a whole, I will continuously compare pre-biblical and biblical traditions (biblical and scriptural are synonymous). For our purposes, "pre-biblical" traditions would include the role of various texts in either the original collection of Isaianic oracles, earlier redactional levels such as AR (Assyrian Redaction) or even the so-called collection of "Second Isaiah." The views of many scholars will not fit our definition of "pre-biblical" and "biblical." For example, the term "final form" has become so problematic because people mean different things when they speak of the book as a whole. When describing the "final form" of Isaiah or the scriptural scroll of Isaiah, some conservatives wish to suggest that Isaiah of Jerusalem wrote every part of Isa 1–66 and therefore reject any historical-critical inquiry. Others anchor the text in the final redaction of the book and treat the final editor as "the author" of the book. Others presume that this book is actually read from beginning to end and that reading strategy provides the key to its meaning.[28] While we will treat various scholars who attempt to interpret the book as a whole, we may disagree with that claim.

In my opinion, several features accompany the formation of scripture, the first of which concerns the relationship of the book of Isaiah to the Torah. Therefore, in the post-exilic period, the later editors betray a consciousness of the Torah, which the book of Isaiah introduces in its prologue (1:7). This sets the stage for how one reads a biblical book as a scriptural book and becomes relevant to the interpretation of Isa 7:14 and 9:1–6 where the text exhibits a shift from prophetic "torah" to Mosaic Torah and at the same level of editing from non-messianic to messianic. Therefore, part of my work here will include the relationship of Torah to the other biblical books and how the Torah sets the precedent for all biblical books. In Chapters 2, I argue that the final editors of the book of Isaiah, probably working within the shadow of the editors of Torah, shift the original significance of the former things not only to the isolated prophecies of Isaiah but to the Mosaic Torah and the legacy of the prophets. In other words, the book of Isaiah cannot be read as a scriptural book apart from the Torah and other prophets.

---

27. Wilfred Cantwell Smith, *What is Scripture? A Comparative Approach* (Minneapolis: Fortress, 1993).

28. Patricia Tull Willey, *Remember the Former Things: The Recollection of Previous Texts in Second Isaiah* (SBLDS 161; Atlanta: Scholars Press, 1996).

Another differentiation between pre-biblical and biblical traditions influences how we view the material of Isa 40–66. The editorial design of Isa 40–66 does not depend on the so-called "Second" and "Third Isaiah" distinctions. Another design to these traditions orders them by the refrain "there will be no peace for the wicked" (48:22; 57:21) and the depiction of the "peacelessness" (i.e. restlessness) of the raging sea (48:18; 57:20), which ignores the modern distinctions of First, Second and Third Isaiah. I am convinced that Isa 40–66 has been editorially organized essentially into three equal parts by this refrain. That structure has been superimposed on whatever could be our conjecture of Second Isaiah and Third Isaiah. Hence, this refrain tri-sects Isa 40–66, concluding the work of Cyrus and any mention of Babylon (48:18), and, as Delitzsch argues, "seals" the second book by directing the prophecies to "the heathen…estranged from God, within Israel itself."[29]

Moreover, several texts that originally may have been primarily referential take on an ambiguity when they become a part of the tapestry of Isaiah. Gerald Sheppard distinguishes "systemic vagueness" from "functional ambiguity": systemic vagueness characterizes various items in the text that were intelligible to its writers or editors but, because of the distance between ancient writers and the modern reader, certain words, persons or things have become unintelligible. By contrast, functional ambiguity occurs when the writers or editors strategically leave the original referent of persons, events or things obscure as a rhetorical feature of the poetry.[30] Just as a metaphor would lose its rhetorical power when translated into "proper" language, the ambiguity that has been established by later editors loses the rhetorical force that lies in the genius of functional ambiguity when modern scholars try to establish the original historical referent. A skilled rhetorician in the pre-modern era would not attempt to locate the original historical referent of Isa 7:14; 9:1–6; 52:13–53:12 or 61:1–3 anymore than one would translate the "figurative" usage of a metaphor into a "proper" usage. Both the metaphor and ambiguity would lose their rhetorical force. Therefore, we need to consider this old rhetorical distinction between the "proper" and

29. This is a position that was primarily argued in pre-modern commentaries, but see F. Delitzsch, *Biblical Commentary on the Prophecies of Isaiah* (trans. James Martin, 3d ed.; 2 vols.; Edinburgh: T. & T. Clark, 1875), 1:256, 383, and Sheppard, "Isaiah 40–66."

30. Gerald T. Sheppard, "Issues in Contemporary Translation: Late Modern Vantages and Lessons from Past Epochs," in *On the Way to Nineveh: Studies in Honour of George M. Landes* (ed. Steven L. Cook and S. C. Winter; Atlanta: ASOR/Scholars Press, 1999), 257–85.

"figurative" use of words. The "proper" usage implies their straight-forward meaning but the "figurative" usage involves metaphor, similes and the like. Both the proper and figurative usage of words function within what the Christianity has called "the literal sense of scripture" (see below). For that reason, Northrop Frye encourages the reader to take the Bible literally but also to take it metaphorically.

However, we may distinguish between "figural" and "figurative" usage. The figural speaks of typological interpretation of a figure or type that consists of either a person, event or thing whose plastic form adumbrates other future events and things. This can be confusing because both the figurative and figural belong to the literal sense of scripture. For example, Hos 3:5 states: "Afterward the Israelites shall return and seek the LORD their God, and David their king; they shall come in awe to the LORD and to his goodness in the latter days." In this passage, David is the type of the New King who prefigures the Messiah. After the birth of the modern era, several scholars used typology to compensate for what may be lost due to modern historical criticism.[31]

Within this distinction of pre-biblical and biblical levels of tradition history, I will demonstrate how the late editors contribute to the forma-tion of this book that now invites the readers to hear some of the words of the pre-exilic prophet in a manner that testifies to a promise of a Davidic king in the post-exilic period. I aim to show that one cannot fully understand the messianic promises within Isa 1–39 without reading them along with Isa 40–66, whereby the final shape or scope of the book sets the limits for interpretation.

Finally, because the book of Isaiah shares texts in common with other biblical books, we have evidence that it was probably edited alongside these other books of Jewish scripture. For example, Isa 2:1–5 is virtually identical with Mic 4:1–5 and Isa 36–39 occurs elsewhere in 2 Kgs 18–20. One becomes aware that the Isaiah text has been carefully edited to place Hezekiah in a positive light (Isa 36–37) indicating that the editors had a motive for this arrangement. This is why, in the pre-modern era, some attributed the writings of Joshua through 2 Kings to Isaiah because of what is shared by both. More specific to our topic, I will demonstrate how the editors invite the readers to hear both references to Torah and messianic interpretation beyond the context of the pre-exilic situation because both comment on Torah and messianic promise at the same late level of editing in this scriptural scroll.

31. See Sheppard's description in his "The Book of Isaiah as a Human Witness." See also Charles Briggs, *Messianic Prophecies* (2d ed.; New York: Scribner's Sons, 1893), 196–97.

This work does not seek to establish the origins of messianism nor describe some sort of evolution or trajectory by which the portrait of an ideal king represented in royal enthronement hymns developed into messianic promise. Neither will I focus on whether or not messianic texts in Isaiah establish the prophet's ability to predict. Rather than focusing on the eighth-century prophet's ability or inability to predict, our inquiry instead seeks to establish how the scriptural book of Isaiah (as a whole) testifies to messianic hope.

III. *Rationale for Selecting Messianic Passages in Isaiah*

I do not claim to address every possibility that Judaism imagined about the Messiah but the one element of Judaism that Christianity picked up. The earliest Christian interpretations that identify Isaianic texts with messianic promise can be found in New Testament citations of the Old Testament. New Testament citations that employ many different modes of interpretation (midrash, pesher, allegory and spiritual senses) may ignore the significance of the larger context. However, I partially want to focus what Christianity later called the "plain" or "literal sense," which became the primary basis for doctrinal interpretation since the mid-second century C.E. I am aware that there are distinctions in rabbinic Judaism between *peshat* and midrash but will not pursue this study.

Each of my core chapters will begin with a history of interpretation regarding the selected passage. My rationale for presenting a history of interpretation seeks not merely to show my research but to provide a fresh empathetic re-description of the issues from the perspective of the current "post-modern" debate. One of the challenges we face, at this time, is to redescribe the many efforts to interpret the book of Isaiah in light of what we now know to be pre-modern and modern positions. The evidence that this is necessary can be seen in the remarkable but misguided effort of Farrar's *History of Interpretation*.[32] In that book, drawn from his famous Bampton Lectures, he declares that pre-modern interpretation could be viewed essentially as a history of errors. Likewise, he treated Jewish interpretation derisively. The only things of value that he found in pre-modern interpretation amounted to what he regarded to be anticipations of the new modern critique of his day. Yet, looking back on the modern era, we have found that the climate created by the Enlightenment has produced a myopia that has failed to see the merits of pre-modern interpretation. Now that the modern era lies in the immediate

32. Frederic W. Farrar, *History of Interpretation* (Bampton Lectures Series; Grand Rapids: Baker, 1961).

past, I aim to redescribe familiar and unfamiliar efforts at messianic interpretation. Therefore, my treatment of secondary literature does not consist of one more modern *Forschungsbericht*, nor the results of my research put on paper, but it offers a novel approach to the history of interpretation on the subject of messianism in Isaiah.

I will show chapter by chapter that there are several ways in which the scroll of Isaiah warrants a messianic reading even when some of the standard features from the above mentioned consensus definition are missing. In some passages, the editors have shown themselves to be conscious of messianic interpretation in the way that they have shaped the texts in order to highlight the possibility of a messianic reading. Other texts were not foreseen even by the later editors to be messianic, yet within the warrants of the text have provoked Jewish readers to identify a certain figure in order to make sense of them. Finally, within the entire Isaianic corpus, the noun משיח only appears in the context of Isa. 45:1 to describe Cyrus. Therefore, we must consider this text as well.

Using these criteria, in my second chapter, I will begin this study by describing Cyrus' role within the book of Isaiah. In Chapter 3, I will focus on messianic interpretation in Isa 7:14; 9:1–6 and 11:1–9. In Chapter 4, I will treat The Suffering Servant (Isa 52:13–53:12). My fifth chapter will focus on Isa 61:1–3, which Jesus read in the temple and about which he proclaimed, "Today this scripture has been fulfilled in your hearing" (Luke 4:18–19). In my final chapter, I will summarize the results of this study and raise other related issues. This section will also focus on a few early examples of Christian and Jewish interpretation of Isaianic passages (Pseudepigrapha, Targum, Qumran and New Testament citations) to provide a comparison with my results. I also plan to discuss the outlook of the nature of prophecy in the pre-modern and modern eras and compare my findings with these perspectives. Finally, I will discuss the implications of this work in the ongoing search for the literal sense within contemporary Christian interpretation.

Chapter 2

CYRUS: YHWH'S ANOINTED

Introduction

Isaiah 45:1 is the only text in Isaiah that overtly mentions the phrase, "his messiah" or "his anointed" (משיחו). Since a few modern scholars have suggested that Isa 45:1 presents Cyrus as a Messiah, we need to consider this passage carefully. As with the other texts discussed in this study, I will initially examine how scholars have tried to describe the original function of this text in what we have called pre-biblical tradition(s) and then how its place within the scroll of Isaiah invites a different assessment of it. In each case, I will present my own conclusions after considering those of others. This chapter makes no attempts to resolve all the redactional issues of Isa 40–55, but aims to show that pieces belonging to one level of tradition have been re-historicized within the scriptural form of Isaiah.

I. Cyrus within Pre-biblical Traditions

A. *Scholarly Efforts to Reconstruct the Traditions around Cyrus*
The mention of Cyrus as "his anointed" (משיחו) or "my anointed" (LXX, τῷ χριστῷ μου) has inspired a wide range of interpretations. Scholars have tried to imagine how Isa 45:1 and the traditions associated with Cyrus functioned originally. In other words, if we try to reconstruct the pre-biblical traditions, what options do we face?

1. *Perspectives that reject Cyrus as Messiah.* Some view the name of Cyrus in Isa 45:1 as a later editor's interpolation that was not part of the original material in Second Isaiah. For example, James D. Smart maintains that the name "Cyrus" is an intrusion which reinterprets Second Isaiah's original messianic hope that dramatically left the servant figure unnamed when pertaining to Israel.[1] Similarly, Charles Torrey asserts

---

1. James D. Smart, *History and Theology in Second Isaiah: A Commentary on Isaiah 35, 40–66* (Philadelphia: Westminster, 1965), 120.

that לכרש in 45:1 is a gloss that disrupts meter and changes the original context from a traditional messianic promise of justice (42:1, 4) to a senseless and unsuitable designation of Cyrus.[2] Isaiah 41:13; 42:6 and 48:14 originally spoke of Abraham and Israel fulfilling David's royal line as Abraham's seed (55:3–5), both having a relationship of love with YHWH (41:8; 43:4) but not Cyrus (45:1) who could not fulfill this messianic roll because "the coming warrior imagined could only be the promised scion of David's royal line." However, Torrey cannot so easily isolate a single, timeless messianic hope without recognizing how messianic expectations in Judaism changed over time. Nor can meter and the Targum determine glosses to emend a *lectio difficilior*.[3]

Others interpret Cyrus typologically so that he serves not as a type of Messiah but as the antitype of Moses or Abraham. Bernard Anderson suggests that the description of Cyrus was fashioned after the Exodus and "the juxtaposition of the 'former things' and 'things to come' refers to God's one and same work, which started with Abraham and is now fulfilled in Cyrus" who ushers in a "new Exodus."[4] Gwilym Jones designates Abraham as the type and Cyrus as the anti-type, whereby the "former things" refer to YHWH's election of Israel via Abraham and the "latter things" to the "outcome" of Israel's election after the exile by acting on its behalf through Cyrus. The heroic figure in 41:2, 25; 46:11 and 48:14 might be reminiscent of both Abraham and Moses but the context depicts Cyrus who will defeat Babylon.[5]

2. Cf. Charles C. Torrey, "Isaiah 41," *HTR* 44 (1951): 121–36.

3. More recent studies have demonstrated that meter itself is not as predictable as scholars had thought during the time of Torrey, especially when pertaining to editorial or textual corrections. Cf. Michael O'Connor, *Hebrew Verse Structure* (2d ed.; Winona Lake, Ind.: Eisenbrauns, 1997), 54–86; Adele Berlin, *The Dynamics of Biblical Parallelism* (Bloomington: Indiana University Press, 1992), 142–43; Paul Dion, *Hebrew Poetics* (2d ed.; Mississauga, Ont.: Benben, 1992), 9–10; David Noel Freedman, "Strophe and Meter in Exodus 15," in *A Light Unto My Path: Old Testament Studies in Honor of Jacob Myers* (ed. H. Goedicke and J. J. M. Roberts; Baltimore: The Johns Hopkins University Press, 1974), 163–203; James L. Kugel, *The Idea of Biblical Poetry* (New Haven: Yale University Press, 1981), 287–304; B. Hrushovski, "Note On the System of Hebrew Versification," in *Hebrew Verse* (ed. T. Carmi; New York: Penguin, 1981), 65–67; idem, *Style in Language* (ed. T. Sebeok; Cambridge, Mass.: M. I. T. Press, 1960), 189; P. Casetti, "Funktionen der Musik in der Bibel," *FZPhTh* 24 (1977): 366–89; D. K. Stuart, *Studies in Early Hebrew Meter* (HSM 13; Missoula, Mont.: Scholars Press, 1976).

4. Bernhard W. Anderson, "Exodus Typology in Second Isaiah," in *Israel's Prophetic Heritage: Essays in Honor of James Muilenburg* (ed. B. W. Anderson and W. Harrelson; New York: Harper, 1962), 177–95.

5. Gwilym H. Jones, "Abraham and Cyrus: Type and Anti-Type," *VT* 22 (1972): 304–19.

Others do not regard Cyrus as Messiah but imagine through comparing Isa 44:24–45:13 with Mesopotamian royal inscriptions that he is a
royal figure on a par with Israelite kings who are often described by
exaggerated language. John Gray argues that God is both universal and
Israel's king and the momentous rise of Cyrus and the subsequent fall of
Babylon is a manifestation of God's rule as King of Israel (41:9, 25;
45:1–7; 46:11; 47:5–15; 48:14–15).[6] Rudolph Kittel concludes that the
material surrounding Isa 45:1 was drafted as if it were in "the Babylonian court style."[7] Shalom Paul then, building on a century of scholarship, argues that the Cyrus oracle imitates Akkadian royal inscriptions on
the basis of themes and vocabulary, calling him "shepherd" (רעה) in
44:28, which often serves as a royal epithet in ancient Near Eastern
inscriptions,[8] but he neglects its biblical usage.[9] Paul's proposal relies on

6.   See J. Gray, *Biblical Doctrine of the Reign of God* (Edinburgh: T. & T. Clark,
1979), 167.
7.   Rudolph Kittel, "Cyrus und Deuterojesaja," *ZAW* 18 (1898): 49–64. Hugo
Gressmann followed this view about thirty years later in *Der Messias* (FRLANT 43;
Göttingen: Vandenhoeck & Ruprecht, 1929). See also Friedrich Stummer, "Einige
keilschriftliche Parallelen zu Jes. 40–66," *JBL* 45 (1926): 171–89; J. W. Behr, *The
Writings of Deutero-Isaiah and the Neo-Babylonian Royal Inscription: A
Comparison of the Language and Style* (Arts 3/3; Pretoria: Publications of the
University of Pretoria, 1937); Morton Smith, "II Isaiah and the Persians," *JAOS* 83
(1963): 415–21; H. M. Dion, "Le genre litteraire Sumerien de 'l'hymne à soi-même'
et quelques passages du Deutéro-Isaïe," *RB* 74 (1967): 215–34; Nahum M.
Waldman, "A Biblical Echo of Mesopotamian Royal Rhetoric," in *Essays on the
Occasion of the Seventieth Anniversary of Dropsie University* (ed. Abraham Isaac
Katsch and Leon Nemoy; Philadelphia: Dropsie University, 1979), 449; J. B. White,
"Universalization of History in Deutero-Isaiah," in *Scripture in Context* (ed. Carl D.
Evans; Pittsburgh: Pickwick, 1980), 180.
8.   See also William Hallo's compilation of Mesopotamian royal titles and
epithets, especially *re'um* and *wardum* in his *Early Mesopotamian Royal Titles: A
Philological and Historical Analysis* (New Haven: Yale University Press, 1957),
132–42. The King of Sumer is often called "the faithful shepherd of the land."
In some of the Sumerian city-laments, Išme-Dagan is termed "beloved shepherd"
(sipa-ki-ag-ga-ni-ir). The image of a ruler who will rebuild the capital city and the
temple is also prominent in Akkadian Royal inscriptions. See also S. N. Kramer and
John Maier, *Myths of Enki, the Crafty God* (Oxford: Oxford University Press, 1989),
157; R. Borger, "Babylonisch-assyrische Lesestücke," *AnOr* 54 (1979): 51–52, 125–
26; D. O. Edzard, *Die "zweite Zwischenzeit" Babylonians* (Wiesbaden: Harrassowitz, 1957), 124–25; V. Hurowitz, "The Literary Structures in Samsuiluna A," *JCS*
36, no. 2 (1984): 191–205.
9.   The epithet, which the tribes of Israel apply to David (2 Sam 5:2) and YHWH
applies idealistically to future rulers (Jer 3:15; 23:4–5; Ezek 34:23), seems to have
"a salvific or messianic sense"; see Antoon Schoors, *I Am God Your Saviour*

Cyrus being the Servant and overlooks how Isa 45:4 declares that YHWH has appointed him "for the sake of my Servant."[10]

John McKenzie argues that "Cyrus is given the place in the history of salvation which in pre-exilic Israel was given to the king."[11] Richard Clifford suggests that Cyrus is a typical king who rebuilds the temple as YHWH's unwitting instrument.[12] Similarly, William Holladay, equating the term משיח as "king" but not "Messiah," refers to him as a "king of a foreign empire who might be thought to be far from Israel's ken," yet on Israel's behalf only takes on the "office of God's agent." Cyrus is "unexpected" evidence that "God is innovative beyond all of Israel's traditional assumptions."[13]

Without drawing heavily on comparative ancient Near Eastern studies, some scholars posit that Cyrus does not function as a Messiah in Isa 45:1. Building on Ivan Engell's work, Aage Bentzen argues that Second Isaiah portrays a universalism and royal ideology in the Cyrus oracle but the *'Ebed YHWH* is the true Messiah and messianic language represents him as a "bye-motif."[14] G. A. F. Knight argues that Cyrus being a "pagan king" disqualifies him as Messiah.[15] C. R. North calls Cyrus an "anointed prince" and the term "*māšiªḥ*" was "shocking" to the prophet's audience because he is a non-Israelite king. He asserts, "we may easily read into it more than was intended because the word 'messiah' had not yet acquired

(VTSup 24; Leiden: Brill, 1973), 269–70; also Carroll Stuhlmueller, "Deutero-Isaiah: Major Transitions in the Prophet's Theology and in Contemporary Scholarship," *CBQ* 42 (1980): 13–14.

10. Shalom Paul calls Cyrus the "servant of Deutero-Isaiah" arguing that Deutero-Isaiah uses much of the royal inscription language to describe Cyrus: "I have called you by your name" (43:1); "He designated my name" (49:1); עבדי (41:8; 42:1; 43:10; 44:1, 21; 45:4; 49:5 etc.); the call of the designated servant, "I YHWH have graciously called you"—a sign and seal of the divine call (42:6) and YHWH calls him from the womb (49:1). See his "Deutero-Isaiah and Cuneiform Royal Inscriptions," in *Essays in Memory of E. A. Speiser* (ed. W. Hallo; New Haven: American Oriental Society, 1968), 180–86.

11. John L. McKenzie, *Second Isaiah* (AB 20; Garden City, N.Y.: Doubleday, 1968), 76.

12. Richard J. Clifford, *Fair Spoken and Persuading* (New York: Paulist, 1984), 117.

13. William L. Holladay, *Isaiah: Scroll of a Prophetic Heritage* (Grand Rapids: Eerdmans, 1978), 138.

14. Auge Bentzen, *King and Messiah* (Lutterworth Studies in Church and Bible; London: Lutterworth, 1955), 49, 51; Ivan Engell, *Studies in Divine Kingship in the Ancient Near East* (Uppsala: Almqvist & Wiksell, 1967).

15. George A. F. Knight, *Deutero-Isaiah: A Theological Commentary on Isaiah 40–55* (ITC; Grand Rapids: Eerdmans, 1965), 87–100.

2. *Cyrus: YHWH's Anointed* 19

all the eschatological content which it came to have in later messianic dogma" and it is never used in the Old Testament to speak of a future messianic king.[16] Yet he fails to see that Ps 2, as just one example, has already been reinterpreted within the post-exilic Psalter to describe the Messiah.[17]

Similarly, J. J. M. Roberts asserts that none of the thirty-nine occasions where משיח appears in the Old Testament refers to an anticipated future figure whose coming will initiate an era of salvation. Second Isaiah used a peculiar term that signified the same royal characteristics to describe any Israelite king newly ascended to the Davidic throne at his coronation, thus expressing a special relationship with YHWH to shock his "Israelite audience into looking into history in a new way." While the Cyrus oracle is modeled after Israelite coronation oracles, the term משיח does not convey messianism in the later sense of the term.[18]

Hans Barstad argues that Second-Isaiah's hearers were not ready to embrace this portrait of Cyrus, a Gentile Persian king, as YHWH's anointed—one who epitomized their national and spiritual identity and who would serve as the agent of restoration:

> The Cyrus figure must have made an enormous impact on the subdued Jews both Babylonian and at home. To Second-Isaiah, the great master of language and rhetoric, the Cyrus event offers a wellcome [*sic*] ingredient, an ingredient of which he makes the most. In fact the Cyrus story makes such an impression on the prophet that he not only refers to his activities through his well known mastering of poetic expressions, but he is also able to include Cyrus in Yahweh's salvation plans for Israel. For this purpose he uses a language about the Achaemenide ruler that may not only seem astonishing, but that must have had a dramatic, if not shocking, effect on the prophet's audience.

For Barstad, what is astonishing is not that Cyrus is "Messiah" but that Cyrus performs a salvific act for Israel. Likewise, Philip R. Davies asserts that "the poems here take for granted that the role of the 'anointed' has not just passed to Cyrus but to the Persians..."[19]

---

16. Christopher Richard North, *The Second Isaiah* (Oxford: Oxford University Press, 1964), 150.

17. Cf. Sheppard, *The Future of the Bible*, 65. See also Erhard Gerstenberger, *Psalms: Part 1 With an Introduction to Cultic Poetry* (FOTL; Grand Rapids: Eerdmans, 1987), 44–50.

18. Roberts, "Messianic Expectations."

19. See Hans Barstad, "On the So-Called Babylonian Literary Influence," *SJOT* 1 (1987): n.p. Philip R. Davies, "God of Cyrus, God of Israel," in *Words Remembered, Texts Renewed: Essays in Honour of John F. A. Sawyer* (ed. Wilfred G. E. Watson; JSOTSup 195; Sheffield: Sheffield Academic Press, 1995), 218.

Westermann asserts that Isa 44:24–45:7 is a royal oracle where Cyrus is "anointed" but never refers to him as the Servant—a term that implies a mutual relationship of permanence. The phrase "anointed" provided the "most shocking news to Second Isaiah's audience" because the term was used at a king's coronation but its later messianic meaning is not operative here since Cyrus merely performs the office of the king for a limited purpose.[20] Similarly, Whybray regards מָשִׁיחַ to serve as an honorific-formal expression that transfers an Israelite royal title for the rhetorical purpose of a "calculated shock."[21]

2. Perspectives that portray Cyrus as Messiah. Some argue that Mesopotamian royal inscriptions prove Cyrus to be Messiah at the original level of Isa 44:24–45:13. Klaus Koch asserts that the Cyrus Cylinder borrows the concept of the ideal king from Babylonian descriptions and Isa 45:1 confers on Cyrus the title of "Messiah" to acknowledge the uniqueness of the Israelite God to evoke cultic worship of YHWH throughout the world. Though not "converted to YHWH," the main purpose of his messiahship was Cyrus' military and political efforts to conquer Babylon.[22]

Paul Hanson contends that Second Isaiah envisioned a "new exodus" through a "Persian Messiah" to fulfill the promise to David, and that calling him "shepherd" and "messiah" gave the office a new significance, showing "confluence between confessional heritage and new event" to carry out YHWH's plans.[23] Similarly, Graham Ogden asserts that Cyrus functions as a new Moses and that "the notion of Cyrus as the elect and empowered *messiah* of YHWH is a point of great issue."[24] Antti Laato argues that Second Isaiah describes Cyrus as a "political Messiah" to

---

20. Claus Westermann, *Isaiah 40–66* (trans. David M. G. Stalker; OTL; Philadelphia: Westminster, 1969), 159–60.

21. Ibid., 159–60; Roger Norman Whybray, *Isaiah 40–66* (NCNC; Grand Rapids: Eerdmans, 1975), 105; Roberts, "Messianic Expectations," 39.

22. Klaus Koch, *The Prophets* (trans. M. Kohl; 2 vols.; London: SCM Press, 1982), 128–30.

23. Paul D. Hanson, *Dynamic Transcendence: The Correlation of Confessional Heritage and Contemporary Experience in a Biblical Model of Divine Activity* (Philadelphia: Fortress, 1978), 39–41; idem, *The Diversity of Scripture* (ed. Walter Brueggemann; OBT 11; Philadelphia: Fortress, 1982), 72; idem, "Messiahs and Messianic Figures in Proto-Apocalypticism," in Charlesworth, ed., *The Messiah*, 67–75.

24. Graham Ogden, "Moses and Cyrus: Literary Affinities Between the Priestly Presentation of Moses in Exodus Vi–Vii and the Cyrus Song in Isaiah Xliv 24–Xlv 13," *VT* 27 (1978): 195–203 (202).

whom he assigns various traits of the Messiah.[25] Aiming to find "kerygmatic content" in Akkadian and Old Testament royal ideology in the Servant and Cyrus texts, he wishes to establish a hermeneutical rationale for understanding the "exilic messianic program" that took place in the same era.[26]

Others argue that Second Isaiah views Cyrus as a Messiah in a manner that predates messianism in early Judaism. G. Adam Smith imagined that the original setting of Isa 40–55 involved a prophetic contest between Second Isaiah and "worshipers of heathen idols...to predict their issue" in the "near future."[27] Eighth-century Isaiah was not predicting 140 years beforehand because Cyrus is prophetic "proof" that "the former things," which may be lost or prophecies of Jeremiah, have now come to pass. Why else would Second Isaiah make a sharp distinction between the former and the latter things?[28] Cyrus "the Gentile Messiah" "is the new thing which is being created while the prophet speaks and which has not been announced beforehand." Since Cyrus is not described by the virtues found in Isa 7–11, his messianic role remains limited and ephemeral—to "lead the petty Jewish tribe back to their obscure corner of the earth."[29]

In *He That Cometh*, Mowinckel argues that while some viewed Cyrus as Messiah, Second Isaiah and his unsure disciples transferred the older idea of political Messiah to a servant who brings salvation:

25. Antti Laato, *A Star is Rising: The Historical Development of the Old Testament Royal Ideology and the Rise of the Jewish Messianic Expectation* (University of South Florida International Studies in Formative Christianity and Judaism 5; Atlanta: Scholars Press, 1997), 176, 179, 181–84.

26. Laato, building on his earlier *Josiah and David Redivivus: The Historical Josiah and the Messianic Expectations of Exilic and Postexilic Times* (Sweden: Almqvist & Wiksell, 1992), treats Isa 40–55 as a literary unity composed during the Babylonian exile to reflect new messianic expectations (inaugurated by the death of Josiah), revealing a shift from a Davidic to pagan Messiah. Since no potential Davidic Messiah had emerged at Babylon's fall, Deutero-Isaiah redefined Israel's messianic hopes through the Servant and Cyrus about whom language is taken from Akkadian and Israelite royal ideology and inscriptions. Cf. Laato's *The Servant of YHWH and Cyrus: A Reinterpretation of the Exilic Messianic Programme in Isaiah 40–55* (ConBOT 35; Stockholm: Almqvist & Wiksell, 1992).

27. G. A. Smith suggests that the prophet dialogues with men who have a national heritage of truth about God but have forgotten it and have turned to false gods. See *The Book of Isaiah* (rev. ed.; 2 vols.; Expositor's Bible; London: Hodder & Stoughton, 1927), 92, 120 and note on 121.

28. Around this line of thinking, Smith maintained that if these prophecies were ancient then it would not matter what was the exact content of these prophecies but that they could not have contained anything so definite as Cyrus (ibid., 9, 11, 12).

29. Ibid., 164, 169, 170, 207.

It is at this point that we may speak of the importance of these Songs for the Messianic expectation. They are not Messianic, in either the earlier or later Jewish sense of the term. But they look for and predict a figure who actually replaces the Messiah, or rather, who will be what the Messiah in the earlier period was never thought of as being, namely a true mediator of salvation, one who brings salvation to the people, who mediates that religious and moral conversion and transformation, without which there can be no salvation, and in which salvation supremely consists.[30]

Second Isaiah temporarily designates Cyrus to fulfill the earlier messianic expectation but later finds another more complete figure to supersede him when a salvific servant Messiah replaces a political Messiah. Earlier messianic expectation was so limited that many contemporary Jews thought that Cyrus fulfilled it, but "Deutero-Isaiah had intended that Cyrus should lead back the exiles, and gather together the dispersed. In these [Servant] Songs, it is the Servant who is to do this."[31]

Similarly, Ralph Klein suggests that Second Isaiah claimed the Persian king to be "God's effective and controversial Messiah" appointed to defeat nations, kings and cities. Certainly the Cyrus oracle evoked consternation since a term which had always applied to a Davidic king was now given to an "avowed pagan like Cyrus." On these grounds, the series of "disputations" (44:24–28; 45:9–13; 46:5–11; 48:12–15) refute those who would question YHWH's choice of Cyrus for this role.[32] Joachim Becker maintains that Isa 45:1 reflects a "compromising situation for the traditional messianic expectation" where all the earthly power and Davidic throne has been transferred to Cyrus.[33] John Watts states that calling Cyrus "Yahweh's anointed, his Messiah," must have been "a shock to Israel" because the term משיח, which described one anointed with oil as a sign of being chosen for some special assignment, like David who was set apart to subdue nations, now is assigned to Cyrus.[34]

Kenneth E. Pomykala claims that both Chronicles and Isa 44:28–45:1 reflect the same messianic outlook during the Persian period, each heralding Cyrus as the Lord's "designated messiah and world ruler."[35]

30. Mowinckel, *He That Cometh*, 243–44.

31. Ibid.

32. Ralph W. Klein, *Israel in Exile: A Theological Interpretation* (OBT 6; Philadelphia: Fortress, 1979), 105–6.

33. Joachim Becker, *Messianic Expectation in the Old Testament* (trans. David E. Green; Philadelphia: Fortress, 1980), 53.

34. John D. W. Watts, *Isaiah 34–66* (ed. David Hubbard and Glenn W. Barker; WBC 25; Waco, Tex.: Word, 1987), 156.

35. Kenneth E. Pomykala, *The Davidic Dynasty Tradition in Early Judaism: Its History and Significance for Messianism* (SBLEJL 7; Atlanta: Scholars Press, 1995), 73, 228.

Second Temple Judaism did not reflect the expectation of a Davidic messianism, which, differing over time, would eventually become traditional in both rabbinic Judaism and Christianity, but Second Isaiah regards Cyrus as "the messiah of the Jews."[36]

Among those who argue that the משיח applies to Cyrus to describe a temporary office or a specific purpose, Calvin contests that משיח was not a perpetual title but that this office of redeemer was discharged for a time.[37] Morgenstern reasons that Cyrus ascends to the throne as a "Babylonian Messiah" who is set aside for a "specific purpose."[38] Similar to Mowinckel, Richard Schultz asserts that Isa 40–48 shifts focus from a Davidic to Persian king whereby "Cyrus is Yahweh's Messiah" who "offers only a temporary solution to Israel's problem" after whom "the Suffering Servant emerges as the only solution for a recalcitrant people."[39]

B. *Rethinking the Evidence*
In agreement with most scholars, who attribute the greater part of Isa 40–55 to "Second Isaiah," we may ask: Why does Isa 45:1 use the term משיח in 45:1 to describe Cyrus? If we view the Cyrus oracle in light of Mesopotamian royal inscriptions, we must realize that this form does not dominate Isa 44:24–45:7 and Cyrus' approval comes from YHWH the God of Israel rather than from the Babylonian "chambers of destiny." Form-critically Westermann designates Isa 45:1–7 as a prophetic oracle adorned by royal language,[40] which may help define Second Isaiah's usage of the term משיח in light of its historical development. Scholars are correct that Isa 45:1 used a "shocking" term to an Israelite audience that implied the kings' special relationship with YHWH.[41] The use of משיחו ("His anointed") would have shocked any reader because this term had never before been used to describe a pagan king. Though astonishing

36. Ibid., 257, 264.
37. Jean Calvin, *Commentary on the Book of the Prophet Isaiah* (trans. W. Pringle; 4 vols.; Grand Rapids: Eerdmans, 1948), 3:395.
38. Julian Morgenstern, "The Message of Deutero-Isaiah in Its Sequential Unfolding," *HUCA* 29 (1958): 1–67.
39. Richard Schultz, "The King in the Book of Isaiah," in *The Lord's Anointed: Interpretation of Old Testament Messianic Texts* (ed. Philip E. Satterthwaite, Richard S. Hess and Gordon J. Wenham; Carlisle: Paternoster, 1995), 158–59.
40. Westermann, who finds form-critical similarities between Isa 45:1–7 and Ps 2, more accurately appraises 45:1–7 as a "royal oracle." See his *Isaiah 40–66*, 153–55.
41. North, *The Second Isaiah*, 150; Whybray, *Isaiah 40–66*, 105; Watts, *Isaiah 34–66*, 156; Roberts, "Messianic Expectations," 39.

to many, the use of משיח in the development of messianism marks the termination of the monarchy but did not have the significance that "Messiah" had in later Judaism.

While the traditions of Second Isaiah could not have implied the same full-blown eschatological meaning that accompanied messianism in later Judaism, the prophet probably perceived Cyrus's acts of deliverance at the very least to resemble the salvific acts of any anointed king according to the pre-exilic meaning of משיח. The historical context of Cyrus' role as the deliverer who sent the Judeans back to their land certainly invoked this response. Now, for the first time ever in written form, the prophet shifts the traditional function of "Messiah" to one other than the Israelite king, a concept that must have been fairly new in his day. If Second Isaiah were the first to use this term as a way of describing such a salvific deliverer, who functioned beyond the standard limits of a temporal king, then perhaps the description of Cyrus may have formed a transition that influenced how early Judaism would establish its own messianic expectation. Therefore, Isa 45:1 celebrated YHWH's use of Cyrus in a significant way while not making the messianic claims of later Judaism since a full eschatological hope of a Messiah had not yet developed. Perhaps Second Isaiah saw no one else to fulfill the "anointed" role of deliver or savior so he applied a title to Cyrus that was reminiscent of the king who served as Israel's champion. In light of the empty Davidic throne about which Ps 89 so poignantly laments in a Midrash on 2 Sam 7, "you have renounced the covenant with your servant" (Ps 89:39) this scenario quite possibly provided an incentive to redefine messianic hope for the very first time in Isa 45:1.

Comparing the use of משיח in Isa 45:1 with the rest of the Old Testament, this term seldom if never speaks of the future eschatological messianic expectation that arises in early Judaism. From Roberts' perspective that none of the thirty-nine usages of משיח in the Old Testament *originally* referred to an anticipated Messianic future figure, we can be sure Isa 45:1 does not meet our definition of messianism, where an eschatological event must take place after the monarchy has ceased to exist.[42] On four occasions, "P" uses the term in the post-exilic era to specify anointed priests הכהן המשיח (Lev 4:3, 5, 16; 6:15) representing another shift from its traditional reference to kings. This usage was probably not available to Second Isaiah who was not thinking about the priests in Isa 45:1. On two occasions, it pertains to prophets representing another shift from the traditional reference to an "anointed king"

---

42. Roberts, "Messianic Expectations," 39.

(1 Chr 16:22; Ps 105:15). The term משיח most often relates to kings in general (1 Sam 2:10; 12:3, 5); one other than the priest (1 Sam 2:35); Saul (1 Sam 12:5; 24:7 [Eng. 6], 11 [Eng. 10]; 26:11, 16, 23; 2 Sam 1:14, 16); Eliab (1 Sam 16:6); David (2 Sam 19:22; 22:51; 23:1; 2 Chr 6:42; Ps 18:51). Four times the usage is more ambiguous but probably concerns the king (Pss 20:7; 28:8; 84:10; Hab 13:13). The traditional pre-exilic use of the term conventionally pertains to temporal kings and the post-exilic usages seem to compensate for the fact that no king sits on the throne. Although these original usages may not signify an eschatological figure whose coming would initiate an era of salvation, within the latter formation of biblical books, some passages were reinterpreted by later editors to be heard as messianic (Pss 2:2; 89:39, 52; 132:10, 17; Lam 4:20; Dan 9:25, 26).[43] What then is the significance for Isa 45:1?

Probably the earliest pre-biblical level of Second Isaiah reveals a prophetic dispute where the prophet gains leverage against the other prophets.[44] Cyrus then serves as a proof of fulfilled prophecy and the oracles around the former and latter things seem to imply superiority of one prophet over other prophets by the fact that prophecy has come to pass.[45] Therefore, the confirmation of the true prophet rests on his claim to give true prophecy. The Cyrus oracle then serves as a confirmation that the "former things" have been fulfilled and now Second Isaiah is going to announce "new things." Not only does Cyrus appear as a prophetic proof but he will return the exiles to their land, an expectation of any deliverer king.

If messianic promise in part originated as a response to the exile and end of the monarchy, then the Messiah's first order of business would embody the restoration of the Jewish people to their land. Cyrus actually carried out a version of that agenda by saving the Judean exiles from the hand of Babylon, inviting them to go back to Jerusalem and rebuilding their capitol city and temple. Yet there is no sense that Cyrus ever permanently liberated them since in Nehemiah the returned exiles claimed

43. While Walter C. Kaiser argues that these passages were originally messianic in their pre-exilic context (*Toward an Old Testament Theology* [Grand Rapids: Zondervan, 1978], 148–49), Gerstenberger a century earlier argued that Ps 2 was originally post-exilic and messianic (*Psalms*, 44–50).

44. Christopher R. North, "The Former Things and the New Things in Deutero-Isaiah," in *Studies in Old Testament Prophecy: Presented to Professor Theodore H. Robinson by the Society for Old Testament Studies on His Sixty-Fifth Birthday, August 9, 1946* (ed. H. H. Rowley; Edinburgh: T. & T. Clark, 1950), 111–26; idem, *The Second Isaiah*, 2–3.

45. Smith, *Isaiah*, 9.

to be slaves under the Persians (Neh 9:36). Cyrus was not a Davidic king who could fulfill the promises to David in 2 Sam 7, he did not serve the God of Israel, and never converted to Judaism. The idea that a Gentile could fulfill the promises to David is rather "shocking." Why then is he is called "anointed"?

Several observations can be made regarding Isa 45:1 and its relationship to the "former things." First, there is no evidence to justify that the original argument about the former and latter things were about messianic promise. Second, the function of the former things reduces Cyrus' role to a proof of true prophecy but does not serve as a messianic proof. Third, the term מְשִׁיחוֹ ("his anointed") implies that Cyrus assumes the role of deliverer (41:2–3, 25–26; 45:1–2; 46:13; 48:20 etc.), which once belonged to the now extinct Davidic kingship. Although God can still be called "king" when Israel has a human king, the meaning of מָשִׁיחַ in Isa 45:1 most likely does not imply that Cyrus is the King of Israel because elsewhere the pre-biblical traditions of Second Isaiah call YHWH Israel's "Creator and King" (43:15; 44:6). Yet Cyrus is called "Messiah!"

For Second Isaiah, Cyrus functions as YHWH's instrument, but more specifically, Isa 45:1 clearly marks a transition in the meaning of the word "Messiah" whereby the use of this term has shifted the significance of מָשִׁיחַ from its earlier pre-exilic reference to one other than a contemporary Davidic king. In the historical context of Cyrus sending the Judeans back to their land, Isa 45:1 has provided the very first use of the term מָשִׁיחַ to describe a salvific deliverer, who exceeds the standard limits of a temporal Davidic king and has formed the earliest transition that influenced how early Judaism would establish its own messianic expectation and understanding of the meaning of מָשִׁיחַ.

II. *Isaiah 45:1 within the Book of Isaiah as a Whole*

While historical criticisms reveal a pre-biblical tradition history around the meaning of מָשִׁיחַ in Isa 45:1, this does not fully answer the question of messianism within the book as a whole. The so-called Second Isaiah material merely constitutes one level of tradition history that predates the scriptural form of the composite book. The book of Isaiah as a whole pushes the meaning of messianism to even greater dimensions whereby clarifying the actual role of the Messiah because the units of tradition take on new force and become rehistoricized within the scriptural scroll of Isaiah.

A. *Efforts to Describe Cyrus and the Former Things in the Book as a Whole*

Since Duhm asserted that Isa 40–55 originally accompanied some extant body of literature other than Isaiah (e.g. Jeremiah), scholars became interested in historical origins rather than the book as a whole.[46] However, during the past twenty-five years, scholars have redirected their inquiry to the book as a whole. Ever since Childs' ground-breaking inquiry in his 1979 *Old Testament Introduction*,[47] much study has focused on the greater book of Isaiah. Few works have either built on or exceeded his original argument concerning the "former things."[48]

Only a few modern scholars argue that the entire book was written by eighth-century Isaiah, Walter C. Kaiser representing this belief, argues that the term *"messiah"* was used by Isaiah for Cyrus in a more general sense as an epithet that did not have Messianic implications.[49] He concludes that only nine references to "Messiah" or "anointed" in the Old Testament (1 Sam 2:10, 35; Pss 2:2; 20:6; 28:8; 84:9; Hab 3:13; Dan 9:25, 26) refer to Messiah while the others refer to anointed kings or priests. Cyrus is "anointed" in the sense that he is designated by God to carry out his will. Although Kaiser claims to read the book of Isaiah as a whole, I would argue that he is actually reading it pre-biblically as an inerrant source of historical reference because he tries to establish eighth-century Isaiah as the author of the whole book long before it had reached its scriptural form. Thus, he cannot interpret Isaiah as a biblical book but only the history to which it refers. His norms for messianism

---

46. D. Bernhard Duhm, *Das Buch Jesaja* (HKAT 3; Göttingen: Vandenhoeck & Ruprecht, 1892).

47. Childs, *Introduction to the Old Testament as Scripture*, 316–17.

48. Edgar Conrad, *Reading the Book of Isaiah* (OBT; Minneapolis: Fortress, 1991); Marvin Sweeney, "On Multiple Settings," in Lovering, ed., *SBL Seminar Papers, 1992*, 267–73; Christopher R. Seitz, "How is the Prophet Isaiah Present in the Latter Half of the Book? The Logic of Chapters 40–66 Within the Book of Isaiah," *JBL* 115, no. 2 (1996): 219–40; idem, *Zion's Final Destiny* (Minneapolis: Fortress, 1991); Ronald E. Clements, "The Prophecies of Isaiah and the Fall of Jerusalem in 587 B.C.," *VT* 30 (1981): 421–36; idem, "Beyond Tradition History," *JSOT* 31 (1985): 95–113; Wegner, *An Examination of Kingship*; Sheppard, "Anti-Assyrian Redaction"; idem, "Book of Isaiah as a Human Witness"; idem, "The Scope of Isaiah"; Rolf Rendtorff, "Zur Komposition des Buches Jesaja," *VT* 34 (1984): 295–320; idem, "Jesaja Jesaja 6 im Rahmen der Komposition des Jesajabuches," in *Le livre d'Isaïe* (ed. Jacques Vermeylen; BETL 81; Leuven: Duculot, 1989), 73–82; idem, *Canon and Theology*; Tull Willey, *Remember the Former Things*; H. G. M. Williamson, *The Book Called Isaiah: Deutero-Isaiah's Role in Composition and Redaction* (Oxford: Clarendon, 1994).

49. Kaiser, *The Messiah in the Old Testament*, 16.

derive from later Christian interpretation, again from a conservative historical perspective that does not account for the end of the monarchy in his definition of messianism.

Other modern historical conservatives argue that Cyrus cannot be a Messiah since he is not a Davidic figure. For example, Edward J. Young proposes that when eighth-century Isaiah wrote chs. 1–66, he probably thought of Cyrus as "a type of Messianic Servant of the Lord."[50] Oswalt T. Allis argues that the prophet's ability to predict guarantees messianism in Isaiah. As Isaiah predicted Cyrus as "a type of the Messiah" who "freed Israel from a grievous bondage which was the penalty and punishment of sin," he predicted Jesus Christ, who is the true Messiah.[51] Yet G. Adam Smith laid the prediction theory to rest over a century ago.

Claiming to interpret the book as a whole, Edgar Conrad claims to use a "synchronic approach," arguing that Isaiah's message was preserved as a testimony for the time to come by creating a relationship "between that past vision of Isaiah in chs. 6–39 and the present setting of the implied community in 40–66" testified in the trial scenes.[52] Within this framework, Cyrus is the "new foreign Messiah on the scene (44:28 and 45:1)" since the Davidic kingship no longer exists.[53] Conrad's major problem is that he professes to be reading scripture synchronically but within this framework he makes historical claims about the tradition history of the book. Hence, the category of "implied reader" would not apply to the first readers of the scroll of Isaiah since they would not see these various levels of interaction within the book that are only self-evident to esoteric-minded readers and not a public who first heard this book read.[54]

In her dissertation, "Remember the Former Things," Patricia Tull Willey has shown convincingly "intertextuality" between "Second-Isaiah" and other biblical books. Yet she argues, as her subtitle suggests, that the "former things" entail Second Isaiah's recollection of "previous texts" of "Israel's past," but never demonstrates the function of the "former things" either within their original setting, redactional framework or the book as a whole.[55] For her, Cyrus does not function as a

---

50. Edward J. Young, *The Book of Isaiah: The English Text with Introduction: Exposition, and Notes.* Vol 3, *Chapters 40 through 66* (NICOT; Grand Rapids: Eerdmans, 1972), 195.

51. Oswalt T. Allis, *The Unity of Isaiah* (Philadelphia: Presbyterian & Reformed Press, 1950), 87–101.

52. Conrad, *Reading the Book of Isaiah*, 135, 140, 141.

53. Ibid., 145. His reason is that "there will be no new Uzziahs, Ahazes, or Hezekiahs."

54. See Sheppard's probing analysis of Conrad in "The Book of Isaiah," 558–61.

55. See Tull Willey, *Remember the Former Things*, 72–74.

Messiah, but "anointed" in Isa 45:1 reflects how such monarchial roles have been distributed among YHWH, Israel, Cyrus and Zion, since Jerusalem has no earthly king.

H. G. M. Williamson cleverly argues that the "former things" refer to Isa 8:23b, representing Deutero-Isaiah's call to reopen the sealed testimony of Isaiah (8:16) and announce the turning aside from judgment to salvation through the agency of Cyrus. [56] Isaiah 13:17 serves as a *post eventum* prophecy of Cyrus depicting his Median connection on his mother's side and earlier conquest when he became king of Media.[57] Assuming that "Deutero-Isaiah" borrows the idea of the former things from "Proto-Isaiah," he anchors the meaning of the older Isaianic traditions in Second Isaiah's redaction and does not consider that a later redactor may have reworked Isa 7–9 to present 8:23–9:6 in light of a deliverer who would shed light on the darkness of exile (see my Chapter 3). For Williamson, Cyrus is not a Messiah but God's "agent of deliverance" and "liberator."[58] Although claiming to treat the "redactional unity" of the greater book, he tries to solve too many problems by an appeal to Second Isaiah's intent and fails to differentiate Second Isaiah from the book's later editors.[59] While he connects Cyrus with the former things and even claims that Third Isaiah plays a role in holding parts of Isaiah together, Williamson fails to treat Cyrus in relation to the former things in Isa 65.

Childs argues from the "canonical context" that the "former things" include Isaiah's prophecies in Isa 1–39 and Second Isaiah "bears testimony to the history of the prophetic word" so that "its meaning does not derive from a referential reading based on events recorded in the sixth century" but "its message turned on the fulfillment of the divine word in history."[60] While modern scholarship has attempted to describe the original setting of the former and latter things, it has disregarded "the basic theological witness by disregarding its new canonical shape."[61] Therefore, Second Isaiah's original circumstances have been editorially dehistoricized in order to hold together the book of Isaiah as a whole. Hence, Childs does not regard Cyrus to be presented as a Messiah because the term should "not be construed according to its later usage as

56. Williamson, *The Book Called Isaiah*, 70–77, 107.
57. Ibid., 158, 172.
58. Ibid., 71, 158.
59. Ibid., 18.
60. Childs attributes this observation to Clements and yet Clements credits this observation to Childs; see Clements, "Beyond Tradition History," 32, 97.
61. Childs, *Introduction*, 329.

the promised eschatological messianic deliverer. Rather the term was used originally in reference to the consecration of Israel's rulers..."[62] While he was the first to explain how the former things function beyond their original historical setting, Childs does not bring together his brilliant observation of the former things in the book as a whole with the "anointed" role of Cyrus in Isa 45:1.

Following Childs' description of the former things and how Second Isaiah has been editorially "dehistoricized" to hold together the book of Isaiah as a whole, Seitz, showing little interest in 13:17 as a "former thing," has tried to develop this evidence by a more detailed appeal to statements in chs. 36–39 (37:35; 39:5–7).[63] Unlike Childs and Seitz, Sheppard and I find the question of how these traditions have been "*re-historicized*" within the scriptural scroll of Isaiah to be more helpful than the description of "de-historicizing" of traditions in chs. 40–66 and a key to understanding messianism within the scriptural scroll of Isaiah.

B. *Rethinking the Evidence*
Part of the problem of Isa 45:1 involves the definition and change of meaning in the word משיח. The discussion about Cyrus presupposes the former things not only in the older modern categories of "First," "Second" and "Third Isaiah," but in the evolution of the whole scriptural scroll where the shift in the meaning of the former things will also reflect the changing meaning of the word משיח. Since at least some of the former things are found in Isa 1–39 (8:23; 36–39) and reiterated in "Third Isaiah" (65:16b–17), this alters the presentation of Cyrus. If the argument around the former and latter things has been extended to the book as a whole, then the interpretation of Cyrus as YHWH's anointed must also extend to these dimensions. At this level, Cyrus and the former things conform to a new dimension, where they have been rehistoricized within the book of Isaiah and the discussion about Cyrus and messianism must account for this formation.

Along these lines, the former things appearing in Isa 1–39 relate to the question of messianism, where Isa 8:23 seems to contrast the "former" events (הראשון), which occurred when Tiglath-pileser annexed "Zebulun" and "Naphthali," with the latter things (האהרון) when the territory would be restored to Israel. While Williamson has argued that Second Isaiah borrows from this passage, I will argue (in my Chapter 3) that a later editor has inserted these expressions, which proves to be significant in

62. See Childs' latest commentary on *Isaiah* (OTL; Louisville, Ky.: Westminster John Knox, 2001), 353.
63. Seitz, *Zion's Final Destiny*, 37–46.

the relationship between "Second" and "Third Isaiah" (41:22; 42:9; 43:9, 18; 46:9; 48:3; 65:16, 17), in establishing a bridge between the language of exile in 8:21–22 and the promise of a Davidic deliverer in 9:1–6. Within the framework of the book of Isaiah (whether or not Williamson is correct), this construction pushes the former and latter things to be understood according to the motif of light cast upon the "darkness" of the exile (8:22; 9:1; 60:1; 63:9; 65:16). Now the former and latter things in the context of Isa 1–39 alter a royal enthronement hymn (9:1–6) that may originally have spoken about Josiah or Hezekiah to be reinterpreted messianically.

Furthermore, just as YHWH has "stirred up" (עורׄ√) Cyrus against Babylon in Second Isaiah (41:2, 25; 45:13), the same terminology in Isa 13:17 shows that YHWH is "stirring up the Medes" against Babylon also placing the former things in Isa 1–39.[64] This is important because it moves the discussion about Cyrus to the book as a whole. Yet the idea of "stirring up" one from the east/north is never found within a traditional messianic context. From this perspective, the one "stirring up" from the east/north does not seem to be a Davidic Messiah but an agent in the hand of God, any more than Assyria had been used earlier by God to bring judgment to northern Israel. Since the former things in Isa 8:23 alter a royal enthronement hymn to be reinterpreted messianically and are fulfilled in the person of Cyrus (13:17; 41:2, 25; 45:13), does this strengthen the case that Second Isaiah considered Cyrus as the Messiah mentioned in 9:1–6? Perhaps! But if the Second Isaiah traditions originally did employ the former things messianically in relation to Cyrus, they no longer do so in the book as a whole.

Within the scriptural scroll of Isaiah, the rhetoric around the "former things" no longer centers on the pre-biblical contest of prophet against prophet during the time of Second Isaiah within a setting of ancient Near Eastern power politics, but now serves as a confirmation of God's word within scripture itself. Isaiah 40, serving as an introduction to the material that follows, invites the reader to keep in mind that "YHWH's word endures forever" (v. 8) and that "the mouth of the LORD has spoken" (v. 5). Isaiah 40:21 reminds us that this prophetic legacy goes back to the beginning when the foundations of the earth are laid. YHWH himself "establishes the word of his servant, and fulfills the prediction of his messengers," YHWH himself "says of Jerusalem, 'It shall be inhabited,' and of the cities of Judah, 'They shall be rebuilt, and I will raise up their ruins.'" The word that comes out of YHWH's mouth "shall not return

---

64. See Childs, *Introduction*, 330; Note also that YHWH "stirred up the enemies" of Ephraim and the inhabitants of Samaria in 9:11.

empty" (45:23; 55:11). Finally, the reader is summoned to hearken to this word (66:5).

Therefore, the trial speeches (41:1–5, 21–29; 43:8–13; 44:6–8; 45:18–25), which may have involved an original conflict of prophet against prophet, are not so evident because no prophet appears overtly in the foreground. The original conflict now remains esoteric in the prehistory of scriptural context, so that modern scholars must read between the lines to find it and can speculate on that basis about the pre-biblical interpretation of Cyrus. In fact, Cyrus himself plays a minor role within the latter formation of the book of Isaiah and never again appears after ch. 48. Cyrus, who is called the most shocking term in Isa 45:1, disappears from the context of scriptural scroll of Isaiah after Isa 48. What, then, is the scriptural function of calling Cyrus משיח when he, like every other Israelite king, dies and cannot fulfill the promises to David in 2 Sam 7?

The "former things," appearing in the so-called Third Isaiah corpus (65:16, 17), have now pushed these references to another level.[65] In Isa 46:9, the prophet reminds his reader to "remember the former things" in order to prove the reliability of God's word. Nevertheless, in 65:17 we find the Niphal verbal phrase, תזכרנה הראשנות ("the former things shall not be remembered"). In 65:18–25, past fulfillments including the work done by Cyrus are passé, because we are encouraged now to think only about the new thing that God will do by ushering in the messianic era. Isaiah 65:25 makes this situation clear by taking up the portrayal of a Davidic Messiah by citing Isa 11, thus indicating a messianic hope which finds no fulfillment in the earlier role of Cyrus. Though functioning like a temporal king in the pre-exilic era by fulfilling a specific "anointed" task of deliverer, because of his mere death but all the more by sheer lineage, Cyrus in the face of the terminated monarchy cannot fulfill the promises to David: "I will raise up your seed after you, who shall come forth from your loins, and I will establish his kingdom… I will establish the throne of his kingdom forever" (2 Sam 7:12–13); and "…your throne shall be established forever" (2 Sam 7:15–16). So, then, what role does Cyrus play in Isa 45:1 as it relates to the book as a whole?

The book of Isaiah does not present Cyrus as a Messiah since the expectations for a future ruler in the first part of the book (esp. chs. 9–11) presuppose characteristics about which Isa 45:1 says nothing. The post-exilic community can forget the former things (65:17) because they have been fulfilled in Cyrus' by releasing the people from exile and rebuilding their temple, but one must not forget the messianic prophecy in its eschatological dimensions (11:6; 65:25). These new things, which speak

65. See Chapter 4 of this monograph.

of a period after the Babylonian captivity and appearance of Cyrus, supersede those former events around the captivity. Cyrus then functions in a manner similar to Pekah and Rezin, "the two smoldering stumps of firebrands" (7:4, 16); each unwittingly (45:4) confirms the prophet's ability to fulfill God's word. In light of the eradicated monarchy, no longer can the term "Messiah" speak of a temporal Israelite king and so Cyrus fulfills a temporary role as YHWH's anointed by responding to the crises that there would never again be an earthly king who would fulfill that role. But he cannot "forever" fulfill the promises to David. Therefore, the community of faith can forget the former things that announce the appearance of Cyrus but not the messianic concept that belongs to the end of time.

Even if Laato, Hanson, Pomykala and Becker are correct in speculating that Second Isaiah viewed Cyrus as a Messiah, then we must ask how the later formation of the book changes the portrait of him laid out in the pre-history of the book. Clearly, Cyrus does not conform to the portrait of a Messiah depicted in the book of Isaiah as a whole, nor in the greater framework of scripture and early Judaism. First, he does not offer a solution in a supernatural way to activate and restore within this world the promises made to David after the monarchy has ended. He is not a Davidic figure, as described in Isa 7, 9, 11; 65:25 and in 2 Sam 7. Second, beyond our definition of messianism, Cyrus is not assigned the moral attributes of the Messiah (i.e. righteousness, justice etc.) but righteousness stems from YHWH's divine acts of raising him up.[66] Third, Cyrus is never called to a relationship of covenant loyalty to God.[67] Finally, there is no indication in scripture that he became a Jew or even a "God-fearer" within the socio-religious tradition.[68] While these are beyond the definition listed in the Introduction, they do apply to Cyrus in relation to messianism.

Cyrus was chosen for a specific service and his election had no meaning outside his becoming God's instrument, as did the Assyrian of Isa 10. Cyrus carries out YHWH's purpose by rebuilding Jerusalem and

66. On this point, see Joachim Begrich, *Studien zu Deuterojesaja* (BWANT 77; Stuttgart: W. Kohlhammer, 1938), 128–30.

67. Cf. H. H. Rowley, *The Biblical Doctrine of Election* (London: Lutterworth, 1950), 137.

68. See G. Ogden's remarks on this score in his "Cyrus Song [Isaiah 44:24–45:13] and Moses: Some Implications for Mission," *South East Asia Journal of Theology* 18, no. 2 (1977): 43–44. Also note Mary Boyce's argument that since Achaemenide agents influence Zoroastrianism, Cyrus must have been a Zoroastrian; see Boyce, *A History of Zoroastrianism* (Handbuch der Orientalistik 2; Leiden: Brill, 1982), 45.

its temple (44:28; 45:13). YHWH has taken his right hand (הַחֱזַקְתִּי בִימִינוֹ) so that he will defeat the enemy, Babylon (41:2, 25; 45:1–7), and the nations will know that there is no other god besides YHWH (45:6). The difference between Cyrus and the Assyrian is that one destroyed and the other restored. However, Cyrus functions as YHWH's unwitting agent, as did the Assyrians and later Babylonians, because he does not know YHWH (44:5).

Another problem centers on the role of Cyrus vis à vis the Servant. Supposing that one could argue that the Servant in some case functions as the Messiah, then Cyrus is not a candidate since he is not called God's servant because God calls him for the sake of the Servant who in this context is Israel (45:4). Therefore, Cyrus is distinguished from the Servant and could not perform any messianic role that might be assigned to the Servant. So, at least within an early Christian definition of the Servant as the Messiah (Matt 8:17; Luke 22:47; John 12:38–41; Acts 8:32–33; Rom 15:21; 1 Pet 2:22), Cyrus would be ruled out from this office. The fact that Cyrus is never mentioned again after Isa 48 and that the Servant texts usually cited by Christians as messianic occur most often after ch. 49 (namely 52:13–53:12), would exclude him from the office at least within the framework of early Christian interpretation.

C. *Cyrus' Role within Other Biblical Scrolls as Compared with the Scroll of Isaiah*

Childs is correct that, within the book as a whole, the former things include Isa 1–39, but he does not consider how the description of Cyrus and the logic of the "former things" extend beyond the book of Isaiah to other biblical books. Isaiah 40 reframes the original conflict of prophet against prophet to be heard within the broader context of scripture, whereby the prophetic word comes from the beginning (40:21). Even the former things now come from creation (41:4, 8; 44:24–28) and may explicitly have the Mosaic Torah and Genesis in mind. Israel is called to look back to its beginning, even to Abraham the first prophet, to Sarah (51:1–2) to Noah (54:9) and of course to Moses (63:11, 12). Moreover, two times we hear the words repeated, לֹא בַסֵּתֶר דִּבַּרְתִּי ("I did not speak in secret," 45:19; 48:16), the second of which tells us that YHWH's revelation has not been concealed "from the beginning" (מֵרֹאשׁ). This phrase is probably related to the oral reading of the Torah or YHWH's revelation through the prophets and reminiscent with the Torah's own definition of revelation: "the secret things (הַנִּסְתָּרֹת) belong to YHWH our God, but the revealed things belong to us and to our children forever, to observe all the words of this Torah" (Deut 29:29). Even the repetition of

the expression "you are my witnesses" (43:10, 12) is only found elsewhere at Josh 24, during the covenant renewal, where the people are
called to witness the conditions of the Torah. The former things within
the book of Isaiah preclude the Torah traditions (42:4, 24). Cyrus once
served as proof of the former things but within the scripture scroll of
Isaiah these things now serve as a confirmation of God's word (40:8) and
more precisely the Mosaic Torah (1:10; 42:21; 43). What does this have
to do with messianism?

Within the scroll of Isaiah, now the former things clarify the post-
exilic sense of messianism (65:17–25) and rehistoricize Cyrus's role by
de-messianizing him in order to re-express the hope of an eschatological
Davidic king who will usher in the messianic era. Since Second Isaiah
merely constitutes one level of tradition history that predates the scriptural form of the composite book of Isaiah, later editing now moves the
discussion around YHWH's anointed to an even greater dimension, where
clarifying the actual role of Cyrus in relation to the function of the
former things in the post-exilic age. Therefore, interpretation of Isa 45:1
must extend to the dimensions of the scriptural scroll of Isaiah as a whole
and not the prophet that we can reconstruct behind the book.

Because the discussion about Cyrus presupposes these former things,
which are also found in Isa 1–39 (8:23; 13:17; 36–39) and reiterated in
some traditions of so-called Third Isaiah (65:17), this alters how Cyrus is
presented within the scroll of Isaiah as a whole and beyond. Not only
does Cyrus serve as proof of Isaianic prophecy, but Cyrus' prophetic
fulfillment presupposes a greater prophetic legacy. Isaiah even shares
texts with Micah (Isa 2:1–5; Mic 4:1–5) and Kings (Isa 36–39; 2 Kgs
18–20), and YHWH also "stirs up" Cyrus in other biblical books (2 Chr
36:22–23 = Ezra 1:1–2):

> In the first year of King Cyrus of Persia, in order that the word of the
> LORD by the mouth of Jeremiah might be accomplished, YHWH stirred up
> (הֵעִיר) the spirit of King Cyrus of Persia so that he sent a herald
> throughout all his kingdom, and also in a written edict declared: "Thus
> says King Cyrus of Persia: The LORD, the God of heaven, has given me
> all the kingdoms of the earth, and he has charged me to build him a house
> at Jerusalem in Judah."

Although the Isaianic portrait of the Persian paints a picture different
from Ezra and Chronicles, in each text Cyrus stands as proof for the
divine word. While in Isaiah, Cyrus confirms the prophecies of Isaiah,
both Ezra and Chronicles locate this divine word in the prophecies of
Jeremiah, which in scripture belong to the same prophetic legacy.

One cannot talk about the Cyrus apart from the inner-witness of biblical books that demonstrate such signs of intertextuality. Isaiah, Jeremiah and Moses all belong to the same scriptural prophets of Israel. The final editors of the book of Isaiah, probably working within the shadow of the editors of Torah, shift the original locus of the former things not only to the isolated prophecies of Isaiah but to the Mosaic Torah and the legacy of the prophets where Cyrus proves the reliability of God's word but does not meet early Judaism's messianic expectation. Not only has the inter-testimony of biblical books re-historicized Cyrus's role within scripture, but the post-exilic scroll of Isaiah has de-messianized the earlier exilic reference to him in Isa 45:1 that names him as "his messiah" or "his anointed" (מְשִׁיחוֹ).

Conclusion

Although the word "Messiah" is not used in Isa 65:17–25, the citation from Isa 11, which early Judaism interpreted messianically, implicitly redefines and reinterprets the concept of messianism as a response to the only Isaianic passage that uses the term מָשִׁיחַ (Isa 45:1). While royal oracles were sometimes reinterpreted as messianic (8:23b–9:6; 11:1–9), the one that uses the term מָשִׁיחַ to describe Cyrus within the scriptural scroll of Isaiah has been de-messianized. If Second Isaiah did describe Cyrus messianically, the book of Isaiah has reinterpreted this pre-biblical messianic tradition as non-messianic. Therefore, just as later editors may reinterpret non-messianic texts messianically, they could just as well reinterpreted messianic texts as non-messianic, showing that this shift can move in both directions as a result of the changing meaning of "Messiah."

We also see instances in royal enthronement oracles, such as Ps 2, where the meaning of מָשִׁיחַ must change in the post-exilic era to accommodate for the promises made to David when a king no longer sat on the throne. On these grounds, the "Messiah" is not the next king fulfilling a temporal role, nor Cyrus, but one who takes on an eschatological function and in a superhuman way fulfills the promises given to David after the monarchy has ended.

Therefore, whether or not Cyrus originally fit a messianic role in the pre-biblical history, he does not fulfill the messianic description within the book of Isaiah (chs. 7–11) and within the greater corpus of scripture or later Judaism. An Achemenide king cannot fulfill the expectation of the Davidic deliverer, as we are reminded in 65:25. Just as we are called to forget the "former things" (43:18; 65:17), prophecies of which Cyrus unwittingly fulfils, this Persian ruler disappears from the drama of Isaiah after Isa 48 and is eclipsed by a more precise description of the messianic age (Isa 65:25 cites 11:6). Within the book as a whole, Cyrus serves merely as an instrument of YHWH in a manner similar to the Assyrians and the Babylonians, but not as a Messiah. Theoretically, at the level of Second Isaiah, it is possible that Cyrus was called "Messiah" to compensate for an empty throne but that the formation of the book has nullified this pre-biblical messianic expectation. Later editing provides evidence that the origins of post-exilic messianism may very well have begun within the formation of the scriptural scroll of Isaiah itself, initially by calling a non-Davidic king "Messiah," and subsequently de-messianizing him to present a new definition that looks beyond the temporal and assumes an eschatological expectation.

Chapter 3

MESSIANIC INTERPRETATION
IN ISAIAH 7:14; 9:1–6 AND 11:1–9

Introduction

Within the history of pre-modern biblical interpretation, Jewish scholars have always been divided regarding whether or not to interpret Isa 7:14; 9:1–6 and 11:1–9 messianically, while Christians almost consistently have interpreted these texts messianically. Since the modern era, Christian scholars have debated over whether these texts should be interpreted as messianic. Much of this controversy centers on the problem of locating messianic hope within pre-exilic Isaianic traditions. As indicated in my introductory chapter, I will work within a dominant modern definition of messianism, one which suggests that this hope arose during the post-exilic period.[1] Therefore, one cannot regard a pre-exilic, ideal kingship as messianic since our definition requires an eschatological event that takes place after the end of the Davidic monarchy. So, even if a scholar describes a tradition as messianic, it may fail to meet these significant criteria.

This chapter will initially examine how scholars have tried to describe the original "pre-biblical" function of Isa 7:14; 9:1–6 and 11:1–9 and then will re-evaluate their place within the scroll of Isaiah. Pre-biblical traditions for these verses would include their role in either the original

---

1. See Mowinckel, *He That Cometh*, 3–4, 20; P. Grelot, "Le Messie dans les Apocryphes de l'Ancien Testament.état de la question," in *La venue du Messie. Messianisme et eschatologie* (ed. E. Massaux; Rech. Bib. 6; Bruges: Desclée de Brouwer, 1962), 46–47; Becker, *Messianic Expectation*; J. C. L. Coppens, *Le messianisme royal: Ses origines son développement son accomplissement* (LD 54; Paris: Cerf, 1968), 33–34, 119–25; U. Kellermann, *Messias und Gesetz. Grundlinien einer altestamentlichen Heilserwartung: Eine traditionsgeschichtliche Einführung* (BibS[N] 61; Neukirchen–Vluyn: Neukirchener, 1971), 91–106; S. Talmon, "Typen der Messiaserwartung um die Zeitenwende," in *Problem biblischer Theologie. Gerhard von Rad zum 70. Geburtstag* (ed. H.W. Wolff; Munich: Kaiser, 1971), 571–88.

collection of Isaianic oracles or earlier redactional levels such as the (anti-Assyrian) Josianic redaction (hereafter AR [the conventional abbreviation for Assyrian Redaction]). On the other hand, the book as scripture describes the completed text of Isaiah in the post-exilic period, when the later editors are conscious of the Torah which is evident in the introduction (1:7). This becomes relevant to messianic interpretation in ch. 9, where the text exhibits a shift from prophetic teaching to Mosaic Torah and from non-messianic to messianic. This chapter makes no attempts to resolve all the redactional issues of Isa 7–11 but aims to show that pieces that belonged to one historical level of tradition have been rehistoricized within the scriptural form of Isaiah.

In my third section, "Rethinking the Evidence," I will discuss problems raised by theories of multiple redactions and will show how the pre-biblical traditions of Isa 7:14 and 9:1–6 function differently in scripture. I will also examine the relationship between Isa 9:1–6 and the "Former Things" in Isa 40–66, especially since we have already shown how Cyrus has been de-messianized in light of the former things to redefine messianic hope in the post-exilic era. Finally, I will consider the placement of Isa 11:1–9 within the context of scripture. I will treat Isa 7:14; 9:1–6 and 11:1–9 together in one chapter because the later editors have set up these verses to be read together (e.g. Isa 8:8, 10 reinterprets the name Emmanuel, thus linking Isa 7 with Isa 8 and 9:1–6). If one reads Isa 7:14; 9:1–6 and 11:1–9 in isolation of each other, one has not heard their scriptural form. While, in theory, I want to interpret these texts together, I must treat them independently, because that is what scholars have already done. I will then redescribe how they are related together at the end of this chapter.

I. *Isaiah 7:14; 9:1–6 and 11:1–9 as Pre-biblical Traditions*

A. *Non-messianic Assessments*
There are no perspectives that interpret the pre-biblical traditions of Isa 11:1–9 as non-messianic without also regarding 7:14 and 9:1–6 as non-messianic, but several scholars regard the pre-biblical traditions of Isa 7:14 and 9:1–6 as non-messianic apart from 11:1–9.

1. *Perspectives that interpret the pre-biblical traditions of Isaiah 7:14 as non-messianic.* Martin Buber calls Isa 7:14 the "most controversial passage in the Bible" probably because of difficulty in determining both the original meaning and messianic interpretation of the passage.[2] For

---

2.   M. Buber, *Der Glaube der Propheten* (Zurich: Manesse, 1950), 201.

example, Aage Bentzen argues that the formula that Isaiah employs in 7:14 is non-messianic and originally derives from fertility rites of the royal Canaanite cults.[3] H. Wheeler Robinson maintains that Isa 7:14 was probably not originally messianic but depicts a normal birth which would later "acquire prophetic meaning."[4] Likewise, Robert H. Pfeiffer suggests that Isa 7:14 is not messianic but that Gentile Christians used the Greek Bible as a "weapon" against the Jews, claiming "the virgin birth of Jesus through the incorrect Greek rendering of Is. 7:14."[5]

Similarly, Mowinckel thinks that through "traditio-historical and literary criticism...we discover whether there was any conception of a Messiah in the pre-exilic age."[6] Isaiah related "a well known popular belief of the time, about a supernatural woman who would bear a son whose birth would be an omen of happy transformation" to the Davidic dynasty endangered by the Syro-Ephraimite coalition:[7]

> The prophet does not here predict a Messiah, but a prince who realizes the idea of the king as the connecting link between God and the people... To this extent there is a measure of truth in the old Jewish interpretation of the Immanuel prophecy as a promise of the birth of King Hezekiah. He is the prince for whose birth everyone is waiting, and who, according to custom, will be greeted with shouts of exultation as rapturous as those with which, in the Ugaritic poem, King Dan'il receives the news of the birth of his son; he will be hailed with the cultic shout, "With us is God," and receive the honorable name Immanuel.[8]

Yet, Emmanuel did not come to Judah since Ahaz disregarded God's prerequisite, but later Jewish-Christian interpreters understood Isa 7:14 as the messianic hope, which "was truly fulfilled only in Jesus."[9]

Most scholars, who focus strictly on the original historical context, contest any messianic interpretation of Isa 7:14 because its referent in v. 16 was originally set within the circumstances of the Syro-Ephraimite War.[10] I. W. Slotki rules out "Christological interpretation" because the

---

3. Auge Bentzen, *Jesaja* (Copenhagen: G. E. C. Gads, 1943), 62.

4. H. Wheeler Robinson, *Inspiration and Revelation in the Old Testament* (Oxford: Clarendon, 1946), 35, 171.

5. Robert H. Pfeiffer, *Introduction to the Old Testament* (New York: Harper & Brothers, 1948), 75, 437.

6. Mowinckel, *He That Cometh*, 15.

7. Ibid., 109–13.

8. Ibid., 118.

9. Ibid., 119.

10. This has been a common interpretation as far back as D. Bernhard Duhm, *Das Buch Jesaja* (4th ed.; Göttingen Handkommentar Zum Alten Testament; Göttingen: Vandenhoeck & Ruprecht 1922), 70.

birth of the child functions as a sign to convince Ahaz of fulfilled prophecy in his own time of a young woman and child who cannot be identical with persons who lived 700 years later.[11] A. S. Herbert disclaims Isa 7:14 as messianic since 7:10–17 portrays the young woman as Ahaz's contemporary.[12] Similarly, William Holladay asserts that "Isa 7:1–17 is not that of the birth of a Messiah but the reassurance of a weak young king in the eighth century B.C.E. who was threatened by an invasion led by two kings from the north." Isaiah 7:14–17 refers to either Hezekiah or Isaiah's Son during the Syro-Ephraimite War and Matthew relies on the LXX.[13]

Most scholars believe that עלמה refers only to an anonymous young woman and her child during the time of Isaiah and Ahaz.[14] Others speculate that עלמה refers to Ahaz's wife and that her child is his son Hezekiah, the future king who would be obedient to YHWH.[15] Others

11. I. W. Slotki, *Isaiah: Hebrew Text and Hebrew Translation with an Introduction and Commentary* (4th ed.; Soncino Books of the Bible; London: Soncino, 1961), 35.

12. Arthur S. Herbert, *The Book of the Prophet Isaiah 1–39* (CBC; Cambridge: Cambridge University Press, 1973), 64.

13. Holladay, *Isaiah*, 73.

14. J. G. Eichhorn, *Die hebräischen Propheten* (3 vols.; Göttingen: Vandenhoek & Ruprecht, 1816–19), 1:176–77; Abraham Kuenen, *The Prophets and Prophecy in Israel: An Historical and Critical Enquiry* (trans. A. Milroy; London: Longmans, Green & Co., 1877); Duhm, *Jesaja*, 75; George B. Gray, *A Critical and Exegetical Commentary on the Book of Isaiah I–XXVII* (ICC 10a; repr., Edinburgh: T. & T. Clark, 1956), 124; Karl Budde, *Jesaja's Erleben. Eine Gemeinverstandliche Auslegung der Denkschrift Des Propheten (Kap 6:1–9:6)* (Gotha: L. Klotz, 1928), 22–54; W. C. Graham, "Isaiah's Part in the Syro-Ephraimitic Crisis," *AJSL* 50 (1933/34): 207; Ludwig Köhler, "Zum Verstandnis von Jes 7,14," *ZAW* 67 (1955): 48–50; Georg Fohrer, "Zu Jes 7,14 im Zusammenhang von Jes 7,10–22," *ZAW* 68 (1956): 54–56; idem, *Das Buch Jesaja* (3 vols.; Zurcher Bibelkommentare; Zurich: Zwingli, 1966), 1:114; W. McKane, "The Interpretation of Isaiah VII,14–25," *VT* 17 (1967): 213–15; Michael E. W. Thompson, "Isaiah's Sign of Immanuel [Isa 7:10–17]," *ExpTim* 95, no. D (1983): 70–71.

15. Hans-Joachim Kraus, *Die Königsherrschaft Gottes im Alten Testament. Untersuchungen zu den Lieden von Jahwes Thronbesteigung* (BHT 13; Tübingen: J. C. B. Mohr [Paul Siebeck], 1951), 97; W. Vischer, *Die Immanuel-Botschaft im Rahmen des königlichen Zionsfestes* (ThSt 45; Zurich: Zollikon, 1955). Christopher R. Seitz, *Isaiah 1–39* (Interpretation 31/1; Louisville, Ky.: John Knox, 1993); H. Junker, "Ursprung und Grundzüge des Messiasbildes bei Isajas," in *Congress Volume: Strasbourg, 1956* (VTSup 4; Leiden: Brill, 1957), 181–96; Erling Hammershaimb, *Some Aspects of Old Testament Prophecy from Isaiah to Malachi* (Teologiske Skrifter 4; Copenhagen: Rosenkilde og Bagger, 1966), 19–23; Mowinckel, *He That Cometh*, 110–19; John J. Scullion, "Approach to the Understanding of Isaiah 7:10–17," *JBL* 87 (1968): 288–300; Hans Wildberger, *Isaiah 1–12: A Commentary* (trans. Thomas H. Trapp; Continental Commentaries; Minneapolis:

suggest that the young woman is merely one of the "the *'almôth* of the kings harem."[16] Gleason Archer contends that עלמה implies "virgin," designating Isaiah's fiancée soon to marry him.[17] Still others propose that the term alludes to the prophet's wife and Emmanuel is one of Isaiah's sons.[18] These positions rule out any original messianic significance of Isa 7:14.[19]

Fortress, 1991), 291–94. The general disagreement of this theory rests on evidence that Hezekiah was already born at the time that this oracle was given.

16. Franz Delitzsch, *Biblical Commentary on the Prophecies of Isaiah* (trans. James Martin; 3d ed.; 2 vols.; Edinburgh: T. & T. Clark, 1875), 1:17.

17. Gleason Archer, "Isaiah," in *The Wycliffe Bible Commentary* (ed. Charles Pfeiffer and Everett Harrison; Chicago: Moody, 1962), 618; idem, *Encyclopedia of Bible Difficulties* (Grand Rapids: Zondervan, 1982), 267–68.

18. Hölscher even thought that the definite article in the word העלמה refers to a definite woman who would most likely be Isaiah's own wife and that Emmanuel was born between Isaiah's other two sons Shear-Jashub and Maher-Shalal-Hash-baz. Cf. Gustaf Hölscher, "Des Buch der Könige, Seine Quellen und Seine Redaktion," in *Eucharistérion: Studien zur Religion und Literatur Des Alten und Neuen Testaments: Hermann Gunkel zum 60. Geburtstage dem 23. Mai* (ed. H. Schmidt; FRLANT 36; Göttingen: Vandenhoeck & Ruprecht, 1923), 106, 110; idem, *Die Profeten. Untersuchungen zur Religionsgeschichte Israels* (Leipzig: J. C. Hinrichs, 1914), 229. See also J. Meinhold, *Studien zur israelitischen Religionsgeschichte*. Vol. 1, *Der heilige Rest*. Part 1, *Elias Amos Hosea Jesaja* (Bonn: A. Marcus E. Weber, 1903), 116–18; H. Donner, *Israel unter den Völkern. Die Stellung der Klassischen Propheten des 8. Jahrhunderts v. Chr. Zur Aussenpolitik der Könige von Israel und Juda* (VTSup 11; Leiden: Brill, 1964), 1–193. Cheyne contests, "…how can Isaiah have called his wife by a name so liable to be misunderstood as *'almah*, especially as in the very next chapter he gives her what was probably her recognized title, 'the prophetess' (vii. 3)." See T. K. Cheyne *The Prophecies of Isaiah: A New Translation with Commentary and Appendices* (5th ed.; 2 vols.; London: Kegan, Paul, Trench & Co., 1889), 1:47.

19. In the same manner, several scholars have contended that Isa 9:1(2)–6(7) originally comprised a royal enthronement oracle to a Judean king; see M. B. Crook, "A Suggested Occasion for Isaiah 9:2–7 and 11:1–9," *JBL* 48 (1949): 213–24; J. Lindblom, *A Study on the Immanuel Section in Isaiah, Isa Vii:1–Ix:6* (Scripta Minora Regiae Societatis Humaniorum Litterarum Lundensis 4; Lund: C. W. K. Gleerup, 1957–58), 33–41; S. Herrmann, *Die Prophetischen Heilserwartungen im Allen Testament. Ursprung und Gestaltwandel* (BWANT 5; Stuttgart: Kohlhammer, 1965), 132–33; Gerhard von Rad, "The Royal Ritual in Judah," in *The Problem of the Hexateuch and Other Essays* (trans. E. W. Trueman Dicken; London: Oliver & Boyd, 1966), 222–31; P. Auvray, *Isaïe 1–39* (ed. J. Gabalda et al.; Sources Bibliques; Paris Library Lecoffre, 1972), 125; Walter Zimmerli, *Old Testament Theology in Outline* (trans. D. E. Green; Edinburgh: T. & T. Clark, 1978), 195; Becker, *Messianic Expectation*, 45; Ronald E. Clements, *Isaiah 1–39* (NCBC; Grand Rapids: Eerdmans, 1982), 104; Koch, *Prophets*, 1:133; John Hayes and Stuart A. Irvine, *Isaiah, the Eighth-Century Prophet* (Nashville: Abingdon, 1987), 180–82.

Obviously, if these efforts to describe the original historical settings are correct, then no messianic interpretation seems to pertain to Isa 7:14. Yet, even approaches that depend more on semiotic than strictly historical perspectives can interpret Isa 7:14 non-messianically. For example, Lars Rignell argues that the young woman symbolizes Israel and Emmanuel is Shear-Jashub who signifies the remnant as a symbol that will find future fulfilment of the new Israel but not the Messiah.[20] Similarly, H. Kruse interprets Emmanuel as the remnant who will enjoy future circumstances of paradise (7:15, 22) but, in contrast to Rignell, regards the woman as Zion rather than Israel.[21] These approaches interpret this passage symbolically and non-messianically.

2. Perspectives that interpret the pre-biblical traditions of Isaiah 9:1–6 (NRSV, 9:2–7) as non-messianic. Several scholars regard Isa 9:1–6 to be originally a pre-biblical royal accession oracle for a Judean king. Albrecht Alt, who influences several others on this point,[22] suggests that "the expectation of the Messiah has its origin in this complex of ideas" but the figure in 9:1–6[7] is not in "any sense the bringer of the longed-for time of salvation, independently of Yahweh. He is only a gift of Yahweh to that time…"[23] Lindblom asserts that Isaiah anticipates Hezekiah to usher in the new age but Isa 9:1–6 is not messianic because "the Messiah…is alien to Isaiah, as to all the prophets of the eighth century."[24] More recently, Christopher Seitz argues that Isa 9:1–7 speaks of the "defeat of the Syro-Ephraimite coalition with the accession of Hezekiah," which provides "concrete fulfilment of Emmanuel."[25]

Mowinckel, using traditio-historical methodology to study messianism, which he regards eschatological in nature, maintains that Isa 9:1–6

20. Lars G. Rignell, "Isaiah Chapter I," *ST* 11 (1957): 113, 117.

21. H. Kruse, "Alma Redemptoris Mater: Eine Auslegung der Immanuel Weissagung Is 7:14," *TTZ* 74 (1965): 27–28.

22. Crook, "A Suggested Occasion"; von Rad, "Royal Ritual"; Auvray, *Isaïe 1–39*; Herbert, *The Book of the Prophet Isaiah 1–39*, 75; Zimmerli, *Old Testament Theology in Outline*, 195; Becker, *Messianic Expectation*, 45; Hayes and Irvine, *Isaiah*, 180–82.

23. Albrecht Alt, "Jesaja 8,23–9,6. Befreiungsnacht und Krönungstag," in *Festschrift A Berthelet zum 80. Geburtstag* (ed. W. Baumgartner; Tübingen: J. C. B. Mohr, 1953), 29–49; idem, *Essays on Old Testament History and Religion* (ed. David E. Orton; trans. R. A. Wilson; The Biblical Seminar 9; Sheffield: JSOT Press, 1989), 235, 258–59.

24. Lindblom, *Isa Vii:1–Ix:6*, 33–41; idem, *Prophecy in Ancient Israel* (Oxford: Blackwell, 1962), 369.

25. Seitz, *Isaiah 1–39*, 85.

and 11:1–9 "come as near as possible to being 'Messianic expectation'"
but "did not exist as a hope until restoration was to be accomplished."[26] If
we read Isa 9:1–6 without our preconceived Christian understanding, it
describes an event that has already occurred. Divine titles and metaphor
of light and darkness speak of the birth of the sun god and describe an
ideal royal child's birth that only much later would produce a messianic
hope.[27] If Isa 11:1–9 is Isaianic, then we are dealing with "the prepara-
tory ideological background of the Messianic faith…[and]…the passage
presupposes the fall of the monarchy."[28]

Therefore, Isa 9:1–6 and 11:1–9 are pre-messianic passages that warrant messianic interpretation only through a shift in the ideology of the
people but not within scripture.

Slotki denounces "Christological interpretation by the Church" because
non-Jewish exegetes interpret the royal figure in Isa 9:5 (Heb.) to be a
"contemporary" person whom the Talmud and later Jewish commentators understood to reference Hezekiah. The phrase לסרבה המשרה in 9:6
(NRSV, 9:7) speaks of Ephraim passing over to King Hezekiah, the first
ruler since the division of the Northern and Southern Kingdoms to
combine the entire nation as in the days of David and Solomon.[29]

3. *Perspectives that interpret all three pre-biblical traditions as non-
messianic.* Some scholars perceive an ideological shift in Isa 7:14; 9:1–6
and 11:1–5, one which builds upon an expectation of an ideal ruler that
evolves as messianic hope develops. For example, R. B. Y. Scott views
Isa 7:14; 9:1–6 and 11:1–5 as messianic only within a limited modern
definition of the terminology. He discerns "later 'messianic interpretation'" of Isa 7:14 to rest only on the conviction that the messianic hope
had been fulfilled in the virgin birth of Jesus, which "is based on an
inaccurate translation of the Hebrew text." This "prediction of miraculous birth of a Messiah more than seven centuries later could hardly have
served as a sign to Ahaz." The king is "messianic" only because "every
monarch of the Davidic dynasty was then an anointed representative of
Yahweh, and a sacred, even semi-divine, person." Isaiah 9:1–6 is "a
dynastic oracle uttered on the occasion of the anointed of a new king, or
at the anniversary celebration of this event."[30] Isaiah 11:1–9 serves as its
companion piece where "the king is 'messianic'" because he is a new

26. Mowinckel, *He That Cometh*, 155.
27. Ibid., 102–10.
28. Ibid., 16.
29. Slotki, *Isaiah*, 44, 45.
30. On this point he follows the argument of Crook, "A Suggested Occasion."

monarch in the Davidic dynasty."[31] Similarly, John Watts asserts that Isa 7:14 was originally messianic because the passage depicts a threat to the Davidic throne, concluding that "whatever deals with the Davidic promises of the throne to his heirs must have relevance to 'Messiah.'" Isaiah 7:14; 9:5–6 and 11:1–5 are messianic only as far as they "deal with messianic themes...related to the Davidic Dynasty."[32] Both Scott and Watts seem to have reinvented a minimalist definition that defines "Messiah" in its standard pre-exilic usage to speak of a temporal "anointed" king but not according to our definition.

Other scholars claim that later redactors have reinterpreted earlier Isaianic materials in light of various Israelite kings but not messianically. For example, Hermann Barth dates Isa 7:21–22 in 701 B.C.E., as a reinterpretation of 7:14–15 in light of Sennacherib's destruction, but later editing during the time of Josiah describes him as an ideal king after the removal of Assyrian domination.[33] Barth considers how the tradents have reworked the earlier Josianic redaction in light of the collapse of the Southern Kingdom but never to interpret any of these texts messianically.[34] Isaiah's *Denkschrift*, a term which describes the original words

31. Scott, *The Book of Isaiah*, 231–32, 247.

32. Watts, *Isaiah 1–33*, 102, 137–38, 174–76.

33. Barth focuses on an Assyrian Redaction (AR) during the time of Josiah where the central thrust is God's impending destruction of Assyria and the rebuilding of the Davidic empire under Josiah. He finds AR in six different passages (8:23b–9:6; 10:5–34; 14:6–21, 24–27; 30:27–33; 31:1–9); the *Völker* texts (8:9–10; 17:12–14; 29:1–8); occasional phrases (1:9; 5:14–17, 30; 6:12–13; 7:8b; 8:8b) and glosses about Assyria (7:17b, 18b; 8:7b) that are used to reinterpret Isaiah's message. Barth identifies four major congruities that run throughout this material: (1) themes of destruction and salvation from Assyria, the removal of Assyrian domination, the ability to repel future Assyrian threats and peace under the reign of a future king; (2) seventh-century phenomena; (3) AR reinterprets original Isaianic materials by naming Assyria as the object of destruction; (4) since redacted material customarily includes original Isaianic passages, Isaiah wrote two original documents with the intention of preserving Isa 8:16–18 and 30:8: first his *Denkschrift* during the Syro-Ephraimite War (6:1–11; 7:1–8a, 9–17; 8:1–8a, 11–18) and subsequently a document in 701 B.C.E. during Sennacherib's invasion of Judah (Isa 28:7b–22; 29:9–10, 13–14; 30:8–17). These evolved into two separate collections (chs. 2–11 and 28–32). During Josiah's time, an anti-Assyrian redactor reworked and consolidated these collections and another incorporated a core of oracles against the nations (14:4b–21, 24–27, 28–32; 17:1–18, 12–14; 18:1–6). See Hermann Barth, *Die Jesaja-Worte in der Josiazeit. Israel und Assur als Thema einer produktiven Neuinterpretation der Jesajaüberlieferung* (WMANT 48; Neukirchen–Vluyn: Neukirchener, 1977), 226–32.

34. This level of redaction describes the death of Josiah, Egyptian domination, destruction of Jerusalem, deportation of Jews to Babylon and the end of the Davidic

of Isaiah or so-called Isaianic "memoir," ends in 8:16–18 and serves as a foundation for the later development of 8:23b–9:6 during the time of the AR, which celebrates Josiah's accession and not the coming of a Messiah.[35] Fully aware of the many arguments for a post-exilic dating of Isa 11 (i.e. the termination of the Davidic dynasty), Barth questions the conventional chapter divisions between Isa 10 and 11, positing an early date for Isa 11:1–5 and regarding 10:33b–34 and 11:6–9 as later additions.[36] Emphasizing only how AR reinterprets 8:23b–9:6 and 11:1–5, Barth notes in passing the later exilic and post-exilic levels but, similar to Sweeney, has not explained how AR has changed in its significance due to these later levels of editing around 8:23–9:6 and 11:1–9.

Using *relectur* to describe how editors may have reinterpreted earlier traditions, Jacques Vermeylen does not think that any level reflects messianic interpretation. Dating most of Isa 7 during the Syro-Ephraimite War, he regards 7:18–25 and 8:8b–10 as later additions that restructure 7:1–8:10 as a "palistrophe" that is superimposed on the central core of the "Isaianic memoir."

Originally the child's arrival and identity remained unimportant. It served as a sign to inform Ahaz that his unbelief had annulled the promises that required belief replacing them with judgment. Isaiah 9:5–6a was composed much later than the Isaianic memoir, which ends in

---

kingdom. The "Massa," which was incorporated into the oracles against the nations (1:2–20; 33), is exilic. Isa 34–35 and some additions in chs. 1–11 and 28–32 are post-exilic (ibid., 286–91).

35. He makes this observation because YHWH is the subject matter in both 8:16–18 and 8:23b–9:6, which answers the complaint of 8:17 with a song of thanksgiving. The *Denkschrift* responds to the Syro-Ephraimite War to show that Assyria was against the North (8:23b) and both units deal with the nation of Israel as a whole. Hence, Barth posits distinct connections between 8:23b and the poem that follows for three reasons: (1) the phrase חקל (8:23b) serves as the source for the terms צלמות and חשך in Isa 9:1b; (2) Isa 9:3 descends from the phrase about the North's release from foreign domination in 8:23b; (3) the northern orientation of 8:23b finds its parallel in 9:6 (i.e. the throne of David). Isaiah wrote 8:23b–9:6 because it is unlikely that he would speak of both judgment and salvation but the message of salvation described in 8:23–9:6 reflects the time of Josiah (*Die Jesaja-Worte*, 62–63, 145–48).

36. Since the hope communicated in Isa 11:1–5 finds structural and thematic similarities with original Isaianic material (Isa 7:9b, 17), Barth thinks that 11:1–5 and 10:33a come from the pen of Isaiah, but that 10:27b–32, 33b–34 is a later addition. The word הנה, followed by a nominal clause, functions as a "prophecy of the present" (10:33a) and was originally followed by the *wāw* perfect in 11:1, but 33b–34 elaborates on the tree imagery in 10:33a and 11:1 (*Die Jesaja-Worte*, 62–63, 73–74).

8:18, and 8:16–18. It consisted of a "postscript" of the memoir along with 8:19–23 and appeared ostensibly different from the preceding material.[37]

Like Barth, Vermeylen considers Isa 9:1–6 to reflect a later Josianic redaction that was composed during his accession (like Pss 2; 45; 72; 110), but he understands Isa 8:23–9:6 to have offered a later rereading of "Emmanuel" in light of Josiah (announcement of the coming child and the repetition of the first person plural draws attention to עמנו אל).[38] The prepositional phrase לנו (9:5) recalls the name Emmanuel (7:14); "a child has been born to us, a son has been given to us" (9:5a) reinterprets "the children that Yahweh has given to me" (Isa 8:18); the child no longer serves as a sign to encourage faith in YHWH but rather describes an ideal Davidide unlike Ahaz, yet not a Messiah. Isaiah 9, which finds similarities with the very early Pss 89 and 132, is a pre-deuteronomistic rereading of 2 Sam 7:14 that could not have undergone post-exilic remodeling.[39]

Likewise, Vermeylen suggests that Isa 11:1–5, which depends upon the preceding oracles, comes from the second half of the seventh century and gives them a new interpretation.[40] Isaiah 10:33–34 refers to Assyria as trees that are cut down but to Israel as a shoot which comes out of the stump of Jesse, as the disjunctive *wāw* (וְיָצָא) makes apparent. Isaiah 11:2–5 offers an antithetical response to the abuses imposed by the leaders of Judah (5:19–23) and Assyria (10:5, 13). The new king who receives his wisdom from God is contrasted with the Assyrian's false claim of wisdom (10:13). The Assyrian oversteps his role as the rod of the Lord (10:5) but the figure in 11:1–5 will "strike the earth with the rod of his mouth" (10:4). Isaiah 11:1–5 was added to contrast 5:19–21; 10:1–3, 5–14, 27b–32, 33–34 in the later seventh century (on the basis of vocabulary and ideology—glorious future without reference to faith as compared to 7:9, 13–17). After 11:1–5 was composed, the editors added

---

37. J. Vermeylen, *Du prophète Isaïe à l'apocalyptique, Isaïe I–XXXV*, vol. 1. *Miroir d'un demi-millenaire d'experience religieuse en Israel* (EBib; Paris: Lecoffre, 1977), 233–34. Elsewhere in his work (pp. 245–49), Vermeylen proposes six levels of redaction in "the book of Immanuel": (1) threat (7:17); (2) Isaiah's threats against Samaria (vv. 18–25); (3) a reading of the Assyrian invasion (8:6b–14) in light of belief in inviolability of Zion during 587 B.C.E.; (4) the linking of the birth of Immanuel with Josiah (9:1–6); (5) Deuteronomistic school after 587 inserted a prediction (6:11) and a reason for punishment upon Judah (8:19, 21–22 [7:23–25 may belong to this layer]); (6) by the Jewish community during the second temple to define a "holy remnant."

38. Ibid., 233–36.

39. Vermeylen rejects the view of Marti and others who think that Isa 9:5b has a post-exilic origin; see Karl Marti, *Das Buch Jesaja* (KHC 18; Tübingen: J. C. B. Mohr [Paul Siebeck], 1900), 34ff.; Vermeylen, *Du prophète Isaïe*, 234–36.

40. Vermeylen, *Du prophète Isaïe*, 252–62.

10:27b–34 along with an edited collection of texts that he calls "the book of Immanuel" during the Exile as an "eschatological" rereading. While Vermeylen shows how 10:33–34 may have reinterpreted 11:1–5 as messianic,[41] Wegner observes that Vermeylen's reconstruction depends very heavily upon the supposition that the "book of Immanuel" was inserted after it was a complete unit, which is very speculative.[42]

Marvin Sweeney asserts that the Isaianic core of Isa 7:2–17 and 20 presupposes the consequences of Ahaz's actions so that Isaiah sought by this account to persuade Hezekiah that he must not rely on Assyria, as did Ahaz, and that YHWH would re-establish the hegemony of the Davidic monarchy over the previous Northern Kingdom of Israel.[43] However, the later edited form of Isa 5–12 results from Isa 7:10–17 and serves as a Josianic rereading of the original reassurance of the Emmanuel sign, that Ahaz would be delivered from the Syro-Ephraimite coalition (7:3–9). Now the "present form" announces a threat of Assyrian intervention in the land even during the time of Hezekiah![44] Isaiah 9:1–6 is a "psalm of thanksgiving" contrasting light and darkness and presupposing the enthronement of a new Davidic king who is undoubtedly Hezekiah.[45] This threat to the Davidic dynasty in 11:1–5 cannot refer to Hezekiah's time since his kingship was not threatened, but "such a scenario fits well with Josiah." Therefore, 11:1–5 and 6–9 and the phrase "a small boy shall lead them" (11:6b) are "an allusion to the boy king Josiah, one of the youngest ruling monarchs of the Davidic dynasty." Sweeney settles on this non-messianic interpretation of all three passages because he concludes that the Josianic redaction produces the "final form of chs. 5–12" when no messianic expectation had yet arisen.[46]

B. *Messianic Assessments*

No scholars treat Isa 7:14 as the only messianic passage in Isa 7–11. All messianic interpretations of 7:14 depends on appeals to 9:1–6 and 11:1–9 or are at least concurrently interpreted that way.

41. Wegner questions that נצר is a reference to Josiah since the order of chs. 10–11 suggests that a shoot rises up subsequent to the destruction of the Assyrian, whereas Assyria fell after Josiah's death (*An Examination of Kingship*, 32). However, the burden of proof is on Wegner to demonstrate that the order of a prophetic text determines chronology?

42. Ibid., 33.

43. Marvin A. Sweeney, *Isaiah 1–39 with an Introduction to Prophetic Literature* (FOTL 16; Grand Rapids: Eerdmans, 1996), 150.

44. Ibid., 156–58.

45. Ibid., 175–87.

46. Ibid., 150.

1. *Perspectives that interpret the pre-biblical traditions of Isaiah 9:1–6 as messianic.* Several significant scholars during the twentieth century have regarded Isa 9:1–6 to be messianic on the grounds that it has a post-exilic oracle origin.[47] John Barton, who describes the problems of interpreting Isa 7:10–14; 9:2–7 (NRSV) and 11:1–9 as messianic, reasons that messianic expectation began in the 530s after the monarchy had ceased and the exiles had returned to the land. The short-lived hope for a renewed monarchy "detached from realistic fulfilment, was transmuted into a hope for a deliverer whom God himself would send in a more or less miraculous way."[48] If Isa 9:2–7 (the English NRSV of 9:1–6) were pre-exilic, it would not invoke messianic interpretation because the royal city was still occupied by the king. Isaiah would have be "foretelling first the collapse and then the miraculous restoration of the dynasty of David." If Isa 9:2–7 (NRSV) were composed after the dynasty had already fallen in the exilic age, "then it can be taken as messianic; though it might still be better to regard it as a realistic expression of the hopes that focused on Zerubbabel, or some other descendant of David."[49]

Similarly using Isa 9:1–6 as an example for messianic interpretation, Robert Wilson employs a social-scientific approach, regarding Isaiah to be a "peripheral prophet with a small support group," who promised the restoration of an ideal king after judgment.[50] Isaiah 8:11–12 tells that YHWH delivered to Isaiah a private oracle warning him not to follow popular opinion, a warning which implies that Isaiah was promoting a minority view and that he was being urged to change his message because he had ceased to be a central prophet. Isaiah was a prophet who was linked to "the Jerusalemite royal ideology of election of the city and election of the Davidic house." Yet in light of the social opposition, "the group withdraws into itself, and the prophet's public activities cease until the reign of Hezekiah…" Hence, "Isaiah accepts the idea of election of the Davidic line and then expands on it to include the concept of a

---

47. Duhm, *Jesaja*, 88; Marti, *Das Buch Jesaja*, 91; Hölscher, *Die Profeten*, 348; Gray, *Reign of God*, 174; Mowinckel, *He That Cometh*, 102–10; Fohrer, *Das Buch Jesaja*, 1:1–38; Wolfgang Werner, *Eschatologische Texte in Jesaja 1–39: Messias, Heiliger Rest, Völker* (FB 46; Würzburg: Echter, 1982), 202; Otto Kaiser, *Isaiah 1–12: A Commentary* (trans. J. Bowden; 2d ed.; OTL; London: SCM Press, 1983), 204–6.

48. Barton, *Isaiah 1–39*, 115.

49. Ibid., 116.

50. Note that Robert R. Wilson (*Prophecy and Society in Ancient Israel* [Philadelphia: Fortress, 1984], 270–73) treats only Isa 9:6 (Eng. 9:7) but has not discussed the possibilities of 7:14 or 11.

Davidic messiah (Isa 16:5; 9:6 [9:7]).”[51] Wilson equates Davidic election of a pre-exilic king such as Hezekiah with messianism, but does not differentiate between pre-exilic ideology and post-exilic messianic expectation.

2. Perspectives that interpret Isaiah 9:1–6 and 11:1–9 as messianic. Some view the pre-biblical traditions of Isa 9:1–6 and 11:1–9 as messianic on the basis that these texts are post-exilic in origin. For example, R. H. Pfeiffer asserts that the description of the righteous rule of the messianic king (9:1–7 and ch. 11) could only have been written after the collapse of the Davidic dynasty (587).[52]

Others claim that Isa 9:1–6 and 11:1–9 became messianic through the later interpretation of the community of faith but that this view is not necessarily warranted by the context of these passages in Isaiah. Although it is “virtually impossible for a Christian to read” 9:2–7 “without Christian associations (the lines of Handel’s messiah ringing in one’s ears),” William Holladay asserts that Isa 9:7 and 11:6 speak of a coronation ode to a king over Israel (Hezekiah) or the anniversary of his coronation. However, after Jerusalem fell in 587, “the old songs of Isaiah’s became a nucleus for Jewish dreams of interpretation.”[53] Finding warrants for messianic interpretation within the shift of the people’s expectation but not in the book of Isaiah itself, he concludes that these passages outlived their context and provided “hopes for the future”

Others regard Isa 9:1–6 and 11:1–9 as messianic because ch. 11 reinterprets 9:1–6 accordingly. For example, Paul Hanson suggests that Isa 9 portrays a royal psalm about an ideal king, which possibly was used for Hezekiah’s enthronement, but ch. 11 shifts the attention from that of an eternal, royal and sovereign Davidic king to an ideal ruler who upholds righteousness and equity. Even though fervent Yahwists originally believed that Josiah upon his enthronement (640 B.C.E.) was “God’s chosen Davidic Messiah,” the discouraging events of Josiah’s death in 609 and eventually the fall of Jerusalem in 587, engender more grandiose messianic hopes (thus, Second Isaiah believed that Cyrus was the Messiah). Therefore, Hanson asserts that Matthew connects Jesus of Nazareth with “Isaiah's messianic ideal in the birth narrative...”[54]

51. Wilson, *Prophecy and Society in Ancient Israel*, 270, 273.
52. Pfeiffer, *Introduction*, 75, 437.
53. Holladay, *Isaiah*, 105–10.
54. Hanson, *The Diversity of Scripture*, 67–74.

3. *Perspectives that interpret only Isaiah 11:1–9 as messianic.* Some scholars regard only 11:1–9 but not 7:14 or 9:1–6 as messianic because of the post-exilic use of "the stump of Jesse" in 11:1, which implies to them that David's dynasty has been destroyed.[55] For example, S. R. Driver asserts that Isa 7:14 and 9:1–6 are both set in the Syro-Ephraimite War and refer to Hezekiah, but interprets 11:1–10 as messianic since this text originates in the post-exilic period.[56]

Others consider Isa 11:1–9 to be an eighth-century messianic prophecy.[57] Slotki claims that 11:1–9, like 7:14 and 8:23–9:6, specifically belongs to "the reign of Ahaz" or even "later days of Isaiah's life." Yet 11:1–9 is different from 7:14 and 8:23–9:6 because it portrays an "ideal ruler" governing in "the messianic age." For him, 8:23–9:6 but not 7:14 refers to Hezekiah, while 11:1–9 is messianic because it possesses an eschatological nature that is not present in 7:14 and 8:23–9:6.[58]

Others regard Isa 11:1–9 to have gained messianic status after the exile when a messianic expectation originated. Herbert considers 11:1–9 to be messianic since the word "anointed…is implied in the description of the investiture of the Davidic king."[59] Isaiah 11:1–9 may have an eighth-century origin but has "acquired new depths of meaning in the post-exilic age when the Jews waited for the consolation of Israel."[60] Hence, Herbert finds a warrant for messianic interpretation within the history of messianic thought rather than in Isaiah.

4. *Perspectives that interpret all three pre-biblical traditions as messianic.* Some scholars claim that messianic expectation began with eighth-century Isaiah. R. P. Carroll suggests that eighth-century Isaiah speaks of

55. Cf. Marti, *Das Buch Jesaja*, 113; Gray, *Isaiah I–XXXIX* (1956), 213–14; Karl Budde, "Über die Schranken, die Jesajas Prophetischer Botschaft zu Setzen," *ZAW* 41 (1923): 189; Sigmund Mowinckel, *The Psalms in Israel's Worship* (trans. D. R. Ap-Thomas; 2 vols.; Oxford: Blackwell, 1951), 2:22; Fohrer, *Das Buch Jesaja*, 1:166; Jochen Vollmer, *Geschichtliche Ruckblicke und Motive in der Prophetie Des Amos, Hosea und Jesaja* (BZAW 119; Berlin: de Gruyter, 1971), 180–81; Werner, *Eschatologische Texte in Jesaja 1–39*, 49–50.

56. Samuel R. Driver, "Introduction," trans. James Martin, in *F. Delitzsch's Biblical Commentary on the Prophecies of Isaiah*, vol. 1 (4th ed.; Edinburgh: T. & T. Clark, 1892), 208–10.

57. This is contrary to Hermisson and Barth who regard only 11:1–5 as Isaianic, with vv. 6–9 as a later addition; see H. J. Hermisson, "Zukunftserwartung und Gegenwartshritik in der Verkündigung Jesajas," *EvTh* 33 (1973): 58–59; Barth, *Die Jesaja-Worte*, 73–74.

58. Slotki, *Isaiah*, 56, 58.

59. Herbert, *The Book of the Prophet Isaiah 1–39*, 89–90.

60. Ibid., 90.

a Messiah, whom the prophet anticipates to be born in the imminent future.[61] Similarly, Bernard Duhm claims that messianic promise surfaces in authentic Isaianic material (9:1–6; 11:1–5) but that 7:14 becomes messianic through editorial interpretation. The prophet gives Ahaz a sign that will operate after nine months because Ahaz will later meet children by that name, which will invoke a memory of his disbelief. Pregnancy and birth cannot serve as a sign alone but must be accompanied by the giving of the name. However, because "any woman" might yell "God is with us" when she is giving birth, belief is more important than content in the case of this revelation. Isaiah 7:14 operates messianically only when vv. 17 and 21 reinterpret vv. 1–17 in light of the Babylonian exile and both vv. 15 and 22a project these verses into the last days during the age of the Messiah. Duhm separates the "authentic" from the later "inauthentic" verses (vv. 18–25), which provide merely an artificial addition to Isaiah.[62]

Nevertheless, Duhm thinks that Isa 9:1–6 and 11:1–5 were drafted after the defeat of Assyria and do not belong to Deutero-Isaiah who uses verbs only in the perfect instead of imperfect aspect (if Isaiah did not write this then it must belong to the Maccabean period). Isaiah 9:1–6 constitutes pure poetry and not prophecy because Isaiah does not refer to his call in this oracle as a license to proclaim judgment, nor does he use "thus says the Lord." Apparently for Duhm, unless a prophet says, "thus says the Lord," he merely speaks poetically. Isaiah 9:1–6 describes a promise that belongs to a genuine messianic hope of one who would sit upon the throne "similar to David."[63] Duhm regards 11:1–5 to be one of Isaiah's 'Swan Songs' (the others being 2:2–4; 32:1–5, 15–20) written at an old age after Sennacherib's invasion describing a distant hope of the messianic age that it is not reminiscent of Isa 9:1–6 but of 2:2–4; 32:1–15, 15–20.[64] Isaiah foresaw both the destruction and restoration of the Davidic house, which had become old like a tree that no longer had fruit. The threat to the Davidic house had not yet been fulfilled because the people had not yet gone through the exile.[65] Before the Messiah would come, Judah would be punished (compare 3:7 and 7:9) but a second David would grow from the root of David.[66] For Duhm, Isa 65 offered the only evidence of later hope that this prophecy was coming to

61. Robert P. Carroll, *When Prophecy Failed: Reactions and Responses to Failure in the Old Testament Prophetic Traditions* (London: SCM Press, 1979), 138–40.

62. Duhm, *Jesaja*, 74–75.

63. Ibid., 88–89.

64. Ibid., 103.

65. Ibid., 105.

66. Ibid., 104.

pass. Isaiah 9:1–6 and 11:1–5 convey a pre-exilic messianic perspective, while the monarchy was still intact, but 7:14 was reinterpreted messianically by the editorial addition in 7:15, 17, 21 and 22. This, of course, lies beyond a definition of messianism that regards this hope to have originated after the exile.

Others believe that this portrait of the Messiah unfolds more clearly through the succession of Isaianic texts (7:17; 9:1–6; 11:1). For example, Edmond Jacob asserts that Isa 7 shows how "a righteous, faithful and pious king, walking in the footsteps of David was a sign of the Messianic king." Isaiah 7 contrasts "the hope and figure of the ideal king" with an unfaithful, weak and hesitant king Ahaz, who seeks salvation through Assyria. Emmanuel's mission is merely announced in ch. 7 but described in detail in chs. 9 and 11. "By insisting on the birth of the Messiah, the prophet seeks to declare his complete participation in the course of history" whereby "the Messianic sovereign must prove that his reign is a faithful reflection of the reign of Yahweh himself."[67]

Others use traditio-historic approaches to describe a pre-exilic messianic expectation in Isaiah. For example, Hugo Gressmann proposes that Isaiah was compelled to prophesy the birth of a divine child (7:14; 9:1–6; 11:1–9) in reaction to the conditions of the Syro-Ephraimite War. This messianic idea stems from myths taken from other cultures about the birth of a divine child, who eats curds and honey (v. 15), which are the foods of the gods.[68] Isaiah 9:1–6 (Heb.) then interprets Emmanuel to be a Davidic king.[69] In his later monograph, Gressmann plainly identifies "Emmanuel" in 7:14 as the Messiah.[70] He also asserts that 9:1–6 and 11:1–5 is from 9:5 (Heb.) was taken from the fivefold accession titles given to Egyptian kings.[71] Although some of these specific titles in 9:5 were never used to describe humans (except in royal psalms), he regarded these titles as mythological and traditional. The shoot in 11:1 portrays a Davidic king who will reign righteously and bring about peace and prosperity. Although Gressmann does not state whether or not this king is a Messiah, he considers the paradisal elements in 11:6–9 to be post-exilic and provide possibilities for messianic interpretation.[72]

67. Edmond Jacob, *Theology of the Old Testament* (trans. Arthur W. Heathecote and Philip J. Allcock; New York: Harper & Row, 1958), 336.

68. Gressmann, *Der Messias*, 245.

69. Hugo Gressmann, *Der Ursprung der Israelitisch-Judischen Eschatologie* (FRLANT 6; Göttingen: Vandenhoeck & Ruprecht, 1905), 215, 272–84.

70. Gressmann, *Der Messias*, 238–42.

71. Ibid., 245.

72. Ibid., 246–47.

Others understand the messianic idea from an eschatological perspective, whereby in the post-exilic age the community looks forward to a time when the present age is done away with and the Messiah reigns over a restored kingdom in the future age. This framework creates the possibilities for messianism. For example, Lindblom asserts that the figure of the Messiah "is alien to Isaiah" at its original level but Isa 9:1–6 and 11:1–5 are either "exilic or post-exilic" references to the Emmanuel child in 7:14 "after the end of the monarchic period."[73] Therefore, Lindblom thinks that messianic interpretation in Isaiah belongs not to eighth-century Isaiah but to the exilic or post-exilic editors.

Others maintain that messianism in Isaiah cannot be eschatological. For example, Hans Wildberger argues that Isa 7:14; 8:23–9:6 and 11:1–19 cannot foretell an eschatological Messiah because they are from the hand of Isaiah. One should not attribute 7:14 to the birth of the Messiah because "Isaiah does not await the birth of the Messiah 'at the end of days' but in the very near future." He thinks that Emmanuel could very well be the son of Ahaz and even Hezekiah, and that v. 15 constitutes a later addition to reinterpret the Emmanuel prophecy as messianic.[74] Wildberger deems the term "messianic" to be problematic, but understands messianic interpretation to have taken place (e.g. 8:23ab–9:6) through a succession of events, which the community has seen to be fulfilment of prophecy:

> There is no place in the OT which speaks of a משיח (Messiah) as a savior figure who comes forth out of the transcendent regions and brings world history to an end... The child, about whose birth Isaiah speaks in this passage, will sit upon the throne of David in Jerusalem. Yet, without a doubt, his birth is a salvation event. The future ahead of him will be more than just a drawn out continuation of the present; it is indeed skilled history in the normal earthly–human realm, but it is at the same time fulfilled history. What is expected is an on-going condition of salvation (שלום, peace, shalom); cf. the majestic conclusion מעתה ועד עולם (from now on even into eternity). In this connection, the terms messianic and eschatological take on their proper sense...
>
> ...And whoever the ילד (child) and בן (son) might have been, the hopes which had been brought to life by his birth were only partially fulfilled. But Isaiah's predictions about a ruler from the house of David were not simply put on a shelf after the downfall of the Davidic Kingdom, not even when the attempt to restore the Davidic Kingdom under the influence of Haggai and Zechariah went for naught. The author of the gospel of

73. Lindblom, *Isa Vii:1–Ix:6*, 80–82, and *Prophecy in Ancient Israel*, 368–69.
74. Hans Wildberger, *Jesaja 1–12* (BKAT 10; Neukirchen–Vluyn: Neukirchener, 1980), 264, 291–92, 295–96, 299–300; Eng. ed., *Isaiah 1–12*, 318.

Matthew saw the fulfilment of 8:23aβb and 9:1 when Jesus appeared publicly in Galilee (Matt. 4:15f.) without, of course, making use of the overall witness provided by this pericope, and Zechariah's song of praise (Luke 1:79) refers to 9:1 but once again, without giving this passage a specific christological interpretation. On the other hand, Luke 1:32f. alludes to v. 6 and makes the claimed that the fulfilment of the prediction of Isaiah took place when the son of Mary was born.[75]

Wildberger also regards Isa 11:1–9 to be Isaianic and v. 10 to belong to vv. 1–9 thematically, but that a "different hand at work here" added v. 10 in order to reinterpret the figure in vv. 1–9 as a worldwide messianic figure. He is an ideal future ruler who would come from the house of David. Isaiah 11:1–9 appears very similar to Ps 72, though in the latter the psalmist petitions on behalf of a present ruler while Isaiah predicts a future ruler, whose coming would bring about a time of salvation.[76] The descriptions of Paradise, the Davidic ruler, the spirit of God resting on the anointed one and the continuation of his family line provide a foundation for messianic interpretation.[77] Though Isa 11 depicts a deeper crisis in the Davidic Dynasty than does ch. 7, both texts show that "the prophet is certainly...not thinking in terms of a far distant future."[78] Since Hezekiah did not pay attention to the prophetic word but continued "the fateful policies of his father, who had turned to Assyria for help" by turning to Egypt/Ethiopia in the same way, Isaiah speaks in defiance of the ideology of kingship in Jerusalem and no longer uses the nomenclature about "a house or the kingdom of David" (9:5), speaking now of the line of Jesse.[79] Wildberger does not consider this text to be eschatological because the prophet speaks of the future within his own present era. The designation "Messiah," which never appears in Isa 11, "can be justifiably used, insofar as this future ruler will bring about a fulfilment of that which Israel's faith had conceived to be the ideal ruler who was to sit upon the royal throne in Jerusalem." The messianic hopes of Isaiah himself are limited to Israel but the editorial remarks in v. 10 envision a Messiah who is closer to the heart of the people.[80]

Others claim that no Isaianic oracles were originally messianic but that messianic interpretation occurs within a shift in the interpretive traditions of the community of faith. For example, Walter Brueggemann argues the legitimacy of "two readings" to identify the child in Isa 7:14 and

75. Wildberger, *Isaiah 1–12: A Commentary*, 409–10.
76. Ibid., 463, 467.
77. Ibid., 466.
78. Ibid., 470.
79. Ibid., 469.
80. Ibid., 485.

9:1–7: (1) an "*historical reading*" identifies Hezekiah as the child and (2) a "*christological reading*" draws the text to the story of Jesus and his virginal mother.[81] He reasons that the identity of the עלמה is not important because the "focus is not on the birth but on the child."[82] Isaiah 11 provides "messianic flavor" upon which the reader can draw "an illumination of Jesus."[83] Therefore, Brueggemann seems only to interpret Isa 7:14; 9:1–6 and 11:1–9 messianically through an ideological shift of the reader rather than from the warrants of the text.

Others assert that the Isaianic text itself reflects a development from kingship to messiahship as the meaning of משיח takes on new dimensions over time. John Gray suggests that the messianic interpretation of 7:14 belongs to the Christian community[84] but that 9:1–6 represents a guarantee to stabilize Davidic rule, which subsequently develops into messianism.[85] Isaiah 11 then presents a later application of the eschatological Messiah.[86]

Daniel Schibler argues that the prophetic book of Isaiah illustrates a difference between "messianic prophecy" and "messianism." Early prophetic messianism expresses a hope headed by a prophet with regards to a Jerusalemite king. Messianism occurs "whenever the king and the remnant practised justice and righteousness as David did" (2 Sam 8:15).[87] Hence, Isa 7:14 and 9:6–7 "is a form of dynastic messianism, that is, it expresses a belief and hope that all descendants of David will match him in practising justice and righteousness... As David was the king *par excellence*, so there will always be a descendant of David like him..."[88] On this basis, Schibler reasons that Hezekiah embodies the arrival of this new heir to the Davidic throne and is "without doubt Isaiah's first Messiah."[89] Yet he overlooks that an ideal king does not make a Messiah. He argues, that because of a "gradual opaqueness" in the text, Isa 7:14 and 9:5–6 function as messianic prophecies that point beyond the figure of Hezekiah in the same way that 11:1–4 points "to a new David." All three "messianic prophecies have an expectancy about them that sets them

81. Walter Brueggemann, *Isaiah 1–39* (Westminster Bible Companion; Louisville, Ky.: Westminster John Knox, 1998), 74, 85.
82. Ibid., 69–70.
83. Ibid., 101.
84. Gray, *Reign of God*, 265.
85. Ibid., 122.
86. Ibid., 127–28.
87. Daniel Schibler, "Messianism and Messianic Prophecy in Isaiah 1–12 and 28–33," in Satterthwaite, Hess and Wenham, eds., *The Lord's Anointed*, 89.
88. Ibid., 97.
89. Ibid., 98.

apart from the rest of the texts that express hope in Isaiah 1–12."
Schibler does not find messianic interpretation from the warrants of the
text but tries to show how a pre-exilic hope can evolve into a messianic
expectation through a shift in the community's own ideology. This again
is contrary to our definition of messianism.

Others have argued that this shift takes place within the evolution of
Isaiah's own thinking. G. Adam Smith views 7:14 with Hezekiah as the
most likely the original referent for Isa 9:1–6. Nonetheless, Smith argues
that Isaiah's prophecy had not "been exhausted in Hezekiah."[90] He therefore infers that Isaiah's own description of the exile creates the possibility for messianic interpretation.

> Isaiah foretells his Prince on the supposition that certain things are ful-
> filled. When the people are reduced to the last extreme, when there is no
> more a king to rally or to rule them, when the land is in captivity, and
> revelation is closed, when in despair of the darkness of the Lord's face,
> men have taken to them that have familiar spirits and wizards that peep
> and mutter, then, in that last sinful, hopeless estate of man, a Deliverer
> shall appear.[91]

Consequently, Smith asserts that a disconnectedness exists between the
various messianic oracles. Isaiah 11 serves as evidence that "Isaiah has to
grow in his conception of His hero" until Isaiah conceived of a "Messiah
who is no more a mere experience as Immanuel was nor only outward
deed and promise like the Prince-of-the-four-Names but at last, and very
strongly a character."[92]

Many scholars are convinced that these texts gain messianic significance through the redaction history of the Isaianic text. As early as the
1800s, Thomas K. Cheyne asserts that when the Emmanuel prophecy
was uttered in Isa 7, Isaiah could not have had a full conception of the
events that precede the coming of the Messiah because Isa 6 concludes
with a later editorial description of exile that gives rise for messianic
interpretation.[93] Although there is no mention of Emmanuel's Davidic
origin, Cheyne recognizes that there is also no mention of this in Isa 11.
Yet Isa 8:23–9:6 is set in a "factitive" Hebrew "tense," whereby the
Messiah emerging from the Davidic family "shall appear, and bring
tyranny of Israel's foes to an end. Under him the empire of David shall
be restored on an indestructible foundation."[94] Therefore, Isa 8:23–9:6

90. Smith, *The Book of Isaiah*, 1:138, 140.
91. Ibid., 1:141–42.
92. Ibid., 1:180–82.
93. Cheyne, *Isaiah*, 1:48.
94. Ibid., 1:59, 60.

presents a picture of the Messiah, who shall live an immortal life and peacefully establish the Davidic kingdom.[95] Cheyne notes that as the Egyptians used five names in accession hymns, "the Messiah here receives not one but five names." Yet he asserts that

> Isaiah held the metaphysical oneness of the Messiah with Jehovah, but he evidently does conceive of the Messiah, somewhat as the Egyptians, Assyrians, and Babylonians regarded their kings, as an earthly representation of Divinity... No doubt this development of the Messianic doctrine was accelerated by contact with foreign nations; still it is in harmony with fundamental Biblical ideas and expressions.[96]

Isaiah 11 supplements "the vague predictions" in 7:14–16 and 9:6–7, making clear that the Messiah must belong to the family of David, not indicating that Isaiah thought of Hezekiah because 11:1–5 portrays one who is a monarch of the whole world.[97]

Though some read vv. 6–9 "allegorically" (Calvin), or in a "secondary allegorical sense" (Hengstenberg) or "realistically" (the Rabbis) or as "typology" functioning within "realistic" interpretation (Naegstrom), Cheyne thinks that "it is more natural to continue the realistic interpretation and we are bound to do so by lxv. 25." Because of the "improved condition of the human world...the evil propensity of lower animals will die out," Cheyne anchors vv. 6–9 in the distant future since nothing is said of the products of earth in vv. 6–9, "which generally furnish such striking features to descriptions like the present."[98]

C. *Rethinking the Evidence*

In sum, we have demonstrated several options for the interpretation of the pre-biblical traditions of Isa 7:14; 9:1–6 and 11:1–10. I agree with most scholars that the original pre-biblical tradition of 7:14 pertained only to the conditions of the Syro-Ephraimite War but was not originally messianic because the woman who would give birth to a child anticipated a fulfilment that would take place during the time of Ahaz and Isaiah (vv. 14–16). Many interpret 9:1–6 as a royal enthronement psalm that might have spoken of any king but most likely Hezekiah or Josiah (Alt, Crook, Gerbert, Becker, Clements, Seitz et al.). Others assert that messianism can only have originated in Isaiah at the post-exilic level of tradition history (Driver, Duhm, Marti, Hölscher, Gray, Lindblom, Mowinckel, Fohrer, Pfeiffer, Werner, Kaiser, Wildberger), some of whom

95. Ibid., 1:63.
96. Ibid., 1:61–62.
97. Ibid., 1:76.
98. Ibid., 1:77.

view the texts as messianic due to their eschatological nature (Lindblom and Mowinckel). Others consider the possibilities of a pre-exilic messianic hope either because of its eschatological nature (Slotki's solution for ch. 11) or because traditio-historical methods ferret out whether or not there is a pre-exilic messianic expectation in 7:14; 9:1–6 and 11:1–9 (Mowinckel, Gressmann). Others assign messianic status to these texts only because the community of faith interpreted them accordingly (Holladay, Hanson, Gray, Herbert, Brueggemann, Schibler). Likewise, others regard the original expectation of an ideal king to have become more fully defined as a messianic expectation developed within Israel and the reader responded to the text from that ideology (R. B. Y. Scott, John Watts, John Gray). Nonetheless, others do not even differentiate between an "ideal king" and "Messiah," but use both terms interchangeably (Wilson, Hanson, Slotki, Jacob, Wildberger, Scott, Schibler). Others think that messianic hope unfolded in Isaiah's own thinking through a progression of texts that ultimately found messianic significance through Isaiah's own description of the exile (G. A. Smith). Still others assert that through redaction history some texts became messianic (Cheyne, Duhm, Wildberger), but others claim the opposite because the latest level of redaction in these texts have been rendered in light of Josiah (Barth, Sweeney).

Any claim that eighth-century Isaiah originally imagined a Messiah when he uttered the words "a young woman shall conceive..." proves to be implausible. In my opinion, Clements and Oswalt provide a strong argument that, at the pre-biblical level of tradition history, the Emmanuel child is Maher-shallel-haz-baz because 8:4 elaborates on 7:15–16 almost as if the writer is naming the Emmanuel child as Maher-shallel-haz-baz in 8:4 (see below).[99] Similarly, the pre-biblical tradition of 9:1–6 may very well have originated as a pre-exilic royal accession oracle but was not originally messianic. Therefore, the original traditions of 7:14 and 9:1–6 would most likely describe the next king but not an eschatological deliverer after the throne lay empty. On the other hand, scholars can legitimately claim that Isa 11 was originally messianic if they date this oracle in the post-exilic age when the "stump of Jesse" refers retrospectively to the destruction of the monarchy. Yet, if 11:1–9 originally described Josiah and his reign, then it would not have been messianic.

Those who regard an ideal kingship as messianic do not satisfy our definition that requires an eschatological event to take place after the

99. "For before the child knows how to call 'My father' or 'My mother,' the wealth of Damascus and the spoil of Samaria will be carried away by the king of Assyria."

monarchy has already terminated. Any attempts to interpret any of these texts as messianic through ascribing the meaning to "reader response" completely disregards the warrants of the text. Messianism is absent within pre-biblical traditions that originated while the monarchy still endured. From this perspective, scholars have atomized the book into originally small units but have failed to examine how the later context of the book of Isaiah has altered the significance of the same units of tradition from non-messianic to messianic.

II. *Interpretation within the Biblical Scroll of Isaiah*

A. *Non-messianic Assessments of the Biblical Testimony*
1. *Perspectives that interpret the biblical testimony of Isaiah 7:14 as non-messianic.* Similar to several pre-biblical examples, some scholars believe that Isa 7:14 is non-messianic but only interpreted messianically not from the warrants of the Isaianic text but on the basis of Matthew's own citation. For example, John F. A. Sawyer views the messianic interpretation of 7:14 as something different from "what Isaiah actually meant when he first uttered the words of the Immanuel Prophecy." He asserts that Jewish, Christian, and Muslim interpretations of the prophets "have gone far beyond the biblical sources themselves..." Matthew's interpretation divorces Isa 7:14 from its original context because it expresses his belief that "Jesus was born of a virgin." In Jesus "God is with us" in a special way and the coming of Jesus is the fulfilment of prophecy, which has been altered from its original context of judgment to one of salvation.[100] Since the early church relied on "scriptural authority" for every doctrine, the New Testament writers have applied these passages to the person of Jesus.[101]

2. *Perspectives that regard all three biblical testimonies as non-messianic.* John Hayes and Stuart Irvine treat Isa 1–39 (with the exception of chs. 34–35) as the words of Isaiah that have been preserved in the larger book of Isaiah. For Hayes and Irvine, Isa 34–35 and 40–66 play no semantic role for interpretation but merely represent a kind of supplement that does not take away from the original meaning of chs. 1–39. The pristine meaning of these chapters does not change in any significant way within the book as a whole. Hayes and Irvine are merely interpreting the eighth-century part of the book of Isaiah within the original context

---

100.   John F. A. Sawyer, *Prophecy and the Biblical Prophets* (rev. ed.; Oxford Bible Series; Oxford: Oxford University Press, 1993), 139.
101.   Ibid., 144, 145.

of 735/4 B.C.E. Although I have argued that Seitz does not interpret the book of Isaiah as a whole in his commentary on Isa 1–39, he claims that he does.[102] His commentary does not really interpret the book as a whole because he comprehends Isa 7:14; 9:1–6 and 11:1–9 only in light of the original traditions of the Syro-Ephraimite. If we do concede that Seitz interprets the book as a whole, it is curious that his position resembles that of Hayes and Irvine, who assert that not even Isa 11:1–5 "looked forward to a future messiah…"[103]

B. *Messianic Assessments of the Biblical Testimony*
No studies treat the biblical testimony of Isa 7:14 or 9:1–3 as messianic apart from the testimony of 11:1–9.

1. *A perspective that interprets only the biblical testimony of Isaiah 11:1–5 as messianic.* Similar to his treatment of the Cyrus oracle, Edgar Conrad, who claims to read the text synchronically, reaches historical conclusions regarding the interpretation of Isa 7:14–25 and 9:2–7. On this basis, he reasons that the "Ahaz narrative" (7:14–25) finds fulfilment in the "Hezekiah narrative" (9:2–7) through the person of Hezekiah. Yet, he claims that Isa 11 portrays the restoration of the people "in a more magnificent way…"[104] While Conrad distinguishes between the "promised ideal king (9:2–7) and his realization in Hezekiah,"[105] his historical claims go well beyond a "synchronic reading." By anchoring the text in a moment when a king still sits on the throne, Conrad rules out the possibility of any messianic expectation that may be implied in his terminology, "ideal king."

2. *Perspectives that interpret the biblical testimony of Isaiah 9:1–6 and 11:1–5 as messianic.* Sawyer suggests that Isa 9:1–6 originally referred to the Assyrian invasions of northern Israel (734–732) but gains messianic status because 11:1 depicts the Davidic king who "would emerge from the ruins to save his people."[106] Both passages are "legitimately known as messianic prophecies," 9:2–7 is from "early stocks of Davidic tradition" and 11:1–9 is "certainly later" expressing a vision of peace and justice that expands to the whole world.[107] The New Testament writers,

---

102. Seitz does seek to interpret the book as a whole in his later *JBL* article: "How is the Prophet Isaiah Present?"
103. Hayes and Irvine, *Isaiah*.
104. Conrad, *Reading the Book of Isaiah*, 47.
105. Ibid., 45.
106. Sawyer, *Prophecy*, 84, 89.
107. Ibid., 61.

who searched their scriptures to explain their experience, have interpreted these Isaianic texts in light of the person of Jesus.[108]

3. *Perspectives that regard all three biblical testimonies as messianic.*
A small minority of modern scholars, including E. J. Young and Walter
Kaiser,[109] argue that the eighth-century Isaiah was the "author" of the
entire book and originally prophesied about a Messiah in Isa 7:14; 9:1–6
and 11:1–6. At the dawn of the modern era, E. W. Hengstenberg still perceives eighth-century Isaiah to be a foreteller of Christ and an explicator
of Torah. Therefore, he regards all that precedes Isa 7:14 as "an historical
introduction." Because Ahaz refuses a sign, "a sign is then *forced* upon
him." Hengstenberg asserts that "the future appearing of the Messiah was
at that time the *general belief* of the people."[110] Moreover, he maintains
that עלמה implies "*the particular virgin,* who was present in the inward
perception of the prophet."[111] He overcomes the seven centuries between
the overthrow of the two northern kingdoms (v. 16) and the birth of the
Messiah (vv. 14–15) because the prophet beholds all visions in the
present.[112] "Every prediction of the Messiah was at the same time *both
old and new.*" This sign pointed toward "the second predicted event,
whose earlier fulfilment then becomes a certain pledge of the fulfilment
of the former, on which it properly depends."[113] Hengstenberg thinks that
Hezekiah cannot be the subject of Isa 7:14, but "the coming of the
Messiah shall be preceded by severe divine judgments and afflictions of
the people."[114] Hengstenberg concludes that both Isa 7:14 and 7:15–16
were spoken by the prophet in the same "*ecstasy*" so that the prophet had

108.   Ibid., 144–45.
109.   Edward J. Young, "The Immanuel Prophecy: Isaiah 7:14–16," *WTJ* 15/16
(1953): 97–124, 23–50; idem, *Isaiah,* 1:293–94, 324–46, 378–93; Kaiser, *The
Messiah in the Old Testament,* 158–67.
110.   E. W. Hengstenberg, *Christology of the Old Testament and a Commentary
on the Messianic Predictions* (trans. Thomas Arnold; Grand Rapids: Kregel, 1970
[first printed 1847]), 142, 158.
111.   Ibid., 152–53.
112.   Ibid., 154.
113.   His rationale is based on the following aspects: (1) the testimony of the
New Testament; (2) the fact that Hezekiah never ruled over Galilee, which belongs
to the ten Northern tribes; (3) the fact that Isaiah ascribes divine attributes to the
Messiah which a mortal king would not have; (4) the testimony of the Psalms,
provide a description of the same characteristics that are found in Isa 9:1–6; (5) the
observation that Hezekiah cannot be the figure in either 7:14 or 9:1–6 because he
was already born when these prophecies were given. Ibid., 181–81.
114.   Ibid., 158, 159.

no concern for time.[115] The phrase "Emmanuel" (7:14) along with Isa 9:5, "where the Messiah is called the mighty God," both testify to God made flesh.[116]

For Hengstenberg, Isa 9:1–6 "connects the prediction of the deliverance from captivity with that of the times of the Messiah." He argues that 9:1 "gave rise to the opinion of the Jews that the Messiah would appear in Galilee."[117] He also asserts that the "blessings immediately after the exile and the blessings of the Messiah's time are not carefully separated." First of all, he uses an old rhetorical distinction between "the proper" use of words and "the figurative" use of words. He argues that there is no sufficient ground for "a double reference" if we recognize "the figurative character of the prediction." In his view, "most of the prophecies of the Messiah, the feeble beginning of his kingdom is closely connected with its glorious completion."[118]

Hengstenberg asserts that Isa 11 invokes messianic interpretation through the picture of a shoot arising from the devastated house of David, with the text functioning as a "foretelling" rather than the modern understanding of prophesy as a "forthtelling." However, he maintains that Isa 11 describes Judah's defeat but not utter destruction because the promise of the Messiah "had not yet been fulfilled." He argues that the prophet uses the name "Jesse" instead of David because the family of David has declined. The Davidic house "shall be exalted when sunk to the lowest." This image predicts that "the Messiah, before he should attain to glory, would be obscure and lowly."[119] Hengstenberg thinks that Isa 11:1–5 speaks of the Messiah in general terms but vv. 6–9 speak of a figure taken from the theocracy who will accomplish for the covenant people restoration which has already begun but shall be completed at the end of the world."[120] Similar to Isa 9:1–6 (NRSV, 9:2–7), ch. 11 mentions only a few "perfections of the Messiah" (righteousness, wisdom, strength, etc.). He asserts that one must determine whether words are to be interpreted as "metaphorical or literal," whether the prophet represents only metaphorically the cessation of all hostility among human beings or whether he expected it in the time of the Messiah to include the actual cessation of all enmity, all destruction, all that is hurtful, even in the irrational part of creation. In other words, he argues that the figurative

115.   Ibid., 161.
116.   Ibid., 155.
117.   Ibid., 174.
118.   Ibid., 175.
119.   Ibid., 184, 186, 187.
120.   Ibid., 185.

characteristics of Isa 11 point to a spiritual deliverance by the Messiah and future conversion of the Jews. Using figurative language, the prophet describes a spiritual Messiah, who will search the heart of humans, set up a kingdom of peace and fulfill his main objective of removing inward sin.[121]

Roland K. Harrison regards Isa 7:14; 9:1–6 and 11:1–9 to be the eighth-century prophecies of Isaiah about a Messiah.[122] He thinks that Isaiah's earliest prophecies (7:1–9:7) originated during the Syro-Ephraimite conflict, while Isa 11:1–9 was composed by Isaiah between 715 and 711 B.C.E. Accepting Isa 1–66 as the words of the prophet Isaiah, Harrison asserts that there is "no extraneous material at all in the prophecy of Isaiah."[123] He finds little difficulty interpreting Isa 40–66 as Isaianic and 7:14; 9:1–6 and 11:1–9 as messianic because the prophet projected himself into the future and described anterior events as though they had already happened.[124]

Dispensational-Fundamentalist, Clarence E. Mason, who takes an approach similar to Harrison, believes that in all three "prophecies," Isaiah spoke of a Messiah. Yet his work demonstrates the quandary that modern historicism has created even for conservative approaches to Isa 7:14 since v. 16 sets the "historical" birth of the child during the Syro-Ephraimite conflict. Consequently, he argues for a "double fulfilment" of the prophecy in order to hear the "plain sense" of the texts without sacrificing their Christology. This position of a double fulfilment can also be found similarly in the positions of Barnes, Lattey and Moody.[125]

E. J. Young solves the problem of reference differently. He asserts that the word העלם clearly implies that "the prophet beholds the virgin with child" whereby v. 14 "constitutes a definite prophecy of the birth of Immanuel" but claims that the nature of the prophecy changes between v. 14 and vv. 15–16. Verse 14 prophesies the birth of the Messiah but vv. 15–16 speak of an entirely different person since "language of prophecy

121. Ibid., 189, 191, 192, 199.
122. Roland K. Harrison, *Introduction to the Old Testament* (Grand Rapids: Eerdmans, 1969), 784, 924.
123. Ibid., 780.
124. Ibid., 775.
125. A. Barnes, *Notes on the Old Testament: Critical, Explanatory, and Practical: The Book of the Prophet Isaiah* (London: Blackie & Son, 1845); C. Lattey, "The Emmanuel Prophecy: Isa 7:14," *CBQ* 8 (1946): 369–76; D. Moody, "The Miraculous Conception," *RevExp* 51 (1954): 495–521; Clarence E. Mason, *Prophetic Problems with Alternative Solutions* (Chicago: Moody, 1973), 47–50. See also Richard D. Patterson, "A Virgin Shall Conceive [Isa 7:14; Treasures from the Text]," *Fundamentalist Journal* 4, no. 11 (1985): 64.

is filled with mystery and is sometimes obscure."[126] Young then reasons that both 7:14 and 9:6 lay stress on the child's names and uses New Testament proof texts to show that these descriptions are messianic.[127] Young reasons that since Hezekiah was already born, Isa 9 and 11 cannot refer to him.[128] Therefore, he envisions a timeless messianic expectation that began with eighth-century Isaiah.

Alec Motyer, who refers to the 66 chapters as "Isaiah's book," offers a rather opaque description of how he views the book to function as a unity. He asserts that there are three messianic portraits in Isaiah that function as different facets of the one Messiah: the King (chs. 1–37); the Servant (chs. 38–55) and the anointed conqueror.[129] He contends that each are messianic predictions. Isaiah 7:14 speaks of an "expectation of a divine Messiah" who was born of a virgin, since in Motyer's mind " *'almâ* is not a general term meaning 'young woman' but a specific one meaning 'virgin.'" "Immanuel" will be born within the "immediate threat" and the "undated future" since "Isaiah does nothing to resolve this tension between immediacy and remoteness." Therefore, he regards 7:14 to speak of a messianic expectation for which "every next king in David's line was the focus of a longing that he would be the Messiah, and every actual king was guardian of that longing inasmuch as he might be the Messiah's father." Ahaz's unbelief jeopardized this messianic hope resident in the house of David.[130] Motyer thinks that out of the tension between Isa 1:25–27 (which he interprets to be "the predicted Davidic glory") and 7:17 (which he considers to be "the predicted Davidic downfall") emerge "such prophecies as 9:1–7 and 11:1–16."[131] He regards 9:1–7 to be a prediction that is "couched in past tenses; the future is written as something which already happened."[132] Comparing Ps 2 with Isa 9:1–7 (Heb. 8:23–9:6), Motyer argues that the psalm is non-messianic, depicting the sonship of the king as "wishful thinking" or "at best…adoption," but in his assessment 9:1–7 portrays the Messiah as a "born king" who is

126. Young, "Immanuel Prophecy," and *Isaiah*, 1:293–94.

127. Young's include: New Testament proof texts "a son is given" (John 3:16); "the government shall rest on his shoulders" (Matt 11:27; 28:18; John 5:22); "prince of peace" (Luke 2:14); "Immanuel" (Matt 1:21); see Young, *Isaiah*, 1:329–31.

128. Ibid., 1:380.

129. J. Alec Motyer, *The Prophecy of Isaiah: An Introduction and Commentary* (Downers Grove, Ill.: Intervarsity, 1993), 13.

130. Ibid., 87.

131. Ibid., 122.

132. Ibid., 98. See Galia Hatav, *The Semantics of Aspect and Modality: Evidence from English and Biblical Hebrew* (Studies in Language Companion 34; Amsterdam: John Benjamins, 1997).

"actually divine." Therefore he asserts that "the Old Testament Messianic enigma" ("how can a veritable son of *David* be *Mighty God* and 'father of eternity?'") is precisely what the New Testament portrays in the person of Jesus Christ.[133] Consequently, Motyer deems the root of Jesse in ch. 11 as the "root support and origin of the Messianic family…" In order to sustain his perspective that these texts are firsthand messianic predictions from Isaiah himself, he asserts that this "prediction" does not require "the historical fall of the monarchy to prompt it."[134]

Walter Kaiser, who claims that every verse of Isaiah was written by Isaiah Ben Amoz, asserts that "virgin" is the "only conclusion one can arrive at" when translating עלמה. Hezekiah, who is not born of a virgin, is the "near fulfilment" because "rarely does the near event meet most, much less all the details and expectations that the ultimate even completes."[135] Like Isa 7:14, 9:1–7 reflects the same context of the Syro-Ephraimite coalition, which poses threats of extinction against the Davidic dynasty and will find ultimate fulfilment in the messianic age. Similarly, the stump in 11:1 may have referred to King Ahaz himself but also speaks of the Davidic dynasty that will be cut down. The shoot that comes forth from the stump "will be the son of the virgin named Immanuel" (7:17) and the figure of 9:6. Like Motyer, Kaiser's line of thinking not only ignores all the research on the term עלמה, but also his explanation of Hezekiah as a "near fulfilment" and the Messiah as a "double fulfilment" is not convincing.

Although these individuals claim to read the book of Isaiah as a whole, as I have argued in the previous chapter, they often interpret it "pre-biblically" as an inerrant source for reconstructing historical events. In such cases, they are interpreting Isaiah less as a biblical book and more in terms of the prophet's own intent and the history to which Isa 7–11 refers. The problems of interpreting 7:14–16 reveal clearly the dilemma that "conservative" Christians have acquired from bringing a modern understanding of history to the text. Hence, their norms for interpretation must derive from a conservative historical perspective where the end of the monarchy is not necessary in their definition of messianic hope.

Others who use modern historical-critical methods also describe messianic interpretation as a kind of double fulfilment. Seitz asserts that Isa 1–39 has "undergone a 'Babylonian redaction' whereby Assyria is interpreted as a type for the later Babylonians and the sparing of Jerusalem in 701 B.C.E. is seen here as just a postponement of the prophet's larger

133.   Motyer, *Isaiah*, 99, 103.
134.   Ibid., 122.
135.   Kaiser, *The Messiah in the Old Testament*, 160–61.

vision of judgment."[136] On the one hand, he desires to find "coherence in the final form of the material," but, on the other hand, puts all of the weight of his research on the pre-biblical traditions. For example, Seitz views the Emmanuel child in 7:14 and of the royal figure in 9:1–6 to be none other than Hezekiah. On the other hand, after placing all emphasis on the identification of this child as Hezekiah, he makes a faint gesture about how ch. 11 has re-interpreted chs. 7 and 9 "but not so severely that the original historical referent is lost."[137] Seitz identifies a kind of "doubled fulfilment" (my words) whereby the text has two referents, one of which is the original and the other a secondary messianic referent that can be found only through the agency of ch. 11. His conclusions do not move far from those of Duhm, who sees messianic interpretation only as a secondary result of the editors and not as significant as the original meaning of the text. Seitz finds himself in a predicament similar to the modern conservatives, who try to make the text fit orthodoxy through a sort of double fulfilment. He does not take the whole book of Isaiah as seriously as much as he focuses on history to which it points.

Franz Delitzsch, who in his fourth edition acknowledges the dia-chronic features of the Isaianic text, claims that the young woman in 7:14 could very well be Abijah (2 Kgs 18:2; 2 Chr 19:1) the mother of Hezekiah but was "at the same time…the Messiah."[138] It is probable that

> the believing portion of the nation did concentrate their messianic wishes and hopes for a long time upon Hezekiah and even Isaiah's prophecy may have evoked such human conjectures and expectations, through the measure of time which it laid down, it would not be a prophecy at all, if it rested upon no better foundation in this, which would be the case if Isaiah had a particular maiden of his own day in his mind that time.[139]

This figure would be the "pledge of Judah's continuance" and "would not arrive without the present degenerative house of David, which brought Judah to the brink of ruin, being altogether set aside."[140] Regarding Isa 7:14, Delitzsch suggests that "if, therefore, we adhere to the letter of prophecy, we may easily throw doubt upon its veracity; but if we look at the substance of the prophecy, we soon find that the complex character by no means invalidates its truth." From this perspective, Delitzsch solves "the discrepancy between the prophecy in the history of fulfilment." This prophecy is "directly messianic; it is a divine prophecy within human

136. Seitz, *Isaiah 1–39*, 6.
137. Ibid., 75.
138. Delitzsch, *Isaiah*, 1:218.
139. Ibid., 1:218.
140. Ibid., 1:220.

limits."[141] Even though "the Jews" attempt to reduce the figure in 9:1–6 by eliminating the messianic sense of the passage and removing any notion of the Messiah's deity, 9:1–6 points to the Messiah, whom many have considered to be Hezekiah.[142] Isaiah 11:1–5 also refers to the Davidic Messiah who shall rise up after the ending of the monarchy.[143]

Others, who employ historical-critical methods to understand the book of Isaiah, describe a messianic expectation that began through Jerusalem-ite traditions while the monarchy was still intact. For example, Brevard Childs understands Isa 7:14; 9:1–5 and 11:1–5 to be messianic since "the prophet Isaiah formulates his promise for the future in terms of the Jerusalem traditions, that is, the election assigned to David." The fact that "a remnant would survive the judgment was not just a distant hope, but had already appeared as a guarantee in the sign of the child, Immanuel (7:14)." Within the context of Assyria's destruction of the North, "Isaiah developed his message of the divine promise to the house of David." Although the promised ruler would establish his throne eternally, he would come "only after the 'stump to Jesse' had been cut down (11.1ff.)."[144] Essentially, David's kingship became "a type of eschatological rule of God himself" in the context of the prophets' rejection of "the false and arrogant rule of Israel's kings" who would be replaced by "God's true representative."[145] Therefore, this righteous Davidic king took on characteristics that "transcended human qualities (Isa 9:6)."[146]

Other scholars, who interpret the biblical traditions of Isa 7:14; 9:1–6 and 11:1–6 messianically, describe an evolution of messianism through an ideological shift that transforms Isaiah's original description of kingship into messiahship, not due to later redaction but when the meaning and expectation of משיח takes on new dimensions over time. For example, John Oswalt, who treats the book of Isaiah as a "theological and ideological unity," argues against the view that the primary fulfilment of 7:14 occurred during Ahaz's time and was later cleverly applied to Christ. He states that if "the sign did not occur in any sense until 725 years after the fact [it] flies in the face of the plain sense of the text."[147]

141.   Ibid., 1:227, 228.
142.   Ibid., 1:243–44.
143.   Ibid., 1:281–82.
144.   Brevard S. Childs, *Biblical Theology of the Old and New Testaments* (Philadelphia: Fortress, 1993), 177.
145.   Brevard S. Childs, *Old Testament Theology in a Canonical Context* (Philadelphia: Fortress, 1986), 119.
146.   Ibid., 242.
147.   John Oswalt, *The Book of Isaiah 1–39* (Grand Rapids: Eerdmans, 1986), 25, 208.

He concludes, that "the most attractive option in Isa 7 and 8 is that Immanuel and Maher-shalal-hash-baz were one and the same."[148] Since Ahaz rejects God's sign to be "with us," God's promise becomes negative for Ahaz but salvific for Israel. God is with us in judgment and salvation. Hence, ch. 9 moves beyond the ordinary sign to a cosmic scale, which no longer portends future events or situations as do Shear-jashub and Maher-shalal-hash-baz. These names do not convey the relationship between God and his people as does Emmanuel. Instead, they express the amazing character of the Messiah and his reign.[149] Therefore, the juxtaposition of light and darkness portrays a situation that awaits the delivering power of the future king. Isaiah 11:1–9 then expresses a mature messianic hope, which originally began in the description of kingship in 7:14 and which was amplified in 9:1–6. At this ripened level of messianic promise in 11:1–9, this hope rests on what Oswalt considers to be a "realistic" portrait of a "superhuman" Messiah.[150]

In a similar fashion, Shemaryahu Talmon differentiates between the epithet of מָשִׁיחַ, which refers to an actual king or his immediate successor, and the concept of messianism, which is credal and visionary in nature and transcends "the original terrestrial signification of the term *māšîaḥ*."[151] Talmon locates three successive ways of expressing messianic expectation: historical realism, conceptualization and idealism. Historical realism consists of a socio-political expectation that must be evaluated in the historical setting and the theoretical understanding of the biblical institution of kingship. Conceptualization must be understood within the existential context of the historical people who conceptualized a messiah and whose societal and creedal evolution simultaneously was mainly determined by their concepts. The final stage culminates in an idealization of the anointed after 70 C.E. in the Christian period when "the Messiah" takes center stage and ushers in the eschatological era of salvation.[152] Within a succession from "historical realism" to "idealism," Talmon interprets Isa 7:14 messianically since the name "Immanuel" functions as a "prolepsis of the Davidic visions assembled in the ensuing chapters" and like 7:14–16, 9:1–6 speaks of Ahaz's unborn son who is

---

148.   Ibid., 25, 213.

149.   Ibid., 213.

150.   Ibid., 278.

151.   Shemaryahu Talmon, "Concept of Mashiah and Messianism in Early Judaism," in Charlesworth, ed., *The Messiah*, 80.

152.   Talmon also asserts that none of the thirty-nine occurrences of מָשִׁיחַ in the Hebrew canon refer to an anticipated figure of the future whose coming will concur with the inauguration of an era of salvation (ibid., 80–83).

destined to "ring in an eon of bliss."[153] While 9:1–6 speaks of the near future, 11:1–10 offers a futuristic perspective, unbounded by historical reality" after "ideation had replaced the earlier historical realism."[154] Isaiah 11:1–10 then functions as one of the several passages that grew out of 2 Sam 7 (Jer 23:5–6; Hos 3:4–5; Amos 9:11–15; Mic 5:1–8; Hag 2:20–23 et al.), "unbounded by historical reality," exhibiting the "ideation" that emerges after the events of 586 B.C.E., when a king no longer sits on a throne. These three Isaiah oracles for Talmon reflect three stages in the development of the *māšîaḥ* historicity (7:14–16), ideation (9:5–6), and idealization (11:1–10), thus reflecting a "progressive dehistorization of the *māšîaḥ* notion."[155]

Others aim to show that messianic interpretation can only be understood within the inner-biblical testimony. This is how James Luther Mays aims to trace "the trajectory of messianic theology in the Bible." He argues that, just as one needs to comprehend Deuteronomy to understand Jeremiah and Torah to understand Ezekiel, one needs to know the Psalms (namely the so-called enthronement psalms) to understand Isaiah. The prophet speaks the words of Isa 9:6 from an already existent conception of the identity and role of the Davidic king which is spelled out in the royal Psalms. When reading Isaiah, one is "supposed to know that Ahaz was installed in rituals represented by the royal Psalms" (Ps 2).[156] Therefore, to understand these passages in context we must view Isaiah within the framework of a "trajectory of messianic thought concerns with the role in the reign of God of the figure who is called King, seat of David, servant of God, Messiah, son of God." Psalm 2 provides a foundation from which we may understand this trajectory that is transformed by such prophets as Isaiah and eventually understood by the writers of the Gospels as king, Messiah, and son of God.[157] These enthronement psalms would be spoken at the time of the change of rulers to assert the authority of the king's new office whereby he is named son of God as a confession that he was the representative and agent of the deity.[158] The house of David becomes the Dynasty which the Lord builds for him (2 Sam 7).[159] Therefore, Isa 9:6 speaks of the entire reign of the

153.   Ibid., 92, 97.
154.   Ibid., 93, 97.
155.   Ibid., 97.
156.   James Luther Mays, "Isaiah's Royal Theology and the Messiah," in *Reading and Preaching the Book of Isaiah* (ed. Christopher R. Seitz; Philadelphia: Fortress, 1988), 39–40.
157.   Ibid., 41–43.
158.   Ibid., 44–45.
159.   Ibid., 47.

king in Judah and 11:1–9 indicates that this promise endured while the instruments failed.[160] Mays' contribution serves a very important role in showing the relationship between messianism in the book of Isaiah and the Psalter.

Others argue that Isa 7:14; 9:1–6 and 11:1–5 are each messianic on the basis that 11:1–5 functions to reinterpret 7:17 and 9:1–6 as messianic.[161] Ronald Clements, who attempts to describe the unity of the book of Isaiah,[162] while giving careful consideration to the diachronic dimensions of the text, maintains that the few actual words that Isaiah ben Amoz spoke were composed shortly after the Syro-Ephraimite crisis was settled. However, a group collected, preserved and reflected upon Isaiah's original writings briefly after he died (e.g. the "Isaianic memoir" serves as the core of the larger collection of 5:1–14:27).[163] He argues that the Isaianic Memoir originally ended in 8:18 but was developed and reinterpreted. An editor added the accession oracle (8:23–9:6) to the memoir so that Emmanuel (Isa 7:14), who originally appeared as one of a succession of descriptions about Isaiah's sons (vis à vis Shear-jashub [7:3] and Maher-shalal-hash-baz [8:3]), now was reinterpreted by 8:23–9:6 as a royal child from David's dynasty, namely Hezekiah. The editors then added 7:2 and 9b to draw a contrast between "Ahaz's lack of faith and Hezekiah's victorious faith," thus changing "the whole character of the Immanuel prophecy…"[164] Finally, after the events of 587 B.C.E., when the Davidic dynasty had come to an end, there arose the hope of an eschatological deliverer, of whom Isa 11:1–5 attests. Hence, Isa 11 directly reinterprets 9:1–6 (and indirectly 7:14) as messianic.

Others, who employ older historical-critical methods, maintain that Isa 7:14; 9:1–6 and 11:1–9 were originally non-messianic but became messianic when the editors reinterpreted the book of Isaiah. While several scholars think that it is unnecessary to equate messianism with eschatological hope, Joachim Becker maintains that, although עלמה (7:14) originally referred to Isaiah's wife, a later redactor placed this text within post-exilic circumstances and interpreted the text as messianic.[165] Becker

---

160. Ibid., 42, 48.

161. Seitz (*Isaiah 1–39*, 84–87) previously argued similarly but also describes a type of double fulfilment of these texts in a different manner.

162. Clements, *Isaiah 1–39*, 19–21.

163. Ibid., 4.

164. Ibid., 8. Also see his "The Immanuel Prophecy of Isa 7:10–17 and Its Messianic Interpretation," in *Die Hebräische Bibel, Festschrift for Rolf Rendtorff* (ed. Erhard Blum et al.; Neukirchen–Vluyn: Neukirchener, 1990), 234–35.

165. Joachim Becker, *Isaias. Der Prophet und Sein Buch* (SBS 30; Stuttgart: Katholische Bibelwerk, 1968).

also asserts, "Vorexilischer Messianismus ist ein Anachronismus, fast etwas wie eine contratictio in terminus."[166] Likewise, Isa 8:23–9:6 was originally read against the background of Pss 2; 45 and 110 as a royal accession oracle to portray the adoption of the king (probably Hezekiah) but not his actual birth. However, the redactors have fashioned the material in such a manner that now it is followed by a period of restoration in the poem of ch. 9, thus transforming the passage to be read messianically. During the post-exilic period, the birth of a Davidic king would give rise to reading the text as messianic promise. Becker also claims that the original intent of 11:1–5 was similar to ch. 9, but composed in the post-exilic era, after the termination of the Davidic dynasty, and was originally read messianically. Thus he would place 11:1–5 in a new context of restoration which increases the possibility of a messianic reading.

In his latest edition, Otto Kaiser suggests that the main concern of the book of Isaiah is to explain the collapse of the kingdom of Judah as a direct "consequence of the people's refusal to listen to the prophet and to trust in Yahweh instead of Egypt (cf. 30:12ff.; 30:1ff.; 31:1ff.)." He believes that the redactors have so thoroughly reworked the book that it would be impossible to find any element that came from Isaiah ben Amoz.[167] While Kaiser argues that the New Testament interpretation of Isa 7:14 "goes beyond the horizons of Old Testament thinking,"[168] he still tries to understand it as messianic in some sense because the Emmanuel child will grow up in the time of salvation described in 7:15a.[169] He thinks that 7:10–17 might be post-Deuteronomic and that 7:10–14a and 17 were later interpreted in terms of messianic eschatology leaving the

166.   Ibid., 20: "Pre-exilic messianism is an anachronism, nearly something like a contradiction in terms" (my translation).

167.   Kaiser has completely changed his position in the second edition of his commentary. In the revised edition, he posits that in the sixth century an editor added a *Denkschrift* (6:1–8:18) to the basic material (chs. 28–31) in order to propagate Deuteronomistic theology, namely, that the people have received punishment because of their faithlessness and ingratitude towards God. Following this were redactions pertaining to judgment followed by an Assyrian revision that took place in the fifth century B.C.E. and probably gave rise to Zion theology. Consequently, the book came together as a whole by three final redactions: (1) a redaction responsible for 2:1–17 that also ties together Third and First Isaiah; (2) a late eschatological redaction, whereby 5:25 served as a bridge that created eschatological significance, 14:24–27 providing a foundation for reshaping 10:5–12:6; (3) a redaction during the Maccabean period that has a wisdom character (purified Zion). See Kaiser, *Isaiah 1–12* (2d ed.), 1–5, 117–18, 234.

168.   Kaiser, *Isaiah 1–12* (2d ed.), 155.

169.   A time of salvation rather than the catastrophe of 587 (ibid., 163).

"situation of Ahaz far behind."[170] Kaiser, who in his first edition assigned an earlier pre-exilic date to 8:23b–9:6,[171] has now abandoned his earlier form-critical findings and argues in his revised edition that this passage was composed in the post-exilic era after 587 when the monarchy had come to end. On this basis, 8:23b–9:6 functions messianically and also provides a messianic context for our hearing of the Emmanuel prophecy in 7:14–16. In a similar fashion, he considers 11:1–9 to have been composed after "the downfall of the Davidic empire" whereby the text describes an "eschatological David" as opposed to the expectations in ch. 9 of "liberation from the yoke of the enemy."[172] While his earlier form-critical descriptions led him to conclude that these texts were non-messianic, Kaiser seems to have reclaimed messianism for these texts in his later edition by dating them and their promise in the post-exilic period.

Some scholars believe that Judaism's messianic expectation began with Isaiah himself but that the expectation changed when the book of Isaiah reached its final form. In his dissertation, entitled "Who is Immanuel: The Rise and the Foundering of of Isaiah's Messianic Expectations," Antti Laato argues that originally Isa 7:14; 9:1–6 and 11:1–5 had a messianic intent[173] but that a Deuteronomistic editor attempted to remove this expectation from the writings of Isaiah ben Amoz so that they may refer to Hezekiah. In Laato's recent study, he shows how Jewish interpreters came to rely on this presentation of Hezekiah.[174] Laato uses Carroll's notion of cognitive dissonance to prove this idea.[175] Most fascinating, Laato's view suggests the reverse of conventional scholarship, which finds the shift to occur from non-messianic to messianic. In this early work, Laato does not account for the fact that if a messianic idea

170. Ibid., 163–64.

171. Remember that while Gunkel's form-critical arguments aimed at correcting the notion that most Psalms were originally post-exilic, he argued that they were indeed pre-exilic (Hermann Gunkel, *Die Psalmen* [Göttinger Handkommentar zum Alten Testament 4; Göttingen: Vandenhoeck & Ruprecht, 1926]). In the second endition of his commentary (*Isaiah 1–12*), Kaiser has moved back into the opposite direction.

172. Kaiser, *Isaiah 1–12* (2d ed.), 254–55.

173. Antti Laato thinks that the eighth-century prophet had some notion of a messianic figure who would free the nation of Israel from Assyria. See Laato's description of why the Israelite situation would give occasion for such an expectation in *Who is Immanuel?* (Åbo Akademi Dissertation; Åbo: Åbo Akademi Press, 1988), 48–100, 192–96.

174. Antti Laato, *"About Zion I Will Not Be Silent"*: *The Book of Isaiah as an Ideological Unity* (ConBOT 44; Stockholm: Almqvist & Wiksell, 1998), 30–44.

175. Robert P. Carroll, "Inner Tradition Shifts in Meaning in Isaiah 1–11," *ExpTim* 89 (1977/78): 301–4.

originally were to fail and secondarily refer to Hezekiah, then why were these prophecies preserved? How, then, was the messianic idea later reincorporated into Israel's messianic expectation? Laato attempts to answer these questions in his later work, *"About Zion I Will Not Be Silent"*. He shows that, although several rabbinic texts consider Hezekiah to be the referent of Isa 7; 9 and 11, Hezekiah is a "typos" or "model" for the coming Messiah and righteous servant who brings future salvation.[176] Isaiah 65:25 indicates that this "promise of peace...will be fulfilled in the restored Zion." Isaiah 40–55 announces this salvation but chs. 56–66 reiterate that the fulfilment has been postponed because of the people's disobedience.[177]

Under the direction of Ronald Clements, Paul Wegner argues in his published dissertation that the edited book of Isaiah provides warrants that invite messianic interpretation. Wegner asks, "Does the final form contain any message of its own or is it merely an anthology of various writers inspired by Isaiah Ben Amoz?"[178] This question finds its answer when later editors "reread" the original texts in light of the promise of a Davidic king. Wegner's approach to Isaiah moves in the same direction as recent studies on messianism in the biblical book of Psalms.[179] He demonstrates that although it is "unlikely that the original Isaiah 7:10–17 was intended to be understood messianically," the redactional shaping of the text prepared a way for the passage to be heard in that way.[180] Wegner argues that Isa 7:14 was originally linked to the circumstances of the eighth century B.C.E.,[181] but asserts that 7:18–25 serves as a modification related to the events of 722 or perhaps 701 so that it began to be understood proto-messianically.[182] Later editors build on this possibility and refine it in terms of traditional messianism. Therefore, Matthew can quote this passage to apply it to his Messiah, because this material had already been shaped to be heard accordingly.[183]

However, Wegner's description of how vv. 18–25 function as a "rereading" (722 or 701 B.C.E.) of earlier material is crucial to his greater

176.   Laato, *"About Zion I Will Not Be Silent"*, 35, 142.
177.   Ibid., 167, 209.
178.   Wegner, *An Examination of Kingship*, 15.
179.   Mays, "Torah Psalms"; Sheppard, *Wisdom as a Hermeneutical Construct*; idem, *The Future of the Bible*.
180.   Wegner, *An Examination of Kingship*, 134, 136.
181.   The child serves as a sign for Ahaz and his age corresponds to contemporary events (7:16)
182.   The phrase "Proto-messianic" is my term to describe Wegner's argument. See Wegner, *An Examination of Kingship*, 136.
183.   Ibid., 134.

argument for messianic interpretation in Isa 1–39.[184] Though Wegner thinks that the description of a razor shaving off all of a man's hair indicates severe destruction and humiliation for the land (v. 20), he admits that we cannot easily determine whether this depiction refers to the destruction of the Northern or the Southern Kingdom. Contrary to Clements, he denies that v. 22b is post-exilic.[185] If all editorial layers of Isa 7 remain pre-exilic when a king still sits on the throne, he is forced to argue for a pre-exilic messianism without clear definition.[186]

Wegner attempts to establish a pre-exilic expectation of a future deliverer who would constitute some sort of inchoate form of messianism:

> In several early studies, such as S. Mowinckel (1956) and J. Becker (1980), it has been argued that the completed concept of the Messiah arose during the post-exilic period which may indeed be very correct, but very little attention has been paid to the background and development of this concept. We intend to demonstrate that the actual development of the concept is much more complicated and the basic elements of constituting this concept existed much earlier than the post-exilic period.[187]

He argues similarly for an early dating of the origins and editing of Isa 9:1–6 and 11:1–9.[188] Yet, his own proposal remains unclear about what this "messianism" asserted.

Wegner's work reflects the same problems found in the work of those scholars who proceeded him. One of his main criticisms of secondary literature rests on the assertion that scholars have not taken Isaiah as a whole seriously, and yet he does not treat the book as a whole, as is evident from the title of his dissertation. Moreover, his conservative attempts to find a maximal amount of original Isaianic material does not help to explain how earlier traditions came to be understood as messianic within the "final form" of the later book of Isaiah.[189] Another weakness is that Wegner confuses Child's "canonical approach" with Sander's "canonical criticism."[190] Similar to Sanders, Wegner seeks to establish a "canonical hermeneutic" which aims to identify a consistent factor in the process of tradition history. In this way, he hopes to explain how the same normative tradition might properly lead to vastly different interpretations in

---

184. Ibid., 77–80, 103.
185. Ibid., 105.
186. Ibid., 136.
187. Ibid., 2.
188. Ibid., 136, 211, 212, 268.
189. Wegner accuses his opponents for their failure to acknowledge certain material as Isaianic. Cf. also Vermeylen, "Du prophete Isaïe à l'apocalyptique," 35 and Barth, "Israel und das Asyrerreich."
190. Wegner, *An Examination of Kingship*, 14.

different times and circumstances.[191] He looks for this pattern behind every redactional reinterpretation of preceding tradition.[192] Like Becker, Vermeylen and Clements, Wegner focuses on independent levels of editing without viewing the whole book of Isaiah as scripture. Sheppard's contribution more accurately represents an approach that takes seriously the scriptural function of such texts and their diachronic prehistory, but he does not thoroughly explore all the implications involved, nor does he treat all the related messianic texts within the book.[193]

4. *Perspectives that interpret the biblical Isaiah 7:14 through typological interpretation.* Many scholars who view Isa 7:14 as historically anchored in the events of the Syro-Ephraimite War resort to "typology" to rationalize its messianic role. In the nineteenth century, T. K. Cheyne argues from the history of rhetoric that typology belongs to the literal sense, unlike allegory, but observes how some scholars of his time had already begun to confuse typology with allegory in Isa 7:14.[194] Charles Briggs, who rightly observes that typology and promise both operate within the literal sense, presumes that the child can be either a promise or a type. In the case of 7:14, the name Emmanuel functions as a "pledge" that "God is with us" and remains as a "predicted pledge until the birth of the Messiah" because no child by that name appears anywhere else in the book.[195] Since 7:14 refers to a boy in Isaiah's time, the promise is resolved by his birth and the options for messianic interpretation can now only include multiple fulfillment or typology:

191.   This theory of redaction harmonizes differences in redactional layers that stand worlds apart from one another. Sanders called this factor "the canonical hermeneutic," while acknowledging that not every interpretation found in scripture itself met that standard. See Sanders, *Canon and Community*, and his *From Sacred Story to Sacred Text*.

192.   Wegner's use of *relecture* presupposes that the editors applied the same method at every stage of tradition history. He tries to solve a problem in the environment of change of tradition history by finding a solution within the redactor's intent at each level of change as though a canonical hermeneutic can be found. Not only is it unconvincing that each level of tradition embodies the same kind of theological rereading, but this appears to be a pious accounting or over-theologizing of editorial changes. The things that give rise to changes in the text are not so predictable but are considerably diverse.

193.   See the works of Sheppard: "The Anti-Assyrian Redaction"; "Isaiah 1–39"; "The Book of Isaiah"; "The Book of Isaiah as a Human Witness" (1993); "Two Turbulent Decades"; "The Book of Isaiah as a Human Witness" (1995); "The Scope of Isaiah".

194.   Cheyne, *Isaiah*, 1:48.

195.   Briggs, *Messianic Prophecies*, 196–97.

The names assigned to the children of the prophet are plain enough, but there is no connection of this name with any of his children. If, however, anyone should prefer to think that a child of a prophet or the royal house bore his name as a sign, the prediction would then become typical and cease to be direct prediction, but the Messianic idea would not be lost. This Immanuel would be a type of the great Immanuel, just as David and Moses and Solomon and others have been such types of the Messiah.[196]

Briggs uses typology to compensate for what may be lost due to modern historical criticism.[197]

G. Adam Smith argues that in order "to identify Immanuel with the promised Messaiah of David's house" we would have "to fall back on some vaguer theory of him finding him to be a personification—either a representative of the coming generation of God's people or a type of the promised tomorrow..." Therefore, he allows for interpretation of Emmanuel in terms of Jesus Christ and suggests further that Ahaz is "the Judas of the Old Testament."[198]

S. H. Widyapranawa, who uses the terms "sign" and "symbol" interchangeably, says that "a sign *(ot)* is a physical happening, a material event in the world of physical phenomena that in itself represents an eschatological reality, or the incursion of eternity into time."[199] Essentially, Widyapranawa uses typological logic for his description of the Emmanuel child.[200] Consequently, he considers Isa 9:1–7 to be "a continuation of the message of the Immanuel sign," and Hezekiah, who fits the role of the 'child born to us,' serves as "a prophetic symbol (another 'sign') of a messianic king still to come."[201] Moreover, Widyapranawa maintains that 11:1–10 refers back to 9:6 where the king-deliverer sitting on the throne is Hezekiah. He then asserts that in ch. 11, "Isaiah so much declares that Hezekiah is in fact a sign and a promise of one still greater than he who was still to come."[202] Hence, 7:14; 9:1–7 and 11:1–10 refer to Hezekiah, who is a type of the Messiah.

---

196.   Ibid., 197.
197.   See Sheppard, "The Book of Isaiah as a Human Witness" (1993), on this point.
198.   Smith, *Isaiah*, 1:119.
199.   S. H. Widyapranawa, *The Lord is Savior: Faith in National Crisis. A Commentary on Isaiah 1–39* (ITC; Grand Rapids: Eerdmans, 1990), 41.
200.   See Erich Auerbach, "Figura," in *Scenes from the Drama of European Literature: Six Essays by Erich Auerbach* (Gloucester: Peter Smith, 1977), 11–75.
201.   Widyapranawa, *The Lord is Savior*, 51–52.
202.   Ibid., 68.

C. *A Few Pre-modern Examples*

1. *Targum.* Targum Jonathan interprets Isa 9 and 11 messianically but
not 7:14. The translation in 7:14 simply renders the Hebrew in Aramaic
with no suggestion of messianic import.[203] By contrast, in 9:5 the Targum
volunteers:

> The prophet says to the house of David, behold a boy child has been born
> to us, a son has been given to us; and he has taken the law upon himself
> to keep it; and his name has been called from old, wonderful counsellor,
> mighty God, he who lives forever, the Messiah (משיחא) in whose days
> peace shall increase upon us.[204]

While Samson Levey contests that there is any messianic interpretation
in ch. 9 except maybe indirectly from "throne of David" and "his kingdom" in v. 6,[205] for several reasons he cannot sustain his argument. His
opinion that the past "tense" indicates how the "Targumist may have had
Hezekiah in mind as the Messiah" ignores how Semitic verbs have an
aspect rather than a tense.[206] Second, Levey alleges the Targumist's
expectation of Hezekiah as Messiah in 9:6 without considering that this
same expectation does not work in the other texts which he regards the
Targum to interpret messianically. At most, Levey can claim that the
Targum may have Hezekiah in mind as the referent of selective texts, but
he cannot consistently interpret all the Targumic references to the
Messiah in this way. Therefore, Hezekiah like Cyrus may fulfill a few
but not all aspects of messianic hope. Besides, the Targum's use of
משיחא clearly signifies *"the* Messiah" rather than a variety of possible
Messiahs.

Before the outset of ch. 11, the Targum renders שמן with the Aramaic
משיחא to speak of anointing oil, thereby relating the deliverance in ch. 10
with the Messiah. While it is unlikely that the Targumist views ch. 10 as
a backdrop for messianic interpretation in ch. 11, this paraphrase demonstrates how one can find messianic resonances in ch. 10. The Targum
explicitly interprets 11:1 messianically: "A king shall come forth from
the sons of Jesse, and the Messiah shall grow up from his son's son."

---

203.   The Aramaic reads: בכין יתינן יהוה הוא לכון אותא הא עולימתא מעדיא ותליד
בר ותקרי שמיה עמנו אל ("Therefore, YHWH himself will give you a sign; see a young
woman is with child and shall bear a son and call his name Emmanuel").

204.   My translation from J. F. Stenning, ed., *The Targum of Isaiah* (Oxford:
Clarendon, 1949), 33.

205.   Samson H. Levey, *The Messiah: An Aramaic Interpretation; the Messianic
Exegesis of the Targum* (HUCM 2; Cincinnati: Hebrew Union College/Jewish
Institute of Religion, 1974).

206.   See Hatav, *The Semantics of Aspect and Modality.*

Similarly, v. 6 begins with "in the days of the Messiah of Israel…" In v. 10, the Aramaic paraphrases the Hebrew שרש ישי ("root of Jesse") as בר בריה דישי ("the son of the son of Jesse") in order to make more explicit that the messianic line comes from the ancestry of David. The phrase אליו גוים ידרשו ("the nations shall seek him") has been interpreted as ליה מלכון ישתמען ("the kingdoms shall be subject to him"), thus amplifying with clarity the power of the messianic office (v. 10). Therefore, Levey admits that no messianic interpretation of Isa 11 is "explicit" within the Targum.[207]

2. *Ibn Ezra* (אבן עזרא). Ibn Ezra (Abraham ben Meir) was intent upon understanding the *peshat* of the text of Isaiah and was critical of midrashic, typological and allegorical interpretation. Therefore, he ruled out any view that interpreted Emmanuel as "symbolic (משל) of the kingdom" because he did not regard the depiction of the "lad's knowing good and evil" and Maher-Shalal-Haz-baz's calling "father and mother" to correspond with this interpretation. Ibn Ezra drew a separation between *peshat* and *derash* and thought that halakah contradicted the literal meaning of the text.[208] Hence, he did not interpret Emmanuel in Isa 7:14 to be the Messiah partially because he did not think that the *peshat* of this text warranted such an interpretation. He also denied that עלמה would ever imply virgin (בתולה) on the basis of Prov 30:19, "the way of a man with a young woman (עלמה)." He also argued that "many become entangled[209] and say that Emmanuel is Hezekiah but he is not the same one, even if this prophecy were spoken at the beginning of Ahaz's reign."[210] Such interpretation fails because "the land of Ephraim and Damascus were abandoned in Hezekiah's sixth year…"[211] He argues, "I think (lit. 'it is right in my eyes') that Emmanuel is a son of Isaiah, as is Maher-Shalal, and it testifies 'I went into the prophetess.'"[212] The name Emmanuel, functioning as a sign in 8:10, provides further evidence that

207. Levey, *The Messiah*, 52–53.
208. See Wilhelm Bacher, "Bible Exegesis," *Jewish Encyclopedia* 3 (1901–6): 162–69 (368).
209. This is Jastrow's rendering of the Hithpael of שמט√ for which he uses the lexeme "to run in all directions," or "to blunder" or "to be entangled" in the Qal. See Marcus Jastrow, *Dictionary of the Targum, Talmud Babylonian and Yerushalmi, and Midrashic Literature* (2 vols.; New York: Pardes, 1950), *s.v.*
210. M. Friedländer, ed., *The Commentary of Ibn Ezra on Isaiah*, vol. 3 (edited from MSS and trans., with Notes, Introduction and Indexes; London: The Society of Hebrew Literature by Trübner & Co., 1877], 16 [my translation]).
211. Ibid., 16 (my translation).
212. Ibid., 17 (my translation).

this is the name of the prophet's son, because it functions similarly to the names of Isaiah's other two sons.

However, Ibn Ezra regards the "child" in Isa 9:1–6 to be Hezekiah because the context refers to the invasion of Sennacherib (8:23; 9:4) when Hezekiah was thirty-nine. The term יוֹעֵץ "indeed speaks of Hezekiah" (בן היה חזויה) in 2 Chr 30:10 (ויוֹעֵץ המלך). Isaiah 11 presents problems since "most commentators say that this is the Messiah," but Rabbi Moses Hakkohen thought that this chapter referred to Hezekiah "because it coheres with the previous section." Since Ibn Ezra sees the possibilities of interpreting 11:1 as referring to either Hezekiah[213] or the Messiah,[214] he does not sanction any one view but shows the credibility of both.

3. *Luther.* In his commentary on Isaiah, Martin Luther never uses the appellation "Messiah" but always uses, the Greek synonym "Christ." He realizes the problem of reference and thus asserts that in Isa 7:14 the prophet "foretells two signs: The one is hidden, the other open." The prophet explains that the open sign applies to Ahaz but the hidden one "does not apply to Ahaz because he did not live to see it." Luther asserts that the "Jews" do not understand this passage and say that Emmanuel is Hezekiah. Nevertheless, v. 16 testifies that this sign is hidden and functions as a sign of judgment "for the sake of the ungodly."[215] Luther asserts that even though some say that v. 17 applies to "the removal of Babylon," this verse is speaking about the Assyrians since the Babylonian kingdom "did not yet exist." Yet comparing Assyria with Babylon (7:20), he claims that the hair of the feet speak of the "common people" and the beard the "priestly realm," implying that the "highest to the lowest...both earthly and spiritual kingdoms will be made bald...as was done by Nebuchadnezzar, the king of Babylon."[216]

Luther also reads 9:1–6 as messianic promise but does not suppose that it foresees a physical reign of the Messiah (my words). "David's reign over the Jews was physical, but at length Christ has begun a spiritual reign over the people, which will last forever."[217] Hence, Isa 9:1–6

213.   He argues that 2 Kgs 20:20 portrays Hezekiah as mighty as described in 9:2. This prompted the return of the people after they found that Jerusalem had escaped the snare of Sennacherib. After the loss of the greater part of his army as described in v. 11, Sennacherib died.

214.   Note Ibn Ezra's references to "the Messiah" (vv. 10, 13) and "the Messianic period" (v. 11) in Friedländer, *The Commentary of Ibn Ezra on Isaiah*, 3:24–25.

215.   Martin Luther, *Works* (ed. Jaroslav Pelikan; Saint Louis, Miss.: Concordia, 1955), 84, 85.

216.   Ibid., 85, 86.

217.   Ibid., 101.

signifies that both "Jews and Gentiles were in darkness, that is, in error, unrighteousness...[having] a false understanding of the law," but the "light is the Gospel."[218] Christ, the king born and given to us, has conquered the world through the Cross.[219] Therefore, as a "king different from David," Christ will bring "a resurrection from the dead."

Luther advises that ch. 11 addresses a "different subject." "This," he explains, is "the way the prophets usually contemplate the connection between the earthly and the spiritual kingdom..." Finally, he asserts that Isaiah "is speaking about Christ, not about Hezekiah, as the Jews quibble." The stump of Jesse is "the family of David" whose line is disintegrated and whose shoot is Christ. He then views 11:6 as "allegorical": Paul was a wolf before his conversion; lambs are Christians; leopards are persecuting tyrants; the goats are the martyrs; the calves are the faithful; and lions are the rich. The "savage, wild, irascible, hateful, murderous, ungovernable, and the people of the gentle Christ—come to agreement through the preaching of the Gospel." Therefore the Jews will be scattered into exile so that they can prepare the way for Christ.[220]

4. *Calvin*. Jean Calvin contends that Isa 7:14 is obscure partly because "the Jews, who by much caviling, have laboured...to pervert the true exposition...to torture the prophet's meaning to another sense" by alleging "that the person here mentioned is Hezekiah" or "that it is the son of Isaiah." Moreover, Calvin says that

> those who apply this passage to Hezekiah are excessively impudent; for he must have been a full grown man when Jerusalem was besieged. Thus they are grossly ignorant of history.[221]

Nor does he think that the child can be Isaiah's son because such "frivolous conjecture" fails to see that "we do not read that a deliverer would be raised up from the seed of Isaiah." Recognizing that v. 16 has created problems for messianic interpretation, Calvin concludes that v. 16 speaks of a different child from the one referred to in vv. 14–15.[222] Because this is an obscured picture by which "the Christ was foreshadowed...the name Immanuel could not be literally applied to a mere man; and, therefore there can be no doubt that the prophet referred to Christ."[223]

218. Ibid., 97.
219. Ibid., 100.
220. Ibid., 122–26.
221. Calvin, *Commentary on the Book of the Prophet Isaiah*, 1:244.
222. Ibid., 1:250.
223. Ibid., 1:245.

Because Ahaz rejects the sign, a great destruction would come from the very place from which he expected preservation, creating a problem that only a messiah could solve.[224]

Calvin argues that Isa 9:1–6 envisions a Davidic messiah who will reign eternally. Sometimes the prophets "foretell that David, who was already dead, would be king."[225] He argues that, similar to 7:14, the "Jews imprudently torture this passage [9:6], for they interpret it as relating to Hezekiah, though he had been born before this prediction was uttered." He understands that Isaiah's messianic expectation must be heard against the darkness of exile. Accordingly, 9:2 encompasses the destiny of the people, who in the "captivity of Babylon," experienced "the destruction of the city, in their captivity, and in what appeared to be their utter destruction, [so that] they may behold the light of God."[226] Therefore, 9:6 not only promises that God will "bring back the people from captivity, but he will place Christ on his royal throne."[227]

Calvin perceives the "stump of Jesse" in Isa 11 as a metaphor to speak of Judah's "future desolation" while the term "Jesse" downplays the house of David.[228] This *prediction* applies solely to the person of Christ; for till he came *no such branch arose*." Moreover, he argues that ch. 11 cannot apply to Hezekiah, Josiah or Zerubbabel. If they had fulfilled this messianic expectation, then there would not have been any hope for a Messiah before the time of Christ:

> We see, therefore, that to the wretched and almost ruined Jews, consolation was held out in the Messiah alone, and that their hope was held in suspense until he appeared. At the time of his appearance, there would have been no hope that the kingdom would be erected and restored if this promise had not been added; for the family of David appeared to be extinct. On this account he does not call him *David*, but *Jesse*…[229]

Calvin's understanding of Isaiah's messianic expectation presupposes its fulfilment after the end of the monarchy, which logically rules out Hezekiah. The juxtaposition of "dry *trunk*" and "*forest*" is "more beautiful than if he had said in plain language that the Messiah would come." Christ is this Messiah and his kingdom is "spiritual."[230]

---

224. Ibid., 1:245–61.
225. Ibid., 1:298.
226. Ibid., 1:298, 299.
227. Ibid., 1:306, 307.
228. Ibid., 1:372.
229. Ibid., 1:372 (my italics).
230. Ibid., 1:373, 374.

III. *Rethinking the Evidence*

A. *Problems Raised by Theories of Multiple Redactions*

Many scholars seem to identify several levels of tradition but cannot differentiate between the pre-biblical and biblical level. For example, Seitz claims to be interpreting the biblical text but interprets either the original tradition of the Syro-Ephraimitic or sometimes another tradition from 701 B.C.E. He claims to identify a later Babylonian redaction but has not shown it to have any semantic import in his interpretation of Isa 7:14; 9:1–6 and 11:1–9. Yet Seitz never states when these pre-biblical traditions become scripture and the implications of the same. Quite similar to Hayes and Irvine, Seitz in his commentary treats chs. 34–35 and 40–66 as a type of addendum that does not take away from the original eighth-century meaning nor alter it in any serious way.

Barth, Becker, Vermeylen, Sweeney and others attempt to show how the redactors have reinterpreted earlier traditions in light of later traditions. These attempts may or may not show how a text that was originally non-messianic could later be reinterpreted messianically. For example, Sweeney locates the last redaction of Isa 5–12 no later than the time of Josiah. Since the monarchy would have still existed, he finds no need for messianic expectation. However, his approach fails to explain the significance of these chapters within the final post-exilic edition of Isa 1–39.

On this point, Sweeney has trouble deciding which level of redaction governs the text. On one hand, he tries to evaluate each redactional level as equally significant. On the other hand, he insists that the Josianic redaction produces the "final form of Isa Chs 5–12."[231]

Conversely, Wegner, who regards the "latest" level of redaction in chs. 7–11 to have occurred no later than 701 B.C.E., attempts to describe a pre-exilic messianic expectation. Like Sweeney, he does not attempt to describe the later levels of redaction in chs. 5–12 and its relation to the book of Isaiah as a whole. Something about Isa 7:14; 9:1–6 and 11:1–9 compelled the Targum and New Testament writers to interpret various texts messianically. It is possible that Jewish interpreters began to name Hezekiah as the referent in order to have a strategy for arguing against Christian interpretation of the Old Testament, but have ignored the warrants of the text. Clearly, these modern theories of multiple redactions have failed to find the warrants for messianic interpretation that have been identified by the later Jewish Targum and the New Testament.

---

231. Sweeney, *Isaiah 1–39*, 150.

Oftentimes, modern interpreters do not distinguish between the pre-biblical and biblical levels of tradition but treat the text as though the biblical level may exist at each earlier level of tradition history. Individuals who approach the text in this manner may give precedence to one level of redaction by anchoring the text in that particular time period but ignore the latter formation of the book of Isaiah. For example, Sweeney and Wegner view the redaction of 701 B.C.E. as the "final form" of Isa 7–11 and allow this tradition to govern the meaning of 7:14; 9:1–6; and 11:1–9 (11:1–5), but they disregard the possibility that post-exilic editors reworked these passages when the book of Isaiah reached its completed form. Thus, Wegner attempts to resolve the problem by describing a pre-exilic messianism and Sweeney by assigning to it no messianism at all. On one hand, Wegner falsely reads the messianism that he regards to exist at the scriptural level into this pre-biblical level. His approach is problematic because it seeks to read as "biblical" the pre-biblical traditions of 701 B.C.E. that existed long before the book of Isaiah reached its present form. On the other hand, Sweeney, who recognizes that messianism originated in the post-exilic era, treats the redaction of 701 as though it were the biblical form and rules out messianic interpretation. The view that messianism serves as response to the termination of the monarchy is not a modern invention. Even Luther and Calvin, who do not try to resolve the origins of the text, observe how messianic hope might well address the circumstances of the Babylonian exile when the throne sat empty. Yet, redaction criticism can also explain how post-exilic editing might reinterpret earlier traditions as a response to the destruction of Jerusalem, the exile and the cessation of the monarchy.

In my view, Sweeney has shown that Isa 2–4 serves to exhort "the Jewish community in Jerusalem" during the post-exilic era,[232] though he fails to acknowledge the relationship between chs. 2–4 and 5–11. For example, Isa 3:13–15 appears to have derived from what was originally a juridical parable with the rest of it now found in 5:1–6.[233] Isaiah 1–4 finds similarities with Pss 1–2 that serve as an editorial introduction, which now invites the Second Temple community to read the Psalter as meditations on Torah.[234] Like Ps 1, Isa 2–4 depicts Torah being taught in

232. Yet this logic itself seems to rebut the view of Sweeney, Seitz and others who try to break the book up using ch. 33 on the basis that the later material that they find in ch. 33 already appears in chs. 1–4. Do not chs. 1–4 invite us to read the whole book as a response to the exile?
233. Sheppard, "The Anti-Assyrian Redaction," 204–11.
234. Pss 1–2, separated by no superscription, form an editorial introduction to the Psalms, telling the post-exilic community how to read the book of Psalms as scripture. Ps 1:2 assists the post-exilic community to read this book as meditations

the restored city of Jerusalem (2:3). Isaiah 1:20–26 describes the faithful city after the exile by expanding on the standard invective-threat oracles whereby the threat has been altered to include salvation since "judgement has already fallen and Israel [now] partakes in it."[235] Hence, Isa 2:5–22

on Torah (compare with Josh 1:7, 8). Without v. 2, Ps 1 would have originally been a wisdom psalm. Ps 1:6 summarizes the consequences of wisdom and Torah by means of a proverb. The Psalm as a whole now identifies the source of wisdom as the Torah of the LORD. Ps 2 was originally a royal enthronement psalm, but in the post-exilic era it became linked to 2 Sam 7 as a messianic prophecy. Therefore, this introduction invites one to read the Psalter in light of the three idioms of revelation (Torah, Prophets and Wisdom). The two chapters link both Psalms with *Stichwörter* (keyword connections) ("mediate" [plot]—1:2; 2:1; "sit"—1:1; 2:4; "perish"—1:6; 2:11). Ps 2:11 then rounds off this introduction by answering the opening words ("Blessed [אַשְׁרֵי] is the man") with "Blessed (אַשְׁרֵי) are those who take refuge…" (see 1:1). Not only does the word "refuge" end the introduction (2:11), but is repeated throughout the Psalter (7:1; 11:1; 16:1; 34:8b; 52:7 etc.) as a fulfilment of keeping Torah. See Sheppard, *Future of the Bible*, 59–95.

235.   Although this oracle departs from the standard invective-threat, such a change is not surprising. As Childs demonstrates in *Isaiah and the Assyrian Crisis*, Isaianic invective-threat oracles are characteristically altered. For example, a threat is sometimes built on a disputation (22:12–25; 28:11–17); an invective ends in a lament (1:4–9) or a wisdom saying (10:15); a threat joins with summary appraisal (14:4ff.; 17:12–14). Due to the unity of 1:21–26 (see below) and the fact that Isaianic judgment oracles are characteristically altered (see below), this text reflects the expected Isaianic alteration of the invective-threat whereby the invective is found in vv. 21–23 and the equivalent of the threat in vv. 24–26. While the invective does not begin with the standard causal clause marker עַל, "because you did such and such…," the unit fits the pattern of Gunkel's *Scheltrede* and *Drohwort* by listing the offences of those who stand in judgment. This is followed by the adverb לָכֵן, the announcement of divine word formula ("thus says YHWH") and the particle הוֹי. Isa 1:21–26 is a self-contained unit which is defined by the *inclusio*, קִרְיָה נֶאֱמָנָה in vv. 21 and 26 as well as forming a chiastic pattern. Note also that in an ingenious sort of way, the oracle has been set up so that the very act of judgment itself establishes restoration. It is fascinating that in v. 21, the faithful city has become a whore (זוֹנָה) and in v. 26 she is again "called" קִרְיָה נֶאֱמָנָה. While עִיר is used synonymously with קִרְיָה in vv. 21–26, the phrase קִרְיָה נֶאֱמָנָה ("faithful city") frames the unit in such a manner as to establish restoration within an oracle of judgment. In v. 21, our maiden city used to be righteous (צֶדֶק) but in v. 26 she (you) is again called a city of righteous (יִקָּרֵא לָךְ עִיר הַצֶּדֶק). Thus, in the word pair צֶדֶק מִשְׁפָּט (v. 21), מִשְׁפָּט functions as the *Stichwort* but צֶדֶק frames the oracle. Moreover, her silver (in v. 22) has become the very dross (סִיגִים) that YHWH will remove (v. 25). Even her princes (שָׂרִים) synonymous with שֹׁפְטִים), who are rebels, shall be restored as in the first times. That which is used pejoratively in the invective is transformed into what is favorable within the threat. The positive things (i.e. faithfulness and righteousness), of which she is accused of losing in the invective, she regains in the threat. The negative attributes, for which she is charged in the invective, shall be

similarly describes the future exaltation of Jerusalem, whose former leaders have already been humbled and brought down low (וישׂח...וישׁפל, v. 9), a motif that the editors have carried across Isa 1–12 (2:9, 11, 17; 5:15 and 10:33–34) so that Isa 2–4 cannot be detached from its post-exilic introduction in ch. 1 or its context within chs. 1–12. Similarly, 4:1–6 not only emphasizes the "glory of the Lord" in the restored Jerusalem but describes this glory with Torah imagery: "cloud by day and smoke and shining flame by night" (Isa 4:5; Exod 13:21, 22; 14:24; 40:38; Num 9:16; 14:14; Deut 1:33). Therefore, the post-exilic community could hear the description about the people going into exile in 5:13 in light of the Exodus in the Torah of Moses. Sweeney's isolation of Isa 1–4 overlooks this important relationship within the book as a whole. This approach can only "find lines of harmony and continuity at the expense of understanding the degree to which a canonical context retains historical discontinuities, conflictual inner-biblical interpretations, and persistent vagueness, ambiguities, or contradictory intentions."[236] Therefore, we cannot ignore the impact that this later development might have upon the interpretation of Isa 7:14; 8:23–9:6 (Heb.) and 11:1–9.

On this basis, Isa 1–12 must be read within the context of Isa 1–66. Gerald Sheppard has shown how, through a displacement of texts (Isa 5:25–30 from 9:7–20,[237] 5:15–16 from 2:6–21,[238] and 3:13–15 from 5:1–7[239]), the editors have created a "retrospective synthesis" in chs. 2–12 that

eliminated in the threat. Restoration is promised within a threat of judgment. Hence, in this passage judgment encompasses restoration. See Brevard S. Childs, *Isaiah and the Assyrian Crisis* (SBT, 2d Series 3; London: SCM Press, 1967), 20–38.

236. Sheppard, "The Anti-Assyrian Redaction," 216.

237. Sheppard shows that Isa 5:25–30, having belonged originally after the invective that lacks a threat at the end of 9:7–20, is more than an accidental insertion, as many scholars would assert (e.g. Duhm, Marti, Fohrer, Eichrot, Kaiser), but now stands after six woe oracles and functions as "a literary device used in the time of Josiah to direct the judgement in the original oracle...not only to against the Northern Kingdom (cf. 9:8) but against the southern kingdom as well."

238. Isa 5:15–16, which is recognized by most scholars to have belonged to the tradition history of Isa 2, and which may have originally followed 2:6–22 (O. Kaiser and Sheppard), is now located in a place where humanity (here "the nobility" [5:14]) is depicted to be "going down" to Sheol. This unit now stands before the testimony in ch. 6, which depicts the exaltation of the Lord who is sitting on the throne, "*high and lifted up*." Thus, Barth considers 5:15–16 to belong to the latest stage in post-exilic period.

239. Isa 3:13–15, which originally belonged to 5:1–7 (between 5:1b–2 and 5:3–7) as the "interpretation" and "indictment" in a juridical parable about a vineyard, similar to the one that Nathan told to David in 2 Sam 12, is now set by *Stichwort* connections between "his people" in vv. 13–14 and the twice repeated "my people"

also links chs. 1–39 together through common motifs.[240] The mention of "briers and thorns," which occurs only in chs. 1–39, is originally applied to Judah and then reapplied to either the destruction of Samaria or the exile (7:23, 24, 25—depending on the date of redaction[s]), Ephraim (9:18) and Assyria (10:17), thus connecting various time periods within these chapters. The repetition of the refrain ("For all this his anger has not turned away, and his *hand* is stretched out still…") allows the theme of God's hand as a symbol of judgment to surface across 5:8–10:4. Yet 12:1 ("your anger has turned form me and you comforted me") reinterprets that refrain (5:25; 9:12, 17, 21; 10:4) in light of the exile and explicitly anticipates 40:1. Since םחנ is never used to describe comfort in chs. 1–39 but reverberates throughout chs. 40–66 (40:1; 49:13; 51:3, 12, 19; 52:9; 54:11; 57:6; 61:2; 66:13), we can conclude that the salvation hymn in ch. 12 presupposes 40:1. Moreover, this outstretched hand is reapplied to Babylon in 14:26, 27,[241] where, in the same context about Babylon (13:1, 19; 14:4), the text refers to Cyrus (13:17). Similarly, the prophet's words to Ahaz (7:4; 8:12), "do not fear," resound throughout so-called Second and Third Isaiah (40:9, 10, 13, 14; 43:1, 5; 44:2, 8; 51:7; 54:4, 14; 57:11; 63:17). Further, 65:25 recapitulates 8:23, 11:6–9, includes the "former things," and 61:1 alludes to 11:2. Therefore, chs. 2–12 must be read in light of the book as a whole as a response to the promises that address the post-exilic situation.[242]

B. *Isaiah 7:14 in the Context of the Scriptural Scroll of Isaiah*

The conventional modern view that messianic expectation arose during the post-exilic period ought to influence how we regard messianic interpretation of Isa 7:14; 9:1–6 and 11:1–10. Yet, 7:14 poses a problem for messianic interpretation, which has not only stymied modern but premodern scholars as well. Does Isa 7:14 provide a warrant for the messianic citation in Matt 1:23 or does Matthew merely manipulate the text to refer to Jesus? While Isa 7 was not originally messianic, some scholars try to show how the original levels of tradition provide a foundation for messianic interpretation (Childs, Wegner). The narrative in ch. 7 centers around the conflict between the Syro-Ephraimite coalition and

---

in 3:12 in order to set the word vineyard in ch. 3 so that it links the other sections that contain the same motif. This displacement then contemplates the condemnation of leaders and anticipates what is read in ch. 5.

240. Cf. Sheppard, "The Anti-Assyrian Redaction," 198–216.

241. That is why Barth argues that AR extends from 2:1a to 14:27.

242. Cf. Sheppard, "The Anti-Assyrian Redaction," 193–216, and "The Book of Isaiah."

Ahaz but contain motifs around the institution of kingship upon which later messianic interpretation was established. Therefore, we cannot ignore the retention of pre-biblical traditions upon which the book of Isaiah is built. Although, form-critically, scholars break up Isa 7 into smaller original units of tradition (usually chs. 1–9 and 10–17), the second part depends on the first part and the first part finds its resolution in the second. This is why Wildberger has taken chs. 1–17 as a unit because each part is so heavily dependent on the other.

Prior to the Syro-Ephraimite War against Assyria, Rezin, king of Syria, had aspired to organize an anti-Assyrian campaign and the phrase עַל־אֶפְרַיִם implies that Pekah had consorted with Rezin under compulsion.[243] In Isa 7:3–9, Isaiah addresses an oracle of salvation to the Davidic king and assures him that he has no reason to fear "the two smoldering stumps of firebrands" if he earnestly pays heed to the promise of YHWH (7:4). The fire has already burnt out and is merely "smoldering."[244] Verse 7 reinforces that the coalition "will not stand." Isaiah reminds Ahaz of the covenant with David in 7:13 using language that concerns the monarchy—the "Davidic house" (בֵּית דָּוִד, lit. "the house of David").[245] Wegner asserts that בֵּית דָּוִד refers simply to Ahaz but could this phrase have another nuance to its meaning?[246] The expression בֵּית דָּוִד finds similarities with 2 Sam 7 where David intends to build YHWH a house, but in contrast YHWH promises to build David the house that would be his dynasty.[247] Essentially, the phrase בֵּית דָּוִד either implies the monarchy (1 Sam 19:11; 20:16; 2 Sam 3:1, 6) or David's royal line (1 Kgs 12:20; 17:21). In Jer 21:12, בֵּית דָּוִד is more specifically described in later verses as בֵּית־מֶלֶךְ יְהוּדָה...מֶלֶךְ יְהוּדָה הַיֹּשֵׁב עַל־כִּסֵּא דָוִד (Jer 22:1–2). However, more specific to the Isaianic context, the phrase בֵּית דָּוִד is redefined precisely in Isa 7:17 in terms that imply the succession of an ancestral line: בֵּית אָבִיךְ ("ancestral house," 7:17), whereby the threat in v. 17 is not merely against Ahaz but against the entire dynasty.[248] Similarly, the expression בֵּית דָּוִד in 22:22 is more explicitly explained in 22:23 to be בֵּית אָבִיו. Therefore, the phrase בֵּית דָּוִד in ch. 7 provides the

243. See Wildberger, *Isaiah 1–12*, 293.
244. Wegner, *An Examination of Kingship*, 93; E. G. Kraeling, "The Immanuel Prophecy," *JBL* 50 (1931): 278.
245. This construct clause is definite by virtue of the fact that the absolute is a proper noun.
246. Wegner, *An Examination of Kingship*, 123.
247. Cf. Mays, "Isaiah's Royal Theology," 47.
248. See Hugh G. M. Williamson, *Variations on a Theme: King, Messiah and Servant in the Book of Isaiah* (The Didsbury Lectures 1997; Carlisle: Paternoster, 1998), 107.

framework for the election and downfall of an anointed king. This circumstance provides the basis from which the later expectation of messianism flows and how the change in the meaning of the concept of anointed (משׁיח) gives rise to a later eschatological messianic expectation in the post-exilic era (similar to how a royal enthronement hymns [Ps 2 and Isa 9:1–6] have been reinterpreted messianically).

Although Judah is threatened by the coalition in the north and Assyria in the east, Isaiah tells Ahaz, "fear not" (7:4). Würthwein rightly shows that "fear not" implies that Judah should not call for Assyria's aid against the Syro-Ephraimite coalition because such an act would only be accomplished by a *de facto* submission to Assyria's mighty power.[249] Wildberger asserts that the phrase השׁכירה בעברי נהר ("hired beyond the river," v. 20) even describes Ahaz's cowardly act of hiring Tiglath-pileser at the cost of the temple's silver and palace's gold treasures.[250] For Ahaz to call upon Tiglath-pileser is an act at variance with the promises made to the "Davidic house." The efforts by Ephraim and Syria to install the Ben Ṭabĕal in place of Ahaz (7:6) were undoubtedly threats to permanence of the monarchy. Yet, the promise continues in v. 7, assuring Ahaz that the efforts of the coalition "shall not stand, and it shall not come to pass." After vv. 8–9 give the reason for Ahaz's replacement,[251] various scholars assert that the text sets up the reader to expect a repetition built on vv. 7–8:[252]

(ו)ראשׁ יהודה ירושלם	The head of Judah is Jerusalem,
(ו)ראשׁ ירושלם בן־דויד	and the head of Jerusalem is the son of David.

Yet instead we find the words: אם לא תאמינו כי לא תאמנו ("if you do not stand firm in faith, then you will not stand at all"). Wildberger asserts that "This faith is grounded in the history of YHWH's relationship with

---

249. E. Würthwein, "Jes. 7,1–9. Ein Beitrag zu dem Thema: Prophetie und Politik," in *Theologie als Glaubenswagnis. Festschrift für Karl Heim zum 80. Geburtstag* (Hamburg: Furche-Verlag, 1954), 47–63.

250. Wildberger, *Isaiah 1–12*, 325.

251. "For the head of Aram is Damascus, and the head of Damascus is Rezin. The head of Ephraim is Samaria, and the head of Samaria is the son of Remaliah."

252. Ever since von Ewald's *The History of Israel* (3d ed.; London: Longmans, Green & Co., 1876–86], 79), scholars have suggested this reading because the force of the text elicits this response of the reader. See Vischer, *Die Immanuel-Botschaft*, 18; J. Skinner, *Isaiah Chapters I–XXXIX* (The Cambridge Bible for Schools and Colleges; Cambridge: Cambridge University Press, 1896), 54; Wildberger, *Jesaja 1–12*, 273; idem, *Isaiah 1–12*, 291. However, this in itself provides no warrant for emending the text. This factor is merely an outgrowth of the rhetorical force of the text itself.

the Davidic house, as it had been formulated theologically on the basis of the tradition about the election of the dynasty ruling in Jerusalem."²⁵³ Along with the admonition "fear not," the prophetic word warns Ahaz not to overlook the protection that has been offered to Jerusalem and its king. In other words, Ahaz should not forget the covenant made with David.²⁵⁴ Wegner suggests that if Ahaz fails to trust in YHWH, "a long period of vassalage will begin."²⁵⁵ Ahaz disobediently rejects YHWH's promise because he trusts in or relies on the Assyrian rather than YHWH. Therefore, his refusal to believe incites judgment rather than salvation. He will reap bitter consequences.

The editors of Isa 40–66 have reapplied God's original warning to Ahaz, "fear not" (7:4; 8:12), to the exilic and post-exilic circumstances (40:9; 41:10, 13, 14; 43:1, 5; 44:2, 6–8; 51:7; 54:4, 14; 57:11; 63:17). The "fear not" motif is never used in contexts about Cyrus but it is used in the messianic material, first in the original Syro-Ephraimite tradition (7:4) and also in a later reinterpretation of 7:14 (7:25; 8:6, 12, 13; 35:4). Therefore, these re-applications of "fear not," both in Isa 1–39 and 40–66, summon the post-exilic community to look back at Isa 7 in light of the exile when the monarchy had been reduced to naught. Although the original advice of "fear not" to Ahaz once served as a prophetic warning not to forget the covenant made with David or to overlook the protection that has been offered to Jerusalem and its king, this later use of the admonition now invokes a portrait of restoration for Jerusalem after judgment. In a time after the decline of the "house of David," people may very well have seen Emmanuel to be a restorer of what Ahaz had forfeited.

Verse 10 underscores that YHWH again spoke to Ahaz and offered a sign (אות) that has no limits (v. 11).²⁵⁶ Citing Helfmeyer, Wegner argues that a sign "by its very nature points to something beyond itself and its main function is 'to mediate an understanding or to motivate a kind of behavior.' "²⁵⁷ He even cites Gunkel that "a sign is a thing, a process, an event by which one recognizes, learns or remembers something or realizes the credibility of a matter."²⁵⁸ Yet these isolated definitions do not account for the semantic range of the word, which extends beyond these

253. Wildberger, *Isaiah 1–12*, 317.
254. Ibid., 298.
255. Wegner, *An Examination of Kingship*, 94.
256. This unlimited sign is הַעְמֵק שְׁאָלָה אוֹ הַגְבֵּהַּ לְמָעְלָה ("let it be deep as Sheol or high as heaven").
257. F. J. Helfmeyer, "אות 'Ôth," in *TDOT* 1:167–88 (169, 170); Wegner, *An Examination of Kingship*, 94.
258. See Wegner, *An Examination of Kingship*, for the German.

definitions, encompassing both profane and religious spheres. In prophetic literature, אוֹת functions to legitimize the prophetic word as a "technical device for gaining recognition and belief from his hearers."[259] Yet Ahaz does not want an incentive to believe the prophetic word, and both his refusal to ask YHWH for a sign and his pseudo-spiritual words "I will not ask, and I will not put the LORD to the test" (v. 12) nullify the promise. In v. 13, Isaiah addresses the "house of David." Slotki adds an interesting twist to v. 13, asserting that "Isaiah turns away from the king in indignation and addresses the court or members of the royal family present."[260] Whatever the case, Isaiah responds:

> Therefore the Lord himself will give you a sign. Look, the young woman is pregnant and shall bear a son, and shall name him Emmanuel. He shall eat curds and honey when he knows how to refuse the evil and choose the good. For before the boy knows how to refuse the evil and choose the good, the land before whose two kings you are in dread will be forsaken." (7:14–16)

God can give a sign even if Ahaz rejects it, and so God gives the sign of Emmanuel. Wildberger appropriately observes that "one must speculate about which associations would have involuntarily sprung into the minds of those who were partners in the discussion with Isaiah, as they heard the name Immanuel."[261] Scholarly efforts to reconstruct the traditions around Isa 7:14 have clearly demonstrated that this text could not have originally been viewed as messianic. Verses 15 and 16 increase this improbability by placing the birth of this child within the context of the Syro-Ephraimite War. Certainly the work of pre-modern theologians, like Calvin, illustrate the major obstacle that v. 16 has created for messianic interpretation when reading the book as a whole.

Even if Emmanuel were from the line of David, this would not guarantee that he is a Messiah. Although Justin Martyr argued that there is nothing here to exclude Emmanuel from a Davidic origin, one reason supporting this notion is that the prophecy is addressed to the house of David.[262] This operation does not resolve the way v. 16 describes a figure

259. See H. Donner and W Röllig, *Kanaanäische und Aramäische Inschriften* (Wiesbaden: Otto Harrassowitz, 1962–64), 412–13; R. Payne Smith, *Thesaurus Syriacus* (Oxford: Clarendon, 1897), no. 141.4; Helfmeyer, *TDOT*, 1:167–88; Ernst Jenni and Claus Westermann, *Theologisches Handworterbuch zum Alten Testament* (2 vols.; Munich: Kaiser, 1971), 67–69.
260. Slotki, *Isaiah*, 34.
261. Wildberger, *Isaiah 1–12*, 311.
262. Justin Martyr, "Dialogue with Trypho," in *Œuvres completes*, vol. 20 (trans. G. Archambault; Paris: Migne, 1994), 68.

born during Isaiah's time, who could possibly have referred originally to Hezekiah or any other Davidic king, but not a Messiah. Are there then warrants for messianic interpretation of Isa 7:14 or does Matthew merely force this passage to refer to Jesus?

In my view, later editors reinterpreted Isa 7 messianically from the perspective of the exile, which presupposes the end of the monarchy. For instance, the call report in ch. 6 describes Isaiah's mission to proclaim the destruction of Judah. In 6:11, YHWH responds to Isaiah's query "How long, O Lord?" saying, "until the cities lie waste without inhabitant." While several scholars do not assign this verse to the exile,[263] Kaiser regards Isa 6 to be an introduction to chs. 7 and 8 whereby the narrator calls attention to the events of 587.[264] Although one cannot solve redactional problems solely on the basis of vocabulary, the word שְׁמָמָה is used predominantly in prophetic literature to speak of the destruction of 587 or later disasters.[265] Wildberger rightly notes that the statement about

263. Clements thinks that this text must primarily have been applied to Judah and Jerusalem but is not ready to assign this to the exile (Clements, *Isaiah 1–39*, 77–78; cf. Wegner, *An Examination of Kingship*, 131–32). However, Clements does concede that v. 13c might direct attention to "the impact of Babylonian imperialism after that of Assyria" (Clements, "The Prophecies of Isaiah," 426). Seitz compares these verses with 7:18–25 when "Assyria will come against Judah itself" and regards Jerusalem as the tenth that remains in v. 13a (Seitz, *Isaiah 1–39*, 58). Sweeney regards vv. 12–13 as "later additions" but also believes that "there is no evidence that this addition is post-exilic" (*Isaiah 1–39*, 138). See also Hayes and Irvine, *Isaiah*, 112–13.

264. See, Kaiser, *Isaiah 1–12* (2d ed.), 121, 132. Kaiser finds support from a preponderance of scholars: Duhm, *Jesaja*, 70; W. H. Brownlee, "Text of Isaiah VI 13 in Light of DSIa," *VT* 1 (1951): 296–98; Fohrer, *Das Buch Jesaja*, 1:30; Rudolf Kilian, *Die Verheissung Immanuels. Jes 7,14* (SBS 35; Stuttgart: Katholisches Bibelwerk, 1968), 51; Herbert, *The Book of the Prophet Isaiah 1–39*, 60; Barth, *Die Jesaja-Worte*, 196; John D. W. Watts, "The Formation of Isaiah 1: Its Context in Chapters 1–4," in *SBL Seminar Papers, 1978* (ed. Paul Achtemeier; SBLSP 13/14; Missoula, Mont.: Scholars Press, 1978), 51; Clements, *Isaiah 1–39*, 78; John A. Emerton, "The Translation and Interpretation of Isaiah VI,13," in *Interpreting the Hebrew Bible: Essays in Honour of E. I. J. Rosenthal* (ed. J. A. Emerton and S. C. Reif; Cambridge: Cambridge University Press, 1982), 114.

265. At least three of the four other times that the word שְׁמָמָה appears in Isaiah (1:7; 17:9; 62:4; 64:9) are post-exilic. When the word appears in Jeremiah, it speaks principally of the events of 587 (6:8; 12:10, 11), specifically of the destruction of Jerusalem and/or the cities of Judah (4:27; 9:10; 10:22; 34:22; 44:6), depicting Babylon as the destroyer (25:12; 32:43; 50:13; 51:26, 62 [of Hazor, 49:33]). One time it appears in an oracle against the nations: Ammon (49:2). Ezekiel also predominantly uses this word to depict the destruction of "Jerusalem," "the house of Israel" or "the cities" of Judah in 587 (6:14; 14:15–16; 15:8; 33:28–29; 36:34; note

deportation (v. 12a) could describe either Isaiah's time in 721 B.C.E. or the Babylonian exile.[266] Moreover, the description in Isa 6:13 seems to recall the tree-cutting imagery in 10:33–11:1 (see below). Brueggemann relates the stump in v. 13b with the "the stump of 587."[267] Though the vocabulary differs, the imagery of a stump (מַצֶּבֶת) in v. 13 invokes a connection with the "stump of Jesse" (יִשַׁי מִגֶּזַע) in 11:1. One could even speculate that the details from 2 Kgs 16:5 that were inserted into Isa 7:1 may betray the same hand that added these other later reflections in ch. 6. The call account in ch. 6 seems to serve as an editorial introduction that invites the reader to hear Isa 7 as anticipating the exile when Judah and its king were reduced to a mere "stump" and an expectation had already arisen of a Messiah who would bring deliverance.

In a similar fashion, Isa 7:18–25 offers clues of editorial additions analogous to those found in 6:12–13. Sheppard argues that these "editorial changes in the 'context' of Isaianic traditions produced changes in their meaning for later readers."[268] Clearly vv. 18–25 speak of severe devastation to the land that points to a period much later than the Syro-Ephraimite War. Wegner argues that vv. 18–25 reinterpret vv. 1–17 messianically by virtue of the fact that they describe the devastation which was brought on by the Assyrians.[269] However, a pre-exilic messianic

that in Isa 10:4 Jerusalem is named to drink the same cup of destruction that Samaria has already drunk and is later mentioned in 23:13); the royalty (of the land of Israel [53:2]) "shall be clothed in destruction (or despair)" (7:27). Otherwise, Mount Seir faces destruction because she rejoiced over the destruction of the house of Israel (35:3, 4, 7, 9, 14, 19) and also faces destruction Egypt (29:9, 10, 12; 32:15). Zephaniah speaks of the destruction of Jerusalem (1:13), Ashkelon (2:4) and of Moab for taunting Judah over her destruction (2:9, 13). Micah might be speaking from the pre-exilic times about the destruction of Samaria and Jerusalem (1:7) or Egypt (7:13). See also Joel 2:20; 4:19; Mal 1:3.

266. Wildberger, *Isaiah 1–12*, 258–59.
267. Brueggemann, *Isaiah 1–39*, 63.
268. Sheppard, "Isaiah 1–39," 543–49.
269. See Wegner, *An Examination of Kingship*, 132. We can agree that Isa 7:18 might serve as a pre-exilic editorial addition. Because of its mention of Egypt, who at the time of the Syro-Ephraimite war posed no threat to Judah, it must be an addition. However, as a beekeeper "whistles" (שָׁרַק) to attract a bee (דְּבוֹרָה), YHWH will whistle at Assyria. Apart from the name "Deborah" (דְּבוֹרָה) the word "bee" (דְּבוֹרָה) appears four times in the Old Testament (Deut 1:44; Judg 14:8; Ps 118:12; Isa 7:18) three times of which refer to the enemy (Deut 1:44; Ps 118:12; Isa 7:18) who in these three contexts is Assyria. Wildberger argues that the writer compares bees with the stinging Assyrians who are warlike and bent on victory (Wildberger, *Isaiah 1–12*, 323). Since this verse implies a threat and the enemy here is clearly defined, v. 18 cannot refer to any other event later than 701.

expectation is unlikely. The description in v. 20 of a razor shaving off all the hair of a person's head, beard and feet (the latter a euphemism for genitalia) possibly portrays the brutal humiliation of the exile and probably refers to the exile of both the Northern and Southern Kingdoms.[270]

The description of poverty and destitution in vv. 21–25 might also reflect the circumstances of the exile because the inhabitants must keep alive a cow to survive. In my view, "curds and honey" (חמאה ודבש) are foods of privation for a people whose land has been depopulated by the enemy and has been turned into pasture,[271] despite other scholarly efforts to see here an abundant and fortunate times.[272] Sweeney argues cogently that these are the foods that Emmanuel will eat until he is weaned.[273] Whether or not the phrase "He shall eat curds and honey..." (v. 15) *originally* spoke of "good times" or "bad times," vv. 21–22 reinterpret v. 15 in light of impoverished times. Can there be prosperity in the midst

---

270. This is Wegner's point, but he is more inclined to favor the Northern Kingdom. See Wegner, *An Examination of Kingship*, 103.

271. Cheyne says that "cornfields and vineyards having been destroyed, there will be a superabundance of pastureland, and the few survivors will have to subsist on sour milk and natural honey" (*Isaiah*, 1:51). Others think that curds and honey speak of foods of poverty, deprivation or from the conditions of devastation. See von Ewald, *The History of Israel*, 89–90; Delitzsch, *Isaiah*, 1:221; August Dillmann, *Der Prophet Jesaia* (5th ed.; Kurzgefasstes Exegetisches Handbuch zum Alten Testament 6; Leipzig: S. Hirzel, 1890), 71; Skinner, *Isaiah Chapters I–XXXIX*, 57; Marti, *Das Buch Jesaja*, 78; Duhm, *Jesaja*, 76; Smith, *The Book of Isaiah*, 1:115; Kraeling, "The Immanuel Prophecy"; Fohrer, "Zu Jes 7,14"; Johann Jakob Stamm, "La prophétie d'Emmanuel," *Revue de Theologie et de Philosophie* 32 (1944): 113–15; Fohrer, *Das Buch Jesaja*, 1:115; Widyapranawa, *The Lord is Savior*, 42; Seitz, *Isaiah 1–39*, 68; Motyer, *The Prophecy of Isaiah*, 86.

272. Curds and honey have been interpreted as foods of paradise; see Rignell, "Isaiah Chapter I"; Kruse, "Alma Redemptoris Mater"; William Lowth, *A Commentary Upon the Prophet Isaiah* (London: W. Taylor & H. Clements, 1714), 187–88; Gray, *Isaiah I–XXXIX*, 129–31 (1956); J. A. Bewer, "The Hellenistic Mystery Religion and the Old Testament," *JBL* 45 (1926): 1–13; Erling Hammershaimb, "Immanuel Sign [Isa 7:10]," *ST* 3 (1951): 136; Lindblom, *Isa Vii:1–Ix:6*, 23; Hammershaimb, *Some Aspects of Old Testament Prophecy*, 21; Martin Rehm, *Der königliche Messias im Licht der Immanuel-Weissagungen des Buches Jesajas* (Eichstöter Studien n.s. 1; Kevelaer: Butzon & Bercker, 1968), 66–67; Kaiser, *Isaiah 1–12* (2d ed.), 160–62; Brueggemann, *Isaiah 1–39*, 74, 85. Curds and honey have even been understood as "messianic foods"; see Gressmann, *Der Messias*, 156. Wildberger argues that curds and honey was a food of "abundance in the time of salvation"; see Wildberger, *Isaiah 1–12*, 314. Wegner argues that "the Syro-Ephraimite coalition is defeated and Ahaz and the Southern Kingdom need not worry about starvation which was a primary concern in time of war"; see Wegner, *An Examination of Kingship*, 129.

273. Sweeney, *Isaiah 1–39*, 147.

of humiliation (7:20) and "briers and thorns" (7:23, 24, 25)? If v. 15 may have originally implied abundance and prosperity, vv. 21–22 provide the negative side of this abundance of curds and honey: "On that day, one will keep alive a young cow and two sheep and will eat curds because of the milk that they (the cow and sheep) give." Since the Piel of חיה√ operates very similar to the Hiphil, the Piel imperfect יְחַיֶּה functions here as a causative, "to keep alive."[274] These two verses portray such difficult times that one must try to "keep alive" one cow or one sheep to provide milk. Moreover, the Niphal participle of יתר√ (הַנּוֹתָר) in v. 22 isolates "all who are left in the midst of the land" from all others who have either deserted the land or been taken into exile. Those who are left shall eat curds and honey. Because these conditions pertain to the fate of Judah, Clements and Kaiser properly identify this text with Nebuchadnezzar's conquest of Jerusalem in 587 as an "eschatological-messianic prophecy of salvation."[275]

Most scholars date 7:23–25 during either the events of 701 or 587.[276] Verses 23–25 describe a disaster so harsh[277] that "a thousand vines worth a thousand shekels will become briers and thorns" (v. 23). The land will be so barren that the cattle and sheep run loose (v. 25). While some scholars wish to connect this imagery of "briers and thorns" (a motif that is repeated also vv. 24 and 25) to AR, there is nothing compelling about this imagery that would force one to believe that vv. 23–25 must be regarded as pre-exilic. Sheppard demonstrates that a succession of editors has consistently built on the motifs of briers and thorns (שָׁמִיר and שַׁיִת).[278] Reapplied to multiple situations and different moments of discourse, it

274. Jenni, *Theologisches Handworterbuch zum Alten Testament*, 1:414.
275. Clements asserts that this explains why the Emmanuel child will eat honey and curds. Since the grain crops are destroyed, people will be "left to eke out a livelihood from the few cattle and sheep that remain"; see Clements, *Isaiah 1–39*, 92, and cf. Kaiser, *Isaiah 1–12* (2d ed.), 164. Wildberger (*Isaiah 1–12*, 328) claims that these verses could refer to either the events of 701 or 587.
276. Hayes and Irvine do ascribe these verses to eighth-century Isaiah and date them in 735–32 B.C.E. (*Isaiah*, 140). Clements regards vv. 23–25 to be a later addition that describes "the fate of the Northern Kingdom" (*Isaiah 1–39*, 93) and is followed by several others on this point (e.g. Herbert, *The Book of the Prophet Isaiah 1–39*, 66; Widyapranawa, *The Lord is Savior*, 44; Wegner, *An Examination of Kingship*, 132–33). Seitz too assigns these verses to the siege of Assyria (*Isaiah 1–39*, 80). Wildberger, who regards vv. 18–25 as one kerygmatic unit, argues that vv. 23–25, like the preceding verses, could also refer to either the events of 701 or 587 (*Isaiah 1–12*, 328). Kaiser views vv. 18–25 as a post-exilic redaction that interprets vv. 1–17 messianically (*Isaiah 1–12* [2d ed.], 164–65).
277. Wildberger, *Isaiah 1–12*, 328.
278. Sheppard, "The Anti-Assyrian Redaction," 210–11.

would not at all be surprising that later editors reapplied "briers and thorns" to the exile.

Wegner asserts that since the "briers and thorns" speak of Judah in Isa 5:7, 7:23–25 must refer to Sennacherib's invasion but he fails to mention that Isa 5:7 also includes Israel.[279] Wildberger suggests that the repetition of "on that day" does not serve as an eschatological day of judgment but a day of disaster.[280] Not only do vv. 21–25 appear to reinterpret the "curds and honey" in 7:15, but also the briers and thorns. A standard editorial formula, the phrase "on that day" (vv. 18, 20, 21, 23)[281] and the repetition of "briers and thorns" hold together all of vv. 18–25 in such a manner that if only one portion of these verses were indeed post-exilic, then the whole would be reinterpreted accordingly. Although one cannot prove either view conclusively, there remains a possibility that the editing at the end of ch. 7 comes from the aftermath of Nebuchadnezzar's invasion or the Assyrian Crisis. Nevertheless, we cannot overlook how Isa 1–4 provides a framework for interpreting the chapters that follow (Isa 7:14 included) in retrospect to the events of 587 B.C.E., when a messianic expectation had arisen.

Furthermore, if later editing is present in ch. 6, and possibly ch. 7, then we should also not at all be surprised that ch. 8 contains material that comes from an exilic or post-exilic editor. In fact, Wegner argues that the structure and description of destruction and restoration in 8:1–9:6 reveals an editorial arrangement similar to 6:12–7:25.[282] While a few scholars have regarded Isa 8:19–9:6 as part of Isaiah's original "*Denkschrift*" (or "memoir"),[283] other scholars believe that 8:19–22 were added either after the exile of the Northern Kingdom (722),[284] or the exile of the

279.   Wegner, *An Examination of Kingship*, 106.

280.   Wildberger, *Isaiah 1–12*, 323.

281.   See also Isa 2:11, 12, 20; 3:7, 18; 4:1, 2.

282.   Wegner, *An Examination of Kingship*, 202–203.

283.   Skinner, *Isaiah Chapters I–XXXIX*, 71–75; Budde, "Über die Schranken"; idem, *Jesaja's Erleben*, 46–51. More recently, Jeppesen, Hayes and Irvine and Laato argue that the memoir extends to 9:6; see K. Jeppesen, "Call and Frustration: A New Understanding of Isaiah Viii 21–22," *VT* 32 (1982): 145–57 (148–49); Hayes and Irvine, *Isaiah*, 170–84; Laato, *Who is Immanuel?*, 100–101.

284.   Cf. Lindblom, *Isa Vii:1–Ix:6*, 33–34; Godfrey R. Driver, "Isaianic Problems," in *Festschrift für Wilhelm Eiler* (ed. G. Wiessner; Wiesbaden: Otto Harrassowitz, 1967), 43–44; Charles F. Whitley, "The Language and Exegesis of Isaiah 8,16–23," *ZAW* 90 (1978): 41–42; J. T. Willis, *Isaiah* (The Living Word Commentary on the Old Testament; Austin: Sweet, 1980), 78–79; Jan Ridderbos, *Isaiah* (trans. John Vriend; BSC; Grand Rapids: Zondervan, 1985), 98–99; Oswalt, *Isaiah 1–39*, 238–39; Wegner, *An Examination of Kingship*, 78, 202–3; Sweeney, *Isaiah 1–39*, 182.

Southern Kingdom (587).[285] The problem with linking 8:19–22 with the fall of Samaria is that the Northern Kingdom never experiences deliverance or restoration as described in 8:23–9:6, which would leave this section as an eternally unfulfilled prophecy.[286] Yet for the post-exilic community, these verses, when applied to Judah, may very well describe the exile, thus explaining how they came to be interpreted messianically.

Several clues appear in ch. 8 that illustrate a confluence of later material, some of which provide evidence that the editors reinterpreted these verses in light of the exile. First, vv. 19–22 present a change from first person singular forms to second and third person plural forms, which probably indicates that vv. 19–22 constitute an editorial addition.[287] Since v. 23 also appears to be an editorial addition, Wegner posits that 9:1 may have originally followed 8:18 and vv. 19–22 were inserted here to explicate the destruction promised in earlier oracles.[288] Second, 8:20 shows signs that a fifth-century editor later reinterpreted an earlier reference to the "torah" (8:16) as the Mosaic Torah. In 8:16, we hear the words "Bind up the testimony (תְּעוּדָה), seal the teaching (תּוֹרָה) among my disciples." This early reference to "torah" was originally employed merely in the sense of the prophet's teaching. Yet 8:20 reverses the order of testimony and torah in 8:16 to "Torah and testimony," thus giving the Torah precedence. The testimony is now subordinate to the Torah. Since 8:19–20

285. Some take this view on the basis that בה (v. 21) may refer to Jerusalem (Barth, *Die Jesaja-Worte*, 153; Clements, *Isaiah 1–39*, 91), while others oppose this view because they think that v. 22 defines בה as the land. See Skinner, *Isaiah Chapters I–XXXIX*, 72; George B. Gray, *Isaiah I–XXVII* (1959), 160; Hayes and Irvine, *Isaiah*, 171; Joseph Jensen, *Isaiah 1–39* (OTM 8; Wilmington, Del.: Michael Glazier, 1984), 109; Scott, *The Book of Isaiah*, 230; Watts, "The Formation of Isaiah 1," 125; Wegner, *An Examination of Kingship*, 78.

286. Similarly, Wegner asserts that 8:23 indicates that the Northern Kingdom would be glorified (*An Examination of Kingship*, 160) but the problem is that the Northern Kingdom never was glorified in the manner described in 8:23–9:6. Carroll would suggest that the natural reflex to failed prophecy would be to project into the future with hope that some day it would be fulfilled; see Carroll, *When Prophecy Failed*, 142–44. This view is not much different from that held by Marx, who, in a series of letters to Engels, said that Jew and Christian could abide with present sufferings because they attached chiliastic visions to them to suppress the pain of suffering. See Karl Marx and Friedrich Engels, *On Religion* (New York: Schocken, 1964). The Jehovah's Witnesses are a prime example of a group whose leader had prophesied that Jesus would return in 1914 but salvaged the prophecy by keeping the date but saying that Jesus returned to his heavenly temple. However, the post-exilic editor did more than merely try to salvage a meaningless prophecy. He found genuine fulfilment when the exiles returned as these verses spoke to their own situation.

287. See Wegner, *An Examination of Kingship*, 161.

288. Ibid., 203.

also seem to add comments to vv. 16–18 that invoke a picture of exile (see below),[289] at this later editorial level, the Torah of God becomes "reminiscent of the Mosaic law." The "torah" of the prophet has now been "identified with divine Torah, known most clearly in the books of Moses."[290] For example, Sweeney states that 1:10 belongs to the "introduction" of the book:

> Although it is unlikely that the author of this passage intended "Torah" to refer to the Five Books of Moses, it would be understood as such in a late 5th-century context (cf. Sheppard, Book of Isaiah," esp. 578–82). In this respect, the final form of the book of Isaiah presents itself as an expression of YHWH's Torah to Israel at a time when the postexilic Jewish community was reconstituting itself on the basis of Mosaic Torah.[291]

Since Sweeney allows for a fifth-century redaction of this scroll, the significance of the Torah as that of Moses *belongs* to the level of late redaction when this scriptural book was constructed. In the post-exilic period, the later editors are conscious of the Torah because, as my previous chapter demonstrated, the biblical scroll of Isaiah has been edited in the shadow of the Torah. Consequently, the book of Isaiah has a prologue that introduces the Torah as the subject matter against which one reads the words of the prophet (1:10). Hence, we see, within the book of Isaiah itself, a warrant for later rabbinic efforts to interpret the book as a commentary on Torah. Therefore, if the word "Torah" has indeed changed in its meaning, then we should not at all be surprised that the meaning of texts about kingship are reinterpreted messianically in the post-exilic period. Most likely, messianic warrants belong to the same late levels of editing as those passages in Isaiah that draw attention to Torah.

C. *Isaiah 9:1–6 in Relation to the "Former" and "Latter" Things in Isaiah 40–66*

The term עֵת הָרִאשׁוֹן ("the former time") in Isa 8:23 resonates with the "former things" in chs. 40–66 (41:22; 42:9; 43:9, 18; 46:9; 48:3; 65:17).

---

289. Sheppard, "Isaiah 1–39," 579.

290. See ibid., 548. This stands in opposition to Jensen's view that these references to "torah" in Isaiah never meant the Mosaic Torah or prophetic teaching but rather instruction with wisdom overtones. While we must grant that Jensen leaves aside any "torah" references that he thinks are later than the time of Isaiah, Jensen does consider 8:20 to be irrelevant, since he deems this verse either to be a gloss or else to derive from the same tradition history that lies behind 8:16—in either case, v. 20, for Jensen, adds nothing to the meaning of the term "torah." See Joseph Jensen, *The Use of Tôrâ by Isaiah: His Debate with the Wisdom Tradition* (CBQMS 3; Washington, D.C.: The Catholic Biblical Association of America, 1973), 5–6.

291. Sweeney, *Isaiah 1–39*, 53.

Yet, this word appears in the singular in 8:23 rather than in the plural as in chs. 41–48. In 8:23, it refers to one "former" event or time period rather than a plurality of prophecies as in chs. 41–48. Scholars have pointed out that הָרִאשׁוֹן and כָּעֵת do not agree in gender but only in number and definiteness. Some have attempted to solve the problem by assigning the temporal clause as the subject of the sentence.[292] Some believe that the adjectives (הָרִשׁוֹן and הָאַחֲרוֹן) function substantively and refer to kings[293] and more specifically Israelite kings.[294] Williamson convincingly argues that Deutero-Isaiah borrows the idea of the former things from Proto-Isaiah, thus representing a summons to reopen the sealed testimony of Isaiah (8:16) and to announce God's repeal of judgment and re-enactment of salvation through the agency of Cyrus.[295] However, he overlooks how ch. 40 has altered the former things to include creation and the written Torah (see Chapter 2 above). In the same way that the former things have been altered by this later reading in ch. 40, 8:20 similarly calls the reader to hear Isaiah as a scriptural book and thereby read this text in light of the Mosaic Torah. Therefore, we cannot overlook the role of Torah (8:20) and its juxtaposition with the "former" and "latter things," especially in relation to messianic interpretation. While the "former" (הָרִאשׁוֹן) in 8:23 may have originally contrasted the "former time" of Tiglath-pileser annexing "Zebulun" and "Naphtali" with the "later time" (הָאַחֲרוֹן) when the territory would be restored to Israel, these words have taken on new dimensions within the book as a whole.

Another indicator of editorial reinterpretation may be found in a contrast that is drawn in vv. 22 and 23. Wegner rightly explains the "logical play on words" between מָעוּף and צוּקה in v. 22 and מוּעָף and מוּצק in v. 23, which, he maintains, draws a stark contrast between two time periods (namely, the campaign of Tiglath-pileser and the fall of the Northern Kingdom) in order to interpret 9:1–6 messianically.[296] Weger assumes that a pre-exilic addition can function as messianic interpretation. He maintains that 9:1–6 combined with royal ideology gave rise to

292.   Wildberger, *Jesaja 1–12*, 363; Laato, *Who is Immanuel?*, 173.

293.   Budde, *Jesaja's Erleben*, 99; Herbert, *The Book of the Prophet Isaiah 1–39*, 73; John A. Emerton, "Some Linguistic and Historical Problems in Isaiah VIII.23," *JSS* 14 (1969): 160–68.

294.   Hayes and Irvine (*Isaiah*, 177) regard the הָרִאשׁוֹן ("former one") as referring to Jeroboam and הָאַחֲרוֹן ("the latter one") to Menahem. H. L. Ginsburg ("Pekah and Hoshea of Israel [Isa 8:23]," *ErIsr* 5 [1958]: 61–65) suggests Hoshea and Pekah.

295.   Williamson, *The Book Called Isaiah*, 70–77, 107.

296.   For further details on exegesis and the many views of the history of interpretation on this point, see Wegner, *An Examination of Kingship*, 151–52.

the "concept" of a "future deliverer" who would liberate the people from the yolk of Assyria but later developed into the traditional understanding of the Messiah.[297] However, the editor's juxtaposition of light and darkness in 8:22–9:1, a motif characteristic of chs. 40–66, might also provide a way to describe light being shed on the darkness of the exile. This is typified in the way that light and darkness speak of exile and deliverance (42:7, 16; 60:1).[298] God's ability to create light to overcome the darkness provides an image for restoration and the return of the exiles (42:16; 45:7). The captives are depicted as coming out of the darkness of exile (49:9). Moreover, the darkness of Babylon's own exile is described in terms of darkness (47:5, 14). The image of light breaking forth as the dawn depicts restoration (58:8). God's people hope for and anticipate the light of justice and righteousness in order to overcome the darkness and gloom of injustice and unrighteousness (59:9). Light shall rise in the darkness to whomever gives food to the hungry, and their gloom *will become* like midday (58:10). The light becomes dark to portray the day of the Lord (judgment) against Babylon in the post-exilic era: "For the stars of the heavens and their constellations will not give their light; the sun will be dark at its rising, and the moon will not shed its light" (13:9, 10). The nations shall come to YHWH's light (60:3) and God's people will no longer require the light of the sun by day nor the moon at night because YHWH himself is their everlasting light (60:19, 20). Therefore, the editors call the post-exilic community to walk in the light (2:5).

The juxtaposition of light and darkness in 8:22–9:1 finds close similarities with the same imagery in 60:1–2. In the messianic age, God's light arises upon his people: "For darkness shall cover the earth, and thick darkness the peoples; but the LORD will arise upon you, and his glory will appear over you" (60:2). However, the terms for "dark gloom" (מעוף) in 8:22 and מועף in "8:23," which appear nowhere else in the Old Testament, are different terms than the thick darkness (ערפל) found in 60:2. The term ערפל characterizes ("thick cloudy darkness"), which appears fifteen times in the Old Testament, speaks of concealment (Job 38:9). It describes a darkness that is severely thick in order to obfuscate the presence of God (Exod 20:21; Deut 4:11; 5:22; 2 Sam 22:10 = Ps 18:10; 1 Kgs 8:12; 1 Chr 6:1; Job 22:13; Ps 97:2) or the way one should go (Jer 13:16; Ezek 34:12). ערפל even describes God's judgment (Joel 2:2; Zeph 1:15). Because this darkness provides such a compelling

297. Ibid., 199.
298. Mauchline acknowledges that Isa 9:2 immediately recalls 8:22 and 9:1, which also makes the reader think of 60:1. He does not regard this passage as referring to the events of 587 but to the Assyrian damage to Jerusalem in 701. See his, *Isaiah 1–39: Introduction and Commentary* (TBC; London: SCM Press, 1962).

description of the exile like so many other motifs in Isa 60–62, several scholars have attributed chs. 60–62 to Second Isaiah[299] or his disciples.[300] This major motif of light and darkness appears chiefly in Isa 40–66, except for sparse examples in chs. 1–39, which appear to be exilic or post-exilic editorial re-interpretations.[301] Therefore, a later hand is at work in 8:20–9:1 to portray light that is shed on the darkness of exile. In the same manner, such "scripture-conscious" editing has altered the meaning of תּוֹרָה (v. 20), so the *Stichwörter* (מָעוּף and צוּקָה in v. 22 and מוּצָק and מוּעָף in v. 23) provide a contrast between the light of the messianic age[302] and the darkness of exile.[303]

Scholars, who have been puzzled by how 9:1–6 can be messianic, often overlook how the later editing in ch. 8 seems to invite messianic interpretation. Williamson comments that this passage is not "particularly suitable to a post-exilic date" but completely overlooks the later import of this level of editing.[304] Some explain messianism in 9:1–6 by alleging that these verses originally were post-exilic.[305] More recent scholarship

---

299. Cheyne, *Isaiah*, vol. 1; Abraham Kuenen, *Historisch kritische Einleitung in die Bücher des Alten Testaments hinsichtlich ihrer Entstehung und Sammlung*. Vol. 2, *Die Prophetischen Bucher* (Leipzig: O. R. Reisland, 1892).

300. Some believe that a student of Second Isaiah composed this work since there are numerous citations which are narrowly connected to the "grand master." Around this group, slowly other prophets from the same time were called. Consequently all this material was welded together into one redactional framework which we now call Trito-Isaiah. See G. C. Workman, *The Servant of Jehovah* (New York: Longmans, Green & Co., 1907), 245, cited by W. A. M. Beuken, *Jesaja*, vol. 2 (Nijkerk: Callenbach, 1989), 157; see also, among others, Westermann, *Isaiah 40–66*, 352–53, and K. Pauritsch, *Die neue Gemeinde: Gott sammelt Ausgestossene und Arme. Jesaia 56–66* (AnBib 47; Rome: Pontifical Biblical Institute, 1971), 105–7.

301. Isa 10:17 describes light that will become a fire that will burn even the briers and thorns but does not include a juxtaposition of light and darkness. Isa 2:5 and 30:26 also describe light but without darkness. See also 13:10–11, whose description of Babylon leads many to date as exilic or post-exilic.

302. See further my remarks on 8:23–9:6.

303. Verses 19–22 depict a time of great distress when the people will be encouraged to conjure up "familiar spirits" (הָאֹבוֹת) and "mediums" or "necromancers" (הַיִּדְּעֹנִים). The narrator asks, "should not a people consult their God (אֱלֹהָיו)...for Torah and testimony?" Because of their disobedience to Torah, "they have no dawn" (v. 20). "They will pass through it (the land) distressed and hungry, and when they become hungry, they will make themselves outraged and will curse their king and their God" (v. 21). "They will only see distress, darkness [and] the gloom of anguish and they will be driven into deep darkness" (v. 22).

304. Williamson, *Variations on a Theme*, 45.

305. See Marti, *Das Buch Jesaja*, 94–95; Duhm, *Jesaja*, 92; Hölscher, *Die Profeten*, 348; E. König, *Das Buch Jesaja* (Gütersloh: Bertelsmann, 1926), 139–40;

acknowledges that 9:1–6 could function form-critically as a hymn of thanksgiving[306] or a royal enthronement hymn either to Hezekiah[307] or Josiah,[308] and might not be originally messianic.[309] Granting that 9:1–6

Mowinckel, *He That Cometh*, 138–43; Theodor Lescow, "Das Geburtsmotiv in den messianischen Weissagungen bei Jesaja und Micha [Isa 7:14; 9:5,11; Mic 5:1–3]," *ZAW* 79 (1967): 180–88; Jochen Vollmer, "Zur Sprache von Jesaja 9,1–6," *ZAW* 80 (1968): 343–50; W. Dietrich, *Jesaja und die Politik* (BEvT 74; Munich: Kaiser, 1976), 120, 207; Kaiser, *Isaiah 1–12* (2d ed.), 205–6.

306.   Mowinckel, *He That Cometh*, 102; Lindblom, *Isa Vii:1–Ix:6*, 34–35; Wildberger, *Jesaja 1–12*, 168–76, 366; F. Crüsemann, *Studien zur Formgeschichte von Hymnus und Danklied in Israel* (WMANT 32; Neukirchen–Vluyn: Neukirchener, 1969); Barth, *Die Jesaja-Worteer*, 148–52; Vermeylen, *Du prophète Isaïe*; J. P. Olivier, "The Day of Midian and Isa 9:3b," *JNSL* 9 (1981): 143; Laato, *Who is Immanuel?*, 176–78; Kaiser, *Isaiah 1–12* (2d ed.), 207; Sweeney, *Isaiah 1–39*, 179–83. Note that Lindblom (*Isa Vii:1–Ix:6*, 4, 34) and Gressman (*Der Messias*, 244–45) think that this purported "thanksgiving hymn" mainly has to do with Hezekiah. Wegner identifies weaknesses in labelling this either a hymn of thanksgiving or a royal enthronement oracle, but does show that vv. 6–7 find affinity with a birth announcement. He wants to show that this passage does not conform to one specific form. See Wegner, *An Examination of Kingship*, 168–76; followed by Williamson, *Variations on a Theme*, 32.

307.   This is the view of Alt ("Jesaja 8,23–9,6," 235, 258–59) and has been followed by others: Crook, "A Suggested Occasion"; Vischer, *Die Immanuel-Botschaft*, 40–54; Lindblom, *Isa Vii:1–Ix:6*, 33–34; Hans Peter Müller, "Uns ist ein Kind geboren. Jes. 9.1–6 in traditionsgeschichtlicher Sicht," *EvT* 21 (1961): 414; von Rad, "The Royal Ritual in Judah," 222–31; Herbert, *Isaiah 1–39*, 75; Zimmerli, *Old Testament Theology in Outline*, 195; Becker, *Messianic Expectation*, 45; Hayes and Irvine, *Isaiah*, 180–82; Seitz, *Isaiah 1–39*, 85. Ever since the early twentieth century, scholars who did not necessarily refer to Isa 9:1–6 as a "royal accession hymn" have linked these verses to Hezekiah's accession. See R. H. Kennett, "The Prophecy in Isaiah IX,1–7 (Heb. VIII,23–IX,6)," *JTS* 7 (1906): 330; William Foxwell Albright, *Yahweh and the Gods of Canaan* (Jordan Lectures 1965; London: Athlone, 1968), 22; J. M. Miller and J. H. Hayes, *A History of Ancient Israel and Judah* (Philadelphia: Westminster, 1986), 683.

308.   This is part of a redaction to refer to the accession of Josiah (Barth, *Die Jesaja-Worte*, 145–48; Vermeylen, "Religieuse en Israël," 233–36). Herbert (*The Book of the Prophet Isaiah 1–39*, 74) suggests that this text may have received prophetic fulfilment through individuals such as Hezekiah and Josiah but was reinterpreted messianically by the community after the exilic when no king reigned in Jerusalem.

309.   Other than the datings ascribed to Isaiah during the Syro-Ephraimite war or AR during Josiah's reform, or somewhere in the post-exilic period, scholars suggest two other time frames: pre-Isaianic (Crook, "A Suggested Occasion"; idem, "Did Amos and Micah Know Isaiah 9:2–7 and 11:2–9?," *JBL* 73 [1954]: 144–51) or Maccabean (Kennett, "The Prophecy in Isaiah IX,1–7"; M. Treves, "Little Prince

originally might derive from a royal accession or thanksgiving oracle to either Hezekiah or Josiah, we can still ask: How did these verses gain messianic import?[310] Wegner moves in the right direction by arguing that the text has been editorially reinterpreted as messianic. On the basis of our prerequisite that messianism must have arisen during the post-exilic period, we must question his proposal for a 722 or 701 "rereading." It makes better sense that post-exilic editors reinterpreted this royal accession oracle with imagery that belongs to this later time (light cast on the darkness of exile, torah interpreted as Mosaic Torah, and the "former things" reinterpreted in the time of Cyrus).

Within this later editorial context (8:19–23), 9:1–6 concurs with this image of light and darkness since 9:1 opens using this metaphor: "The people who walked in darkness have seen a great light…" Who are these people (העם) in 9:1? Wegner argues that since v. 23b was not originally a part of the poem, then we could assume that "the people must refer to Judah since the child is later described as sitting upon the throne of David." In order to interpret this as Judah, Wegner seems compelled to "atomize" this text to its original pre-biblical unit of tradition history. He ignores his foundational question, "Does the final form contain any message of its own…?"[311] Wegner is correct that 9:1–6 on its own speaks of Judah but this level of tradition history cannot determine the meaning of the "final form." The context provides more likelihood that editors have retained both the traditions about the Northern and Southern Kingdoms in order to include both kingdoms together in the messianic hope. Therefore, the woe oracles that were originally applied to Ephraim, beginning in 5:8 and ending in 10:5, now have been applied to both Israel and Judah in 5:7. That is why the summary appraisal in 5:7 spells out that the Song of the Vineyard is about Judah and Israel. The original juridical parable before 3:13–15, which was editorially detached from the original song (5:1–2; [3:13–15;] 5:3–6), does not require such a detailed explanation.[312] The original function had been lost by such editing and the editors could interpret what remains in 5:1–6 as an allegory pertaining to both Judah

---

Pele-Joez," *VT* 17 [1967]: 464–77). Duhm (*Jesaja*, 88–89), who ascribed these verses to Isaiah, asserted that the Maccabean period was the only other alternative (see above).

310.   Clements (*Isaiah 1–39*, 104) regards this unit to have originally been an oracle for the accession of either Hezekiah or Josiah.

311.   Wegner, *An Examination of Kingship*, 15.

312.   Nathan's juridical parable (1 Sam 12:1–4) does not include an explanation but is followed by David's anger and oath to kill the guilty (12:5) and Nathan's words "you are the man."

and Israel. Similarly, any redactor(s) who leave(s) traces of prose connecting links in ch. 10 (vv. 12, 20, 23 and 24–27)[313] has/have framed
oracles, which were originally against Israel, now to Judah as well
(10:11, 12, 24, 32). In addition, the imagery of briers and thorns, which
originally applied to Judah, now pertains to Israel (9:18; 10:17). Likewise, 11:10–16 speaks of a time when the nations will seek after the ruler
described in 11:1–9. Isaiah 11:12 resounds: "he will gather the dispersed
ones of Israel, and shall assemble the scattered ones of Judah from the
four corners of the earth." Isaiah 13 relates the Babylonian situation back
to these earlier chapters. Aware of the exile and dispersion in both the
south and north, the editors cannot specify either Judah or Israel but seek
to combine both into the tapestry of judgment and promise since the
Messiah will draw all nations and tribes to YHWH. Therefore, Sweeney
rightly suggests that 9:1–6 anticipates an ideal Davidic king who will
reunite the Northern and Southern Kingdom[314] but in his portrayal of a
multilayered redaction history, he fails to acknowledge the import of
post-exilic editing for 9:1–6. An ideal Judean king, whom the community of faith celebrated in the pre-exilic era, now appears as a Davidic
king in the post-exilic period—a king Messiah who shall bring light to
darkness for both the Northern and Southern Kingdoms.

This contrast of light and darkness is followed by a threefold repetition of כי that describes why the light is significant to the people who
have walked in darkness.[315] The preposition כי in vv. 3, 4 and 5 seems to
imply that the people rejoice (v. 2) "because" their burden has been lifted
(v. 3), the peace that the king brings causes peoples to destroy their
weapons (v. 4),[316] and a royal child is born who will establish this peace
(v. 5). Williamson asserts that vv. 3–4 speak of God's work of deliverance without any reference to human agency.[317] However, messianic

313. For further discussion on the redaction history of theses verses, see O. C.
Whitehouse, *Isaiah I–XXXIX* (2 vols.; The Century Bible; London: Thomas Nelson
& Sons, 1905), 1:163; Kemper Fullerton, "The Problem of Isaiah, Chapter 10," *AJSL*
34 (1917/18): 170–84; Childs, *Isaiah and the Assyrian Crisis*, 41–44; Vermeylen,
"Religieuse en Israël," 263–64; Barth, *Die Jesaja-Worte*, 23–25, 40–41; Clements,
Isaiah 1–39, 114; Kaiser, *Isaiah 1–12* (2d ed.), 230, 240; Wegner, *An Examination
of Kingship*, 234–35; Sweeney, *Isaiah 1–39*, 198–211.
314. Sweeney, *Isaiah 1–39*, 175–88.
315. Ibid., 178.
316. Wegner states: "Normally the accession of the king inspired hope for
peace, but would anyone even in his wildest hopes be so convinced that the king was
going to bring peace that he would destroy valuable military equipment which could
be reused?" (*An Examination of Kingship*, 179).
317. Williamson, *Variations on a Theme*, 35.

interpretation functions through the description of how this Davidic deliverer brings light to the darkness of exile.

Similar to Ps 2, Isa 9:1–6, which probably was originally a royal enthronement oracle, gained messianic significance when read within the post-exilic shaping of the text. From this perspective, Mays correctly demonstrates that the Psalter provides a foundation for understanding how messianism functions in Isaiah.[318] Contrary to the views that describe messianism in Isa 9:1–5 only in terms of some post-exilic reader's response, warrants for messianic interpretation lie within the edited context of the biblical text itself (8:20–22). This is why the Qumran Thanksgiving Scroll (Hôdayôt) can employ a poem (3.15–18) that both portrays the birth of the Messiah and refers to the "wonderful counselor" of 9:5.[319]

In the pre-exilic period, Isa 9:5–6 may have included epithets to describe an ideal or successor king. Sweeney asserts that the redactor of chs. 36–39 has shaped this text to place Hezekiah in a favorable light.[320] Yet Hezekiah neither offered anything beyond temporary peace nor brought about any lasting deliverance that would spare the nation the events of 587.[321] Even if this passage were to use exaggerated language to speak of an ideal king at the pre-biblical level, in the post-exilic era when messianic hope had arisen, the community could reinterpret these verses as a "proper usages" that make actual claims rather than exaggerated language about a king who sits on the throne. In my Introduction, I have shown that the "proper" usage of words implies their straightforward meaning but the "figurative" usage involves metaphor, similes and the like.

Isaiah 9:6 cannot describe a king with exaggerated language (Hezekiah, Josiah or any other) because the termination of the monarchy has set the climate for messianic hope of one who will bring about endless peace (שלום אין־קץ) to the throne of David (על־כסא דוד) throughout eternity (ועד־עולם). Whoever sits upon the throne of David merely perpetuates the Davidic promises to the next generation[322] but, since the phrases אין־קץ and מעתה ועד־עולם imply that this monarch will reign for

318. Mays, "Isaiah's Royal Theology," 39–51.

319. Cf. Lawrence H. Schiffman, *From Text to Tradition* (Hoboken, N.J.: Ktav, 1991), 123.

320. Sweeney, *Isaiah 1–39*, 13–17.

321. See Wegner, *An Examination of Kingship*, 204, on this point.

322. Wildberger, *Jesaja 1–12*, 380; Kaiser, *Isaiah 1–12* (2d ed.), 214; H. Kruse, "David's Covenant," *VT* 35 (1985): 139–64; Oswalt, *Isaiah 1–39*, 248; Watts, *Isaiah 1–33*, 134; Wegner, *An Examination of Kingship*, 180; Rehm, *Der königliche Messias*, 168; Kaiser, *Isaiah 1–12* (2d ed.), 214; Jensen, *Isaiah 1–39*, 1–39.

eternity,[323] this verse cannot merely describe the reigns of ideal kings or the hier apparent. The figurative use of these phrases cannot warrant messianic interpretation, but when applied as a proper usage, one must interpret this king messianically. The Messiah is invested with super-human powers from God that past kings have not possessed.

Moreover, the repetition of the uncommon term הַמִּשְׂרָה (from vv. 5 and 6) seems to imply that both vv. 5 and 6 refer to the same person[324] whose "names in 9:5 extend beyond human capabilities."[325] The name אֵל גִּבּוֹר portrays a supernatural deliverer. Further, the proper usage of the name אֲבִיעַד, which is most commonly translated "eternal Father," again points beyond the ephemeral reign of a king like Hezekiah or Josiah into eternity. It is not uncommon to find the term אֲבִי in names.[326] Wegner inaccurately refers to the *yôdh* in אֲבִי as a first common singular suffix[327] but this limited scope of the morphology completely overlooks that אָב like אָח irregularly become אֲבִי in the construct singular "father of eter-nity."[328] The translation "father forever" finds similarities with גְּבֶרֶת עַד[329]

---

323.   Gressmann, *Der Messias*, 245; Otto Procksch, *Jesaia. Übersetzt und erklärt* (KAT 9/1; Leipzig: A. Deichertsche Verlagsbuchhandlung D. Werner Scholl, 1930), 149; Oswalt, *Isaiah 1–39*, 248; Seitz, *Isaiah 1–39*, 87; Sweeney, *Isaiah 1–39*, 179. Others think that this language refers to a kingdom whose rule will be for a long time but not for eternity. See G. W. Wade, *The Book of the Prophet Isaiah: With Introduction and Notes* (2d ed.; Westminster Commentaries 20; London: Methuen & Co., 1929), 66; Willis, *Isaiah*, 186; Hayes and Irvine, *Isaiah*, 184.

324.   Wegner, *An Examination of Kingship*, 182.

325.   John D. Davis, "The Child Whose Name is Wonderful," in *Biblical and Theological Studies* (Princeton Centenary Volume; New York: Scribner's, 1912), 93–108; Lars G. Rignell, "A Study of Isaiah 9:2–7," *LQ* 7 (1955): 31–35; Joseph C. L. Coppens, "L'interprétation d'Is, VII, 14, a la lumière des études les plus récentes," in *Lex Tua Veritas: Für H. Junker* (ed. H. Gross and F. Musser; Trier: Paulinus-Verlag, 1961), 31–45; Oswalt, *Isaiah 1–39*, 245–46;Wegner, *An Examination of Kingship*, 181. See also Wegner's in-depth description of the significance of these names (pp. 183–201).

326.   Note: Abialbon (1 Sam 9:1); Abiasaph (Exod 6:24 etc.); Abiathar (1 Sam 22:23 etc.); Abida (Gen 25:4 etc.); Abidan (Num 1:11 etc.); Abiel (1 Sam 9:1 etc.); Abiezer (Num 26:30 etc.); Abigail (1 Sam 25:30 etc.); Abihail (1 Chr 2:29 etc.); Abihu (Exod 6:23 etc.); Abijah (1 Chr 7:8 etc.); Abimael (Gen 10:26 etc.); Abimelech (Gen 20:2–18 etc.); Abinadab (1 Sam 7:1 etc.); Abinoam (Judg 4:6 etc.); Abiram (Num 16:1 etc.); Abishag (1 Kgs 1:3 etc.); Abishai (2 Sam 3:30 etc.); Abishalom (1 Kgs 15:2 etc.); Abishua (1 Chr 8:4 etc.); Abishur (1 Chr 2:28 etc.); Abital (2 Sam 3:4 etc.); Abitub (1 Chr 8:11 etc.).

327.   Wegner, *An Examination of Kingship*, 188.

328.   This irregular form of the construct should be taught in any elementary Hebrew Grammar. For example, see Choon-Leong Seow, *A Grammar for Biblical Hebrew* (rev. ed.; Nashville: Abingdon, 1995), 121.

("mistress forever," Isa 47:7) or עֶבֶד עוֹלָם ("slave forever," 1 Sam 27:12; Job 40:28).[330] Similar to the above verse, these names signify a proper use of one who transcends human abilities and not the exaggerated language of an ideal king.

The appellation שַׂר־שָׁלוֹם invokes a portrait of peace brought about by this deliverer. Harrelson argues that שַׂר is used to replace מֶלֶך because the writer was unhappy with the Davidic king so he refrained from using the nomenclature.[331] Others contend that שַׂר is used here instead of מֶלֶך to show the king's sub-ordinance to God[332] or that YHWH is the true king.[333] Is it not also logical that a child would be born a prince (שַׂר) before he became a king, even if the birth of the "child" served as a figurative description of king at his enthronement? Not only does this designation take up a picture of peace brought by royalty, but the next verse describes this peace as eternal (לְשָׁלוֹם אֵין־קֵץ). Verses 5–6 also seem to affirm the promises made to David in 2 Sam 7:12, "I will establish his kingdom" both passages using מַמְלַכְתּוֹ and the Hiphil of the verb כון.[334] This language may have included exaggerated epithets for a king, which in themselves cannot guarantee messianism, but later, after the exile, we can hear them as actual claims rather than figurative expressions.

Within the framework of post-exilic editing, this messianic hope could not be fulfilled by Hezekiah or Josiah because, from a post-exilic editing of this scroll, their reigns were transitory and do not meet the description of Isa 9:5–6, which portrays a deliverer who brings light to the darkness of Judah's exile. Since no monarch inhabited the throne in the post-exilic era, many Jewish interpreters came to anticipate a figure whose reign would last throughout eternity. Even if this oracle once depicted the

329.   This segolate noun typifies how pure long vowels do not reduce (*hôlem* to *šewa*) except in originally closed syllables, as in this case where the noun is in the construct.

330.   Kaiser, *Isaiah 1–12* (2d ed.), 128; Wegner, *An Examination of Kingship*, 188.

331.   Harrelson, "Nonroyal Motifs in the Royal Eschatology," 151.

332.   Von Rad, "The Royal Ritual in Judah," 230–31; Wildberger, *Jesaja 1–12*, 380; Wegner, *An Examination of Kingship*, 181.

333.   Theodoro Vriezen, "Essentials of the Theology of Isaiah," in Anderson and Harrelson, eds., *Israel's Prophetic Heritage*, 142–43; Wegner, *An Examination of Kingship*, 181.

334.   Williamson also suggests that the phrase "rod such as mortals use" (2 Sam 7:14) finds similarities with "rod of their oppressor" in v. 4. Yet the term in 2 Samuel is used to speak of YHWH's discipline of the king in 7:4, and his punishment of the oppressor in Isa 9. Williamson, *Variations on a Theme*, 36.

enthronement ceremony of either Hezekiah or Josiah, the post-exilic circumstances and ambiguity of 9:1–6 rules out these kings as possible candidates. In contrast to the "former time" in 8:23b, this kingdom is described here in eschatological dimensions. This is why Sheppard argues that a hymn originally spoken at the accession of a king could gain messianic import:

> AR's own eulogy of Josiah in Isa 9:1–6 gains messianic proportions for post-exilic interpreters. They capitalize on the ambiguity of the promissory context, which does not name a specific historical king and which points in florid terms to one who can turn the "darkness," even that of exile (8:21–23), into light (9:1). Such "reinterpretations," rather than being pious deceptions, reveal a confidence that the vitality of the voice of God in ancient Israel lent a depth of meaning to Isaiah's oracles that could be extended to times and places beyond the imagination of the living prophet…[335]

Likewise, Wegner rightly acknowledges that "the ambiguity here helps to engender messianic expectations and suggests that this ruler is not simply another Davidic king, but the *last* Davidic king," unlike Hezekiah or Josiah.[336] The later editors have exploited the ambiguity of the text within the context of promise in 7:14 and Isa 9:1–6 by leaving the explicit historical monarch unnamed. In ch. 7, the ambiguity of the child creates the possibilities for messianic interpretation. Talmon has called attention to what he calls "progressive dehistorization,"[337] just as Schibler suggests "gradual opaqueness"[338] to describe some sort of ambiguity that functions within the warrants of the text to invite a later messianic interpretation. What distinguishes the Emmanuel child (7:14) from Shear-jashub (7:3) and Maher-shalal-hash-baz (8:3) is the ambiguity of the child. The texts makes clear that Shear-jashub and Maher-shalal-hash-baz are children of Isaiah but the identity of Emmanuel is not so clear. Thus, some scholars identify the child as Isaiah's child[339] others as the son of Ahaz—namely Hezekiah, the future king who would be obedient to the revealed laws[340]—and others as an anonymous child during the

---

335.   Sheppard, "The Anti-Assyrian Redaction," 215.
336.   Wegner, *An Examination of Kingship*, 183.
337.   Talmon, "Concept of Mashiah," 97.
338.   Schibler, "Messianism and Messianic Prophecy," 103.
339.   Meinhold, *Studien zur israelitischen Religionsgeschichte*, 116–18; Hölscher, *Die Profeten*, 229; idem, "Des Buch der Könige," 106, 110; Stamm, "La prophétie d'Emmanuel"; C. Kuhl, *The Prophets of Israel* (Edinburgh: T. & T. Clark, 1960); Donner, *Israel unter den Völkern*, 225–40.
340.   Kraus, *Die Königsherrschaft Gottes im Alten Testament*, 97; Vischer, *Die Immanuel-Botschaft*; Seitz, *Isaiah 1–39*; Junker, "Ursprung und Grundzüge des

time of Isaiah and Ahaz.[341] Only the ambiguity of the Emmanuel child can substantiate Clements' argument that the accession oracle in 9:1–6 adds "emphasis to original prophetic birth announcement of 7:14 with the intention of reinforcing the reader's awareness that the reputation and future of the Davidic dynasty was at stake."[342] Not only does this ambiguity function to invite messianic interpretation of 7:14, but serves similar purposes in 9:1–6 where an unnamed royal heir from David's line will bring light and peace to the post-exilic era as Messiah. Within the framework of post-exilic reinterpretation (6:11–13; 7:18–25; 8:19–23), the editors have utilized this ambiguity as a cornerstone for reinterpretation. The use of the "light and darkness" motif, former and latter things, and a role for the Mosaic Torah are all major motifs in chs. 40–66 that reinterpret the earlier Isaianic material and "capitalize on the ambiguity of the promissory context."[343]

On these grounds, the ambiguous child (יֶלֶד) "born to us" in Isa 9:5 resonates with the ambiguous child (הַנַּעַר) who "knows how to refuse the evil and choose the good" in 7:16 and whom the young woman bears (יֹלֶדֶת) in 7:14.[344] Wegner argues that it is unnecessary for 7:14–17 and 9:1–6 to describe the same child and that the time period is different for each passage.[345] However, I agree with Mauchline, who perceives 7:14 to

Messiasbildes bei Isajas"; Hammershaimb, *Some Aspects of Old Testament Prophecy*, 19–23; Mowinckel, *The Psalms in Israel's Worship*, 78–84; idem, *He That Cometh*, 110–19; Scullion, "Approach to the Understanding of Isaiah 7:10–17," 288–300; Wildberger, *Isaiah 1–12*, 291–95.

341. Duhm, *Jesaja*, 75; Eichhorn, *Die Hebraischen Propheten*, 176; Gray, *Isaiah I–XXVII*, 124 (1956); Budde, *Jesaja's Erleben*, 22–54; Graham, "Isaiah's Part in the Syro-Ephraimitic Crisis," 7; Köhler, "Zum Verstandnis von Jes 7,14," 48–50; Fohrer, "Zu Jes 7,14," 54–56; idem, *Das Buch Jesaja*, 1:114; McKane, "The Interpretation of Isaiah VII,14–25," 213–15; Thompson, "Isaiah's Sign of Immanuel,' 70–71.

342. Clements, "The Immanuel Prophecy," 233.

343. Sheppard, "The Anti-Assyrian Redaction," 215.

344. Though the vocabulary that speaks of the child fluctuates, there are similarities in each passage. In 7:14, "the young woman…shall bear a son" (וְיֹלֶדֶת בֵּן) in the same manner that the prophetess shall bear a son (וַתֵּלֶד בֵּן) in 8:3. While 8:18 uses הַיְלָדִים to describe Isaiah's children and 9:6 יֶלֶד, which is indeed similar to the verb of 7:14 and 8:3, 7:16 uses the articular נַּעַר (7:16; 8:4). However, נער without the article is more common: "a child shall lead them" (11:6); "boys be made princes" (3:4); "youth shall be insolent" (3:5); a "child" in general (10:19); "a child will be slaughtered" (13:18); "young men shall be naked" (20:4); "boys of Assyria" (37:6); "even boys will be faint" (40:30); "youth shall die at the age of a hundred" (65:20).

345. Wegner, *An Examination of Kingship*, 131.

speak of the future birth of the Messiah but in 9:5 (9:6 NRSV) speaks of the child after he has been born.[346] More specifically, Vermeylen has argued that the prepositional phrase לָנוּ in 9:5 recalls that the name Immanuel in 7:14 in order to call attention the earlier passage.[347] Seitz suggests that the combination of לָנוּ and אֵל גִּבּוֹר perform this purpose.[348] From one perspective Wegner is correct that originally the child referred to in 9:5 may very well be different from the Emmanuel child, but Vermeylen and Seitz rightly show how 9:5 calls attention to 7:14. The editors have not only "reshaped" the context around 7:1–17 and 9:1–6 by reinterpreting earlier traditions in light of the exile, but have also united what was originally Isaiah's *denkschrift* (his original oracles) and a royal enthronement oracle through various editorial makers (i.e. 6:11–13; 7:18–25; 8:19–23). Isaiah 6:11–13 and 7:18–25 provide a new framework that introduces and concludes "the Ahaz narrative" (7:1–17) in light of the exile. This new context also invites the reader to hear 9:1–6 in conjunction with 7:14.

Similarly, Isa 7:18–25 and 8:19–23 also function in this capacity by framing 8:1–16 in light of the exile (587 B.C.E.) while also bridging these verses together with 9:1–6 in a new reinterpreted context. The formula "again YHWH spoke to me *saying*" (וַיּוֹסֶף יהוה דַּבֵּר אֶל־אָחָז לֵאמֹר), employed in 7:10 to join together 7:1–9 with 11–17, is also used in 8:5 to join vv. 6–8 to 1–4. Isaiah 8:6–8 originally consisted of an invective-threat oracle that was set within the conditions of the Syro-Ephraimite War. A textbook case for an invective-threat oracle can be seen here. The invective opens in v. 6 with the preposition כִּי to indicate a causal clause: "because this people has refused the waters of Shiloah that flow gently, and melt in fear before Rezin and the son of Remaliah" (v. 6). The threat, beginning with the standard לָכֵן, announces a "flood" of judgment:

> therefore, the Lord is bringing up against them the mighty and numerous waters of the River…it will rise above all its channels and overflow all its banks; it will sweep on into Judah; it will overflow and pour over. It will reach up to the neck; and its outspread wings will fill the breadth of your land… (8:7–8)

Whether or not the vocative, "O Emmanuel," was added as an editorial addition,[349] Emmanuel is now interpreted within the context of judgment. Because this storm of judgment "will sweep on into Judah as a flood,"

346. Mauchline, *Isaiah 1–39*.
347. Vermeylen, "Religieuse en Israël," 223.
348. Seitz, *Isaiah 1–39*, 87.
349. Kaiser, *Isaiah 1–12* (2d ed.), 185; Clements, *Isaiah 1–39*, 97.

Kaiser suggests that "the tendency of the memorial is to think not only of the Assyrians, but also of the Babylonians, whose attack finally put an end to the kingdom of Judah in 587."[350] While the phrase "the king of Assyria and all his glory" (v. 7) betrays that this text may have once been reinterpreted by AR,[351] within the later editorial context (8:19–23), Emmanuel would likely have been reinterpreted in light of 587 B.C.E. with the imagery of the storm portraying Nebuchadnezzar's invasion.[352] In these verses, Emmanuel now portends that "God is with us" in judgment.

While vv. 6–8 align the phrase עִמָּנוּ אֵל with judgment, vv. 9–10 associate this appellation with salvation. Wildberger argues that the "Jerusalem salvation traditions" serve as the original setting for vv. 9–10.[353] Clements argues that these verses offer the assurance of YHWH's protection for Judah and Jerusalem from the hand of the Assyrians.[354] No matter what nations come against Judah, v. 10, in the imperative, commands that they, "Take counsel together, but it shall be brought to naught; speak a word, but it will not stand, for God is with us" (עֻצוּ עֵצָה וְתֻפָר דַּבְּרוּ דָבָר וְלֹא יָקוּם כִּי עִמָּנוּ אֵל). In vv. 9–10, the later editors have retained a tradition antithetical to v. 8 as God's response to judgment. Even if vv. 9–10 originally spoke of the time of Assyrian domination, the later editing in

---

350. Kaiser, *Isaiah 1–12* (2d ed.), 184.

351. Clements, *Isaiah 1–39*, 97.

352. In the Mesopotamian city-laments, we find the storm which is connected prototypically with Enlil operating as the divine agent of destruction. Enlil fulfills this role as chief antagonist in LSUr 184ff. In Northwest Semitic mythology, Enlil finds his parallel in the Ugaritic Lôton or Môt. The storm often serves as a metaphor for the enemies' destructive forces (see Herman L. J. Vanstiphout, "Death of an Era: The Great Mortality in Sumerian City Lament," in *Death in Mesopotamia* [Copenhagen: Akademisk, 1980], 86), and even a battle chariot (see Mark Cohen, *The Canonical Lamentations of Ancient Mesopotamia* [Potomac: Capital Decisions, 1988], 88). In LSUr destruction occurs at the word of Enlil, who is the "shepherd-destroyer":

> On that day, the word (of Enlil) was an attacking storm—
> who could fathom it?
> The word of Enlil is destruction on the right, is [ ] on the left,
> This is what Enlil did in order to decide the fate of mankind:
> Enlil brought down the Elamites, the enemy, from the highlands.

Storm imagery also appears several times in Isaiah ("storm," 9:7–8; "windstorm," 21:1; "storm" and "heat," 25:4; YHWH "has measured the waters in the hollow of his hand," 40:12; Yahweh controls the storm, 40:21–24; 44:24–28; Yahweh dries up the storm, 50:2; Zion is "storm-tossed," 54:10).

353. Wildberger, *Isaiah 1–12*, 353.

354. Clements, *Isaiah 1–39*, 97–98.

8:19–22 underscores that God's judgment was ultimately achieved in 587 B.C.E., thus temporarily setting YHWH's protection in abeyance. In the aftermath of Nebuchadnezzar's invasion, Judah would have understood vv. 6–8 as having been fulfilled, and 8:9–10 would now present "God with us" as a sign of future salvation. Now a tension between judgment and promise has been left by the editors so that the role of Emmanuel stands within this dialectic. Now Isa 7:14 cannot be heard isolated from 8:8 and 10. After the events of 587, this eschatological tension of judgment and promise provides occasion for Judaism's early messianic expectation and thereby provides a warrant to interpret 7:14 messianically.

One could also imagine that the notion of "God with us" may extend beyond the immediate context of Isa 7:14 to chs. 40–66. While the appellation אֵל is common throughout the Isaianic corpus,[355] the combination of אֵל with עִם is not. We do find the affirmation of "God with (or 'among') us" using the preposition בְּ instead of עִם: "God is with you (בָּךְ אֵל) alone" (45:14).[356] Nevertheless, using the preposition עִם, Isa 41:10 incorporates the idea that "God is with you" (אַל־תִּירָא כִּי עִמְּךָ־אָנִי אַל־תִּשְׁתָּע כִּי־אֲנִי אֱלֹהֶיךָ, "fear not, for I am with you, be not dismayed for I am your God"). On these grounds, 41:10 refers to the Emmanuel prophecies in 7:14.

In terms of rhetorical analysis, we have differentiated between "proper" and "figurative" usage. When 9:1–6 operated independently from the book of Isaiah within an original social context of a royal enthronement ceremony, the exaggerated language functioned "figuratively" to describe an historical Davidic king such as Hezekiah or Josiah. Since kings in ancient Israelite religion were not considered divine, the exaggerated language of the original oracle ("Almighty God") must have been "figurative" rather than "proper." However, within a later context of the book as a whole, the attributes of the "child born to us" in Isa 9:1–6 describe more than just an earthly king. The language itself begins to be heard as "proper" language because, after the monarchy has ended, messianic expectation includes eschatological elements whose exaggerated features can be attributed to this character's description. Although Christians may have traditionally understood the "proper" usage of "Almighty

355. Cf. Isa 7:14; 8:10; 9:5; 10:21; 12:2; 14:13; 40:18; 43:10, 12; 44:10, 15, 20, 21, 22; 46:6, 7, 9, 12.

356. Isa 43:12 provides the negation of "god with (or 'among') us" but using the preposition בְּ instead of עִם: "there was no strange [god] with (or among) you…I am *El*" (אֵין בָּכֶם זָר…וַאֲנִי־אֵל). See also 45:21, 22; 46:9, which also claim that there is no god other than El.

God" to speak of the incarnation, the Jews have not shared the same view but have assumed that the Messiah is invested with powers from God that past kings have not possessed. Therefore, the latter formation of the book presents hope in a superhuman royal figure who will fulfill the promises made to David in the eschatological era. Features that were originally intended to be "figurative" now have become "proper" and must describe a Davidic Messiah if his name really is called "Almighty God."

D. *Isaiah 11:1–9 in the Context of the Biblical Scroll of Isaiah*
Just as Isa 7:14 and 9:1–6 depend on ch. 8 for messianic interpretation, ch. 10 sets the framework for ch. 11 and ties it together the book as a whole. The prose connecting links in 10:5–34 provide evidence that this material has been editorially organized.[357] The conventional view has been that ch. 10 represents later editing around original Isaianic material.[358] Isaiah 10:1–4 originally comprised a woe oracle but now 9:21, which describes the northern assault on Judah[359] and the refrain, "For all this his anger has not turned away, and his hand is stretched out still," connects this unit with the preceding material. Since 10:4 then repeats the refrain from 5:25, 10:1–4 has been edited to be heard within the preceding framework of God's judgment. While the woe oracles speak of leaders in Judah, the invective threat oracles with the refrain speaks to Northern Israel. This is why the invective threats in 5:8–24 have been displaced from 9:7–21 in order to allow the refrain to surface across

357. For further discussion on the redaction history of theses verses, see White-house, *Isaiah I–XXXIX*, 1:163; Fullerton, "The Problem of Isaiah, Chapter 10"; Childs, *Isaiah and the Assyrian Crisis*, 41–44; Vermeylen, "Religieuse en Israël," 263–64; Barth, *Die Jesaja-Worte*, 23–25, 40–41; Clements, *Isaiah 1–39*, 114; Kaiser, *Isaiah 1–12* (2d ed.), 230, 240; Wegner, *An Examination of Kingship*, 234–35; Sweeney, *Isaiah 1–39*, 198–211.

358. See Marti, *Das Buch Jesaja*, 102–10; Gray, *Isaiah I–XXXIX*, 194 (1956); Fohrer, *Das Buch Jesaja*, 1:153–64; Childs, *Isaiah and the Assyrian Crisis*, 39–44, 61–62; Wildberger, *Jesaja 1–12*, 490–30; idem, *Isaiah 1–12*, 411–58; Barth, *Die Jesaja-Worte*, 28–34, 40–41; Vermeylen, "Religieuse en Israël," 251–68; Seitz, *Isaiah 1–39*, 93–94; Sweeney, *Isaiah 1–39*, 196–211. Both in his earlier form-critical commentary and his later redaction-critical work, Kaiser has taken this view (*Isaiah 1–12: A Commentary* [1st ed.; OTL; London: SCM Press, 1972], 141; Kaiser, *Isaiah 1–12* [2d ed.], 230–33). Clements more specifically regards this later editing as a "midrashic developments" (vv. 5–15, 16–19) and characterizes v. 19 as a midrashic exegesis of the remnant in 7:3 in relation to the Northern Kingdom (*Isaiah 1–39*, 113–14).

359. "Manasseh devoured Ephraim, and Ephraim Manasseh, and together they were against Judah"

5:8–10:4a and to direct judgment not only against the Northern Kingdom (9:8–21 [Heb.]) but also against the Southern Kingdom. The woe oracles in 10:1–4 and 10:5–15 counterbalance the six woe oracles in 5:8–24 while the refrain, "For all this his anger...," in 10:4 frames the end of the woe oracle, calls attention to the refrain that follows the woe oracles in ch. 5 (5:25) and serves as a transition from the woe oracle against Judah (10:1–4) to the one against Assyria the "rod of my anger" (10:5–19).[360] Therefore, the editors have not allowed any traditions about either the Northern or Southern Kingdoms to remain isolated but have retained both traditions in order to include both kingdoms together in the messianic hope.

Similarly, Childs argues that 10:10 is a later addition, as shown by an anacoluthon that breaks the interrogative style of vv. 9 and 11 and, more importantly, contrasts Jerusalem and Samaria with other nations contrary to v. 11, which sets Jerusalem only against Samaria.[361] This later level of editing in v. 10 does not specify either Judah or Israel but seeks to combine both into the framework of judgment and promise. Isaiah 11:10 portrays the nations inquiring of "the root of Jesse" and vv. 11–12 depict the Lord extending his hand to gather the dispersed from the four corners of the earth. Therefore, Isa 11:1–9 has been editorially adapted to emphasize the exile and dispersion of the Northern and Southern Kingdoms and peoples coming from every nation to behold this royal figure.

Nevertheless, most parts of 10:5–34 originally fit into the tradition history that proclaims "woe" to Assyria, who is scorned for overstepping the strictures of punishment to which YHWH has called him and for becoming boastful and proud. Verses 8–11 depict the Assyrian's direct speech that takes the form of self-praise.[362] This description of Assyria's hubris culminates in v. 11: "shall I not do to Jerusalem and her idols what I have done to Samaria and her images?" Childs suggests that both vv. 7 and 12 serve to highlight the punishment for Assyria's boast illustrated in vv. 8–11.[363] Therefore, vv. 12–16, which some date very late, portray YHWH's punishment of Assyria after God has used Assyria to punish Jerusalem.[364] The questions in 10:15, "Shall the ax vaunt itself

360. See Sheppard, "The Anti-Assyrian Redaction," 198–216.
361. Childs, *Isaiah and the Assyrian Crisis*, 43.
362. Ibid., 43.
363. Ibid., 43.
364. Vermeylen assigns a post-exilic date to vv. 16–19 ("Religieuse en Israël," 259), Wildberger a Persian date (*Jesaja 1–12*, 238), and Kaiser a post-exilic date (*Isaiah 1–12* [2d ed.], 238). Barth (*Die Jesaja-Worte*, 62–70), however, regards these verses to have been written after Isaiah's time, but considers them to allude to Assyria.

over the one who wields it, or the saw magnify itself against the one who handles it?" (NRSV), rhetorically assert YHWH's sovereignty. Therefore, Assyria will reap the punishment it deserves, which is depicted by a forest fire (vv. 16–19) and the cutting down of trees (vv. 33–34).[365]

The fact that Isa 10:20–22 seems to refer to the Northern Kingdom[366] might possibly indicate that 10:21 originally spoke about a remnant from the Northern Kingdom, though within the book as a whole it now includes Judah as well (5:24; 8:14, 18; 10:17; 11:16).[367] Some scholars think that 10:23 speaks of the destruction that effected only the Northern Kingdom,[368] and others the events of 701.[369] Others think that 10:23 is post-exilic because God's judgment affects the whole world.[370] Clearly, the generalizing nature of v. 23 that includes "all the earth" or "all the land" (כל־הארץ) rules out any isolation of the Northern Kingdom as the only recipient of judgment but includes Israel as a whole and possibly all the nations. Yet God's anger is now redirected against Assyria and his judgment against his people now comes to an end (vv. 24–25).

Isaiah 10:28–32 seems to describe an advance on Jerusalem in 701 from the North[371] but the views vary as to whether these verses refer to either the Syro-Ephraimite War,[372] the fall of Samaria in 722 B.C.E.,[373] the invasion of Sargon II upon Jerusalem during Ashdod's revolt

365. See Clements, *Isaiah 1–39*, 113; Wegner, *An Examination of Kingship*, 226; Kirsten Nielsen, *There is Hope for a Tree: The Tree as Metaphor in Isaiah* (JSOTSup 65; Sheffield: JSOT Press, 1989), 124.

366. Clements, "Prophecies of Isaiah"; Wegner, *An Examination of Kingship*, 240.

367. Wegner, *An Examination of Kingship*, 241.

368. G. F. Hasel, *The Remnant: The History and Theology of the Remnant Idea from Genesis to Isaiah* (Andrews University Monographs 5; Berrien Springs, Miss.: Andrews University Press, 1972).

369. Wegner, *An Examination of Kingship*, 241; Seitz, *Isaiah 1–39*, 95; Sweeney, *Isaiah 1–39*, 198–211.

370. Gray, *Isaiah I–XXXIX*, 206 (1956); Herbert, *The Book of the Prophet Isaiah 1–39*, 87; Wildberger, *Jesaja 1–12*, 417–22; idem, *Isaiah 1–12*, 434 38; Kaiser, *Isaiah 1–12* (2d ed.), 242.

371. See Yohanon Aharoni and Michael Avi-Yonah, *The Macmillan Bible Atlas* (rev. ed.; New York: Macmillan, 1979), 154.

372. Scott, *The Book of Isaiah*, 246; Donner, *Israel unter den Völkern*, 30–38; idem, "Der Feind aus dem Norden. Topographische und Archaologische Erwagungen zu Jes 10:287b-34," *ZDPV* 84 (1968): 46–54; Herbert, *The Book of the Prophet Isaiah 1–39*, 88; Hayes and Irvine, *Isaiah*, 127; Stuart A. Irvine, *Isaiah, Ahaz and the Syro-Ephraimitic Crisis* (ed. David L. Peterson; SBLDS 123; Atlanta: Scholars Press, 1990), 274–79.

373. Cheyne, *Isaiah*, vol. 1.

(712–711),[374] Sargon's later revolt (720),[375] Sennacherib's invasion[376] or even a final eschatological attack on Jerusalem.[377] The Syro-Ephraimite War can be ruled out since vv. 28–32 describe an Assyrian invader rather than Ephraim and Syria. These verses most likely functioned at the original level to announce judgment on Jerusalem by describing an Assyrian advance on Jerusalem.

However, 10:33–34 seem to alter the original meaning and referents. The use of הנה at the beginning of v. 33 could insinuate a later unit of tradition.[378] Scholars think that these verses depict the pruning of the nation of Israel in order to make it more productive,[379] or its punishment before restoration that is described in 11:1–5.[380] Yet some assert that these verses do not apply to Israel at all but to Assyria.[381]

374.   Franz Feldmann, *Das Buch Isaias Übersetzt und Erklärt. Exegetisches Handbuch Zum Alten* (Münster: Aschendorf, 1925), 151; Procksch, *Jesaja: Ubersetzt und erklart*, 175; Wildberger, *Jesaja 1–12*, 423–35; idem, *Isaiah1–12*, 450–58; Dwayne L. Christensen, "The March of Conquest in Isaiah X,27c–34," *VT* 25 (1976): 387; A. K. Jenkins, "Hezekiah's Fourteenth Year: A New Interpretation of 2 Kings Xviii:13–Xix:37," *VT* 26 (1976): 284–98; Vermeylen, *Du prophète Isaïe*, 267; Clements, *Isaiah 1–39*, 117–19; Kaiser, *Isaiah 1–12* (2d ed.), 247; Oswalt, *Isaiah 1–39*, 274; Sweeney, *Isaiah 1–39*, 204. Yet Hayim Tadmor argues that Sargon stayed at home during this campaign; see his "The Campaigns of Sargon II of Assur," *JCS* 12 (1958): 22–40, 92–94. Sweeney (*Isaiah 1–39*, 206) rightly notes that no Assyrian record mentions a campaign against Judah at this time.

375.   Sweeney, *Isaiah 1–39*, 206.

376.   Wade, *The Book of the Prophet Isaiah*, 79; Rehm, *Der königliche Messias*, 190; Ridderbos, *Isaiah*, 121; Willis, *Isaiah*, 201; H. H. Rowley, "Hezekiah's Reform and Rebellion," *BJRL* 44 (1961–62): 395–431; Auvray, *Isaïe 1–39*, 138–41; Kaiser, *Isaiah 1–12* (2d ed.), 245–51; John Bright, *A History of Israel* (Philadelphia: Westminster, 1981).

377.   Marti, *Das Buch Jesaja*, 109; Duhm, *Jesaja*, 103–4.

378.   Wegner, *An Examination of Kingship*, 243.

379.   Kaiser, *Isaiah 1–12* (1st ed.), 157; Watts, *Isaiah 1–33*, 165–67.

380.   Sigmund Mowinckel, "Die Komposition Des Jesajabuches Kap. 1–39," *AcOr* 11 (1933): 283–84; Auvray, *Isaïe 1–39*, 138–40; Kaiser, *Isaiah 1–12* (1st ed.), 157; Fritz Stolz, "Die Bäumes Des Gottesgartens auf dem Libanon," *ZAW* 84 (1972): 141–56; Wildberger, *Jesaja 1–12*, 427; idem, *Isaiah 1–12*, 456–57; Herbert, *The Book of the Prophet Isaiah 1–39*, 88; Barth, *Die Jesaja-Worte*, 70–72; Vermeylen, *Du prophète Isaïe*, 266; Kaiser, *Isaiah 1–12* (2d ed.), 247; Jensen, *Isaiah 1–39*, 129.

381.   F. Huber, *Jahwe, Juda und die anderen Völker beim Propheten Jesaja* (BZAW 137; Berlin: de Gruyter, 1976), 32–33; Vermeylen, "Religieuse en Israël," 266; Clements, *Isaiah 1–39*, 121; Nielsen, *There is Hope for a Tree*, 130; Seitz, *Isaiah 1–39*, 95; Sweeney, *Isaiah 1–39*, 211.

Most important for our study, what relationship does the image of tree-cutting in 10:33–34 have with the sprout in 11:1? Scholarship is divided as to whether 10:33–34 are secondarily connected[382] or originally united.[383] While Barth appraises 10:33–34 to be pre-AR, Clements, Sheppard and Wegner claim that it belongs to AR.[384] Vermeylen argues that 10:33–34 reinterprets an original description of the assault of Sargon II against Ashdod (712 B.C.E.) to portray an Assyrian attack on Jerusalem.[385] Barth argues that 10:33–34 is a rereading of 2:9–17 so that ch. 10 refers to the destruction of Assyrians.[386] K. Nielsen asserts that the pre-biblical and latter reinterpreted levels of tradition history are rather opaque since we only have the final text, but instead regards 10:33–34 and 2:9–17 as related oracles that are from Isaiah.[387]

One significant key for understanding the relationship between Isa 10 and 11 lies in how 10:33–34 has taken up and reapplied the expressions from 2:6–17 and the refrain "humankind is humbled and persons are brought low" (וישׁח אדם וישׁפל־אישׁ) repeated in 2:9, 11, 17 and 5:15. This resonance with Isa 2 represents a level of redaction that the editors have marked by key terminology and repeated across Isa 1–39. As Sweeney has argued, 2:2–4 offers a generalization upon the book whereby the material in 2:6–17 cannot fit into any one event applicable to either Assyria and its downfall, or Israel and its downfall, or Judah and its downfall, or Babylon and its downfall.[388] Most specifically, 10:33–34, which has reapplied this aspect of ch. 2 to chs. 10–11, now transcends the particularity of 701 and broadens the historical horizon of God's judgment. Therefore, one cannot date the eschatological oracles in Isa 2

---

382. Marti, *Das Buch Jesaja*, 113–14; Kemper Fullerton, "Viewpoints in the Discussion of Isaiah's Hopes for the Future," *JBL* 41 (1922): 1–101; Gray, *Isaiah I–XXXIX*, 215–16 (1956); Mowinckel, *He That Cometh*, 17; Fohrer, *Das Buch Jesaja*, 1:166; Vermeylen, *Du prophète Isaïe*, 270–71; Clements, *Isaiah 1–39*, 120–21; Wegner, *An Examination of Kingship*, 246.

383. J. G. von Herder, *Vom Geist der Ebräischen Poesie* (Leipzig: J. R. Barth, 1825), 406–7; Childs, *Isaiah and the Assyrian Crisis*, 62; Kaiser, *Isaiah 1–12* (1st ed.), 157; Wildberger, *Jesaja 1–12*, 425–27; idem, *Isaiah 1–12*, 462–65; Sweeney, *Isaiah 1–39*, 200.

384. Barth, *Die Jesaja-Worte*, 70–77; Clements, *Isaiah 1–39*, 120–21; Sheppard, "Anti-Assyrian Redaction," 202; Wegner, *An Examination of Kingship*, 243–52.

385. Vermeylen, *Du prophète Isaïe*, 265–68.

386. Barth, *Die Jesaja-Worte*, 75–76.

387. Nielsen, *There is Hope for a Tree*, 126–34.

388. Sweeney, *Isaiah 1–4*, passim.

and 4 in light of specific historical events.[389] Similarly, the impact of this material in ch. 10 has relativized the text by the resonances of 2:6–7 and has put the events of 701 within a broader pattern of God's judgment across time. In terms of God's judgment in history, 10:33–34 now belong to the eschatological summaries that one finds in chs. 2, 4 and 11. Therefore, the eschatological nature of 11:6–9 offers a balance to the generalizing nature of 10:33–34 and thereby frames Isa 11:1–5 within this vast perspective. Like 2:2–4, the ending of ch. 10 now situates the events of 701 within this larger pattern of God's eschatological judgment whereby ch. 11 follows immediately with messianic prophecy.

Another key for understanding how ch. 11 functions against the backdrop of ch. 10 lies in the differences between Isa 10 and 11. For example, in 11:9, YHWH is the speaker (בכל־הר קדשׁי), but 10:33–34 uses the third person. Nevertheless, most importantly 10:34 and 11:11 are contrasted by judgment and restoration. Wildberger rightly recognizes that the redactor may have intentionally placed 10:33a, 34 before 11:1–9 in order to arrange the text to have a "very dismal backdrop for the messianic hopes."[390] Therefore, Isa 10–11 provides a sequence whereby YHWH uses Assyria to punish and purify Israel, and delivers a remnant of righteous ones through a messianic figure who will establish a kingdom of peace and justice.

A further explanation to how Isa 10 may advance messianism in Isa 11 can be seen by the way the Targum suggests that שֶׁמֶן denotes "anointing oil" in 10:27 to refer to the Messiah, thereby rendering the Hebrew מִפְּנֵי־שָׁמֶן with the Aramaic phrase מן קדם משׁיחא. Therefore, one could argue that the Targumist views ch. 10 to serve as a backdrop for messianic interpretation in ch. 11. The LXX renders the Hebrew as ἀπὸ τῶν ὤμων ὑμῶν ("from your shoulders"). The fact that the LXX uses ὤμως consistently to render שׁכם ("shoulder," twice), כתף ("shoulder," twice), and צד ("side," twice), which could be equated with the shoulder region, but never uses ὤμως for שׁמן, can indicate either its own interpretation, a different *Vorlage* or a scribal error. There is nothing about the "shoulder" that would lead one to believe that the translator used ὤμως to interpret שׁמן. Before assuming that the LXX had a Hebrew text different from the MT, one should allow for the possibility that the translator confused שׁכם for שׁמן. During the time that Isaiah was translated into Greek, the כ might possibly have been confused for the מ but the ן and מ did not look

---

389. This is partially why Barth assigns 5:15–16 to the post-exilic period (*Die Jesaja-Worte*, 64).

390. Wildberger, *Isaiah 1–12*, 463.

at all alike, thus ruling out graphic similarity.[391] However, the translator rendered מֵעַל שִׁכְמֶךָ in the first line as ἀπὸ τοῦ ὤμου and could very well have rendered the second line through parablesis as ἀπὸ τῶν ὤμων ὑμῶν. Therefore, we will prefer שְׁמֶן in MT, which provides a lexical warrant for messianic interpretation in the Targum.

Several other editorial markers in Isa 10 call attention to chs. 7 and 9 in a way that links 11:1–9 to previous messianic passages. Isaiah 10:20–23 duplicates terminology from 7:3 and 9:5 (שְׁאָר יָשׁוּב and אֵל גִּבּוֹר), which has led some scholars to regard vv. 20–23 as a reinterpretation of 7:3 and 9:5.[392] Clements finds such striking similarities between vv. 24–27 and 9:3 that he regards vv. 24–27 as "midrashic" interpretation of 9:3.[393] YHWH's words to Ahaz, אַל־תִּירָא ("do not fear"), are repeated in v. 24. The phrase "on that day" in v. 27 calls an end to the judgment that is announced in the "on that day" oracles in 7:18–25, and 11:1–9 is followed by the formula "on that day" in 11:12 to announce the return for the exiles from the Southern Kingdom. Isaiah 10, now serving as an introduction to ch. 11, calls attention to key materials in chs. 7 and 9 in order to remind us of the Emmanuel child (7:14) and child born to us (9:5) before embarking into Isa 11.

Some scholars interpret Isa 11:1–9 messianically by either assigning it a post-exilic[394] or Maccabean date.[395] Others claim that vv. 6–9 are later

391. See Emanuel Tov, *Textual Criticism of the Hebrew Bible* (Minneapolis: Fortress, 1992), 8, 200, 343, 361, 410.

392. Duhm, *Das Buch Jesaja*, 102; Fohrer, *Das Buch Jesaja*, 1:160; Wildberger, *Jesaja 1–12*, 415; idem, *Isaiah 1–12*, 435–36; Barth, *Die Jesaja-Worte*, 36; Vermeylen, "Religieuse en Israël," 263; Clements, *Isaiah 1–39*, 115; Kaiser, *Isaiah 1–12* (2d ed.), 241; Wegner, *An Examination of Kingship*, 240; Seitz, *Isaiah 1–39*, 94; Sweeney, *Isaiah 1–39*, 200; Brueggemann, *Isaiah 1–39*, 94–95.

393. Clements, *Isaiah 1–39*, 116.

394. See P. Volz, *Die vorexilische Jahweprophetie und der Messias: In ihrem Verhältnis dargestellt* (Göttingen: Vandenhoeck & Ruprecht, 1897), 60–62; Marti, *Das Buch Jesaja*, 110, 113–14; Hölscher, *Die Profeten*, 348; D. H. Corley, "Messianic Prophecy in First Isaiah," *AJSL* 39 (1922/23): 224; Fullerton, "Viewpoints in the Discussion of Isaiah's Hopes for the Future"; Budde, "Über die Schranken"; Gray, *Isaiah I–XXXIX*, 214 (1956); Wade, *Isaiah*, 81–82; Mowinckel, *He That Cometh*, 17; Scott, *The Book of Isaiah*, 247; Sheldon H. Blank, *Prophetic Faith in Isaiah* (London: A. & C. Black, 1958), 161–70; Fohrer, *Das Buch Jesaja*, 1:166; Lescow, "Das Geburtsmotiv in den messianischen Weissagungen"; Peter R. Ackroyd, "Historians and Prophets," *SEÅ* 33 (1968): 164–66; J. Lust, "Immanuel Figure: A Charismatic Judge-Leader [Is 7:10–17]," *ETL* 47, no. 3–4 (1971): 469; Vollmer, *Geschichtliche*, 180–81; H. W. Hoffmann, *Die Intention der Verkundigung Jesajas* (BZAW 136; Berlin: de Gruyter, 1974), 20; Clements, *Isaiah 1–39*, 121–22; Kaiser, *Isaiah 1–12* (2d ed.), 254–55; Brueggemann, *Isaiah 1–39*, 99.

(post-exilic) additions that reinterpret an original Isaianic passage (11:1–5).[396] On the basis of our definition, messianic hope begins in the post-exilic age after the monarchy has ended, so messianic interpretation would not be possible if Isa 11:1–9 were either Isaianic[397] or Josianic.[398]

395.   This view is a minority one. See R. H. Kennett, *The Composition of the Book of Isaiah in the Light of History and Archaeology* (The Schweich Lectures 1909; London: Oxford University Press, 1910), 68, 85; Treves, "Little Prince Pele-Joez."

396.   See von Ewald, *The History of Israel*, 343; Cheyne, *Isaiah*, 1:75; Duhm, *Jesaja*, 104–5; Brevard S. Childs, *Myth and Reality in the Old Testament* (SBT 21; (Naperville, Ill.: Allenson, 1960), 64; Coppens, *Le messianisme royal*, 82–85; Hermisson, "Verkündigung Jesajas"; Otto Eissfeldt, *The Old Testament: An Introduction* (trans. P. R. Ackroyd; New York: Harper & Row, 1976), 319; Barth, *Die Jesaja-Worte*, 63; Vermeylen, "Religieuse en Israël"; Wegner, *An Examination of Kingship*, 263–64. Duhm regarded 11:1–5 to have come from the same late level of tradition history as Isa 2:2–4 and 32:1–5, 15–20, which he regarded as Isaiah's "Swan Songs," and which would have been composed after Sennacherib's invasion, if he indeed did at all compose them (written in his comments on 2:2–4 in *Das Buch Jesaja*).

397.   See Dillmann, "Der Prophet Jesaia," 104; Skinner, *Isaiah Chapters I–XXXIX*, 94f.; Delitzsch, *Isaiah*, 1:281–82; Duhm, *Das Buch Jesaja*, 104; Gressmann, *Der Messias*, 247; Wade, *The Book of the Prophet Isaiah*, 62; Procksch, *Jesaja*, 151–52; Scott, *The Book of Isaiah*, 247; H. Renard, "Le messianisme dans la premiere partie du livre d'Isaïe," *SP* 1 (1959): 405–6; Martin Buber, *The Prophetic Faith* (New York: Harper & Brothers/Harper Torchbooks/The Cloister Library, 1960), 148; Childs, *Myth and Reality*, 64–67; idem, *Old Testament Theology in a Canonical Context*, 119; idem, *Theological Reflection on the Christian Bible*, 177, 243; Walther Eichrodt, *Der Heilige in Israel: Jesaja 1–12* (BAT; Stuttgart: Calwer, 1960), 137–38; E. J. Kissane, *The Book of Isaiah: Translated from a Critically Revised Hebrew Text With Commentary* (2 vols.; Dublin: Browne & Nolan, 1960), 1:125–26; Slotki, *Isaiah*, 56, 58; Helmer Ringgren, *The Messiah in the Old Testament* (SBT 18; London: SCM Press, 1961), 30–32; Herrmann, *Die Prophetischen Heilserwartungen*, 137–40; idem, *A History of Israel in Old Testament Times* (trans. John Bowden; rev. ed.; London: SCM Press, 1981), 253; Rehm, *Der königliche Messias*, 191–94; Auvray, *Isaïe 1–39*, 141–45; Kaiser, *Isaiah 1–12* (1st ed.), 154–55; K. Seybold, *Das davidische Königtum im Zeugnis der Propheten* (FRANT 107; Göttingen: Vandenhoeck & Ruprecht, 1972), 93–97; Odil Hannes Steck, *Friedenvorstellungen im Alten Jerusalem. Psalmen, Jesaja, Deuterojesaja* (ThSt 111; Zurich: Theologisches Verlag, 1972), 60; Wildberger, *Jesaja 1–12*, 442–46; idem, *Isaiah 1–12*, 462–85; Becker, *Messianic Expectation*, 45; Willis, *Isaiah*, 202–3; Jensen, *Isaiah 1–39*, 130–31; Oswalt, *Isaiah 1–39*, 255–77; Hayes and Irvine, *Isaiah*, 206; Roberts, "The Old Testament's Contribution to Messianic Expectations," 44–45; Charlesworth, "Introduction," 23; Motyer, *The Prophecy of Isaiah*, 3–16, 120–27; Seitz, *Isaiah 1–39*, 96; Kaiser, *The Messiah in the Old Testament*, 155, 164–67; Brueggemann, *Isaiah 1–39*, 99.

Yet if Isa 11:1–9 were post-exilic, the "stump of Jesse" in 11:1 would describe an already severed Davidic dynasty from which a messianic shoot sprouts.[399] Understanding that messianism originated in the post-exilic era, Werblowsky regards the "stump of Jesse" to be a "technical anachronism" to "describe as 'messianic' those scriptural passages that prophesy a future golden age, the ingathering of the exiles, the restoration of the Davidic dynasty, the rebuilding of Jerusalem and the Temple, the era of peace when the wolf will lie down with the lamb…"[400] Wegner argues that this passage falls short of the full concept of the Messiah which later developed because, first, he regards the deliverance as taking place in the present age and not in the future; second, there is no indication that the rule of this king extends to the whole earth; and third, עוד does not imply the termination of the monarchy. Yet I have cited other reasons why early Jewish sources found warrants to interpret Isa 11 as messianic.[401]

Wegner denies a post-exilic date for Isa 11:1–9 because the editors would not have placed "this passage or Isa 8:23–9:6 in the context of the Assyrian conflict if it was actually written in the post-exilic era when Assyria was no longer a serious threat."[402] That assumption is refuted by the way other anti-Assyrian material in chs. 1–39 is interspersed with later material against Babylon. For example, 14:25–27 provides a

398.   Barth, *Die Jesaja-Worte*, 63; Vermeylen, "Religieuse en Israël," 269–76; Sweeney, *Isaiah 1–39*, 204, 209. The strongest reason for ruling out that "shoot from the stump of Jesse" in Isa 11:1 refers to Josiah is that his enthronement (in 640 B.C.E.) occurred before Assyria was destroyed (see Wegner, *An Examination of Kingship*, 266) or even a final eschatological attack on Jerusalem (see Marti, *Das Buch Jesaja*, 109; Duhm, *Das Buch Jesaja*, 103–4).

399.   See, Marti, *Das Buch Jesaja*, 110; Duhm, *Das Buch Jesaja*, 104–5; Gray, *Isaiah I–XXXIX*, 215–16; Kaiser, *Isaiah 1–12* (1st ed.), 157; idem, *Isaiah 1–12* (2d ed.), 254; Clements, *Isaiah 1–39*, 122; Werner, *Eschatologische Texte in Jesaja 1–39*, 63.

400.   R. Werblowsky, "Messianism: Jewish Messianism," in *The Encyclopedia of Religion* (ed. M. Eliade; New York: MacMillan, 1987), 9:472–77 (472).

401.   The Targum Jonathan; *Talmud, Sanh.* 93ab (R. Tanhum [ca. 250–90 CE]); *Sanh.* 93b (Raba [after 200 CE]; *Midrash Gen. Rab.* 2.4 (R. Simeon b. Lakish [ca. 50–90 CE]); *Gen. Rab.* 97; *Num. Rab.* 13:11 (R. Pheneḥ Yair); *Ruth Rabbah* (R. Judah b. Simon); *Song of Songs Rabbah* (R. Ḥuna [ca. 320–50 CE] under the designate of R. Eleazor the Modean [ca. 250–90 CE]); *Ruth Rab.* 5:6 (R. Jonathan [ca. 250–90 CE]).

402.   Wegner, *An Examination of Kingship*, 265. Von Ewald maintained that Isaiah expected the Messiah's advent to synchronize with the Assyrian invasion. See his *Commentary on the Prophets of the Old Testament* (trans. J. F. Smith; 5 vols.; London: Williams & Norgate, 1875–81).

description of YHWH's hand of judgment stretched out against Assyria surrounded by a context of judgment against Babylon. Isaiah 1–39 has been so reworked that one cannot determine with certainty which layer of editing governs the latter formation of the book. Moreover, the generalizing nature of 10:23, 33–34 intentionally prevents one from determining with certainty whether the context of destruction surrounding Isa 11 refers either to the Syro-Ephraimite War (735–732), the fall of Samaria (722), the invasion of Sargon II upon Jerusalem during Ashdod's revolt (712–711), or Sargon's later revolt (720), Sennacherib's assault on Jerusalem (701) or Nebuchadnezzer's invasion (587). Finally, the eschatological character of 11:6–9 counterbalances the generalizing nature of 10:33–34, thus surrounding Isa 11 with material that cannot correspond solely to any one event about Assyria, Babylon, Israel or Judah. Placed within the context of severe destruction, Isa 11 has been primed to evoke messianic interpretation.

Scholars tend to support a post-exilic date for Isa 11:1–9 because גֵּזַע of "stump of Jesse" (גֵּזַע יִשָׁי) assumes that the Davidic monarchy has been terminated.[403] Moreover, the notion of the Spirit resting on individuals[404] and both the paradisal[405] and the eschatological elements of the text[406] all reveal concepts that emerged at a later date.[407] Some scholars seem to think that the nomenclature "Jesse" has been used either to downplay the house of David[408] or more specifically to depict a "new David."[409] Lexicons render the word גֵּזַע with (1) "stump" or "trunk" or (2) "cutting" or "stock" that has been cut off a parent plant for

403. Marti, *Das Buch Jesaja*, 110, 113–14; Duhm, *Das Buch Jesaja*, 104–5; Budde, "Über die Schranken"; Gray, *Isaiah I–XXXIX*, 214–15 (1956); Mowinckel, *He That Cometh*, 17; Fohrer, *Das Buch Jesaja*, 1:166; Vollmer, *Geschichtliche*, 180–81; Clements, *Isaiah 1–39*, 122; Kaiser, *Isaiah 1–12* (2d ed.), 254–55; Brueggemann, *Isaiah 1–39*, 99.

404. Marti, *Das Buch Jesaja*, 113–14; Fohrer, *Das Buch Jesaja*, 166; Vollmer, *Geschichtliche*, 61–63; Werner, *Eschatologische Texte in Jesaja 1–39*, 63.

405. Marti, *Das Buch Jesaja*, 113; Gressmann, *Der Messias*, 246–47; Hermisson, "Verkündigung Jesajas"; Eissfeldt, *The Old Testament*, 319; Barth, *Die Jesaja-Worte*, 60–63.

406. Gray, *Isaiah I–XXXIX*, 214 (1956); Clements, *Isaiah 1–39*, 122.

407. For a more in depth description, see Wegner, *An Examination of Kingship*, 263–64.

408. This is the view of Calvin that was forwarded in the modern era by Oswalt; see Calvin, *Commentary on the Book of the Prophet Isaiah*, 1:372; Oswalt, *Isaiah 1–39*, 278.

409. Cf. Mowinckel, *He That Cometh*, 161–62; Kaiser, *Isaiah 1–12* (1st ed.), 157; idem, *Isaiah 1–12* (2d ed.), 161; Alt, "Jesaja 8,23–9,6," 224; Harrelson, "Nonroyal Motifs in the Royal Eschatology," 154–55.

propagation, as in Isa 40:24.[410] גזע in 40:24 speaks about princes and rulers (v. 23) who are scarcely planted and whose stock (גזע√) has not taken root. While some think that this "stump" (גזע) does not describe an absolute termination of the monarchy,[411] most scholars understand גזע to imply that the Davidic dynasty has been diminished to a stump.[412] Since גזע in 11:1 stands parallel to שרש, as is also the case in Job 14:8, the term in 11:1 is unlikely to describe "cutting" or "stock" but most likely a "stump" from which a new "shoot" or "branch" should sprout. Isaiah 11:1 seems to take up the imagery of the tree felling in 10:33–34, so that the immediate context confirms that גזע implies a "stump." Because גזע is used as a "metaphor" in 11:1[413] to describe the remnant of a royal Davidide who will come forth from this "stump," we can reasonably accept that this verse depicts the collapsed Davidic dynasty.

Furthermore, this metaphor (גזע) resonates with description of a "stump" (מצבת) at the end of Isa 6, which has resulted from the destruction of the cities that now lay waste. The word מצבת, which appears three times in the Old Testament, is used to speak of the "pillar" of Absalom as a memorial stone (2 Sam 8:18) or of sacred "pillars" (2 Kgs 18:4), but in this Isaianic context can only imply "stump" because the term describes the leftover part of an oak tree after it has been cut down. Though the words גזע and מצבת are different, the metaphor is the same.[414] From this perspective, 11:1 uses an image, which alludes to the stump in 6:11–13 that has resulted from a destruction that most likely describes the very events that severed the monarchy (587). Wegner argues that these verses could be a pre-exilic expectation but it would be

410.   BDB, 826; KB 1:631.

411.   Motyer (*The Prophecy of Isaiah*, 122) regards 11:1 as a "prediction" that "does not need the historical fall of the monarchy to prompt it." See also Hayes and Irvine, *Isaiah*, 212. Wildberger thinks that it refers to the instability of the Davidic dynasty (*Jesaja 1–12* [1st ed.], 442–43; *Isaiah 1–12* [2d ed.], 469–70). Vermeylen ("Religieuse en Israël," 232, 269–70) thinks that this has to do with the death of the Davidic king before the new king, Josiah, ascended to the throne. Similarly, Sweeney (*Isa 1–39*, 204) reasons that in Josiah's time when no uncle or Davidic figure exercised authority during his young age, the stump represents how "Josiah was the only Davidic heir to survive the coup."

412.   Driver, "Introduction," 208–10; Marti, *Das Buch Jesaja*, 110; Duhm, *Das Buch*, 104; Budde, "Über die Schranken,"; Gray, *Isaiah I–XXXIX*, 214–15 (1956); Pfeiffer, *Introduction to the Old Testament*, 75, 437; Mowinckel, *He That Cometh*, 17; Fohrer, *Das Buch Jesaja*, 1:166; Vollmer, *Geschichtliche*, 180–81; Clements, *Isaiah 1–39*, 122; Werner, *Eschatologische Texte in Jesaja 1–39*, 49; Kaiser, *Isaiah 1–12* (2d ed.), 254; Wegner, *An Examination of Kingship*, 231.

413.   KB 1:187.

414.   See KB 2:621.

unlikely that the writer would use "stump" if the kingship were still intact.

Outside Isa 11:1, the term חֹטֶר ("shoot") occurs only in Prov 14:3 as a beating stick of discipline. The single context in which the word חטר appears here finds in the parallelism the analogous term נֵצֶר, meaning "shoot", "branch," "sprout" (Isa 11:1; 60:21), or "'dead' "branch" (Isa 14:19; Dan 11:7). Apart from the verb (נצר√), which implies something different than the noun,[415] the term נצר, which appears just a few times in its nominal form, speaks of a "vigorously growing shoot" (Isa 60:21) and exhibits a royal association by applying נצר to the king of Babylon (14:19).[416] Therefore, in the bi-cola of 11:1, חטר in the first colon anticipates something approximating the meaning "shoot," "branch" or "sprout," since this is the meaning of the related term נצר in the second colon. Outside Isa 11:1, one discovers that no other term in *BHS* stands in parallelism with חטר because the only other use of the term in *BHS* (Prov 14:3) employs antithetical parallelism. Third, in light of this, the Near Eastern cognates that could provide a suitable definition for the root חטר are the Akkadian *ḥutartu*, which implies "staff," and the ancient Arabic خطر, which means "lash" or "spear,"[417] each of which are created from a "branch" or "shoot." The LXX uses ῥάβδος, "rod" or "staff," which approximates to the lexemes for the term in parallelism and these other cognates. Since Qumran does not reflect anything different that would help resolve the lexicography of these terms, we can assume that "shoot," "branch," not only express the essence of the parallel term, cognates and translation, but of חטר as well.

The imagery of "the branch" is not unique to later prophetic literature. Vermeylen argues that חטר refers to Josiah, who was a young and powerless branch when he became king.[418] Yet the ambiguity of the text invites other possibilities as well. The "branch" is often interpreted messianically[419] and the synonym for נֵצֶר in 4:2, צֶמַח,[420] seems to reflect

---

415. נצר√ = to "guard" or "watch."

416. Wegner, *An Examination of Kingship*, 253–54.

417. Yet in modern Arabic, خطر means "peril" or "danger."

418. Vermeylen, "Religieuse en Israël," 274.

419. The term כִּפָּה ("branch, leaf, or palm branch," 9:14; 19:5) is not used messianically.

420. The word צֶמַח is found in no other place in Isaiah as a noun. The Akkadian *šamaḫu* implies a "luxurious branch" (*CAD*). The verbal form צמח√ ("to sprout") has to do with promise of either "salvation" (45:8), or YHWH's "blessings" (44:4) or "healing" (58:8) or "righteousness" (55:10; 61:11) or the new things in contrast to the former things that will spring forth (42:9; 43:19) The noun צֶמַח also refers to a "messianic king" (Jer 23:5; 33:15; Zech 3:8; 6:12). Isa 4:2 uses צֶמַח to refer to

"messianic overtones" of 11:1.[421] The Targum interpretively translates
צמח as "the Messiah." While נצר and צמח are different terms, both elicit
the same metaphor.[422] Within the parallelism of 11:1, both the "shoot"
(חטר) or "branch" (נצר), which sprouts from the "stump" of David's
severed dynasty invokes messianic interpretation in the post-exilic age.
The prince of the congregation at Qumran was identified as the "branch
of David" (the two are juxtaposed in 4Q285).[423] That is why Collins
posits that the compilers of "the *Psalms of Solomon* are the first Jews to
see in Isaiah 11 or Psalm 2 the promise of a glorious future glorious
king."[424]

Isaiah 2–5 specifies royal qualities without identifying any particular
king. Isaiah 11:2 describes six spiritual manifestations that are related to
the empowerment of the spirit of YHWH: a "spirit of wisdom and understanding, the spirit of counsel and might, the spirit of knowledge and the
fear of the LORD" (11:2).[425] Both "counsel" and "might" are the first two
theophoric names used in 9:5.[426] These attributes function due to "the
Spirit of YHWH resting upon him" (ונחה עליו רוח יהוה).[427] Mostly in
exilic or post-exilic Isaianic material, the sovereign[428] Spirit of YHWH
empowers or comes upon individuals for service.[429] We are led to ask if

---

a future time after cleansing judgment, when the remnant of Israel will see the
re-establishment of the monarchy, renew their worship and their indentity as
YHWH's covenant people, and enjoy the fruit of the land.

421.   This is the view of Seitz, *Isaiah 1–39*, 42.

422.   Motyer, *The Prophecy of Isaiah*, 122; Seitz, *Isaiah 1–39*, 97.

423.   John J. Collins, *The Scepter and the Star: The Messiahs of the Dead Sea
Scrolls and Other Ancient Literature* (New York: Doubleday, 1995), 64, 71; R. H.
Eisenman and M. Wise, *The Dead Sea Scrolls Uncovered: The First Complete
Translation and Interpretation of 50 Key Documents Withheld Over 35 Years* (Rock-
port, Mass.: Element, 1992), 29; Geza Vermes, "The Oxford Forum for Qumran
Research Seminar on the Rule of War from Cave 4," *JJS* 43 (1992): 88.

424.   Collins, *The Scepter and the Star*, 56.

425.   Note the positive attributes that are related to the word רוח in Isaiah: a
spirit of judgment (4:4); a spirit of justice to one who sits in judgment (28:6). Note
also the negative spiritual attributes: a spirit of confusion (19:14); a spirit of deep
sleep (29:10).

426.   Laato, *Who is Immanuel?*, 204–5; Wegner, *An Examination of Kingship*,
183–201; idem, "A Re-examination of Isaiah IX 1–6," *VT* 42 (1992): 109–12;
Williamson, *Variations on a Theme*, 43.

427.   Wegner, *An Examination of Kingship*, 250.

428.   Note the question "who has directed the spirit of YHWH?" in 40:13.

429.   God will put his spirit in Hezekiah (37:7); the spirit of YHWH gathers them
(34:16); spirit from on high poured out (32:15); YHWH pours forth his spirit (44:3);
YHWH puts his spirit on his servant (42:1); YHWH sends the prophet in his spirit

these qualities in vv. 3–5 describe any king or do they only portray a unique messianic figure.[430] In v. 2, the description of YHWH's Spirit inhabiting this figure is not at all unique since Hezekiah, like any Israelite king, receives this quality (37:7). Moreover, this "fear of the Lord" is again a quality of any good king.

Isaiah 11:3b–4 shows that his ability to judge righteously transcends human abilities (the abilities of his eyes to see and ears to hear). Isaiah 11:4 reads:[431]

> But he shall judge the poor in righteousness,
>> and he shall decide with equity for the afflicted of the earth,
> he shall smite the earth with the rod of his mouth,
>> and with the breath of his lips he shall kill the wicked.

The terms "eyes to see" and "ears to hear" (11:3) may possibly refer back to 6:10, where Isaiah is told to "...stop their ears, and shut their eyes, so that they may not look with their eyes, and listen with their ears..." (NRSV).[432] In the hope that YHWH may give the king his righteousness and justice in Ps 72, the Psalmist petitions, "May he judge your people with righteousness, and your poor with justice" (vv. 1, 2). Yet this justice and righteousness comes through "the rod of his mouth." The term שֵׁבֶט ("rod") is used consistently throughout Isaiah to describe an instrument of judgment or punishment.[433] In 9:4, the royal figure breaks "the rod of the oppressor" but in 11:4 the shoot from Jesse's stump exceeds human efforts by judging with "the rod of his mouth." Unlike 9:5, where אֵל גִּבּוֹר seems to imply that the kings military might will bring about peace,[434] the deliverer in ch. 11 uses the might of this

(48:16); the spirit of YHWH gives rest (63:14); YHWH's "spirit that is upon you" (59:21); "the spirit of the Lord GOD is upon me" (61:1).

430.   For views that maintain that such an endowment is unique, see M. Tate, "King and Messiah in Isaiah of Jerusalem," *RevExp* 65, no. 4 (1968): 409–21; Oswalt, *Isaiah 1–39*, 281; Wegner, *An Examination of Kingship*, 255. For views that argue that these are attributes describing each and every king, see T. N. D. Mettinger, *King and Messiah: The Civil and Sacral Legitimation of the Israelite Kings* (ConBOT 8; Lund: C. W. K. Gleerup, 1976), 233–53; Clements, *Isaiah 1–39*, 123; Wegner, *An Examination of Kingship*, 255.

431.   Wegner argues that "this leader is intended to be a contrast to the blindness and deafness of the nation of Israel" (*An Examination of Kingship*, 255).

432.   Williamson, *Variations on a Theme*, 49.

433.   Note that שֵׁבֶט refers to an instrument of punishment by the oppressor (9:3; 10:24; 14:5, 29); "Assyria, the rod of my anger" as the instrument of judgment (10:5); the instrument of judgment against Assyria (30:31); the instrument for beating culinary herbs (28:27). On two occasions, שֵׁבֶט is used for "tribe" (49:6; 63:17).

434.   See Williamson, *Variations on a Theme*, 42.

one's own words, which outweighs any military prowess or physical beatings that a rod may inflict because he enlists the authority of God's own word.[435] N. A. Dahl submits that 11:4 fits the messianic description of "conqueror" since "the Messiah was often assumed to perform the destruction of hostile forces by his word...rather than with military force."[436] Even the metaphorical description, "righteousness will be the waistband around his loins, and faithfulness the waistband about his waist," describes one who exceeds the limits of an ordinary king (see Isa 9:5–6 and Ps 72). Wegner rightly states:

> This uniqueness is portrayed in two ways: (1) by using terms for this ruler which are commonly applied to God a connection is drawn between them; and (2) the characteristics of this ruler were never totally achieved by any human king but appear to reflect the hopes and expectations surrounding kingship (cp. Ps 72).[437]

This portrait transcends the abilities of any past king by describing a role or expectation that only a messiah can fulfill. Even the finest Israelite kings cannot measure up to the ability of the king to execute righteousness in Isa 11.

What is more, Isa 11 finds similarities with other messianic descriptions in Isaiah. The attributes listed in vv. 3–5 correspond to the series of titles in 9:5.[438] Although each list is not comprehensive, the titles from each enhances the other. The attributes of peace, righteousness and concern for equity for the poor in vv. 3–5 find similarities with 9:1–6.[439] The phrase בצדק in 11:4 seems to reflect the language of "justice and righteousness" (במשפט ובצדקה) in 9:6. The phrase בשבט פיו in 11:4 finds similar language to describe God's exploits (Hos 6:6), the messianic king (Zech 9:10) and the servant (Isa 49:2). The moral qualities described in Isa 9:6 and 11:2–5 (i.e. צדק, "righteousness"; משפט, "justice"; והאמונה, "faithfulness") provide necessary components that

435. See Gressmann, *Der Messias*, 247–48; Kaiser, *Isaiah 1–12* (2d ed.), 257–58.
436. N. A. Dahl, "Messianic Ideas and the Crucifixion of Jesus," in Charlesworth, ed., *The Messiah*, 384.
437. Wegner, *An Examination of Kingship*, 256.
438. Laato, *Who is Immanuel?*, 226; Wegner, *An Examination of Kingship*, 253; Williamson, *Variations on a Theme*, 50.
439. Wegner brings this thought even further in suggesting that these verses reflect the same royal ideology behind 9:1–6 and that this ideology can be found in the Psalter as well, there in reference to peace (Ps 72:3), righteousness (Ps 72:2–4, 12–14) and equity for the poor (Ps 72:2–4, 12–14). See Wegner, *An Examination of Kingship*, 233 n. 93.

would be present in messianic definitions of early Judaism and Christianity but, for example, were absent in the characterization of Cyrus (Isa 41–48).

Isaiah 11 does not even mention historical events that would reveal a more precise dating such as in Isa 9:1–6. This subtle difference may account for the retention of the factors that originally made 9:1–6 a royal enthronement hymn. After the editors reinterpreted this non-messianic enthronement oracle messianically, the text retained the description of historical events that originally surrounded the kings' accession to the throne. However, 11:1–9 was originally messianic and did not describe an Israelite king. Therefore, 11:1–9 does not reflect any historical events that accompanied a king's reign, because, after the "stump of Jesse" had already ceased to exist, this oracle was fashioned to anticipate an eschatological event that did not include such events in human history.

Like Isa 11:2, 61:1 also describes the empowerment of YHWH's Spirit, though ch. 61 makes explicit what was implicit of messianic expectation in 11:2. The very language about the spirit of the Lord "upon him" has been taken up in 61:1 and applied in the first person to a figure who has been "anointed" (מֹשַׁח√). From this perspective, ch. 61 probably is interpreting ch. 11 messianically and placing the Servant within this expectation. The phrase רוּחַ אֲדֹנָי יְהוִה עָלָי ("the spirit of the *'Adōnāy* YHWH is upon me," 61:1) has altered 11:2's וְנָחָה עָלָיו רוּחַ יְהוָה ("the spirit of YHWH shall rest on him," 11:2) since the Servant in 61:1 now speaks in the first person. The reason that the spirit of YHWH is upon him is because (יַעַן) YHWH has "anointed" him. The verb נחה has been replaced in 61:1 by a verbless sentence. The third person suffix pronoun after the preposition עָלָיו (11:2) has been changed to עָלָי (61:1) by the first person suffix pronoun, and the appellation רוּחַ יְהוָה (11:2) has been altered to רוּחַ אֲדֹנָי יְהוִה. Clearly these significant similarities along with the use of the verb משח in 61:1 seem to make a messianic claim on the greater text of Isaiah.

O. Kaiser, who claims in his first edition that Isa 11:1–9 speaks of a king, now regards this passage to be a messianic description because it is heard against the backdrop of the "annihilation of the Davidic monarchy" (587), whereby the Messiah is understood as a shoot from his [David's] family tree."[440] Yet Wegner asks why we could not merely regard these verses as a figurative description or portrait of an ideal ruler?[441] First, this is not a royal enthronement psalm and does not include the same

---

440. Kaiser, *Isaiah 1–12* (1st ed.), 158, and *Isaiah 1–12* (2d ed.), 254–55.

441. Wegner poses this question, which for all intents and purposes he does not answer (*An Examination of Kingship*, 232).

adoration of a king, upon which people interpret figuratively. Instead, we have here a prophecy of rejuvenation of the fallen Davidic dynasty portrayed by a "stump" that only can be fulfilled in the post-exilic era by a Messiah. Further, vv. 6–9 describe eschatological events that never appear in any enthronement psalms. This expectation of universal peace (vv. 6–9) that transcends the earthly realm would only be realized by a supernatural happenstance that was conceived in the minds of people in the post-exilic age where because of the termination of the Davidic monarchy, a messianic hope originated.

Many conflicting interpretations have been assigned to Isa 11:6–9. Modern scholars, among them Cheyne, have noted that 11:6–9 has been interpreted allegorically (Calvin), realistically (the Rabbis), in a secondary allegorical sense (Hengstenberg) or as typology within the literal sense (Naegstrom).[442] Calvin allegorizes 11:6–9 as the spiritual condition within humans.[443] Clements thinks that although this peace is brought to the animal realm, it also has effect on humankind.[444] Some argue that the eschatological elements portrayed in 11:6–9 provide proof that these verses are late,[445] since they paint a picture similar to how early Greek and Latin poets depict the ideal life.[446] Yet others claim that there is evidence for such thinking in other early ancient Near Eastern texts, such as *Gilgamesh* (Tablet 12);[447] and *Enki and Ninhursag*.[448] While theoretically these eschatological images could be old or late, this type of comparative methodology does not address the problem of Isa 11:1–9. What

442. Cheyne, *Isaiah*, 1:77.
443. Calvin, *Commentary on the Book of the Prophet Isaiah*, 3:383–86.
444. Clements, *Isaiah 1–39*, 124.
445. Gray, *Isaiah I–XXXIX*, 219 (1956); Kaiser, *Isaiah 1–12* (2d ed.), 259; Wegner, *An Examination of Kingship*, 257.
446. Such as, the *Eclogues* of Virgil (4:21–22; 5:20); the Sibylline Oracles iii.766–95; Empedocles, fragment 130D–136 and 137b; Porphyry, *Vita Pythogorae* 19; Iamblichus, *De vita pythogoria* 24, 17f.; Aristophanes, *Pax* 1075f; Plato, *Politicus* 271d, 272d; Horace, *Epistles* 16, 50–55; Ovid, *Metamorphosis* I, 101: 50; XV, 96–110; *Fasti* IV, 295–416.
447. *ANET*, 74; Jeffrey H. Tigay, *The Evolution of Gilgamesh Epic* (Philadelphia: University of Pennsylvania Press, 1982), 5–13; William Jones, "From Gilgamesh to Qohelet," in *The Bible in Light of Cuneiform Literature* (ed. William Hallo et al.; Lewiston, N.Y.: Edwin Mellen, 1990), 365.
448. Samuel Noah Kramer, *Sumerian Mythology: A Study of Spiritual and Literary Achievement in the Third Millennium BC* (rev. ed.; Philadelphia: University of Pennsylvania Press, 1972), 54–59. See also Rehm, *Der königliche Messias*, 209–28; Vermeylen, *Du prophète Isaïe*, 275; Laato, *Who is Immanuel?*, 204 Wildberger, *Jesaja 1–12*, 456; idem, *Isaiah 1–12*, 479–80; Wegner, *An Examination of Kingship*, 258.

else about this content would help determine whether it is pre-exilic or post-exilic? The fact that גרע, שרש, נצר and חטר are not familiar expressions but are used very few times in the Old Testament, provides evidence that they are not old terms but new terms that offer specificity to this text in the post-exilic age to describe a messianic shoot that has sprouted from the stump of Jesse's line after the monarchy has terminated. Wegner cannot substantiate his claim that גזע does not imply the termination of the monarchy.

While many scholars argue that 11:6 is antecedent of 65:25,[449] O. Kaiser claims that 11:9 quotes 65:25b in order to relate "the expectation expressed in [11:]6–8 to the notion of the future..."[450] Others contend that 65:25a serves as a brief summary of 11:6–7 and that 65:25b also summarizes Gen 3:14.[451] Duhm asserts that 65:25b originated before 11:6–7 since הר קדשי only appears once in Isa 1–39 but five times in chs. 55–66. Since Seitz is so interested in proving that the deliverer in chs. 11 is Hezekiah, and since Sweeney assumes Josiah, they completely overlook the relationship between Isa 11 and 65:25. In doing so, they fail to describe the book as a whole.[452]

Whether or not Isa 11:6 constitutes the original material from which 65:25 cites, the intra-testimony between chs. 11 and 65 serves as a confirmation of messianic prophecy. Because the "former things," appearing in the so-called Third Isaiah corpus (65:16, 17) have taken on new dimensions in the scriptural scroll of Isaiah, the discussion now moves from the events of the exile and the release of the captives to a new eschatological level. Just as the later editing in Isa 10–11 transforms the discussion around Assyria into a larger pattern of God's eschatological judgment and salvation, 43:18–19 and 65:18–25 render obsolete past fulfilments of prophecy, including the work done by Cyrus, because God will now do a "new thing" (43:19) and is now creating "new heavens and a new earth" (65:17). The "new things," which speak of a period long after the former events of Babylonian captivity and Cyrus's edict, anticipate an eschatological scenario where "the wolf and the lamb shall feed together..." (65:25). In order to embrace the "new things" that God will do, the post-exilic community cannot hold on to temporal images of

---

449.   Skinner, *Isaiah Chapters I–XXXIX*, 242; Kissane, *The Book of Isaiah*, 1:137; Young, *Isaiah*, 1:517; Westermann, *Isaiah 40–66*, 410; A. S. Herbert, *The Book of the Prophet Isaiah 40–66* (CBC; Cambridge: Cambridge University Press, 1975), 188; Whybray, *Isaiah 40–66*, 278–79; Watts, *Isaiah 1–33*, 355.

450.   Kaiser, *Isaiah 1–12* (2d ed.), 253, 260.

451.   Westermann, *Isaiah 40–66*, 410; Whybray, *Isaiah 40–66*, 278; Wegner, *An Examination of Kingship*, 251.

452.   Seitz, *Isaiah 1–39*, 95–108; Sweeney, *Isaiah 1–39*, 196–211.

human champions such as Cyrus because that would fit into the pattern of idolatry spoken of throughout the book. Because YHWH is "about to create new heavens and a new earth," the prophet exhorts the community that these "former things shall not be remembered..." (65:17), but neither should they forget the eschatological description of the shoot who "shall come forth from the stump of Jesse" and who will bring eternal peace when "the lion lies down with the lamb." The end of the Davidic house provides the fulfilment of earlier prophecy about YHWH's judgment, but the latter formation of the book lays the foundation for messianic expectation. The post-exilic community can forget those former prophecies, which were connected to Cyrus because Cyrus has already served his temporal purpose, but God's people cannot forget the messianic concept that belongs to the end of time (11:6–9).

No Israelite king is mentioned in Isa 40–66 because the monarchy had already become a "stump," and when chs. 40–66 was edited chs. Isa 1–39 in the exilic or post-exilic era, the writers presupposed that the monarchy had collapsed with the walls of Jerusalem. From this perspective, 65:25 recollects 11:6, thus negating any interpretation that would connect Hezekiah, Josiah or Cyrus with messianic promise. Similar to Isa 7 and 9, the editors have exploited the ambiguity of this figure who emerges from the lineage of Jesse, and who possesses messianic qualities that provide possibilities for messianic interpretation.

Therefore, Wegner's argument that Isa 11:1–9 falls short of the full concept of the Messiah because the deliverance takes place in the present age and not in the future, overlooks the futuristic nature of 11:6–9 (when the wolf and the lamb shall feed together) and the way 65:17–25 reapplies messianic imagery to old forms.[453] Further, 11:11–16 reflects the exact style and order of the fifth-century oracle in 62:10–12.[454] The way in which the editors have linked these promises of salvation to the nations in 11:10–12, with 11:1–9, shows that the rule of this king now extends to the whole earth (contra Wegner). Even if one could prove that vv. 1–9 were pre-exilic (though this is not likely), vv. 10–12 shape vv. 1–9 by a response to the exile, using some elements that are part of (post-exilic) messianism. For example, vv. 10–11 claim that all the nations will seek "the stump of Jesse," the exiles will return from foreign nations and all of Israel's enemies will be defeated. Finally, the phrase "on that day" in 11:12 resounds the "on that day" formula in 7:20–25 whereby ch. 11 reaffirms that both Emmanuel and Šoreš-Jesse are the answer to the description of exile in 7:20–25 and 11:12.

453. Wegner, *An Examination of Kingship*, 260.
454. Odil Hannes Steck, *Studien zu Tritojesaja* (Berlin: de Gruyter, 1991), 22.

Conclusion

If one takes seriously the juxtaposition that exists in the tension between the original context and later editing, we begin to see how older traditions have at times been overtly reinterpreted in a messianic mode. Isaiah 7:14 invites messianic interpretation within the context of later editing (6:11–13; 7:18–25; 8:20–23) and the reinterpretation of Emmanuel in ch. 8. Isaiah 9:1–6 could very well have originally been a hymn sung at a king's enthronement or during the anniversary of his coronation, but within the later editing, reapplications of the "former things," and the theme of "light and darkness," this oracle takes on messianic proportions. Isaiah 11 seems to be a post-exilic oracle that originally warranted messianic expectation, but which has also been interpreted messianically within the intra-textuality of the book of Isaiah (61:1; 65:25).

Chapter 4

THE SUFFERING SERVANT
(ISAIAH 52:13–53:12)

Introduction

Of all the passages considered here, Isa 52:13–53:12 has inspired the most prolific expositions in the history of interpretation. Paul Hanson says that this song "places images before the reader that elicit deep refection without providing answers to every problem of interpretation."[1] Ever since Duhm's classification of the Servant Songs, modern attempts to solve the identity of the Servant and to try to reconstruct the original pre-biblical traditions behind the biblical composition have rendered as non-messianic what Christians have traditionally interpreted as messianic. In referring to the role of the Servant, H. H. Rowley states,

> I do not like the term "messianic," because it suggests the Davidic Messiah, and so prejudices some questions. Both the Davidic Messiah and the Servant were conceived of as agents in the establishment of the divine rule in all the earth, but they were different conceptions of the means whereby this should be accomplished. They were therefore not related conceptions, and both may have had some roots in the ritual of Jerusalem, though they were not brought together in any vital way before the time of Christ, and we ought to beware of equating them.[2]

Are there warrants to interpret Isa 52:13–53:12 messianically? While the Targum interprets the Servant to be the Messiah, it re-interprets the phrases about his sufferings as referring to Israel or the rival nations. Earlier Jewish readers were already asking, "who is the suffering Servant whose death provides atonement (53:4, 5, 6, 10, 11, 12) for the people?" Jewish interpreters felt compelled to speculate: "Was it Joshua?" "Was it

---

1. Paul D. Hanson, *Isaiah 40–66* (Interpretation; Louisville, Ky.: John Knox, 1995), 153.
2. H. H. Rowley, *The Servant of the Lord and Other Essays on the Old Testament* (London: Lutterworth, 1952), 54.

Moses?" "Was it Jeremiah?" "Was it Isaiah?" Each of these views seem to reflect various speculative strands of early Judaism.

Early Christians had to find warrants for messianic interpretation in the same way as Jews did. When Christians began to interpret the death of Jesus messianically, then the atonement of the Servant matched their descriptions of Jesus' own sufferings well, even though the Servant in Isa 53 is never called a king. Thus, Isa 52:13–53:12 had not been heard earlier as messianic for many Jews because the Messiah would not suffer and die (e.g. Peter could not tolerate a suffering and dying Messiah [Matt 16:22; Mark 8:32]). Were Christians merely imposing this reading on the text or does the text itself provide warrants for messianic interpretation? Did the Evangelists fashion the Gospel narratives to correspond with Isa 52:12–53:13 or did this passages testify to the exaltation, sufferings and intercession of Jesus Christ?

In this chapter, I will treat Isa 52:13–53:13 as a unit because the majority of scholars have treated these verses together even within pre-modern interpretation. Since all that has been written on 52:13–53:12 would fill a large house from basement to attic, I will selectively survey scholars who illustrate efforts to describe the function of both the origi-nal pre-biblical tradition(s) and then the scriptural form of the book of Isaiah. I will examine the ambiguity of the Servant's identity and clarity of his exaltation, intercession and act of suffering for the sins of many, exploring whether or not the testimony of the text warrants messianic promise or if such interpretation belongs solely to the liberties of the reader. I will also explore whether the New Testament quotations of Isa 52:13–53:12 are cited from context or betray atomistic exegesis that does not necessarily take the context seriously but attaches the term מָשִׁיחַ to single words or phrases even if the larger context does not suggest it. This chapter makes no attempts to resolve all the redactional issues of Isa 40–55, but serves to question whether or not 52:13–53:12 provides warrants for messianic interpretation within the scriptural book of Isaiah.

I. *Isaiah 52:13–53:12 within Pre-biblical Traditions*

A. *Non-messianic Assessments*
1. *Views that interpret the Servant as Israel.* Since the early 1900s, sev-eral modern Christian scholars have adopted the common Jewish view that the Servant is the nation of Israel.[3] Since the Holocaust, it has been

---

3. Karl Budde, "The So-Called 'Ebed-Yahweh Songs' in Isaiah," *AJTh* 3 (1899): 499–500; Marti, *Das Buch Jesaja*, 344–41, 360–66; Friedrich Giesebrecht, *Der Knecht Jahwes Des Deuterojesaia* (Königsberg: Thomas & Oppermann, 1902);

said that "Auschwitz was worse than Golgotha."[4] The manner in which scholars interpret the Servant as Israel varies with regards to methodology and purpose. Norbert Lohfink argues that Israel's concept of God as a bringer of peace gradually evolved from a model of the total destruction of the enemy and their property (*ḥērem*) to the idea that it is better to be oppressed than to be the oppressor because God can bring the Servant (Israel) back from death to new life.[5] Recently, John Collins asserts that the Servant of YHWH for "Second Isaiah" is Israel and cannot be a messianic king because the prophet who identified a "Gentile Messiah" in Cyrus and "who celebrated the deliverance of Israel by the Persians had no role for a Davidic king."[6] Since Isa 53 has been cited so few times in the New Testament, Collins argues that this must imply that pre-New Testament Judaism had no understanding of a suffering eschatological figure.[7] Yet to many, such a position is far from clear.

Early in the twentieth century, other scholars tried to explain how the portrait of an individual Servant was used for rhetorical purposes to present Israel in a nuanced role. For example, George H. Box and J. Skinner referred to the Servant as the "ideal Israel," but Box thought that the fourth song consciously reminisced of Jeremiah.[8] R. H. Kennett argued that the Servant Songs, which were written in the Maccabean period, referred to the Hasidim who were a select group in Israel.[9] Consequently, Whitehouse regarded the Servant to be Israel within Israel.[10] Paul Volz claimed that the Servant personified the mission of Israel to the world.[11] Arthur S. Peake contended that Servant was the actual

Arthur S. Peake, *The Problem of Suffering in the Old Testament* (London: R. Bryant, 1904), 34–72; G. W. Wade, *The Book of the Prophet Isaiah* (London: Methuen & Co., 1911), 345–48.

4. J. L. Koole, *Isaiah*. Vol. 3, *Isaiah 49–55* (Leuven: Peeters, 1998), 251.

5. Norbert Lohfink, "Der 'Heilige Krieg' und der 'Bann' in der Bibel," *IKZ* 18 (1989): 104–12.

6. Collins, *The Scepter and the Star*, 28.

7. Ibid., 208.

8. George H. Box, *The Book of Isaiah: Translated from a Text Revised in Accordance with the Results of Recent Criticism* (London: Sir Isaac Pitman & Sons, 1908), 194–99, 265–68; J. Skinner, *Isaiah Chapters XL–LXVI* (The Cambridge Bible for Schools and Colleges; Cambridge: Cambridge University Press, 1922), lvi–lxii, 132–50, 263–81.

9. Kennett, *The Composition of the Book of Isaiah*, 72.

10. Owen C. Whitehouse, *Isaiah: Introduction* (The Century Bible; Edinburgh: T. C. & E. C. Jack, 1912–13), 18–25.

11. P. Volz, "Jesaja 53," in *Beitrage zur alttestamentlichen Wissenschaft Karl Budde zum siebzigsten Geburtstag am 13. April 1920* (ed. Karl Marti; BZAW; Giessen: A. Töpelmann, 1920), 181–90 (184).

empirical Israel and not the ideal Israel but that the prophet discerned it from an ideal perspective.[12] Adolphe Lods also perceived the Servant to be the actual Israel but added that perhaps the second song differentiated the Servant from Israel and the fourth song depicted him as the remnant of people, who was aware of Israel's calling and suffered on behalf of "my people."[13] Yehezkel Kaufmann argued that the Servant represented those humble and faithful ones, who constitute the "true Israel."[14]

Hence, Johannes Pedersen maintained that, although the Servant had been assigned for the sake of Israel, the nation took on a "persona" of its own and was personified in the individual identity of the Servant.[15] More specifically, H. Wheeler Robinson, who described the "corporate personality" of Israel, argued that Israel as a whole had been "so impressively individualized…in Isaiah Isa liii…that it had often been taken to refer to a single Israelite."[16] Explaining this form-critically, Charles Torrey argued that the Servant Songs originally found their *Sitz im Leben* in the public days of national lamentation but were inserted into Deutero-Isaiah by a later hand. Therefore, he propounded that, although the personification is startlingly real, "the servant in this case is not the imaginary representative of Israel, the Messiah, but rather the personified nation itself or a representative of Israel."[17]

Likewise, scholars distinguish the Servant as Israel and portray him as a metaphor to describe Israel's function or role within the purposes of YHWH. William Holladay argues that "many" and "we" in 52:13–53:12 is "the kings, the nations" and that the Servant receives the punishment that kings deserve from their crimes (e.g. 1:5–6).[18] The kings have been

12. Peake, *The Problem of Suffering*, 34–72; idem, *The Servant of Yahweh: Three Lectures Delivered at King's College, London* (Manchester: Manchester University Press, 1931), 1–74.

13. Adolphe Lods, *Les Prophètes d'Israël et les débuts du judaïsme* (Paris: A. Michel, 1935), 275–80; idem, *Histoire de la littérature hébraïque et juive: Depuis les origines jusqu'à la ruine de l'état juif* (Paris: Payot, 1950), 472–75.

14. Yehezkel Kaufmann, *The Religion of Israel from Its Beginnings to the Babylonian Exile* (trans. and abridged Moshe Greenberg; London: George, Allen & Unwin, 1961), 155–62.

15. Johannes Pedersen, *Israel: Its Life and Culture*, vols. 3–4 (London: Oxford University Press, 1940), 603–5.

16. Robinson, *Inspiration and Revelation*, 71; idem, *Corporate Personality in Ancient Israel* (Facet Books. Biblical Series; Philadelphia: Fortress, 1967); idem, *Suffering, Human and Divine* (Great Issues of Life Series; New York: Macmillan, 1939); idem, *The Cross in the Old Testament* (London: SCM Press, 1955).

17. Charles C. Torrey, *Second Isaiah: A New Interpretation* (New York: Charles Scribner's Sons, 1928), 34–35, 410–23.

18. Holladay, *Isaiah*, 148–60.

guilty (53:5), but now they are pronounced innocent, acknowledging God's resurrection of his Servant, who is exalted, lifted up and rewarded (52:12, 13).[19] Using imagery that speaks of Jeremiah's career, Second Isaiah is mute regarding the identity of the Servant in order for his hearers to search for an identification, which cries out to Israel, "if the shoes fits, put it on." Holladay argues that "the shoes fit" for Jesus "and he put it on" because although the Servant does not fit Jesus in every detail, "it fits because it became Jesus' own self-understanding of his task."[20]

John Gray specifies how the role of the Servant in Isa 52:13–53:12 "describes how the mission of the true Israel, the saving remnant, will be achieved, by atoning suffering and here is the disclosure of the ultimate implications of the election of Israel."[21] Wolfgang Roth also argues that the divine voice in 52:13–53:12 draws the audience's attention to "my servant," who is the remnant people whom God has called to restore not only Israel but all descendants of Abraham.[22] Richard Clifford distinguishes the Servant as the faithful part of Israel.[23] The speaker is "unlikely" to be the nations because Deutero-Isaiah only mentions them to show the nations that "what happens to Israel makes visible to them the superiority of Israel's God and the inanity of their own gods." The speaker is Israel and also "'the many' who endlessly schemed to escape the Exile." Israel wanes in proximity to the Servant, who bears the burden that Israel once had to bear through "a minority of the exiles," who have a "conscious awareness of the purpose of the Exile coupled with a lively hope of return." Therefore, the "servant's suffering is accepted as valid for the whole people" while "the nations look on astonishment as Israel rises from disgrace to salvation."[24]

Like Clifford, George A. F. Knight construes the Servant as Israel within the context of the exile. He regards the Servant to be Israel, whose historical situation was one of suffering but also one that all people must necessarily meet.[25] God reveals himself as Israel's husband, who also suffered when Israel suffered, because Israel could not fulfill her calling

19. Ibid., 155–56.
20. Like John Goldingay, William Holladay presents the Servant almost as a "role waiting to be fulfilled"; cf. John Goldingay, "The Arrangement of Isaiah Xl–Xlv," *VT* 29 (1979): 292; Holladay, *Scroll of a Prophetic Heritage*, 156, 158.
21. Gray, *Reign of God*, 180.
22. Wolfgang Roth, *Isaiah* (ed. John H. Hayes; Knox Preaching Guides; Atlanta: John Knox, 1988), 150.
23. Clifford, *Fair Spoken and Persuading*, 175–81.
24. Ibid., 180–81.
25. George A. Knight, *Servant Theology: A Commentary on the Book of Isaiah 40–55* (Grand Rapids: Eerdmans, 1984), 171.

alone.[26] Just as the word "rich" in 53:9 refers to the wealth of the Babylonian empire, "Nebuchadrezzar in destroying Israel is likened to Israel's death."[27]

Rikki E. Watts, who claims to interpret "the present form of the book as a whole," argues that "while chapters 1–39 pronounce judgement upon the nation they are not without a future hope for a purified remnant."[28] However, Isa 40–55 shows that "Jacob-Israel is declared to be Israel in name only in a statement which seems tantamount to divesting Jacob-Israel of her servant office."[29] On one hand, Jacob-Israel is presented as Servant (41:8, 9; 44:1; 45:4), and, on the other hand, "she is blind, deaf and devoid of understanding." Against this backdrop, Watts argues that "the fourth song describes the way in which Yahweh's ultimate agent, the unknown עֶבֶד, will realize the new Exodus."[30] The unknown Servant in 52:13–53:12 cannot be Jacob-Israel because the Servant is "spurned" by his own people (49:4; 50:8; 53:8). Therefore, Watts argues that the collective Jacob-Israel failed in his Servant calling and has been reduced to a faithful remnant, whereby "the true Israel has been reduced to one."[31] Watts concludes that, within the book as a whole, Isa 40–55 explains the "failure of the return from exile" and that within this context, "the New Exodus is still in the future."[32]

Klaus Baltzer, who claims that Isa 42:1–25 constitutes a scene before the "heavenly court" which resumes and concludes in Isa 53,[33] asserts that the "Servant Songs" constitute a biography which was secondarily incorporated into Isa 40–55:

> Unter den Voraussetzungen der vorliegenden Untersuchung ist es wahrscheinlich, dass die Biographie, wie sie sich aus den sogenannten Gottesknecht-Texten zusammensetzen lässt, dem Deuterojesaja-Buch bereits vorgelegen hat. Die entscheidende Veränderlich des "Knechtes". Dass "Israel" Knecht ist, ist die ausdrückliche Meinung in übrigen Deuterojesaja-Buch.[34]

26. Ibid., 172.

27. 176.

28. Rikki E. Watts, "Consolation or Confrontation: Isaiah 40–55 and the Delay of the New Exodus," *TynBul* 41 (1990): 31.

29. Ibid., 35.

30. Ibid., 52.

31. Ibid., 55.

32. Ibid., 59.

33. Klaus Baltzer, "Zur Formgeschichtlichen Bestimmung der Texte Vom Gottes-Knecht im Deuterojesaja Buch," in Wolff, ed., *Probleme Biblischer Theologie*, 40–42.

34. In paraphrase, Balzer is saying that, assuming that the basic assumptions of this (= Baltzer's) study are right, then it follows that the biography (of the Ebed

Baltzer and others, who understand the Servant to be Israel, are partially correct about the identification of the Servant as he appears in Isa
40–48.

2. *Views that interpret the Servant as an individual distinct from Israel.*
Some scholars assert that the Servant in Isa 49–55 cannot be identified
with Israel as in chs. 40–48 because the portrait of the Servant varies
from song to song. Hence, Bruston claims that the first Servant Song
speaks of Israel, the second and third songs along with Isa 61:1–3 refers
to the prophet and the fourth song to a future individual who will continue the same work.[35] James D. Smart asserts that the Servant is both
corporate and an individual because 42:1–7; 49:1–6 and 52:13–15 speak
of Israel while 53:1–2 refers to Second Isaiah himself.[36] Smart suggests
that the Servant figure in chs. 40–48 is dramatically left unnamed when
pertaining to Israel in order to present it as restored and transformed.[37]
Similarly, Kaiser asserts that both the Servant and Israel share these
attributes of one who is a Davidic king and has obtained royal office.[38]
C. R. North posits that Israel cannot be the Servant because in the songs,
the Servant assumes an "active mission," but outside of the Songs,
Deutero-Isaiah portrays Israel as a "passive recipient of salvation."[39]

YHWH), which underlies the "*Gottesknecht-Texten*" and can be reconstructed on the
basis of the given texts, was an independent, coherent work before it was included in
(and simultaneously divided into parts and spread all over) the book Deutero-Isaiah.
As the *Gottesknecht-Texte* now stand, namely as parts of the book Deutero-Isaiah,
the Ebed YHWH must be the same figure as in the rest of the book, that is, "Israel."
This shift of meaning is most important, even "decisive." See Baltzer, "Zur Form-
geschichtlichen," 42. See also von Waldow whom Baltzer followed on this point
(H. E. von Waldow, "Analass Hintergrund der Verkuendigung Des Deuterojesaja"
[Ph.D diss., University of Bonn, 1953], 57), and who is followed by Preuss (H. D.
Preuss, *Deuterojesaja. Eine Einführung in seine Botschaft* [BWANT; Stuttgart:
Kohlhammer, 1971], 99–100).
    35. H. Bruston, "Le serviteur de l'éternel dans l'avenir," in *Vom Alten Testament
Karl Marti zum Siebzigsten Geburtstage* (ed. Karl Budde; Giessen: A. Töpelmann,
1925), 37–44.
    36. James D. Smart, "A New Approach to the 'Ebed-Yahweh Problem," *ET* 45
(1933–34): 168–72.
    37. Smart, *History and Theology*, 67–68, 77–78.
    38. Otto Kaiser, *Der königliche Knecht: Eine traditionsgeschichtlich-exegetisch
Studie über die Ebed-Jahweh-Lieder bei Deuterojesaja* (FRLANT 52; Göttingen:
Vandenhoeck & Ruprecht, 1959), 18–31.
    39. Christopher Richard North, *The Suffering Servant in Deutero-Isaiah: An
Historical and Critical Study* (2d ed.; London: Oxford University Press, 1956), 206.
Yet North says that the fourth song is the most difficult to interpret because form-

Similarly, Whybray renounces Israel as the Servant because Israel's role as Servant is always passive but the Servant's role is active. If the Servant were Israel then it would have been made explicit, as in 41:8; 44:2, 21; 45:4; 48:20. Therefore, the Servant is "given the task of bringing Israel back to Yahweh" and is clearly "distinct from the nation."[40] John McKenzie, who does not identify the Servant, distinguishes the Servant from Israel because his work denotes a future saving act, which does not refer to the past (e.g. Exodus) nor to the "saving act in Second Isaiah." McKenzie concludes that he is the "one who will restore Israel as an enduring reality."[41] Likewise, Wilcox and Patton-Williams argue that a Servant who has a mission to Israel plainly cannot be Israel himself and ask, if the Servant were Israel, how does Israel die (52:13–53:12)?[42]

Therefore, many scholars have regarded the Servant to be an historical individual. For example, Duhm himself speculated that the four Servant Songs were not written by the "author" of the rest of Deutero-Isaiah, but that they depicted a Rabbi who was contemporary with this prophet and died of leprosy.[43] Arthur Marmorstein imagined that the Servant was a pious sufferer of Second Isaiah's time.[44] Fred A. Farley suggested that all of the Servant Songs looked back on the career of Jeremiah.[45] Sheldon Blank held that career of Jeremiah served as a personification for the whole nation of Israel.[46] At the beginning of the last century, Richard Kraetzschmar maintained that the Servant was Ezekiel.[47]

3. *Views that interpret the Servant in light of the Tammuz myth.* Since the Ras Shamra and other archaeological discoveries, some scholars

---

critics cannot agree on a category. Thus he concludes that YHWH is the speaker but the song consists of human words of one or more human speakers set in a framework pronounced by YHWH.

40. Whybray, *Isaiah 40–66*, 71, 137.

41. McKenzie, *Second Isaiah*.

42. Peter Wilcox and David Patton-Williams, "The Servant Songs in Deutero-Isaiah," *JSOT* 42 (1988): 80, 94.

43. Duhm, *Jesaja*, 284–86, 365–67, 393–406. Buber (*Der Glaube der Propheten*, 227–28) agreed that the Servant is described as a leper. Note also Schoeps on Symmachus's rendering of Isa 53:4; see Hans Joachim Schoeps, *Aus frühchristlicher Zeit, religionsgeschichtliche Untersuchungen* (Tübingen: Mohr, 1950), 107–9.

44. Arthur Marmorstein, "Zur Erklärung von Jes 53," *ZAW* 3 (1926): 260–62.

45. Fred A. Farley, "Jeremiah and the 'Suffering Servant of Jehovah' in Deutero-Isaiah," *ET* 38 (1926–27): 521–23.

46. Sheldon H. Blank, "Studies in Deutero-Isaiah," *HUCA* 15 (1940): 1–4, 18–27.

47. Richard Kraetzschmar, *Das Buch Ezechiel* (Göttingen: Vandenhoeck, 1900), 46.

have used comparative methodology to interpret the Servant Songs. H. S. Nyberg, who compared Ugaritic Baal texts and Canaanite Tammuz liturgies with the patriarchs, Moses, David and the prophets, argued that the Servant belonged to the past, present and future, and oscillated between the individual and collective. Yet, Nyberg did not view the songs as messianic, nor could they refer to a king because they were written during the exile when Israel had no king.[48] Similarly, Rudolph Kittel had already conceded that the fourth song imitated Babylonian rituals but also denied that the Servant was a king.[49] Similarly, Samuel H. Hooke argued that the cultic idea of a dying and rising god applies to the Servant. He rejected the option of messianic interpretation and instead propounded that Second Isaiah transformed this ancient ritual pattern of the death of an individual into the vicarious death of the Servant who portrayed the political death of Israel.[50]

4. *Views that compare the Servant with Moses.* Others have argued that the Servant functions as a new Moses. For example, Sigmund Freud adopts Sellin's theory that the Servant Songs depict the martyrdom of Moses.[51] Von Rad regards the Servant to be a "second Moses or a *Moses redivivus*," but a prophet "like Moses" because both Deuteronomy and Deutero-Isaiah "stood within a tradition which looked for a prophet like Moses." Yet Deutero-Isaiah does not draw upon Deuteronomy but "both used an existing Mosaic tradition, about his office as mediator, and about the prophet who was to come."[52] Anthony Phillips argues that "the theology" in Isa 40–55 reflects the ideas of the exilic-age prophet who expects a new superior Exodus under a new superior Moses who would establish justice throughout the earth. The prophet urges the faithful exiles to follow the Servant's vicarious sufferings because even if they die in Babylon, their Children will enjoy a secure future even beyond their graves in a heathen land. The Servant never develops into such an autonomous figure as the "messiah" or the "son of man" and plays no

48. H. S. Nyberg, "Smärtornas Man: En Studie Till Jes. 52:13–53:12," *SEÅ* 7 (1942): 5–82.

49. Rudolf Kittel, *Geschichte Des Volkes Israel* (Gotha: Friedrich Andreas Perthes, 1909), 256–57.

50 Samuel H. Hooke, *Prophets and Priests* (London: T. Murby & Co., 1938), 40–42.

51. Sigmund Freud, *Moses and Monotheism* (London: Hogarth Press and the Institute of Psycho-Analysis, 1939), 59–60.

52. Gerhard von Rad, *Old Testament Theology* (trans. D. M. G. Stalker; London: SCM Press, 1975), 259–62.

such role in the Old Testament Apocrypha, Pseudepigrapha or in the narratives about Jesus and in the New Testament.[53]

5. *Views that interpret the Servant in relation to Cyrus.* Others note uncanny similarities between the "Servant Songs" and the "Cyrus songs," seeking to define Cyrus' role in light of the Servant Songs. Some argue that the Cyrus Cylinder provides evidence that Cyrus was the Servant.[54] Sidney Smith argues that the Servant in the first song refers to Cyrus, but in the other three songs to the prophet Deutero-Isaiah, and that the fourth song was written about him after his death. Yet Smith asserts that it is impossible to discriminate between the actions of Cyrus and of the prophet in all four songs.[55] Influenced by Mowinckel, M. Haller also argued that the prophet at first regarded Cyrus to be YHWH's divinely appointed Servant to deliver Judah but was subsequently dissatisfied with Cyrus and hence substituted himself as Servant.[56] W. E. Barnes argued that Cyrus originally was the Servant, but that the prophet came to realize that a spiritual agent must take up the work of the Servant.[57] H. H. Rowley argues that "there is *prima facie* ground for the view that the prophet at first thought of Cyrus as the Servant.[58]

Shalom Paul, who regards Cyrus to be the "servant of Deutero-Isaiah," claims that Deutero-Isaiah uses a great deal of royal inscription language, which he thinks relates to Cyrus. Paul claims that some of the things said about עבדי (41:8; 42:1; 43:10; 44:1, 21; 45:4; 49:5 etc.) also apply to Cyrus, as in the phrase, "I have called you by your name" for the servant Israel (43:1), and the phrase הזכיר שמי ("He designated my name") for

---

53. Anthony Phillips, "The Servant Symbol of Divine Powerlessness," *ExpTim* 90 (1979): 370–74.

54. Robert William Rogers, *Cuneiform Parallels to the Old Testament* (New York: Eaton & Mains, 1912), 380–84.

55. Smith, *Isaiah Chapters XL–LV*, 174–75. See also Rogers, *Cuneiform Parallels*, 380–85. W. Caspari argued that Isa 42:1–4 originally constituted the third Cyrus song and opposes Mowinckel's belief that this did not refer to Cyrus. See his *Lieder und Gottessprüche de Rückwanderer (Jes 40–55)* (BZAW 65; Giessen: Töpelmann, 1934): 196–97.

56. M. Haller, "Die Kyroslieder Deuterojesaja," in Schmidt, ed., *Eucharistérion*, 261–77. See also August Freiherr von Gall, *Basileia Tou Theou: Eine Religionsgeschichtliche Studie zur Vorkirchlichen Eschatologie* (Heidelberg: C. Winter, 1926), 187; C. E. Simcox, "The Role of Cyrus in Deutero-Isaiah," *JAOS* 57 (1937): 158–60; Buber, *Der Glaube der Propheten*, 221–22.

57. W. E. Barnes, "Cyrus the 'Servant of Jehovah,' Isa 42:1–4 (7)," *JTS* 32 (1931): 32–39.

58. Rowley, *The Servant of the Lord*, 29.

Cyrus (49:1). Paul also thinks that the words, אני יהוה קראתיך בצדק ("I
YHWH have graciously called you")—a sign and seal of the divine call
[42:6])—corresponds to YHWH's calling Cyrus from the womb יהוה
מבטן קראני (49:1). Paul can only claim that Cyrus is the Servant if he
can isolate any form-critical units (i.e. Servant Songs) that originally
existed apart from "Second Isaiah" but not within the greater context,
because 45:4 declares that YHWH has appointed him for the sake of the
servant (למען עבדי).[59]

From this perspective, Millard Lind argues that the Servant is seen as
an individual within Israel or a combination of the two.[60] Claiming that
the "roots of servant poems" stem from the same tradition history as do
the trial speeches and that the Servant takes on kingly characteristics,
Lind notes the similarities between the Servant and Cyrus. Yet Deutero-
Isaiah cannot construe Cyrus as the Servant because "the Servant himself
fulfills that positive function of kingship from which Cyrus was cut
short." The "kingly task is not peripheral but central" to the person of the
Servant and would thereby stand in "direct competition to the reign of
kingly rulers such as Cyrus." Only in the Servant can YHWH's oath—that
he will bring forth justice to the nations—be fulfilled and will the moral
quality of his rule of Torah justice guarantee that YHWH alone is God,
creator and redeemer.[61]

6. *Views that interpret the Servant as an Israelite king.* Early in the past
century, others regarded the Servant to be Jehoiachin, who presumably
represented the death of the Davidic monarchy when he surrendered
Jerusalem and was carried off into captivity. Rothstein thought that the
Servant originally was the Davidic dynasty, personified by its concurrent
emissary Jehoiachin.[62] Hoonacker supposed that the Servant referred to
Jehoiachin.[63] Sellin raised the possibility that the Servant might be the
historical figure Jehoiachin serving as a portrait of a future Messiah.[64] W.
Staerk argued that the four songs could not be interpreted identically

59. See Paul, "Deutero-Isaiah and Cuneiform Royal Inscriptions."
60. Millard Lind, "Monotheism, Power, and Justice: A Study in Isaiah 40–55,"
CBQ 46 (1984): 442.
61. Ibid., 432–46.
62. J. Wilhelm Rothstein, *Die Genealogie des Königs Jojachin und seiner Nachkommen (1 Chron. 3, 17–24) in geschichtlicher Beleuchtung: Eine kritische Studie
zur jüdischen Geschichte und Litteratur* (Berlin: Reuther & Reichard, 1902).
63 Albin van Hoonacker, "L'ébed Jahvé et la composition littéraire des chapitres
Xl. ss d'Isaïe," *RB* 18 (1909): 497–528.
64. Ernst Sellin, *Das Rätsel des deuterojesajanischen Buches* (Leipzig: A.
Deichert'sche verlagsbuchhandlung nachf [G. Böhme], 1908), 131–33.

because the first three songs referred to Jeremiah but the fourth song only referred to Jehoiachin.[65] Sellin merely raised the possibility of Zerubbabel but John Watts more recently argued that Isa 52:13–53:12 described the murder of Zerubbabel, whose executed body was mutilated and innocent death mourned.[66] More recently, C. Begg regarded the language of ch. 53 to allude to Zedekiah, whom the Babylonians appointed to the throne when his nephew Jehoiachin abdicated.[67] All these views attempted to pinpoint a royal referent who represents the death of the monarchy after the exile. More wisely identifying the role but not the referent, Brian Peckham explains how Second Isaiah portrays the Servant's "returning to Zion after the exile [and] becomes in the manner of David, the source of justice and peace for all the nations of the world."[68] Similarly, some scholars argue for a "Royal Servant" but do not specify any referent.[69]

7. *Views that interpret the Servant as the Prophet Second Isaiah.* Others argued that the fourth servant song describes Second Isaiah's own sufferings.[70] G. Adam Smith, who understood Isa 53 to be about Second Isaiah, argued that "the Prophet had inevitably become martyr" and within a tension between the words of God and human, "his sufferings were not explained, and the Servant was left in them."[71] Israel is the speaker who confesses that the Servant provides a guilt offering and bears their sins. Therefore, Smith asserts that "his death was no mere martyrdom or miscarriage of human justice: in God's intent and purpose, but also by its own voluntary offering, it was an expiatory sacrifice."[72] Though the description of the Servant does not correspond perfectly with Jesus Christ, Smith concludes that the similarities are striking

65. Willy Staerk, *Die Ebed Jahwe-Lieder in Jesaja 40ff.: Ein Beitrag zur Deuterojesaja-Kritik* (Leipzig: J. C. Hinrichs, 1913), 129, 137–38.

66. Ernst Sellin, *Serubbabel, ein Beitrag zur Geschichte der messianischen Erwartung und der Entstehung des Jedentums* (Leipzig: A. Deichert, 1898), 148–50; Watts, *Isaiah 34–66*, 223–33.

67. C. Begg, "Zedekiah and the Servant," *ETL* 62 (1986): 393–98.

68. Brian Peckham, *History and Prophecy: The Development of Late Judean Literary Traditions* (ABRL; New York: Doubleday, 1993), 216.

69. W. A. M. Beuken, "*Mišpat*: The First Servant Song and Its Canonical Context," *VT* 22 (1972): 2–4; Richard Clifford, "Second Isaiah," in Mays, ed., *Harper's Bible Commentary*, 575.

70. Begrich, *Studien zu Deuterojesaja*; Karl Elliger, *Die Einheit des Tritojesaia Jesaia 56–66* (BWANT 63; Stuttgart: W. Kohlhammer, 1933), 198–221; Whybray, *Isaiah 40–66*.

71. Smith, *The Book of Isaiah*, 2:345–46.

72. Ibid., 2: 360, 363, 364, 384.

and "in Jesus Christ of Nazareth the dream [secondarily] becomes a reality."[73]

Early in his career, Sigmund Mowinckel drew a sharp contrast between the four Servant Songs where the Servant is active and the rest of Deutero-Isaiah where the Servant is always passive. While the Servant is Israel in the songs, he is also as a passive individual none other than the prophet himself.[74] Like some of his contemporaries (Smith, Haller, Barnes), he pointed out that there were uncanny similarities between Cyrus and the Servant but that Cyrus and the Servant were "the obverse and reverse" of divine means to deliverance since Cyrus was given the political task and the Servant the spiritual one.[75] Nevertheless, ten years later, Mowinckel changed his opinion and proposed that the Servant Songs were not the oracles of Deutero-Isaiah but were collected by his disciples, who together formed a Third Isaiah circle, and later inserted them into Second Isaiah. In 1956, suggesting that the speakers were Jews who had seen the Servant grow up in their midst, Mowinckel asserted that the fourth song took the form of an inverted funeral dirge because, unlike a funeral dirge, which celebrated and mourned the loss of the dead man's beauty, courage and manly attributes, "this song tells how unimpressive, hideous and despised the Servant was."[76] Mowinckel concluded that the Servant was not Israel "because Israel deserved to suffer as the logical results of her sins."[77] The Servant could not be the Messiah because, first, he will not renew the covenant and, second, the idea of one

73. Ibid., 2:367.
74. Sigmund Mowinckel, *Der Knecht Jahwäs* (Ausgegeben als Beiheft 2 zu Norsk Teologisk Tidsskrift; Giessen: A. Töpelmann, 1921), 9. This view was also followed by E. Balla, as well as by S. A. Cook who purported that he had independently reached the same conclusions as Mowinckel; see E. Balla, "Das Problem des Leides in der israelitisch-jüdischen Religion," in Schmidt, ed., *Eucharistérion*, 9; Stanely A. Cook, "The Servant of the Lord," *ET* 34 (1922–23): 440–42. Hermann Gunkel (*Ein Vorläufer Jesu* [Zurich: Orell Füssli, 1921]), who offered similar ideas, fervently applauded this view of Mowinckel's.
75. Both were "called by name" (45:3; 49:1), "called in righteousness" (42:6; 45:13), called to free prisoners (42:7 [note that Mowinckel, in *Der Knecht Jahwäs*, considered the first Servant Song to consist of Isa 42:1–7]; 45:13; 49:6), and taken by the hand of YHWH (42:6; 45:1).
76. Mowinckel, in his volume *He That Cometh*, 199–200, to some degree followed the work of H. Jahnow, *Das hebräische Leichenlied im Rahmen der Völkerdichtung* (BZAW 36; Giessen: A. Töpelmann 1923), 256–58.
77. He makes this claim on the basis that "this is emphasized by Deutero-Isaiah" (Isa 40:2; 44:18, 22; 43:8, 22–25; 45:9–10; 48:1–11; 51:17–20; 54:9; 55:7); see Mowinckel, *He That Cometh*, 214.

suffering for others is too "novel" a concept to be equated with messianic hope.[78] Therefore, he must be the prophet Deutero-Isaiah.[79]

While many others have shown that the referent of the Servant changes from song to song, Roger N. Whybray claims that "the servant who is given the task of bringing Israel back to Yahweh…must clearly be distinct from the nation."[80] Second Isaiah begins with a "heavenly council" narrative (40:1–8), where YHWH presents his prophet, Deutero-Isaiah, before the heavenly beings, setting the framework for the prophet in all of the songs to fulfill the task of the Servant.[81] In the fourth song, Whybray identifies the Servant with both Israel (52:13–15) and the prophet of Second Isaiah (53:1–12), who, like Ezekiel, "bears the punishment of Israel" (Ezek 4:4–6). Yet his text-critical argument that יַשְׂכִּיל is an allusion to Israel does not provide convincing evidence that 52:13–15 speaks of Israel and 53:1–12 of the prophet. Whybray's claim, that Isa 53 describes how Second Isaiah was put into prison for preaching against Babylon, does not explain how this incident relates to the sins of his fellow exiles, nor how his imprisonment creates reconciliation or healing for them. Neither could an act of preaching cause his people to be ashamed of how they regarded him.[82]

Similarly, Terrence Fretheim claims that, throughout the Old Testament, human beings suffer for the iniquities of others (Num 14:33; Pss 69:7; 89:50; Lam 5:7) just as representatives of Israel bear the sins of the people such as the scapegoat (Lev 16:21–22), the priest (Exod 28:38; Lev 10:17) and the Servant (Isa 53:4, 11–12). In Ezekiel, the prophet

---

78. Mowinckel builds his argument on the fact that such suffering is not a part of any other messianic description (*He That Cometh*, 238), and this renewal of the covenant is what Mowinckel argued would take place when the Messiah comes (Jer 31:31–34; Ezek 11:19; 36:25–38; 38:31). See ibid., 239–40.

79. In earlier writings, Mowinckel claimed that since Deutero-Isaiah was now dead, it was not as probable that the Servant was this prophet, but if the songs did refer to him, then the description was nuanced by this later circle in mythological terms; see Sigmund Mowinckel, "Die Komposition des deuterojesajanischen Buches," *ZAW* 8 (1931): 87–90, 242–50; idem, "Neuere Forschungen zu Deutero-jesaja, Tritojesaja un dem Äbäd-Jahwä-Problem," *AcOr* 16 (1938): 1–10, 40. However, in 1956, he more clearly states that the Servant was the "Prophet, not Messiah." Cf. Mowinckel, *He That Cometh*, 213–41.

80. Whybray, *Isaiah 40–66*, 137.

81. Ibid., 71.

82. Ibid., 169–83; idem, *Thanksgiving for a Liberated Prophet: An Interpretation of Isaiah Chapter 53* (JSOTSup 4; Sheffield: JSOT Press, 1978). See John Oswalt's fine evaluation of Whybray in his *The Book of Isaiah: Chapters 40–66* (NICOT; Grand Rapids: Eerdmans, 1998), 394.

himself bears the punishment or guilt of the people, but in the Servant Songs, the suffering of the prophet is raised to a new level in his suffering vocation and his vicarious death, which is a sin offering as in 53:10.[83]

One of the most compelling arguments for the identification of the Servant lies in the work of Wilcox and Patton-Williams, who identify the Servant as Israel in chs. 40–48, while in chs. 49–55 he is the prophet himself who has been given a dual mission to his people Israel and to "all the nations." The Servant accepts his suffering and fulfills his mission through the songs. Early Christians, including Philip (Acts 8:34), connected the songs with the salvific value of Christ. The reference in 49:3, 6 is critical because it oscillates between Israel and the prophet but here the prophet, who is called "Israel," is now re-commissioned to take on what has been Israel's mission to the nations:[84]

> Nowhere in chs. 40–48 was the prophet referred to as "servant of the Lord." That identification is clearly made in 49.5, 6, It is our contention that identification is intended at 49.3 too. For in effect, by the re-definition of his mission to include the nations, and by his designation as "servant of the Lord," the prophet has become [the true] Israel.[85]

Although they regard the Servant of the fourth song to be the prophet, Wilcox and Patton-Williams admit that there is a "deliberate ambiguity" and "mystery" that does not make this role definite. While the Servant Israel has suffered for his own sins, the Servant prophet teaches Israel that suffering is a part of the Servant vocation. Hence, the deliberate ambiguity and "paradigmatic character of the suffering servant…makes possible the Christian identification of the servant figure made by Philip."[86] While this extremely helpful contribution may shed light on the pre-biblical traditions of "Deutero-Isaiah," it does not consider how the trisected chapters of Isa 40–66, based on a repeated refrain ("there is no peace for the wicked"), present the Servant within the book as a whole.

8. *Views that appeal to figurative usages or spiritual senses.* Others have understood the word "Servant" to function as figurative rather than a proper usage. Hence, Stanley A. Cook argues that the question—"who is

83. Terrence Fretheim, *The Suffering of God: An Old Testament Perspective* (OBT 14; Philadelphia: Fortress, 1984), 134, 163.

84. Wilcox and Patton-Williams, "The Servant Songs," 88–93. See also Alwin Renker, *Propheten—das Gewissen Israels* (Freiburg: Herder, 1990).

85. Wilcox and Patton-Williams, "The Servant Songs," 92.

86. Ibid., 79.

the servant?"—is as foolish as "who is the prodigal son?"[87] Yet, Lind-hagen describes "the Servant–Wife relationship" in Second Isaiah.[88] Leland Wilshire boldly argues that "the fourth song" found in 52:13–53:12 constitutes a city-lament over the destruction of Zion-Jerusalem whereby the Servant is indeed Zion. Christopher Seitz also finds this position to be attractive.[89]

Paul Hanson argues that the fourth Servant Song "places images without providing answers to every problem of interpretation."[90] While he warns against anachronistically imposing Christian views on a pre-Christian text, Hanson argues that there is an interplay between the original message and contemporary reflections on scripture.[91] The Servant serves as an "alternative" because "the sacrifice of animals has not proven capable of atoning for their sin" because "like the lamb led to slaughter, the servant was a victim of a sacral decision over which he had the no control." So Hanson decides that "by bearing the sin of others and pouring himself out to death, the Servant has become the human vehicle through whom those others are healed."[92] Taking the Niphal verb נִמְנָה ("he let himself be numbered with transgressors," 53:12) as a reflexive rather than a passive, Hanson asserts that "the Servant was not a pawn in the hands of an arbitrary god but one who had committed himself freely to a deliberate course of action."[93] Yet, stymied by how "Second Isaiah" sometimes speaks of the Servant as an individual and other times as Israel, Hanson argues that Second Isaiah describes two offices in relation to God's purpose: the offices of Messiah and Servant. On one hand, Cyrus has been "appointed God's Messiah." On the other hand, God's covenant with David was now extended to the entire nation (55:3), whereby Israel's purposes would be defined not through the royal terms of the traditional Messiah-King from the house of David, but through

87. Stanely A. Cook, *The Cambridge Ancient History* (Cambridge: Cambridge University Press, 1923–39), 492.

88. C. Lindhagen, *The Servant Motif in the Old Testament: A Preliminary Study of the 'Ebed Yahweh Problem in Deutero-Isaiah* (Uppsala: Almqvist & Wiksell, 1950), 174.

89. Leland E. Wilshire, "The Servant City: A New Interpretation of the 'Servant of the Lord' in the Servant Songs of Deutero-Isaiah," *JBL* 94 (1975): 356–67; see also Seitz, *Zion's Final Destiny*, 203. Beuken asserts that Zion more clearly takes on the function of the Servant in Third Isaiah. Cf. W. A. M. Beuken, "The Main Theme of Trito-Isaiah," *JSOT* 47 (1990): 70–71. Cf. also Carroll Stuhlmueller, "The Theology of Creation in Second Isaiah," *CBQ* 21 (1959): 8.

90. Hanson, *Isaiah 40–66*, 153.

91. Ibid., 157.

92. Ibid., 158–61.

93. Ibid., 160.

"the rich symbolism of the Servant." Since Christians have interpreted the Servant as Christ, Hanson regards any messianic interpretation to be the Christian community's response to "the spiritual meaning" of Isa 53.[94]

B. *Messianic Assessments*

Throughout the twentieth century, a major problem turned on whether the Servant Songs should be treated separately from or within the context of Isa 40–55. On one hand, Johann Fischer argued that Deutero-Isaiah later inserted the Servant Songs because the role of the Servant in the songs was different from that of encompassing passages. Fischer examined the identity of the Servant and denounced the collective theory because it could not be proven consistently throughout the songs and therefore claimed that supporters of this view had to alter their hypothesis to explain the texts that described an individual. However, he also found similar difficulties with theories that identified an individual referent in 52:12–53:13. On these grounds, Fischer saw a unique parallel between events of the Servant and of Christ, thereby concluding that these similarities were *not* coincidental but that the fourth song was messianic.[95]

On the other hand, F. X. Pierce claimed that the songs did not need to be interpreted together but each should be treated as an individual unit and not as one song that had been broken up into four parts. He considered the first song to refer to Israel but the latter three to the Messiah.[96]

Others underscored how royal elements of the Servant Songs allowed them to be interpreted as messianic. Franz M. Th. de Liagre Böhl argued that 52:12–53:13 referred to Jehoiachin's release by Evil-merodach who put him to death the next year as a royal substitute.[97] Böhl thought that

94. Ibid., 165–67.

95. Johann Fischer, *Isaias 40–55 und die Perikopen vom Gottesknecht: Eine Kritisch-Exegetische Studie* (Munster: Aschendorff, 1916): 102–3; idem, *Wer ist der Ebed in den Perikopen Js 42,1–7; 49,1–9a; 50,4–9; 52,13–53,12? Eine Exegetische Studie* (Munster: Aschendorff, 1922), 4–5. See also Feldmann, *Das Buch Isaias*, 16–20; idem, *Der Knecht Gottes in Isaias Kap. 40–55* (Freiburg: Herder, 1907); J. S. van der Ploeg, *Les chants du serviteur de Jahvé dans la seconde partie du livre d'Isaïe* (Paris: Gabalda, 1936).

96. F. X. Pierce, "The Problem of the Servant in Is. 40–66," *Ecclesiastical Review* 92 (1935): 83–95.

97. Franz Marius Theodore de Liagre Böhl, "Profetisme en Plaatsvervangend Lijden in Assyrië en Israël," *NedTT* 4 (1949–50): 81–91, 161–76; idem, "Propheten und Stellvertrendes Leiden in Assyrien und Israel," in *Opera Minora: Studies en*

the Servant took on the characteristics of both Tammuz and the Davidic dynasty, combining both elements into one messianic expectation.[98] Joseph Coppens also claimed that the songs emphasized the Davidic dynasty; the first three referred to Zedekiah and fourth to Jehoiachin; each characterized the Messiah through the recollection of these monarchs.[99] Lorenz Dürr considered the Servant to be the Messiah-king on grounds that the songs were based on the Babylonian Akitu (New Year's) festival where the high priest ritually struck the king who made expiation for the people.[100] G. H. Dix even alleged that the Babylonian Tammuz laments influenced the prophet's concept of the suffering Servant, whom he called a "Messianic Angel."[101]

In his early work, Hugo Gressmann interpreted Isa 53 messianically, but regarded the exilic writer of chs. 40–55 as reminiscing about the qualities of Josiah to describe the figure of the Servant and imminently anticipate his advent.[102] In his later work, Gressmann rejected the theory that the Servant was the nation of Israel and argued from a traditio-historic approach that the songs reflected the cult of a dying and rising god. Hence, he argued that the resurrection of the Servant in the fourth song illustrated that this myth was the source of the prophet's messianic ideas.[103] However, A. R. Johnson argued that there was no evidence that ceremonies about a dying and rising god (as known, e.g., from Tammuz and Ras Shamra texts) existed in Israelite ritual, but concluded that the king was annually delivered from death in ritual combat. On these grounds, he interpreted 52:13–53:12 as the "Suffering Servant" and a "Davidic king."[104]

Bijdragen Op Assyriologisch en Oudtestamentlisch Terrein (Groningen: J. B. Wolters, 1953), 76–80; idem, "Nebukadnezar en Jojachin," in *Opera Minora*, 423–29.

98.   Franz Marius Theodore de Liagre Böhl, *De "Knecht Des Heeren" in Jesaja 53* (Overdruk-Uitgaaf Onze 7; Haarlem: Erven F. Bohn, 1923).

99.   Joseph C. L. Coppens, *Nieuw licht over de Ebed-Jahweh-Liedern* (ALBO 2/15; Gembloux: Duculot, 1950), 118–25.

100.   Lorenz Dürr, *Ursprung und Ausbau der Israelitischen-Judischen Heilandserwartung: Ein Beitrag zur Theologie des Alten Testamentes* (Berlin: Schwetschke & Sohn, 1925), 27.

101.   G. H. Dix, "The Influence of Babylonian Ideas on Jewish Messianism," *JTS* 26 (1925): 241–56.

102.   Gressmann, *Der Messias*, 287–39.

103.   Gressmann, *Der Ursprung der Israelitisch-Judischen Eschatologie*, 302–6. See also Hermann Gunkel, "Knecht Jahvehs," in *Die Religion in Geschichte und Gegenwart* (Tübingen: J. C. B. Mohr [Paul Siebeck], 1912).

104.   A. R. Johnson, "The Rôle of the King in the Jerusalem Cultus," in *The Labyrinth: Further Studies in the Relation Between Myth and Ritual in the Ancient*

Ivan Engell suggested that a "royal" or "king ideology" served as the essential aspect of the Servant Songs and explained how the Servant may be interpreted as a *Davidic* Messiah. His argument centered on the merging of royal strands of the Tammuz and Ras Shamra cultic materials with the concept of the Servant. Yet Engell did not think that the Servant was a king or substitute for God in cultic ceremonies; rather, he was the Messiah because all other biblical passages about the Davidic Messiah paralleled the songs in such a way that they established the Servant as the Messiah.[105]

Helmer Ringgren also argued that the vicarious suffering of the Servant drew on the Canaanite "Tammuz" religion and that the death imagery of this deity influenced the religious language of Israel.[106] Isaiah 53 is based on the portrait of the Babylonian king, who did penance and vicariously atoned for the people's sins at the New Year's festival. Isaiah 53 is messianic because the passage anticipates a Messiah who is to bear the sins of many. In Jesus Christ, the idea of the Servant of YHWH becomes a reality.[107]

J. Lindblom described the Servant Songs as the prophet's "revelations from Yahweh" and thinks that the collectors placed these oracles within Deutero-Isaiah. He argued that the Servant was "a vassal king in service of Yahweh, the king of heaven, entrusted with the mission of making the nations subject to the laws of his Sovereign." The Servant also became "an example in the description of the Messianic king" similar to the one found in Isa 11.[108] While the original *Sitz im Leben* for the Servant Songs was public days of lamentation, "*the collector* of the Deutero-Isaianic revelations thought that the Ebed of the Songs referred to Israel in some sense" and that "these Songs have been appropriately placed among other poems concerning the people of Israel, the servant of Yahweh, its contemporary situation, and its prosperous future." Since the collectors placed the "fourth Servant Oracle" within this framework, Lindblom argues that "the idea of the exaltation and glorification of the Servant and

World (ed. S. H. Hooke; London: SPCK, 1935), 100, 111. Aage Bentzen (*Messias-Moses Redivivus-Menschensohn* [London: Lutterworth, 1955], 43n, 80n) argued that Johnson provided no proof of a correlation between the suffering king and the suffering Servant but that he basically recapitulated Engell's view.

105. Ivan Engell, *Studies in Divine Kingship* (Uppsala: Almqvist & Wiksell, 1943), 9, 40; idem, "The 'Ebed Yahweh Songs and the Suffering Messiah in 'Deutero-Isaiah,'" *BJRL* 31 (1948): 56, 57, 68–69.

106. Ringgren, *The Messiah in the Old Testament*, 49–51.

107. Ibid., 51–53, 65–67.

108. Lindblom, *A Study on the Immanuel Section in Isaiah*, 33–41; idem, *Prophecy in Ancient Israel*, 176.

the revealing of Yahweh's arm upon him corresponds to the thought of the triumphal progress of the exiled Jews and the baring of God's holy arm in the sight of the nations."[109] The original Servant Songs were messianic but were reinterpreted by the collectors to speak of exiled Israel as their referent.

Others describe the Servant as a Mosaic figure, who is indeed a Messiah. Aage Bentzen argued that Isa 53 constituted an "autobiographical interpretation" whereby Deutero-Isaiah himself became *Moses redivivus* and the "I" in the Servant Songs spoke of a sort of prophet Messiah, who took up the new task of David as in 55:3–5.[110] More recently, Gordon Hugenberger discerned the Servant to be a second Moses in order both to solve the problem of reference and also to preserve a messianic reading.[111]

Others have addressed the similarities between the Servant and Cyrus, claiming that both individuals were viewed as the Messiah by various parties during the Persian era. Antti Laato, for example, builds on his earlier work, *David Redivivus*, treating Isa 40–55 as a literary unity that was composed during the Babylonian exile. His traditio-historical work aims to show that new messianic expectations (in which the death of Josiah played a significant function) arose during the exile, where there was a shift from a Davidic Messiah to a pagan one. Since no potential Davidic Messiah had emerged by the eve of Babylon's fall, Deutero-Isaiah may have recast Israel's messianic hopes to either the Servant or Cyrus. Laato understands most of the Cyrus and Servant passages (including texts outside of the Servant Songs) to be based on language drawn from either Akkadian royal inscriptions or traditional Israelite royal ideology.[112]

C. *Rethinking the Evidence*

The history of interpretation has demonstrated various efforts to reconstruct the original setting of the four "Servant Songs" or their placement within "Second Isaiah" in order to describe the identity of the Servant. Many have been stymied by how some texts overtly refer to the Servant as Israel, while others present him as an individual who either gathers up

---

109.   Ibid., 268–70.

110.   Aage Bentzen, "The Ebed Yahweh Songs and the Suffering Messiah in Deutero-Isaiah," *Rylands Bulletin* 31, no. 1 (1948); idem, *Messias-Moses Redivivus-Menschensohn*, 54, 64, 67.

111.   Gordon P. Hugenberger, "The Servant of the Lord in the 'Servant Songs' of Isaiah," in Satterthwaite, Hess and Wenham, eds., *The Lord's Anointed*, 105–40.

112.   Cf. Laato, *The Servant of YHWH and Cyrus.*

and restores Jacob-Israel or provides atonement for the many. Traditio-historical attempts to locate the Servant Songs within the cultic drama of a king, who vicariously atones for the sins of the people, represent the attempts of many to describe the Servant Songs within the integrity of their original setting, but still maintain a warrant for messianic interpretation. Redaction-critical approaches that aim to interpret the Servant Songs within the context of Second Isaiah have argued that the Servant Songs cannot be isolated from this context because their meaning has changed at this level of tradition history. Wilcox and Patton-Williams have made a strong argument that within Isa 40–48, the Servant is Israel and within chs. 49–55 he is the prophet.[113] Indeed, Wilshire, who is not alone in his attempts to identify Isa 53 as a city lament over the Servant city Zion-Jerusalem, presents a fascinating argument that is not completely implausible.[114] Historical-critical studies have made a strong case that the original level of tradition history in 52:13–53:12 may not have been messianic. Yet scholars' preoccupation with the origins of the text has obfuscated the book as a whole because they have atomized the text into pre-biblical traditions that antecede the scriptural form of the book of Isaiah.

113. Wilcox and Patton-Williams, "The Servant Songs."
114. F. W. Dobbs-Allsopp, *Weep, O Daughter of Zion: A Study of the City-Lament Genre in the Hebrew Bible* (Rome: Editrice Pontificio Istituto Biblico, 1993); C. J. Gadd, "The Second Lamentation for Ur," in *Hebrew and Semitic Studies Presented to Godfrey Rolles Driver* (ed. D. W. Thomas and W. D. McHardy; Oxford: Clarendon, 1963), 59–71; W. C. Gwaltney, Jr., "The Biblical Book of Lamentations in the Context of Near Eastern Lament Literature," in *Scripture in Context*. Vol. 2, *More Essays on the Comparative Method* (eds. W. W. Hallo, J. C. Moyer and L. G. Perdue; Winona Lake, Ind.: Eisenbrauns, 1983), 191–211; Delbert Hillers, *Lamentations* (Garden City: Doubleday, 1992). Samuel Noah Kramer, *Lamentation Over the Destruction of Ur* (AS 12; Chicago: University of Chicago Press, 1940); idem, "Sumerian Literature and the Bible," *AnB* 12 (1959): 185–204; idem, *The Sumerians: Their History, Culture, and Character* (Chicago: University of Chicago Press, 1963); idem, "Lamentation Over the Destruction Over Ur" (*ANET*, 455–63); idem, "Lamentation Over the Destruction Over Sumer and Ur" (*ANET*, 611–19); idem, "Lamentation Over the Destruction of Nippur," *EI* 9 (1969): 89–93; idem, "Lamentation Over the Destruction of Nippur," *ASJ* 13 (1991): 1–26; Raphael Kutscher, *Oh Angry Sea (a-ab-ba hu-luh-ha): The History of a Sumerian Congregation Lament* (YNER 6; New Haven: Yale University Press, 1975); Leland E. Wilshire, "Jerusalem as the Servant City' in Isaiah 40–66: Reflections in the Light of Further Study of the Cuneiform Tradition," in *The Bible in the Light of Cuneiform Literature* (ed. William W. Hallo, B. W. Jones and G. L. Mattingly; Lewiston, N.Y.: Edwin Mellen, 1990), 231–55.

While these pre-biblical studies are quite interesting and the identity of the Servant has evoked a great deal of curiosity, this is not our pursuit here. First, there is no proof that the "Servant Songs" ever existed apart from Second Isaiah (a hypothesis that rests upon a hypothesis) but even if they originally did, our concern here is not to remove them from their scriptural context but to inquire into their purpose within the form and function of the book as a whole. Second, the meaning of the pre-biblical traditions often semantically changes at the scriptural level. Finally, even if these songs were originally part of the larger corpus of "Second Isaiah" (or whatever one wishes to call this material), this level of tradition history is still pre-biblical and predates the later formation of the book as a whole in the Persian era. Therefore, we must ask: What does the role of the Servant play within the book as a whole?

II. *Interpretation within the Biblical Scroll of Isaiah*

A. *Non-messianic Assessments of the Biblical Testimony*
Recent modern attempts to interpret the book of Isaiah as a whole have shown that some interpret Isa 53 messianically and others non-messianically. Edgar Conrad argues that while Cyrus is the new foreign Messiah, YHWH referred to Hezekiah, the Davidic King, as "my servant," but after the vision of Isaiah, "my servant" in 52:13–53:12 now becomes the community Jacob-Israel.[115] Again we see the circular reasoning of Conrad, who makes historical claims by discriminating between the "vision of Isaiah" and the latter material of 52:13–53:12, which is contradictory to his premise that he is employing a synchronic approach.

Patricia Tull Willey, who claims to be reading the book of Isaiah as a whole but views Second Isaiah as the author of chs. 40–55, suggests that Isa 53 alludes to Lam 3. She reasons that one should not ask "who is the Servant of YHWH?" but "who are the people in relation to YHWH?" She then argues that the "children of Zion," who are envisioned as the servants of YHWH regaining their heritage in Jerusalem, have received their own Davidic promise of divine protection.[116] Therefore, the Servant for her is not the Messiah.

Likewise, Hugh G. M. Williamson, who asserts that the Servant Songs "have often been treated in isolation from their wider context in Isaiah and exclusively in relationship to one another, fails to talk about their placement within the book of Isaiah as a whole because he aims to

---

115. Conrad, *Reading the Book of Isaiah*, 145.
116. Tull Willey, *Remember the Former Things*, 226–28.

consider them in a way that they are not "distinguished from Deutero-Isaiah."[117] He argues that Deutero-Isaiah transferred the (messianic) promises given to David on behalf of Israel through a "'democratization' of the Davidic role..." (e.g. 55:3–5, which ends Deutero-Isaiah).[118] Benjamin Sommer argues that the songs emulate Jeremiah's afflictions, but that Deutero-Isaiah transfers the imagery and vocabulary that describes the torment of Jeremiah to the Servant.[119] The fourth song depends on Jer 11, where the Servant models after the prophet and resonates with Isa 6, while comparing the Servant with Isaiah himself.[120]

B. *Messianic Assessments of the Biblical Testimony*
1. *Approaches that view Isaiah 52:13–53:12 as messianic prophecy.* Relying on a modern view of biblical prophecy that aims to locate the time, circumstances, contemporary audience and the ethical claims of the very prophet who is speaking, some historically conservative scholars try to locate the "author" of Isa 53 in the person of the eighth-century prophet Isaiah in order to justify the book of Isaiah as a whole. For example, Oswalt T. Allis, who argues against G. Adam Smith's view that Cyrus is a proof rather than a prediction, contends that the watershed of messianism in Isaiah lies in the prophet's ability to predict the sufferings of Christ, and that if Isa 53 is truly messianic, then the eighth-century Isaiah would also be the "author" of the prophecies about Cyrus. He argues that there is an important difference between the prophecies about Cyrus and those which concern the Servant because the prophecies about the Servant find their fulfillment in Jesus Christ.[121]

Similarly, Edward J. Young refers to Isa 53 as the "fourth servant passage" rather than "Servant Song" because he does not wish to use language that would exclude the authorship of eighth-century Isaiah. The crux of his argument is that the Servant became our substitute and the New Testament relies on the prophecy of Isa 53. Yet, for Young, 53:5 secondarily refers to the actual death of crucifixion, because the Piel participle, מְחֹלָל ("pierced through"), emphasizes how the Servant bore punishment in our stead.[122] Isaiah 53:6, then, states that the reason why he had to suffer: "because all of us have gone astray." Isaiah's comparing

117. Williamson, *Variations on a Theme*, 130–31.
118. Ibid., 165–66.
119. Benjamin Sommer, *A Prophet Reads Scripture: Allusions in Isaiah 40–66* (Stanford: Stanford University Press, 1998), 64.
120. Ibid., 93.
121. Allis, *The Unity of Isaiah*, 87–101.
122. Young, *Isaiah*, 3:348.

the Servant with the lamb ("he opens not his mouth"), may possibly
reflect the sacrificial lamb of Exod 12:3 in the same way that John the
Baptist claims that Jesus is the lamb of God (John 13:3; cf. also Acts
8:32–35; 1 Pet 1:18, 19). Young claims that the Gospel account of Jesus
being put into prison and given an unjust trial serves as a fulfilment for
the words from prison (53:8). He argues that the Servant sharing his
death with criminals and his grave with a rich man adumbrates Christ's
crucifixion between two criminals and Joseph of Arimathea. Young
concludes that the reason the Servant is so gloriously exalted (as the
Messiah) is because he laid down his soul to death.[123]

Similarly beginning with a christological *a priori*, Walter Kaiser
asserts that in order to understand messianism in Isaiah, "the solution
comes in its fulfillment." Isaiah 52:14 describes the Messiah's first
advent and 52:15 his second advent. The second and fourth stanzas
portray the drama of the cross, while the third and fourth provide the
meanings and explanations.[124] Kaiser maintains that this passage can
never be attributed to Israel because it can never be said that the Israelites had no violence or deceit in their mouths. The death of the servant is
no misadventure or accident but the deliberate plan and will of God
because the very life of a Messiah constitutes a guilt offering.[125] Therefore, 52:13–53:12 was a prophecy about the atoning Messiah.[126]

Locating the "authorship" of Isa 53 as the words of the eighth-century
prophet, Joseph Alexander asserts that it is a fundamental error to suppose that "the book is susceptible of distribution into detached and
independent parts." Instead, he regards the whole as a continuous composition. The Servant is a "mysterious Person whose expiatory sufferings
and spiritual triumphs form the great theme of the subsequent context"
(Isa 53). Yet, in response to the question of whether or not the Servant is
an individual or a collective body, Alexander uses Tyconius' head and
body designations, maintaining that when described as blind and deaf,
the "Servant of Jehovah" is the body (42:19), but in 52:13–53:12 he is
the head.[127] "The objection, that the title *Servant* is not applied elsewhere
to Messiah, would have little force if true, because the title in itself is a

123.   Edward J. Young, "Of Whom Speaketh the Prophet [Acts 8:26ff; Isa 42:1–
4; 49:1–6; 52:13–53:12]," *WTJ* 11, no. 2 (May 1949): 135–55; idem, "The Origin of
the Suffering Servant Idea," *WTJ* 13 (Nov. 1950): 19–33; idem, *Isaiah*, 3:341–73.
    124.   Kaiser, *The Messiah in the Old Testament*, 79.
    125.   Ibid., 181.
    126.   Kissane, *The Book of Isaiah*, 2:183–91.
    127.   Joseph Addison Alexander, *Commentary on the Prophecies of Isaiah*
(Grand Rapids: Zondervan, 1953), 283–309.

general one, and may be applied to any chosen instrument."[128] Isaiah 53 represents the voluntary humiliation of the Messiah, whereby he becomes a savior only by becoming a substitute who was stricken by God for the purpose of saving humanity. This proves the divinity of Christ.[129] Alexander concludes that since סבל means "to pardon" and נשא means to "take away" by "bearing" or "removing (sin)," the text shows that a holy God can only take away sin by bearing it and can only forgive it by providing atonement for it.[130]

Similar to Alexander, Delitzsch uses Tyconius' head and body descriptions but describes the Servant as "the center of the circle, the heart and head and of the body of Israel."[131] Delitzsch argues that the Servant of "servant songs" constitutes both "spiritual Israel" and "the mediator of salvation who arises out of Israel." Therefore, Delitzsch states:

> There is something very striking in this figure. Here, in the very centre of this book of consolation, we find the idea of the Servant of Jehovah at the very summit of its ascent. It has reached the goal. The Messianic idea, which was hidden in the general idea of the nation regarded as "the servant of Jehovah," has gradually risen to in the most magnificent metamorphosis from the depths in which it was less concealed. And this effusion has generated what was hitherto altogether strange to the figure of the Messiah, viz. the *unio mystica capitas et corporis*. Hitherto Israel has appeared simply as the nation governed by the Messiah, the army which he conducted into battle, the commonwealth ordered by him. But now, in the person of the servant of Jehovah, we see Israel itself in personal self manifestation: the idea of Israel is fully realized, and the true nature of Israel shines forth in all its brilliancy. Israel is the body, and He the head, towering above it. Another element, with which we found the messianic idea enriched before ch. vii. was the *munus triplex*. As early as ch. vii–xii. the figure of the Messiah stood for as the figure of a King; but the prophet likened them to Moses, promised in Deut. xvii. 15, was still wanting. But, according to ch. xlii., xlix.,l., the servant of Jehovah is first a prophet, and as the proclaimer of the new law, and the mediator of the new covenant, really second Moses; at the close of the work appointed Him, however, He receives the homage of kings, whilst, as ch. liii. clearly shows, that self-sacrifice lies between, on the ground of which He rules above as a priest after the order of Melchizedek—in other words, a Priest and also a King. From this point onward there are added to the Messianic idea the further elements of the *status duplex* and the *satisfactio vicaria*. David was indeed the type of the twofold state of his

128. Ibid., 287.
129. Ibid., 289, 294, 295.
130. Ibid., 308.
131. Delitzsch, *Isaiah*, 2:302.

> antitype, inasmuch as it was through suffering that he reached the throne;
> but where have we found, in all the direct Messianic prophecies anterior
> to this, the suffering path of the *Ecce Homo* even to the grave? But the
> servant of Jehovah goes through shame to glory and through death to
> life.[132]

Therefore, he explains that no longer are the prophecies of the Messiah
merely of a king, for he is also a priest upon his throne.[133] Hence, "God
does not suffer those who have sinned to be overtaken by the sin they
have committed; but it falls upon his servant, the righteous One."[134]

Alec Motyer, who refers to Isa 38–55 as "the book of the Servant"
and argues that there are three facets or portraits of the one Messiah in
the book of Isaiah (King, Servant, and Anointed Conqueror).[135] He lists
themes that are similar between both the Servant and anointed conqueror.[136] Motyer claims that "while the Servant suffers we are still
straying, and the Lord, acting as high priest in relation to the Victim-
Servant (Isa 53:6c; cf. Lev 16:21), loads him with our wrong." God
himself "superintends" the priestly duty (Lev 16:21) of "transferring the
guilt of the guilty upon the Servant" so that he makes "satisfaction" for
sin. Therefore, "Isaiah uses 'healing' in a total sense; the healing of the
person, restoring fulness and completeness, a mark of the Messianic day
(19:22; 30:6)."[137] Substitutionary sacrifice lay at the heart of 52:13–53:12
because, as Heb 10:4 puts it, "the blood of bulls and goats cannot take
away sins."

Barry G. Webb argues that, since the previous chapters have repeatedly
drawn attention to Israel's endemic sinfulness, Isa 52:13–53:12 describes
forgiveness whereby the Servant is pictured as a priest, "sprinkling" the
unclean as a guilt offering. Webb claims that Isaiah's portrait of the
Servant, who is a sage, priest, sacrifice, servant, sufferer, conqueror and
intercessor, will be complete when 61:1–3 is fulfilled. The picture of a
Servant-Messiah is clear, "when all the relevant data are in, we will see
the whole in the light of the New Testament."[138] Although Motyer and

132.   Ibid., 2:340–41.

133.   Ibid., 2:342.

134.   Ibid., 2:320–21.

135.   Motyer, *The Prophecy of Isaiah*, 122–36.

136.   Isa 53:2 reintroduces "the Messianic imagery of 4:2, the 'holy seed'
imagery of 6:13 and the royal imagery of 10:33–11:1," but he fails to note that 4:2
uses צמח and not יונק and this "shoot" or "sucker" does not come out of a stump but
out of "dry ground" (ibid., 423, 428).

137.   Ibid., 429.

138.   Barry G. Webb, *The Message of Isaiah* (The Bible Speaks Today; Downers
Grove, Ill.: Intervarsity, 1997), 204–14.

Webb are not completely ignorant about the diachronic tensions in the text of Isaiah, they locate Isa 53 in the eighth century by naming the prophet of this chapter, "Isaiah."[139] This approach harmonizes dissimilar texts and different voices speaking from different situations and times but fails to respect the implications of modern historical criticism, including the tensions and differences that belong to biblical prophecy.

Others, who try to view the book as a whole, locate Isa 53 within its exilic or post-exilic circumstances by naming that prophet Deutero-Isaiah. For example, John McFayden asserts that there were many people who fill the role of YHWH's Servant but the greatest of them all, is "Jesus," who was "likewise rejected by his people." He interprets the Servant Songs within the "book as a whole," which for him are the pre-biblical traditions of Deutero-Isaiah, whose genre in Isa 53 changes from a funeral dirge to prophecy anticipating "Good Friday and Easter morning…"[140] McFayden does not show how 52:13–53:12 on its own engenders christological possibilities but such interpretation of this text for him seems to rely on the New Testament's usage of the Servant Songs.

Similarly, Józef Homerski, who aims to read Isa 52:13–53:12 within the context of scripture, emphasizes how the Servant's salvific mission, death and resurrection in "the fourth Servant song" may be interpreted as messianic. He pays careful attention to the relationship between Deutero-Isaiah's Servant and Deutero-Zechariah's Shepherd and claims that several texts in the Old Testament provide images of a suffering Messiah (Isa 50:4–9; 52:13–53:12; Zech 12:10; 13:7; Ps 22:2–22).[141] Though it is not clear how these texts influenced the description of the sufferings of Christ, Homerski argues that the fourth Servant song among these other texts shows that it is the will of God to redeem the world through the humiliation, suffering and the Messiah's sacrificial death for the sins of the guilty.[142]

Likewise, John Sawyer argues that we need to "treat each passage as we come to it, in its own context, and try to understand what it is about it, rather than who the Servant is."[143] Claiming to interpret the book as a

139. Motyer, *The Prophecy of Isaiah*, 21–34, 426, 431–35; Webb, *The Message of Isaiah*, 214.
140. John E. McFayden, "The New View of the Servant of the Lord," *ET* 34 (1922–23): 294–96.
141. Józef Homerski, "Cierpacy Wybawca i Oredownik," *RocTKan* 24, no. 4 (1977): 75–90.
142. Józef Homerski, "Cierpacy Mesjasz w Startestamentalnych Przepowied-niach Prorockich," *RocTKan* 27 (1980): 27–42.
143. Sawyer, *Prophecy and the Biblical Prophets*, 78.

whole, he criticizes modern interpreters for exploiting or lifting the Servant Songs from their context (Isa 40–55) and argues that through the process of atomization, certain passages, like ch. 53, lose their "christological" meaning.[144]

Roy A. Rosenberg, who compares the image of the "slain Messiah" (Dan 9:26) with the portrait of the "righteous sufferer" (Isa 53; Zech 3:8; Jer 23:5), maintains that the destiny of "the Messiah ben David" was death. This view was used to bolster the exegesis of some Jewish sectarians, who eliminated the Messiah ben David and championed the cause of the priestly Messiah as the solitary eschatological ruler.[145]

John Oswalt breaks up "the poem" into five stanzas, whereby the first and last contain "commendation of the Servant in the voice of God" and "the middle three speak of the Servant's humiliation and suffering..."[146] While Cyrus was anointed to restore exiled Israel, the Servant is anointed to the task of restoring sinful Israel ("we" and "us"). This act finds "true fulfillment in the realization of what the whole sacrificial system prefigured."[147] The poem ends describing the exaltation of the Servant as "a victory parade with the Servant, of all people, marching in the role of conqueror, bringing home the spoils of conquest."[148] In his "very exalted" state, the Servant is not Israel, nor the prophet, but "this is the Messiah or no one."[149]

Walter Brueggemann asserts that neither Christian nor Jew can decode the poetry of Isa 52:13–53:12, but agrees with "the common assumption of Jewish interpretation" that the Servant is "the *humiliated (exiled) people* who by the powerful intervention of Yahweh is about to become *the exalted (restored) people of Zion*."[150] Brueggemann insists that "this poetry does not in any first instance have Jesus on its horizon..." The Church cannot determine how Easter's "miracle" of the "humiliated Jesus" being exalted "to the right hand of God" works any more than "we know how to move from 52:14 to 52:15, any more than the Isaiah tradition knew how to get from 'former things' of punishment to 'latter things' of deliverance." He concludes that "in understanding *the servant*

144.   John F. A. Sawyer, *The Fifth Gospel: Isaiah in the History of Christianity* (Cambridge: Cambridge University Press, 1996), 187–88.

145.   Roy A. Rosenberg, "The Slain Messiah in the Old Testament," *ZAW* 99 (1987): 259–61.

146.   Oswalt, *Isaiah 40–66*, 376.

147.   Ibid., 376, 381, 404.

148.   Ibid., 394.

149.   Ibid., 378–79.

150.   Walter Brueggemann, *Isaiah 40–66* (Westminster Bible Companion; Louisville, Ky.: Westminster John Knox, 1998), 149 (italic in original).

as Israel—or as an unnamed one at work in ancient Israel—or derivatively using the servant imagery to understand *Jesus as servant* points to the definitional mark of both faiths, a claim both faiths have in common in their common trust in a common God to do something new."[151]

In his careful study, Jan L. Koole shows similarities between the Servant, David and the Messiah. He calls attention to how both the Servant and David "shall succeed" (יַשְׂכִּיל, Isa 52:13; 1 Sam 18:5, 14).[152] The Hiphil of the root שכל (52:13) is also used to describe "the Messiah in Jer 23:5f., where שכל parallels the making of 'justice and righteousness' (עָשָׂה מִשְׁפָּט וּצְדָקָה) in the world…"[153] The "shoot" and "sucker" in 53:2a "alludes to the davidian descent of the Servant." The verb נכה in Isa 53:4 refers to 2 Sam 7:14, where the Servant is smitten but only with the rod of men.[154] The phrase חלק שלל ("to divide the spoil," 53:3) reflects the "warrior" image of 9:2, and so Koole argues that "the suffering Servant will prove to be a triumphant Messiah."[155] Yet, the political ruin of Israel appeared to camouflage all messianic expectation and the Servant even appeared to be "the opposite of a messianic king."[156] While claiming to treat the "final canonical stage" of Isaiah, Koole does not differentiate between the pre-biblical "Songs of the Servant" written by "Deutero-Isaiah" and the scriptural form of Isaiah, thus demonstrating how scholars often do not distinguish between pre-biblical and biblical traditions.[157]

Gerald Sheppard treats the "scriptural testimony in Isa 52:13–53:12" rather than the what "may have been a prebiblical tradition belonging to a Second Isaiah." While this text offers a "very deficient historical narrative," Sheppard affirms that "it succeeds in confronting us with an ingenious chiaroscuro, a half-revealed portrait of someone who has the needs of Israel and the world at heart." Since Jewish and Christian scripture is a testimony to revelation, 52:13–53:12 "reminds us that it is the revelation and not necessarily the testimony that gives us clarity." As Christians found an "astonishing possibility" in 52:12–53:12, "solely from the perspective of the risen Lord," the "literal sense" became "a testimony to the Gospel." Sheppard, who searches for warrants from scripture's own testimony to revelation, states:

151.   Ibid., 144.
152.   Koole, *Isaiah*, 251.
153.   Ibid., 264.
154.   Ibid., 292.
155.   Ibid., 339.
156.   Ibid., 255.
157.   Ibid., 249–43.

The play between the one and the many, as well as the language making
the many righteous, provided an ideal correspondence to explain the
equally enigmatic and unexpected death of the Messiah, Jesus's death
could be seen as an act of atonement and his resurrection corresponded to
the language of the servant's elevation in 52:13. In brief, when by the light
of the revelation of Jesus Christ's resurrection, Christians held together the
obscure pattern of meaning in 52:13–53:12 and the senseless death of
Jesus, the mystery of both receded. If we hear both as testimonies to the
same revelation, then the revelation itself is what shines through. The
scripture promise and its fulfilment can now be known in an unexpected
way.[158]

After being placed within the testimony of scripture, Isa 52:13–53:13 no
longer refers to the original historical events that surrounded it, "but now
as Jewish scripture it testifies prophetically to a revelation of the Torah"
and now "raises new historical issues about the identity of the servant,
unforeseen in the original tradition." Therefore, "the movement from
prebiblical to biblical in this case was not a dehistoricizing movement
but a rehistoricizing one, a shift from an earlier reference to a known
historical figure to a testimony about a mysterious unspecified historical
figure."[159] In its ambiguity, the text now "points to truth still hidden from
us and wrapped in mystery" helping us to understand why "so many
Jewish interpreters imagined so many different possibilities for the
identity of the 'servant.'" For Jews, "Isa 52:13–53:12 can logically
remain an obscure testimony to an unresolved mystery of God's revelation" but, for Christians, this testimony "clarifies a historical truth
about Christ's suffering, death, and resurrection." Sheppard concludes,
"since the testimony of the cross and the testimony of Isaiah both live
from the same revelation, they illuminate the historical nature of each by
means of that revelation."

2. Perspectives that interpret through typological interpretation. George
Workman claimed that the ideal king occupies a prominent a role in the
first half of Isaiah but has no place in the second half because here the
Servant is analogous to the presence of the Messiah, of whom David was
the princely representative.[160] Using Tyconius' head and body descriptions, Israel is called to be the ideal Servant just as the Church is summoned to be the body, to "put away" its sinful ways and become "an

158. This paragraph was edited out of his final draft of his commentary
submitted to HarperCollins. Gerald Sheppard, "Commentary on Isaiah," in Mays,
ed., *HarperCollins Bible Commentary*, 489–537.
159. See Sheppard's description, ibid., 489–501.
160. Workman, *The Servant of Jehovah*, 27, 46, 50.

elect race, a royal priesthood, a holy nation, designed by him to manifest or declare his excellences." The Servant in the singular, idealizes all "worshipers of Jehovah" as one person, but since few loyal God-fearing Israelites sought restoration, the prophet shifts from using "Servant" to "Servants" to characterize individuals within the nation who are true worshippers. Therefore, the movement from corporate to individual Servant represents a progression in thought and not a change in subject. The culmination of the description of the Servant develops into the conception of the Messiah" (Isa 53), thus separating the "ideal" Servant Israel from the Servant Messiah.[161] While Workman's description appears to interpret the Servant as Messiah through a prophetic use of words, this is not the case, since he closes his essay on this subject claiming that the "Servant of Jehovah" was "a type of Jesus of Nazareth."[162]

3. *A few reflections of New Testament scholarship.* Many New Testament scholars who use historical-critical methods think that concept of the Suffering Servant and the Messiah came together as one expectation before the time of Jesus Christ.[163] Whether or not Jesus himself was influenced by the Suffering Servant passages, apart from any reference to Isa 53 and Dan 7, J. D. G. Dunn argues that Jesus' self-understanding "anticipated suffering and rejection" and he saw his death in conjunction with the coming kingdom and not a defeat. Yet all this strengthens the likelihood that Isa 53 and Dan 7 influenced the utterances that Jesus himself made when he entertained the expectation of rejection, suffering and death.[164] W. D. Davies argues that "apart from the great enigma of Isa 53, so important for Matthew, I suggest that the presentation of Jesus

161. Ibid., 83–94.
162. Ibid., 95.
163. Joachim Jeremias, *Abba: Studien zur Neutestamentlichen Theologie und Zeitgeschichte* (Göttingen: Vandenhoeck & Ruprecht, 1966), 106–10; idem, "Παῖς Θεοῦ," trans. G. W. Bromiley (*TDNT* 5:677–700); Nils Johansson, *Parakletoi, Vorstellungen von Fürsprechern für die Menschen vor Gott in der Alttestamentlichen Religion, im Spätjudentum und Urchristentum* (Lund: Gleerupska Universitetsbokhandeln, 1940), 113–15; Harald Riesenfeld, *Jésus transfiguré: L'arrière-plan du récit évangélique de la transfiguration de notre-seigneur* (ASNU 16; Copenhagen: Ejnar Munksgaard, 1947), 81–83, 314–18; William David Davies, *Paul and Rabbinic Judaism: Some Rabbinic Elements in Pauline Theology* (London: SPCK, 1911), 275–77; William Manson, *Jesus, the Messiah: The Synoptic Tradition of the Revelation of God in Christ—With Special Reference to Form-Criticism* (London: Hodder & Stoughton, 1944), 171–75.
164. J. D. G. Dunn, "Messianic Ideas and Their Influence on the Jesus of History," in Charlesworth, ed., *The Messiah*, 378–80.

as a Greater Moses probably itself carries within it the notion of suffering," yet it is "not surprising that scholars discovered his lineaments in Isaiah 53."[165]

Howard Clark Kee argues for a wide range of messianic titles in Judaism, from the post-exilic era to the second revolt under bar Kochba, for depicting divine agents (anointed king, anointed priest, anointed prophet, and Cyrus is called Yahweh's "Shepherd").[166] Nebuchadnezzar is described as Yahweh's servant (Jer 25:9). The word "servant" applies to the nation of Israel (Isa 41:8; 44:1; 48:20; 65:8–9) but also to the individual Servant, "the righteous one" (52:13; 53:11), whose sufferings work to benefit the many. What these "motifs of messianic, revelatory, and predictive figures in the prophetic and apocalyptic traditions" show is "that the Messiah or redeemer is in every case a mediator between the divine purpose and the aspirations of a community."[167] On these grounds, Kee argues that the Jesus of Mark defied and redefined the definition of ritual purity as a new way to provide covenantal identity for the Jewish people. Although Peter misunderstood Jesus' messianic role, Mark's linking Jesus to a range of explicit messianic and redemptive roles shows how "the woman with the alabaster flask who anoints Jesus…perceives that his death is essential to his messianic mission." Therefore, "the messianic figure does not merely model the Davidic paradigm but surpasses David in a transcendent manner."[168]

Yet, others argue against this position and posit that there is no proof for a suffering Messiah in Judaism or that Isa 52:13–53:12 had any influence on the New Testament concept of messianism.[169] For example, Kenneth D. Litwak asserts that of the seven quotations of the "fourth Servant song" in the New Testament, most citations follow the LXX, but that in Matt 8:17 notable departures from LXX prove useful. Isaiah 53 has been used for three distinct but overlapping purposes: passion apologetic, justification for preaching to the Gentiles and moral admonition of believers. Litwak argues that the writer's motive moved from passion to apologetics the further the New Testament moves from the original

165.   William David Davies, "The Jewish Sources of Matthew's Messianism," in Charlesworth, ed., *The Messiah*, 507.

166.   Howard Clark Kee, "Christology in Mark's Gospel," Neusner, Green and Frerichs, eds., *Judaisms and Their Messiahs*, 187–208.

167.   Ibid., 192.

168.   Ibid., 203.

169.   M. D. Hooker, *Jesus and the Servant* (London: SPCK, 1959); Sam K. Williams, *Jesus' Death as a Saving Event* (Missoula, Mont.: Scholars Press, 1975), 111–20; Marinus de Jonge, *Jesus, the Servant Messiah* (New Haven: Yale University Press, 1991), 48–50.

meaning of Isa 53, but Litwak is not sure whether the New Testament writer did not understand the "real" meaning of Isa 53 or whether he was applying it in a different way. This perspective causes Litwak to think that the New Testament writers in general did not understand the "fourth Servant song" messianically and fulfilled in Jesus, thus explaining why the New Testament and early Church *testimonia* made such little use of it.[170]

C. H. Dodd argues that messianic citations of the Old Testament are cited from context,[171] but Donald Juel consistently treats them as examples of a midrashic atomistic exegesis.[172] Midrashic interpretation does not necessarily take the context seriously but may attach the term משיח to a single word or phrase even if the larger context does not suggest it. In Isa 52:13, for example, the Targum renders the passage as "my Servant, the Messiah" but reapplies the phrases about his sufferings either to Israel or his adversaries. This does not necessarily imply that the Targumist interprets the Servant figure as a Messiah but only that he can interpret isolated words or phrases. However, this is similar to the head/ body distinctions of Tyconius, though it has been applied to a different view of the Messiah. Juel contends that a similar midrashic interpretation of 52:13–53:12 in the New Testament confirms a pre-modern atomistic exegesis that does not imply that the Servant is understood messiani- cally.[173] While I am aware that many modes of interpretation (midrash, pesher, allegory and spiritual senses) may ignore the significance of the larger context, I want to focus in part on what Christianity later called the "plain" or "literal sense," which became the primary basis for doctrinal interpretation since the mid-second century C.E. I will argue that Dodd and Juel offer two extremes on the continuum and that while some pas- sages were cited atomistically, others presupposed the larger literary context of the text that is quoted.

C. *A Few Pre-modern Examples*

1. *Non-messianic assessments.* Unlike other texts that we have presented as candidates for messianic interpretation (Isa 9:1–6; 11:1–5), a much larger percentage of pre-modern efforts within Judaism describe the Servant in 52:13–53:12 as non-messianic than these other texts. While

---

170. Kenneth D. Litwak, "The Use of Quotations from Isaiah 52:13–53:12 in the New Testament," *JETS* 26, D (1983): 385–94.

171. C. H. Dodd, *According to Scripture: The Sub-Structure of New Testament Theology* (Digswell Place: James Nisbet & Co., 1961), 74–88.

172. Donald Juel, *Messianic Exegesis: Christological Interpretation of the Old Testament in Early Christianity* (Philadelphia: Fortress, 1988), 119–33.

173. Ibid., 119–33.

the Targum refers to the Servant as the Messiah, it reclassifies his sufferings as referring to Israel or the rival nations in order to segregate the Servant from the sufferings that describe him. Ibn Ezra, whose era was full of massacres in the Rhineland by crusaders on their way to the holy land, posits that עבדי ("my Servant") refers to "the Israelite" or "the whole nation of Israelites." While the nations deserved to be afflicted because their religion was false, it came upon Israel who followed the true religion.[174] As long as the heathen have peace, Jerusalem will not find mercy, concluded this Medieval rabbi. History itself was enough evidence for him to claim that the Niphal נגש ("he was oppressed") spoke of "every Jew in exile." Every nation will think that "Israel was stricken because of our sins" (53:8). Distinguishing the Servant from the Messiah, Ibn Ezra considers the phrase "he shall see his seed, he shall prolong his days" to speak of "the generation which will return to God, that is, to the Torah of God, in the days of the Messiah." Since he explains that עבדי ("my Servant") refers to Israel, he concludes that עבדי mentioned in 52:13 is the same figure who appears in 42:1; 49:3 and 53:11 because all these chapters are connected to each other.[175]

However, R. Sh'lomoh Yiṣḥaqi ("Rashi") maintained that, in Isa 53, Israel suffered for the atonement of the nations: "The prophet constantly speaks of the whole people as one man." Israel suffered in order to atone for other nations. The phrase "cut off from the land of the living" implied that the people were exiled from the land of Israel.[176] Likewise, Radak, an acronym for Rabbi David Qimḥi, argues that "this Parashah refers to the captivity of Israel, who are here called 'my servant.'" Following Ibn Ezra, Qimḥi suggests that there are "so many nations in the world who believe that the features of the Jew are disfigured and unlike those of other men..." The pains that Israel endured in captivity cannot be attributed to their own iniquity. "*My servant* Israel, who will be *righteous* and know the Lord, *will by his knowledge, make righteous* many nations, as it was written" (see Isa 2:3). "He will teach us his ways, and we will walk in his paths and by his righteousness will bear the iniquities of the gentiles, for by it there will be peace and prosperity in the world even for the gentiles."[177] In response to Christian interpretation, Qimḥi states:

---

174. Friedländer, *The Commentary of Ibn Ezra on Isaiah*, 3:242.
175. Ibid., 241–47.
176. Samuel R. Driver and Adolf Neubauer, trans., *The "Suffering Servant" of Isaiah According to the Jewish Interpreters* (Oxford: James Parker & Co., 1877), 37–39.
177. Ibid., 49–56.

I should like to ask the Nazarenes [Christians] who explain this Parashah of Jesus, how the prophet could have said, "He shall be lifted up and lofty exceedingly?" If this alludes to the flesh, Jesus was not "lifted up" except when he was suspended upon the cross; if it refers to the Godhead, then he was mighty and lifted up from the beginning [so that it could not be said, he *will* be lifted up]. Moreover, the prophet says *to them* (למו), ver. 8, but then he ought to have said *to him* (לו), for למו is plural, being equivalent to להם. Again he says, "He shall see seed": if this refers to his flesh, then he had no seed; if to his Godhead, as the literal sense is inappropriate, they explain the word *seed* as alluding to his disciples, although his disciples are nowhere spoken of as either *sons* or *seed*. He says, too, "He shall lengthen days"; but in the flesh he did not lengthen days, and if he says of his Godhead that as a reward [for suffering] he will have long life, are not the days of God from everlasting to everlasting (cf. Ps 90:2). Lastly, he says, "And he interceded for transgressors"; but if he is God himself, to whom could he intercede?[178]

Trying to argue on the terms of Christian interpretation, Qimḥi holds Christians to the "literal sense" of the text, but Qimḥi does not and need not confine himself to *peshat*. For example, he interprets the referent of the Servant to be Israel in some verses but Moses as the referent of the very same Servant in other verses. This is demonstrated in Qimḥi's agreement with the Rabbis, who assert that 53:12 represents the work of Moses, who resigned himself to death (Exod 32:23), was "numbered among transgressors" and "poured out his soul to death" because he was numbered with those who died in the wilderness. Moses also "bore the sins of many" when he made atonement for their making of the golden calf, and he "interceded for the transgressors" when he sought mercy for the transgression of Israel.[179]

Throughout the Middle Ages, many Rabbi's claimed the same interpretation. For example, Rabbi Isaiah Ben Mali (the Elder) interprets that "Israel shall prosper (ישכיל as 1 Sam 18:14)."[180] Rabbi Shem Tobh Ben Shaprut says that "the whole Parashah has reference to Israel."[181] Rabbi Mosheg Kohen Ibn Crispin cites the scribe Ibn Danân, who seeks to keep himself at "the doors of the learned" and speaks out "against the heretics who interpret it of Jesus" because he does not deem it "right or permissible to apply the prophecy to the King Messiah (for reasons which any intelligent man will easily find out): it must in fact refer to either Israel as a whole or Jeremiah."[182] Ibn Crispin himself claims that ישכיל in

178. Ibid., 55–56.
179. Ibid., 56.
180. Ibid., 78.
181. Ibid., 94.
182. Ibid., 114.

52:13 refers to how "all the nations were in astonishment and wonder at the depression of Israel in captivity, when their countenance and form were marred beyond those of other nations.[183] Rabbi Naphtali Ben Asher Altschuler said this about Christians, who interpreted the Servant to be Jesus Christ: "the Gentiles have heaped upon this Parashah a heap of vanity..."[184] These few examples indicate that the non-messianic interpretation of the suffering Servant in the pre-modern era belonged primarily to Jewish scholarship.[185]

2. Messianic assessments. While a large segment of scholars ruled out Isa 52:13–53:12 as a candidate for messianic interpretation throughout the history of Judaism, we can be sure that some segments of early Judaism seriously considered this passage as a candidate for messianic interpretation since the Targum applies the exaltation of the Servant to the Messiah (עבדי משיחא). Yet, because the Targum transfers any sufferings to Israel or the nations, we can assume that suffering was not a part of that expectation. Levey asserts that "this is an excellent example of Targumic paraphrase at its best. It is not a translation...but a reworking...of Deutero-Isaiah's conception of the Suffering Servant into an exalted proud, and aggressive personality, a champion who takes up the cudgels for the despised and down trodden and suffering Israel." On one hand, Levy is correct in that "he also restores Israel to national dignity, rebuilds its sanctuary and is a champion of Torah, metes out judgement to the wicked, and consigns them to Gehenna."[186] The Servant who in the MT is portrayed as "a root out of parched ground" is emended in the Targum "like a tree which sends its roots by streams of waters..." The Servant's act of being despised, forsaken, acquainted with sufferings and sorrows have been transferred to the glory of all kingdoms (53:3). He pleads for Israel's sins to be pardoned but he does not make vicarious atonement. Certainly the Targum takes liberties to "rework" this text. Yet, on another hand, something about the Hebrew text, especially the description of the Servant's exaltation (52:13), prompted Messianic interpretation in the Targum.[187]

---

183. Ibid., 117.
184. Ibid., 318.
185. See also Joseph Alobaidi, *The Messiah in Isaiah 53: The Commentaries of Saadia Gaon, Salmon ben Yerubam and Yefet ben Eli on Is 52:13–53:12* (Bern: Peter Lang, 1998).
186. Levey, *The Messiah*, 66–67.
187. See Roger Syrén, "Targum Isaiah 52:13–53:12 and Christian Interpretation," *JJS* 40 (1989): 201–12.

Even evidence from Qumran shows that, for some people, Isa 52:13–53:12 resonated with some aspect of messianism within early Judaism. The very fact that 1QIs^a adds a final *yōdh* to מָשְׁחַת making it מָשַׁחְתִּי ("I have anointed") indicates some degree of messianic interpretation (52:14). Probably the original root was שׁחת but the very fact that someone in the Qumran community copied מָשַׁחְתִּי offers proof that in some manner, some parts of the Jewish community were interpreting this text messianically before or during the time of Christ.[188] Jean Starcky has put forward the theory that 4QAaronA (4Q541) draws from the imagery of a suffering Messiah from the perspective opened up by the Servant poems[189] and this view has been followed by several.[190] However, John

188.   William Hugh Brownlee that the original root was מָשְׁחַת was the construct of מָשְׁחָה ("anointing") and was replaced by מָשַׁחְתִּי to make the messianic inference more clear. See his "Messianic Motifs of Qumran and the New Testament," *NTS* 3 (1956–57): 12–30; and his "*Mshty* (Is. 52:14 1QIsa," *BASOR* 132 (1953): 8–15. D. Barthélemy also thinks that the change was intentional; see his, "Le grand rouleau d'Isaïe trouvé près de la Mer Morte," *RB* 57 (1950): 546, and his *Critique textuelle de l'Ancien Testament* (OBO 50/2; Fribourg: Éditions Universitaires; Göttingen: Vandenhoeck & Ruprecht, 1986), 387–90. Others have interpreted 1QIs^a to read מָשַׁחְתִּי as "I have anointed." See also Edward Yechezkel Kutscher, *The Language and Linguistic Background of the Isaiah Scroll (1QIsaᵃ)* (STDJ; Leiden: Brill, 1974), 262. Barr and Guillaume read מָשַׁח as the root of מָשַׁחְתִּי; see A. Guillaume, "Some Readings in the Dead Sea Scroll of Isaiah," *JBL* 76 (1957): 42; James Barr, *Comparative Philology and the Text of the Old Testament* (Oxford: Clarendon, 1968), 285. Yet we also must be aware that 1QIs^b supports the MT. See A. Rubinstein, "Isaiah LII, 14—Mišḥat—and the DSIa Variant," *Bib* 35 (1954): 475–79; Gillis Gerleman, *Studien zur alttestamentlichen Theologie* (Heidelberg: Schneider, 1980), 39–40; Koole, *The Prophecy of Isaiah*, 268–69; G. R. Driver refers to this as a *hireq compagnis* ("Isaiah i–ix: Textual and Linguistic Problems," *JJS* 13 [1968]: 92).

189.   "Avant de quitter l'époque d'Alexandre Jannée, nous voudrions signaler un manuscit de notre lot de la grotte 4 (sigle provisoire 4QAhA) dont l'écriture est fort analogue à celle du scribe des *Testimonia*. Les joints effectués, il n'y a a malheureusement qu'une demidouzaine de fragments utiles, dont deux avec phrases continues. Mais leur intérêt est grand, car ils nous paraissent évoquer un messie souffrant, dans la perspective ouverte par les poèmes du Serviteur." Cf. Jean Starcky, "Les quatres étapes du messianisme à Qumran," *RB* 70 (1963): 491–92.

190.   Emil Puech, "Fragments d'une apocryphe de Lévi et le personnage eschatologique. 4QTestLévi(c-d) (?) et 4QAJa," in *The Madrid Qumran Congress* (ed. J. Trebolle Barrera and L. Vegas Montaner; Leiden: Brill, 1992), 492–99; George J. Brooke, "4Q Testament of Levi^d (?) and the Messianic Servant High Priest," in *From Jesus to John: Essays on Jesus and New Testament Christology in Honour of Marinus de Jonge* (ed. M. de Boer; JSNTSup 84; Sheffield: JSOT Press, 1993), 83–100; Martin Hengel, "Jesus der Messias Israels," in *Messiah and Christos: Studies in Jewish Origins of Christianity* (ed. I. Gruenwald, S. Shaked and G. Stroumsa; J. C. B. Mohr [Paul Siebeck], 1992), 164.

Collins thinks that this one about whom 4QAaronA speaks "will atone for all the children of his generation..." and whose "eternal sun will shine, and his light will be kindled in all the corners of the earth..."[191] better describes a priest, namely "the Teacher of Righteousness, who endured the opposition of the man of the Lie."[192]

While Rashi, Qimḥi and Ibn Ezra did not interpret the Servant as Messiah, some medieval rabbis did. In the thirteenth century, Ramban (Rabbi Moshe Ben Naḥman—Nachmanides) states: "*Behold my servant shall understand.* For at that time of redemption the Messiah will perceive and *understand...*" but added that "He will be loftier than Abraham, more exalted than Moses, loftier than ministering angels; the Messiah that is."[193] In the fourteenth century, Ralbag (Rabbi Levi Ben Gershon) identified the Servant as "'a prophet from the midst of thee.' In fact, the Messiah is such a Prophet as it is stated in the Midrash of the verse, 'Behold my Servant shall prosper'" (52:12).[194] Rabbi Moshe El-Sheikh says about ch. 53:

> I may remark then that our Rabbis with one voice accept and affirm the opinion that the prophet is speaking of the King Messiah and we ourselves shall adhere to the same view: for the Messiah is of course David, who, as is well known, was "anointed," and there is a verse in which the prophet speaking in the name of the Lord says expressly. "My Servant David shall be king over them" (Ezek 37:24).[195]

About the same verses, the same Rabbi says that "God declares in these verses how far the merits of those who thus suffer for the sins of their own age extend their efforts, adducing a proof from the case of the Messiah who bore the iniquities of the children of Israel."[196]

Except for occasional views like that of Servetus, who interprets the Servant in Isa 53 to be Cyrus, the vast majority of pre-modern Christians interpreted ch. 53 messianically. About Servetus, Calvin states: "the perfidious scamp wrenches the passage so as to apply it to Cyrus..."[197]

---

191.   4Q541 frag. 9, lines 9–11.

192.   Collins, *The Scepter and the Star*, 125.

193.   Driver and Neubauer, *The "Suffering Servant,"* 78–79.

194.   See John T. Townsend, ed. and trans., *Midrash Tanhuma (S. Buber Recension)* (Hoboken, N.J.: Ktav, 1989), 166–67; Driver and Neubauer, *The "Suffering Servant,"* 568.

195.   Driver and Neubauer, *The "Suffering Servant,"* 258.

196.   Ibid., 259.

197.   See the citation in Roland H. Bainton, *Hunted Heretic: The Life and Death of Michael Servetus 1511–1553* (Boston: Beacon, 1960), 100, 185; Louis I. Newman, *Jewish Influence on Christian Reform Movements* (New York: Columbia University Press, 1925), 582–85.

That is why H. H. Rowley argues that the traditional Christian view down to the end of the eighteenth century was that Isa 53 "was a messianic prophecy."[198] In *Contra Celsum*, Origen cited Isa 53 as proof against the Jewish opposition to a suffering Messiah, which considered this "defeated Messiah" to be an offense.[199] Using head and body imagery to explain the identity of the Servant, Tyconius, who was followed by many, declared that the phrase, "he bears our sins and suffers pain for us; he was wounded for our offenses...applies to the Lord...," who is the head, but wherever the Servant is named as Israel, the prophet speaks of the body.[200]

Luther asserts that Isa 53 speaks of the sufferings of Jesus Christ to "shoulder" the burden of our sin. First, he states that the Messiah will not come with a physical kingdom since his appearance is "so extremely marred."[201] Second, so offensive is the appearance of Christ that few Jews, he claimed, would "believe what we have heard" about a Messiah who would suffer such a loathsome death.[202] Third, Luther thought that the Servant suffered patiently, and fourth that his suffering has the power to remove our guilt.[203]

Jean Calvin contends that the chapter division between chs. 52 and 53 "ought to be disregarded; for it ought to have begun with the thirteenth verse of the former chapter." He professes that the term "Servant" speaks of the "office committed to him." Never using the term "Messiah," but only the Greek synonym "Christ" or the appellations "King" and "supreme King" Calvin argues that "almost the same metaphor was used by the prophet (Is. xi) when he said, 'a branch shall spring out of the stock of Jesse.'"[204] In 53:1, Isaiah declares that there will be few that submit to the Gospel of Christ. He argues that "Matthew quotes this prediction, after having related that Christ cured various diseases; though it is certain that he was appointed not to cure bodies, but rather to cure souls; for it is of spiritual disease that the prophet intends to speak." Moreover, the phrases "He shall see his seed" and "He shall prolong his days" imply that, through the resurrection, "he shall procure a people for

198.   Rowley, *The Servant of the Lord*, 4.

199.   Origen, *Contra Celsum* (trans. Henry Chadwick; Cambridge: Cambridge University Press, 1953), 50, 194, 389, 407.

200.   Karlfried Froehlich, *Biblical Interpretation in the Early Church* (Sources of Early Christian Thought; Philadelphia: Fortress, 1984), 105, 110–14.

201.   Martin Luther, *Lectures on Isaiah 40–66* (ed. Hilton C. Oswald; Saint Louis, Miss.: Concordia, 1972), 216.

202.   Ibid., 219–26.

203.   Ibid., 226–32.

204.   Calvin, *Commentary on the Book of the Prophet Isaiah*, 4:106–32.

himself" and "Christ shall not be hindered by his death...from living eternally."[205] Therefore, the portion which the Lord will divide with him speaks of "the result of the death of Christ" which is "the victory which Christ obtained by his death."[206] Christ "offered the sacrifice of his body, and shed his blood, that he might endure the punishment which was due us; and...in order that the atonement might take effect, he performed the office of an advocate and interceded for all who embraced the sacrifice by faith..." (John 17).[207]

III. *Rethinking the Evidence*

A. *Isaiah 52:13–53:12 within Biblical Prophecy*
While in the pre-modern era, non-messianic interpretation of the Servant belonged specifically to Judaism, in the modern era even Christians came to interpret Isa 52:13–53:12 non-messianically. Certainly, a modern understanding of scripture effected the way Christians interpreted texts. Even late modern scholars, who claim to treat the "final canonical stage" of Isaiah, often fail to differentiate between the pre-biblical "Deutero-Isaiah," the "Servant Songs" and the scriptural book of Isaiah.[208] Other historically conservative or fundamentalist scholars represent the opposite extreme of referring to the writer of chs. 40–66 as "Isaiah"[209] or even the prophet as the eighth-century prophet himself.[210]

Although modern scholarship has also been preoccupied with the identity of the Servant in 52:13–53:12, the scriptural book of Isaiah leaves the prophetic identity, historical circumstances and audience ambiguous but does not specifically identify the Servant or the one depicted as speaking in Isa 53. The function of a prophet in a scriptural book is much different than a modern historical reconstruction of a prophet, which has been adopted by both conservatives and liberals. Within the book as a whole, we cannot simply set the circumstances and audience of 52:13–53:12 within the exile. Having taken form in the shadow of the editors of Torah, the book of Isaiah functions as a scrip-

---

205. Ibid., 4:125.
206. Ibid., 4:129.
207. Ibid., 4:131.
208. Tull Willey, *Remember the Former Things*, 226–28; Williamson, *Variations on a Theme*; Sommer, *A Prophet Reads Scripture*; Koole, *The Prophecy of Isaiah*, xi, 249–43.
209. Motyer, *Prophecy of Isaiah*, 426, 431–35; Webb, *The Message of Isaiah*, 210, 214.
210. Allis, *The Unity of Isaiah*, 1–50, 88–89, 96–101; Alexander, *Isaiah*, 284; Kissane, *The Book of Isaiah*, vol. 2; Young, *Isaiah*, 3:183–191.

tural book that, like the Torah, is "for your children, and your children's children," so that within every generation, the book may be read by the "next generation" as a testimony to revelation. We have already seen how the original locus of the former things has shifted within the book as a whole from Cyrus, who serves as proof of fulfilled prophecy, to that which points beyond the isolated prophecies of Isaiah, and now testifies along with the legacy of the prophets to the Mosaic Torah (see above, Chapter 2). In the same way, whatever may have originally been the original historical references in 52:13–53:12, within the later formation of the book they now have become ambiguous regarding time, circumstances and audience. In the post-exilic age, when the people have returned to the land and the final editors are framing the scroll of Isaiah, the book now testifies that the homecoming and rebuilding have not provided restoration because the sins of the nation still persist, thus creating an eschatological tension within which 52:13–53:12 functions. Therefore, this ambiguity guarantees that the description of the suffering Servant who makes atonement on behalf of a sinful people now transcends the exilic time, circumstances and audience, and speaks, like the book of Torah, "to your children, and your children's children and to all who are far off."[211]

The problem of treating Isa 52:13–53:12 as one among three other Servant Songs is that this level of tradition history at most speaks of a pre-biblical tradition but does not account for the latter formation of the book of Isaiah as a whole.[212] We have demonstrated how, in the 1900s, several scholars argued that the Servant Songs should not be isolated but should be read within the greater context of Isa 40–55, but even this logic functions within the arena of pre-biblical traditions. Scholarship has demonstrated that we cannot determine with certainty whether or not the four Servant Songs ever existed independently from the book. Yet, if they were originally independent, a number of changes have taken place in the latter formation of the book that have altered the meaning of the material. Likewise, they are now set within the context of the book of Isaiah and serve another purpose. When the context of the literature

---

211. See Exod 10:2; 12:24, 26–30; Deut 4:9; 6:2, 7, 20, 21; 12:28; 23:8; 29:29; 31:13; 32:46.

212. Granted, scholarship has shown that there are similarities between the so-called "fourth song" and the other songs. For example, like Isa 42:1, which opens in the first person with הן עבדי ("here is my Servant"), the fourth Servant Song opens with הנה ישכיל עבדי ("Look, my Servant will have success," 52:13). The use of √בזה to describe the Servant also appears in Isa 49:7 in a manner similar to Isa 53:3 (see below). Yet, within the book as a whole, the similarities may very well be resonant indicators of what may have been pre-biblical Servant Songs.

changes, then the meaning of the literature also changes because it now belongs to a larger process of collecting. While it is probable that at the original level of tradition history the writer had the identity of the Servant in mind, these songs have been edited into the larger context, whereby ambiguity now functions rhetorically within the text.

However, pre-modern interpretation demonstrates that the hermeneutical difficulties in Isa 52:13–53:12 are not solely a modern creation. Numerous examples have shown that messianic interpretation in ch. 53 cannot easily be divided by pre-biblical and biblical levels of tradition history since many pre-modern interpreters have explained this chapter both messianically and non-messianically. Early Jewish interpretation yielded clever messianic readings of 52:13–53:12 which were different from that of Christians because Judaism had no expectation of a suffering Messiah. The Targum makes this evident by how it reapplies the phrases about the Servant's sufferings either to Israel or to foreign nations. From this perspective, the Targum has made a distinction similar to Tyconius' head and body description, which allowed Christians to treat various psalms of lamentation as a witness to the head, Jesus Christ, and apply to the body, the Church, any confession of sin in the same psalms.

B. *The Clarity of Isaiah 52:13–53:12*

1. *The Servant Israel and the individual Servant.* Although we have partially discussed ambiguity as a functional feature in Isa 52:13–53:12, the interpretation of this text does not merely rely on some sort of reader-response criticism, but must draw from the warrants of the text. Ambiguity functions as just one of these warrants (see below), but other warrants can be found in the clarity of the text. For example, the editors have arranged the material in ways that clarify and demarcate how to interpret the word עבד throughout chs. 40–66. Yet ever since Duhm first argued that the Servant Songs form a unit (42:1–4; 49:1–6; 50:4–9 [10, 11]; 52:13–53:12),[213] such demarcations have become blurred. Some scholars have interpreted these so-called "songs" in light of each other without a great deal of concern for the greater context.[214] Other studies[215] have

---

213.   Cf. Duhm, *Jesaja*, 284–87, 339–43, 351–54, 365–78.

214.   Duhm (*Jesaja*, 285) isolates the songs from the rest of the context because they are loosely connected to the context of Isa 40–55: "Die Stele, die jetzt Gedicht einnimmt, wird einfach bedingt gewesen sein durch genügenden freien Raum am Rande oder Zwischen grösseren Absatzen der deuterojesaja Schrift." See also North, *The Suffering Servant*, 206; Whybray, *Isaiah 40–66*, 71; Wilcox and Patton-Williams, "The Servant Songs."

noted the difference between chs. 40–48 and 49–55 (e.g. Babylon, Cyrus, idols and the "former things" are no longer mentioned in chs. 49–55).[216] We have even seen how scholars have resorted to psychological and historical efforts to rationalize these differences as a historical progression through which Israel is not able to perform the work of the Servant (chs. 40–48) and now an individual fills the role of the Servant and makes atonement on behalf of Israel. Workman downplays these differences in order to protect the text against those who would ascribe chs. 49–55 to "a different authorship." [217] Yet such a modern view of "authorship" does not illumine the book as a whole. The importance here lies not in whether chs. 40–48 and 49–55 were written by the same or different hands, but on how these distinctions demarcate different pieces of material within the greater tapestry of Isaiah.

Whether one writer ("Second Isaiah") originally composed Isa 40–55 and another ("Third Isaiah") created chs. 56–66, or even two writers formed chs. 40–48 and 49–55 (more likely, ch. 40 was much later than 41–55), the editors have not retained these "Second" and "Third Isaiah" distinctions. The refrain "there will be no peace for the wicked" (48:22; 57:21) cuts across the so-called "Second" and "Third Isaiah" material so that chs. 40–66 has been editorially arranged into three roughly equal trisections (chs. 40–48; 49–57; 58–66). Delitzsch asserts that this refrain organizes chs. 40–66 into three parts and that the end of the first trisection operates to conclude the work of Cyrus and any mention of

215.   For example, P. E. Bonnard aimed to show that after extracting the Servant Songs from the material in chs. 40–55, chs. 40–48 addressed the people of Israel and 49–55 a remnant of Deutero-Isaiah's disciples; see P. E. Bonnard, *Le Second Isaïe*, EBib (Paris: Gabalda, 1972). Spykerboer saw no hiatus between chs. 48 and 49. Hendrik Carel Spykerboer, *The Structure and Composition of Deutero-Isaiah* (Meppel: Krips Repro BV, 1976). Stuhlmueller ("Deutero-Isaiah," 5) claimed that Isa 40–55 took on four stages: chs. 41–48 were written before and chs. 49–55 after the fall of Babylon followed by the Servant Songs and finally ch. 40 as an overture.

216.   Note that one is more likely to find the terms "Jacob" and Israel in chs. 40–48 than in chs. 49–57. While the writer(s) employ(s) the term "Jacob" 19 times in chs. 40–48, twice in 49:1–6 and only once in 49:7–57:21, he employs the phrase "Israel" 35 times in chs. 40–48, three times in 49:1–6 but only five times in 49:7–57:21. When the designations "Jacob" and "Israel" are used in 49:1–6, they never pertain to the people of God but directly to God (i.e. "Holy One of Israel" and "King of Jacob") but in chs. 40–48, they always apply to the people of God (excluding the second Servant Song). The title "Zion" appears three times in chs. 40–48 but eight times in 49:7–57:21. Yet we find the appellation Jerusalem five times in chs. 40–48 and five times in 49:7–57:21. Israel appears to be the Servant in chs. 40–48 but in chs. 49–57 the Servant becomes an individual.

217.   Workman, *The Servant of Jehovah*, 27, 80–81.

Babylon (48:18), and seals what he calls the "second book" by directing the prophecies to "the heathen...estranged from God, within Israel itself."[218]

Moreover, Isa 52:13–53:12 provides evidence that differentiates the Servant from Israel. If the Servant were Israel in this chapter, as Baltzer and others posit, then the collective voice "we" by shear logic would have to imply the nations. However, such an occurrence would be *sui generis* because nowhere in the entire Old Testament does the voice "we" pertain to the nations but always to Israel. Likewise, 53:6 is framed by the *inclusio* כלנו ("all of us" or "we all"), which supports the idea of the Servant being an individual because a comparison is drawn here between one person and "all" others (כלנו) and not between a few who form a faithful minority and an unfaithful majority.[219] Most of the time, when כל alludes to people, it refers specifically to Israel,[220] Since כל itself does not distinguish between the nations and Israel, Koole notes that in the last usages of כל before 52:12–53:13, 50:9 compares those who are called to obey the voice of the Servant[221] and 51:18 speaks of Jerusalem who has lost "all" (כל) of her children.[222] Yet, this does not prove that כלנו speaks of Israel in 53:6. However, the exact form, כלנו, only appearing in chs. 40–66 and only once in chs. 40–55 (53:6), always denotes Israel.[223] Furthermore, the simile (כצאן) ("like sheep") recalls

218. Delitzsch, *Isaiah*, 1:256, 383. This is a position that was primarily argued in pre-modern commentaries (Calvin, Luther et al.).

219. Koole, *Isaiah*, 296.

220. Israel (41:9; 42:22; 43:7; 46:3 [remnant of the house of Israel]; 48:14 [כלכם]; 54:13 ["all your children shall be taught by YHWH"]; 55:1; 56:6, 7 ["all who keep sabbath"], 10; 59:11; 60:21; 61:2, 9; 64:9; 65:8; 65:12; 66:10; 66:20). However, other times כל refers either to the nations who are specifically not Israel: "all the nations" (43:9 [כל־הגוים]; 60:4, 6 ["all those from Sheba"], 14; 61:11; 62:2; 18; 66:20) or to those who may or may not be Israel: "all flesh" (49:26; 66:16, 23; 66:24); "all the ends of the earth" (45:22–25) idol worshipers or false prophets (44:9, 11; 45:16).

221. My observation: Isa 50:9 proclaims judgment to "all of them" (כלם) in a context where YHWH speaks in the first person "I" and to Israel as "you" (vv. 1–3). Another voice speaks in the first person singular "I" and "me" (probably the Servant since v. 10 seems to name the voice as "his Servant") who is differentiated from "all of them" who will wear out like a garment and asked "who among you fears YHWH and obeys the voice of his Servant?"

222. Koole, *Isaiah*, 297.

223. Note how כלנו appears in 59:11 within a context that fluctuates between the first, second and third person to speak of Israel. Note "you" and "your" (59:2–3); impersonal "no one," "they" or "their" (vv. 4–8); "us" or "we" or "we all" (כלנו, vv. 9–11). Note also how in Isa 64:5, 7 where כלנו stands in relation to יהוה אבינו ("YHWH our father"). In Isa 64:8, "we all" (כלנו) are YHWH's people.

how Israel is frequently called the flock צאן and often "the sheep of his pasture."[224] Israel made up one flock who would ultimately be shepherded by a Davidic king who is called the "righteous Branch" (Jer 23:1–5). YHWH "chose his servant David, and took him from the sheepfolds" (Ps 78:70), which serves as the plastic form or type that adumbrated the Messiah. Yet the term צאן is *never* found alongside גוים in the Old Testament. Therefore, within this framework, the "we" of 53:6 can be none other than Israel. This may be seen more clearly in how Isa 40–66 has been trisected to reflect a progression from the corporate description of the Servant to an individual portrait. Finally, 53:9b says that the Servant is without sin but this cannot be said of Israel (Isa 1:3; 5:7; 9:8–14; Ezek 20:21–40; Ps 95:10). Therefore, the Servant in Isa 52:13–53:12 seems to be differentiated from Israel.

Consequently, the Servant in the singular becomes more ambiguous in Isa 49–57 and the individual "my Servant" in 52:13–53:12 becomes an individual who has the possibilities to perform an eschatological task and to invite for Jews and Christians messianic interpretation. The second trisection (chs. 49–57) does not represent a historical progression but it shows that the editors are dealing with different topics and establishing different territories of discourse. In Isa 49–57, the work of the Servant moves beyond the time period and direct historical circumstances of Cyrus and the release from Babylon (chs. 40–48) because these chapters now belong to the period after the release from Babylon unto the end of time. This is why we cannot treat all of the so-called "Servant Songs" as if they all mean the same thing.

What relationship, then, do these songs have to each other within the later formation of the book of Isaiah? Some twentieth-century scholars have tried to correct Duhm's isolation of the Servant Songs by reading them within the greater context of Isa 40–55, but even this logic functions within the arena of pre-biblical traditions. The scriptural form and function of the trisections obliterate any lines which might have existed between "Second" and "Third Isaiah" and redistribute the Servant Songs into these different territories of discourse. While Isa 40–48 explicitly identifies Israel as the Servant of YHWH,[225] only in 49:3 is the Servant

224. See Ps 79:13; cf. also Pss 77:21; 78:52; 79:13; 80:1; 95:7; 100:3; 107:41; Isa 63:11; Jer 23:1–3; 50:6, 45; Ezek 34:2–31; 36:37, 38 etc.

225. See the excellent description of Wilcox and Patton-Williams ("The Servant Songs") but note that they make these distinctions for chs. 40–48 and 49–55 and do not observe that chs. 40–66 has been trisected. In his "The Arrangement of Isaiah Xl–Xlv," Goldingay observes that in comparing 41:1–20 with 41:21–42:12, both passages consistently identify the Servant with Israel. See also his *Isaiah* (NIBC; Peabody, Mass.: Hendrickson, 2001), 301–9.

identified with Israel in chs. 49–57, but that is within a set of verses that seem to make a transition from the first to the second trisection (49:1–6).[226] In 49:1–6, the Servant speaks in the first person: "He (YHWH) said to me, 'You are my Servant, O Israel, in whom I will display my splendor'" (49:3). The first person pronoun in 49:3 denotes Israel whom Yahweh designates as "My Servant." However, in 49:4 a shift occurs which adumbrates the figure of the Servant after he objects to this identification, apparently because he wishes to be differentiated from Israel. In 49:5–7, his role becomes more clearly defined as one who will bring Israel back to Yahweh.[227] Thus the Servant, who is called "Israel," is also differentiated from Israel. Thus, in 54:17, Israel is first called "servants" (plural) rather than "servant." In this progression from a corporate to an individualized Servant (49:1–6), the personal language in this "second song" already is far too specified to pertain to Israel and the clarity of the individual Servant's role cannot be metaphor.[228] The ambiguity and individuality of the Servant in the "third" and "fourth Servant Songs" is much more pronounced. Since the editors have strategically distributed the four Servant Songs across the first two trisections in a manner that transfers the identity of the Servant from Israel to an unidentified individual, we cannot treat 52:13–53:12 as one among four Servant Songs. Illustrating a common function of biblical prophecy, these two

226.   Isa 49:3 also provides the only occasion where the Servant is named in the four songs and the term "Israel" does not stand in parallelism to "Jacob." In this context, the Servant is called Israel and at the same time confesses that YHWH "formed me in the womb to be his servant, to bring Jacob back to him, and that Israel might be gathered to him" and "to raise up the tribes of Jacob and to restore the survivors of Israel" (49:5, 6). Some think that the word "Israel" may be an interpolation in Isa 49:3, but there seems to be little textual evidence to affirm such an assertion. After 49:6, the exiles are invariably named "Zion-Jerusalem" and the names "Jacob" and "Israel" appear merely as components in the names of God. Thus, Wilcox and Patton-Williams assert that the prophet in 49:1–6 takes up the task which has been assigned to the Servant ("The Servant Songs," 92).

227.   And now the LORD says—"he who formed me in the womb *to be his Servant to bring Jacob back to him and gather Israel to himself*, for I am honored in the eyes of the LORD and my God has been my strength." He says: "It is too small a thing for you to be my Servant to restore the tribes of Jacob and bring back those of Israel I have kept. I will also make you a light for the nations, that you may bring my salvation to the ends of the earth." This is what the LORD says—the Redeemer and Holy One of Israel—to him who was despised and abhorred by the nation, to the Servant of rulers: "Kings will see you and rise up, princes will see and bow down, because of the LORD, who is faithful, the Holy One of Israel, who has chosen you" (Isa 49:5–7).

228.   Whybray, *Isaiah 40–66*, 136.

trisections represent different prophetic voices speaking to different times, circumstances and audiences. Therefore, the editors have set these so-called Servant Songs within this trisected material and they have now taken on a different meaning.

Yet, at the biblical level, there remains some sort of correspondence between Isa 52:13–53:12 and the other "songs." What, then, do these similarities existing between the so-called Servant Songs now imply for the scriptural form of the book?[229] In the present form of Isaiah, there is a residual remnant of this original level of tradition history that may indicate that the Songs were once semantically connected or meant to be heard together. Yet, the trisections have rehistoricized these songs so that they must now be read within the new context of the book as a whole.

2. *The clarity of the Servant's exaltation.* Isaiah 52:13–53:12 begins and ends with the phrase עבדי ("my Servant," 52:13; 53:12), while also framing this passage with a description of the Servant's exaltation. Like the Servant in 52:13–53:12, there are many other Servants in the Old Testament, such as "my servant David"[230] and "my servant Moses" (Josh 1:4). Jeremiah even refers to Nebuchadnezzer as "my Servant" (Jer 25:9; 27:6; 43:10). In Isa 1–39, we find "my servant Isaiah" (Isa 20:3), "my servant Eliakim son of Hilkiah" (22:20) and "my Servant David" (Isa 37:35). Zechariah speaks of "my Servant the branch" (Zech 3:8). The phrase "my Servant Jacob" or "my Servant Israel" appears in Isa 40–48. The Messiah is called "my Servant" in *2 Bar* 70:9. Some of these other Servants of YHWH are described as those who will succeed, and the Hiphil of the root שכל is sometimes paired with the root צלח (Isa 53:10), as is the case for Joshua (Josh 1:7–8), David (1 Sam 18:5, 14), Solomon (1 Kgs 2:3) and Hezekiah (2 Kgs 18:7). However, in 52:13 the Hiphil of שכל is paired with the Qal of רום, which distinguishes the Servant of YHWH in 52:13–53:12 from all other Servants and uniquely speaks of his

229. Like Isa 42:1, which opens in the first person with הן עבדי ("here is my Servant"), 52:13–53:12 opens with הנה ישכיל עבדי ("Look, my Servant will have success," 52:13). הנה not only serves as a stylistic feature but, as Oswalt (*Isaiah 40–66*, 378) rightly notes, calls the reader to "pay attention." This is heightened by the appellation עבדי ("my Servant") beginning and ending the song (52:13 and 53:11–12). The use of √בזה to describe the Servant also appears in Isa 49:7 in a manner similar to 53:3. Working with pre-biblical levels of tradition history, Westermann notes that there is a "deliberate" connection between 42:1–4 and 52:13–53:12 and he asserts that the "two songs go together" in that 42:1–4 shows the origin and chs. 52–53 the culmination of the Servant's work (ibid., 258).

230. 2 Sam 3:18; 7:5, 8; 1 Kgs 11:3, 32, 34, 36; 14:8; 2 Kgs 19:34; 1 Chr 13:4; 17:7; Ps 89:3, 20; Isa 37:35; Jer 33:21, 22, 26; Ezek 33:23, 24; 37:24, 25.

exaltation. As Koole has brought to our attention, the Hiphil of שכל (52:13) is also used to describe an eschatological figure, who fits our definition of messianism and will execute justice and righteousness on earth.[231] Moreover, the two consecutive verbs ירום ונשא are also used of YHWH in 6:1 and translated by OG as ὑψωθήσεται καὶ δοξασθήσεται σφόδρα for both.[232] While the root רום can apply to the height, self-exaltation, Yahweh's exaltation of his people,[233] the term refers normally to God, when used in a positive and affirmative sense to declare the exalted state of another.[234] In Ps 89:20, YHWH exalts (√רום) a royal figure, probably fitting our definition of messianism, because this passage, in the post-exilic era, activates and restores the covenant with "my servant David," also recalling Ps 2 and ending with משיחך. Just because רום appears in a messianic passage does not require that Isa 52:13 be interpreted messianically. In the book of Isaiah, רום applies to YHWH's act of *raising up* children (1:2), the *haughty* (2:11, 12, 13, 14, 17; 10:12; 37:23) and the *lofty* trees that are brought low (10:15, 33). The term רום also is used to convey that YHWH will *lift up* highways (49:11; 57:15) and Zion is told to *lift up* her voice (40:9; 58:1; 62:10). YHWH himself is exalted throughout chs. 1–39 and once in chs. 40–66 (6:1; 14:13; 25:1; 26:11; 33:10; 57:15). The verb √רום seems to be used in the fientive sense, which indicates the change of state from humiliation to exaltation.

In both 52:13 and 53:11–12, God himself declares the Servant's exaltation because only a divine voice can proclaim such resplendence. The extremely negative attitude of alarm toward the Servant becomes one of extreme regard. The divine voice again affirms the Servant's exaltation:

231.   Koole, *Isaiah 49–55*, 264.

232.   Origen's *Obelus* has καὶ μετεωρισθησεται = Q, Chrysostum. Aquila, Symmacus and Theodotion read επαρθησεται και μετεωπισθησεται. For discussion on the LXX and 52:13, see Otfried Hofius, "Zur Septuaginta-Übersetzung von 52:13b," *ZAW* 104 (1992): 107–10.

233.   The word √רום is used to speak of the height (Deut 1:28; 2:21; 9:2) or *self-exaltation* of a person (Deut 8:14; 17:20) or king (Dan 11:36), YHWH's exalting (√רום) of the poor or those who serve him (1 Sam 2:7, 8; 2 Sam 22:49; 24:24; Pss 3:4; 9:14; 27:5, 6; 37:34; 75:8; 89:20; 92:11; 113:7), or the prophet Jehu (1 Kgs 16:2). YHWH does not exalt (√רום) the proud (Hos 13:6). Wisdom exalts those who seek wisdom (Prov 4:8). Note also that the word is used many times to speak of lifting or raising up voices, objects, their hands, heads and offerings to YHWH, or to describe "haughtiness."

234.   God is lifted up (Exod 15:2; 1 Sam 2:1, 10; 2 Sam 22:47; 1 Chr 25:5; 2 Chr 5:13; Neh 9:5; Job 22:12; Pss 18:47, 48; 21:14; 30:2; 34:4; 46:11; 57:6, 12; 66:17; 78:69; 99:2, 5, 9; 107:32; 113:4; 118:16, 28; 145:1; Isa 6:1; 14:13; 25:1; 26:11; 33:10; 57:15; Ezek 10:4).

"Therefore I will allot him a portion with the great, and he shall divide the spoil with the strong" (53:12). Oswalt asserts that the poem ends describing the exaltation of the Servant as "a victory parade with the Servant, of all people, marching in the role of conqueror, bringing home the spoils of conquest."[235] The Servant is portrayed as the victor. The adverb, לכן ("therefore"), marks a principal result clause, thus reflecting back on v. 11, which states "the righteous one, my Servant, shall make many righteous, and he shall bear their iniquities." Exaltation is merely the result of the Servant's atoning work.

With the phrase, אחלק־לו ברבים ("I will divide the spoil for him with the mighty"), as Whybray notes, the "spoil" (שלל) functions as the object of both verbs (אחלק and יחלק) but also adds that שלל here is used in the metaphorical sense, "reward."[236] In this ballast structure, not only does שלל add an element to the second colon that is not in the first colon, but the subject switches between the divine voice in the first colon and the Servant in the second colon. Some argue that the Piel יְחַלֵּק ("he will receive") should be emended to the Qal יַחֲלֹק ("he shall distribute").[237] The sense is that the Servant will return from his mission like a conquering warrior laden with spoil.[238] Perhaps חלק plays on חלה to emphasize the ascent from humiliation to exaltation.[239]

While some render the first appearance of רבים as "many,"[240] an even wider group translates רבים in 53:12 as a substantive: "great [ones]," or "mighty [ones]."[241] Muilenburg and others take ברבים as the direct

235. Oswalt, *Isaiah 40–66*, 394.
236. Whybray, *Isaiah 40–66*, 182.
237. Ibid., 182; David J. A. Clines, *I, He, We, and They: A Literary Approach to Isaiah 53* (JSOTSup 1; Sheffield: JSOT Press, 1976), 22; Godfrey R. Driver, "Isaiah 52:13–53:12: The Servant of the Lord," in *In Memoriam Paul Kahle* (ed. G. Fohrer and M. Black; BZAW 103; Berlin: Töpelmann, 1968), 102; Koole, *Isaiah 49–55*, 339.
238. Webb, *The Message of Isaiah*, 213.
239. Koole, *Isaiah 49–55*, 339.
240. Alexander, *Isaiah*, 306–07; McKenzie, *Second Isaiah*, 132, 136; Holladay, *Isaiah*, 156; Clifford, *Second Isaiah*, 181; Watts, *Isaiah 34–66*, 232; Motyer, *The Prophecy of Isaiah*, 343; Oswalt, *Isaiah 40–66*, 399, 405–6.
241. Calvin, *Commentary on the Book of the Prophet Isaiah*, 4:129; Alexander, *Isaiah*, 306; Delitzsch, *Isaiah*, 1:338; Smith, *The Book of Isaiah*, 2:345; Josef Scharbert, *Heilsmittler im Alten Testament und im Alten Orient* (Freiburg: Herder, 1964), 207; Ernst Kutsch, *Sein Leiden und Tod—Unser Heil* (BibS[N] 52; Neukirchen–Vluyn: Neukirchener, 1967), 37–38; Westermann, *Isaiah 40–66*, 255; Driver, "Isaiah 52:13–53:12," 104; Mitchell Dahood, "Phoenician Elements in Isaiah 52:13–53:12," in *Near Eastern Studies in Honour of W. F. Albright* (ed. H. Goedicke; Baltimore: The Johns Hopkins University Press, 1971), 64; Preuss,

object: "...I will divide to him the many as a portion, the countless he will share as booty." The "many" or "mighty" become the Servant's possession.[242] Yet the preposition ב seems to function as an associative instrumental which would rule out this option. In light of the parallelism (עצומים = רבים), the lexemes "mighty" or "great" most likely express the meaning of רבים. Along with NRSV, Koole argues that את (in ברבים) parallels ב (in ברבים), and "undoubtedly means 'with, among...'" Others think that את (in את־עצומים) marks the direct object.[243] Unlike its first appearance in the verse, את (את־פשעים) marks the direct object.[244] The text emphasizes that, even though he suffers and dies, the Servant will divide booty with the mighty ones because he is victorious.

YHWH's act of exalting the Servant occurs after his death on the other side of the grave.[245] This is because the exaltation of the Servant is deeply connected with his humiliation whereby the causal clause affirms that all this is "because he poured out himself to death, and was numbered with the transgressors; yet he bore the sin of many, and made intercession for the transgressors" (53:12).[246] Exaltation rests on the fact

Deuterojesaja, 98; Young, *Isaiah*, 2:358; Bonnard, *Le Second Isaïe*, 265, 282–84; Whybray, *Isaiah 40–66*, 182; W. A. M. Beuken, *Jesaja* (3 vols. in 5; A Nijkerk: Uitgeverij GF Callenbach, 1989), 2A:233–34; Gerleman, *Studien zur alttestamentlichen Theologie*, 43; Hans-Jurgen Hermisson, "Der Lohn des Knechts [Isa 42:1–4; 49:1–4; 50:4–9; 52:13–53:12]," in *Die Botschaft und die Boten: Festschrift für Hans Walter Wolff zum 70. Geburtstag* (ed. Jorg Jeremias and Lothar Perlitt; Neukirchen–Vluyn: Neukirchener, 1981), 286; Douglas A. Knight and Gene M. Tucker, *The Hebrew Bible and Its Modern Interpreters* (SBLCP; Philadelphia: Fortress; Chico, Calif.: Scholars Press, 1985), 179; Hugenberger, "The Servant of the Lord," 114; Schultz, "The King in the Book of Isaiah," 158; Koole, *Isaiah 49–55*, 337; Brueggemann, *Isaiah 40–66*, 149; Oswalt, *Isaiah 40–66*, 405–6.

242.   Skinner, *Isaiah Chapters XL–LXVI*, 133; James Muilenburg, *The Book of Isaiah*, in Buttrick, ed., *The Interpreter's Bible*, 5:631; Raymond J. Tournay, "2d Isaiah [Review]," *RB* 72 (1965): 501; Sh. Porúbčan, "The Word *'OT* in Isaiah 7,14," *CBQ* 22 (1960): 157; D. Winton Thomas, "A Consideration of Isaiah LIII in the Light of Recent Textual and Philological Study," in *De Mari à Qumrân: Festschrift J. Coppens* (BETL 24; Glembloux: Duculot, 1969), 120; Joseph C. L. Coppens, *Le messianisme et sa relève prophétique* (BETL 38; Gembloux: Duculot, 1974), 64; Pierre Grelot, *Les poèmes du serviteur: De la lecture critique a l'hermeneutique* (LD 103; Paris: Cerf, 1981), 54; Koole, *Isaiah 49–55*, 338.

243.   H. Cazelles, "Les Poèmes du Serviteur," *RSR* 43 (1955): 55; Thomas, "Isaiah LIII," 120; Coppens, *Le messianisme et sa relève prophétique*, 64.

244.   Koole, *Isaiah 49–55*, 337.

245.   Westermann, *Isaiah 40–66*, 267.

246.   See Klaus Koch, "Messias und Sündenvergebung in Jesaja 53, Targum: Ein Beitrag zu der Praxis der aramäischen Bibelübersetzung," *JSJ* 3 (1972): 147–48.

that he suffered and died. The causal clause indicator תחת אשר is used always as a causal protasis ("because" or "since")[247] and Motyer claims that תחת אשר is "the strongest causative in Hebrew..."[248] Only because of his suffering unto death can he be exalted or "lifted very high" (52:13), which for Christians becomes the very foundation for the exaltation of their Messiah, Jesus Christ. The Servant will be exalted "because he poured himself out to death...and bore the sin of many" (see below). If we take the Niphal verb וְנִמְנָה ("he let himself be numbered with transgressors," 53:12) as a reflexive rather than a passive, then "he poured out his soul to death" voluntarily. There is a difference between being passively abused and willfully laying down one's life for others. When the Servant lay down his life, he did so from a place of power. Yet the dialectic lies in the occurrence that he was also exalted because he poured out his soul to death.

The exaltation of the Servant (e.g. the use of רום) may have provided one impetus for the Targum to interpret Isa 52:13–53:12 messianically, but the suffering which becomes the very catalyst for his exaltation excludes this passage from the traditional messianic expectation of early Judaism. Moreover, these verses offer no description of a messianic king. From this perspective, we should not be at all surprised that the Targum refers to the Servant as "the Messiah" but reinterprets the phrases about his sufferings as referring to Israel or the rival nations. In light of the description of exaltation, it is not at all surprising that the Targum would have "my Servant, the Messiah" with such exalted language.

3. *The clarity of the Servant's intercession and substitutionary atonement.* The verse that describes the exaltation of the Servant (52:13) is followed by a description of immeasurable revulsion at the abuse of the Servant. Isaiah 52:12 announces Salvation but, as Oswalt states, "instead we hear about suffering, humiliation, and loss..."[249] While many scholars think that the Servant provided atonement on behalf of the people, others have posited something different regarding what his suffering signifies. Levey argues that the Servant pleads for Israel's sins to be pardoned but he does not make vicarious atonement.[250] Rashi believed that this passage had to do with atonement but Israel was suffering for the atonement of the nations (see above). While many Jews could read the Servant's

247. Cazelles, "Les Poèmes du Serviteur"; BDB, 1066; Beuken, *Jesaja*, 2A:232; Koole, *Isaiah 49–55*, 339.
248. Motyer, *The Prophecy of Isaiah*, 443.
249. Oswalt, *Isaiah 40–66*, 375.
250. Levey, *Targum*, 66–67.

role of performing atonement, they could not conceive of a suffering Messiah. Both G. Adam Smith's argument that Servant had become the martyred prophet and Freud's position that this text describes the martyrdom of Moses seem to rule out the atoning work of the Servant.[251] Watts' more recent argument that 52:13–53:12 describes the murder of Zerubbabel, whose executed body was mutilated and innocent death mourned, seems also to rule out the Servant's atoning work.[252] Does the suffering of the Servant involve a substitutionary atonement or does it merely describe the martyrdom of an innocent victim?

Isaiah 52:14, with the comparative כַּאֲשֶׁר, describes one who would not fit the expectation of the exalted Servant: "Just as many were horrified by you, truly, his appearance is marred beyond human appearance and his form beyond that of humans." Though scholars offer different reasons for the awkwardness of 52:14, whether the verse is a tricolon by creating a bicolon through omitting the third colon,[253] or רַבִּים is an added *Stichwort*[254] or an original line has been lost,[255] 52:14 marks a sriking contrast from 52:13.[256] Whether the original transition has been lost in either the process of tradition or transmission history, or a pausal stop marks a transition, thereby allowing the reader to pause and reflect on the exalted state of the Servant, the reader now focuses his or her attention on the locution שָׁמְמוּ that points to the appalling portrayal of the Servant. Certainly, שָׁמְמוּ begins a new thought that causes alarm. According to Fritz Stolz, the verb שׁמם√ implies that "the fate of the suffering servant of God also occasions horror."[257] Kaiser translates שׁמם as "impulsive rigidity" (*"regungslose Starre"*).[258]

251. Smith, *The Book of Isaiah*, 2:345–46; Freud, *Moses and Monotheism*, 59–60.

252. Watts, *Isaiah 34–66*, 223–33.

253. Jean Steinmann, *Le livre de la consolation d'Israël et les Prophètes du Retour de l'exil* (LD 28; Paris: Cerf, 1960).

254. Paul Volz, *Isaiah II* (Leipzig: A. Deichertsche Verlagsbuchhandlung D. Werner Scholl, 1932), 173.

255. Duhm, *Jesaja*, 394; M. Treves, "Isaiah 53," *VT* 24 (1974): 106. G. R. Driver follows the Targum and replaces רַבִּים with עַמִּי רַבִּים יָמִים ("Isaianic Problems," 91). The NEB has four cola "Time was when many (replacing 'great') were aghast at you my people; so now many nations recoil at sight of him."

256. Instead of emending the text without clear textual evidence, Beuken (*Jesaja*, 2A:201–2) aims to preserve the monostich, thus positing a pausal stop in order that v. 13 may settle with the reader before he or she proceeds to v. 14.

257. Fritz Stolz, "שׁמם *šmm* 'to Lie Deserted,'" trans. Mark Biddle (*TLOT* 3:1373).

258. Kaiser, *Der königliche Knecht*, 90.

The prepositional phrase עָלֶיךָ has also aroused different explanations. Tournay argues that "il suffit de vocaliser ici au féminin: עָלַיִךְ" because when speaking about Israel, the context uses a female personification for Zion (people) and he thinks that the gender must match. Not only does he emend the text to fit the interpretation, but also Zion and Israel are not univocal. Driver preserves the masculine suffix by adding עַמִּי to the colon.[259] Others assert that עָלֶיךָ was an old writing error for עָלָיו.[260] Even if one does not choose to emend the text here, the changing of voice and person in ancient Near Eastern poetry sometimes occurs as a stylistic device.[261] Whether this switch in person represents a stylistic device or a corrupt text, it places just one more element of mystery and ambiguity to this passage.

Clearly, "many" (רבים) people experience consternation over his horrifying appearance. Whether these "many" describe Israel compared with an individual Servant, or the heathen of Israel compared with the Servant Israel, or the nations compared with the Servant Israel, the key lies in the characterization of how the many were astonished by his form and appearance. Nevertheless, Koole argues that 52:14 compares closely with 53:2 where the speaker must be Israel and 53:3 describes the same indifference to the Servant's suffering as שמם expresses in 54:14. Moreover, the "many" (רבים) in 53:12 are picked up from 52:14 and are identical to the "we" in 53:4–5. Therefore, Koole does not think that 52:14 refers to nations but to Israel. [262] Further, vv. 14 and 15 distinguish between רבים ("many") and גוים רבים ("many nations"), most likely indicating that with גוים, the adjective רבים speaks of the foreign nations and רבים alone speaks of Israel especially since רבים in 53:11 cannot rule out Israel.[263]

The use of the comparative מן (מאיש, "more than a man," and מבני אדם, "more than the sons of men") conveys the distortion of the Servant from typical human norms. Calvin says that this is not a "מ to be a particle noting comparison" but to denote "among," but he does not seem

259. Driver, "Isaianic Problems," 91.

260. Westermann, *Isaiah 40–66*, 253–54, 258–59; Fohrer, *Jesaja*, 2:158; McKenzie, *Second Isaiah*, 129; Beuken, *Jesaja*, 2A:234–35; Clines, *I, He, We, and They*, 11.

261. Othmar Keel, *The Song of Songs* (trans. Frederick J. Gaiser; Continental Commentaries; Minneapolis: Fortress, 1994), 40.

262. Koole, *Isaiah 49–55*, 267–68.

263. See Hermisson, "Der Lohn Des Knechts," 285; Odil Hannes Steck, "Aspekte Des Gottesknechts in Jes. 52,13–53:12," *ZAW* 97 (1985): 49–52; T. Hartmann, "רב; *Rab* Many," trans. Mark Biddle (*TLOT* 3:1194–201); Koole, *Isaiah 49–55*, 271.

to offer grounds for his reasoning.[264] Dahood translates this מִן as a causal "by," which is reasonable with a passive verb and could point back to the torment of the Servant.[265] The preposition מִן cannot be a privative or separative because along with the adverbial phrase, מִשְׁחַת, the Servant is being *compared* with ordinary human beings.

After describing this unusual appearance, כֵּן ("thus," "even," "so," "indeed"), which is subordinate to כַּאֲשֶׁר (52:14), the next verse opens stating that "Just as there were many who were astonished at him...*so* he shall sprinkle nations..." (52:15). The Hiphil imperfect third person masculine singular יַזֶּה (from נזה√) has invoked several options. Some translate נזה√ as "startle" from the Arabic root أزان ("startle") or ضن ("to leap up," "spring up," or "jump," in the sense that one jumps when startled).[266] This use of comparative Semitics may possibly preserve an older cognate significance of the word נזה, but this idea of importing a cognate is unlikely since this meaning of the word cannot be exemplified anywhere else in the Old Testament. The Targum supplies יבדר ("scatter"); Aquila and Theodotion have ραντίσει; Symmacus reads ἀποβάλλει. Similar to the Peshitta (מדכא) and Vulgate (*asperget*), Rashi reads ירה (Hiphil) for יזה ("to cast down"). Yet these too seem to correct the difficulty of an enigmatic term. On the basis of the parallelism and the usage of the word throughout the Old Testament, the word "sprinkle" best fits the context. Except for one occasion, which still describes blood being spurted against a wall (2 Kgs 9:33), the verb נזה√ is used exclusively to speak of the ceremonial cleansing by the sprinkling of the blood of a sacrifice, anointing oil or water of purification (Exod 29:21 [וְהִזֵּיתָ]; Lev 4:6, 17; 5:9; 6:20; 8:11, 30; 14:7, 16, 27; 16:14, 15, 19; Num 8:7; 19:4, 18, 19, 21; Isa 63:3). The Qal is employed for "splashing" of blood (e.g. Lev: 6:20 [27]) and the Hiphil for "sprinkling" of blood (e.g. Exod 29:21). נזה appears in Isa 63 to depict the act of trodding the wine press and the splattering (נזה) of grape juice (Isa 63:3), serving as a symbol for YHWH trampling the people and pouring out their life blood (63:6) during the year of redemption (63:4) when their savior (63:8) redeemed them (63:9 with נשא√). Used for ceremonial purposes, the word נזה is often accompanied with anointing oil (Exod 8:11, 30; 14:16, 27, 51; 16:14, 15, 19; 29:21) "upon the one who is to be cleansed of the leprous disease" (Lev 14:7). It applies to the "slaying goat" on the day of

264. Calvin, *Commentary on the Book of the Prophet Isaiah*, 4:107.
265. Dahood, "Phoenician Elements," 270.
266. See North, *The Second Isaiah*, 228; Dahood, "Phoenician Elements," 65; Clines, *I, He, We, and They*, 14. Also NRSV, RSV, NBG, NAB, JPS. Note that NEB and REB have "recoil."

atonement: "He shall slaughter the goat of the sin offering that is for the people and bring its blood inside the curtain, and do with its blood as he did with the blood of the bull, sprinkling it upon the mercy seat and before the mercy seat..." (16:15) "...for the uncleanliness of Israel" (16:19). These liquids (blood, oil etc.) always serve as the object or material means of נזה, but never except here in 52:15 does that upon which the liquid is sprinkled become the direct object (יזה גוים רבים).[267] Therefore, most scholars correctly connect the word with the purifying capacity of sprinkling with blood.[268]

Kaufmann says that the Servant did not alone bear the punishment of the speakers, but that "his sufferings were on their, not on his account."[269] If he is correct, then Isa 53:4 describes substitutionary atonement. At the beginning of the verse, the parallelism is synonymous but is set in *Qînāh* meter:

> (A) Surely (B) our infirmities (C) he   (A) אכן (B) הלינו (C) הוא נשא
> bore (B) and our torments (C) he   (B) ומכאבינו (C) סבלם
> carried them

Opening the first colon of Isa 53:4, the term אכן reverses what immediately precedes it in 53:3: השבנהו אכן הלינו הוא נשא ("we did not esteem him, *but* [we were wrong because] he carried our infirmities").[270] If the suffixed pronoun, "*our* infirmities" (הלינו), implies "Israel," then it fits well with Isa 1:4–5 where the prophet indicts the sinful nation whose "whole head is sick" (כל־ראש לחלי). Yet, in the same way that the scapegoat or sacrificial animal "takes away" (√נשא) the sins of the people

---

267.   See Motyer, *The Prophecy of Isaiah*, 425–26.

268.   E. J. Young, "The Interpretation of *yzh* in Isaiah 52:15," *WTJ* 3 (1941): 125–32; ibid., "The Origin of the Suffering Servant Idea"; Johannes Lindblom, *Die Ebed Jahwe-Orakel in der neuentdeckten Jesajahandschrift* (Berlin: A. Töpelmann, 1951), 40–41; Cazelles, "Les Poèmes du Serviteur"; Muilenburg, *Isaiah*, 5:616–17; North, *Second Isaiah*, 228; Preuss, *Deuterojesaja*, 97; Henri Blocher, *The Songs of the Servant* (Downers Grove, Ill.: Intervarsity, 1975), 61; J. H. Eaton, *Festal Drama in Deutero-Isaiah* (London: SPCK, 1979), 76–77; Barthélemy, *Critique textuelle*, 387, 394; Webb, *The Message of Isaiah*, 204–14; Motyer, *The Prophecy of Isaiah*, 426; Oswalt, *Isaiah 40–66*, 374, 379–81; Koole, *Isaiah 49–55*, 272.

269.   Kaufmann, *The Religion of Israel*, 161.

270.   Andrew B. Davidson, *Introductory Hebrew Grammar: Hebrew Syntax* (3d ed.; Edinburgh: T. & T. Clark, 1976), 164; Bruce K. Waltke and Michael O'Connor, *An Introduction to Biblical Hebrew Syntax* (Winona Lake, Ind.: Eisenbrauns, 1990), 670–71; Walter Baumgartner, *Hebräisches und Aramaisches Lexikon zum Alten Testament von Ludwig Koehler und Walter Baumgartner* (3 vols.; 3d ed.; Leiden: Brill, 1967–83), 3:4.

(Lev 5:1, 17; [שא עון] 10:17; 16:22; 17:16; 20:19; Num 9:13; 14:34), the
Servant takes on himself the sin of Israel and the world and "bears" or
"takes away" (נשא√) their sins (53:4).[271] Ceremonially, the word is used
in Lev 10:7 to describe how the sin offering removes the guilt of the
congregation (לשאת את־עון). Most specifically, the scapegoat ritually
bears the iniquities of the people:

> Then Aaron shall lay both his hands on the head of the live goat, and
> confess over it all the iniquities of the people of Israel, and all their trans-
> gressions, all their sins, putting them on the head of the goat, and sending
> it away into the wilderness by means of someone designated for the task.
> The goat shall bear (נשא√) on itself all their iniquities to a barren region;
> and the goat shall be set free in the wilderness. (Lev 16:21–22 [NRSV])

The verb נשא provides a preponderance of examples that explicitly refer
to the ritual bearing of sin.

    The second colon of 53:4 fills out this first bicola with synonymous
parallelism. Clearly the term ומכאבינו, which is parallel to חלינו, confirms Kugel's theory about the A and B cola: if "A is so, and what's
more, B." Therefore, the noun חלי speaks of sickness or illnesses in
general but מכאוב in the second colon is more specific. Except in one
case that describes Israel's "sufferings" in Egypt (3:7), the word מכאוב,
which is translated as "suffering," "sorrow," "torment," "wound," "pain"
or "grief" is consistently used to describe a "suffering" that occurs as a
result of wrongdoing.[272] Isaiah 53:4 says that the Servant has borne

---

271.   In the other three places where נשא√ appears in the book of Isaiah (6:1;
33:10; 57:15), YHWH is lifted up. See Oswalt, *Isaiah 40–66*, 377 n. 71, 386.

272.   The word מכאוב is used in the context of a confession to describe the
"suffering" that accompanies Israel's separation from YHWH (1 Chr 6:29). It is
employed in Elihu's case against Job (33:19) to provide evidence that Job's suffering ("they are chastened with suffering" [במכאוב]) has occurred because of his sin,
though Habel may be pressing the limits to claim that Elihu uses forensic language
(the noun ריב and the Hophal verb והוכח). See his *The Book of Job: A Commentary*
(ed. Peter R. Ackroyd, James Barr and Bernhard W. Anderson; OTL; Philadelphia:
Westeminster, 1985), 469. Note that מכאוב describes the "sufferings" of the wicked
(Ps 32:10) and is used in a lamentation of the individual that directly precedes the
confession of sin (Ps 38:18–19) or to speak of "those whom you [YHWH] have
caused to suffer" and thus charges YHWH to "add [imperative] guilt to their guilt"
(Ps 68:27–28 [NRSV 26–27]). Qohleth challenges the traditional claim that folly
produces such "sorrow" (מכאוב), asserting that there is vanity in wisdom because,
although it should make one complete, when wisdom and knowledge increases,
"sorrow" increases (Eccl 1:18). Jeremiah claims that Israel's "pain" (מכאוב) is
incurable because of her guilt (Jer 30:15) and Baruch too will suffer this "pain"
along with all flesh (45:3). Such "pain" accompanies Babylon's judgment and fallen

(√סבל, "to shoulder") those pains of judgment.[273] It is interesting that the verb נשא√, which is often used to describe a sacrificial act, appears in the first colon, but ומכאבינו, which is primarily connected to wrongdoing, appears in the second colon, thus balancing the entire bicolon with specificity about sacrifice and sin. The suffering described here is strongly connected to guilt. The Servant is not merely suffering justly or unjustly with his people, but is bearing the consequences of their wrongdoing in the same way that a sacrificial animal atones for the sins of the people.[274] Fretheim argues that in 52:13–53:12 it is not God's threat that intended to move people to repentance but God's sorrow.[275]

Westermann rightly points out that, like the book of Job, Isa 53:4 reflects the "orthodox" and "devout" attitude of the ancient world that suffering was considered to be "God's smiting and his wrath."[276] However, in the second bi-cola of v. 4, the parallelism changes to stress that the Servant's suffering is undeserved. The first bi-cola have a predictable *Qînāh* meter: A-B-C//B-C. Yet the second bi-cola are structured differently: A-B-C//C-D-C.

(A) yet we (B) accounted him	(A) ואנחנו (B) חשבנהו (C) נגוע
(C) stricken, (C) smitten	(C) מכה (D) אלהים (C) ומענה
(D) by God, (C) and afflicted	

While the last colon in the second half of v. 4 appears not to balance the previous colon, this may be explained by the isocolic principle which Gordon coined as *ballast variants*.[277] Gordon claims that the *ballast variant* is essentially a *filler*, but in this verse it functions as more than a mere filler.[278] Unlike elliptical structure, there occurs here more than the omission of a term,[279] but also the replacement of another.[280] In this

state (Jer 51:8). The book of Lamentations mourns over the destruction of "the city" (Lam 1:1–4) and Zion-Jerusalem's sufferinf for "the multitude of her transgressions" (1:5–9) and YHWH inflicting "sorrow" upon her "on the day of his fierce anger" (1:12) because Zion has rebelled (1:18).

273. The verb סבל√ has to do with bearing someone else's burden; see Oswalt, *Isaiah 40–66*, 386.

274. See Bernt Janowski, "Er trug unsere Sünden: Jesaja 53 und die Dramatik der Stellvertretung," *ZThK* 90 (1993): 1–24.

275. Fretheim, *Suffering of God*, 134.

276. Westermann, *Isaiah 40–66*, 262–63.

277. Cyrus H. Gordon asserts that "If a major word in the first stichos is not parallelled in the second, then one or more of the words in the second stichos tend to be longer than their counterparts in the first stichos" (*Ugaritic Textbook* [Rome: Pontifical Biblical Institute, 1965], 135).

278. Ibid., 138.

279. Kugel, *The Idea of Biblical Poetry*, 90.

particular case, the par of the "A" pronominal term ואנחנו and the "B" verbal term חשבנהו does not reappear in the second colon, but is replaced by two "C" terms (ומענה and מכה) and a "D" term (אלהים). These words in the second colon not only fill out a line of poetry, which would otherwise be too short,[281] but also place more emphasis on the undeserved afflictions that the Servant received.

The second bi-cola open with *wāw* adversative: "Surely he bore our infirmities...*but* we (ואנחנו),*" which contrasts with "he (הוא), accounted him stricken...by God..." The copula is consequently adversative and can be compared with אך. Moreover, the verbal phrase (חשבנהו, "we accounted him") builds on the logic of v. 3 (ולא חשבנהו, "we held no account of him"), thus clarifying in v. 4 that whatever sufferings he may have received, "we accounted him" deserving of them. This verb (חשב) does not imply the positive sense of "esteem" or appreciate" but the pejorative meaning "to assess as."[282] The repetition of this verb from the previous verse (53:3) signifies that "we did not (initially) esteem him at all but we finally esteemed him in a negative sense." The three passive participles stand in apposition to one another as the objects of חשבנהו, but since the verb has its own object suffix (חֲשַׁבְנֻהוּ), the passive participle נָגוּעַ, which governs the third colon, stands first in this series of passive participles as "a second accusative of product."[283] Since the word נגע√ sometimes applies to leprosy, some have argued that the use נָגוּעַ implies that the Servant too suffered from this illness.[284] The Qal passive participle נָגוּעַ bears the meaning of the verb נגע√. The noun נֶגַע can refer to an "assault,"[285] "blow," "beating,"[286] "wound" or can nuance the meaning of the verb in the extended sense to mean "disaster," "affliction" or "plague,"[287] or more specifically and prevalently describe "leprosy" or

280. Gordon, *Ugaritic Textbook*, 138.
281. See W. G. E. Watson, *Classical Hebrew Poetry: A Guide to Its Techniques* (2d ed.; JSOTSup 26; Sheffield: JSOT Press, 1986), 344–45.
282. Koole, *Isaiah 49–55*, 290–91.
283. *Gesenius' Hebrew Grammar* (ed. Emil Kautzsch; trans. A. E. Cowly; 2d Eng. ed.; Oxford: Clarendon, 1910), 371–72; Davidson, *Hebrew Syntax*, 109–10.
284. Duhm, *Jesaja*, 284–86, 365–67, 393–406; Buber, *Der Glaube der Propheten*, 227–28; Schoeps, *Aus frühchristlicher Zeit*, 107–10; Lindblom, *Die Ebed Jahwe-Orakel*, 44; Raymond J. Tournay, "Les chants du serviteur dans la seconde partie d'Isaïe," *RB* 59 (1952): 494 n. 5.
285. Noun נגע = "assault" (Deut 17:8; 21:5).
286. Noun נגע = "blow" (2 Sam 7:14; Ps 89:33).
287. Noun נגע = "plague" (Exod 11:1; Judg 20:34, 41; 1 Kgs 8:37, 38; 2 Chr 6:28, 29; Job 38:12; 39:11).

some other "disease."[288] However, the passive participle cannot imply "leprosy" because it is only used as a noun. Westermann argues that this cannot imply leprosy because this text portrays a typical sufferer.[289] Most of the time, the proper usage of the verb נגע√ is taken to mean "to touch" and oftentimes is used for purity reasons.[290] Other times, the extended meaning of נגע√ is "to reach" (a place or an amount),[291] or "to come," "draw near" or "approach," but cannot fit 53:4 since this intransitive usage does not apply to a passive voice.[292] The word also is used figuratively with the idea of touching with the intent to harm,[293] "to strike," "to beat"[294] or "to afflict."[295] Yet, the Qal passive participal נָגוּעַ within the parallelism of 53:4 (נָגוּעַ...מֻכֵּה וּמְעֻנֶּה) renders either "beaten" or "stricken" but probably not "afflicted" in the parallelism since that is the default meaning of the third passive participle (מְעֻנֶּה).

The next two passive participles establish the fourth colon (מֻכֵּה אֱלֹהִים וּמְעֻנֶּה). As already discussed, the *ballast variant* functions as more than merely a *filler* because the "C" correlatives (ומענה and מכה) and "D" terms (אלהים) replace the expected correlatives in order to

---

288. Noun נגע = "leprousy" (Lev 13:2, 3, 4, 5, 6, 9, 12, 13, 17, 20, 22, 25, 27, 29, 30, 31, 32, 42, 43, 44, 45, 46, 47, 49, 50, 51, 52, 53, 54, 55, 56, 57, 58, 59; 14:3, 32, 34, 35, 36, 37, 39, 40, 43, 44, 48, 54; 15; Deut 24:8; 2 Chr 26:20).

289. Westermann, *Isaiah 40–66*, 265.

290. נגע√ = "to touch" (Gen 20:6 [sexually]; Exod 4:24; 12:22; 19:12, 13; 29:37; 30:29; Lev 5:2, 3; 6:18, 20; 7:19, 21; 11:8, 24, 26, 27, 31, 36, 39; 12:4; 13:2; 15:5, 7, 10, 11, 12, 19, 21, 22, 23, 27; 22:4, 5, 6; Num 4:15; 16:26; 19:11, 13, 16, 18, 21, 22; 31:19; Deut 14:8; Josh 9:19; Judg 6:21; Ruth 2:9; 1 Sam 10:26; 2 Sam 14:10, 23:7; 1 Kgs 6:27; 19:5, 7; 2 Kgs 13:21; 1 Chr 16:22; 2 Chr 3:11, 12; Job 1:11; 2:5; 4:5; 5:19; 6:7; 19:21; Pss 104:32; 105:15; 144:5; Prov 6:29; Isa 6:7; 52:11; Jer 1:9; 4:10; 12:14; Lam 4:14, 15; Dan 8:5, 18; 10:10, 16, 18; Hos 4:2; Amos 9:5; Hag 2:12, 13; Zech 2:12).

291. נגע√ = "to reach (Gen 28:12; Lev 5:7; 1 Sam 14:9; 2 Chr 28:9; Job 20:6; Ps 32:6; Isa 8:8; 16:8; 30:4; Jer 4:18; 48:32; 51:9; Dan 12:12; Jonah 3:6; Mic 1:9; Zech 14:5).

292. נגע√ = "to come," "draw near" or "approach" (Ezra 3:1; Neh 7:72; Esth 2:12, 15; 4:3, 14; 5:2; 6:14; 8:17; 9:26; Pss 88:4; 91:10; 107:18; Eccl 12:1; Song 2:12; Isa 5:8) with Hiphil to "cast" or "bring down" (Isa 25:12; 26:5; Lam 2:2; Ezek 7:12; 13:14; Dan 9:21).

293. נגע√ = the metaphorical meaning of "harm" and stands parallel with "to do harm to someone" (Gen 26:11, 29; 1 Sam 6:9).

294. נגע√ = "to strike" or "beat" (Gen 32:26, 33; Josh 8:15; 1 Sam 6:9; 2 Sam 5:8; Job 1:19; Ezek 17:10). When God is subject, he "strikes" an individual with sickness (Gen 32:26 [Eng. 25], 33 [Eng. 32]; 1 Sam 6:9; Job 19:21). See G. Botterweck, "נגע *ng‛*," trans. J. T. Willis (*TDOT* 9:203–9).

295. נגע√ = "to afflict or plague" (Gen 12:17; 2 Kgs 15:15; Pss 53:4, 8; 73:5, 14). The word also means "to treat" (Eccl 8:14).

emphasize what "we" considered to be true about the Servant's suffer-ings. While few scholars contend that God is not the instrument of this "smiting,"[296] David J. A. Clines represents the others who think that "by God" goes with all three passive participles and that the phrase "our sins" was in fact the source of the Servant's suffering.[297] This second passive participle opens up the fourth colon and establishes "the con-struct state before a genitive of cause" or "a genitive of agency": מכה אלהים ("smitten by God").[298] From the perspective of theodicy, Kaiser argues that the plural "gods" are implied in אלהים, yet this is unlikely given the context.[299] Beuken follows Kutsch who asserts that YHWH will chasten (Hiphil נכה√) David's son, but only with "the rod of men" (2 Sam 7:14). Yet God strikes the Servant "wie ihn nur ein Gott führen kann."[300] This conclusion would be appealing for those who are searching to equate the Servant in Isa 53 with messianic promise but is highly unlikely since נכה is such a common term.[301]

The parallelism magnifies the speakers initial declaration that "we" esteem him stricken by the appositional phrase מכה אלהים of נגוע, which creates a type of staircase parallelism that more explicitly states that we considered him "smitten by God." The Pual participal מְעֻנֶּה then height-ens the description of the "afflicted," "humiliated," "oppressed" and "wretched"condition of the Servant. Many times, ancient texts assumed that God afflicted people for the purpose of punishment for sin (Isa 64:11 [NRSV 12]; Ps 90:15; Job), but here the Servant suffered not for his own sin but for the sin of those who had regarded him punished for his own iniquities. The intensity builds from our original presumption that the first person plural voice considered him "beaten," what is more "stricken of God," and even more: "afflicted." Yet, in reality, he bore the conse-quences of "our" wrongdoing. The Servant is not merely taking part in "our" suffering, but is bearing it like the scapegoat or any sacrificial animal bears the sins of the people. This was a new and revolutionary concept that a human sufferer would have the power to be a substitute and atone for human sin.[302]

---

296.   W. H. Schmidt, "אֱלֹהִים 'Elōhîm," trans. Mark Biddle (*TLOT* 1:114–26); Helmer Ringgren, "אֱלֹהִים 'Elōhîm," *TDOT* 1:50.

297.   Clines, *I, He, We, and They*, 17.

298.   Gesenius, *Gesenius' Hebrew Grammar*, 359; Davidson, *Hebrew Syntax*, 37; Waltke and O'Connor, *Biblical Hebrew Syntax*, 143, 616–17; Muilenburg, *Isaiah*, 5:622.

299.   Kaiser, *Der königliche Knecht*, 103–4.

300.   Kutsch, *Sein Leiden und Tod*, 22; Beuken, *Jesaja*, 2A:216–17.

301.   Koole, *Isaiah 49–55*, 292.

302.   Westermann, *Isaiah 40–66*, 263.

Isaiah 53:5 only builds on this notion of substitutionary suffering: "We assumed him, stricken, smitten by God, afflicted, *but* he was wounded for our transgressions, crushed for our iniquities; upon him was the punishment that made us whole, and by his bruises we are healed." The participle מְחֹלָל, which is pointed like a Poel instead of a Pual, has been translated in various ways. The verb חלל√ I signifies "to bore" or "pierce," but חלל√ III means "to desecrate" (Isa 43:28).[303] While the LXX reads the passive participle ἐτραυματίσθη, which the LXX uses in the nominal form in several contexts to imply piercing,[304] Aquila reads מחלל as "profaned" (βεβηλωμενός).[305] The Peshitta has מתקטל ("killed"), which is the meaning of חלל in Job 6:9. The parallel Pual participle, מְדֻכָּא ("crushed" or "shattered"), better upholds the lexeme "pierced" for מחלל in this particular context than does "profaned" (and is not surprising that Christian interpreters would equate the lexeme "pierced" [חלל√] with Christ and the cross).[306] Moreover, the term דכא√ can connote "humiliation of spirit" (57:15) which accentuates the dative מֵעֲוֹנֹתֵינוּ where the Servant's suffering had spiritual as well as physical significance.

The מִן in מִפְּשָׁעֵנוּ, indicating cause, insinuates that the Servant suffered "because of our transgressions."[307] This is why Watermann argues that מחלל מפשענו should be translated "wounded from our transgressions" and that "they were the cause of his wounds."[308] The word-pair פשע ("transgression," "rebellion," "guilt" or "punishment for transgression") and עון ("iniquity," "debt" or "guilt") rounds out the concept of sin in a fuller sense than חטא√. Motyer claims that חטא√ may mean "no more than a pity" (53:12). עון√, "sin as a moral defect" (53:5), is distressing but leaves room for argument that what cannot be helped cannot be blameworthy. פשע√ (53:5, 8, 12) implies "willful sin" that cannot be overlooked by God. Perhaps that is why YHWH claims that "I do not delight in the blood of bulls, or of lambs, or of goats" (1:11). Certainly,

---

303. BDB, 319–20.

304. Several Greek words are used to translate חלל: τραυματίας ("wounded," four times—22:2 [by the sword]; 34:3; 51:9 [for מחוללת תנין, "who *pierced* the dragon?"]; 66:16); παραλύω (once for חלל√ in 23:9); ἐμίαναν ("defiled [ceremonial impurity]," twice for חלל√ in 43:28; 47:6); βεβηλόω ("desecrate [in disregarding what is to be kept as holy]," three times for חלל√ in 48:11; 56:2, 6).

305. Aquila: και αυτος βεβηλωμενος απο αθεσμιων ημων συντετριμμενος απο των ανομιων ημων.

306. See also where these terms appear in parallelism elsewhere (Pss 89:11; 94:5 [where, in the parallelism, there is a triplet—עונה, חלל, דכא√]).

307. Davidson, *Hebrew Syntax*, 142.

308. L. Waterman, "The Martyred Servant Motif of Is. 53," *JBL* 56 (1937): 28.

"the punishment that made us whole was upon him." Although the noun מוּסַר really implies "discipline" or "instruction" in wisdom literature (containing the notion of the "rod of correction"), obviously the writer is using it in the sense of punishment in the same way that somebody in our modern culture using corporal punishment would say that he or she is "disciplining" their child for wrong doing, yet they really mean "punish." Whatever the design of these phrases indicates, the first person pronominal suffixes ("our") emphasizes the substitutionary character. Koole asserts that this refers to the sin and guilt of Israel, but, in my opinion, the ambiguity of the unnamed "we" or "our" leaves this category open in a way that all readers can claim that "he has borne our transgressions."[309]

The verbal phrase וּבַחֲבֻרָתוֹ נִרְפָּא־לָנוּ adds a different twist to this notion of substitution and has inspired several ideas of how we must interpret this phrase within the parallelism. Does the suffering of the Servant embody "our" sickness as well as punishment? Cazelles suggests that this affliction, which needs to be healed, is the disease of idolatry (עצב) that the nations aroused in Israel.[310] While he is correct that עצב means both "pain," "sorrow" and "idol" (48:5), עצב is never found in 52:13–53:12, the anti-idol passages only appear in chs. 40–48, and this idolatry is never called a sickness. What kind of "sickness" do these vereses then describe? Does the language of healing (רפא) and sickness (חלי) emphasize that "sin" is like a sickness that needs to be healed? The LXX specifically has translated חלי as "sin" (ἁμαρτίας)[311] and the Targum interprets the "bearing of sin" as intercession for the forgiveness of our transgressions and iniquities (חובנא and עויתנא). Certainly, in later verses, the Servant not only "bears" or "carries" the consequences of sin, but the actual guilt itself (עון, 53:11b; חטא, 53:12b). The term רפא can imply forgiveness or healing from sin since elsewhere it stands parallel to סלח ("to forgive," Ps 103:3). Volz maintains that the Servant is the agent or instrument of healing but does not perform the healing itself.[312] Whether or not he is correct, the emphasis is on the Servant's actions. The prepositions and their suffixcd pronouns עליו and לנו accentuate the contrast between "him" and "us," thus emphasizing the vicarious suffering of the Servant. The לנו does not mark the object of the preposition but designates a *lamed* of specification that governs the subject of the passive verb and, along with the instrumental ב (וּבַחֲבֻרָתוֹ), declares that

309.   Koole, *Isaiah 49–55*, 292–93.

310.   Cazelles, "Les Poèmes Du Serviteur."

311.   See I. L. Seeligmann, *The Septuagint Version of Isaiah: A Discussion of Its Problems* (Mededelingen en Verhandelingen 9; Leiden: Brill, 1948), 288.

312.   Volz, *Isaiah II*, 177–78.

"through his bruises *we* are healed."[313] Most poignant is that here the sin of humanity is described in terms of sickness (Ps 103:3) which only the work of the Servant can heal.[314] The Servant endured the punishment of others in order that he may obtain healing and redemption.

Verse 6 continues to describe this line of thinking through the speakers' confession of guilt ("All we like sheep have gone astray; we have all turned to our own way") and affirmation of the Servant's substitutionary act ("but YHWH has laid on him [בו] the iniquity of us all"). A major problem with connecting the Servant with Israel and "we" and "us" with the nations is that "we" and "us" in this context are compared with sheep, which regularly serve as a metaphor for Israel: "You have made us like sheep for slaughter, and have scattered us among the nations" (Ps 44:11). In this context, the flock, צאן, is differentiated from the Servant (53:6).[315] Therefore, this verse portrays the speakers as those who confess that they "prone to wander" (תעינו) from YHWH's ideal. Most lexicons assume תעה to be the root, but the resonant *yōdh* indicates an original √תעי (CCY). The Qal perfect form, תָּעִינוּ, does not show a true apocopation because the III ה form of the assumed root functions merely as an orthographic representation and hence the third radical returns to its original final semi-vowel *yōdh*.[316] The semantic range of תעה in Isaiah fluctuates in the Qal from the concrete meaning, "wandering," to figurative or ethical wandering: "to err" (29:24); "to wander about" (47:15); "go astray" (16:8; 35:8 [physically]); "to reel" (21:4; 28:7) or "to stagger" (28:7 [from intoxication]). In the Hiphil, תעה means to "lead astray" (3:12; 9:15; 19:13; 30:28; 63:17). In Isa 19:14, the Niphal infinitive construct (בְּהִתְעוֹת) speaks of one "staggering" from intoxication. Both the Qal (47:15) and Hiphil (30:28) stems of תעה also portray one wandering in helpless confusion. In the context of 53:6, where the writer compares the sinner with lost sheep, we can isolate the figurative usage, "to wander," with the understanding that, in this context, the word has ethical implications (Ps 119:176).[317]

---

313.   Waltke and O'Connor, *An Introduction to Biblical Hebrew Syntax*, 210.

314.   Knight, *A Commentary on the Book of Isaiah 40–55*, 180.

315.   See above notes on צאן and בלנו.

316.   The so-called "Lamed-Hê" or "Third Hê" verbs, which have ה as the third radical in the lexical form, are in fact CCW and CCY verbs, but verbs ending in *hê* with *mappîq* constitute a relatively uncommon CCG verbal root (e.g. גבה). See William Stanford LaSor, *Handbook of Biblical Hebrew* (Grand Rapids: Eerdmans, 1978), 113, 123.

317.   See John F. A. Sawyer, "תעה *tʿh*, 'to Wander About,'" trans. Mark Biddle (*TLOT* 3:1431–32).

Likewise, a similar metaphor (לדרכו פנינו) is employed as the parallel term of תעינו. With verbs of motion, such as פנה√, the ל marks the object of the allative motion, "each has turned *to* his own way."[318] The phrase לדרכו פנינו is then the antithesis of דרך יהוה (Gen 18:9; Judg 2:22; Prov 10:29; Isa 40:3; Jer 5:4, 5). This is not speaking of the way from Babylon or return from exile (Isa 42:16; 52:11–12) that is announced before this pericope, but represents the moral failure to walk in the way that has been prescribed through Torah. The speakers have failed to allow YHWH to guide them in the right way and the consequences have been laid on the Servant: ויהוה הפגיע בו את עון כלנו ("but YHWH has caused the iniquity of us all to fall upon him"). Conceivably, the Servant suffered a martyr's death, but 53:6b says that "YHWH has laid on him the iniquity of us all," which describes substitution that transcends mere martyrdom.

Isaiah 53:7 picks up the metaphor of the sheep (53:6a) but the lamb is now slaughtered as a sacrificial lamb. Does the narrative compare the Servant with sheep because they possess a submissive, non-defensive nature, or does this animal figuratively describe his sacrificial nature? The Niphal verb נַעֲנָה is not always used in the passive voice but also has the reflexive meaning "humble oneself" (Exod 10:3). We can also understand why some would construe the Servant as the prophet since Jeremiah refers to himself (Jer 11:19) in a similar fashion, though uses different vocabulary (ואני ככבש אלוף יובל לטבוח). Yet no one can discount that sheep are the primary animals of sacrifice in the Old Testament. Moreover, שה ("lamb") is regularly (e.g. 43:23; 66:3) connected with cultic laws, while רחל ("sheep") has no such application in the Old Testament. Motyer says that, because the parallelism uses one term that does not have to do with cultic ceremony (רחל), then the whole bi-cola must not compare the Servant's death with a Passover lamb but imply that he goes submissively to what awaits him.[319] One could argue this point in the opposite direction, since the term שה is used regularly in the context of the cultic setting and adds a positive element to the parallelism rather than allowing רחל to remove it. Both elements in the parallelism will never be univocal because their equivocal or analogical nature helps create the poetic artistry. Therefore, we conceivably see a double image in 53:7: one of a sacrificial lamb going tolerantly to slaughter, even if it suspects its destiny, and another of a sheep who does not resist even when it faces the hair-pulling shears. Yet, under both circumstances, the lamb does not demur the treatment.

318.   Waltke and O'Connor, *An Introduction to Biblical Hebrew Syntax*, 205.
319.   Motyer, *The Prophecy of Isaiah*, 433.

Verse 8 underscores that the Servant's suffering was caused by oppression and judgment. In the expression מעצר וממשפט, the preposition מן can either be a separative, causal or privative.[320] A causal would suggest that he was taken away because of these things, a separative would imply that he was taken from oppression and judgment, and a privative would insinuate that he was refused of ("from," "apart from" or "without") these things. The separative and privative can be ruled out because such isolation "from" oppression and judgment would not provide a catalyst for suffering. The NRSV and JPS treat the second מן as a genitive ("a perversion *of* justice") but the conjunctive *wāw* (וממשפט) would exclude this possibility. Therefore, the causal clause seems to indicate that he suffered "because of" oppression and judgment. While the term משפט can mean justice or judgment, the servant was judged unto death and yet no justice protected him. When the synonymous terms (משפט, עצר) are used, they cannot carry the positive meaning of justice but must speak of "judgment." Payne and others might be correct that √לקח with ממשפט creates a set formula for "due process of law."[321] No matter which way one looks at this, the Servant died a violent death and this death wielded its final blow.

The Second bi-cola of 53:8 strongly connect this oppression and judgment with death ("cut off from the land of the living") and substitution ("stricken for the transgression of my people"). Delitzsch treats כי as an emphatic "adverbial accusative" ("as for"; NRSV = "for") but JPS, NAS and RSV treat it as a causal "that" or "because."[322] However one renders כי, the narrator relates the oppression and judgment that the Servant suffered with death. Soggin argues that the form of this text argues against the interpretation that the Servant was put to death, and the less prevalent view that he rose from the dead. He argues that נגזר מן always describes a hopeless situation using hyperbole in the individual laments by stating that one has fallen into the hands of death, rather than a real instance of death. In order to describe literal death, the writers would use similar expression נכרת מן instead of נגזר מן. Soggin's argument rests on fragile ground because the Niphal of √גזר appears only five times in the Old Testament, which does not allow enough attestations of this lexeme to establish a pattern, and of these five times, Lam 3:54 is the only

320. Ronald Williams, *Hebrew Syntax* (Toronto: University of Toronto Press, 1988), 125, 319, 321; Waltke and O'Connor, *An Introduction to Biblical Hebrew Syntax*, 212–13.

321. David F. Payne, "The Servant of the Lord: Language and Interpretation," *EvQ* 42, no. 3 (1971): 135; Blocher, *The Songs of the Servant*, 64; Motyer, *The Prophecy of Isaiah*, 434.

322. Delitzsch, *Isaiah*, 1:325.

occurrence that explicitly uses hyperbole.[323] Whybray argues that the speakers imply by the phrase נגזר מארץ חיים ("nearness to death), "he was 'as good as dead.'"[324] However, from the manner in which ארץ חיים contrasts life and death elsewhere in the Old Testament (Pss 28:1; 116:9; 142:5, 6; Isa 38:11; Jer 11:19), we can be confident that the Servant here died and "was separated from the land of the living." The parallel phrase reinforces the two bi-cola in v. 8 suggesting that he actually received the judicial consequences of "my people." Hanson suggests that despite the yearly sacrifices and the prophets' drama of proclaiming a message of repentance and impending judgment, the people still go into exile and the problem of sin still persists.[325] Therefore, the causal מן (מפשע עמי) indicates that the Servant died "because of the rebellion of my people."[326]

Isaiah 53:9 makes further mention of the Servant's death. Some claim that the phrase ויתן...קברו[327] describes the designated place where the Servant's oppressors wanted to bury him, but because they did not really kill him, they did not carry out this plan.[328] However, twice in Ezekiel, קבר appears in conjunction with נתן to speak of people who have clearly died as in this context (Ezek 32:23; 39:11). Having already equated the Servant's death with judgment (53:8), 53:9 uses the substantive רָשָׁע, which classes the Servant with wicked people (רשע). If the parallel phrase ואת־עשיר במתיו ("and his tomb with the rich...") juxtaposes רשע with עשיר, then what does this say about the Servant? It seems that the analogous terms רשע and עשיר underscore the wicked traits of the rich against whom the prophets uttered judgment because they exploited and oppressed the poor. This verse appears to be saying that the Servant was given a grave with criminals and oppressors.[329]

323.   J. Alberto Soggin, "Tod und Auferstehung des leidenden Gottesknechtes: Jes. 53:8–13," *ZAW* 87, no. 3 (1975): 346–55. See also on this point, Oswalt, *Isaiah 40–66*, 396.

324.   Whybray, *Isaiah 40–66*, 177.

325.   Hanson, *Isaiah 40–66*, 157.

326.   Williams, *Hebrew Syntax*, 125, 319, 321; Waltke and O'Connor, *An Introduction to Biblical Hebrew Syntax*, 212–13; Motyer, *The Prophecy of Isaiah*, 435.

327.   Elliger (*Deuterojesaja*, 7) wishes to emend וַיִּתֵּן to Pual וַיֻּתַּן, but Oswalt (*Isaiah 40–66*, 390) follows 1QIsaᵃ, which has ויתנו ("they have assigned" = it was assigned).

328.   Yehezkel Kaufmann, *The Babylonian Captivity and Deutero-Isaiah* (New York: Union of American Hebrew Congregations, 1970), 169; Whybray, *Isaiah 40–66*, 104.

329.   Motyer (*The Prophecy of Isaiah*, 435) contends that עשיר must speak here as a "rich man" and not the collective rich class of persons because עשיר only functions as a collective when it is parallel to another singular representing a different class of person (e.g. the poor). Therefore, he claims that this speaks of a particular

Yet the last bi-cola of 53:9 declares his innocence in order to assert that the Servant did not deserve this punishment: "They made his grave with the wicked and his tomb with the rich, *even though* (עַל)[330] he had done no violence, and there was no deceit in his mouth" (NRSV). The verb חמס implies actively planned hostility (Prov 10:6, 11), ill treatment (Gen 16:5) and even violence performed with weapons against people (Gen 49:5) including weapons used in war (Joel 3:19 [NRSV 4:19]). "Even though" the Servant was judicially condemned, he did no "violence" (חמס). Some scholars argue that this speaks of the sinlessness. Certainly, the New Testament makes the claim that in order to make expiation for others one would have to be sinless (2 Cor 5:21), but Mowinckel asserts that in Jewish thought this cannot mean that he was sinless because no human being is.[331] Although a great deal could be said about the translation techniques applied to the Greek text of Isaiah,[332] using a standard interpretational method to classify various Hebrew words as "lawlessness," the LXX here translates חמס as ἀνομίαν to underscore that "the Servant did nothing unlawful" or did not break Torah.[333] It is safe to say that v. 9 declares his innocence despite that fact that he died the death of a criminal.

---

rich man. This interpretation no doubt supports the notion that this text "prophesies" about Joseph of Arimathea. While North and Wade (among others) object to equating עשיר with the burial of Jesus, Delitzsch reasons that without "the fulfilment it would be impossible to understand verse 9 at all"; see North, *The Second Isaiah*, 231; Wade, *The Book of the Prophet Isaiah*; Delitzsch, *Isaiah*, 1:327. Remember how Irenaeus argued that if it had not been for the fulfillments we would not have known the prophecies (*Ante-Nicene Fathers: Translations of the Writings of the Fathers Down to AD. 325*. Vol. 1, *Against Heresies* (ed. Alexander Roberts and James Donaldson; Grand Rapids: Eerdmans, 1993), 496.

330.   Note, in this context, עַל = "even though" (cf. Job 10:7). See Davidson, *Hebrew Syntax*, 142.

331.   Mowinckel, *He That Cometh*. Cf. also, Job 4:17–21; 15:14–15; 25:4–6.

332.   R. R. Ottley, trans. and ed., *The Book of Isaiah According to the Septuagint (Codex Alexandrinus)* (2d ed.; Cambridge: Cambridge University Press, 1909); Seeligmann, *The Septuagint Version of Isaiah*; Joseph J. Ziegler, ed., *Septuaginta: Vetus Testamentum Graecum* (Academiae Litterarum Göttingensis Editum 14: Isaias. 2d ed.; Göttingen: Vandenhoeck & Ruprecht, 1967), 7–115; Sidney Jellicoe, *The Septuagint and Modern Study* (Oxford: Clarendon, 1968), 67, 155, 299–300, 310; Hofius, "Zur Septuaginta-Übersetzung von 52:13b."

333.   Note that LXX uses ἀνομίαν also to translate other words that may describe the act of breaking Torah: סָרָה (1:5); מַעֲלָל (3:8); מִשְׁפָּח (5:7); חַטָּאָה (5:18); חַטָּאת (58:1); עָאוֶן (6:7; 27:9; 53:5; 64:6); רִשְׁעָה (9:18); † (21:4); פֶּשַׁע (53:12); פֶּשַׁע (24:20; 43:25, 26; 44:22; 50:1; 53:5, 8; 59:12 [2×]); בֶּצַע (33:15); חָמָס (53:9); שֶׁקֶר (59:3); אָוֶן (59:4, 6).

Isaiah 53:10–11 repeats the already mentioned sacrificial motifs (sprinkling, bearing sin, guilt offering, penal substitution, peace with God and mediation). The disjunctive *wāw* distinguishes between what humans did to the Servant and "YHWH's will to crush him" in order to legitimize his atoning work as a divinely inspired act. Verse 10 repeats the words דכא and חלי (vv. 4–5), expressing that his suffering is not due to his own guilt but to God's will. Already, YHWH has claimed that he "does not delight in the blood of bulls, or of lambs, or of goats" (1:11). While some read this verb as חלל,[334] or even less likely חלא,[335] the majority of evidence supports the difficult reading הֶחֱלִי. The word דכא recalls v. 5. Several have argued along the lines of the LXX (which has translated דכא as καθαρίσαι, "to purify") and the Targum (which uses the word pair למצרף ולדכאה, "to refine[336] and to purify") that דכא is being used to speak of spiritual purification.[337] Yet the poet here attributes the Servant's very act of suffering to the will of YHWH. Perhaps the same writer claimed that "YHWH was pleased to make great his Torah" (42:21) and that Cyrus fulfills the pleasure of YHWH to rebuild

---

334.　1QIsaᵃ reads ויחללהו instead of הֶחֱלִי, which Kutscher ascribes to the *šōreš* חלל II, which means "to pierce" or "wound mortally," and could have influenced Symmacus (ἐν τῷ τραυματίσμῳ); see Kutscher, *The Language and Linguistic Background of the Isaiah Scroll (1QIsaᵃ)*, 236; Harald Hegermann, *Jesaja 53 in Hexapla, Targum und Peschitta* (Gütersloh: C. Bertelsmann, 1954). Similarly, Dahood argues for a Hiphil infinitive construct with a third person suffix (החליו) that is subordinate to חפץ: "he desired to pierce him"; see Mitchell Dahood, "Isaiah 53:8–12 and Massoretic Misconstructions," *Bib* 63 (1982): 568–69. Cf. also Julian Morgenstern, "The Message of Deutero-Isaiah in Its Sequential Unfolding," *HUCA* 32 (1961): 318.

335.　Motyer (*The Prophecy of Isaiah*, 439) and others claim that הֶחֱלִי does not derive from √חלה but √חלא, and that "this final aleph can easily drop away as in *heḥeṭî* for *heḥeṭî'*... So here we have *heḥelî* for *heḥelî'*..." See Delitzsch, *Isaiah*, 1:330; North, *The Second Isaiah*, 231; Thomas, "Isaiah LIII," 125; GK 74k, 75ii: While this does not change the meaning of the construction in this case √חלה and √חלא are translated by the same lexemes. However, this argument is untenable, because unlike החליא where the quiescent aleph closes the final syllable, like the previously mentioned תעה, the resonant *yōdh* in √חלה indicates an original √חליה (CCY). Here, the final *yōdh* does double duty, both marking a long "i" class vowel and providing a final radical to the end of the word. This is seen in the Hiphil הֶחֱלִי, which does not show a true apocopation but the so-called "final *hê*" in the lexical form functions merely as an orthographic representation. In fact, it constitutes a CCY verb that returns to its original, final semi-vowel *yōdh*. This resonant *yōdh* does not appear in a III א form. See LaSor, *Handbook of Biblical Hebrew*, 113, 123.

336.　The Targum seems to use √דכא in this way.

337.　Duhm, *Jesaja*, 403; Driver, "Isaiah 52:13–53:12," 96; Coppens, *Le messianisme et sa relève prophétique*, 64.

Jerusalem (44:28), but here "YHWH was pleased (חפץ√) to crush him, he made him sick" (53:10), though this phrase is quite awkward.[338]

The conditional marker אם seems to mark the condition of the guilt offering and to govern the clause that follows: "if" or "when you make his life an offering for sin, he shall see his offspring."[339] The form תשים has yielded several options. Some regard the phrase תשים אשם to be a late interpolation[340] and others delete only אשם from their textual reconstruction.[341] Some take תשים as a passive.[342] Wade emended תָּשִׂים to read as a third masculine singular יָשִׂים, making the Servant the subject (as do Syr., Vulg., Lut., RSV, NASV, CBAT, REB, JPSV), "if" or "when he makes

338. Several scholars attempt to correct the awkwardness of this phrase, among them Wade, who emends הֶחֱלִי to read בָּחֳלִי in order to create a bridge from דֻּכָּאוֹ (Wade, *The Book of the Prophet Isaiah*, 233). In an earlier work, Elliger took הֶחֱלִי to be a noun (Elliger, *Deuterojesaja*, 7; Begrich, *Studien zu Deuterojesaja*, 64; Westermann, *Isaiah 40–66*, 254; Kaufmann, *The Babylonian Captivity and Deutero-Isaiah*, 160; Barthélemy, *Critique textuelle de l'Ancien Testament*, 402), but he later changed his mind regarding this option and took it as a Hiphil perfect. See North, *The Second Isaiah*, 331; Karl Elliger, "Jes. 53:10: Alte Crux—Neuer Vorschlag," *Mitteilungen Des Instituts für Orientforschung* 15 (1969): 228–30; Kaiser, *Der königliche Knecht*, 86; Kutsch, *Sein Leiden und Tod*, 13. Grelot (*Les poèmes du serviteur: De la lecture critique a l'hermeneutique*, 60) asserts an imperfect here. Some emend הֶחֱלִי אם to read as "he revived him" or "healed him"; cf. Begrich, *Studien zu Deuterojesaja*, 64; Driver, "Isaiah 52:13–53:12," 96–97; Coppens, *Le messianisme et sa relève prophétique*, 64; Westermann, *Isaiah 40–66*, 267.

339. Mitchell Dahood, "Textual Problems in Isaiah," *CBQ* 22 (1960): 400–409; Dahood, "Isaiah 53:8–12 and Massoretic Misconstructions"; James R. Battenfield, "Isaiah 53:10: Taking an 'If' Out of the Sacrifice of the Servant," *VT* 32 (1982): 485; I. Sonne, "Isaiah 53:10–12," *JBL* 78 (1959): 335–42. Others take this as a concessive marker, "though YHWH makes his life a guilt offering, he shall…" Cf. V. van der Leeuw, *De Ebed Jahweh-profetieen* (Assen: Van Gorcum, 1956), 251; Thomas, "Isaiah LIII," 125.

340. Marti, *Das Buch Jesaja*, 351; Hans Peter Müller, "Ein Vorschlag zu Jes 53:10f," *ZAW* 81, no. 3 (1969): 377–80.

341. Duhm, *Jesaja*, 403; Sonne, "Isaiah 53:10–12," 363–65; H. L. Ginsburg, "The Arm of YHWH in Isaiah 51–63 and the Text of Isa 53:10–11," *JBL* 77 (1958): 156.

342. Rashi and several modern scholars follow the Peshitta, vocalized as תֻּשַׂם as proposed by *BHS* (see Godfrey R. Driver, "Linguistic and Textual Problems: Isa 40–66," *JTS* 36 [1935]: 403; Thomas, "Isaiah LIII," 125). Regarding this reading in light of 4QIsa^d, see also H. Haag, *Der Gottesknecht bei Deuterojesaja* (EdF 233; Darmstadt: Wisenschaftliche, 1985), 14; Barthélemy, *Critique textuelle de l'Ancien Testament*, 402–3; Islwyn Blythin, "A Consideration of Difficulties in the Hebrew Text of Isaiah 53:11," *BT* 17 (1966): 27–31; I. L. Seeligmann, "Deixai Autō Phōs," *Tarbiz* 27 (1957): 127–41. Dahood ("Phoenician Elements in Isaiah 52:13–53:12," 71) has pointed this as a passive perfect (שָׂם).

himself (soul) an offering for sin." Yet there is no textual evidence for such grounds.[343] If one follows the MT, since there is no sufformative, the *tāw* preformative clearly establishes תָּשִׂים as either a third feminine singular or a second masculine singular leaving different alternatives. Since נַפְשׁוֹ is a feminine it could serve as the subject of תָּשִׂים, "if" or "when his soul makes an offering for sin," but נַפְשׁוֹ seems to sit too far removed from the verb to be its subject. The other alternative would read "when" or "if *you* make his life an offering for sin" (LXX, ASV, NRSV, KJV, NKJV, JPS). Following this reading, either Israel or the nations become the subject of the sentence. Most people treat תָּשִׂים as a Qal,[344] but nothing rules out a Hiphil since both *binyānîm* of שׂים√ are completely indistinguishable, the *hireq yōdh* middle vowel also being the long "i" class vowel marker of the Hiphil. No matter what the stem, however, the verb שׂים√ is unusual to use in conjunction with sacrifice. Gipsen recounts occasions where the verb is used in conjunction with placing offerings somewhere (e.g. placing the bread and cakes in the palms of Aaron [Exod 29:24], placing frankincense on the offering [Lev 2:15], placing sacrificial fruit in a basket [Deut 26:2]) but is not used for אָשָׁם ("guilt offering").[345] Beuken posits that the text does not refer to an offering that the Servant has made, but rather YHWH's acceptance of his submission.[346] Beuken's proposal disregards how the sacerdotal significance of the term אָשָׁם ("guilt offering") is consistent with the expiatory language that is replete throughout the context of Isa 52:13–53:12. The word אָשָׁם ("guilt offering") is a sacrificial term that is used to describe an offering that compensates for an offense when someone's right of ownership has been violated (1 Sam 6:3–4).[347] Von Rad argues that the word אָשָׁם, "whose function is expiation," may have to do with "an offense against the Godhead."[348] The Servant compensates for Israel's guilt toward YHWH in order to place the people in right relationship with him. While the text is ambiguous about who establishes the guilt offering (תָּשִׂים), one thing is clear: "his soul" (נַפְשׁוֹ) becomes the very offering itself.

The protasis then claims that "he shall see his offspring, and shall prolong his days" (NRSV). Lindblom argues that even though the Servant

343.   Wade, *The Book of the Prophet Isaiah*, 343.

344.   Oswalt, *Isaiah 40–66*, 401.

345.   W. H. Gipsen, "Distinctions Between Clean and Unclean," *OtSt* 5 (1948): 195–96.

346.   Beuken, *Jesaja*, 2A:228–29.

347.   Smith, *The Book of Isaiah*, 2:360, 363, 364, 384; Webb, *The Message of Isaiah*, 207–8; Koole, *Isaiah 49–55*, 256.

348.   Von Rad, *Old Testament Theology*, 1:259.

has died, he is able to see the future of his children in the same way that Rachel, who is dead, weeps for her children.[349] Sonne corrects יִרְאָה to read as a Hiphil and זְרַע to read as זרעו, thus, "he will reveal him his arm," but this view is not attested elsewhere and is implausible.[350] Koole argues that these offspring are all the children of the new Zion, while Wilshire also views the Servant as the city of Zion-Jerusalem but asserts that the Servant is still "inextricably bound up with her" (55:1–5). Some argue that 53:10 speaks of resurrection since the Servant could not "see his offspring," and thus prefer to read "prolong his days."[351] Oswalt expresses that "his life will not be futile after all."[352] Koole notes that חפץ speaks of both the Servant's and Cyrus' activity, but while Cyrus is responsible for restoration in a political sense, the Servant brings it in a spiritual sense (44:28; 46:10; 48:14; 53:10).[353] While Cyrus saves Judah from the Babylonian oppression, the Servant saves them from the debt of sin.

Verse 11 continues to show benefits of the Servant's atoning work: "Out of his labor, he shall see; he shall find satisfaction through his knowledge. The righteous one, my servant, shall make many righteous, and he shall bear their iniquities." The preposition מן has a wide range of meanings:[354] it can either function as a separative ("from"),[355] a partitive ("of" or "from"),[356] a genitive ("of"),[357] a temporal ("after the travail of his life")[358] or even ironically a causal ("because").[359] Whatever the

349. Lindblom, *Die Ebed Jahwe*, 45.

350. Sonne, "Isaiah 53:10–12," 335–42. Note that Sonne does not vowel-point the text.

351. Calvin, *Commentary on the Book of the Prophet Isaiah*, 4:125; Young, *Isaiah*, 3:355–56; Homerski, "Cierpacy Wybawca i Oredownik"; Holladay, *Isaiah: Scroll of a Prophetic Heritage*, 155–56; Gressmann, *Der Ursprung der israelitisch-judischen Eschatologie*, 302–6, among others.

352. Oswalt, *Isaiah 40–66*, 403.

353. Koole, *Isaiah 49–55*, 327.

354. For all of these functions of מן, see Williams, *Hebrew Syntax*, 125, 319, 321; Waltke and O'Connor, *An Introduction to Biblical Hebrew Syntax*, 212–13.

355. Gerleman (*Studien zur alttestamentlichen Theologie*) argues for a separative by claiming that "it decreases the importance of his misery" ("*er sieht von seinem Elend ab*"), but this thought defies the entire purpose of the passage.

356. Slotki, *Isaiah*, 264.This view does not fit the context. See Koole, *Isaiah 49–55*, 329.

357. Oswalt (*Isaiah 40–66*, 403) calls this an objective genitive. See also Slotki, *Isaiah*, 264.

358. Skinner, *Isaiah Chapters XL–LXVI*, 132; König, *Das Buch Jesaja*, 441; Volz, *Isaiah II*, 171; Muilenburg, *Isaiah*, 5:629–30; North, *The Second Isaiah*, 233; Whybray, *Isaiah 40–66*, 180; Beuken, *Jesaja*, 2A:231; Hans Walter Wolff, *Jesaja*

variation of מָן, the preposition here names the "labor of his soul" as the source of all which follows in this bicola. The noun עָמָל may signify "labor," "work" or "toil,"[360] but secondarily "trouble," "hardship" or "misery."[361] Often paired with אָוֶן ("iniquity"), עָמָל sometimes suggests "mischief" or "wrongdoing," indicating the pejorative implications.[362] The word עָמָל has a component of suffering, and lexicographers even render it as "suffering" or "oppression." The word cannot mean "travail" as in childbearing (AV) because never on any occasion is this term used in the Old Testament in the context of child birthing.[363] Following 53:10, v. 11 states that from this labor of his very soul, the Servant "shall see…"

Textual difficulties in Isa 53:11 have triggered the reflexes of several textual traditions in order to explain the syntax surrounding יִרְאָה, which many think lacks an object, possibly אוֹר ("he shall see light").[364] While

---

53 im Urchristentum (Berlin: Evangelische, 1952), 25; Blythin, "A Consideration of Difficulties in the Hebrew Text of Isaiah 53:11"; Kutsch, *Sein Leiden und Tod*, 35; Preuss, *Deuterojesaja*, 98.

359.   The following argue that מָן functions as a causal: Friedländer, *The Commentary of Ibn Ezra on Isaiah*, 3:246–47; Young, *Isaiah*, 3:356; Coppens, *Le messianisme et sa relève prophétique*, 64; McKenzie, *Second Isaiah*, 130; Jean Koenig, *L'herméneutique analogique du Judaïsme antique d'après les témoins textuels d'Isaïe* (VTSup 33; Leiden: Brill, 1982), 282; Webb, *The Message of Isaiah*, 213.

360.   עָמָל = "labor" or "work" or "toil" (Deut 26:7; Judg 5:26; 107:12; 140:10; Eccl 1:3; 2:10, 11, 18, 19, 20, 22, 24; 3:9, 13; 4:4, 6, 9; 5:14, 17, 18; 6:7; 8:15; 9:9; 10:15; Jer 20:18). Note that עמל also = "possessions" as the product of labor (Ps 105:44).

361.   עָמָל = "trouble" or "hardship" or "misery" (Gen 41:51; Num 23:21; Job 3:10, 20; 4:8; 5:6, 7; 7:3; 10:14; 11:16; 16:2; 20:22; 25:18; 55:1; 73:5, 16; 90:10; 94:20; Prov 31:7; Hab 1:3).

362.   עָמָל = "mischief," "wrongdoing" (Job 15:35; Pss 7:15, 17; 10:7; Prov 24:2; Isa 59:4; Hab 1:13).

363.   עָמָל = "suffering" (Judg 10:16) or "oppression" (Isa 10:1).

364.   JPS renders "he shall see it (the arm of the Lord)." We can automatically reject Coppens' emendations, יִרְאָה יִשְׂבָּע (*Le messianisme et sa relève prophétique*, 118), or that of Schwarz, יִרְאָה יֵשַׁע יִשְׂבָּע ("'…sieht er…wird er satt': Eine Emendation [Jes 53:11]," *ZAW* 84, no. 3 (1972): 356–58), because these lack textual evidence. However, 4QIsa^a, 4QIsa^b and 4QIsa^d and LXX add אוֹר = φῶς (NAN, NIV, NRSV), thus providing an object for יִרְאָה (see Barthélemy, *Critique textuelle de l'Ancien Testament*, 403–5). It is difficult to know whether these textual traditions have added אוֹר after the verb יִרְאָה due to dittography because of similarities in letters in both words (*BHS*: ראה = רוה) or for interpretational reasons. For example, Koole suggests that perhaps Isa 50:10 could have influenced the addition of אוֹר (Koole, *Isaiah 49–55*, 324, 329; cf. also Wade, *The Book of the Prophet Isaiah*, 344; Volz, *Isaiah II*, 170; Muilenburg, *Isaiah*, 5:629; Westermann, *Isaiah 40–66*, 257–58; Young, *Isaiah*, 3:353; Beuken, *Jesaja*, 2A:230; Koole, *Isaiah 49–55*, 329).

we choose to uphold the MT on the basis that each textual tradition has an integrity of its own, it is fascinating that "light" becomes the object of the Servant's seeing. In two places, רָאָה and אוֹר appear together in Isaiah; a similarity that is most fascinating: "the people who walked in darkness have *seen* a great *light*" (9:1). The addition of אוֹר in 53:11 may have been an interpretive move either to situate the Servant within messianic circumstance or to connect the Servant with Israel who anticipates the light that is shed on the darkness of exile.[365] Moreover, יִשְׂבָּע abruptly follows יִרְאֶה asyndetically, "'he shall see, he shall be satisfied'...for the satisfaction does not come until after the enjoyment of the sight."[366] The verb √שבע seems to be modified by what appears to be either "an accusative, or by an adjunct with בּ" (Pss 65:5; 88:4; Lam 3:30).[367]

This perception of sight is sharpened by his very knowledge (בדעתו) and its relationship to יראה ישבע.[368] Yet the meaning of בְּדַעְתּוֹ and syntax of the verse has generated many opinions. While בְּעַבְדָתוֹ has most often been taken as an infinitive construct, some construe דעת as a noun.[369] Some aim to correct בְּדַעְתּוֹ to read as בְּרָעָתוֹ ("with his calamity")[370] or בַּעֲבֹדתוֹ ("with his Servants").[371] JPS has "devotion." Clearly,

365. See also רָאִיתִי אוֹר in 44:16.
366. Cf. Gesenius, *Gesenius' Hebrew Grammar*, 386. This view is followed by Skinner, *Isaiah Chapters XL–LXVI*, 132–33; Koole, *Isaiah 49–55*, 330. Note also that in order to make sense of יִרְאֶה יִשְׂבָּע with what follows, 1QIsaᵃ adds a conjunctive *wāw*, reading ובדעתו instead of בדעתו. Perhaps this is based on the *Vorlage* of LXX, the same tradition upon which the Peshitta may also be based and about which Koole says "the words thus connected are followed by a new part of the sentence which starts with a copula" (cf. Koole, *Isaiah 49–55*, 330; Hegermann, *Jesaja 53*, 43, 63–64).
367. Koole, *Isaiah 49–55*, 330.
368. We can automatically rule out the position of Dahood, who asserts that ידע III has the meaning "to sweat" (Prov 10:9; 14:33), thereby rendering the colon "he was soaked with his sweat" ("Phoenician Elements," 72) because this idea is too foreign to the parallelism. Williamson's argument ("Daʿat in Isaiah LIII,11," 118–22) that דעת means "rest" and Hans Peter Müller's translation "*sein Gut*" ("his property") ("Ein Vorschlag zu Jes 53:10f," 377–80) can also be rejected sunce these solutions really offer no substantial proof.
369. Skinner, *Isaiah Chapters XL–LXVI*, 133; Barr, *Comparative Philology and the Text of the Old Testament*, 19–21; W. Schottroff, "ידע *ydʿ* to Perceive, Know," trans. Mark Biddle (*TLOT* 2:509); G. Botterweck, "דעת *daʿat*," trans. J. T. Willis (*TDOT* 5:453).
370. Kissane, *The Book of Isaiah*, 2:190; Steinmann, *Le livre de la consolation d'Israël*, 170. Yet this vowel pointing is not found in the Old Testament because, in the near (pretonic) open syllable, the vowel has lengthen to a *qāmeṣ* and is pointed בְּרָעָתוֹ (e.g. Prov 14:32; Eccl 7:15; Obad 1:13). Note, from another perspective, the

the philology behind יָדַע and דַּעַת in the history of Hebrew grammar is very important. D. Winton Thomas argues that בְּדַעְתּוֹ is from an original first *wāw* (ודע√) root, which means "obedient," "submissive" and, consequently, "brought low" or "humbled." This in its noun form means humiliation but does not derive from a first *yōdh* root (ידע√).[372] On these very grounds, Schottroff and others argue that the first *wāw* verbal root יָדַע implies "conquered" or "humiliated" or "humiliation."[373] Others argue that "humiliation" or "obedience" belong to the meaning of ידע√.[375] Bo Reicke asserts that a first *wāw* is not necessary brcause the idea of obedience is inherent in the first *yōdh* root ידע√.[374] Theodore H. Robinson, followed by Oswalt, do not worry about philology but contend that בְּדַעְתּוֹ does not belong to the third colon but to the second one: "he shall be satisfied by his knowledge." This interpretation would parallel the first colon, "he will see..." and having provided atonement, the Servant is now satisfied. Joseph Jensen suggests that, by using the term "knowledge" (דַּעַת), "the author is here adapting to the Servant some of the things said of the Davidic King in 11:1–9."[376] However, this term is too common to link with another context.

---

spirantizing of *tāw* removes the sharpend syllable, thus placing the *'ayin* in an open unaccented syllable which now must take a long vowel (בְּרָעָתוֹ) but with בְּדַעְתּוֹ there is a reduced vowel under the *'ayin* to close the syllable before the *tāw*, which takes the *dāgēsh*.

371. Elliger, *Deuterojesaja*.

372. Thomas, "Isaiah LIII," 120, 126. See also L. C. Allen ("Isaiah LIII,11 and Its Echoes," *Vox Evangelica* 1 [1962]: 24–28) and Schottroff ("ידע *yd'* to Perceive, Know," 2:509) who support this view.

373. Theodore H. Robinson, "Notes on the Text and Interpretation of Isaiah 53:3, 11," *ExpTim* 72 (1959): 383; Thomas, "Isaiah LIII," 120, 126; Allen, "Isaiah LIII,11 and Its Echoes"; Blythin, "A Consideration of Difficulties in the Hebrew Text of Isaiah 53:11"; Driver, "Isaiah 52:13–53:12," 101; Whybray, *Isaiah 40–66*, 180; Clines, *I, He, We, and They*, 21; Schottroff, "ידע *yd'* to Perceive, Know," 2:509; Bo Reicke, "The Knowledge of the Suffering Servant," in *Das Ferne und Nahe Wort: Festschrift L. Rost* (ed. F. Maas; BZAW 105; Berlin: Töpelmann, 1967), 186–92; John Day, "*Da'at* 'Humiliation' in Is 53:11 in Light of Is 53:3 and Dan 12:4, and the Oldest Known Interpretation of the Suffering Servant," *VT* 30 (1980): 97–103; Oswalt, *Isaiah 40–66*, 403–4.

375. Robinson, "Notes on the Text and Interpretation of Isaiah 53:3, 11"; Oswalt, *Isaiah 40–66*, 403–4. See also, Day, "*Da'at* 'Humiliation' in Is 53:11"; Koole, *Isaiah 49–55*, 331.

374. Reicke, "The Knowledge of the Suffering Servant," 186–92. In support of this view, see Day, "*Da'at* 'Humiliation' in Is 53:11." In rejection of this view, see H. G. M. Williamson, "*Da'at* in Isaiah LIII,11," *VT* 28 (1978): 118–22.

376. Jensen, *The Use of Tôrâ by Isaiah*, 132.

How might the syntax of this verse help interpret דַּעַת? Some connect "knowledge" with the first line.[377] Tournay argues that the writer uses an object genitive, which identifies "the knowledge one will have of the Servant" or "familiarity with the Servant."[378] Koole, who follows Skinner's claim that this is not the genitive of the object but of the subject (the knowledge of God and salvation), argues that, in "Deutero-Isaiah," the suffix of this word consistently "has the value of a subject genitive."[379] Note that when √רָאָה and √יָדַע are juxtaposed in the parallelism (41:20; 44:18–19), the terms relate to an ability to perceive YHWH's power to save. Therefore, this verse probably contains a subject genitive, which implies that the knowledge of Servant and his salvation will bring satisfaction.

The act of substitutionary atonement is also depicted in the phrase "The righteous one, my servant, shall make many righteous," but still more difficulties exist in this phrase. Some emend the text to read as either a Hiphil perfect (הַצְדִּיק) or a Qal infinitive absolute (צָדוֹק), but such a reading lacks any evidence.[380] Some argue that צַדִּיק should be deleted because it was added due to dittography from יַצְדִּיק, but there is no textual witness for this assertion.[381] Some move this phrase to the previous line or even emend it to read "by his knowledge, he has made many righteous." Some interpret the verb as a Hiphil intransitive (יַצְדִּיק, "to show himself as righteous") or what Westermann calls an "internal causative."[382] The Hiphil of √צדק usually is followed by a direct object (Deut 25:1; 2 Sam 15:4) but this verse is the only place where this verb takes the indirect object governed by the preposition לְ, "to bring righteousness to" or "to provide righteousness for..." (לרבים).[383] This

377. Jan Schelhaas, *De lijdende knecht des Heeren. Het Ebed-Jahwe-probleem* (Groningen: Wever, 1933), 102; Kaiser, *Der königliche Knecht*, 85; Gerleman, *Studien zur alttestamentlichen Theologie*, 43; Beuken, *Jesaja*, 2A:231; Muilenburg, *Isaiah*, 5:630.

378. Tournay, "2d Isaiah."

379. Skinner, *Isaiah Chapters XL–LXVI*, 133; Koole, *Isaiah 49–55*, 330–32.

380. For the Hiphil infinitive absolute (הַצְדֵּק), see Sonne, "Isaiah 53:10–12." For the Qal infinitive absolute (צָדוֹק), see Müller, "Ein Vorschlag zu Jes 53:10f."

381. Volz, *Isaiah II*, 171, 172; Elliger, *Deuterojesaja*, 13; Morgenstern, "The Message of Deutero-Isaiah"; McKenzie, *Second Isaiah*, 132; Kutsch, *Sein Leiden und Tod*, 36; Davidson, *Hebrew Syntax*, 45; A. Gelston, "Some Notes on Second Isaiah," *VT* 21 (1971): 524–27.

382. Westermann, *Isaiah 40–66*, 267; Mowinckel, *He That Cometh*, 199; Reicke, "The Knowledge of the Suffering Servant," 189–90; Whybray, *Isaiah 40–66*, 180–81; Haag, *Der Gottesknecht bei Deuterojesaja*, 168 n. 5; Beuken, *Jesaja*, 2A:232.

383. Motyer, *The Prophecy of Isaiah*, 442.

construction has been called "a ל paraphrase of the accusative"[384] or "a ל of specification that marks the object of a transitive verb."[385] In 51:1, Israel ("my people" or "my nation," 51:4) was depicted as seeking after righteousness, 51:5 announces "my righteousness is near" and 51:7 that they "know righteousness, you people who have my Torah in your hearts." However, "my Servant" (עבדי), whose designation has been repeated from 52:13, does not refer to the people of Israel who seek righteousness but die to make "many" righteous.[386]

Here the word רבים can only imply "many" or "numerous."[387] Do these "many" (רבים) refer to Israel[388] or to the nations[389] or to both? Are these "many" the same ones who repudiated the Servant in 52:13–15? Since the same "many," who are justified in 53:11, are represented with the third person pronominal suffix in עונתם, we can assume them to be the persons whose debt of wrongs the Servant has borne (53:4–5). In 52:15, the phrase גוים רבים ("many nations") seems to isolate or distinguish the nations, whereas רבים alone does not give such specificity. Clearly, it is true that the description of the Servant has not yet specified any close relationship between the Servant and the nations.[390] Yet if the "many" are Israel, does this mean that the Servant makes atonement only for Israel but not the nations? Koole solves this problem by "cautiously" opting "for the view that it refers to Israel; salvation reaches the world

384.   Koole, *Isaiah 49–55*, 135.

385.   Waltke and O'Connor, *An Introduction to Biblical Hebrew Syntax*, 210.

386.   Clines (*I, He, We, and They*, 22) emends the text to fit LXX and 1QIsaᵃ, where the phrase עבדי is omitted due to orthographic variance. Köhler argues that עבדי serves as an abbreviation for עבד יהוה, but Dahood takes עבדי to imply "his Servant"; see Ludwig Köhler, *Deuterojesaja Stilkritisch Untersucht* (BZAW 37; Giessen: Töpelmann, 1923), 49; Dahood, "Phoenician Elements in Isaiah 52:13–53:12," 72.

387.   Koole, *Isaiah 49–55*, 257.

388.   Ibid., 334.

389.   H. P. Hertzberg, "Die 'Abtrünnigen' und die 'Vielen,'" in *Verbannung und Heimkehr: Beitrage zur Geschichte und Theologie Israels im 6. und 5. Jahrhundert v. Chr.: Wilhelm Rudolph zum 70. Geburtstage* (ed. Arnulf Kuschke; Tübingen: J. C. B. Mohr, 1961), 103–8; Friedrich V. Reiterer, *Gerechtigkeit als Heil:* צדק *bei Deuterojesaja. Aussage und Vergleich mit der alttestamentlichen Tradition* (Graz: Akadem. Druck- u. Verlagsanst, 1976), 110; Ernst Haag, "Die Botschaft vom Gottesknecht: Ein Weg zur Uberwindung der Gewalt," in *Gewalt und Gewaltlosigkeit im Alten Testament* (ed. N. Lohfink; QD 96; Freiburg: Herder, 1983), 166 n. 5; Beuken, *Jesaja*, 2A:232.

390.   Koch, "Messias und Sündenvergebung in Jesaja 53"; Koole, *Isaiah 49–55*, 334.

via Israel."[391] Koole's opinion makes sense at the original level of tradition history, where the identity of the "Servant" and the "many" may very well have been obvious. However, within the book as a whole, this identity has been left ambiguous (see below) so that one does not know clearly whether the beneficiaries of the Servant's atoning work are Israel, the nations or some other party.

Moreover, if the Servant were Israel or the prophet, how could he bear the sins of many? In order to make many righteous, he must first be righteous and second bear their iniquities. Koole states:

> The Servant was treated with horror by the bystanders, 52:14, and counted among sinners, v. 12, but in reality he did not commit violence or speak lies, v. 9, and this recognition of his righteousness is now explicitly by the divine word. He is not betrayed in his trust in the one who would recognize him as righteous and vindicate him, 50:7f. In this is he the model of the suffering righteous man who is defended by Yahweh against his enemies, Ps. 5:13; 7:10 etc... In contrast to these psalms of lament... his innocent suffering here brings about the salvation of those who oppressed him and the justification of others can take place through his mediation. The "righteous one" is also the name of the Saviour of the end of time in 2 Sam 23:3, cf. Jer 23:5; also Isa 11:5 etc.[392]

The phrase יסבל הוא ועונתם ("he shall bear their iniquities") makes more explicit what was stated in v. 4, סבלם ומכאבינו ("our sufferings [that resulted from our wrongdoing] he has borne them"). This type of substitution that makes the offerer acceptable is not novel. The purpose of a burnt offering was so that the offerer might be acceptable (לרצנכם, Lev 19:5; 22:19–21; 23:11). The Servant makes many righteous through bearing their iniquities as a substitution. Using a wide range of words that describe sin, the Servant is portrayed like the scapegoat who ritually bears the sins, transgressions and iniquities of the people (Lev 16:21–22).

Isaiah 52:12–53:13 is loaded with terms that elaborate on the Servant's distorted appearance (52:14): "stricken," "smitten," "afflicted," "pierced," "crushed," "punishment," "wounded," "sickness," and "suffering." All of these images climax in the last three verses with the phrases נפשו אשם תשים ("when you make his soul a guilt offering"),

391. Koole, *Isaiah 49–55*, 335.

392. Ibid., 334. See also Karl Theodor Kleinknecht, *Der leidende Gerecht-fertigte: Die alttestamentlich-jüdische Tradition vom "leidenden gerechten" und ihre Rezeption bei Paulus* (WUNT 13; Tübingen: J. C. B. Mohr, 1984), 48–50; Lothar Ruppert, "'Mein Knecht, der gerecht, macht die Vielen gerecht und ihre Verschuldungen—er trägt sie' (Jes 53,11): Universales Heil durch das stellvertretende Strafleiden des Gottesknechtes?," *BZ* 40, no. 1 (1996): 1–17.

עמל נפשו ("anguish of his soul," 53:11) and תחת אשר הערה למות נפשו
("because he poured out himself to death"). Certainly, the word נפש
creates a verbal link between these last three verses but in v. 12 the
Servant's suffering plummets to the level of death.

Divided into three bicola, 53:12 sums up all that has been stated about
the Servant's humiliation and exaltation. Each of the three bicola begin
with emphatic markers: adverbial (לכן, "therefore"), causal (תחת אשר,
"because"), or *waw* adversative (והוא, "but" or "yet he"). In a result
clause, the first bicolon describes the exaltation of the Servant. The
second bicolon states in a causal clause that he was exalted "because he
poured out himself to death." The third, beginning with a *wāw* adversative, announces that, although the Servant was numbered with trans-
gressor (we know the truth), he truly bore the sin of many and made
intercession for them. This function as a mediator culminates in the
intercession that he makes on behalf of transgressors.

The answer to the question about whether to locate the Servant's
mediation during his humiliation or during his exaltation lies within the
poetry.[393] As demonstrated above, the first bicolon describes the
exaltation of the Servant:

Therefore (A) I will allot for him (B) with the mighty	לכן (A) אחלק־לו (B) ברבים
(B′) and with the strong (A′) he will allot the spoil	ואת־עצומים (B′) יחלק שלל (A′)

With שלל functioning as a *ballast variant* (replacing לכן) and serving as
the object for both verbal forms of חלק√ ("I will allot," "he shall allot"),
the first bicolon describes the exaltation of the Servant within this
principle result clause. As in 53:11–12, God himself speaks in 52:13
because only a divine voice can proclaim the exaltation of the Servant.
Shifting from the first to third person of the same verb, the Servant
performs the same function as God, but note how the causal marker, תחת
אשר, in the third stich, shows the relationship between the Servant's
suffering and exaltation:

(Adv.) because (Hi.) he poured out to death (Dir. Obj.) his soul	(Adv.) תחת אשר (Hi.) הערה למות (Dir. Obj.) נפשו
(prep.) and with the transgressors (V) was numbered	(Ind. Obj.) ואת־פשעים (Ni.) נמנה
(Subj.) yet he (Dir. Obj.) the sin of many (V) bore	(Subj.) והוא (Dir. Obj.) חטא־רבים (Qal) נשא

393. See Koole, *Isaiah 49–55*, 343.

(Adv.) because (Hi.) he poured out to death (Dir. Obj.) his soul	תחת אשר (Hi.) הערה למות (Adv.)
(Ind. Obj.) and for the transgressors, (V) he made intercession	נפשו (Dir. Obj.)
	ולפשעים (Hi.) יפגיע (Ind. Obj.)

These bicola continue the synonymous parallelism that began the strophe, though each coordinate cannot be easily identified in terms of A-B-C. Yet the synonymous cola together isolate the Servant's death, numbering with transgressors, bearing of sin and mediation for transgressors within the locus of his sufferings.

The third colon identifies the Servant's suffering. Out of the thirteen instances where אשר is used, it always functions as a causal protasis ("because" or "since")[394] and every instance is connected to judgment due to some wrong committed.[395] Perhaps this has to do with the Servant taking on the judgment of many. Motyer's claim that תחת אשר is "the strongest causative in Hebrew…" and that it clearly accentuates that the exaltation of the Servant occurs *because* of the very fact that "he poured out his soul to death."[396] The Hiphil form (הֶעֱרָה, "he poured out"), which appears two other times in the Hiphil (Lev 20:18, 19) and reports the demise of the Servant, signifies the verbal usages to "uncover" or "expose" with regards to sexual relations. In the Piel, ערה along with נפש means "to bear," "to become naked" (וְתֵעַר נַפְשִׁי), in the sense of being defenseless (Ps 141:8). Therefore, some think that ערה implies that the Servant "uncovered," "bore" or "exposed" himself to mortal danger.[397] Because, the *life* (נפש) is in the blood (Lev 17:11), others render ערה to signify that he "poured out" his life blood as an expiation for sin.[398] Knight submits that ערה implies that the Servant "emptied out his *nephesh*, that is to say, his whole personality," almost like Paul's notion of the "kenosis" (Phil 2:7, 8).[399] No matter how the word is taken, the Servant's sufferings ultimately culminate in death.

394. Cazelles, "Les Poèmes du Serviteur"; Davidson, *Hebrew Syntax*, 143; BDB, 1066; Beuken, *Jesaja*, 2A:232; Koole, *Isaiah 49–55*, 339.
395. See the 13 times that תחת אשר appears in the Old Testament: Num 25:13; Deut 21:14; 22:29; 28:47, 62; 1 Sam 26:21; 2 Kgs 22:17; 2 Chr 21:12; 34:25; Jer 29:19; 50:7; Ezek 36:34.
396. Motyer, *The Prophecy of Isaiah*, 443.
397. Slotki, *Isaiah*, 264; Driver, "Isaiah 52:13–53:12," 102; McKenzie, *Second Isaiah*, 131; Young, *Isaiah*, 3:359; Coppens, *Le messianisme et sa relève prophétique*, 65; Whybray, *Isaiah 40–66*, 183; Gerleman, *Studien zur alttestamentlichen Theologie*, 43; Koole, *Isaiah 49–55*, 339; Oswalt, *Isaiah 40–66*, 406.
398. Delitzsch, *Isaiah*, 1:339; Skinner, *Isaiah Chapters XL–LXVI*, 133; Westermann, *Isaiah 40–66*, 268; Beuken, *Jesaja*, 2A:234.
399. Knight, *The Hebrew Bible and Its Modern Interpreters*, 179; Motyer, *The Prophecy of Isaiah*, 443.

The next colon accentuates the injustice and humiliation that accompanied this death. The verb √מנה with the particle את functions in this verse to add emphasis and can be attached to a nominative as well as an accusative.[400] If we understand the Niphal verb as a reflexive rather than a passive, then, functioning as a "tolerative Niphal," נִמְנָה would imply that "*he let himself be numbered* with transgressors" and that his suffering was noncompulsory.[401] In other words, the Servant was not a puppet dangling on the strings of an arbitrary deity, but he himself acquiesced to the divine judgment on sin. Clearly, this colon makes the point that he died the death of a criminal.

The fifth colon, והוא חטא־רבים נשא ("yet he bore the sins of many"), almost restates 53:4 (אכן חלינו הוא נשא), which we have already established to imitate the ritual of the scapegoat's bearing of sin. Yet, in v. 4, the Servant bears "our infirmities" (חֳלָיֵנוּ + √נשא) and "the consequences of our wrongdoing" (מַכְאֹבֵינוּ + √סמל), but in the final summing up of the Servant's work, v. 12 makes the implicit explicit that he bore "the sin of many." While the MT has the construct singular noun חֵטְא, the LXX, all other versions and Qumran copies including 4QIs^d have the construct plural חטאי. We cannot ascertain whether the MT dropped the *yōdh* due to haplography or Qumran and the *Vorlage* of the LXX added it, because the Hebrew does not have a large enough cross-section of witnesses. Nevertheless, we can determine that either "sins" as the multiplicity or "sin" as the conglomerate of human iniquities (e.g. all or every), describe the human problem which the Servant solved.

Therefore, this mediation in the final colon, ולפשעים יפגיע ("and for the transgressors, he made intercession"), is set within a synonymous parallelism that correlates his death, treatment as a criminal, sin-bearing and finally intercession for transgressors. In an ingenious sort of way, יפגיע pairs with והוא...נשא ("he bore [sins]") and חטא־רבים pairs with ולפשעים while חטא performs double duty with נשא and רבים. The Servant's work of mediation is synonymous with the act of pouring his soul out to death, being numbered with transgressors and bearing the sin of many. In essence, all these functions perform a mediatory act.

400.　P. P. Saydon, "The Meanings and Uses of the Particle *'et*," *VT* 14 (1964): 192–210; John MacDonald, " *'t* in Classical Hebrew: Some New Data on Its Use with the Nominative," *VT* 14 (July 1964): 264–75; Jacob Hoftijzer, "Remarks Concerning the Use of the Particle *'at* in Classical Hebrew," in *Oudtestamentlich Werkgezelschap in Nederland* (Leiden: Brill, 1965), 1–99.

401.　Westermann, *Isaiah 40–66*, 268–69; Motyer, *The Prophecy of Isaiah*, 443; Hanson, *Isaiah 40–66*, 160.

Therefore, the Servant performs his mediatory role within his suffering and his exaltation is the outcome of his sufferings. The MT has the masculine plural participal פֹּשְׁעִים, but on the basis of 1QIsa[a-b], 4QIsa[d] (פֹּשְׁעֵיהֶם[וֹ]) and the LXX (τὰς ἁμαρτίας αὐτῶν), *BHS* proposes to emend the text to read וּלְפִשְׁעָם,[402] which is not impossible since פִּשְׁעָם appears elsewhere in the Old Testament (Job 8:4; Pss 89:33; 107:17; Isa 58:1). Whether "transgressors" or "their transgression," both convey the same idea of the Servant making intercession or mediation for sin.

Playing on YHWH's causing the Servant to bear the burden of sin (53:6), the Hiphil verb יַפְגִּיעַ in 53:12 recalls 53:6.[403] Often the preposition ב with פגע in the Qal essentially means "to meet" or "encounter," but it can also signify "to urge" (Ruth 1:16), or "to meet with danger," thus conveying the idea "to bother" or "to molest" (Ruth 2:22). The Qal of פגע also carries the meaning of intercede (Gen 23:8). The Hiphil has two meanings, "to intercede" (Isa 59:16; Jer 15:11; 36:25) and "to lay a burden" (Isa 53:6), but the usage of the Hiphil in Job 36:32b is too difficult to determine.[404] Whybray translates פגע here as "plead for, intercede," rejecting any nuances of substitutionary atonement in his identification of the Servant as Deutero-Isaiah himself. He restricts the meaning of the verb merely to the "intercession," which, like Moses (Exod 32:11–13) or Samuel (1 Sam 7:8–9), the prophet makes on behalf of others.[405] Probably the Hiphil יַפְגִּיעַ in its proper usage means "to cause to reach" and hence the figurative idea of "make entreaty" occurs by causing someone's plea to reach someone's ears.[406] However, within the parallelism, יפגיע pairs with נשא, which plays a much more active

402. This reading is followed by Godfrey R. Driver, "Once Again Abbreviations," *Textus* 4 (1964): 80; Kutscher, *The Language and Linguistic Background of the Isaiah Scroll*, 383; Clifford, *Fair Spoken*, 175; Barthélemy, *Critique textuelle de l'Ancien Testament*, 403–7; Karl Elliger, "Nochmals Textkritisches zu Jes. 53," in *Wort, Lied und Gottesspruch: Festschrift für Joseph Ziegler* (ed. Josef Schreiner; Wurzburg: Echter, 1972), 143–44; Koole, *Isaiah 49–55*, 342; Oswalt, *Isaiah 40–66*, 399.

403. Note that Dahood ("Phoenician Elements in Isaiah 52:13–53:12," 72–73) follows 1QIsa[a] = יפגע but distinguishes this consonantal form as a defective Hiphil, but Elliger ("Nochmals Textkritisches zu Jes. 53," 143–44) points to 1QIsa[a] = פגע as a Niphal passive according to OG (παρεδόθη). In my opinion, because 1QIsa[a] may easily be explained by haplography of the *yōdh*, MT stands as a reliable witness.

404. Victor P. Hamilton, "פָּגַע (*pāgaʿ*) Encounter, Meet, Reach, Entreat, Make Intercession," *TWOT* 2:715.

405. Whybray, *Isaiah 40–66*, 183; idem, *Thanksgiving for a Liberated Prophet*, 71–73.

406. See Motyer, *The Prophecy of Isaiah*, 443.

role in mediatorship than Whybray purports. In an ingenious sort of way, והוא...נשא ("he bore [sins]") and חטא־רבים corresponds to ולפשעים with חטא almost performing double duty with נשא and רביב.

Clearly, the Servant has made atonement for many. Ginsburg states that "The sense of the entire composition is that the Servant has suffered in order to expiate the guilt of the many vicariously."[407] Oswalt observes that "this undeserved suffering can only be a revelation of the delivering arm of the Lord, of his ability to restore his people to fellowship with himself, if it is substitutionary, a concept familiar to Jews through the language of the entire sacrificial system."[408] This sacrificial concept has transferred the disturbing procedure of an innocent animal bearing the sins of many to an innocent human being, who would serve as this very sacrifice in order to atone for human sin. The shedding of innocent human blood, which customarily requires vengeance, here reconciles and heals.[409] From this perspective, Hanson, who does not acknowledge any distinctions between pre-biblical and scriptural levels, still seeks to understand the theological purpose of the Servant and rightly argues that the Servant's death is not merely a martyrdom:

> Isaiah 53 is Second Isaiah's contribution to this spiritual quest for an answer to the question of how the tragic pattern of sin and punishment could be broken and replaced by the wholeness that accompanies a hearty embrace of God's compassion and righteousness. It revolves around the notion of a Servant of the Lord whose surrender to God's will was so total that he took the consequences of the sin of the community upon himself, even though he was innocent of any wrong. This of course is the stuff of martyrdom which can be moving but totally ineffective in relation to the human plight unless accompanied by one critically significant dimension: "Yet it was the will of the LORD to crush him with pain" (53:10). The Servant is not acting alone. The Servant is serving God's purpose. Not tragic fate, but obedience to the Lord motivates the Servant to place no limits on self-giving love.[410]

The "arm of YHWH" reveals how God's plan of salvation has been carried out by the suffering of the Servant (53:1). Clearly, the *raison d'être* of the Servant is to perform a work of expiation on behalf of the people, which in many respects explains why several individuals have attributed this portrayal of the Servant to the role of a priest whether or

---

407. H. L. Ginsburg, *The Book of Isaiah* (Philadelphia: The Jewish Publication Society of America, 1973), 21.
408. Oswalt, *Isaiah 40–66*, 377.
409. Koole, *Isaiah 49–55*, 254.
410. Hanson, *Isaiah 40–66*, 156–57.

not they view him as a priestly Messiah.[411] However, we cannot link the Servant with the priestly Messiah of the Maccabean-Hasmonean rulers or Qumran because, first, Isa 52:13–53:12 predates these traditions by too many centuries and, second, the Servant himself becomes the sacrifice rather than merely the one offering it.[412]

This aspect of suffering and making atonement is not part of the traditional messianic expectation of early Judaism as seen in the Targum.

411. Ogden, "Moses and Cyrus"; Fretheim, *Suffering of God*, 134, 163; Rosenberg, "The Slain Messiah"; Hengel, "Jesus der Messias Israels," 164; Puech, "Fragments d'une apocryphe de Lévi," 492–99; Brooke, "4Q Testament of Levi[d]," 2; Motyer, *Isaiah*, 429; Collins, *The Scepter and the Star*, 125; Webb, *The Message of Isaiah*, 209–10. It is highly unlikely, even at the original level of tradition history, that the Servant is a king who made expiation. Cf. two different views on this subject: Dürr, *Ursprung und Ausbau*, 27; Kittel, *Geschichte des Volkes Israel*, 256–57.

412. Note that in Sirach a Messiah would be like this priest, who was not an offspring of David nor a Zadokite but a Maccabean priest (45:1–25; 50:1–24). See André Caquot, "Ben Sira et le Messianisme," *Sem* 16 (1966): 43–68; Jean Carmignac, "L'infinitif absolu chez Ben Sira et à Qumran," *RevQ* 12, no. 2 (1986): 251–61. However, Qumran offers another picture. See the pre-Qumran *Damascus Rule* (CD 12, 19–23, 1; 19, 10–11, 22–25). Note that G. J. Brooke maintains that the pre-Qumran "*Damascus Document* consistently speaks of only one Messiah" ("The Messiah of Aaron in the Damascus Document," *RevQ* 15 [1991]: 215–30). See also *The Community Rule* (1QS 9:5–11); *The War Rule* (1QM/4QM, 2, 1–4; 15, 4; 16, 3–8, 12–14; 18, 5–6; 19, 11–12); *The Messianic Rule* (1QSa 2, 11–20); Raymond E. Brown, "The Messianism of Qumrân," *CBQ* 19 (1957): 53–82; Vermes, *Jesus the Jew*, 135–37; John J. Collins, *The Sibylline Oracles of Egyptian Judaism* (Missoula, Mont.: Society of Biblical for the Pseudepigrapha Group, 1974), 35–45; John Nolland, "Sib. Or. III.:265–94: An Early Maccabean Messianic Oracle," *JTS* 30 (1979): 158–66; Anders Hultgård, "The Davidic Messiah and the Saviour Priest," in *Ideal Figures in Ancient Judaism: Profiles and Paradigms* (ed. John J. Collins and George W. E. Nickelsburg; Missoula, Mont.: Scholars Press for the Society for Biblical Literature, 1980), 93–110; Richard A. Horsley, "Popular Messianic Movements Around the Time of Jesus," *CBQ* 46 (1984): 471–95; idem, *Bandits, Prophets, and Messiahs: Popular Messianic Movements Around the Time of Jesus* (San Francisco: Harper, 1985), 106–27; Emil Schürer, "The Qumran Messiahs and Messianism," trans. T. A. Burkill, in *The History of the Jewish People in the Age of Jesus Christ* (ed. Geza Vermes and Fergus Millar; 3 vols. in 4; Edinburgh: T. & T. Clark, 1973–1987), 2:550–54; idem, in the same volume, "The Qumran Community According to the Dead Sea Scrolls," trans. T. A. Burkill, 2:575–90; Shemaryahu Talmon, "Waiting for the Messiah: The Spiritual Universe of the Qumran Covenanters," in Neusner, Green and Frerichs, eds., *Judaisms and Their Messiahs*, 111–37; Michael A. Knibb, "The Interpretation of Damascus Document VII, 9b–VIII, 2a and XIX, 5b–14," *RevQ* 15 (1991–92): 243–51; Brooke, "4Q Testament of Levi[b]"; Collins, *The Scepter and the Star*, 125.

If one expects a victorious Messiah, who offers a solution in an extraordinary way and insures the promises to David after the monarch has disappeared, the Servant certainly would not fit this category. Most constituents of ancient Judaism would not have considered suffering and death to offer an "extraordinary solution" (53:2–3). In 53:1, the speakers, having already been confronted by the prophetic word ("Was it not YHWH, against whom we have sinned, in whose ways they would not walk, and whose Torah they would not obey?," 42:24) confess their sin. The speakers should have known better but accept the accusation that they have misjudged the Servant: "we held him of no account" (53:3) and "yet we accounted him stricken, struck down by God, and afflicted" (53:4). Each of us acknowledges culpability: "All we like sheep have gone astray; we have all turned to our own way…" (53:6) from YHWH the Good Shepherd (40:11). This confession leads to acquittal in v. 11.[413] Isaiah 49–52 does seem to anticipate the salvation, which the Servant procures in Isa 53 and the people are invited to participate in chs. 54–55 but still anticipate in 56, finally ending the trisection with the words, "There is no peace, says my God, for the wicked."[414] Clearly the ending of exile, which is announced in 40:1–2, did not provide restoration for the nation. Therefore, the later editing of the book describes a problem that finds its fulfillment within an eschatological framework. Yet this alone cannot in itself make Isa 53 messianic. Judaism did not expect a suffering Messiah, but are there warrants for Christians interpret this passage messianically?

4. Similarities and differences between the Servant and the Davidic Messiah. Some scholars have noted various similarities between Isa 52:13–53:12 and other passages that we have been traditionally interpreted messianically. Like the branch that is from the "root" of Jesse's line (מִשָּׁרָשָׁיו) and understood as the termination of the monarchy through the parallel term "stump" in 11:1, the Servant in 53:2 describes a root out of dry ground (וּכְשֹׁרֶשׁ מֵאֶרֶץ צִיָּה). Calvin argues that in 53:2 the שֶׁרֶשׁ ("twig") almost finds the same metaphor that appears in 11:1, "a branch shall spring out of the stock of Jesse."[415] Yet parched ground offers a different metaphor of death than does a stump. Delitzsch argues that, like 11:1–9, "where the shoot springs forth from the proud cedar of the Davidic monarchy after it had been felled, the servant is described as a

413. Koole, *Isaiah 49–55*, 252.
414. See Oswalt, *Isaiah 40–66*, 385.
415. Calvin, *Commentary on the Book of the Prophet Isaiah*, 4:113.

tender shoot."[416] While the imagery created by the word שׁרשׁ appears seven times in chs. 1–39 and twice in chs. 40–55, the nuances are more similar in 11:1 and 53:2 than elsewhere. Moreover, Joseph Jensen suggests that, by using the term "knowledge" (דעת), "the author is here adapting to the Servant some of the things said of the Davidic king in 11:1–9."[417] Peckham's description of one who functions in a manner like David, returning to Zion after after the exile and becoming the source of justice and peace for all the nations of the world, finds similarities with the portraits of the deliverer in Isa 9:1–6; 11:1–5 and 61:1–3.[418] Yet he carefully never calls the Servant "the Messiah."

Since the phrase חלק שׁלל ("to divide the spoil," 53:12) reflects the "warrior" image of 9:2–3, Koole argues that "the suffering Servant will prove to be a triumphant Messiah."[419] While both the Davidic deliverer and the Servant will mightily divide the spoil, the Servant explicitly will do so because (תחת אשׁר) he suffered and died. The word מראה is only found in 11:3; 52:14 and 53:2. Finally, the Servant bears (יסבל) in 53:11d the burden that Israel once had to bear in 9:4 (סבלו).[420] Nevertheless, any attempts to harmonize 52:13–53:12 with 9:1–6 and 11:1–5 does not account for the differences between the two texts. Isaiah 52:13–53:12 separates itself from 9:1–6 and 11:1–5 because the Servant suffers and dies an atoning death. Similar to other passages that have evoked messianic interpretation, the Servant is also called to shut the mouth of kings (52:15), just as he is called in ch. 49 to "restore the survivors of Israel" and to be "a light to the nations" (49:6), which will result in kings standing up and princes prostrating themselves (49:7b). While 52:12–53:13 finds similarities with 9:1–6 and 11:1–5, we cannot harmonize 52:12–53:13 with 9:1–6 and 11:1–6 to interpret the Servant messianically because the Servant is depicted differently. The one who fulfills the promises to David after the monarchy has ended by shedding light on the darkness of exile, and the one who executes righteousness, justice and endless peace because his throne has no end (9:1–6; 11:1–6) does not suffer and die as in 52:13–53:12.

Many features separate the portrait of the Servant in 52:13–53:12 from the Davidic king and for that manner Jesus. Notice that David is described as וטוב ראי ("good looking") but the Servant after his beating is described in an opposite fashion. Isaiah 33:17 states that the

416. Delitzsch, *Isaiah*, 1:312.
417. Jensen, *Tôrâ*, 132.
418. Peckham, *History and Prophecy*, 216.
419. Clifford, *Fairspoken*, 181; Koole, *Isaiah 49–55*, 339.
420. Clifford, *Fairspoken*, 181.

anticipated king must be beautiful but the Servant here is unsightly:[421]
33:17 says "Your eyes will see the king in his beauty," but 52:14 says
"Just as there were many who were astonished at him—so marred was
his appearance, beyond human semblance, and his more than the sons
of men." We have already demonstrated that מִן of comparison in the
phrases מֵאִישׁ ("more than a man") and מִבְּנֵי אָדָם ("more than the sons of
men") conveys the distortion of the Servant from typical human norms.
Unlike David who is depicted in a positive light by use of תֹּאַר (1 Sam
16:18), Isa 53:2 negates the same word (לֹא־תֹאַר) to describe the Servant.
Instead, Isa 53:3 describes the Servant as "despised and rejected" (נִבְזֶה
וַחֲדַל). Oswalt claims that the Niphal masculine singular participle of
בזה√ implies "worthless"[422] and that וַחֲדַל אִישִׁים indicates that humans
have withdrawn from relations with the Servant because they do not
consider him to have any importance for them.[423] Muilenburg argues that
the plural אִישִׁים provides assonance with the immediately following
אִישׁ, but this does not explain the two other instances where this form
appears since אִישׁ does not follow the plural there (Ps 141:4; Prov 8:4).[424]
Koole rightly maintains that "instead of a superhuman he is an under-
dog,"and Oswalt states that "He is not one of the winners, he is one of
the losers."[425] Therefore, this portrait does not coincide with David or
any form of pre-Christian messianic hope. As expected of the Messiah,
the Servant would indeed bring salvation, but the manner in which he
would do it was completely ironic.

The differences between 52:13–53:12 and other passages that have
inspired messianic interpretation are greater than the similarities. We
must conclude that, on this basis of comparison, within the book of

---

421.   Matthias Augustin, *Der Schone Mensch im Alten Testament und im
Hellenistischen* (Frankfurt am Main: Lang, 1983), 179; Koole, *Isaiah 49–55*, 270.

422.   Oswalt, *Isaiah 40–66*, 383. Isa 49:7 is the only other place where בזה√
appears in the book of Isaiah. After the announcement of divine word formula
(כֹּה אָמַר־יהוה), YHWH, who is described by the appositional phrase "the redeemer of
Israel, his holy one," speaks to the Servant in the Qal infinitive construct לִבְזֹה־נֶפֶשׁ
("to the despised one [soul]"), which is intensified by the Piel participle that stands
in apposition, לִמְתָעֵב גּוֹי לְעֶבֶד מֹשְׁלִים ("to the one abhorred by the nation, to the
Servant of rulers..."). In 37:22, the similar term (בוז√) has a sense of scorning or
dismissive mocking.

423.   Whybray, *Isaiah 40–66*, 174; Oswalt, *Isaiah 40–66*, 383. Note that Isaiah
53:3 is the only place in chs. 40–66 where we find the verb חדל√, but it appears a
few times in chs. 1–39 to imply "stop" (1:16; 24:8) and "turn away" in the sense of
rejection (2:22), the second of which fits this context.

424.   Muilenburg, *Isaiah*, 5:620.

425.   Koole, *Isaiah 49–55*, 251; Oswalt, *Isaiah 40–66*, 383.

Isaiah as a whole this passage does not fit the usual criteria for messianic interpretation. Does the Targum, then, have any warrant to interpret the exalted Servant as "the Messiah" but the suffering Servant as the nations? Do early Christians have any justification in linking this passage with their suffering and risen Messiah, Jesus Christ? Does the biblical text provide any built-in warrants for messianic interpretation or have those who have cherished this text as a testimony to their Messiah merely done so by some sort of "reader response" hermeneutic?

C. *Messianic Interpretation and Functional Ambiguity*

1. *Functional ambiguity.* Messianism in Isa 52:13–53:12 is not self-evident because the text itself creates the problem of clear gaps in an interpretation that must be bridged, either by messianism or some other view. The text functions as an arena whereby certain things may be ruled out and others made clear. Rikki Watts poses a question not realizing that the answer lies within the question itself: "How is the relationship between Jacob-Israel as Servant and the *unknown* Servant to be resolved?"[426] Watts' question or dilemma unwittingly provides the answer to the problem because this area of the unknown essentially functions as part of the rhetoric of the text. Clines says that, the Servant's identity is not a "puzzle to be solved, a code to be cracked."[427] That is why early in the last century, Gunkel and Gressmann, working from a traditio-historic approach, still pointed out the "vagueness" or element of "mystery" that enveloped the Servant.[428] Likewise, Wilcox and Patton refer to a deliberate ambiguity.[429]

In his article "Issues in Contemporary Translation," Gerald Sheppard distinguishes between "systemic vagueness" and "functional ambiguity." Systemic vagueness describes those things in the text that made sense to its writers or editors but not to its readers because of the distance between especially the modern reader and ancient writers. Functional ambiguity, however, operates as a rhetorical feature of the poetry that has been strategically placed within the text and is essential to the poem. Just as a skilled rhetorician would not translate the figurative usage of a metaphor into a proper usage because the metaphor would then lose its rhetorical power, Isa 53 cannot afford any attempts to resolve the ambiguity of the Servant and the voices that surround him. Otherwise, the poetry would lose the rhetorical force that lies in the genius of functional ambiguity.

---

426. Watts, "Consolation or Confrontation," 50–51 (my italics).
427. Clines, *I, He, We, and They*, 25.
428. Gressmann, *Der Ursprung*, 317–20; Gunkel, "Knecht Jahvehs."
429. Wilcox and Patton-Williams, "The Servant Songs."

Modern attempts to locate the original or historical meaning of Isa 53 and thus identify the Servant as Deutero-Isaiah, Jehoiachin, Zion etc., have removed the rhetorical force that lies in the ambiguity of the text. Motyer and others, who refer to the prophetic voice as "Isaiah," falters at a "canonical" level in his conception that the parties can be identified, but his claims are more inaccurate than older historical-critical approaches because at least the older modern approaches are making more plausible historical claims (though speculative).[431] As do most modern critics, Motyer's designation obliterates the rhetorical force that lies in the ambiguity of the text but also creates an historical error and ignores the clear-cut differences between chs. 1–39 and 40–66 even at the level of the book as a whole. In the context of the book of Isaiah, the editors have relied upon and have helped to create a functional ambiguity in Isa 53. Probably the pre-biblical writer, whom modern critics have referred to hypothetically as "Second Isaiah," knew the original identity of the suffering Servant who also could have been Second Isaiah himself or some other person of his time. However, this designation no longer exists at a scriptural level. When individuals try to resolve the ambiguity of the text on a purely grammatical basis, they forfeit the rhetorical force, which permits various messianic and non-messianic interpretations that have been integral to both Judaism and Christianity.

The history of interpretation demonstrates a modern tendency to identify and isolate each change of voice in Isa 53, such as when the voice refers to YHWH (53:1, 6, 10), which leads many commentators to remark that "the prophet is speaking now" because YHWH cannot be referring to himself.[432] Yet the specificity of 49:3 breaks the logic used here to claim that the voice switches between YHWH and the prophet since in 49:3 the speaker is neither YHWH nor the prophet: "And he said to me, 'You are my servant, Israel, in whom I will be glorified.'"

This segregation of the various voices (e.g. the prophet and the voice of YHWH) may not prove fruitful for the study of Isa 53 because such a clever identification not only fails to solve the problems of the text, but also may overlook how this feature functions as a rhetorical device that helps establish the functional ambiguity of this text.

Ambiguity functions within 52:13–53:12, and both Jews and Christians have impressively capitalized upon it. Essentially, this text depends on an extra-biblical view of the Messiah when it comes to decoding which way to exploit that ambiguity. As early as the second century C.E., Irenaeus argued: "Every prophecy is enigmatic and ambiguous for

431.   Motyer, *Isaiah*, 426, 431, 432, 433, 434, 435, etc.
432.   Koole, *Isaiah 49–55*, 318.

human minds before it is fulfilled. But when the time is arrived and the prediction has come true, then the prophecies find their clear unambiguous interpretation."[433] In Isa 53, Christians began with the reality of a fulfilment and from there sought to find the biblical promises. Therefore, Christians have unfairly belittled Jews for not seeing Christ in the testimony of Isa 53 (e.g. Calvin, Luther et al.). For this very reason, the suffering Servant has been traditionally interpreted messianically within Christianity, but not in Judaism.

What, then, protects this text from some sort of reader response criticism? First, this ambiguity cannot provide the only basis for interpretation but must function in combination with *clarity* in order to create an arena, where the different communities of faith have interpreted the text to describe different types of messianism. Jews, on the one hand, have exploited the text to describe one type of messianism, and Christians, on the other hand, use it to depict a suffering Messiah. For Christians, the Servant must be understood as one who suffers for sin or he is not a Messiah at all. Therefore, the ambiguity of the text warrants messianic interpretation for Christians because the text clarifies an ambiguous figure who is oppressed, afflicted and interceeds for the sins of many (52:13–53:12). Moreover, the text clarifies the Servant as "the righteous one" who victoriously "divides the spoil with the mighty," and is "high and lofty" (52:13; 53:11, 12). In this sense, we could say that the text itself rises up and meets the expectations of the community of faith rather than the reader imposing a particular interpretation upon the text.

2. New Testament citations of Isaiah 52:13–53:12. The earliest Christian interpretations that identify Isaianic texts with messianic promise can be found in New Testament citations of the Old Testament. Furthermore, C. H. Dodd argues that these New Testament citations of the Old Testament are cited from the context of the whole book of Isaiah,[434] though Donald Juel consistently treats them as examples of a midrashic atomistic exegesis.[435] Midrashic interpretation does not necessarily take the context seriously but may attach the term משיח to a single word or phrase even if the larger context does not suggest it. In 52:13, for example, the Targum renders the passage as "my servant, the Messiah," but reapplies the phrases about his sufferings either to Israel or his adversaries. Juel contends that this does not necessarily imply that the Targumist interprets the Servant figure as a Messiah, but only that he can interpret isolated

433. Irenaeus, *Ante-Nicene Fathers*. Vol. 1, *Against Heresies*, 496.
434. Dodd, *According to Scripture*, 75–80.
435. Juel, *Messianic Exegesis*, 119–33.

words or phrases. He argues that similar midrashic interpretation of 52:13–53:12 in the New Testament confirms a pre-modern atomistic exegesis that does not imply that the servant is understood messianically.[436] While various modes of interpretation (midrash, pesher, allegory and spiritual senses) may have been used, modes which ignored the significance of the larger context, we are interested in what Christianity later called the "plain" or "literal sense" and how this became the primary basis for doctrinal interpretation since the mid-second century C.E.

Did the New Testament cite Isa 52:13–53:12 from the context of the whole book or atomistically? Dodd and Juel offer two extremes on this continuum. While some passages were cited atomistically, others presupposed the larger literary context. Since the majority of the verses in the so-called "fourth Servant song" (52:15; 53:1, 4–5, 7–9, 12) have been cited in the New Testament as prophetic evidence for the messiahship of Jesus Christ, this implies much more than atomistic exegesis but that the context itself has inspired this interpretation. Romans 15:20 names Jesus as the Christ by claiming to build on someone else's already existent foundation (Isa 52:15).[437] John 12:38 cites Isa 53:1 to name Jesus as the Messiah (ὁ Χριστὸς), "who must be lifted up" (12:24), and "to fulfill the word spoken by the prophet Isaiah: 'Lord, who has believed our message, and to whom has the arm of the Lord been revealed?'"[438] Matthew 8:17 links Jesus' healings with those of the Servant, whose act of "taking away" or "carrying away" the afflictions of those who were sick is described as carrying those afflictions vicariously.[439] In Acts 8, Philip replies to the perplexities of the Ethiopian eunuch and explains that Isa 53:7–8 testifies to Jesus as the Messiah. First Peter 2:22–25 specifically interprets Isa 53 messianically by connecting 53:9b with the crucifixion

---

436.   Ibid., 119–33.

437.   Properly cited from LXX, the New Testament has renedered ראו and התבוננו as futures in order to render them as prophetic perfects. See Gleason Archer and G. Chirichigno, *Old Testament Quotations in the New Testament* (Chicago: Moody, 1983), 120.

438.   See also Rom 10:16, which cites Isa 53:1 for various rhetorical purposes other than messianic.

439.   This view is promoted by W. F. Albright and C. S. Mann, *Matthew* (AB 26; Garden City, N.Y.: Doubleday, 1971), 94. Albright and Mann also claim that: "In the total context of Isa liii, the identification of Jesus with the Servant would appear to demand far more than a mere removal of suffering. Indeed, the healings here seem to be a 'typical' colection, designed to illustrate the Servant-Messiah theme of the the Old Testament quotations. In that case, the omission of details, if the evangelist knew them, would be deliberate, as tending to obscure the empowering act or word of the Servant-Messiah in his bearing of the sufferings of men."

of Christ: "He himself bore our sins in his body on the cross, so that, free from sins, we might live for righteousness; by his wounds you have been healed." Within the context of "the Lord's supper," Jesus foretells his suffering unto death as a fulfillment of scripture (53:12): "his scripture must be fulfilled in me, 'And he was counted among the lawless'; and indeed what is written about me is being fulfilled." Since the New Testament has cited from such a wide range of Old Testament verses in 52:13–53:12 for the very same purpose, we can assume that the early Christian community understood the greater context to be messianic.

Hence, when the New Testament writers present Jesus as the Messiah, who prayed the lament psalms while dying on the cross, many parts of the psalms of lamentation were obviously being heard by Christians as messianic. Yet, as Sheppard has noted, in the light of Jesus' suffering and death, Christians traditionally interpret these psalms of lamentation as a witness to Jesus Christ and, using Tyconius' head and body imagery, they reapply any confession of sin in the same psalms to the Church and not to Jesus Christ. Early Christians regarded Isa 53 as testifying to the atoning death of Jesus, the Messiah on the cross. As the first early Christians looked into scripture to make sense of that event, they found elements that caused them to hear the text messianically. Therefore, within the clarity and functional ambiguity of Isa 52:13–53:12, these texts logically warranted messianic promise to a community of faith only if its Messiah has died and made atonement for many.

3. *The Servant and Cyrus.* How then can we interpret Isa 53 messianically and rule out Cyrus when the Servant meets very few expectations of a Messiah but the text explicitly calls Cyrus מְשִׁיחוֹ ("his anointed," 45:1)? Although the original level of tradition history might have distinguished Cyrus as a messianic deliverer and the Servant as an identifiable individual such as Second Isaiah himself, the book as a whole has no longer retained the specificity of these traditions. Just as the scriptural form of Isaiah has left the Servant ambiguous, 65:16b–25 has altered the presentation of Cyrus within the book as a whole because the former things, which God's people were once told to remember (46:9), now conform to a new dimension and must not be remembered (65:17). The eschatological elements of prophetic promise rule out Cyrus as a Messiah because YHWH is "going to create a new heaven and a new earth and the former things shall not be remembered or brought to mind" (65:17). Because YHWH is doing a "new thing" (43:19) that exceeds the limits of the former things, the book as a whole now takes on a new eschatological dimension that excludes Cyrus but recalls the promise to prolong

David's line when the monarchy has ended by citing from ch. 11: "the wolf and the lamb shall feed together, the lion shall eat straw." Now, while 65:16b–25 tells the post-exilic community to forget the former things (65:17) that have been fulfilled in part by Cyrus releasing the exiles and rebuilding the temple, this text provides no admonition that would rule out the Servant as Messiah.

Conclusion

In sum, while Isa 52:13–53:12 was not originally messianic and probably not even viewed as messianic by the later editors, within the warrants of the text, this passage has provoked early Christians and some Jewish readers to identify the Servant messianically. Similar to 61:1–3, the ambiguity of the Servant's identity allows this passage to be heard by Christians as messianic within the latter formation of the book of Isaiah. The second tri-section presents the Servant as individual deliverer, who makes atonement for many. The loss of the original historical setting and the way the reference shifts from Israel to an indefinite individual, who is distinct from Israel, creates an ambiguity for the identity of the Servant that pushes the text into eschatological dimensions. Contrary to the Cyrus passage, which provides enough information to exclude him as the Messiah, the ambiguity in 52:12–53:13 would allow the Servant to be understood as Messiah—but *only if* the conception of that Messiah includes "suffering," as is the case of Christianity and even some views of later Judaism after the death of Simon Bar Kosiba (135 C.E.).[440] If one exploits the ambiguity of the text to interpret 52:13–53:12 messianically, then the portrait of the suffering Servant completely alters how the witness of the whole book of Isaiah testifies to Israel's Messiah. No longer is the Messiah merely a Davidic king who fulfills the promises to David after the monarchy has ended, but he is one who suffers and atones for the sins of the people. In light of the book as a whole, it is understandable that once the role of the Servant is applied to the Messiah, the Servant himself would then be *ipso facto* a king.

---

440.   While Christians may have referred to this leader as Kokhba, he is usually referred to as Ben or Bar Koziba. Rabbinic writings present him as בודרה, כוסבא‎ or כסבה‎, and its Greek transliteration is κωσιβα. *Lam. Rab.* 2:4 says, "My teacher used to expound, 'There shall step forth a star out of Jacob (Num 24:17)—thus, read no *kokab* (star), but *kozeb* (liar).' When R. Akiba saw Bar Koziba (read, Kokhba), he cried out, 'this is King Messiah.'" See Schürer, "The Qumran Messiahs and Messianism"; Salomon Buber, *Midrash Rabbah: Lamentations* (Vilna, 1899), 101.

Chapter 5

"THE SPIRIT OF YHWH IS UPON ME"
(ISAIAH 61:1–3)

Introduction

Throughout the ages, Isa 61:1–3 has elicited many different interpretations. Since 61:1–3 uses the verb √משׁח to speak of an individual who announces salvation, this texts has evoked a great deal of attention. The New Testament interprets these verses messianically in its claim that Jesus Christ is the Messiah (Luke 14:18–19). While the Targum regards the speaker of this passage to be "the prophet," Qumran literature (11QMelch) interprets it messianically, as will be considered later. Some Jews and Christians have interpreted Isa 61:1–3 messianically and others have not. As in previous chapters, I will initially examine how scholars have tried to describe the original function of 61:13 as a prebiblical tradition and then how its place within the book of Isaiah may invite a different consideration of it. In each case, I will present my own conclusions after considering those of others. This chapter makes no attempts to resolve all the redactional issues of Isa 56–66, but aims to show how this text within the latter formation of the book may or may not warrant messianic interpretation.

I. *Isaiah 61:1–3 within Pre-biblical Traditions*

A. *Non-messianic Assessments*
Many scholars think that the speaker in Isa 61:1–3 is the prophet.[1] John Gray suggests that "the prophet" declares his commission to proclaim an

1. Karl Elliger, *Die Einheit Des Tritojesaia Jesaia 56–66*, 24–26; Muilenburg, *The Book of Isaiah*, 709–10; G. W. H. Lampe and K. J. Woollcombe, *Essays on Typology* (SBT 22; Naperville, Ill.: Allenson, 1957); Lindblom, *Prophecy in Ancient Israel*, 176, 192, 271; Norman H. Snaith, *The Distinctive Ideas of the Old Testament* (New York: Schocken, 1973), 157; Westermann, *Isaiah 40–66*, 299; Juel, *Messianic*

era of grace.[2] G. Adam Smith considers that the speaker in 61:1 "may be the Prophet himself, or he may even be the Servant."[3] Since Elijah is called to anoint three men in order to wipe out the house of Omri (Hazael king of Syria, Jehu king of Israel and Elisha the prophet), D. S. Russell observes that Elisha's anointing of others exhibits for 61:1–3, "a wider use of anointing in the setting apart of prophets."[4] Julian Morgenstern argues that 61:1 and 10 were originally "integral parts of the Suffering Servant drama" which somehow "came to be dislocated from their original setting and transferred to their present setting in Isa 61."[5] Douglas Jones argues that "the prophet" is the speaker and the anointing is used "figuratively."[6] I. W. Slotki claims that the herald is probably "the prophet" himself who receives "metaphorical anointing" (1 Kgs 19:16).[7] James Sanders asserts that Isa 61:1–11 comprises a hymn which explains "the prophet's mission" in the consolation of Zion.[8] Klaus Koch argues that the prophet "presents himself as Yahweh's plenipotentiary (though without the title *'ebed*; cf. 61:1–6)."[9] Gordon Hugenberger says that Isa 61 has taken on a "prophetic identification."[10]

Others more specifically identify the speaker in Isa 61:1 as either Second or Third Isaiah, but not a Messiah. This consideration goes back to Duhm, who differentiates between what he coined as *"Deuterojesaja"* and *"Tritojesaja"* because the latter reflects consistently post-exilic writing style and setting that resemble portraits and ideas of writers in the latest times of Israel.[11]

Exegesis, 9; Claus Westermann, *Prophetic Oracles of Salvation in the Old Testament* (trans. Keith Crim; Louisville, Ky.: Westminster John Knox, 1991), 188; Roberts, "The Old Testament," 40.

2. Gray, *Reign of God*, 214.

3. Smith, *The Book of Isaiah*, 3:436.

4. D. S. Russell, *The Method and Message of Jewish Apocalyptic* (OTL; Philadelphia: Westminster, 1964), 305.

5. Morgenstern, "Isaiah 61," 109–10.

6. Douglas Jones, *Isaiah 56–66 and Joel* (London: SCM Press, 1964).

7. Slotki, *Isaiah*, 526–29.

8. James A. Sanders, "From Isaiah 61 to Luke 4," in *Christianity, Judaism and Other Greco-Roman Cults* (ed. J. Neusner; SJLA 12; Leiden: Brill, 1975), 75–106.

9. Koch, *The Prophets*, 2:157.

10. Hugenberger, "The Servant of the Lord," 112.

11. Duhm (*Jesaia*, xiii) thinks that the heathen have rebuilt the Jerusalem wall, the temple has been erected and the people are now living in Jerusalem. Isa 56:7 makes mention of post-exilic sacrifices and no human is directly mentioned as a tool *(werkzeug)* of God used to avenge the enemy as Cyrus in Second Isaiah (p. 394). In 58:1b, "Trito-Isaiah" announces the people's sins and there is no more mention of the sun and the moon in chs. 56–66 (pp. 406–7). Duhm asserts that the writer

Duhm aims to squelch the notion set forth by Cheyne and Kuenen that chs. 60–62 belongs to "Second Isaiah," but maintains that here we have a "Third" whose relationship with Second Isaiah is evident by the way that the redactors leave distinct pieces of each that are not identical.[12] Before the editors dislocated the original independent text of Third Isaiah material, the original scroll of Third Isaiah opened with Isa 61–66 and provided a proper call narrative. According to Duhm, chs. 56–60 originally closed Third Isaiah. This original order more effectively sets forth Third Isaiah's prophetic program.[13] Duhm draws this assumption from the fact that both halves of chs. 56–66 are the same size with the same peripheral seams, which appear to have been turned around and divided into two roles.[14] There is an interruption after 60:22, which indicates that a different order now exists.[15] Blame for sins occurs at the beginning and end of chs. 56–66. The despairing language which now ends ch. 66 would better mesh with the context of chs. 56–59.[16] Thus, the striking words, "the spirit of the Lord is upon me," would more appropriately open Third Isaiah[17] as Third Isaiah's call report, and the promise, "I am the Lord; in

---

distinguishes himself from his predecessor (*Vorgänger*) because he speaks from himself in the first person moving more in the direction of Haggai, Ezekiel and Zechariah (ibid., xvii, xiv, 390, 391, 425, 431). Sekine has considered Duhm's work as the basis for Third Isaiah research; see Seizo Sekine, *Die tritojesajanische Sammlung (Jes 56–66) redactiongeschichtlich untersuch* (BZAW 175; Berlin: de Gruyter, 1989), 1.

12. On this point, see Duhm, who claims that since Isa 60 and 62 quote phrases from Second Isaiah, we have all the more evidence against Cheyne and Kuenen that Third Isaiah is utilizing already existent material (*Jesaia*, xviii, 425). Yet, in a lengthy commentary, which did not come out until three years following Duhm's commentary, Cheyne indeed praises Duhm for these observations (for discussion on this, see Sekine, *Die Tritojesajanische Sammlung*, 4). Duhm also argues that a number of things are odd in ch. 61, which does not lend to its placement. Isa 61:10 is alien to its context and the opening phrase, "the Spirit of Yнwн is upon me," does not support that *Ebed Yнwн* is speaking. The task of *Ebed Yнwн* is to teach Torah but he is not even mentioned here once. Duhm argues that "Trito-Isaiah" mistakes the bringer of good news with the prophet but not Deutero-Isaiah because the repeated mention of the day of vengeance does not fit into his portrait of *Ebed Yнwн's* actions and sufferings. The similarities are not strong enough to ascribe chs. 60–62 to the penmanship of Deutero-Isaiah and the quotations weaken this notion all the more (*Jesaia*, 425).

13. Duhm, *Jesaia*, 425.

14. See ibid., 391, 424, 425, 458.

15. See Pauritsch for further comment, *De Neue Gemeinde*, 105.

16. See Duhm, *Jesaia*, 458.

17. See Duhm's comments on 61:1 (ibid., 425).

its time I will hasten," would offer a more fitting conclusion.[18] Therefore, Duhm views 61:1–3 as the call of the prophet Third Isaiah and rules out messianic interpretation.

John McKenzie asserts that Isa 61 reflects the Servant Songs and is uttered by "the prophet…Third Isaiah" (vv. 1–7), Yahweh (vv. 8–9) and Zion (vv. 10–11). The prophet considers himself to be fulfilling the mission of the Servant and hence interprets the Servant Songs. His task is to proclaim salvation to Israel. The brokenhearted captives and prisoners denote the post-exilic Israelite community, though the poor and brokenhearted do not speak of Israel as a whole but only the faithful ones.[19] More specifically, William Holladay suggests that 61:1–4 resembles the "triumph" seen in Second Isaiah but refers to Isa 61 as "the work of Third Isaiah."[20] Since kings and priests were anointed but the anointing of a prophet was rare, as in the case of Elisha, Holladay regards the anointing in 61:1 to function in a "figurative sense" to legitimize Third Isaiah's words.[21] A. Joseph Everson argues that Third Isaiah clarified "his own calling as a messenger with the specific language describing the servant."[22] Richard Horsley asserts that with the monarchy destroyed and perhaps discredited, Third Isaiah provides a vivid expression of how there may have been a shift from the expectation of a kingly deliverer to that of a prophet, but that "there is little evidence that expectations of an eschatological prophet were very prominent in Jewish society."[23] David Meade argues that 61:1–3 is a "'call' narrative" that provides "a glimpse into the self-consciousness" of Second Isaiah's disciples who possibly carry out the tradition of their mentor and proclaim the unfulfilled message until it is fulfilled.[24] K. Koenen asserts that Isa 61:1–3 forms the call of Third Isaiah because, like Isa 6:8, the verb שלח, followed by a series of infinitives, emulates the commissioning of a prophetic individual (1 Sam 15:1; 2 Kgs 2:2–6; Jer 7:25; 25:17; 26:12–15; Zech 2:12–15; 4:9; 6:15).[25]

---

18. See ibid., 424–26 on 60:22 and following.

19. McKenzie, *Second Isaiah*, 181. Procksch, *Jesaja*, 152; Rowley, *The Servant of the Lord*, 6, 31.

20. Holladay, *Isaiah*, 19, 179.

21. Ibid., 179–80, 216.

22. A. Joseph Everson, "Isaiah 61:1–6 (To Give them a Garland Instead of Ashes)," *Int* 32 (1978): 70.

23. Horsley, *Bandits, Prophets, and Messiahs*, 148–49.

24. David G. Meade, *Pseudonymity and Canon* (WUNT 39; Tübingen: J. C. B. Mohr [Paul Siebeck], 1986), 39–40.

25. K. Koenen, "Textkritische Anmerkungen zu schwierigen Stellen im Tritojesajabuch," *Bib* 69 (1988): 564–73.

Several scholars argue that the Servant is speaking in Isa 61:1–3 (42:1–9; 49:1–9; 50:4–9; 52:13–53:12).[26] Sigmund Mowinckel contends that the speaker in 61:1–2 speaks in a manner similar to the speaker of the Servant Songs, who is a prophet in Deutero-Isaiah's circle. The prophet reinterpreted the words of Deutero-Isaiah so that the Servant Songs convey the new revelation, which amplified what the master had said. The prophet, who is the Servant, accomplishes what was not achieved by Cyrus, or the governor of David's line, the restoration of the temple. Otherwise the glad tidings of the full salvation and restoration of Israel could not be realized. Thus the message about the Servant far surpasses everything in the Old Testament message about the Messiah (the future king), his person and his work. Mowinckel thinks that the speaker in 61:1–2 may very well be the Servant and the passage may depict his prophetic call. He thinks that "The speaker is not the king but the king's herald, i.e., the prophet. The royal functions cannot simply be transferred to the herald or prophet." The Servant's task exceeds the expectation of a future king because he will bring salvation to Zion through "his suffering and death."[27] Mowinckel concludes that it was not until Jesus proved himself to be "something much more than a Jewish Messiah" that the figure of the Servant influenced messianic thought.[28]

Claus Westermann regards Isa 60–62 to be the "nucleus" of "Trito-Isaiah" and to contain nothing but a message of salvation. Since 60:13 says that the temple has not yet been rebuilt and Haggai describes a time period about whose beginning Third Isaiah only proclaims, Westermann specifies a date "previous to Haggai and Zechariah, before 521."[29] He argues that Isa 59 forms a lament that becomes part of the framework of chs. 60–62 and the oracles of judgment in 56:9–57:13. The charges that Isa 59 makes against transgressors constitute part of the same strand that allows 56:9–57:13 to transform earlier oracles of doom into charges brought against transgressors.[30] Following older modern approaches, Westermann thinks that this salvation is "not spoken to the exiles but to

26.   Torrey, *Second Isaiah*, 452; van Hoonacker, "L'ébed Jahvé"; George E. Cannon, "Isaiah 61, 1–3 as Ebed-Jahweh Poem," *ZAW* 40 (1929): 284–88; Otto Procksch, *Theologie des Alten Testaments* (Gutersloh: Bertlesmann, 1950), 290; John Bright, *The Kingdom of God* (Nashville: Abingdon, 1953), 146, 153, 198, 209–11; Walter Zimmerli and Joachim Jeremias, *The Servant of God* (rev. ed.; Studies in Theology 20; Naperville, Ill.: Allenson, 1965), 26, 29.

27.   Mowinckel, *He That Cometh*, 226, 255.

28.   Ibid., 255–57.

29.   Westermann, *Isaiah 40–66*, 295–96.

30.   Ibid., 301–2.

the people who, long after the return to Judah and Jerusalem, were still looking to the future for this."[31] Therefore, Westermann thinks that chs. 60–62 refer to a "prophet active in Jerusalem and Judah not long after the return."[32] Deutero-Isaiah's disciple, "Trito-Isaiah," ministered in the early post-exilic period primarily "to reawaken Deutero-Isaiah's message of salvation for a small band of people living in disillusionment after the end of the exile and return."[33] Isaiah 61:1–3, then, witnesses to Trito-Isaiah's prophetic self-consciousness but not to a Messiah.[34]

Others assert that Isa 61:1–3 assumes a prophetic genre without specifically naming the speaker as "the prophet." For example, Robert Wilson refers to Isa 61 as a "so-called prophetic liturgy."[35] David L. Petersen refers to Isa 61 as "tradent-prophecy," whereby Third Isaiah performed an "exegetical" role in response to an already existing prophetic tradition but did not make an original prophetic contribution.[36] Petersen regards the speaker here to be a traditionalist, who is one of the "preservers and interpreters of authoritative traditions…"[37]

Others claim that the speaker in 61:1–3 is the Servant. John Bright, who regards 61:1–2 to be one of the Servant passages, argues that the Servant "proclaims good tidings of God's redemption" but was never considered by Judaism to be the Messiah. The Servant gained messianic status as the Church understood Jesus to unite the Servant with other messianic concepts.[38] Similarly, Norman Whybray suggests that 61:1–3 finds close similarities with the Servant Songs and the speaker in 61:1–3, who, like the Servant, claims to have received YHWH's Spirit.[39] He thinks that Isa 61 has undergone a process of development that originated from the same tradition history as did Isa 60 whereby a disciple of Second Isaiah borrows themes from the Servant Songs. He applies them to himself believing the Servant to be Second Isaiah.[40] While he does not confirm a direct connection between the Servant and the Messiah, Whybray acknowledges the problems posed if the speaker in 61:1–3 is intentionally identifying himself with the Servant. Nevertheless, the phrase

31.   Ibid., 297.
32.   Ibid., 353.
33.   Ibid., 299.
34.   Ibid., 367.
35.   Wilson, *Prophecy and Society in Ancient Israel*, 260.
36.   Petersen, *Late Israelite Prophecy*, 213–30.
37.   Ibid., 25. On this point, Peterson follows the view of D. Michel, "Zur Eigenart Tritojesajas," *ThViat* 10 (1965/66): 213–30.
38.   Bright, *The Kingdom of God*, 146, 153, 198, 208–14.
39.   Whybray, *Isaiah 40–66*, 239.
40.   Ibid., 240.

"has anointed me," like in 45:1, is used "metaphorically, but not to speak of a Messiah."

Others assign 61:1–3 to the people of Israel whether or not they have assumed the prophetic role. James D. Smart resists associating the speaker with a prophetic role in 61:1–3 and identifies this figure with Israel, whom he calls "the servant of God."[41] On the other hand, Joachim Becker argues that this prophetic role "is transferred theocratically to the entire nation."[42] George Knight even argues that "me" in 61:1 is both "Trito-Isaiah and Israel."[43] "Consequently," Knight concludes that "all the Servant people are anointed here" so that "in the power of the Spirit Israel might set all other peoples free."[44] Similarly, Wolfgang Roth asserts that 61:1–63:6 contains "the servant people's announcement of Israel's release into a new creation," and that 61:1–11 announces that the hour has come for the servant people to be "filled with the spirit of the Lord."[45] Edgar Conrad contends that the community is speaking in the first person singular.[46]

More recently, P. A. Smith argues that 61:1–3 speaks of the whole people using terms in the plural.[47] Here, Third Isaiah "refers to the Jerusalem community as a whole."[48] Smith argues that the usage of the word "comfort" may betray a connection between various passages but "by no means signifies common authorship" because the term is too common in chs. 40–66.[49] The notion of divine spirit and the portrait of his occupation marked by the infinitive construct with the preposition ל recalls the description of the Servant in 42:1–2 whose mission was to the exiled Israel as a whole. Trito-Isaiah understood his mission to the Jewish community as a whole.[50]

Others underscore the priestly dimensions of Isa 61. Morgenstern, claims that ch. 61 originated "about 450 BC" during a time when the priesthood was evolving into the "dominant" group. While claiming that 61:1 and 10 were dislocated from the Servant Songs (see above), he

41. Smart, *History and Theology in Second Isaiah*, 259–60.
42. Becker, *Messianic Expectation*, 51.
43. George A. F. Knight, *The New Israel: A Commentary on the Book of Isaiah 56–66* (Grand Rapids: Eerdmans, 1985), 50.
44. Ibid., 51.
45. Roth, *Isaiah*, 168.
46. Conrad, *Reading the Book of Isaiah*, 147.
47. P. A. Smith, *Rhetoric and Redaction in Trito Isaiah: The Structure, Growth and Authorship of Isaiah 56–66* (VTSup 62; Leiden: Brill, 1995), 89.
48. Ibid., 25.
49. Ibid., 160.
50. Ibid., 24–25.

asserts that the rest of Isa 61 speaks of Israel as YHWH's priest people, who minister "to Him in His sanctuary as the chosen intermediary between them and Him."[51] From a different perspective, P. Grelot asserts that the speaker in Isa 61 is the newly "anointed" high priest and his anointing is metaphorical and not literal.[52]

Identifying a schism between priestly and prophetic groups, Paul Hanson posits that the units found in Isa 60–62 form the heart of "Third Isaiah," depicting a visionary (prophetic) group's plan of restoration and reflecting what the disciples have learned from Second Isaiah.

In 61:1–3, a prophetic voice reasserts the old themes of Second Isaiah to a new situation, which, according to the structure and metric patterns in chs. 60–62, is located somewhere between the time of Second and Third Isaiah. Yet this community moves out on its own in chs. 56–59 and 63–66 as "Third Isaiah" takes a shape of its own.[53] Using social analysis to identify two groups (the hierocratic [priests] and the visionary [prophets]),[54] Hanson thinks that the visionary program based in Second Isaiah, emerges in chs. 60–62 to oppose the Zadokite-led hierocratic group, who claimed that only the Zadokites possessed holiness and the right to priesthood. Thus, the disciples of "Second Isaiah" have cultivated their own policy of restoration in chs. 60–62, which appointed "the whole nation" to be holy and to be priests.[55] Using the language, style and themes of Second Isaiah, chs. 60–62 became "proto-apocalyptic" emerging out of failure for the glorious redemptive promises uttered in Second Isaiah to find fulfillment in the politics of the post-exilic community. Therefore, 61:1–3 applies "the words used to describe the Servant in 42:1 to a new time and situation" to claim "inheritance of the office of that important figure in Second Isaiah's prophecy." The Servant Songs (at their pre-biblical level) possess an intentional ambiguity, which allow them to be applied to 61:1–11, not for the purposes of messianic

51.   Morgenstern, "Isaiah 61."

52.   P. Grelot, "Sur Isaïe LXI: La première consécration d'un grand-prêtre," *RB* 97 (1990): 414–31.

53.   Paul Hanson, *The Dawn of Apocalyptic: The Historical and Sociological Roots of Jewish Apocalyptic Eschatology* (Philadelphia: Fortress, 1979), 60.

54.   Hanson says that, in the polarized nature of the cultic enterprise, the Hierocratic scheme aims to control the culture and life of the community but the visionary idealizes the entire community and wishes for Zion to be restored as the focus of YHWH's presence in place of a centralized temple. The post-exilic Zadokite leaders used Ezek 40–48 as a blueprint regarding their plans for restoration, which are found in Isa 40–55 and 60–62 (ibid., 71, 79–100). See also Childs, *Biblical Theology*, 182.

55.   Hanson, *Dawn of Apocalyptic*, 71–76.

interpretation, but to establish the role of the Servant to one of Second Isaiah's disciples ('a visionary'), who would be YHWH's instrument to bring about reconciliation and healing to the community. He concludes, "if we can speak here of messianism, it is a democratized form of messianism, perhaps inspired by Second Isaiah's concept of a democratization with David (55:3), and reinforces an apparent democratization of priestly prerogatives as well (Isa 61:6; cf. Zech 14:20–21)."[56] In sum, Hanson establishes the sociological context largely from the studies of Weber, Mannheim and Troeltsch rather than from the biblical texts themselves. I believe that he has also misappropriated the term "apocalyptic" and has built on a taxonomy that does not define its essential nature or clarify its historical and sociological matrix. John Collins defines apocalyptic as that which must be mediated by an "other worldly" being to a human recipient and offers a thorough view of the cosmos through the order of the heavens or predetermined course of history.[57] Form-critically, "Second" and "Third Isaiah" materials do not meet this definition (contra Hanson).[58]

John Watts atypically identifies three speakers in Isa 61:1–11: the first is a preacher, healer and messenger (vv. 1–3), the second an administrator or ruler (vv. 4–7) and the third is YHWH himself.[59] Watts likens the "royal factors" of Isa 61 with "the spirit" in 11:2 which was upon a king and present at the "anointing" of Cyrus in 45:1, but regards this anointing as "figurative for a commissioning for a specific task." For Watts, this task includes the proclamation of "liberty to the captives and an opening to those imprisoned."[60] Watts, therefore, does not regard this passage as messianic.

---

56.   *Isaiah 40–66*, 223–24. It must be noted that Gerhard von Rad speaks of "democratizing" a messianic tradition. See his *The Message of the Prophets* (London: SCM Press, 1968), 208.

57.   J. J. Collins' definition reads: "Apocalypse is a genre of revelatory literature with a narrative framework, in which a revelation is mediated by an otherworldly being to a human recipient, disclosing a transcendent reality which is both temporal, insofar as it envisages eschatological salvation, and spatial insofar as it involves another, supernatural world." See his "Apocalypse: The Morphology of a Genre," *Semeia* 14 (1979): 59–67; idem, *Introduction to Apocalyptic Literature* (Grand Rapids: Eerdmans, 1984); idem, *The Apocalyptic Vision of the Book of Daniel* (Ann Arbor: University of Michigan, 1977), 9.

58.   See Collins' from-critical description of apocalypses (*Introduction*, 20), but also notice how Hanson lucidly lays out cautions to which he himself cannot adhere (Hanson, *The Historical and Sociological Roots*, 43).

59.   Watts, *Isaiah 34–66*, 305.

60.   Ibid., 305.

B. *Messianic Assessments*

Some scholars aim to align the "royal features" that exist in 61:1–3 with traditional messianic interpretation. G. Widengren maintains that 61:1–3 is a royal self-praise hymn (*königliche Selbströhmungshymne*).[61] Yet others try to explain how a prophetic identification of the speaker in 61:1–3 can be heard messianically. Selman thinks that texts that speak of "anointing by God's Spirit led to prophetic activity (Is. 61:1–2; Joel 2:28–32 [3:1–5])." These, for him, are "sufficient warrant for regarding prophecy in a messianic light."[62] Rowley argues that the prophet is the joyous messenger and the mediator of salvation.[63] Others argue that Isa 61:1–3 provides a warrant for a prophetic Messiah. For example, some claim that when 61:1 was applied to Jesus, it spoke of him as a prophet but not a king.[64] Joseph Alexander asserts that Isa 61 describes the prophetic "office" of the Messiah. If the speaker were the prophet, he could only function as a type of the Messiah, but the person presented here *is* the Messiah.[65] At the same time, the text can solicit "a subordinate and secondary reference to Israel as a representative of the Messiah, and to the Prophets as in some sense the representatives of Israel, as well as of Messiah in their prophetic character…" In any case, Alexander suggests that we are always brought back to Christ who is the "ideal prophet."[66]

Similarly, John Collins argues that the speaker in 61:1 is "a prophet, who makes his proclamation in the name of God" but one "who also claims to be anointed, and so he is a משיח, or anointed one."[67] He is evidently a human, who says "the spirit of the Lord God is upon me," but also God, since 61:6 reads "I the Lord love justice."[68] He reasons:

61. G. Widengren, *Sakrales Königtum im Alten Testament und im Judentum* (Stuttgart: Kohlhammer, 1955), 56–58. See also von Waldow, "Analass Hintergrund," 54; Kaiser, *Der königliche Knecht*, 54–56.

62. Martin J. Selman, "Messianic Mysteries," in Satterthwaite, Hess and Wenham, eds., *The Lord's Anointed*, 296.

63. Rowley, *The Biblical Doctrine of Election*, 112.

64. Russell, *The Method and Message of Jewish Apocalyptic*, 305; K. Berger, "Zum Problem der Messianität Jesu," *ZThK* 71 (1974): 1–30; idem, "Die Königlichen Messiastraditionen des Neuen Testaments," *NTS* 20 (1973–74): 1–44; Anthony E. Harvey, *Jesus and the Constraints of History* (Philadelphia: Westminster, 1982), 120–53.

65. Alexander, *Commentary on the Prophecies of Isaiah*, 397.

66. Ibid., 398. See also, Jamieson, Fausset and Brown who, in a similar vane, assert that eighth-century Isaiah is the "author" of Isa 40–66 and 61:1–3 describes a messianic office. See Robert Jamieson, A. R. Fausset and David Brown, *Commentary on the Whole Bible* (Grand Rapids: Zondervan, 1945), 428, 499.

67. Collins, *The Scepter and the Star*, 118.

68. Ibid., 120–21.

We now have a text from Qumran (4Q521) that has a remarkable parallel to Jesus' answer to the Baptist and that also refers to a messiah, whom heaven and earth obey. While it is apparently God who heals the wounded, gives life to the dead, and preaches good news to the poor in that text, the role of preaching is usually assigned to an agent. The mention of the messiah suggests that God acts through an agent here, too. It is quite likely, then, that these words were considered "works of the messiah," as well as of God, before the Gospels. Since the works in question are typical of what is attributed to Jesus in the Gospels, this text strengthens the case that the epithet "anointed" or "messiah" could have been attached to him because of his words and deeds. The "messiah" in 4Q521 is not perceptibly royal, however, and is best regarded, like the "anointed" speaker in 61, as a prophet not a king.[69]

Hence, Collins concludes that this supports the view that YHWH will accomplish his eschatological intention through a prophetic Messiah.[70]

Others aim to define the speaker as a Servant Messiah. For example, Charles C. Torrey identifies Isa 61 as a "'Servant' poem" that presents "the figure of the Servant Messianically…as in chapter 42 (first part), 45, and 49." "The picture of the sympathetic and magnanimous helper… takes us back to 42:1–7…"[71] The verb "anoint" is not accidental, nor insignificant because "the Servant, who is the speaker, is *The Messiah*." The "year of favor" in 61:2 speaks of "the dawn of the Messianic age."[72] Walther Eichrodt asserts that Deutero-Isaiah portrays the Servant in 42:1 and in 61:1, which may very well be a "fragment of the Servant Songs," as "the messianic king, who is portrayed as the favoured bearer of the spirit…"[73]

More recently, scholars assert that the meaning of 61:1–3 relies on how Isa 60–62 has been edited into the greater context of "Third Isaiah," but not necessarily the book as a whole. For example, Karl Pauritsch uses "rhetorical criticism" to propose that the pre-redactional order of chs. 60–62 was originally fixed in a different sequence (chs. 61, 62 and 60), which presented the book so that contextually chs. 56–60 and 62–66 would contain about the same number of verses.[74] His central question

69. Ibid., 205.
70. Ibid., 117–22.
71. Torrey, *Second Isaiah*, 452.
72. Ibid., 453.
73. Walther Eichrodt, *Theology of the Old Testament*, vol. 2 (trans. J. A. Baker; London: SCM Press, 1967), 59.
74. Pauritsch seeks to explain why the editor made this change and that 60:1–22, 61:1–7 and 62:1–9 and constitute the original primary units. Isa 60:22 would have formed the conclusion but 62:10 was added before the final redaction and made a transition from ch. 60 to 61:10 in view of the whole context. The summarizing

turns on whether "these chapters have an internal coherence, a common plan and a specific relation to one another."[75] Isaiah 61:1–3 and 62:1 speak of the prophet in the first person and 61:1 has the characteristics of a call narrative (*Berufungserlebnisses*) that contains the prophet's own consciousness, intention and authorization by God. Hence ch. 61 serves as the first stage followed by chs. 62 and 60 which proclaim an urgent promise from God that entreats his audience to maintain a covenant relationship with God.[76]

Pauritsch asserts that Isa 61, forming three strophes (vv. 1–3, 4–7 and 8–9, 11), is one of the most important units of proclamation. Form-critically, 61:1–3 makes up a *königliche Selbstrühmungshymne* (royal self-praise hymn) where the speaker does not function as a prophet but as a king.[77] In what he labels an "edifying prophetic sermon of salvation" (he seems to contradict himself because he said that the speaker is *not* a

---

nature of 62:11–12 was added during the final redaction of Third Isaiah. By placing ch. 60 before ch. 61, 62:10 would have been incomprehensible when isolated from 62:11–12. Hence 62:10–12 made a smoother transition into 66:3–4. See his *Die Neue Gemeinde* (AnBib 47; Rome: Biblical Institute Press, 1971), 105–7. See also Sekine, *Die Tritojesajanische Sammlung*, 19.

75.   Pauritsch agrees with Westermann that chs. 60–62 consist of the three elements which form a complaint: *Feindklage* ("Lamentation about enemies," ch. 60), *wirklage* ("complaint," ch. 61), and *Anklage Gotts* ("accusation," ch. 62). In the center of ch. 62, God has again turned to his people but Pauritsch cautions that it would be premature to suppose that these chapters are a unity; "Nur wenige Exegeten sprachen von Kap. 60–62 als einer größeren Einheit. Niemand bezweifel allerdings dieselbe Verfasserpersönlichkeit. Meist spricht man von einer, kleineren Sammlung" (*Die Neue Gemeinde*, 105).

76.   Pauritsch suggests that Isa 62 is made up of six strophes each comprising seven lines: vv. 1–3, 4–5, 6–7, 8–9, 10 (a short strophe) and 11, 12. Verse 12 cannot be viewed as the original unit. The chapter really ends with v. 9 but a redactor added v. 10 so that he could attach ch. 60 to the end. Isa 62:11–12 were then added as a summary after chs. 60–62 were arranged in their final form. Isa 62:10–12 serves as the original conclusion of Third Isaiah (*Die Neue Gemeinde*, 114, 115). Generally, Isa 60 is a non-problematic passage (yet vv. 6c, 12, 14a, 17b, 19c are glosses) that is made up of ten strophes with four lines each (vv. 1–3, 4–5, 6–7, 8–9, 10–11, 13–14, 15–16, 17–18, 19–20, 21–22). In vv. 1–3, the "prophet" formulates or summarizes his main thesis and the rest of the chapter refutes those who would hold God responsible for the exile. Verses 10–16 place the blame on the enemy and vv. 17–22 warn against accusing themselves. In the last strophe, 60:20–22 addresses Zion for the first time as the people are unified in the eschatological time, while 60:22b provides the horizon, guarantee and fulfillment of the entire message of chs. 60–62. Therefore, one cannot view Isa 61 apart from this greater context (ibid., 106, 126, 127).

77.   Ibid., 108–14, 128.

prophet), the speaker is an individual different from Second Isaiah himself, calling on the hearers to see their need to pray to God that he might speed up salvation and demonstrate his love for Zion.[78] The release of the captives reflects this task of bringing glad tidings. Isaiah 61 would then open the entire block of chs. 61, 62 and 60 with a proclamation of salvation. Following Elliger, Pauritsch argues that ch. 60 is a promise but adds that it closes the block. Within this context, ch. 61 deals with the future, but the use of the perfect aspect suggests that the future is already fixed (a so-called "prophetic perfect"). Pauritsch states that it is not clear from the context who the speaker is, but from the content it is implied that it must be a king, presumably the messianic king. However,

> the (political) release of the prisoners in order to demonstrate royal humanity seems to be an important argument, but the function to bring a glad message is assigned rather to a Herald. There is a final point to make: that Isa 61:1–3 does not intend to pronounce an independent message, but rather has a certain function in its context (60–62) to fulfill.[79]

Pauritsch finds himself stymied by the tension between the herald of good tidings, an hypothetical Third-Isaiah's own call narrative and a king Messiah who releases the captives. It is interesting that, within this tension, he does not conclude that Third Isaiah originally spoke these words to describe his own call narrative and that the later royal Messiah would speak the same words as a fulfilment.

Referring to all of Isa 40–66 as Deutero-Isaiah, Benjamin Sommer claims that 60:17–61:1 alludes to ch. 11. His evidence is based on the vocabulary similarities in each (נצר, 11:1//60:21; רוח, 11:2//61:1; צדק, 11:3–5//60:17; ארץ, 11:4//60:21). Moreover, he asserts that Deutero-Isaiah makes an "allusion" to kingship without mentioning it.[80] By presenting these similarities, Sommer raises the possibilities for messianic interpretation. However, except for the possibility of נצר, these vocabulary items are so common that his argument is not convincing. Because he addresses various "inner-biblical allusions" in a way that seems to treat "Deutero-Isaiah" as an entity separate from the book of Isaiah, Sommer has not treated the book of Isaiah as a whole.

78. Ibid., 134–36.
79. The German: "Die Freilassung der (politischen) Gefangenen zum Zeichen königlicher Humanität scheint zwar ein wichtiges Argument zu sein, doch is die Aufgabe, 'frohe Botschaft zu bringen,' eher einem Herold zuzuordnen. Endlich ist zudenken, daß 61,1–3 kein selbständiges Verkündigungsstück sein will, sondern eine bestimmte Funktion im Kontext zu erfüllen hat" (ibid., 129).
80. Benjamin Sommer, "Scroll of Isaiah as Jewish Scripture, Or, Why Jews Don't Read Books," in *SBL Seminar Papers, 1996* (SBLSP 35; Atlanta: Scholars Press, 1996), 239; idem, *A Prophet Reads Scripture*, 20, 86–87, 113, 141.

C. *Rethinking the Evidence*

At the original level of tradition history, 61:1–3 could have referred to either the prophet, the Servant or even a Messiah (by the use of משח). The fact that scholars speculate such a wide variety of referents for 61:1–3 demonstrates how the ambiguity of the text may illicit polyvalent interpretations. By treating this material as the work of "Trito-Isaiah," individuals have not only anchored the text in a pre-biblical level of tradition history, but have ignored the later stages of development, whereby the book of Isaiah became a whole product. Therefore, any pre-biblical level of tradition history, whether or not the original intent of 61:1–3 presupposes messianic interpretation, does not identify the meaning of the scriptural scroll of Isaiah but at best interprets a pre-biblical messianism set forth by either Second or Third Isaiah.

II. *Interpretation within the Biblical Scroll of Isaiah*

A. *Non-messianic Assessments of the Biblical Testimony*

In more recent years, several scholars have tried to consider the biblical book of Isaiah as a whole, and their interpretation of 61:1–3 has depended on the way that they understand chs. 60–62 to have been edited into the greater book of Isaiah. Yet many individuals, who claim to interpret the book as a whole, do not necessarily interpret 61:1–3 messianically. For example, by describing the formation of the book of Isaiah as a concatenation of *relecteurs*, Vermeylen argues for several layers of redaction in chs. 60–62.[81] He asserts that 61:1–4 is not the speech of a prophet, but the community of faith's hopeful reply to the phrase in 60:1, "the glory of YHWH has risen upon you." Isaiah 61:1–4 "rereads" 60:1–11, 12 in light of the faithful Israel's duty, but does not do so messianically. Although he claims to be reading the book as a whole, Vermeylen does not allow the scriptural form to govern meaning of the text but anchors the meaning of each unit in the redactor's "rereading."

W. A. M. Beuken argues that it is necessary to read "Trito-Isaiah" as a part of the whole book and in relation to "a hermeneutical framework."[82] He contends that such a unity bears the mark of intentionality.[83]

---

81. Vermeylen, *Du prophète Isaïe*, 2:471–89.

82. Beuken, *Jesaja*, 3A:158. See also Ulrich Berges, *Das Buch Jesaja. Komposition und Endgestalt* (Herder Biblische Studien 16; Freiburg: Herder, 1998).

83. Emphasizing the book as a whole, Beuken first explains the role of Isa 60–62 within the scheme of chs. 56–66 and how 61:1 and 61:11b are emphatically anchored in "Third Isaiah." The name "YHWH" (62:1 and 11b) surrounds the entire chapter and the word-pair "righteousness" and "praise" refers back to 61:3 where

Consequently, the writer of *Tritojesaja* is a disciple of *Deuterojesaja* and carries on the tradition.[84] Following what he refers to as Westermann's "*Klage* Theory," Beuken thinks that chs. 60–62 is a herald or announcement of salvation which follows a pattern of a lamentation: after ch. 60, there is a complaint about the enemies; after ch. 61, a complaint about their personal circumstances; and after ch. 62, a complaint about God. Isaiah 60–62 forms a unity within the heart of Third Isaiah, and chs. 60 and 62, which are about Zion, surround the central chapter (ch. 61) where a prophetic character comes to the stage.[85] On these grounds, Beuken suggests that the term "to send" in 61:1 corresponds to the anointing, which in this text is the prophet.[86] He rules out messianic interpretation in 61:1–3 because, in his view, the book of Isaiah does not refer to a savior beyond history but to one within the boundaries of our world time.[87] In chs. 60–62, "the author" arouses in the reader's mind that something is missing in chs. 60–62 and at the same time needs to be separated from it: namely, that the salvation of Zion assumes the

both characteristics form part of the comfort. Hence, Beuken refers to 60:18 where praise parallels salvation with righteousness in 62:1; 63:1; 56:1; 59:17, which he says form the new defense of Zion (compare with 6:6). Righteousness and praise is situated in Zion, which is not mentioned in ch. 61 except by a gloss in v. 3. But according to numerous commentators, righteousness and praise form an important background to the chapter, whereas in 62:1 it is immediately announced. Therefore these chapters cannot be isolated (*Jesaja*, 3A:219). Beuken thinks that chs. 60–62, leaving out 60:10 and 62:1–7, is the *"oorsponkelijke"* (original) *"literarische Fortschreiben* of Js 40–55," which he argues never existed by itself. The other chapters of *Tritojesaja* would have found their place before and after chs. 60–62 in the process of the formation of the whole book of Isaiah. Isa 63:1–6 along with 59 would then have been added to this central core of the collection during the final redaction (ibid., 3A157). Beuken then asserts that the relationship between 63:1–6 and ch. 59 plays an important role in the redaction-critical theory that 63:1–6 and 56:9–59:20 form the first expansion (*uitbreiding*) on Isa 40–55 and 60–62. Both 63:1–6 and ch. 59 form the framework for chs. 60–62 even though chs. 60–62 interrupt an original connection between 63:1–6 and 56:9–59:20 (ibid., 3A:246).

84.   Regarding chs. 60–62, Beuken (*Jesaja*, 3A: 164) states: "…The imagery of light and darkness does service to the theme of the revelation of God's salvation. Third Isaiah has employed the heritage of his predecessors with a new idiom (to arise). He paints the fulfillment of all the promises which were earlier made, as the coming of YHWH to Zion."

85.   Ibid., 3A: 157.

86.   W. A. M. Beuken, "Servant and Herald of Good Tidings: Isaiah 61 as an Interpretation of Isaiah 40–55," in Vermeylen, ed., *Le livre d'Isaïe*, 415–16.

87.   See his article "Did Israel need a Messiah?" in *Messianism Through History* (ed. W. Beuken, Seán Freyne and Anton Weiler; London: SCM Press; Maryknoll, N.Y.: Orbis), 3–13.

punishment of God's enemies.[88] The effectiveness of Beuken's proposal lies in his efforts to show the link between chs. 60–62 and its exterior blocks, chs. 56–59 and 63–66. He adequately portrays the dialectic between chs. 60–62 and the text which surrounds it. Yet he really does not explain its connection with the greater book of Isaiah as he claims.

Odil Hannes Steck describes a multi-layered process of redaction history in Isa 55–66 (which, for him, do not form a unity) whereby on a grand scale the editors betray early intentions for a unified Isaiah. He argues that various themes taken from ch. 40 appear in ch. 49 and have been distributed throughout chs. 60–62, which do not appear in chs. 56–59 and 63–66.[89] Therefore, Isa 60–62 is a literary extension of Second Isaiah (not a successor prophet) which betrays previous knowledge of chs. 40–55.[90] Steck asserts that chs. 60–62 do not really add anything

88.   Beuken argues that, through the oration of 63:1–6, the same issues for chs. 56–59 apply to chs. 60–62 because there exists a tight redactional framework, which ties together chs. 59 and 60 (*Jesaja*, 3A:58) with 63:1–6, adding to chs. 60–62 in light of ch. 59. Isa 63:1–6 displays a connection with chs. 60–62 but displays a different nature than the internal relationship of chs. 60, 61 and 62. However, if one accept 60:1–63:6 as at least one redactional whole, then the internal boundaries (*"afbukening"*) will present no literary difficulty. Isa 63:1–6 is closely connected with 59:15–20 and at the same time is separated by 60–62, and, since it has a disputation, it is an account about something that has already happened, giving it the literary character of an *inhaalmanoeuvre* ("a narrator who catches the audience up with the drama"). Thus, he compares this text with a messenger story in classical drama. So "the author" rouses the impressions in chs. 60–62 that something is missing, which at the same time must be separated from it (*Jesaja*, 3A: 256).

89.   Following Cheyne, Pauritsch and Westermann, Steck (*Studien zu Trito-jesaja*, 16, 27–28) argues that Isa 56–59 and 63–66 were not originally part of Third Isaiah. Isa 56–59 provides the cultic opening for the announcement of gentiles and cannot belong with the announcement of chs. 60–62, which speaks about the coming of the Gentiles and their effect on God's people. The Zion appeal (*"Aufforderung"*) in Isa 60:1 makes no reference to chs. 56–59. Unlike Isa 60–62, the healing in chs. 56–59 depends on the repentance of the people. The speech about the judgment of God's people (63:1–6), the great prayer (63:7–64:11) and the division of Israel's domination (chs. 65–66) do not correspond to chs. 60–62. Isa 56–59 and 63–66 not only fit together with each other, but appear as though they have been placed into an already existent *Großjesaja* book at a much later time because they show grave internal differences with chs. 60–62. Although chs. 60–62 form a foundation for Third Isaiah, chs. 60–62 is separated from Third Isaiah and was added at a different time.

90.   This is evident since 60:1 refers to the appeals that begin with קוּמִי in 51:17; 52:2 and 54:1, but which are never found in chs. 56–59 (Steck, *Studien zu Tritojesaja*, 16). Isa 60–62 has been arranged in five redactional stages as the greater book of Isaiah has grown: (1) 60:1–9, 13–16; 62:1–11; (2) 60:10–11; 62:1–7; (3) 62:10–12; (4) 60:17–22; 61:2; 62:8–9; (5) 60:12a; 61:3 (Steck, *Studien zu*

new to Second Isaiah except that an editor brings together the whole through 62:10–12.[91] He argues that chs. 35, 40 and 60–62 (all belonging to the same stock) were added together in the fifth century to the nucleus the greater Isaiah book by the help of 62:10–12.[92] Isaiah 40–55 and 60–62 have been bridged by chs. 35 and 40 to a *Protojesaja* corpus to create a new composite. At this level the corpus has reached what Steck calls "Großjesanisches proportions," because it stretches across First, Second and Third Isaiah.[93] Rather than applying typical redaction criticism,

---

Tritojesaja, 119). Stages 1 and 2 serve as a literary extension to Second Isaiah and stages 3–5 are drawn from the three final redactions in 60–62. Isa 60:1–9, 13–16 and Isa 61 to be the *Grundtext* of not only chs. 60–62, but all of chs. 56–66. Isa 60 is modeled after ch. 49, whereby 49:6 has influenced 60:1–3 by emphasizing restoration (pp. 77–80). Isa 60:4 almost reduplicates 49:18, which calls Zion to "lift up your eyes round about and see...all gather together, they come to you" (pp. 76, 77). The second half of Isa 60:4 emulates 49:22b, "Your sons will come...and your daughters will be carried in the arms." The small difference between the two passages is that in 60:4 the sons "come from afar" but in 49:22b they "they will bring your sons in their bosom." Also, in 60:4 the daughters are carried in the "arms" (צד) but in v. 22b they are carried on "shoulders" (כתף) (pp. 75–77). Isa 60:5–13 then seems to imitate the theme of 49:23a where nations and kings will serve them (p. 68) and 49:26a where the afflictors of Zion will bow down to her (p. 77). Isa 60:15–16 makes reference to the statement in 49:26b: "know that I am the savior" (pp. 49, 55, 77, 78). Isa 60:17–22 does not fit into Steck's *Grundtext* because it does not belong to the previous verses nor the sections that immediately follow, but is entirely different material. Steck would assert that 60:17 is too dissimilar from 60:1–16 to be a part of the *grundtext* (p. 62). In 60:17a, YHWH himself brings blessings to Zion, but, in 60:1–3, YHWH's glory appears rather than YHWH directly. Steck says that, "others bring something to Zion (61:3, 14), come to Zion (4b, 5b, 6a, 13) or they bring something (9a and 11b)." This is quite different than Yahweh's appearing in v. 17. Since vv. 17b–18 are accompanied by prophesies which have conditions for restoration, Steck argues that that vv. 17b–18 are from a different hand because these conditions are not present in vv. 1–16 (p. 51).

91. See Steck's explanation (ibid., 18, 26.).

92. According to Steck (ibid., 50), Isa 60:12 does not belong to the original *Grundtext* because v. 12a provides the precise wording of Jer 27:8–10, and 12b is influenced by 2 Kgs 19:17 and Jer 37:18 (p. 51). Isa 62:10–12 unravels the knot (*problemknoten*) for how "Third Isaiah" fits into the greater Isaiah book. The previously mentioned second and third redactional layers are significant in how "Third Isaiah" became connected to the greater Isaiah book. Accordingly, Steck suggests that 40:1–11 and 34 are the two passages to which v. 35 finds the theological bridge where no cross-references are found in chs. 56–59 and 63–66, but is convinced that these references do appear in chs. 60–62 (p. 20).

93. Like Vermeylen, Steck argues that Isa 35 prophesies about the homecoming of the Israelites and also appears in chs. 40–55+60 and 62:10–12. Steck asserts that these are all a retelling of 11:11–16 and 27:12–13. Isa 62:10–12 reflect the exact

Steck performs a *Tendenz Kritik*, tracing similarities, allusions and even quotations quite effectively.

Steck argues that Isa 60–62 is not merely a reiteration of "Second Isaiah" or a foundation for "Third Isaiah," but the unifying catalyst. This view emphasizes the importance of reading chs. 60–62 in light of the greater book of Isaiah. Hence, for Steck, chs. 56–66 cannot be understood apart from the whole. Nevertheless, at this later level of tradition history 61:1–3 remains non-messianic and its referent is Zion. Steck suggests that the speaker in Isa 61 would only be the prophet if one speculates that the text were independently created and yet influenced by Deutero-Isaiah.[94] Yet, he asserts that the book of Isaiah was not composed by a prophetic school but by literary redoing whereby the direct references in chs. 56–66 to chs. 40–55 are not the work of a disciple "pulling them out of his hat," but the work of a redactor.[95] On this basis, Steck neither interprets 61:1 as referring to the Messiah, nor to the prophet (just as 62:1 refers to YHWH and not the prophet), but to Zion.[96]

Antti Laato argues that 61:1–11 presents the "prophetic Servant" or "prophetic persona who is speaking in Isaiah 56–66."[97] Laato claims that Isa 61 provides an "important text in the Deutero-Isaianically formulated proclamation of salvation (chs. 60–62) because it describes the figure who performs the same function as the loyal servant of Isaiah 40–55."[98] He then assumes that "this prophetic Servant delivers a comforting message to his audience, showing that the task of the loyal servant in Isaiah 40–55 has not yet been completed but will continue until the promised salvation for Zion will be fulfilled" (compare 61:1 with 42:1). He notes that Isa 60–62 corresponds to 2:2–4 (with its future vision of the glory of Zion), and chs. 56–69 to 2:5 (which is an exhortation to live according to YHWH's commandments). Therefore, Laato contends that the editor, who combined 2:2–4 and 2:5 to provide an "analogy" to chs. 56–62, "was influenced by the composition of 56–59 + 60–62."

---

style and order of the oracle in 11:11–16, yet without messianic interpretation in mind (ibid., 22). Hence, he posits that all these references are formed with one unit in mind. They are reiterations of the proto-Isaiah text. In fact, these texts would be incomprehensible if they were read outside the context of *Großjesaja* (p. 23). On this point, Steck concludes that in the early "*Diadochenzeit*," two independent bodies exist which comprise all three areas of "*Proto, Trito und Deuterojesaja*" (p. 26).

94.   Odil Hannes Steck, "Tritojesaja Im Jesajabuch," in Vermeylen, ed., *The Book of Isaiah*, 375 n. 29.

95.   See Steck, *Studien zu Tritojesaja*, 1–19, 119–20.

96.   Ibid., 16.

97.   Laato, *"About Zion I Will Not Be Silent"*, 203.

98.   Ibid., 162.

Isaiah 40–55 then declares that the salvation is at hand, while chs. 56–66 repeat that its fulfilment was postponed because of the people's disobedience.[99] On the same grounds, Laato aims to prove that 62:1–2 parallels ch. 60 because both passages share the same vocabulary (נגה, צדקה, צלפיד יבער, etc.). Although such lines of continuity may be drawn by themes and vocabulary in many different texts, these are weak grounds for showing the *Tendenz* or "influence" of the redactor.

Some, who do not claim that the warrants for messianic interpretation lie in 61:1–3, aim to show messianic interpretation in the Gospel accounts through a sort of reader response application. Ulrich E. Simon argues that Gospel becomes "the terminus technicus" for Isa 61. In ch. 61, "the Evangelist" (i.e. herald of good tidings) and Gospel unite "in the Messianic task of procuring God's reign." In Isa 61, the Evangelist and Gospel portray a close union, but the exact relationship between the two remains flexible. Attempting to locate Isaiah within the whole of scripture, John Sawyer asserts that in saying "the Spirit of the Lord is upon me…" the speaker uses "messianic words," but he never states that this passage is messianic or that the speaker is the Messiah.[100]

Similarly, Walter Brueggemann suggests that 61:1–11 "continues the primary accents of ch. 60 concerning the coming reversal of the fortunes of Jerusalem, the coming abundance and prosperity of Jerusalem, and the corresponding subservience of the nations." [101] Yet, distinct from ch. 60, Isa 61 depicts the importance of the human agency of a poet who speaks in the first person in vv. 1–7 and 10–11, and whom he differentiates from YHWH in vv. 8–9. Brueggemann argues that we do not know the identity of the speaker, who is a poet that exercises enough "theological authority" to transform "the community of emerging Judaism." Whether the "'spirit anointing' is a concrete liturgical act in the community or simply a metaphorical claim of authority," Brueggemann rightly asserts that:

> Either way, the juxtaposition of "spirit" and "anoint" is bound to recall in Israel the old narrative of the authorization of David with the same two features: "Then Samuel took the horn of oil, and *anointed* him in the presence of his brothers; and the *spirit* of the Lord came mightily upon David from that day forward" (1 Sam. 16:13; see 2 Sam. 23:1–2). As David was a massive *newness* in Israel, so now this speaker is to effect a deep social newness.[102]

99.   Ibid., 138, 141, 155, 178, 194, 209.
100. Sawyer, *The Fifth Gospel.*
101. Brueggemann, *Isaiah 40–66*, 212.
102. Ibid., 213.

Brueggemann notes that the lead verb "to bring good news" is the verbal form of "gospel" and describes "one anointed to 'gospel' the world of Judaism."[103] While he never makes a claim for messianism and even states that 61:1–4 is "not directly an anticipation of Jesus," Brueggemann thinks that this passage describes Davidic figure who re-enacts David's *anointing* by the *spirit* (1 Sam 16:13).

B. *Messianic Assessments of the Biblical Testimony*

1. *Modern approaches.* Some scholars do not interpret Isa 61:1–6 in light of Judaism's messianic hope, but begin with a Christian *a priori*. Edward J. Young concludes that 61:1–3 speaks of Christ. Although, when reading this passage in the temple, Christ "does not explicitly declare that He is the speaker, it is difficult to interpret otherwise, for the work described is such that only God can accomplish." He claims that it is not warranted to limit the speaker to Isaiah, or generally to the prophets: "The speaker is the Messiah."[104] Young also asserts that 61:1–3 places a "dominant emphasis" on the Servant and agrees "admirably" with what is described elsewhere about the Servant's work and vocation.[105] Walter Kaiser argues that 61:1–3 provide the credentials of the coming Messiah, who will be endowed with the Spirit of the Lord so that he can carry out his prophetic role. He ingeniously argues that since "Yahweh appoints the Servant and the Spirit anoints him," this passage provides "one of the earliest constructs of the doctrine of the Trinity." Kaiser concludes that "rather than being anointed with oil as many priests and kings in the Old Testament, this Servant is anointed by the Holy Spirit."[106]

On the other hand, Alec Motyer asserts that "without appeal to the gospels…Isaiah displays here a Messianic figure." Similar to the second Servant song (49:1–6), this figure "speaks in his own person about himself and his God-given ministry."[107] This passage relates to the endowment of the Spirit the Lord's own endeavor to bring favor and vengeance in 59:16–21. When Jesus quoted this passage (Luke 4:16–22), he stopped at the word "favor" and did not continue to "vengeance" because his messianic task was to save the world and not to condemn it (John 3:17). So, "Isaiah sees a double-faceted ministry that the Lord Jesus apportions respectively to his first and second comings, the work of the Servant and the Anointed Conqueror." Thus, Motyer asserts that

103.   Ibid., 214.
104.   Young, *Isaiah*, 3:458.
105.   Ibid., 3:459.
106.   Kaiser, *The Messiah in the Old Testament*, 183.
107.   Motyer, *The Prophecy of Isaiah*, 499.

the year of favor expresses the compassion that the Lord has shown to Israel and the Gentiles, and "the Anointed One proclaims that this year has now come."[108]

Others find a strong resemblance between Isa 61, the Servant Songs and 11:1–6. For example, Franz Delitzsch argues that the speaker "is the very same 'servant of Jehovah' of whom and to whom Jehovah speaks in ch. xlii. 1sqq., lii. 13–liii and therefore not the prophet himself…"[109] He argues that the use of משח hints "that the Servant of Jehovah and the Messiah are one and the same."[110]

Similarly, Barry G. Webb asserts that individual who speaks in Isa 61:1 is "both the Servant of chapters 40–55 and the Messiah of chapters 1–35 because the phrase, "*The Spirit…is on me*' recalls Isa 42:1 ('I will put my Spirit on him'), but also 11:1 ('The Sprit of the Lord will rest on him')."[111] Therefore, Webb asserts that Isaiah's vision of a suffering Messiah was to be fulfilled in Jesus Christ. Isaiah 61:1–6 consists of a "speech by the Servant-Messiah" who "speaks as an anointed preacher" mainly about the Year of Jubilee, which had begun for the restored community with their release from captivity and return to their own land."[112] The "*comfort* they receive is not just release from exile, but release from condemnation through the forgiveness Jesus has won for them."[113] John Oswalt refers to the speaker in Isa 61:1–3 as "the Servant/ Messiah" who announces his role, and calls the people "to enter into the salvation that God has made available to them and to embrace their role to be holy people (62:10–12)." He maintains that "the centrality of this figure in this obviously eschatological section of the book argues for someone more than one of the prophets…" He provides evidence for such an assertion by tracing the similarities between the speaker in 61:1–3, the Servant (42:1–9; 49:1–9; 50:4–9; 52:13–53:12) and "the Messiah in ch. 11" (e.g. the Spirit of the Lord in Isa 11:2; "an anointing to speak" in Isa 61:1–3, similar to the word of his mouth being his most powerful instrument [11:4], and righteousness being his virtue [11:5]). Oswalt concludes that "this synthesis of the Servant and the Messiah is of the greatest importance, and provides another example…of the synthetic function of chs. 56–66 in relation to the book as a whole.[114] Childs asserts that "the prophetic vision of the messianic Sabbath was thus couched in the terms

108. Ibid., 500.
109. Delitzsch, *Isaiah*, 1:424.
110. Ibid., 1:425.
111. Webb, *The Message of Isaiah*, 233–34.
112. Ibid., 234–35.
113. Ibid., 235.
114. Oswalt, *Isaiah 40–66*, 563.

of goodness to the afflicted, liberty to the captives, and freedom to those bound in prison (Isa 61:1ff.)."[115]

More recently, Hugh G. M. Williamson, who claims to be interpreting the book of Isaiah as a whole, argues that chs. 60–62 "are the closest to the outlook of Deutero-Isaiah" and therefore underscores the resemblances between chs. 60–62 and "Deutero-Isaiah."[116] He concludes that there is "little that is new" in chs. 60–62 "beyond the bare fact of the extension of promise." On this basis, he claims that 61:1–3a "stands at the centre of this material" and "has the claim above all others in the last part of Isaiah to be considered a cardinal messianic passage…"[117] He alleges that "although this figure is not called a "servant," many of the uncertainties that confronted us in discussion of the servant of 40–55 are present here too."[118] He attempts to determine that the speaker in 61:1–3 fulfills the messianic task of "a variety of figures in Deutero-Isaiah: Cyrus, the servant, the herald of good news, God's ministers in the heavenly court, and the prophet himself."[119] On this basis, Williamson assumes that the speaker "expects to complete the as yet unfinished work of the servant, just as we have already seen that he expects to complete part of the works of Cyrus." Williamson attempts to prove this connection by locating the same vocabulary in chs. 40–55 and 60–62.[120] Apart from

---

115.   Childs, *Theological Reflection on the Christian Bible*, 401.

116.   Williamson (*The Book Called Isaiah*, 169–90) relies on Westermann (*Isaiah 40–66*, 295–96) on this point, but overlooks how Westermann considers chs. 60–62 to be the "nucleus" of "Trito-Isaiah."

117.   Williamson, *The Book Called Isaiah*, 174.

118.   For example: (1) Spirit being upon him is "probably a specific reference to the new David" (11:1; 42:1); (2) anointing similar to the noun used of Cyrus which explains "obviously royal overtones" (54:1); (3) the phrase "he has sent me" recalls the commissioning of 6:8 especially in light of how "Deutero-Isaiah's commissioning was understood as in some sense an extension of that of his eighth-century predecessor" (Isa 40); (4) "'bringing good news (*lebaśśēr*)' is prominent in Deutero-Isaiah" (40:9; 41:27; 52:7); (5) the verb 'to proclaim (*qārā'*)' might possibly refer to 40:2–6 and Isaiah 6; (6) "'to comfort (*nahēm*)' is the last in a series of emphasized infinitives" which are "related to the very first words of Isaiah 40…" (also 49:13; 51:3, 12, 19; 52:9; 54:11); (7) the "noun (*'ānāw*)" does not occur anywhere else in Isa 40–66, but its related adjective *'ānî* is used in Deutero-Isaiah in the plural as a description of Israel (41:17; 49:13; 51:21; 54:11); "'the captives (*šebûyīm*)…are used generally for people in their Babylonian captivity" (49:24, 25; 52:2); "'the prisoners (*'asûrîm*)…is used at 42:7 and 49:9 for those whom the servant is to release from prison…" etc. (Williamson, *The Book Called Isaiah*, 175–180).

119.   Ibid., 185–86.

120.   Some of these resemblances include: the subservience of the nations who bring tribute to Zion (51:5; 60:9); the promise of salvation is unconditional; royal

the words משׁח and נחם,[121] the vocabulary, which Williamson identifies as common to 61:1–3 and chs. 40–55, extends fairly evenly across chs. 1–66 and for that manner all prophetic literature.[122] Therefore, his argument has been built on weak evidence. Finally, Williamson's attempts to describe merely the "outlook" of "Deutero-" and "Trito-Isaiah," without viewing the book of Isaiah as a whole. He simply negotiates between hypothetical pre-biblical "authors" (to use his terminology), who at best loom from the pre-history of the book of Isaiah.[123]

2. *Perspectives that interpret Isaiah 61:1–3 through typological interpretation.* G. Adam Smith acknowledges that the speaker in Isa 61 might be either the prophet himself or the Servant. Overlooking the fact that the Old Testament records few anointed prophets (e.g. Elisha; cf. Ps 105:15), Smith asserts that the gift of the Spirit and anointing correspond well to any prophet or a unique Servant. The fact that Jesus Christ fulfilled this role does not decide the question one way or the other. Thus Smith resorts to typology to explain messianic interpretation in that "a prophet so representative was as much the antitype and foreshadowing of Christ as the Servant himself was…and…Jesus of Nazareth so plainly fulfilled it…"[124]

---

language (chs. 40–48; 62:3); everlasting covenant (55:3; 61:8); promise extending to seed or offspring (53:10 [picking up on 44:3 and 48:19; 61:9). Williamson tries also to harmonize the one-time appearances of משׁפט in chs. 60–62 (at 61:8) by equating this term with the appearance צדקה with and without ישׁוע (and related forms) in chs. 40–55 (41:2; 45:8, 21; 46:13; 48:18; 51:5, 6, 8). Yet this plethora of צדקה in chs. 40–55 and paucity of משׁפט in chs. 60–62 makes his argument unconvincing. Although he correctly shows that צדקה appears with ישׁוע or parallel to it (61:10, 11; 62:1) and without ישׁוע (60:21; 61:3).

121.   The word נחם appears three times in chs. 1–39 (once for positive comfort), eight times in chs. 40–55, and three times in chs. 55–66.

122.   For example, רוח appears 25 times in chs. 1–39, nine times in chs. 40–55, and 13 times in chs. 55–66. Even Rabshakeh uses the phrase "he has sent me." בשׁלח√ appears 21 times in chs. 1–39, six times in chs. 40–55, and five times in chs. 55–66. קרא appears 30 times in chs. 1–39, 33 times in chs. 40–55, and 23 times in chs. 55–66. The noun ענו appears six times in chs. 1–39 and once in chs. 55–66 but does not appear in Isa 40–55 except as Williamson acknowledges in the similar term עני, which appears seven times in chs. 1–39, five times in chs. 40–55 and twice in chs. 56–66. שׁבר appears once in chs. 1–39, and once in chs. 55–66. אסר appears once in chs. 1–39, once in chs. 40–55 and once in chs. 55–66.

123.   Even the fact that Williamson refers to *"lebaśśēr"* in 41:27 as "the climax of one of the trial speeches" find their setting in a pre-biblical tradition around the former things rather than the scriptural form (Williamson, *The Book Called Isaiah*, 180).

124.   Smith, *The Book of Isaiah*, 435–36.

Similarly, Workman argues that there are affinities between the self-delineation in 61:1–3, and both 49:1–6 and 50:4–11, purely because the Servant and the speaker in 61:1–3 are both represented by a man endowed with the divine spirit and appointed to the prophetic office. However, the figure in 61:1–3 is not called "Servant." The Servant is a mediator of Salvation, but the speaker in 61:1–3 describes his own prophetic mission and is only a herald of salvation. Yet, "like the Servant, he was a type of Jesus of Nazareth, who is said by Luke to have one occasion applied a portion of the passage to himself as being typically applicable to him."[125] Similarly, George Lampe argues that Isa 61:1 refers to the prophet, this passage functions typologically in terms of the Messiah.[126]

3. *A few reflections from New Testament scholarship.* New Testament scholarship has also struggled to explain how Isa 61:1–2 could be cited as messianic. J. D. G. Dunn argues that Jesus' quoting from 61:1–2 indicated that he accepted the category of prophet to describe himself rather than Messiah.[127] W. H. Brownlee identifies Jesus as a priestly Messiah.[128] E. Earle Ellis regards 61:1–2 to be messianic inasmuch as the speaker, with whom Jesus identifies himself in 61:1 and 58:6, is "the servant of the Lord (and not the people)." In Luke 4, Jesus' claiming to be a prophet "probably carried messianic connotations."[129] José Mariá Casciaro claims that Luke cites from Isa 61 to demonstrate Jesus' first messianic declaration by recalling blessings that come through the Messiah.[130] While these scholars think that the New Testament cites Isa 61:1 messianically, many New Testament scholars do not argue the same.

Roger Stronstadt suggests that the Isaianic text used in Nazareth and cited in Luke 4 may have appeared similar to the Targum, "the Spirit of Prophecy from before the Lord God is upon me," but that this character of the text disappeared when Luke (or his source) assimilated the text to the Greek LXX translation of Isaiah.[131]

125.   Workman, *The Servant of Jehovah*, 94–95.
126.   Lampe and Woollcombe, *Essays on Typology*, 45–49.
127.   Dunn, "Messianic Ideas," 378.
128.   Brownlee, "Messianic Motifs," 12–30, 195–210.
129.   E. Earle Ellis, *The Gospel of Luke* (The Century Bible; London: Nelson, 1966), 97; idem, *Eschatology in Luke* (ed. John Reumann; Biblical Series 30; Philadelphia: Fortress, 1972), xiii, 1–20.
130.   José Mariá Casciaro, et al., *The Navarre Bible: Saint Luke's Gospel* (trans. Brian McCarthy; Dublin: Four Courts, 1987), 75.
131.   Roger Stronstad, *The Charismatic Theology of St. Luke* (Peabody, Mass.: Hendrickson, 1984), 42–43.

C. H. Dodd tries to explain that Isa 61:1–2 "refers to the prophet Isaiah" and functions as a source of *testimonia* in kerygmatic passages in a manner that cites "all allusions to the Old Testament in context."[132] Although the rest of ch. 61 does not function as a testimony, the context, which describes the ideas of priestly people (61:6), eternal covenant (61:8) and the people of God as bride (61:10), is "directly related to the central role of Christ." Therefore, the New Testament quotes 61:1–2 as "the programme of the ministry of Jesus in Luke iv. 1–19, and echoed in Acts x. 38, Mt. xi 5 = Lk. vii. 22, Mt. v. 4." The speaker in Isa 61:1–2 is not designated by the title "Servant" but he "functions" in the same way as the Servant. However, Isa 61:1–2 alone warrants messianic interpretation in the sense that Jesus' "endowment of the Spirit is in fact his 'anointing.'"[133] Although other Isaianic passages are also messianic, Isa 61 is the only one "which speaks of 'anointing' at all."[134]

Others believe that Isa 61:1–3 was originally not messianic but attempt to explain how it began to be interpreted messianically. Jacques Dupont claims that Q refers to eschatological times and portrays consolation promises without a messianic claim.[135] Similarly, Zimmerli argues that Q refers to Isa 61 in a manner that describes human conditions in eschatological times and provides a messianic promise.[136] J. Schmitt argues that 61:1–3 originally spoke of "the prophet," and that the Beatitudes are the first place in the New Testament to that make use of it. He asserts that Jesus is by nature non-messianic, that he never claimed to be a Messiah and that he did not justify this identification by Judaic "spiritual unction" (*onction spirituelle*). So, Jesus himself did not cite messianic biblical texts or the Targum. Messianic interpretation of 61:1–2 and the title "Christ" begin with the later community, a development found in the Gospel of Luke and in Acts (Luke 4:18; Acts 4:27; 10:38).[137]

132. Dodd, *According to Scripture*, 52, 53.
133. Ibid., 94–95.
134. Ibid., 105.
135. Jacques Dupont, *Les Béattitudes* (Bruges: Abbaye de Saint-André, 1969), 39–51.
136. Walter Zimmerli, "Die Seligpreisungen der Bergpredigt und das Alte Testament," in *Donum Gentilicium: New Testament Studies in Honour of David Daube* (ed. E. Bammel, C. K. Barrett and W. D. Davies; Oxford: Clarendon, 1978), 17–20.
137. J. Schmitt, "L'oracle d'Is. LXI 1 ss. et sa relecture par Jésus," *RSR* 54 (1980): 97–108. See also H. Heller, "Acht Christusämter nach Is. 61:1–3," *Wort und Geist* 32 (1938): 43–48, 57–67; S. Lassalle, "Y-a-t-il dans Isaïe un cinquieme chant du serviteur?," *Bullétin Renan* 98 (1963): 3–4; Paul Hoffmann, *Studien zur Theologie der Logienquelle* (Münster: Aschendorff, 1971), 114, 205, 212; Heinz Schürmann, *Das Lukasevangelium I* (Freiburg: Herder, 1969), 326, 330, 332; Siegfried Schulz, *Q-Die Spruchquelle der Evangelisten* (Zurich: Theologischer

Joseph Fitzmeyer agues that Isa 61 originally referred to "prophetic anointing" but was later applied to Jesus. He refers to Luke's omission of the phrase "the day of vengeance for our God" as a deliberate suppression of a negative aspect of the Deutero-Isaian message.[138]

Others understand the role of Jesus Christ in Luke–Acts to have combined the offices of prophet and Messiah. For example, Donald Juel asserts that Luke–Acts understands the role of the prophet and Messiah to "have been harmonized" in Isa 61. The use of "anoint" in ch. 61 and the Spirit of the Lord "makes it possible to attribute to the anointed One functions normally ascribed to prophets—like teaching and healing."[139]

Others think that Luke has cited and merged together different Isaianic texts in order to create a composite messianic portrait. Patrick Miller asserts that Luke has merged Isa 61:1–2 and 58:6 to serve as a "Messianic confirmation," since "the coming of Jesus is the coming of God's anointed to release and set free those who are captive and oppressed" (Luke 4:18 cites Isa 61:1 but adds ἀπόστελλε τεθραυσμένους ἐν ἀφέσει from 58:6). He maintains that the New Testament meaning relies on the merging of these two combined texts and the use of ἀφέσις to show how Jesus sets people free from sin and oppression of the evil one.[140] Similarly, Frederick Danker asserts that Luke 4:18, citing words originally ascribed to the prophet, reflects a merging of Isa 42:6 and 58:6 as well as 61:1–2.[141] It cannot be determined whether or not 61:1–2 is a Servant passage, but these passages together were cited to present Jesus as "the Servant of the Lord, anointed by the Spirit."[142]

4. *A few pre-modern examples.* Many Jewish sources do not consider that Isa 61:1–3 speaks of a redeemer but relates it to the prophet.[143] For example, the Targum adds the words אמר נביא ("The prophet said," or

Verlag, 1972), 78–84; Eduard Schweizer, *The Good News According to Matthew* (trans. David E. Green; Atlanta: John Knox, 1975), 71; Gerhard Schneider, *Das Evangelium des Lukas* (Gütersloh: Gütersloher Verlagshaus Mohn, 1977), 152.

138.   Joseph A Fitzmeyer, *The Gospel According to Luke (I–IX)* (AB 28; Garden City, N.Y.: Doubleday, 1981), 532.

139.   Juel, *Messianic Exegesis*, 83–84; Joel Marcus, *The Way of the Lord: Christological Exegesis of the Old Testament in the Gospel of Mark* (Louisville, Ky.: Westminster John Knox, 1992), 74–75.

140.   Patrick D. Miller, Jr., "Luke 4:16–21," *Int* 29 (1975): 417–21.

141.   Frederick W. Danker, *Luke* (Proclamation Commentaries; Philadelphia: Fortress, 1976), 25, 35.

142.   Ibid., 38, 74.

143.   See the *Midrash Rabbah* (Lam 3:49–50, 59), which does regard Isa 61:12 as speaking of a redeemer.

"The spirit of prophecy is upon me").[144] Oswalt suggests that "perhaps this is an attempt to contradict the messianic interpretation stemming from Jesus' use of the passage (Luke 4:16–21).[145] Yet the Targum seems to be exploiting the ambiguity of the text in a manner similar to how Christians interpret it messianically. On the basis of the Targum, Ibn Ezra argues that Isa 61:1 refers to the prophet(s), who is/are anointed *"for the reason of"* (יען)—bringing good tidings.[146]

On the other hand, a number of scholars claim that 11QMelch presents the herald of Isa 52:7 as the one who proclaims the good news of 61:1–3 before Melchizedek comes as the eschatological judge, and that 11QMelch interprets Isa 61 messianically.[147] Line 6 has the words וקרא להמה דרר, which might find similarities with the phrase לקרא לשבוים דרור in 61:1, but the Qumran text does not seem to cite the biblical text in the way that Laato argues.[148] In my opinion, Laato may be relying too much on speculation when he claims that יקום נקמת in line 9 alludes to ויום נקם לאלהינו. However, Laato certainly appears to be correct that line 18, which reads והמבשר הו[א] מ[שיח הרו]ח and uses the principal verbs בשר and משח and the noun רוח, refers to 61:1:

רוח אדני יהוה יען משח יהוה אתי לבשר ענוים שלחני

The traditional Christian view interprets 61:1–3 with the conviction that it testifies to Jesus Christ. Origen posits that 61:1 spoke of the

144. See Bruce Chilton, *The Glory of Israel: The Theology and Provenience of the Isaiah Targum* (JSOTSup 23; Sheffield: JSOT Press, 1983), 52–56.

145. Oswalt, *Isaiah 40–66*, 561.

146. Friedländer, ed., *The Commentary of Ibn Ezra on Isaiah*, 3:281.

147. For the pesher fragment, see J. T. Milik, "Milki-sedek et Milki-resa' dans les ancient écrits juifs et chrétiens," *JJS* 23 (1972): 97–99. See also M. de Jonge and A. S. van der Woude, "11QMelchizedeq and the New Testament," *NTS* 12 (1966): 306; Paul J. Kobelski, *Melchizedek and Malchiresha* (CBQMS 10; Washington, D.C.: The Catholic Biblical Association of America, 1981), 3–23; Michael A. Fishbane, *Biblical Interpretation in Ancient Israel* (Oxford: Clarendon, 1985), 483; D. R. Schwartz, "On Quirinius, John the Baptist, the Benedictus, Melchisedek, Qumran and Ephesus," *RevQ* 13 (1988): 635–46; J. Thurén, "Lukas evangeliets Cantica im Krytans Bruk," in *Academia et Ecclesia: Studia in Honorem Frederic Cleve* (Åbo: Åbo Akademis Förlag, 1991), 175–93; E. Puech, "Notes sur le manuscrit de XIQMelkîsêdeq," *RevQ* 12 (1987): 483–513; T. H. Lim, "11QMelch, Luke 4 and the Dying Messiah," *JJS* 43 (1992): 90–92; E. Puech, "La figure de Melkisedeq et la fin des temps (11QMelk—4Q180–181—4QViscAmr—4QTestQah—4Q280—286–287)," in *La croyance des Esséniens en la vie future : immortalité, résurrection, vie éternelle? : histoire d'une croyance dans le judaïsme ancien* (Paris: Gabalda, 1993), 2:515–62; Sawyer, *The Fifth Gospel*, 24; Laato, *A Star is Rising*, 326.

148. Laato, *A Star is Rising*, 312.

persons of the Trinity (the *Spirit* of YHWH is upon *Me*) but that the anointed one was Christ.

Jean Calvin argues in a subtle fashion that Isa 61:1–3 refers to both the prophet Isaiah and Christ. Calvin acknowledges that Jews laugh at the notion that Christ speaks of himself, but thinks that the phrase "anointed" may apply to Isaiah and other prophets in that they were anointed of YHWH and spoke his words under his authority. Using the "head" and "body" distinctions of Tyconius, Calvin argues that since Christ is the head prophet, this passage applies "chiefly" to him. This description is similar to that of other prophets, whom the Lord anointed.[149] They did not speak on their own but were anointed into the "office of Christ" and were endued with gifts that were necessary for that office. Isaiah 61 provides "a seal" to ch. 60 to confirm that Christ will bring about restoration of the church of Christ. Through the faithful proclamation of the prophets, Christ accomplished the purposes set forth in this passage.[150]

Martin Luther asserts that "Christ" received "spiritual" rather than "physical" anointing in Isa 61:1–3, which "separates this king from all worldly pontiffs." He claims that this anointing indicated that he was made "King and Priest." Luther asserts that the word משׁח did not need to be included because the prophet adds the phrase, "the spirit of the Lord is upon me," so "that we may see that Christ comes anointed not with human unction but with a divine one, to be Messiah, king and priest." Luther understands this passage to operate messianically because from "the verb משׁח, that is, 'He anointed'…we get 'Messiah.' " It is interesting that Luther does not refer to this anointing as that of a prophetic office; rather, he sees that the prophet is describing "the proper office of this *King* to preach."[151] Here, Luther distinguishes between the prophet and the messianic king.

C. *Rethinking the Evidence*
Pre-modern biblical interpretation, especially on the Jewish side, suggests diverse interpretations for Isa 61:1–3 because the ambiguity of the text provides warrants for identifying who spoke these words or who is described.[152] The Targum identifies the speaker in 61:1–3 as the prophet,

---

149. On Tyconius' "head" and "body" distinctions, see Froehlich, *Biblical Interpretation in the Early Church*, 104.

150. Calvin, *Commentary on the Book of the Prophet Isaiah*, 4:303–4.

151. Luther, *Lectures on Isaiah 40–66*, 329–30 (italics mine).

152. It is possible that this phenomenon exists because the Qumran text pre-dates Jesus Christ but the Targum and Rabbis might be a reacting to Christian messianic claims.

while the Qumran community (judging by 11QMelch) and later Christians exploit the same ambiguity in a different direction. Because of the ambiguity of the speaker, the Targum has as much warrant to speculate that 61:1–3 refers to the prophet as do Christian interpreters who view 61:1–3 as messianic. While modern scholars have sought greater control by seeking to establish the original intent of "authors," they have not found agreement due to the text's ambiguity, which has evoked numerous different interpretations.

More recently, scholarship has focused on the placement of Isa 61 (chs. 60–62) within the book as a whole. For example, Steck finds connections between chs. 60–62 and chs. 35, 40 and 49, without making any effort to examine how the book of Isaiah functions as a scriptural book. Laato is correct that Isa 60–62 awaits a day of salvation that was promised in chs. 40–55 that "has not yet come," though he does not account for how this creates a tension that may or may not prepare the grounds for messianic expectation.[153] Sommer tries to find royal features in 60:17–61:1 by comparing words of other royal-messianic texts that are duplicated in 60:17–61:1, but he is not convincing because he identifies words that are very common throughout chs. 1–66.[154] Many scholars have tried to show similarities between 61:1–3 and 11:1–6 and the so-called Servant Songs, often referring to similarities in vocabulary and identifying terms that are too common to prove that there is any editorial *Tendenz*. Williamson shows how "the savior" in 61:1–3 fulfills an expectation that Cyrus failed to accomplish and harmonizes separate texts together without emphasizing their differences. The major problem with each of these approaches is their reliance on the divisions of "Second" and/or "Third Isaiah" and/or the "Servant Songs," which are at best pre-biblical designations and do not speak do justice to the context of the scriptural book of Isaiah.

Modern scholars, who have interpreted 61:1–3 within this framework of "Third Isaiah," have anchored the meaning of the text within a modern perspective of this hypothetical prophet's authorship, but have failed to interpret 61:1–3 within the book as a whole (no matter what they claim).[155] The editorial pattern in chs. 40–66 does not depend on "Second" and "Third Isaiah" distinctions. For example, the refrain "there will

---

153. Laato, *"About Zion I Will Not Be Silent,"* 55, 200.

154. Sommer, *A Prophet Reads Scripture*, 20, 86–87, 113, 141.

155. Note that several scholars claim to be interpreting the book of Isaiah as a whole but still rely on this diachronic category within their definition of the book as a whole (e.g. Beuken, *Jesaja*, 3A:158–60; Steck, *Studien zu Tritojesaja*, 16, 27–28; Williamson, *The Book Called Isaiah*, 180).

be no peace for the wicked" (48:22; 57:21) resonates with the depiction of the restlessness of the raging sea (48:18; 57:20) and cuts across the so-called Second and Third Isaiah distinctions. As argued in my introductory chapter, I am convinced that Isa 40–66 has been editorially divided in roughly three equal parts by the refrain. That structure has been superimposed on whatever could be our conjecture of Second Isaiah and Third Isaiah. Delitzsch, who argues from this very perspective that this refrain trisects Isa 40–66, argues that the refrain concludes the work of Cyrus and any mention of Babylon (48:18), and seals the "second book" by directing the prophecies to "the heathen...estranged from God, within Israel itself."[156]

Moreover, scholars have tried to find connections between the individual speaker who says, "the spirit of YHWH is upon me" (61:1–3), "the shoot from the stump of Jesse" (11:1–6) and "the Servant" (42:6). Yet they have not made a strong case for these links because their methodology rests on vocabulary similarities, which alone cannot establish such a relationship.[157] For example, Oswalt asserts that the emphasis is on the Messiah's speaking here in 61:1–3, which he thinks agrees with 11:4 where the Messiah's "most potent instrument is the word of his mouth." He also purports that "oaks of righteousness" (אילי הצדק) recalls the words "righteousness shall be the belt around his waist" (11:5).[158] Yet these words and concepts are so common in Isaiah that Oswalt has proven nothing. The word רוח ("spirit") is too common to demonstrate an intentional connection between 11:2 and 61:1–3 especially since 11:2 uses רוח יהוה and 61:1 employs רוח אדני יהוה.[159] These similarities of vocabulary between the 61:1 and 11:2 have proven nothing.

156.   Delitzsch, *Isaiah*, 1:256, 383. This is a position that was primarily argued in pre-modern commentaries.
157.   Williamson, *The Book Called Isaiah*, 185–86; Oswalt, *Isaiah 40–66*, 563; Sommer, *A Prophet Reads*, 20, 86–87, 113, 141; Jacob, *Theology of the Old Testament*, 94.
158.   Oswalt, *Isaiah 40–66*, 563.
159.   The Spirit of YHWH rests on the "shoot [who] shall come out from the stump of Jesse" in order that he judge righteously (11:1–5). The "Spirit from on high is poured out" to establish eternal righteousness and justice (32:15–17). YHWH puts his Spirit to establish righteousness and bring liberty to the captives (42:1–9). YHWH will pour forth his Spirit on future generations so that they flourish (44:3–4). YHWH will send the Spirit in order that the prophet teach people to keep the Torah (48:16–18); "my Spirit that is upon you, and my words that I have put in your mouth, shall not depart out of your mouth, or out of the mouths of your children, or out of the mouths of your children's children says the LORD, from now on and forever" (59:21).

One cannot prove any relationship between the phrases ונחה עליו רוח יהוה ("the spirit of YHWH shall rest on him," 11:1) and רוח אדני יהוה עלי ("the spirit of YHWH is upon me," 61:1), beyond noting commonplace similarities in vocabulary and syntax. Several significant differences between these texts work against viewing them together. First, the verbal sentence in 11:2 (ונחה) contrasts with the non-verbal sentence in 61:1. Second, the pronominal suffix and preposition עליו ("upon him," 11:2) differs from עלי ("upon me," 61:1). Finally, 61:1 uses the phrase יען משח יהוה אתי ("because YHWH has anointed me"). Because the word √משח does not appear in 11:2, we are left with the ambiguity of whether 61:1 makes explicit a messianism that was already implicit in 11:1–6, or whether the texts offer two distinct portraits of an individual deliverer.

Scholars argue that the speaker in Isa 61:1–3 is a Davidic figure because of similarities with 1 and 2 Samuel. Oswalt argues that 61:1–3 recalls 1 Sam 10:1, 6–7; 16:13 and 2 Sam 23:1–2.[160] Brueggemann mentions that Isa 61:1–3 "recalls" both 1 Sam 16:13 and 2 Sam 23:1–2 including the words "spirit" and "anoint."[161] He does not mention that the only other places in the whole Old Testament where Spirit filling and anointing appear together is during both Saul's (1 Sam 10:1, 6–7) and David's (1 Sam 16:13) anointing for kingship. In any case, these passages in Samuel do not speak about the Messiah because they use figurative or exaggerated rhetorical language about Saul or David that does not require an eternal kingdom to be fulfilled. Messianic texts can reflect a royal resonance with Saul and David but they far exceed what a king could do even while using exaggerated language. Our definition of messianism recognizes the difference between exaggerated language that depicts the hope of an ideal king and eschatological messianic expectation after the kingship has been destroyed.

In terms of rhetorical analysis, we have differentiated between "proper" and "figurative" usage in the introduction. Isaiah 9:1–6 and Ps 2 in their original social contexts, may have functioned as royal enthronement psalms that "figuratively" used exaggerated language to describe an historical Davidic king (e.g. Hezekiah or Josiah).[162] Yet, in the latter

160.   Oswalt, *Isaiah 40–66*, 564. See also Westermann, *Isaiah 40–66*, 365–66.
161.   Brueggemann, *Isaiah 40–66*, 213.
162.   In the original setting, the exaggerated language of the original oracle ("Almighty God") must have been taken as "figurative" rather than "proper" usage since Israelite religion did not consider its king to be divine. However, within a later setting of the book as a whole, the divine attributes attributed to the "child born to us" in Isa 9:1–6 describes more than just an earthly king, but in its "proper" use, after the monarchy has ended, the text invokes messianic interpretation. Although Christians may have traditionally understood the "proper" usage of "Almighty God"

formation of the book, when the monarchy is ended, the greater scrip-tural context presents hope in a superhuman royal figure who will fulfill the promises made to David in the eschatological era. Some features that were originally intended to be "figurative" now have become "proper" in the context of scripture, so that they have come to describe a Davidic Messiah whose name really can non-figuratively be "Almighty God." We can only consider a text as messianic if it uses "proper" language that describes an eschatological event where a superhuman person activates and restores the promises made to David within this world after the monarchy has ended. Therefore, 61:1–3 describes an ambiguous single individual who functions within the eschatological framework of chs. 60–62, possessing characteristics that are to be taken as a "proper" usage reminiscent of, though exceeding, David's *anointing* by the *Spirit* (1 Sam 16:13; 2 Sam 23:1–2).

Whether trying to identify the pre-biblical or biblical levels of tradi-tion history, some people attempt to make the speaker in Isa 61:1–3 and the Servant one and the same,[163] while others maintain that 61:1–3 uses language similar to the oracles about the Servant.[164] Oswalt maintains that "this synthesis of the Servant and the Messiah is of the greatest importance, and provides another example…of the synthetic function of chs. 56–66 in relation to the book as a whole."[165] Williamson aims to show that the speaker in Isa 61:1–3 fulfills the messianic task through a composite sketch of "a variety" of characters in Deutero-Isaiah (Cyrus, the Servant, the herald of good news) but this conflation of separate texts does not account for the differences of each.[166] His claim that the Hebrew verbs √חקפ (42:7) and √רמא (49:9) are also found in 61:1–3 proves nothing since this vocabulary is found many times outside of the Servant Songs and Isa 61. Moreover, the nomenclature "Deutero-Isaiah" does not

to speak of the incarnation, the Jews have not. Jewish interpretation, however, assumed that the Messiah possessed divine powers that past kings did not possess.

163. Hoonacker, "L'ébed Jahvé"; Smith, *The Book of Isaiah*, 436; Torrey, *Second Isaiah*, 452; Cannon, "Isaiah 61, 1–3 as Ebed-Jahweh Poem"; Procksch, *Jesaja*, 152; idem, *Theologie*, 290; Rowley, *The Servant of the Lord*; Bright, *The Kingdom of God*, 146, 153, 198, 209–11; Zimmerli and Jeremias, *The Servant of God*, 26, 29; Eichrodt, *Theology of the Old Testament*, 59; Morgenstern, "Isaiah 61"; McKenzie, *Second Isaiah*, 181; Kaiser, *The Messiah in the Old Testament*, 183; Webb, *The Message of Isaiah*, 233–34; Oswalt, *Isaiah 40–66*, 563.

164. Delitzsch, *Isaiah*, 1:425; Mowinckel, *He That Cometh*, 255–57; Young, *The Book of Isaiah*, 459; Everson, "Isaiah 61:1–6…"; Whybray, *Isaiah 40–66*, 239; Motyer, *Isaiah*, 499; Laato, *"About Zion I Will Not Be Silent,"* 162.

165. Oswalt, *Isaiah 40–66*, 563.

166. Williamson, *The Book Called Isaiah*, 185–86.

identify the book as a whole. We can grant that both the person in Isa 61:1–3 and the Servant speak in the first person (49:1–9; 50:4–5, 7), profess to have been empowered by the Spirit (in 42:1) and open "the eyes that are blind, to bring out the prisoners from the dungeon" (42:7; 49:9). Even the attempt to identify the speaker in 61:1–3 with the ability of the Servant to execute righteousness and justice responds to the ambiguity while it also exceeds the warrants of the text.

More importantly, scholarship needs to show the differences between Isa 61:1–3 and other possible messianic texts. Instead of the harmonizing these differences, one needs to let this text retain its own limited context and allow the unharmonized dimensions of the text stand. One thing that makes 61:1–3 different from other texts is that the figure here is neither named as a Davidid, nor the Servant, nor any other historical figure. The text remains ambiguous about such an identity. That is why the Targum can interpret ch. 53 messianically but present ch. 61 as a statement by the prophet. Wilcox and Patton have brought to our attention that the Servant is an individual in chs. 40–56 but plural in chs. 57–66.[167] Therefore the speaker in 61:1–3 is an individual who can be distinguished from the Servant people.

Furthermore, 61:1–3 describes a herald of glad tidings (לבשר של חני), making this text different from the other passages that refer to the herald of glad tidings (40:9; 41:27; 52:7; 60:6). Williamson argues that in 40:9, "Zion/Jerusalem becomes herself the herald rather than the recipient of good tidings." However, the herald in 40:9 cannot imply a messenger to the city because the text is not telling another mountain (Zion) to "get up to a high mountain" to announce good news. Instead, this messenger in 40:9 announces good tidings *to* Zion which makes perfect sense if one understands the word מְבַשֶּׂרֶת in a manner similar to קֹהֶלֶת, which functions not as a marker of the feminine gender, but as a *nomen unitatis*.[168] However, the speaker in 61:1–3, is both someone who brings good news and has power "to give to them" (לתת להם) or bring them about:

> to give to them a garland instead of ashes, the oil of gladness instead of mourning, the mantle of praise instead of a faint spirit. They will be called oaks of righteousness, the planting of the LORD, to display his glory. They shall build up the ancient ruins, they shall raise up the former devastations; they shall repair the ruined cities, the devastations of many generations. (61:2–3, NRSV)

167. Wilcox and Patton-Williams, "The Servant Songs."
168. See Waltke and Connor, *An Introduction to Biblical Hebrew Syntax*, 101–5.

The fact that לבשר in Isa 61:1–3 is the infinitive of משח makes this passage a stronger candidate for messianic interpretation than the other references to a herald of glad tidings, in 40:9; 41:27; 52:7; 60:6. These other four passages that use בשר do not necessarily speak of "Messiah" or use the verb or noun (משיח or משח) but of a forerunner.[169] Isaiah 61:1–3 paints a different portrait of a herald of good tidings who announces more extraordinary things than the end of the exile. Therefore, this passage is much more evocative of messianic interpretation than 40:9. Isaiah 61:1–3 provides more reason than any of these other texts in Isaiah for interpreting the herald of good tidings as a messianic figure.

The warrants for interpreting this figure as either the Servant or the Messiah or both cannot be justified less by what is in the text than by what is not. The Targum exploits the possibility that the 61:1–3 portrays the word of the prophet, but Christianity exploits another possibility that invites messianic interpretation. From this perspective, some modern scholars speculate that this unknown speaker is "Third Isaiah." When Jesus reads from Isa 61 in the temple and claims that "Today this scripture has been fulfilled in your hearing," we may wonder whether he claims to be an extraordinary prophet or the Messiah. Both the Targumist and Christians seize upon the ambiguity. Even the debate over whether Jesus was John the Baptist, Elijah, Jeremiah, one of the prophets or the Messiah (Matt 16:14–16; Mark 8:27–29; Luke 9:19–20), or whether John the Baptist might be Elijah, the prophet or the Messiah (Luke 3:15; John 1:25), shows how the language of the text and its ambiguity has created pressure to interpret it in certain ways.

Traditionally, older modern scholarship has described Isa 56–66 as a work that was written after the punishment of the exile to pronounce the judgment of transgressors after the exiles have come home. Westermann argues that "proclamations concerning historical events have been replaced by promises of a more general and abstract kind…"[170] In his opinion, Second Isaiah proclaims salvation "within the historical realm itself" but the subsection of chs. 60–62 does not anticipate salvation "to be inaugurated by a definite historical event, but by the divine, miraculous transformation of a condition, the nation's oppression and its impoverishment, into its opposite." Therefore he states:

> Trito-Isaiah finds himself unable to point in advance to a definite historical event, the divine advent now more dissociated from history. For this reason he does not, like 40:9ff., identify God's advent with the return of

169.   See Oswalt, *Isaiah 40–66*, 565.
170.   Westermann, *Isaiah 40–66*, 299.

those still living in foreign lands. Instead, the latter is included in the counter move of the nations to Zion which ensues on God's coming in salvation.[171]

However, Westermann argues that pre-exilic oracles occur in Isa 56:9–57:13, so that chs. 40–66 includes pre-exilic, exilic and post-exilic texts whose hopes are not anchored in one time and place.[172] Essentially, Westermann describes an anthology of texts that hold in abeyance a dialectic between eras that either await the first judgment and the destruction of the cultic center (56:9–57:13), or endure the aftermath of this destruction when the temple has not yet been rebuilt (60:13) or live in a Second Temple period when sacrifices are again offered in Jerusalem (56:7; 66:1–3). Since 61:1–3 is set within a context where there is no realized salvation, Westermann reasonably suggests that the post-exilic community viewed the speaker within the context of an eschatological expectation of a single individual who will bring about salvation. However, this eschatological perspective is not merely the preoccupation of "Trito-Isaiah," for it belongs at various places in the book of Isaiah as a whole. This deepens the ambiguity and eschatological framework, which Isa 60:19–22 depicts as an age of salvation and something an individual announces in the subsequent verses (61:1–3).

From this perspective, the individual speaking in 61:1–3 fulfills the hope in chs. 60–62, which looks beyond the return from Babylon to an eschatological salvation at the end of time (60:19–20) and paints a landscape of the eschaton: "Your sun shall no longer go down, or your moon withdraw itself; for YHWH will be your everlasting light, and your days of mourning shall be ended" (60:20).[173] Isaiah 60 uses the metaphor of light and the darkness, which resembles 9:1–6 where the people in darkness are promised light. The light here compares to the light that has been shed on the darkness of exile in 8:23–9:6. This eschatological element in chs. 60–62 allows the text to be heard and applied far beyond the time when it was first uttered to the Jewish community after the exile into the present day. The speaker of 61:1–3 can be heard within this later context of Jewish scripture.

The way that the text exceeds the terms of ordinary history becomes evident in the role of Zion and the restored cities within these chapters. If Zion ever were the concrete subject of a lament over a destroyed city, now Zion as a city is replaced as a spiritual realm (60:18). Isaiah 61:4

171. Ibid., 357.
172. Ibid., 302.
173. That is why Westermann even argues that Isa 60 takes for granted that the temple forms a part of the new Jerusalem of the era of salvation (ibid., 304).

possesses a sort of timelessness where even the promise that ancient ruins, former devastations and the ruined cities shall be built up cannot be located in one particular time in history. In 61:4, the two terms in parallelism, זר and נכר, are not synonymous because זר is used to describe one who is not a member of the "in group,"[174] while נכר is used only of a non-Israelite (Gen 17:12; Exod 12:43; Neh 9:2; Lam 5:2). Therefore, זר on its own can refer to someone outside of the clan, and the parallel term נכר similarly declares that a non-Israelite will come and tend to their land.[175] Here, the verb does double duty for the second colon and thus frees space to augment the parallel term (or "ballast variant") with a kind of periphrastic substitution for ערי חרב ("ruined cities") by the phrase שממות דור ודור. This semantic elaboration of the first term adds a timeless dimension to the "ruined cities" so that they may be characterized in the second colon as ruins that have outlasted any human memory (דור ודור).[176] Dan Cohn-Sherbok argues that "Third Isaiah" depicts how "through Israel's redemption all nations will be blessed, and the temple will be a focus of worship for all peoples." After Isa 60 describes Zion's glory and how Jerusalem will be honored throughout the world, "Isaiah focuses on the individual who will bring this about."[177] Isaiah 63:3b–4 in the book of Isaiah corresponds to the program of restoration that the speaker has announced in vv. 1–3a.

By the time that the book of Isaiah reached its scriptural form, this proclamation of a coming salvation (Isa 60–62) had not been directly fulfilled, so the passage gained an eschatological dimension. Therefore, this individual speaking in 61:1–3 would be understood within this context. Oswalt rightly states that "the centrality of this figure in this obviously eschatological section of the book argues for someone more than one of the prophets, or as is more popular today, a personification of the hypothetical 'Levitical-visionary group.'"[178] Just as the post-exilic community can look back on the collapse of the monarchy and the limited function of Cyrus, the warrants of the text now allow them to anticipate the speaker in 61:1–3 to assume eschatological qualities. In the relationship between prophecy and fulfilment, that which has not yet

174. This is the case whether a member of the household (1 Kgs 3:18) or the priesthood (Num 1:51 and passim), or one's society as a whole (Job 15:19), or a relative (Deut 25:5).

175. See Berlin, *The Dynamics of Biblical Parallelism*, 27–28.

176. See Robert Alter, *The Art of Biblical Poetry* (New York: Basic, 1985), 23–25.

177. Dan Cohn-Sherbok, *The Jewish Messiah* (Edinburgh: T. & T. Clark, 1997), 13.

178. Oswalt, *Isaiah 40–66*, 563.

been fulfilled might look forward to the eschaton. Therefore, 61:1–3 (within chs. 60–62) cannot not be anchored in one historical time or event, but has a trans-historical quality that allows the possibility of messianic interpretation.

Similar to 11:10–16, where the "root of Jesse" shall gather all of the nations unto himself, chs. 60–62 reflects this action on behalf of Zion because of the act of one individual (61:1–3) who is anointed to announce liberty. Pomykala argues that the "nations pay homage to the glory of YHWH through a sanctified Jerusalem" (11:10; 60:1–4; 66:18).[179] Like the Servant whom YHWH appointed to be a light to the nations (49:6, 9; see also 42:6, 16), Isa 60 stresses the movement of the nations to the light of Zion.[180] In 60:3, the nations and kings shall come to the light that will rise upon YHWH's people (Ps 102:15 [NRSV 16]). Isaiah 60:4, beginning exactly like 49:18, says that the nations shall bring gifts. The wealth of nations will be brought to Zion and foreigners shall plough their fields (61:5b–6). Foreign nations shall bring treasures that advance restored worship, such as incense, sheep and rams for the altars, that the house of YHWH will be glorified (60:6–7).[181] The safety of all nations depends on serving Zion ("For the nation and kingdom that will not serve you shall perish; those nations shall be utterly laid waste," 60:12). Isaiah 60:10–22 describes the new state of salvation,[182] when these foreigners and their kings shall rebuild the walls of earthly Jerusalem (60:10, 18; 61:4) and "they shall possess the land forever" (60:21). The larger context depicts the rebuilding of Jerusalem (60:10–14), the transformation of Zion (vv. 15–18) and the cosmos as well (vv. 19–22). The nations both take part in the salvation that is breaking out in Zion by bearing gifts and serving, and acknowledge that Zion is the holy place where by God sheds his light. Within this eschatological dimension, the nations in the future acquiesce to Israel and the leadership of a single individual who announces salvation. As a result of his anointing, the nations now have their role defined by his presence.

Set within this eschatological framework, the speaker in 61:1–3 claims to do what no other king can do (e.g. David, Hezekiah, Josiah or Cyrus).[183] Any other "anointed one," such as Cyrus, can rebuild ancient

179. Pomykala, *The Davidic Dynasty Tradition*, 164.
180. See Westermann, *Isaiah 40–66*, 353.
181. Ibid., 298.
182. Ibid., 356.
183. Oswalt (*Isaiah 40–66*, 563) says that "only a king greater than all those others who hold his people captive can make such an announcement. This is the Messiah at work, bringing in his reign of justice and righteousness (11:3–5; cf. also 1:27)." Yet the figure in this passage is anointed to do much more.

ruins and destroyed cities but cannot announce release to the captives in the Diaspora, bind up the brokenhearted, proclaim both the favorable year of YHWH and God's day of vengeance, and comfort all who mourn. Though 57:18 describes contrition that accompanies mourning (אבל√) in order for the people to obtain comfort, 61:1–3 goes further by declaring an outcome of God's "anointing" and "sending." The speaker himself has been "anointed" and "sent" to comfort those who mourn. Rendtorff argues that comfort (נחם) is a thread that holds the larger book of Isaiah together and has been promised at crucial locations of the book (such as 12:1; 40:3; 49:13; 52:9). Here YHWH anoints the speaker to fulfill this appointment.[184] Oswalt asserts that only "because he is the Lord's designee, and can he speak for God, to announce the year of favor and a day of vengeance," can he proclaim liberty.[185]

By what limits has this figure been designated? The word פקח usually applies to the opening of ears and eyes (42:20) but in 42:7 speaks of bringing people out of the darkness of prison, which probably serves as an answer to exile. In the post-exilic era, after the exiles have come home, the phrase ולאסורים פקח־קוח ("release from darkness," 61:1) refers to an event beyond the return of the exiles (see 58:6). Similarly, the phrase ויום נקם ("day of vengeance") "has nothing to do with violent punitive actions against the enemy" because here it "can only mean *deliverance* of the Lord = 'year of the Lord's favor'" (34:8; 61:2; 63:4). These events cannot derive from the actions of an earthly king because a person proclaims comfort, and the word "vengeance" seems to imply salvation.[186] The word דרור is employed selectively in the Old Testament in context with the year of Jubilee (Lev 25) to speak of emancipation from slavery every fifty years. This "acceptable year" has eschatological possibilities because no king had ever announced the year of Jubilee. Therefore, Isa 61:1–3 cannot be restricted to an ordinary historical person or event since these promises anticipate a deliverer whose presence transcends the time.

---

184.   Rendtorff, "Zur Komposition des Buches Jesaja," 298–300, 315–17; idem, *Canon and Theology*, 149–51.

185.   Oswalt, *Isaiah 40–66*, 565.

186.   George E. Mendenhall, *The Tenth Generation: The Origins of the Biblical Tradition* (Baltimore: The Johns Hopkins University Press, 1973), 102 n. 84. All of the texts where the word נקם appears are either exilic or post-exilic. Only once (35:4) does this term function in a message of salvation with no mention of the destruction of the enemy (and perhaps vengeance *on the enemy* might very well be implied in the verbiage), but on all other occasions the term appears in a context where destruction of the enemy is mentioned (1:24; 34:8; 47:3; 59:17; 63:4). Clearly, the writer understands salvation to take place in response to his own time.

This deliverer will bring about salvation in a manner that exceeds the limits of a normal king. That is why Isa 65:17–25 sets the fulfilment of the book of Isaiah's messianic expectation during an eschatological time when YHWH will create "a new heaven and new earth" as opposed to Cyrus whose liberation is set in time and space (65:17–25). Clearly, Isa 65:17–25 dispels any notion, which may have arisen in the post-exilic era, that Israel's messianic promise would be fulfilled by an earthly prophet, priest or king such as Cyrus or a prophetic figure like the so-called Second or Third Isaiah. Such hope anticipates a time when the "wolf and the lamb shall feed together and the lion shall eat straw like the ox..." (65:25). Sekine examines connections between 65:16b–25 and chs. 60–62 in order to make a case that both passages derive from the same tradition history.[187] Nevertheless, whether or not chs. 60–62 and 65:16b–25 may have originated at the same level of tradition history, 65:17–25 strategically responds to the various portraits of a messianic deliverer in Isaiah and rules out former fulfilments of prophecy (e.g. Cyrus as proof of the "former things") and places the fulfilment of this expectation within an eschatological perspective.

In sum, this chapter has focused on what makes Isa 61:1–3 different from other texts. While our definition of messianism relies on an eschatological event in which a superhuman person fulfills the promises made to David within this world after the monarchy has ended, 61:1–3 never mentions David. However, in its uniqueness, this passage also provides warrants for messianic interpretation. First, the speaker, who has been called to announce good news (לבשר) in 61:1–3, in some ways is different from the herald of good tidings in other passages. Especially significant is that the infinitive describing his act of proclaiming good news (לבשר) is subordinate to the verb משח. Second, this individual pronouncing salvation in 61:1–3 fulfills the hope in chs. 60–62, which looks beyond the return from Babylon to an eschatological salvation at the end of time. Third, this one announces a salvation that exceeds the limits of a normal king. Fourth, the spirit of YHWH rests upon him very similarly to the Davidic figure in 11:1–6 and the Servant in 42:1–2, though the speaker here is explicitly described by the word משח. Finally, 61:1–3, being disconnected from any identifiable historical events, possesses an ambiguity that invites several interpretations, one of which is messianic. Whether or not 61:1–3 originally was intended to be interpreted messianically, this text within the scriptural scroll of Isaiah as a whole provides warrants for messianic interpretation.

187. Sekine, *Die Tritojesajanische Sammlung*, 177–78.

Chapter 6

SUMMARY AND CONCLUSIONS

I. *Review of Findings*

As stated in my Introduction, I am working with the definition of messianism that anticipates that a person or persons offer a solution in an extraordinary way to activate and restore within this world the promises made to David in 2 Sam 7 after the monarchy has disappeared. This definition distinguishes between an ideal king and the Messiah because idealism about the king cannot provide a rationale for messianism, though it only fits a very broad definition. Moreover, expectation of an ideal king before the eradication of the monarchy would only fit a pre-exilic definition of מָשִׁיחַ, which would speak of a pre-exilic, Israelite or Judean king who contemporaneously sat on the throne but who had no eschatological attributes. For example, Wegner treats Isa 32:1–8 as a messianic passage but we do not consider this text to be messianic because it describes an ideal king but not a Messiah.[1] The hope of an ideal king uses exaggerated language but texts that provide messianic hope use eschatological language, about a superhuman deliverer.

Therefore, modern scholars, who attempt to reconstruct historically the original Isaianic traditions, would no doubt rule out various pre-exilic texts as messianic. However, I have demonstrated that some texts, which were not originally messianic in their pre-biblical traditions, have been altered by the scriptural context to warrant messianic interpretation.

I have observed in preceding chapters of this study how several editorial devices have been employed to cause pre-biblical and pre-messianic traditions to become messianic biblical testimonies. These devices wed pre-exilic hope to a post-exilic expectation and sometimes the ambiguity of the text gains clarification. In certain cases, post-exilic traditions in the book, some of which are messianic, have been placed next to pre-exilic and pre-messianic traditions.

---

1. Wegner, *An Examination of Kingship*, 275–98.

Among the editorial devices used to warrant messianism, some of the features are post-exilic messianic reinterpretation of non-messianic texts, the relationship between ambiguity and clarity and the placement of eschatological features within the scroll as a whole.

A. *Post-exilic Editing*

Post-exilic editing in Isa 1–39 has altered the significance of some pre-exilic texts that were originally heard non-messianically. These later levels of post-exilic editing look back on the exile when Jerusalem was destroyed, the people were removed from their land and the monarchy was removed, thus providing warrants to re-interpret various texts messianically. In my third chapter, I demonstrated that at this level of scripture-conscious editing, the formation of the book as a whole confirms the pattern of messianic interpretation in the book of Isaiah.

I have not tried to argue that there are lines of continuity between each original tradition and the later editing that provides warrants for messianic interpretation. For example, the original Isaianic traditions did not anticipate a messianic hope upon which the later editors built. Instead, this latter level of editing semantically transformed earlier non-messianic traditions so that they may be re-interpreted by the editors as messianic. Now, within the book of Isaiah as a whole, Emmanuel exceeds the limits of the Syro-Ephraimite War and consequently becomes an answer to the exile when a king no longer sits on the throne. Similarly, within the latter formation of the book, a royal enthronement oracle, which was probably originally uttered at coronation of Hezekiah or Josiah, now within the latter editing describes an eternal royal figure who casts light on the darkness of exile. I have shown that these traditions were not originally messianic but became messianic within what I have called the "biblical" or scriptural form of the book of Isaiah and now they warrant messianic interpretation. Therefore, my approach does not attempt to locate lines of continuity or even trajectories between the original oracles and the latter levels of editing. Neither have I attempted to pinpoint the exact moment in the post-exilic age when messianism originated in order to find lines of continuity between such origins and the "final form" of scripture. Instead, I have demonstrated that post-exilic levels of editing occur at a time when the monarchy has been terminated and hopes for an ideal king may now be replaced by new messianic hopes of one who will extraordinarily activate and restore within this world the promises made to David. Along these same lines, I have not tried either to prove or disprove the prophet's ability to predict, but have established how the scriptural form of Isaiah testifies to messianic hope.

B. *Functional Ambiguity*

I have also demonstrated how ambiguity functions as a rhetorical feature that provides warrants for messianic interpretation. In my third, fourth and fifth chapters, I have demonstrated how in the original level of tradition history, some texts were not messianic but within the latter formation of the book of Isaiah, the editors have guaranteed that the referent of these texts remained ambiguous. Both Judaism and Christianity have exploited that ambiguity, oftentimes in two different directions.

I have also shown that modern attempts to locate the original or historical meaning of passages, which Judaism or Christianity had traditionally interpreted as messianic, have rendered ineffective the rhetorical force that lies in the ambiguity of the text. Therefore, this rhetorical feature includes the listener in multiple ways within the poetic discourse. The reader responds to the various ambiguous roles in the text and may feel as if he or she is being addressed, and gains intimacy with the poetry. Attempts to resolve the ambiguity through an historical reconstruction of its unambiguous origins not only damage the effects of this striking literary feature but nullify any messianic interpretation that the ambiguity may invite.

C. *Eschatological Features and Messianic Interpretation*

Pre-exilic levels of tradition history, such as traditions that speak of ideal kingship, cannot be interpreted as messianic unless they assume that an eschatological event will take place after the monarchy has ceased to exist. I have demonstrated how, after the events of 587, the eschatological tension of judgment and promise provides occasion for Judaism's early messianic expectation and thereby creates a warrant to interpret various texts messianically (see my Chapters 3, 4 and 5). Texts speaking of a king, which are placed next to oracles that use eschatological language and do not present an historical referent, elicit the reader's messianic interpretation (see Chapters 3 and 5).

Throughout this composition, I have referred to an old rhetorical distinction between "the proper" and "the figurative" use of words. I explained in my Introduction that the "proper" usage of words implies their straightforward meaning, while the "figurative" usage involves metaphor, similes and the like. Some texts that use figurative or exaggerated language to speak of a king cannot at the pre-biblical level be interpreted messianically. However, after the monarchy has ended, the community begins to hear these passages as proper uses that can only include the eschatological elements that invite messianic expectation. For example, the Messiah is invested with superhuman powers from God that past kings had not possessed. Within Christianity and Judaism, the book of Isaiah presents hope in a figure, one who will fulfill the promises made to David in the eschatological era. In a very similar fashion, we can only consider a text as messianic if it uses "proper" language that describes an eschatological event where a superhuman person activates and restores the promises made to David within this world after the monarchy has ended.

Even for Christians of the third millennium, who look back at the event of their Messiah's coming, and who affirm that Jesus is the Messiah, Christian hope is still held in abeyance within an eschatological tension. Paul Hanson argues:

> If the Messiah has come, where is the messianic reign of peace and justice? They will rather be moved by this question to pray all the more fervently, "Thy Kingdom come. Thy will be done, on earth as it is in heaven." In this way they can be cleansed of the triumphalism and attending history of lies that claims with Christ all has been finished...[2]

From this perspective, the New Testament was the greatest disappointment to the early Christians next to the death of Christ because they wanted their Messiah to return a second time and set up a kingdom of peace and justice. Therefore, just as messianism within ancient Judaism required an eschatological element, this eschatological expectation still looms over the heads of both Judaism and Christianity to this very day as each sect awaits the coming of a Messiah who will set up a kingdom of peace and justice here on earth.

II. *Other Isaianic Passages Not Treated*

The way that image of "the branch" (צמח) in Isa 4:2 resonates with the "branch" (גזע) or "root" (שרש) of David in Isa 11 has caused some to translate 4:2 messianically. This image reminds us of other images of the "branch" that describe the Messiah in various Old Testament passages (e.g. Isa 11:1; Zech 3:8; 6:12) but this term alone does not fit our definition of messianism. The "cornerstone in Isa 28:16 evokes the same type of interpretation but again does not fit our definition of messianism (see below).

While most scholars regard the promises to David in Isa 55:3–5 to have been reapplied in an untraditional way and transferred to Israel,[3] a

2. Hanson, *Isaiah 40–66*, 163

3. Volz, *Isaiah II*, 139–43; Otto Eissfeldt, "The Promises of Grace to David in Isaiah 55:1–5," in Anderson and Harrelson, eds., *Israel's Prophetic Heritage*, 206–7; Muilenburg, *The Book of Isaiah*, 5:645; Westermann, *Isaiah 40–66*, 283–86; Frank Moore Cross, *Canaanite Myth and Hebrew Epic* (Cambridge, Mass.: Harvard

few think that this passage invokes messianic promise.[4] Walter Kaiser argues that Isa 55:3b distinctly refers to 1 Sam 7:11–16; 23:5 and Ps 89 by mentioning the everlasting covenant (ברית עולם), which was rooted in YHWH's steadfast love for David (חסדי דוד הנאמנים). He argues that the promise given to David is not transferred to Israel in these verses, but "is shared in the inception of the Davidic Covenant."[5]

Isaiah 55:4 differentiates David from the peoples: "See, I made him a witness to the peoples." Only in Josh 24:22; Ruth 4:9–10; Isa 43:10, 12 and 44:8 do we find the phrase "you are witnesses." In Josh 24:22, the people of Israel are witnesses to the swearing in of the covenant. In the first trisection (chs. 40–48), where Israel is overtly called "the Servant" (43:10–12), "my Servant" Israel is told "you are my witnesses." In 44:6–8, YHWH is king and Israel is told "you are my witnesses." In the second trisection where the Servant becomes differentiated from Israel (chs. 49–57), YHWH says that he made David "witness" to Israel (55:4). It is not self-evident in the context of the material that the Servant fulfills the promises made to David as described in 55:3–5 (contra Kaiser).[6] So the promises are not transferred to the Servant either. While I would agree with Kaiser that "the promise given to David in 55:3–6 is not transferred to Israel; it is *shared* with Israel in the inception of the Davidic covenant in 2 Samuel 7," I would disagree that this passage is messianic.[7] Clearly 55:3–5 is speaking of David and not the Messiah, who could at most be a type of the Messiah but not the Messiah himself.

III. *The Terms Messiah and Messianic and the Implications for this Study*

Although the word "Messiah" is an English transliteration of the word משיח, not every text that includes this word משיח will fit the definition(s) of messianism, which I have already described and which arose in early

---

University Press, 1973), 265; Karl Martin Beyse, *Serrubbabel und die Königser-wartungen der Propheten Haggai und Sacharja* (Stuttgart: Calwer, 1972); von Rad, *Old Testament Theology*, 2:240; Petersen, *Late Israelite Prophecy*, 21; Wilcox and Patton-Williams, "The Servant Songs," 87; Pomykala, *The Davidic Dynasty Tradition*, 39. Von Rad (*The Message of the Prophets*, 208) calls this "democratiz-ing" the tradition.

    4. Kaiser, *The Messiah in the Old Testament*, 182; idem, "The Unfailing Kind-nesses Promised to David: Isaiah 55:3," *JSOT* 45 (1989): 91–98.

    5. Kaiser, "Unfailing Kindnesses."

    6. Kaiser, *The Messiah in the Old Testament*, 182. See also Bentzen, "The Ebed Yahweh Songs"; idem, *King and Messiah*, 54, 64, 67.

    7. Kaiser, "Unfailing Kindnesses."

Judaism. Oftentimes the word was used in a context that pre-dated the Jewish hope of a Messiah. Most usages of "Messiah" in the Old Testament/Hebrew Bible merely speak of a contemporary king who sits on the throne in the pre-exilic era. In the case of Cyrus, the later editors rule him out as a Messiah even though the earlier pre-biblical traditions of Second Isaiah had named him מְשִׁיחוֹ ("his anointed," 45:1; 65:16b–25). I have also demonstrated that a passage does not require the word מָשִׁיחַ to be classified as messianic because most biblical texts interpreted as messianic by Jews and Christians do not include the term מָשִׁיחַ, but include other pertinent ideas that describe a Messiah without naming him as one.

I have shown that several Isaianic texts describe the messianic idea of one who would supernaturally fulfill the promises to David after the monarchy has ended, and express a hope that was held by many adherents of early Judaism. Certainly, a biblical passage does not need to use the word מָשִׁיחַ for us to classify it as messianic, and I have shown that texts in Isaiah interpreted as messianic by later Jews and Christians have lacked the term מָשִׁיחַ, while containing other pertinent ideas. At the same time, 45:1 uses מָשִׁיחַ to describe Cyrus whom I have shown cannot fit the role of a Messiah within the scriptural context of Isaiah.

IV. *Biblical Prophecy and Its Implications for Messianism*

In his *Oracles of God*, John Barton charges that the late post-exilic views of prophecy were non-historical and that any concept of prophecy other than a modern historical reconstruction of ancient Israelite prophecy is incorrect. His subtitle, *Perceptions of Ancient Prophecy in Israel after the Exile*, aims "in a systematic way" to address "the perceptions of prophecy in Judaism of the Second Temple period"[8] and "what Jewish writers of the post-exilic age thought about prophecy."[9] He concludes that these later readers connected Isaiah to an historical setting very much like modern fundamentalists "know" these things. Barton dismisses the idea that scripture is prophetic and regards these later views of prophecy to be non-historical. He does not define prophecy in a way that elevates fulfilment in light of later events but reduces prophecy to what he thinks he can prove to be the ethical teaching of the very prophet who is speaking, his time and circumstances, and his contemporary audience.

---

8. John Barton, *Oracles of God: Perceptions of Prophecy in Israel After the Exile* (New York: Oxford University Press, 1986), 3.

9. Ibid., 7.

Barton, like many biblical scholars (both conservative and liberal) is tempted by a modern view of prophecy whereby he must identify: (1) the very prophet who is speaking (a modern view of an author), (2) out of what time and circumstances he is speaking, (3) to what contemporary audience he speaks, and finally, (4) that the prophet is making ethical claims.[10] Like Barton, therefore, modern critics have attempted to attach every segment of Isaiah to a contemporary prophet and his contemporary audience, thus construing the book of Isaiah as written by three historically consecutive "authors": Proto-Isaiah, Deutero-Isaiah, and Trito-Isaiah. This outlook epitomizes modern attempts to acknowledge a diachronic tension in the text, while also preserving the "true" prophetic core. From this modern view of prophecy, scholarship became so preoccupied by these historical origins that most scholars viewed the later levels of tradition history as non-prophetic. For example, we saw how Duhm championed this view of prophecy and dismissed later editing of non-prophetic materials. This understanding of prophecy did not include any idea of the prediction of a Messiah. Consequently, scholars began to

10. Eichhorn, *Die Hebraischen Propheten*, vol. 1; von Ewald, *Commentary on the Prophets of the Old Testament*; D. Bernhard Duhm, *Die Theologie der Propheten als Grundlage für die Innere Entwicklungsgeschichte der Israelischen Religion* (Bonn: Adolph Marcus, 1875); Kuenen, *The Prophets and Prophecy in Israel*; Kuhl, *The Prophets of Israel*; E. Gerstenberger, "The Woe-Oracles of the Prophets," *JBL* 81 (1962): 249–63; von Rad, *The Message of the Prophets*; Hermann Gunkel, "The Prophets as Writers and Poets," in *Prophecy in Israel* (ed. David L. Petersen; Philadelphia: Fortress, 1987), 22–73; Hooke, *Prophets and Priests*; L. Festinger, H. W. Riecken and S. Schacter, *When Prophecy Fails: A Social and Psychological Study of a Modern Group That Predicted the Destruction of the World* (Minneapolis: University of Minnesota Press, 1956); Lindblom, *Prophecy in Ancient Israel*; Eissfeldt, "The Promises of Grace to David"; Ackroyd, "Historians and Prophets"; James L. Crenshaw, *Prophetic Conflict: Its Effect Upon Israelite Religion* (BZAW 124; Berlin: de Gruyter, 1971); Mason, *Prophetic Problems*; James A. Sanders, "Hermeneutics in True and False Prophecy," in *Canon and Authority: Essays in Old Testament Religion and Theology* (ed. G. W. Coats and Burt O. Long; Philadelphia: Fortress, 1977), 20–41; Peter R. Ackroyd, *Isaiah I–XII* (VTSup 29; Leiden: Brill, 1978); Robert P. Carroll, "Second Isaiah and the Failure of Prophecy," *StTH* 32 (1978): 119–31; idem, *When Prophecy Failed*; David L. Petersen, *The Roles of Israel's Prophets* (JSOTSup 17; Sheffield: JSOT Press, 1981); Koch, *The Prophets*, vol. 2; Wilson, *Prophecy and Society in Ancient Israel*; Barton, *Oracles of God*; S. Dean McBride, "Prophetic Vision and Mosaic Constitution," in Mays, ed., *Harper's Bible Commentary*, 22–23; Klass A. D. Smelik, "Distortions of Old Testament Prophecy: The Purpose of Isaiah Xxxvi–Xxxvii," *OtSt* 24 (1989): 70–93; C. von Orelli, *The Old Testament Prophecy of the Consummation of God's Kingdom, Traced in Its Historical Development* (trans. J. S. Banks; Edinburgh: T. & T. Clark, 1889); Sawyer, *Prophecy and the Biblical Prophets*.

construe texts, which were interpreted as messianic throughout Christianity and Judaism, as non-messianic. From this vantage point, pre-exilic prophecies in "Proto-Isaiah" (Isa 7:14; 9:1–6; 11:1–9) could not be messianic to a pre-exilic audience, whose king still sat on the throne. This was not a part of the ancient understanding of prophetic books or the definition of prophecy.

When we affirm the book of Isaiah as prophecy, we are speaking of the book as a whole and not the prophet(s) that we can reconstruct behind the book. Because of the way that modern epistemology has shaped and defined biblical exegesis, after historically reconstructing the original traditions of Isaiah, scholars have attempted to salvage the rest of the book by assigning chs. 40–55 and 56–66 to other prophets. While this may provide a heuristic for describing different levels of tradition history, we cannot divide chs. 1–39; 40–55 and 56–66 by editorial levels because Isa 1–39 is layered with exilic and post-exilic editing (e.g. Isa 1–4; 6:13; 7:20–25; 8:20–22; 12:1–6; 13, etc.) and even, as Westermann argues, pre-exilic oracles may possibly occur in 56:9–57:13.[11] Even scholars who claim to be reading the book of Isaiah as a whole still consider the prophet in chs. 40–55 to be "Deutero-Isaiah," or the prophet in chs. 56–66 to be "Trito-Isaiah." More tendentiously, on the conservative side, some scholars regard all of chs. 40–66 as eighth-century "Isaiah." This reflection of a modern form of knowing also explains the tension felt by some twentieth-century exegetes who think that we should not isolate the Servant Songs from the context of chs. 40–55 as if these chapters represent a scriptural designation on their own.

Contrary to these modern presumptions, within the history of biblical interpretation, Christianity and Judaism have regarded the Bible as a prophetic testimony. Obviously, the book of Isaiah is a prophetic book and not just the original words of the prophet Isaiah. In other words, every part of the book of Isaiah is prophecy and prophecy cannot be reduced merely to the prophets we can historically reconstruct behind the book. We affirm the whole book of Isaiah as a prophetic testimony to revelation. The later levels of editing are no less prophetic but are just as genuine as the original levels. The book of Isaiah offers a parallel to the Torah of Moses, which also has been edited to be read as a prophetic book (see, e.g., Deut 34:10–12).

When attempts are made to describe a biblical prophetic book, there is no obligation to confine an historically reconstructed prophet to his or her time, circumstances and audience. Even pre-modern commentators felt no obligation to identify the prophetic figure who was speaking in

11. Westermann, *Isaiah 40–66*, 302.

chs. 40–55 or 56–66 as the eighth-century prophet Isaiah. Yet pre-modern interpreters could speak about the testimony of Isaiah, whose human words bear witness to God's word, while an audience is being addressed centuries later through different voices. Isaiah 1–39 contains traditions of voices that are speaking, which cannot be confined to the eighth-century prophet. For example, in 1:1 the superscription refers in the third person to "the vision of Isaiah son of Amoz, which he saw…" Moreover, Isa 13 provides an oracle against Babylon. Therefore, the editors and pre-modern interpreters do not share the same view of prophecy, which has caused scholars to think that if we read a prophetic book properly, we have to identify the prophet within his time, circumstances and the audience to whom he is speaking. This was not necessary for the ancient understanding of prophetic books or the definition of prophecy. Perhaps this is why such a voice remains ambiguous in 52:13–53:12 or 61:1–3. In other words, within biblical prophecy, voices that are different from that of the designated writer (Isaiah) often speak from different times, circumstances and to different audiences, but still belong to the testimony of Isaiah. Unlike the modern idea where a written piece is the sole property of the author, Child's rightly asserts that scripture never ruled out a later voice adding to the compositions because the Old Testament is "traditional, communal and developing."[12]

While we affirm the necessity of historical criticisms, we also recognize that after one brings a method as far as possible, the process may still leave an unfinished project. For example, many modern critics have the tendency to confuse redaction-historical reconstructions with the scriptural form of Isaiah. Modern critics even treat the final editors as authors. Sheppard argues that modern critics exhibit "a tendency to confuse a redaction-historical reconstruction with a canonical approach or as a proof of a structural unity." He concludes that "again redactional features in biblical books…reflect esoteric, self-conscious rules of poetic beauty and an anxiety of influence often serving as strong semantic indicators." That is why David Carr argues that editing alone cannot adequately establish "literary unity" or what Sheppard describes as a "macrostructural conception inherent in the formation of the book of Isaiah."[13]

---

12. Childs, *Introduction to the Old Testament as Scripture*, 574.

13. David Carr, "Reaching for Unity in Isaiah," *JSOT* 57 (1993): 61–80; Sheppard, "The Book of Isaiah as a Human Witness," 276; idem, "Canon Criticism"; idem, "Childs, Brevard," in *Historical Handbook of Major Biblical Interpreters* (ed. Donald McKim; Downers Grove, Ill.: Intervarsity, 1998), 575–84. Contrary to the title "canon criticism" imposed on his article, Sheppard himself clarifies that our scripture approach is "certainly not a 'canonical criticism'—as if we now simply

There is even a temptation to re-anchor each layer of tradition history within a specific tradition. For example, Sanders seeks to establish a "canonical hermeneutic" which aims to identify a consistent factor in the process of tradition history. In this way, he hopes to explain how the same normative tradition might properly lead to vastly different interpretations in different times and circumstances.[14] He searches for this pattern behind every redactional reinterpretation of preceding tradition. One main problem with this approach is that the formation of scripture is merely one incidental phase in the process of tradition history. Certain moments of reinterpretation constitute a "canonical hermeneutic." This is unconvincing because every single change in tradition cannot operate under the same pattern. This line of criticism seems to be a pious accounting for all the changes in tradition history. The things that give rise to changes in the text are not so predictable but are tremendously diverse. If the biblical level is one more moment of actualization, namely the "final" redactor as "author" and his or her post-exilic audience, it must be irrelevant to us in the twenty-first century.[15] If we reduce the text to one level of editing—even if it is the latest level—we rule out all other levels of tradition history and anchor the text in one time frame that has no application to successive generations. The Torah clearly becomes a model for all biblical books in the way that it establishes the biblical witness for all future generations (Gen 45:10; Exod 10:2; 12:4–26; Deut 6:2; 7:20–21; 11:19, 21; 12:28; 29:22ff.; 30:1–5; 32:46).

Since Torah sets the precedent for the rest of scripture, other biblical books, including the book of Isaiah, will presume that precedent without needing to redefine what was prescribed by the Torah. For example, the editorial introduction of the Former Prophets and the Psalter begin by admonishing the reader to study these books as meditations on Torah (Josh 1:7, 8; Pss 1:1–3; 2:1 [הגה√]). The Torah defines revelation accordingly: "the secret things belong to YHWH our God, but the revealed things belong to us and to our children forever, to observe all the words of this law" (Deut 29:29). Therefore, defining the Torah as a testimony to revelation, Moses instructs the Levites, "Take this book of the law and

---

need to add one more methodology on top of an already unstackable accumulation of modern methods" (Sheppard, "Biblical Wisdom Literature," 369.

14. This theory of redaction harmonizes differences in redactional layers that stand worlds apart from one another. Sanders called this factor "the canonical hermeneutic," while acknowledging that not every interpretation found in scripture itself met that standard. Sanders, *Canon and Community*; idem, *From Sacred Story to Sacred Text*.

15. Meade, *Pseudonymity and Canon*, 22–26, 211–12.

put it beside the ark of the covenant of the LORD your God; let it remain there as a *testimony* against you" (Deut 31:26). Deuteronomy 32:44–47 states:

> When Moses had finished reciting all these words to all Israel, he said to them: "Take to heart all the words that I am giving in witness against you today; give them as a command to your children, so that they may diligently observe all the words of this law. This is no trifling matter for you, but rather your very life; through it you may live long in the land that you are crossing over the Jordan to possess."

Since the formation of the book of Isaiah seems to have taken place within the shadow of the editors of Torah, as I have described in my Chapter 2, it speaks, like the book of Torah, "to your children, and your children's children and to all who are far off,"[16] so that within every generation, the book may be read by the "next generation" as a testimony to revelation. What does this have to do with Messianism in Isaiah?

I have shown that messianic interpretation occurs at the same late level of scripture-conscious editing as the book of Isaiah has been shaped to be heard as a testimony to revelation. I have also demonstrated in my third chapter how the fifth-century editors of the book of Isaiah have reinterpreted earlier references to the prophet's "torah" (8:16) as the Mosaic Torah (8:20), while also giving the Torah precedence over the testimony of Isaiah. Isaiah's testimony now becomes subordinate to the Torah. At this later level of editing, the Torah of God becomes "reminiscent of the Mosaic law" and the "torah" of the prophet now functions as a prophetic testimony to the "divine Torah, known most clearly in the books of Moses."[17] In the post-exilic period, the later redactors have edited the biblical scroll of Isaiah in the shadow of the Torah whereby the prologue invites the reader to hear "the Torah of our God" in order to "hear the word of God…" (1:10). Similar to how Pss 1–2 make up an editorial introduction that now invites the Second Temple community to read the Psalter as meditations on Torah, Isa 1–4 portrays Torah being taught in the restored city of Jerusalem (2:3).[18] Isaiah 4:1–6 not only

---

16. See Exod 10:2; 12:24, 26–51; Deut 4:9; 6:2, 7, 20, 21; 12:28; 23:8; 29:29; 31:13; 32:46.

17. Sheppard, "Isaiah 1–39," 548, 579.

18. Pss 1–2, separated by no superscription, form an editorial introduction to the Psalms, telling the post-exilic community how to read the book of Psalms as scripture. Ps 1:2 assists us to read this book as meditations on Torah (compare with Josh 1:7, 8). Without v. 2, Ps 1 would have originally been a wisdom Psalm. Ps 1:6 summarizes the consequences of Wisdom and Torah by means of a proverb. The Psalm as a whole now identifies the source of wisdom as the Torah of YHWH. Ps. 2 was originally a royal enthronement Psalm, but in the post-exilic era becomes linked

emphasizes the "glory of the Lord" in restored Jerusalem, but describes this glory with Torah imagery: "cloud by day and smoke and shining flame by night" (Isa 4:5; cf. Exod 13:21, 22; 14:24; 40:38; Num 9:16; 14:14; Deut 1:33). Therefore, the post-exilic community could hear the description of the people going into exile (Isa 5:13) in light of the Exodus found in the Torah of Moses. Just as the Torah defines itself as a testimony to revelation (Deut 31:19, 26), it sets the precedent for the book of Isaiah's testimony to revelation.

V. *The Psalms and Messianism*

Just as the present study has shown how non-messianic traditions in Isaiah came to be reinterpreted as messianic within the latter formation of the Isaiah Scroll in the post-exilic era, there is also promise for such study in the Psalms. Using the same historical-critical methods that have been applied in the preceding chapters to the Isaiah Scroll, but without providing the same lengthy *Forschungsberichten*, I will here describe briefly how a number of the scriptural psalms might also warrant messianic interpretation.

Last century, Dietrich Bonhoeffer posed an important question about the Psalms: "How do the ordinary words of men and women become God's word to me?"[19] Again, the answer to this question lies in how we understand the ways in which pre-biblical traditions have taken on a new scriptural meaning in their placement within the Psalter as a whole. Many Christians consider some Psalms as messianic merely because the New Testament writers treat them as such. Yet, simply because the New Testament quotes a Psalm messianically does not necessarily imply that the text itself warrants messianic interpretation, at least not according to the definition that has been spelled out in the present study.[20]

---

to 2 Sam 7 as a messianic prophecy. Therefore, this introduction invites one to read the Psalter in light of the three idioms of revelation (Torah, Prophets and Wisdom). The two chapters link both Psalms with *Stichworten* ("mediate" [plot]—1:2; 2:1; "sit"—1:1; 2:4; "perish"—1:6; 2:11) Ps 2:11 then rounds off this introduction by answering the opening words ("Blessed [אַשְׁרֵי] is the man") with "Blessed (אַשְׁרֵי) are those who take refuge..." (see 1:1). Not only does the word "refuge" end the introduction (2:11), but is repeated throughout the Psalter (7:1; 11:1; 16:1; 34:8b; 52:7 etc.) as a fulfilment of keeping Torah. See Sheppard, *Future of the Bible*, 59–95.

19. Dietrich Bonhoeffer, *Psalms: The Prayer Book of the Bible* (Minneapolis: Augsburg Fortress, 1974), 13. See also his *Life Together: Prayerbook of the Bible* (ed. B. Kelly; trans. Daniel W. Bloesch; Philadelphia: Fortress, 1995).

20. Remember that while Henry Ainsworth recalled how New Testament writers cited some Psalms christologically, he did not obligatorily use this as a warrant for

Form-critically, Ps 1 was originally a wisdom Psalm and Ps 2 was originally a pre-exilic royal enthronement oracle that celebrated the contemporary king's accession to the throne. However, within the latter formation of the Psalter, these two psalms have been semantically transformed to form an editorial introduction to the Psalter. They tell the readers how to pray the Psalms as scripture. Psalms 1 and 2 are now meant to be read together as one introduction because there is no super-scription that divides Pss 1 and 2. Since Ps 1 is so late that it does not even appear at Qumran, we can assume that the two chapters were united very late.

Several Hebrew phrases have been repeated in both Psalms, which provide "key word connections" (*Stichwörter*) that bring the two Psalms together. The word "happy" or "blessed" (אשר) begins and ends this introduction. Psalm 1:1 begins "Happy are those who do not walk in the council of the wicked," and Ps 2:12 rounds off the introduction with "Happy are those who take refuge..." The verb הגה ("meditate" or "plot") appears in 1:2 and 2:1, contrasting those who meditate on Torah and those who "meditate" or "plot" in vain in order to let the worshipers know that all prayer and meditation needs go be grounded in its subject matter. In addition, those who lower themselves from the position of walking to the position of "sitting" in the seat of the scoffer (1:1) are distinguished from the Lord, who "sits" in the heavens and laughs at their kings (2:4). Finally, the wicked "perish" (√אבד) in 1:6, evidently because their delight is not in the Torah; comparably, the kings and rulers of the earth are told in 2:12 that they must serve the Lord or they will perish. Not only does the word "refuge" end the introduction (2:12), but it is repeated throughout the Psalter as a whole (7:1; 11:1; 16:1; 34:8b; 52:7; 91:2, 4, 9 etc.). When a person is faithful to Torah, he or she trusts in God's promises and reads and prays the Psalms wisely— thereby, he or she finds refuge in YHWH. It thus becomes evident that these key word connections and the lack of superscriptions have been used to bring the two psalms together to form a single introduction that guides the community of faith in its reading of the Psalms as scripture. How, then, are the Psalms to be read?

Without Ps 1:2, Ps 1 would have originally been a wisdom Psalm. However, by means of what Gerald Sheppard and I termed "publishers' notes"—that is, later scripture-conscious editorial additions that guide the reading of the Jewish scriptures as a testimony to Torah—Ps 1:6

interpretation because he thought that the writers had special dispensation to make such interpretational decisions under the influence of the Holy Spirit. See Sheppard, "Pre-modern Criticism in the English Protestant Translations."

functions to summarize the consequences of Wisdom and Torah via the use of a proverb: "for the LORD watches over the way of the righteous, but the way of the wicked will perish." Just as Isa 1:10 instructs the readers that they must hear the scriptural testimony as a witness to Torah in order to hear God's word, and just as Isa 8:20 has been editorially organized to subordinate the prophet's teaching to the Mosaic Torah, so now Ps 1 as a whole in its latter scriptural form identifies the source of wisdom as the Torah of YHWH, with Ps 1:2 assisting the readers/hearers in their understanding of the scriptural psalms as meditations on Torah (cf. Josh 1:7, 8). Similar to Isa 9:1–6, Ps 2 was originally a royal enthronement Psalm that celebrated the king's accession to the throne. In the post-exilic era, however, after the Davidic monarchy had been destroyed, this psalm became linked to 2 Sam 7 as a messianic prophecy, one in which God promised David that his descendants would inhabit the throne forever. Since the kingship had been eradicated and no king sat on the throne, the late post-exilic editors of this introduction to the Psalter could only have understood the Hebrew word משיחו ("His Messiah" or "His anointed") as an eschatological Messiah who would fulfill the prophetic promises to David after the monarchy had ended.

Therefore, these "publishers' notes" tell the readers that the Psalter must be read in light of the three idioms of revelation in the Old Testament: Torah, prophecy and wisdom (cf. Sir 24:23–25). The Psalter as a scriptural book thus serves as a collections of meditations on Torah, identifying the Torah as the source of wisdom, also implying that one must read these Psalms wisely in light of biblical wisdom, and in light of the messianic promise. The Psalter, then, serves as an interpretation and resource for Torah, prophecy and wisdom.

Moreover, the five books conventionally understood to exist in the Psalter emulate the five books of the Torah. At the end of each book of Psalms, the editors give a brief doxology and state "Amen" or "Amen, Amen." Book 1 ends with the last Psalm of David of the first collection. Book 2 ends the second collection of David Psalms with the Solomon Psalm, where Solomon seems to offer a prayer for the Davidic kings, appearing to stand directly by the promises stated in Ps 2. By referring to the "gold of Sheba" in v. 15 (and it cannot be a coincidence that this parallels 1 Kgs 3:29–34; 10:10 and 10:23–25), this Psalm also sets Solomon within wisdom traditions and informs the reader's spirituality and prayers in light of the wisdom traditions that are shared by all cultures. Since Solomon is clearly the referent of Ps 72, one cannot read this Psalm messianically. We can, however, understand how ancient and medieval Christians came to see Solomon here as a messianic type who adumbrates one who will eschatologically fulfill the promises to David just as his father David serves as a messianic type.[21]

Book 3 ends with Ps 89 recalling the promises to David at the end of the double framework of the Asaph Psalms, which recalls Ps 2 as a messianic Psalm that rests on God's promises to David. Unlike the pre-exilic historical circumstances that link Solomon in Ps 72 with Ps 2, Ps 89 reflects on a time when the monarchy had been terminated, when Babylon had destroyed Jerusalem. In Ps 89:2–3, God says that "I have made a covenant with my chosen one, I have sworn to my servant David: 'I will establish your descendants forever, and build your throne for all generations.'" Yet in Ps 89:39, a human prayer anticipates a sharp lamentation over the death of the monarchy in the next part of the very same psalm, saying, "you have renounced the covenant with your servant; you have defiled his crown in the dust." Psalm 89 offers an apropos conclusion to the collection of Davidic lament Psalms, playing on the promises of God that Nathan brought to David, reiterated in the introduction in Ps 2 (see also Ps 132). Thus, we should not be surprised that the editors have arranged this psalm to be followed in Book 4 by the only Psalm to "Moses, the man of God." Not only does it come after the lament Psalms and before Psalms of praise, it also recalls Moses' function in Torah as one who intercedes on behalf of the people (v. 13): "Turn, O LORD! How long? Have compassion on your servants!" Sheppard says that, "Just as Ps 1 refers to Torah, Ps 90 links all of the Psalms to the Prayer tradition of Torah."[22]

After the intercessory prayer of Moses that presents the severe wrath of God (90:7–8), Ps 91 picks up the theme of "refuge" established in the introduction (91:2, 4, 9). Whoever "dwells in the shelter of the Most High" addresses the Lord in v. 2 as "My refuge and my fortress; my God, in whom I trust." Verse 4 then offers affirmation to those who pray this prayer, assuring them that "under his wings you will find refuge." Following this, vv. 9 and 10 affirm that, "Because you have made the LORD your refuge…no evil shall befall you." Therefore, we should not be surprised that in the pre-modern era, Jews and Christians associated these promises with messianic hope. We should also not be surprised that Satan urges Jesus to demonstrate that he can fulfill these promises in Ps 91, if he is truly the Messiah. Matthew 4:11 has Satan quoting Ps 91:11–12 when he tempts Jesus: "he will command his angels concerning you to guard you in all your ways… On their hands they will bear you up, so that you will not dash your foot against a stone." Even Satan knows how

21. See Auerbach, "Figura."
22. Sheppard, *Future of the Bible*, 79.

to read the Psalms scripturally! Jesus withstands Satan's directive to act messianically, citing the Torah in Deut 6:16: "Do not put the LORD your God to the test." Just as the readers of Isaiah must hear the Torah in order to hear the word of God, all of the Psalms must be subject to Torah.

Psalm 45, like Ps 2, is another likely case of a scriptural psalm being read messianically in the post-exilic era. Psalm 45:6, a non-messianic royal enthronement oracle that was recited at the king's accession, reads "Your throne, O God, endures forever and ever," and seemingly reflects the ancient Near Eastern belief that a king was adopted as the deity's son and became divine upon his ascent to the throne (Ps 2:7). Yet, even if one were to read the description of the king in Pss 2:7 and 45:6 as merely a "figurative," exaggerated use of language in the pre-exilic era, when the throne sat vacant in the post-exilic era, the community would have interpreted Ps 45 in light of YHWH's eternal promises to David in 2 Sam 7 as a "proper" use.

If Gunkel is right that Ps 110 is a very old pre-exilic, royal-coronation Psalm, then we can see how, within a final, stabilized Psalter, the later editors may have interpreted this psalm messianically in a manner similar to Pss 2, 45, and Isa 9:1–6.[23] The prophetic formula, "says YHWH" (נאם יהוה), has caused some to speculate whether this psalm originated in a prophetic setting.[24] In v. 1, the Psalmist calls the king "my Lord" (לאדני), and speaks of him sitting at YHWH's right hand. The language of "scepter" and "ruling the enemy" addresses a king (v. 2). Since the superscription implies that this psalm "belongs to David" (לדוד), we can see how v. 4 ("The LORD has sworn and will not change his mind") refers to YHWH's irrevocable promises to David in 2 Sam 7, which responds to the lament of Ps 89. And yet v. 4 says that this messianic figure is also a "priest forever according to the order of Melchizedek," to whom the book of Hebrews refers by citing this verse (Heb 5:6, 10; 7:17, 21). Psalms 89:4 might be a reference to David's priestly functions in 2 Sam 6:14, 18; 24:17, where, like a priest, David wears a linen ephod, offers sacrifices, and blesses the people in the name of YHWH of Hosts. We can easily see how, late in the post-exilic era, when the Psalter reached stabilization, when no king sat on the throne, and when messianic expectations were diverse and many, some anticipation of a king, priest or other prophetic figure may have motivated the editors of the

23. Gunkel, *Die Psalmen*, 5–7; Hans-Joachim Kraus, *Psalms 60–150* (A Continental Commentary; trans. Hilton C. Oswald; Minneapolis: Fortress Press, 1993), 343–60.

24. E.g. Kraus, *Psalms 60–150*, 348.

Psalter to reinterpret the originally non-messianic Ps 110. Notably, it is from this messianically reoriented psalm that the New Testament eventually cites, testifying to the messianic office of Jesus Christ as prophet, priest and king (Matt 22:4; Mark 12:36; Luke 20:42–43; Acts 2:34–35; Heb 1:13; 5:6, 10; 7:17, 21).

We can see how the original prayers of men and women were scriptures to no one, and how they became scripture as they became woven into the greater tapestry of the Psalter as a whole, all the while bearing testimony to the Torah as revelation and God's eternal promises to David. Therefore, David's role as one of several designated writers in the Psalter, along with Solomon, Moses, Korah, Asaph and Ethan, is not much different than other biblical figures whose names are attached to scriptural books, Isaiah included. Sheppard reminds us that the presence of David in the Psalms "provides the key sign of the book's coherence, as well as the context of its interpretation as a part of larger scripture." "We begin to realize that the pre-scriptural hymns can be heard scripturally only when they are heard in association with David." Many of the superscriptions that begin individual psalms refer to the events in the life of David in 2 Samuel.[25]

Modern historical-critical studies have obfuscated this aspect of scripture. At the beginning of the last century, most liberal modern scholars using source criticism thought that the majority of the Psalms were post-exilic, and so determined that David could not have written them. Accordingly, some scholars then wanted to remove the superscriptions. Later, form criticism led scholars to a contrary conclusion that the majority of Psalms originated in pre-exilic times. Many scholars using modern historical-critical methods were preoccupied with the historical origins of the Psalms and so ignored the superscriptions, deeming them inauthentic. It is very interesting to note that Today's English Version and the Good News Bible eliminate the superscriptions and place them in footnotes. This logic has diminished the relationship between David and the Psalms and has in essence provided a concatenation of disconnected prayers of ordinary men and women. On one hand, modern historical-critical analyses have reduced the ability of the Psalms to find their application in connection with the situation and lives of biblical figures. On the other hand, fundamentalist Christians have made an unconvincing attempt to defend the historicity of the superscriptions. And yet this too can be foolish. Just as Isaiah is a writer by designation but could not have written the immense exilic and post-exilic materials that bear his name, the Hebrew superscriptions classify many Psalms as "belonging to

25. Sheppard, *Future of the Bible*, 89–90.

David" (לדוד), thereby identifying him as the "designated writer" rather than conveying a modern notion of authorship. The superscriptions provide an excellent example of inner-biblical interpretation where scripture refers to scripture, just as the prophet Isaiah appears fifteen times in Kings and Chronicles.

For example, Ps 51:1–17 functions form-critically as a penitential prayer of an individual. Verses 1–2 form a plea, vv. 3–6 form a confession of sin, vv. 7–12 offer a petition, and vv. 13–15 make up a customary vow. The note about sacrifices in vv. 16–17 may have belonged to the original petition or it may have been a later addition. The superscription tells us that this is "A psalm of David when Nathan the prophet came to him, after he had gone to Bathsheba." From a modern historical perspective, we would assert that this statement was probably added in the post-exilic period. Verses 18–19 certainly appear to be another editorial addition that contemplates the rebuilding of the walls of Jerusalem and the re-institution of sacrifice, and these verses update an earlier prayer in terms of later hope during the post-exilic period after the destruction of Jerusalem. What is interesting is that the superscription situates this Psalm in David's life, while vv. 18–19 talk about rebuilding the walls that had not yet been built in David's time. The editors were not piecing together the material carelessly here, nor were they piously deceiving anybody. Historical-critical studies of Ps 51 can help us to dismantle the text and find within it earlier and later traditions. Historical criticism ought to help us explain the vagueness and heighten the realism of whatever text we interpret. How, then, do we read Ps 51 as part of scripture? A simple solution, of course, would be to suggest that David was speaking prophetically of a future time when the walls would have fallen. However, historical-critical methods can elevate this anachronism by anchoring the origins of each part of the Psalm in two different time periods.

What a modern historian may call a blatant anachronism may indeed play a greater role in depicting the realism of Ps 51. Notice that the petition form of discourse, and the use of imperatives in vv. 18–19—"Do good to Zion...rebuild the walls of Jerusalem"—links back to earlier verses. In v. 1, the Psalmist pleas, "Have mercy on me, O God...," and in v. 2 we read "Wash me thoroughly from my iniquity, and cleanse me from my sin..." In v. 7 the Psalmist urges, "Purge me with hyssop, and I shall be clean; wash me, and I shall be whiter than snow...," and v. 15 pledges a pious, personal response, "Open my lips, and my mouth will declare your praise..." And yet, within the latter scriptural formation of the Psalter, David is no longer concerned only with his own person, but with Zion and the walls of Jerusalem. There exists a common thread that ties together the pieces of the quilt in the petition that God should "wash," "cleanse," "create," "restore," "deliver" and in v. 18 "do good" and "rebuild." While David says earlier that God desires a "broken spirit" and a "contrite heart" instead of sacrifices, v. 19 portrays David as longing for a time when right sacrifices would be offered once more in Jerusalem. The superscription calls us to contemplate David's life and reign, the latter part of which were tarnished by deleterious acts of adultery and his killing of Uriah the Hittite. We are reminded of Nathan's words to David: "Now therefore the sword shall never depart from your house, for you have despised me, and have taken the wife of Uriah the Hittite to be your wife" (2 Sam 12:10). We remember David's words "I have sinned" (2 Sam 12:10). 2 Samuel 21–24, which assesses David's life on the basis of Torah, prophecy and wisdom, reminds us again of David's failure by naming "Uriah the Hittite" (2 Sam 23:39). The sword did not only affect David personally, but had direct implications for the future of Jerusalem. Thus, David's confession of sin in Ps 51 and his pleading for "a new and right spirit" and a return to "the joy of your salvation" is presented here along with his knowledge of the city walls, which he had so carefully constructed, and of how they are now in shambles, as is his personal life. In a prophetic sense that is typical of scripture (e.g. the distinction between Isa 1–39 and 40–66), the walls are as good as fallen and David now stands within the ruins of the glorious city that he had once built.

Just as David pleads with God in Ps 51, Israel in Ps 89 pleads for God to restore what has been destroyed, while reinterpreting the promises of 2 Sam 7 in light of the exile and referring back to the messianic promise in Ps 2. The words of David do not pretend to predict the future as much as they interpret a whole spectrum of ordinary events from an extraordinary prophetic perspective, one outside the purview of the modern historian. In the broken heart of David, we see the breached walls of Jerusalem during the time of the Judean exile. Therefore, historical-critical analyses perform a necessary heuristic function and caution the readers against harmonizing ancient traditions from a modern view of history. While the "liberal" becomes fascinated with the pre-biblical traditions that lie behind the text and their non-historicity, the conservative "literalist" confuses the realism of the Bible with a conservative-modern account of history. When we speak of the biblical realism in the Psalms, we cannot measure it against that which would satisfy a modern appetite for history and reality. To use Erich Auerbach's language, "the

Biblical testimony is a mimesis…it mirrors reality."[26] The reality is in the text and does not necessarily depend on ostensive reference. That is why von Rad thought that the books of Samuel were so much like modern history that he saw these narratives as the beginning of historical writing.[27] That is probably also why some ancient and medieval writers were prone to think that Isaiah wrote Joshua through Kings.

Just as one cannot find warrants for messianism in the book of Isaiah apart from understanding scripture-conscious editing within the book as a whole, one must push beyond the limits of modern critical methods to understand the Psalter. We must see how the superscriptions can make different impacts within the greater tapestry of scripture, how Pss 1 and 2 form an introduction that calls one to read the Psalms as meditations on Torah, how a royal enthronement oracle can be reinterpreted as messianic promise and how other idioms of revelation function, among them Torah, prophecy and wisdom. David could not be praying psalms that describe the conditions of the post-exilic period. David could not be the "author" who describes the rebuilding of the walls of Jerusalem and its temple. Yet, David is the designated writer of the numerous Psalms that belong to him in a different sense. Just as the traditions that comprise the Pentateuch belong to Moses, who is considered prophet *par excellence* and witness to Torah, and the wisdom books belong to Solomon, the sage *par excellence*, so the Psalter shares this same feature with David, and for that matter Korah, Asaph and Ethan. In the same way, Isaiah is the designated prophet of a book that bears his name. David's presence in the Psalter, a man after God's own heart and repentant sinner, holds the Psalter together. David's presence in the Psalms also underlies all later messianic hopes that anticipate one who would serve as an antitype for David, who is the Messianic type just as his son Solomon in Ps 72 is such a type. Sheppard says that "because the words of these psalms are, on one level, David's words, the text itself is never allowed to float free from its constitution as a human witness to divine revelation."[28]

Therefore, within Christian scripture, the Psalter becomes the prayer book of Jesus Christ because these Psalms are spoken by Jesus Christ and are about Jesus Christ. The claim of the New Testament is that the Psalms are about Jesus the Messiah. Psalm 2:7, "You are my son; today I have begotten you," is reiterated at Jesus' baptism. Childs suggest that Gen 22 lies behind the phrase "my beloved son" which appears in

26. See Erich Auerbach, *Mimesis: The Representation of Reality in Western Literature* (Princeton: Princeton University Press, 1953).
27. Von Rad, *Old Testament Theology*, 1:50–56, 127–28, 316–54.
28. Sheppard, *The Future of the Bible*, 87.

Ps 2 and in the formula used at Jesus' baptism. In 2 Sam 7 (cf. Pss 2 and 89), David is called God's "beloved son," but without any notion of faith as a source of grace (a feature it shares with Gen 22). The use of the "beloved son" terminology functions in 2 Sam 7, Pss 2 and 89 purely as a Messianic formula.[29] Yet in the Gospels, Christ, the Messiah, the beloved son, is the one who takes the faith of Abraham and offers himself up as the sacrifice. Unlike David, who is a type of Messiah, Isaac is not a type of Christ—what is praised is the faith of Abraham, to which God responds with the superabundance of grace for Israel. Comparing Christ's sacrifice with the Binding of Isaac, Rom 8:32 says "God did not spare his only son," which is almost identical to Gen 22:16. In Judaism, a parallel was drawn between Abraham's conduct and the conduct expected in return from God. Paul does not contest that Abraham was rewarded, but in his mind the sacrifice of Jesus the Messiah was given according to grace. Therefore, Acts 4:23–28 also can cite Ps 2 messianically to show how the nations will relate to Jesus, the Lord's anointed or "Messiah" (Ps 2:1–2).

Within the literal sense of Christian scripture, the Psalter becomes the prayer book of Jesus Christ because Jesus prays through the Psalter. Bonhoeffer has brilliantly identified that the new claim of Christianity is that Jesus Christ, the Messiah, prays these prayers with Christians. By this reasoning, when a Christian prays the Psalter, he or she is not alone because Jesus Christ prays the Psalms with them. Within the greater context of Christian scripture, the meaning of the suffering Messiah imagery of Isa 52:13–53:12 becomes clearer when Christ on the cross recites Ps 22 ("My God, my God, why have you forsaken me?"). Yet he too was not alone praying from the Psalter because within the testimony of the Psalter, the saints (Moses, David and Solomon et al.) prayed with him.

Moreover, Christians have understood Ps 69 to be the words of Jesus Christ and about Jesus Christ, interpreting v. 21 as Jesus' words adumbrating from the cross, "They gave me poison for food, and for my thirst they gave me vinegar to drink" (Matt 27:34; John 19:28–29). John 2:17 interprets Ps 69 messianically when, after Jesus had cleansed the temple, "his disciples" recall 69:9 and identify this scriptural text to be messianic prophecy: they "remembered that it was written, 'Zeal for your house will consume me.'" Yet, in Ps 69:5, where there is confession of sin, "O God, you know my folly; the wrongs I have done are not hidden from you,"

29. Childs, however, argues that in the account of Jesus' baptism there is a wedding together of this Messianic promise with an echo of Isaac as a sacrifice. See Childs, *Biblical Theology of Old and New Testaments*, 325–28.

Christians have traditionally applied Tyconius' head and body imagery to explain that Christ *the head* did not sin; rather, the confession actually belongs to *the body* of Christ, the Church.[30] The Psalter, then, is the vicarious prayer of Christ for his Church. Members of the body of Christ can pray these psalms through Jesus Christ, from the heart of Jesus Christ. Christians therefore read the Psalms both as a way of cherishing the rich heritage of the word of God in Judaism, and also as a way of understanding how Jewish scripture has the capacity to testify to Jesus Christ as messianic fulfillment.

VI. *Citations from Isaiah in Early Judaism and Christianity*

While several texts from the Pseudepigrapha, Targum, Qumran and the New Testament cite the book of Isaiah, I maintain that these cannot serve as proof cases to legitimize messianic interpretation. While New Testament citations of the Old Testament do not set a norm for how to interpret the Old Testament, neither do Pseudepigraphical, Talmudic or Qumran citations. In his *Biblical Interpretation in Ancient Israel*, Michael Fishbane tried to show that inner-biblical interpretation set a precedent for the *middoth* of rabbinic midrashic interpretations as prescribed by the Mishnah.[31] However, Fishbane concedes that inner-biblical citation of scripture within scripture does not provide a precise antecedent for midrash and hence resorts to describing the relationship in terms of a trajectory. Just as Rabbinic midrash does not find a clear and complete precedent in Jewish scripture, Christian interpretation cannot rely on the New Testament citations of the Old Testament to establish the norms for biblical interpretation. In some places the New Testament interprets the book of Isaiah messianically and in other places it does not.

A. *A Few Citations of Isaiah in Pseudepigraphical and Other Jewish Literature*
The Sibylline Oracles (657–808 B.C.E.) depict "the Messiah" as a savior king, who is probably a descendent of David.[32] In third Sibyl, the transformation of the earth during the messianic age 785–95 is obviously dependant on Isa 11:

---

30. On Tyconius' "head" and "body" distinctions, see Karlfried Froehlich, Biblical *Interpretation in the Early Church* (Sources of Early Christian Thought; Philadelphia: Fortress, 1984), 104.

31. Fishbane, *Biblical Interpretation in Ancient Israel*, 275.

32. Collins, *The Sibylline Oracles*, 38–39.

Wolves and lambs will eat grass together in the mountains.
Leopards will feed together with kids.
Roving bears will spend the night with calves.
The flesh-eating lion will eat husks at the manger like an ox.
and mere infant children will lead them with ropes.
For he will make the beasts on the earth harmless.
Serpents and asps will sleep with babies
and will not harm them
for the hand of God will be upon them.

Some claim that the "king" in lines 286 and 288 describes Cyrus and/or Zerubbabel.[33] Nolland suggests that the Messiah in this text is neither Cyrus nor Zerubbabel but a "messianic figure of the royal tribe [who] would soon come as the eschatological Temple restorer."[34] He thinks that this hope for a Davidic Messiah is suitable to a dating of 70 C.E. or an early Maccabean period prior to the significant Maccabean success but would be inconsistent with the later Maccabean uprising as a beginning point for messianic hope.[35] Though the description in this text may cause one to speculate about the identity of this Messiah king, Third Sibyl is interpreting Isa 11 messianically.

Within *The Testament of the Twelve Patriarchs*, the *Testament of Levi*, which presents the "Anointed one" and his priesthood (*T. Levi* 17:3) in a way that submits a priestly candidate for the Messiah, describes him as having "a spirit of understanding" (Isa 11:2; *T. Levi* 2:3).[36] Howard Clark Kee argues that this passage is "linked with the spirit of the Lord and promised as a divine gift to the shoot from the royal Davidic line in Isa 1–3."[37] Although the writer of the *Testament of Levi* has a definition of messianism that accommodates a setting and expectation quite different from what we have considered to be appropriate to the book of Isaiah, the messianic imagery here is the same.

The Psalms of Solomon 17 and 18, deriving from the first century B.C.E., has emphatic anti-Hasmonean political overtones. After Alexandra left the kingship to her brighter son Aristobulus and the priesthood to her insensible and less ambitious son Hyrcanus, Antipater, who is the power behind the throne, colludes with Hyrcanus because he can

---

33. See J. J. Collins, *The Sibylline Oracles*; Valentin Nikiprowetzky, *Le troisième Sibylle* (Paris: La Haye, 1970), 17–36.

34. John Nolland, "Sib. Or. III.:265–94," 166.

35. Ibid.

36. Note that "the Testament of Issachar" presents Judah and Levi as "glorified" (5:4–5; 8:1–2).

37. Howard Clark Kee, "Testament of the Twelve Patriarchs: A New Translation and Introduction," *OTP* 1:788 n. 2b.

control him. Pompey is dispatched by Rome to bring order to the eastern Mediterranean and put it under the control of Rome. He conquers Mithridates VI of Pontus, who had been fighting the Romans in Asia Minor, brings the Selucid monarchy to an end and then comes and conquers the Hasmoneans because Aristobulus and Hyrchanus were having a civil war with each other. Looking back on this Hasmonean interlude, which was neither Zadokite nor of the line of David, the Jewish people see that their hopes had been misplaced and they needed to return to a traditional kingship and priesthood. Hence, the *Psalms of Solomon* repudiate the Hasmoneans: "with pomp they set up a monarchy because of their arrogance; they despoiled the throne of David with arrogant shouting" (17:6). Likewise, the same text calls Pompey "a man alien to our race" and "the lawless one [who] laid waste our land" (17:7, 11).

Therefore, the kind of Messiah we can expect in this setting and text would be a Zadokite priest or a Davidic king. This explains why the *Psalms of Solomon* 17 and 18 take up the traditional messianic picture of the final ruler portrayed by Isa 11:1–5.[38] "The king shall be the Lord Messiah" (17:32). "He shall strike the earth with the rod of his mouth forever" or "by the strength of his word" (*Pss Sol* 17:35, 36; Isa 11:4). "He (the Messiah [18:5]) will do (good things [18:6]) for the coming generation under the rod of discipline of the Lord Messiah" (*Pss Sol* 18:6, 7; Isa 11:4). "He will be a righteous king over them" (17:32; Isa 11:4). "He will bless the LORD's people with wisdom and happiness" and "God made him…wise in counsel and understanding" (17:35, 37; 11:2). He will inculcate the "fear of the LORD" (18:7, 8; Isa 11:3). "For God made him powerful in the Holy Spirit, and with strength and righteousness (17:37; Isa 11:2). Similar to how Isa 65 tells the reader to forget the former things about Cyrus because he does not provide the answer for Israel's future messianic hopes, *Psalms of Solomon* cites Isa 11 to remind them that the Messiah is that answer (65:25). The *Psalms of Solomon* reject the rule of the Hasmoneans and cite Isa 11 to remind the Jewish people of their messianic hope. John Collins speculates that "the *Psalms of Solomon* are the first Jews to see in Isaiah 11 or Psalm 2 the promise of a glorious future glorious king."[39]

The *Testament of Solomon* speaks of the "angel of the wonderful counselor" who "foresaw that I would suffer…" The phrase "and he will dwell publicly on the cross" (12:3) seems to be a later Christian interpolation to suggest that Christ would suffer and thus fulfill Isa 9:5

38. Cf. Vermes, *Jesus the Jew*, 130–31.
39. Collins, *The Scepter and the Star*, 56.

(Heb.).[40] Apart from messianic interpretation, the wonderful counselor clearly exceeds the limits of a typical king.

In the *Similitudes of Enoch*, "the Messiah" (*1 En* 48:10; 52:4) is also called the "Son of Man" (46:2; 48:2; 62:7), "Chief of Days" (46:2; 47:3; 48:2; 55:1) and "the elect one" (49:2; 51:3). Furthermore, "the elect one on the throne of his glory" (62:2) "shall be a light to the Gentiles" similar to the Servant (*1 En* 48:4; Isa 49:6).[41] Drawing inspiration from Isa 11, 1 Enoch describes the Messiah accordingly:

> And in him dwells the spirit of wisdom,
> And the spirit which gives insight,
> And the spirit of understanding and might,
> And the spirit of those who sleep in righteousness. (49:2–3)[42]

While Pseudepigraphic literature and other texts of early Judaism cite mainly Isa 11 messianically, other texts have been considered. In his description of eight pretender Messiahs, Josephus alludes to Isa 61:1–3 in order to describe the messianic claims of Simon son of the proselyte Gioras, "by proclaiming liberty for slaves and rewards for free" (Bell IV, 508).

The Pseudepigrapha seldom cites Isa 9:1–6 and does not cite 7:14 messianically. However, in the "Haggadic-type fairytale" about Solomon's building of the temple in Jerusalem, the *Testament of Solomon*, equates "Emmanuel" (Greek Εμμανουελ) and "Wonderful Counselor" from Isa 7:14 and 9:5 (Heb.) as one and the same.[43] The Angel who thwarts Beelzebul exercises power over demons and delivers God's people from Beelzebul's power. Although this does not reflect messianism, it does indicate that Emmanuel and the Wonderful Counselor in Isa 7:14 and 9:5 were viewed as a deliverer who transcends humanity.

B. *The Targum*
Targum Jonathan interprets Isa 9 and 11 messianically but not 7:14. At Isa 9:5, the Targum reads:

> The prophet says to the house of David, behold a boy child has been born to us, a son has been given to us; and he has taken the law upon himself

---

40. D. C. Duling, "Testament of Solomon: A New Translation and Introduction," *OTP* 1: 973 n. 12b.

41. Nickelsburg ("Salvation Without or With a Messiah," 58, 61) argues that titles "chosen one" and "righteous one" in both the *Book of Parables* and here in 1 Enoch "are the titles of the Deutero-Isaianic Servant of the Lord."

42. See ibid., 60.

43. See Duling's notes in "Testament of Solomon," 1:935.

to keep it; and his name has been called from old, wonderful counselor, mighty God, he who lives forever, the Messiah (משיחא) in whose days peace shall increase upon us.[44]

The Targum also renders שמן (Isa 10:27) with the Aramaic משיחא ("the Messiah") to speak of anointing oil, thereby relating the deliverance in ch. 10 with the Messiah. Isaiah 11:1 states: "A king shall come forth from the sons of Jesse, and the Messiah shall grow up from his son's son." Similarly, v. 6 begins with "in the days of the Messiah of Israel..." In 11:10 the Targum renders שרש ישי ("root of Jesse") as בר בריה דישי ("the son of the son of Jesse") in order to make more explicit that the messianic line comes from the ancestry of David. The Targum interprets the Servant in 52:13–53:12 to be the Messiah, but re-interprets the phrases about his sufferings as referring to Israel or the rival nations. However, in 61:1, the Targum adds the words אמר נביא ("The prophet said" or "The spirit of prophecy is upon me"), therefore not interpreting 61:1–3 messianically.[45]

C. *Qumran Literature*

A few passages from Qumran cite the book of Isaiah messianically. The Qumran Thanksgiving Scroll (Hôdayôt) can employ a poem (3.15–18) that both portrays the birth of the Messiah and refers to the "wonderful counselor" of 9:5.[46] The prince of the congregation at Qumran was identified as the "branch of David" (the two are juxtaposed in 4Q285).[47] 1QIs[a] adds a final *yōdh* to משחת making it משחתי ("I have anointed"), which indicates some degree of messianic interpretation (52.14). Since a scribe in the Qumran community copied משחתי, this establishes that some segments of early Judaism were interpreting this text messianically before the time of Christ.[48] Several scholars[49] argue that 4QAaronA

---

44. My translation from Stenning, ed., *The Targum of Isaiah*, 33.

45. See Bruce Chilton, *The Glory of Israel*, 52–56.

46. Cf. Schiffman, *From Text to Tradition*, 123. See my Chapter 3.

47. Collins, *The Scepter and the Star*, 64, 71; Eisenman and Wise, *The Dead Sea Scrolls Uncovered*, 29; Vermes, "The Oxford Forum for Qumran Research Seminar," 88. See also my Chapter 3.

48. William Hugh Brownlee claims that משחת derives from the construct, משחה ("anointing"), and that it was subsequently replaced by משחתי to make the messianic inference clearer. See his "Messianic Motifs," and his "*Mshty* (Is. 52:14 1QIsa)". D. Barthélemy also thinks that the change was intentional. See his "Le grand rouleau d'Isaïe trouvé près de la Mer Morte," 546, and his *Critique textuelle de l'Ancien Testament*, 387–90. Others have interpreted 1QIs[a] to read משחתי ("I have anointed"). See also Kutscher, *The Language and Linguistic Background of the Isaiah Scroll*, 262; Barr (*Comparative Philology*, 285) and Guillaume ("Some Readings in the

(4Q541) draws from the imagery of a suffering Messiah from the perspective opened up by the Servant Songs.[50] 11QMelch presents the herald of Isa 52:7 as the one who proclaims the good news of 61:1–3 before Melchizedek comes as the eschatological judge. Hence, 11QMelch interprets ch. 61 messianically.[51]

D. *New Testament Citations*

Several New Testament citations of Isaiah are overtly non-messianic.[52] Other texts, however, present greater ambiguity whether or not they are cited messianically.[53] Some of the passages that I have here presented as

Dead Sea Scroll of Isaiah," 42) read מֹשֶׁה as the root of מֹשׁחְתִי. Yet we also must be aware that 1QIs^b supports the MT. See A. Rubinstein, "Isaiah LII, 14"; Gerleman, *Studien zur alttestamentlichen Theologie*, 39–40; Koole, *The Prophecy of Isaiah*, 268–69. G. R. Driver ("Isaiah i–ix: Textual and Linguistic Problems," 92) refers to this as a *hireq compagnis*. See also my Chapter 4.

49. Puech, "Fragments d'une apocryphe de Lévi"; Brooke, "4Q Testament of Levi^d"; Hengel, "Jesus der Messias Israels," 164. See my Chapter 4.

50. This view was first proposed by Starcky: "Avant de quitter l'époque d'Alexandre Jannée, nous voudrions signaler un manuscit de notre lot de la grotte 4 (sigle provisoire 4QAhA) dont l'écriture est fort analogue à celle du scribe des *Testimonia*. Les joints effectués, il n'y a malheureusement qu'une demidouzaine de fragments utiles, dont deux avec phrases continues. Mais leur intérêt est grand, car ils nous paraissent évoquer un messie souffrant, dans la perspective ouverte par les poèmes du Serviteur." Cf. Starcky, "Les quatres étapes du messianisme à Qumran," 491–92.

51. For the pesher fragment, see Milik, "Milki-sedek et Milki-resa." See also de Jonge and van der Woude, "11QMelchizedeq and the New Testament," 306; Kobelski, *Melchizedek and Malchiresha*, 3–23; Fishbane, *Biblical Interpretation in Ancient Israel*, 483; Schwartz, "On Quirinius"; Thurén, "Lukas evangeliets Cantica"; Puech, "Notes sur le manuscrit de XIQMelkîsêdeq"; Lim, "11QMelch, Luke 4 and the Dying Messiah"; Puech, "La figure de Melkisedeq et la fin des temps"; Sawyer, *The Fifth Gospel*, 24; Laato, *A Star is Rising*, 326. See my discussion in Chapter 5.

52. See, *Isa 8:12–13* as cited in 1 Pet 3:14–15. *Isa 28:11–12* in 1 Cor 14:21. *Isa 29:13* in Matt 15:8–9; Mark 7:6–7. *Isa 29:16* in Rom 9:20. *Isa 40:6–8* in 1 Pet 1:24–25. *Isa 40:13* in Rom 11:34; 1 Cor 2:16. *Isa 45:23 and 49:18* [Ezek 5:11; Jer 22:24] in Rom 14:11; *Isa 52:5* in Rom 2:24. *Isa 52:7* in Rom 10:15. *Isa 52:11* in 2 Cor 6:17. *Isa 54:1* in Gal 4:27. *Isa 56:7* [Jer 7:11] in Matt 21:13; Mark 11:17; Luke 19:46. *Isa 59:7–8* in Rom 3:15–17. *Isa 65:1–2* in Rom 10:20–21. *Isa 66:1–2* in Acts 7:49–50.

53. As opposed to false Messiahs in Matt 24:24, 24:29 cites *Isa 13:10* to describe the coming of the Son of Man. In the context of Jesus concealing his messiahship, Matt 12:18–21 cites *Isa 42:1–4* to imply that he is the "son of David" (v. 23). 1 Cor 15:54 cites from *Isa 25:8* (κατέπιεν ὁ θάνατος ἰσχύσας [LXX]; Κατεπόθη ὁ θάνατος εἰς νῖκος [New Testament]) to affirm the resurrection as fulfilled prophecy and from Rev 7:17 to show that the lamb on the throne will be shepherd and will wipe away

candidates for messianic interpretation (Isa 7:14; 9:1–6 [Heb.]; 11:1–5, 6–9, 10), the New Testament cites as testimony supporting the identification of Jesus as the Messiah. For example, within context Matt 1:23 cites Isa 7:14 messianically (ἡ παρθένος ἐν γαστρὶ ἕξει καὶ τέξεται υἱόν, καὶ καλέσουσιν τὸ ὄνομα αὐτοῦ Ἐμμανουήλ). Matthew 1:18 speaks of "the birth of Jesus the Messiah." Matthew 1:1 provides a superscription or title for Matt 1:1–17: "the genealogy of Jesus the Messiah son of David" (γενέσεως Ἰησοῦ Χριστοῦ υἱοῦ Δαυὶδ). Matthew 1:17 list three pivotal stages in the messianic line, each consisting of fourteen generations: (1) from Abraham to David; (2) from David to the deportation to Babylon; (3) from the deportation to Babylon to the Messiah (τοῦ Χριστοῦ). Abraham begins Israel's line and David begins the messianic line. The deportation to Babylon is pivotal to this description because it marks the end of the monarchy, when messianic hope begins. Matthew's Gospel account cites Isa 7:14 to show that the birth of Jesus was "to fulfill what had been spoken by the Lord through the prophet" (Matt 1:22). For Matthew, the name Emmanuel is a messianic title.

After his baptism and temptations, Matt 4:12–17 links Jesus' ministry and the course that he took with messianic hope in Isa 8:23–9:1. Hence, Matt 4:15–16 cites Isa 8:23–9:1 (NRSV, 9:1–2). The MT, LXX and Matt 4:15–16 agree on all but four occasions.[54] First, on two occasions, Matt

every tear (καὶ ἐξαλείψει ὁ Θεὸς πᾶν δάκρυον ἀπὸ τῶν ὀφθαλμῶν αὐτῶν). Acts 13:34 cites *Isa 55:3* to speak of the resurrected Christ, who fulfills the promises made to David. Several passages cite *Isa 6:9–10*; some non-messianically and one messianically. Matt 13:14–15 and Mark 4:12 cite Isa 6:6–9 non-messianically, but do so in order to declare that this prophecy has been fulfilled. In Luke 8:10, Jesus cites Isa 6:9 to reveal that his apostles know "the secrets of the kingdom of God; but to others I speak in parables, so that 'looking they may not perceive, and listening they may not understand.'" Acts 28:26–27 cites this passage as a rhetorical device to compare those who reject the Gospel with their ancestors to whom Isaiah first spoke. These passages are cited to establish the prophetic word but not for messianic purposes. To affirm Jesus' kingship, Matt 21:5 cites *Isa 62:11* (Zech 9:9). In the context of accepting Jesus as the Christ and him crucified, 1 Cor 2:9 cites *Isa 64:3* (64:4). Referring to the "day of the Lord," 1 Pet 3:13 cites Isa 65:17 (66:22). Finally, Isa 40:3 is cited in Matt 3:3; Mark 1:3 and John 1:23 to underscore John the Baptist's role as the *meḇaśśēr*. Referring to the "costly corner stone," Rom 9:33; 10:11 and 1 Pet 2:6 cite Isa 8:14 and 28:16 to speak of Jesus Christ. Rom 11:26–27 cites Isa 59:20–21 to establish Jesus Christ as "the deliverer" who comes "out of Zion," saves Israel and "will take away their sins."

54. *BHS* Isa 8:23 reads: בֵּילָא מוּעָף לַאֲשֶׁר מוּצָק לָהּ כְּעֵת הָרִאשׁוֹן הֵקַל אַרְצָה זְבֻלוּן וְאַרְצָה נַפְתָּלִי וְהָאַחֲרוֹן גְּלִיל הַגּוֹיִם הָעָם הַהֹלְכִים בַּחֹשֶׁךְ רָאוּ אוֹר גָּדוֹל יֹשְׁבֵי בְּאֶרֶץ צַלְמָוֶת אוֹר נָגַהּ עֲלֵיהֶם:

LXX Isa 8:23–9:1 reads: καὶ οὐκ ἀπορηθήσεται ὁ ἐν στενοχωρίᾳ ὢν ἕως καιροῦ τοῦτο πρῶτον ποίει ταχὺ ποίει χώρα Ζαβουλων ἡ γῆ Νεφθαλιμ ὁδὸν θαλάσσης καὶ οἱ λοιποὶ

4:15–16 follows the MT, which Stendahl understands to be "a N.T. preference of Semitic monotony as against the LXX's fondness for synonyms."[55] Second, both the LXX and Matt 4:15 omit the words והאחרון הכביד ("but in the latter time he will make glorious") before דרך הים ("way of the sea," ὁδὸν θαλάσσης). Matthew follows the LXX, as opposed to Aquila and Symmachus, in order to stress the local, geographical climate for the ministry of Jesus Christ. Third, beginning Isa 9:1, the LXX uses the default term πορεύομαι for √הלך (העם ההלכים = ὁ λαὸς ὁ πορευόμενος, "the people who walk…"), but Matt 4:16 diverges from the LXX and MT and has ὁ λαὸς ὁ καθήμενος ("the people sitting…"). This reading may have crept into some LXX texts. Isaiah recalls the invasion of Northern Israel by Tiglath-pileser in 733–732 B.C.E. Matthew, who uses the past tense, sees fulfilment of Isa 9:1–2 in Jesus coming to this region and there the light of the Messiah shines not in the darkness of Assyrian invasion nor even the darkness of exile but in relationship to human sin and salvation (4:17).[56]

Romans 15:12 cites Isa 11:10 to establish Jesus Christ as the Messiah to the Gentiles. Two phrases seem to establish this: "Welcome one another as the Christ (ὁ Χριστός) has welcomed you" (15:7) and "For I tell you that Christ (Χριστός) has become a servant of the circumcised on behalf of the truth of God in order that he might establish the promises of the fathers" (15:8). Romans 15:9–12 cites from the Torah (Rom 15:10 from Deut 32:43), Prophets (Rom 15:12 from Isa 11:10), and Psalter (Rom 15:9 from Ps 38:9; Rom 15:11 from Ps 117:1) in order to establish messianic promise to the Gentiles in all portions of Jewish scripture. Most specifically, Rom 15:12, leaving out the phrase καὶ ἔσται ἐν τῇ

οἱ τὴν παραλίαν κατοικοῦντες καὶ πέραν τοῦ Ιορδάνου Γαλιλαία τῶν ἐθνῶν τὰ μέρη τῆς Ιουδαίας. ὁ λαὸς ὁ πορευόμενος ἐν σκότει ἴδετε φῶς μέγα οἱ κατοικοῦντες ἐν χώρᾳ καὶ σκιᾷ θανάτου φῶς λάμψει ἐφ' ὑμᾶς
Matt 4:15–16 reads: Γῆ Ζαβουλὼν καὶ γῆ Νεφθαλίμ, ὁδὸν θαλάσσης, πέραν τοῦ Ἰορδάνου, Γαλιλαία τῶν ἐθνῶν, ὁ λαὸς ὁ καθήμενος ἐν σκότει φῶς εἶδεν μέγα.

55. Krister Stendahl, *The School of St. Matthew and Its Use of the Old Testament* (Philadelphia: Fortress, 1968), 104–6. Note that, first, Matt 4:15 uses γῆ ("land") for ארצה, before both Ζαβουλων and Νεφθαλιμ, but the LXX uses χώρα ("region") for ארצה before Ζαβουλων, but γῆ before Νεφθαλιμ. Second, in Isa 9:1 (NRSV, 9:2), although the LXX has changed the Qal perfect *third* person common plural verb in אור גדול to a *second* person aorist active ἴδετε φῶς μέγα, Matt 4:16 follows the MT and uses φῶς εἶδεν μέγα.

56. Henry Barclay Swete, *An Introduction to the Old Testament in Greek* (Cambridge: Cambridge University Press, 1914), 396–97; Archer and Chirichigno, *Old Testament Quotations*, 98–99; Albright and Mann, *Matthew*, 38–39; Floyd Filson, *The Gospel According to St. Matthew* (New York: Harper, 1960), 72–73; Stendahl, *The School of St. Matthew*, 104–6, 115, 127, 153, 173.

ἡμέρα (והיה ביום ההוא), cites directly from the LXX, ἡ ῥίζα τοῦ Ἰεσσαί καὶ ὁ ἀνιστάμενος ἄρχειν ἐθνῶν, ἐπ' αὐτῷ ἔθνη ἐλπιοῦσιν ("The root of Jesse shall come, the one who rises to rule the Gentiles, in him the Gentiles shall hope"). Paul cites these words underscored by "the root of Jesse" in order to establish Christ as a Messiah to the Gentiles. Perhaps this citation confirms that the post-exilic editors of the book of Isaiah have succeeded in the way in which they have linked the promise of salvation to the Gentiles (11:10–12) to the messianic oracle (11:1–5, 6–9). Possibly, this citation reflects how the book of Isaiah sets a precedent for how messianism in early Judaism included salvation to the Gentiles (Isa 11:10; 42:6, 16; 49:6, 9; 60:1–4, 6–7, 10–14; 61:5, 11; 66:18; etc.).

The New Testament also cites Isa 52:13–53:12 seven times. While some verses do not seem to be cited in a way that shows messianic interpretation,[57] other New Testament writers cite 52:13–53:12 as a testimony to Jesus the suffering Messiah. This indicates that not all New Testament writers cite this passage from the context of the book of Isaiah as a whole but other writers do. In John 12:27–43, where Jesus speaks about his death as the "son of man" (12:34) and the people exhibit their unbelief, the writer cites Isa 53:1 and 6:10 in response to the crowds objection to Jesus' claim, "The hour has come for the Son of Man to be glorified" and "when I am lifted up from the earth, will draw all people to myself." The crowd responds to Jesus, "We have heard from the law that the Messiah remains forever. How can you say that the Son of Man must be lifted up? Who is this Son of Man?" (John 12:34). John 12:37–41 reads:

> Although he had performed so many signs in their presence, they did not believe in him. This was to fulfill the word spoken by the prophet Isaiah: "LORD, who has believed our message, and to whom has the arm of the LORD been revealed?" (Isa 53:1).[58] And so they could not believe, because Isaiah also said, "He has blinded their eyes and hardened their heart, so that they might not look with their eyes, and understand with their heart and turn—and I would heal them" (Isa 6:10). Isaiah said this because he saw his glory and spoke about him. (NRSV)

John 12 cites from Isaiah to depict either the acceptance or rejection of Jesus' claims that he is "the Son of Man" or "Messiah," who will suffer and die.

---

57. Within a context of his preaching the Gospel of the Christ (τὸ εὐαγγέλιον τοῦ Χριστοῦ, 15:19), Paul cites Isa 52:15 in Rom 15:21. Similarly, Rom 10:16 quotes Isa 53:1 to reinforce that some have not received the Gospel. Matt 8:17 cites Isa 53:4–5 to support Jesus' healing ministry and not obtrusively to make claims that Jesus was a suffering Messiah.

58. Isa 53:1 cites the LXX, which reads: κύριε τίς ἐπίστευσεν τῇ ἀκοῇ ἡμῶν καὶ ὁ βραχίων κυρίου τίνι ἀπεκαλύφθη, whereby the divine appellation κύριε is added.

Similarly, the citations from the so-called fourth Servant song in 1 Peter have clearly been taken from the context of the scroll of Isaiah. First Peter 2:22 cites Isa 53:9 ("He committed no sin, and no deceit was found in his mouth") to corroborate the claim that "Christ suffered for you, leaving you an example, so that you should follow in his steps" (1 Pet 2:21). In the same passage, not only does the writer describe the atoning work of Christ but alludes to Isa 53:5, "He himself bore our sins in his body on the cross, so that, free from sins, we might live for righteousness; *by his wounds you have been healed*" (1 Pet 2:25). More-over, 1 Pet 2:25 alludes to the next verse of Isa 53: "For you were going astray like sheep" (Isa 53:6). Clearly, 1 Peter cites from the literary context of Isaiah and not atomistically.

In the book of Acts, the Ethiopian Eunuch reads from the book of Isaiah (Isa 53:7–8 in Acts 8:32–33) and Philip interprets for him that Jesus was the suffering Servant who "like a sheep, he was led to the slaughter..." While the context of Acts seems to imply that he was read-ing from the book as a whole, one thing is clear: the New Testament addresses the problem that the ambiguity of the Servant creates for an objective reader.

Finally, Luke 22:37 quotes Isa 53:12 in order to proclaim that Jesus' own sufferings would "fulfill scripture," which predicted that the Messiah would suffer as a criminal ("'And he was counted among the lawless' and indeed what is written about me is being fulfilled.").[59] However, while this does not indicate that Luke is citing this passage messianically or that this Gospel account is indeed citing *a canonical* Isa 52:13–53:12, it does profess that Jesus fulfills scripture. While some passages were cited atomistically, others presupposed the larger literary context of the text that is quoted and interpreted Isa 52:13–53:12 as a testimony to Christ's sufferings on the cross.[60] Therefore, these citations offer hints to how early Christians were interpreting this text but they do not offer a precedent for interpretation of the Old Testament because the various ways that the New Testament writers cite the book of Isaiah do not always illumine the literal sense of scripture (see below).

Likewise, Jesus read Isa 61:1–2 in the temple (Luke 4:18–19), he rolled up the scroll, sat down to teach, and "then he began to say to them, 'Today this scripture has been fulfilled in your hearing'" (4:21). Since Jesus remarked, "Doubtless you will quote to me this proverb, 'physician

59. See R. T. France, "The Servant of the Lord in the Teachings of Jesus," *TynBul* 19 (1968): 22–52.

60. This view offers middle ground between C. H. Dodd and Donald Juel's view. See Dodd, *According to Scripture*; Juel, *Messianic Exegesis*.

heal yourself!,'" this states that they essentially expected him to perform miracles in his hometown that they heard he had done at Capernaum (4:23). Instead, he recites the proverb, "no prophet is accepted in the prophet's hometown" (4:23). Jesus claims to be the one fulfilling Isa 61:1–2 in their hearing, and the text describing the crowds driving him out of town and trying to throw him off a cliff (4:29) indicates that the narrative presents him making extremely bold assertions, whether or not messianic.[61]

The answer to whether some first-century Jews and Christians interpreted Isa 61 messianically becomes more clear in response to John the Baptist's question posed by the so-called Q, Σὺ εἶ ὁ ἐρχόμενος ἢ ἄλλον προσδοκῶμεν ("Are you the one to come or should we expect another?"). Q cites Isa 61:1:[62] "the blind receive their sight, the lame walk, the lepers are cleansed, the deaf hear, the dead are raised, and the poor have good news brought to them" (Matt 11:5; Luke 7:22). Here, "freedom for the captives" is replaced by the LXX's sight for the blind. The Targum reinforces the captivity motif but the LXX and Q completely eliminate it. Perhaps the phrase ὁ ἐρχόμενος ("the one who is to come") indicates that Q is asking a messianic question that finds its positive affirmation by alluding to 61:1. Definitely, the Q source never uses the term ὁ Χριστός or Χριστός, but it does apply other messianic titles like "Son of Man." Nevertheless, the later editors of Matthew make explicit any messianic interpretation that was implied in the question, "Are you the one to come...?" They do this by attaching τοῦ Χριστου to the non-Q preamble: Ὁ δὲ Ἰωάννης ἀκούσας ἐν τῷ δεσμωτηρίῳ τὰ ἔργα τοῦ Χριστοῦ πέμψας διὰ τῶν μαθητῶν αὐτοῦ ("When John heard in prison what the Messiah was doing, he sent word by his disciples"). While Q was probably interpreting Isa 61:1 messianically, the shapers of the book of Matthew clearly read Isa 61 as messianic by using ὁ Χριστός.

After surveying several New Testament citations of the Old Testament, it becomes plain that there were no established norms for how to

---

61. Miller, Jr., "Luke 4:16–21"; Violet Bruno, "Zum Rechten Verständnis der Nazarethperikope Lc 4,14–30," *ZNW* 37 (1938): 251–71; Hugh Anderson, "Broadening Horizons: The Rejection at Nazareth Pericope of Luke 4:16–30 in Light of Recent Critical Trends," *Int* 18 (1964): 259–75; Robert F. O'Toole, "Does Luke Also Portray Jesus as the Christ in Luke 4,16–30," *Bib* 76 (1995): 498–522; Margaret Rodgers, "Luke 4:16–30: A Call for a Jubilee Year," *RTR* 40 (1981): 72–82; B. J. Koet, "'Today this Scripture has been fulfilled in your ears': Jesus' Explanation of Scripture," *Bijdragen* 47 (1986): 368–94; Heinrich Baarlink, "Ein Gnädiges Jahr Des Herrn—und Tage der Vergeltung : [Lk 4:18–19]," *ZNW* 73, no. 3–4 (1982): 204–20.

62. This citation alludes to parts of Isa 26:19; 35:5–6; 42:18, as well as 61:1.

cite the Old Testament. New Testament writers were not appealing to the literal sense of scripture because they often did not cite the Old Testament from canonical context. While it is logical that some New Testament writers cite the book of Isaiah in a manner that would correspond with the literal sense that originated in the second century C.E. (see below), other New Testament interpretations of the Old Testament cite from Isaiah atomistically. Just because the New Testament does not cite a passage messianically does not abrogate messianic interpretation, and just because the New Testament cites a passage messianically does not make it messianic according to the literal sense of scripture. The New Testament cannot set a precedent for the literal sense of scripture because some messianic interpretation in the New Testament cites the book of Isaiah atomistically. For example, several New Testament writers cite Isa 28:16 messianically, "I am laying in Zion a foundation stone, a tested stone, a precious cornerstone, a sure foundation: One who trusts will not be dismayed" (Rom 9:33; 10:11; 1 Pet 2:6 citing Isa 8:14 and 28:16). However, this passage in no way fits our definition of messianism. First, it says nothing about fulfilling the promises of David after the monarchy has ended. Second, it provides none of the images that have appeared in any other messianic texts within the book of Isaiah. It merely provides an image that prompts New Testament writers to attach it to Jesus, but it does not invoke messianic imagery.

I conclude that the way New Testament scripture cites Old Testament scripture cannot set the norms for biblical interpretation. The warrants used by the New Testament for messianic interpretation cannot set a precedent for interpreting the Old Testament (contra Hays).[63] I have found that the New Testament and other early Jewish sources are helpful because they show that ancient Judaism and early Christianity were already viewing these Isaianic passages messianically. However, one does not need them to establish messianism. I have established messianism within the book of Isaiah by appealing to the literal sense of scripture.

VII. *The Literal Sense of Christian Scripture*

At the time of the publication of Christian scripture, Christians as early as Iranaeus began to claim that the literal sense of scripture was the only normative sense for doctrine. The meaning of literal sense has varied over generations. Early on in Christianity, Irenaeus said that one could

63. Richard B. Hays, *Echoes of Scripture in the Letters of Paul* (New Haven: Yale University Press, 1993).

not hear the literal sense of the text apart from the *regula fidei* ("the Rule of Faith"). In his description of the literal sense, Irenaeus argued that although one knew the stories of the Old Testament, he or she could confuse "the fox's portrait for the King's" if one did not have "the Rule of Truth steadfast in himself, which he received at his Baptism."[64] Having recited this Rule ("of Truth" or "of Faith") at one's initiation into Christianity during Baptism, it became the most elementary aspect of Christian faith. Therefore, when reading the scripture, a Christian did not start *de novo* each time but she or he had the Rule of Faith to inform his or her interpretation.

In her book *Virtuoso Theology*, Frances Young shows the difficulty in pinpointing what exactly constitutes the Rule of Faith.[65] Similar to the old creeds, perhaps the Rule of Faith "arose in the context of training for baptism" but the creeds are a kind of nuanced development of the Rule of Faith. The Rule of Faith was *not* originally a fixed creed, though the later ecumenical creeds and confessions often came to play that role for community of faith. Irenaeus even provided us with several different versions of the Rule, and others can be found in the writings of Tertullian and Origen. The Rule of Faith did not come from canon or derive from the narrative as some sort of secondary product of scripture, but this Rule confirmed the pattern of scripture and accompanied the formation of scripture and the process of recognizing scripture. The Rule of Faith was what one inherited from the apostles, recited at his or her baptism and this Rule existed for those who came to scripture as Christians. The Rule of Truth or Rule of Faith for Irenaeus "outlines the simple orthodox 'system' which alone gives the key to the scriptures..."[66]

I have not tried to deal with the complexities or differences between Jewish and Christian messianic interpretations, but what should be clear is that one cannot simply equate Jewish interpretation with the literal sense of Christian interpretation. For example, the Jewish meaning and application of *peshat* is not the same as the Christian understanding of the literal sense of scripture (Torah or Gospel), the *regula fidei*. We have seen how medieval rabbis argued against traditional Christian messianic readings by utilizing and modifying Christian interpretative techniques. Thus, by appealing to or dismissing the *regula fidei*, and by bringing this to bear on their differing norms and perspectives, the Jewish and

64. *Adv. Haer.* I.9.4.
65. See this careful review of the historical evidence from the second century in Frances Young, *Virtuoso Theology: The Bible and Interpretation* (Cleveland, Ohio: Pilgrim, 1993), 26–65.
66. Ibid., 49.

Christian readers were/are able exploit the text in opposite directions. The literal sense establishes norms for Christians to read the Bible as scripture and holds together the testimony of the text by its revealed subject matter, which is the Gospel of Jesus Christ.[67] Augustine said that the purpose of all interpretation was to engender love for God and neighbor. Only if an interpreter found a text that did not fulfill this goal when read literally should she or he move on to another sense.[68] Therefore, one cannot hear the literal sense of the text apart from the Gospel. Obviously, one can interpret the Bible "literalistically" without hearing its literal sense if one ignores how the testimony of the text must be held together by the Gospel as its subject matter. The literal sense of Christian scripture provides a way, through the Gospel, for Christians to read the Bible within the framework of God's unique message to his people.

St. Thomas Aquinas and the Protestant reformers agreed that for one to know the plain or literal sense of a text was to know the author's intent or the historical sense. However, by the rise of historical criticisms, the scholarly community had mistaken the literal sense with the original historical sense of the text. In his *Divino Afflante Spiritu*, Robert Robinson demonstrates that in the modern era, the interpretative process has been reversed so that the modern reader must first know the author's intent to know the literal meaning. Because of scholarly attempts to find a way to get behind the text to some historical reality, the literal sense of the scripture lost all significance.[69] Even if we could get back to the original meaning of the pre-biblical history behind the book of Isaiah, it cannot determine the literal sense or convey the meaning of scripture apart from the text testifying to its subject matter. In the modern era, the historical sense of the text was construed as being the original meaning of the text as it emerged in its pristine situation. Therefore Brevard Childs says, "the aim of the interpreter was to reconstruct the original occasion of the historical reference on the basis of which the truth of the biblical text could be determined. In sum the *sensus literalis* had become *sensus originalis*."[70]

---

67. Ibid., 38, 41–44.

68. Brevard S. Childs, "The Sensus Literalis of Scripture: An Ancient and Modern Problem," in *Beiträge zur Alttestamentlichen Theologie. Festschrift für Walther Zimmerli zum 70. Geburtstag* (ed. H. Donner; Göttingen: Vandenhoek & Ruprecht, 1996), 80–93.

69. Robert Robinson, *Roman Catholic Exegesis Since Divino Afflante Spiritu: Hermeneutical Implications* (SBLDS 111; Atlanta: Scholars Press, 1988), 24.

70. Childs, "Sensus Literalis."

How, then, can historical criticisms inform our understanding of the literal sense? Northrop Frye encourages his readers to pursue the literal sense of the scripture but completely opposes historical criticism.[71] I, however, have demonstrated how historical-critical methods can help distinguish between such pre-biblical traditions of eighth-century Isaiah, the so-called Second Isaiah and Third Isaiah, and the scriptural form of the book of Isaiah as a whole. The original traditions of Isa 7:14 and 9:1–6 were clearly non-messianic, but where the later editors are conscious of the form and function of the book of Isaiah in relation to the Mosaic Torah, the passages warrant messianic interpretation. Although the identity of the Servant may have been explicit within the original traditions of Second Isaiah, the scriptural form of 52:13–53:12 provides the ambiguity that functions as a warrant for Christians to read the text in light of Jesus as their Messiah who suffered, died and made atonement for sin. While we cannot determine with certainty whether or not 11:1–9 and 61:13 were originally messianic, I have established through historical-critical methods and other contextual methods that, within the pattern of scripture-conscious editing, these passages warrant messianic interpretation.

I have exemplified how historical criticisms are necessary to locate messianic interpretation within the book of Isaiah as a whole while also recognizing their limits. Therefore, it is my claim that Christian scholars need to rely on the help of both historical-critical methods and the literal sense of scripture as it has been passed down to us from the apostles. While I have established through modern methods that the text of Isaiah contains a variety of traditions that reveal an historical disunity, Christians also must affirm that through the literal sense of scripture, they can confess with Irenaeus that "Every prophecy is enigmatic and ambiguous for human minds before it is fulfilled. But when the time is arrived and the prediction has come true, then the prophecies find their clear unambiguous interpretation."[72]

---

71. Northrop Frye, *The Great Code: The Bible and Literature* (Toronto: Academic Press Canada, 1982), 39–65, 78–138, 216.

72. Irenaeus, *Ante-Nicene Fathers*, 1:496.

BIBLIOGRAPHY

Ackroyd, Peter R. "Historians and Prophets." *SEÅ* 33 (1968): 18–54.

—*Isaiah I–XII.* VTSup 29, Leiden, Brill, 1978.

Aharoni, Yohanon, and Michael Avi-Yonah. *The Macmillan Bible Atlas.* Rev. ed. New York: Macmillan, 1979.

Albright, W. F. *Yahweh and the Gods of Canaan.* Jordan Lectures 1965. London: Athlone, 1968.

Albright, W. F., and C. S. Mann. *Matthew.* AB 26. Garden City, N.Y.: Doubleday, 1971.

Alexander, Joseph Addison. *Commentary on the Prophecies of Isaiah.* Grand Rapids: Zondervan, 1953.

Allen, L. C. "Isaiah LIII,11 and Its Echoes." *VE* 1 (1962): 24–28.

Allis, Oswalt T. *The Unity of Isaiah.* Philadelphia: Presbyterian & Reformed Press, 1950.

Alobaidi, Joseph. *The Messiah in Isaiah 53: The Commentaries of Saadia Gaon, Salmon Ben Yerubam and Yefet Ben Eli on Is 52:13–53:12.* Bern: Lang, 1998.

Alt, Albrecht. "Die Staatenbildung der Israeliten in Palästina." Reformationsprogramm der Universität Leipzig. Reprinted in *Kleine Schriften* 2 (1953): 1–65.

—*Essays on Old Testament History and Religion.* Edited by David E. Orton. Translated by R. A. Wilson. The Biblical Seminar 9. Sheffield: JSOT Press, 1989.

—"Jesaja 8,23–9,6. Befreiungsnacht und Krönungstag." Pages 29–49 in *Festschrift A Berthelet zum 80. Geburtstag.* Edited by W. Baumgartner. Reprinted in *Kleine Schriften* 2:206–25. Tübingen: J. C. B. Mohr, 1953.

Alter, Robert. *The Art of Biblical Poetry.* New York: Basic, 1985.

Anderson, Bernhard W. "Exodus Typology in Second Isaiah." Pages 177–99 in Anderson and Harrelson, eds., *Israel's Prophetic Heritage.*

Anderson, B. W., and W. Harrelson, eds. *Israel's Prophetic Heritage: Essays in Honor of James Muilenburg.* London: Harper & Brothers, 1962.

Anderson, Hugh. "Broadening Horizons: The Rejection at Nazareth Pericope of Luke at Nazareth Pericope of Luke 4:16–30 in Light of Recent Critical Trends." *Int* 18 (1964): 259–75.

Archer, Gleason. *Encyclopedia of Bible Difficulties.* Grand Rapids: Zondervan, 1982.

—"Isaiah." Pages 605–54 in *The Wycliffe Bible Commentary.* Edited by Charles Pfeiffer and Everett Harrison. Chicago: Moody, 1962.

Archer, Gleason, and G. Chirichigno. *Old Testament Quotations in the New Testament.* Chicago: Moody, 1983.

Auerbach, Erich. "Figura." Pages 11–75 in *Scenes from the Drama of European Literature: Six Essays by Erich Auerbach.* Gloucester: Peter Smith, 1977.

—*Mimesis: The Representation of Reality in Western Literature.* Princeton: Princeton University Press, 1953.

Augustin, Matthias. *Der Schone Mensch im Alten Testament und im Hellenistischen.* Frankfurt am Main: Lang, 1983.

Auvray, Paul. *Isaïe 1–39*. Sources Bibliques. Paris: Gabalda, 1972.

Baarlink, Heinrich. "Ein Gnädiges Jahr des Herrn—und Tage der Vergeltung: [Lk 4:18–19]." *ZNW* 73, nos. 3–4 (1982): 204–20.

Bacher, Wilhelm. "Bible Exegesis." *Jewish Encyclopedia* 3 (1901–6): 162–69.

Bainton, Roland H. *Hunted Heretic: The Life and Death of Michael Servetus 1511–1553.* Boston: Beacon, 1960.

Balla, E. "Das Problem des Leides in der Israelitisch-Jüdischen Religion." Pages 214–60 in Schmidt, ed., *Eucharistérion.*

Baltzer, Klaus. "Zur Formgeschichtlichen Bestimmung der Texte Vom Gottes-Knecht im Deuterojesaja Buch." Pages 24–43 in Wolff, ed., *Probleme Biblischer Theologie.*

Barnes, A. *Notes on the Old Testament: Critical, Explanatory, and Practical; The Book of the Prophet Isaiah.* London: Blackie & Son, 1845.

Barnes, W. E. "Cyrus the 'Servant of Jehovah,' Isa. 42:1–4 (7)." *JTS* 32 (1931): 32–39.

Barr, James. *Comparative Philology and the Text of the Old Testament.* Oxford: Clarendon, 1968.

Barstad, Hans. "On the So-Called Babylonian Literary Influence." *SJOT* 1 (1987): 90–110.

Barth, Hermann. *Die Jesaja-Worte in der Josiazeit. Israel und Assur als Thema einer Produktiven Neuinterpretation der Jesajaüberlieferung.* WMANT 48. Neukirchen–Vluyn: Neukirchener, 1977.

—"Israel und das Assyrerreich in den nichtjesanischen Texten des Protojesajabuches: Eine Untersuchung zur produktiven Neuinterpretation der Jesajauberlieferung." Ph.D. diss., University of Hamburg.

Barthélemy, Dominique. *Critique textuelle de l'Ancien Testament*, vol. 2. OBO 50/2. Fribourg: Éditions Universitaires; Göttingen: Vandenhoeck & Ruprecht, 1986.

—"Le grand rouleau d'Isaïe trouvé près de la Mer Morte." *RB* 57 (1950): 530–49.

—*Isaiah 1–39*. OTG. Sheffield: Sheffield Academic Press, 1995.

Barton, John. *Oracles of God: Perceptions of Prophecy in Israel After the Exile.* New York: Oxford University Press, 1986.

Battenfield, James R. "Isaiah 53:10: Taking an 'If' Out of the Sacrifice of the Servant." *VT* 32 (1982): 485.

Baumgartner, Walter. *Hebräisches und Aramaisches Lexikon zum Alten Testament von Ludwig Koehler und Walter Baumgartner.* 3 vols. 3d ed. Leiden: Brill, 1967–83.

Becker, Joachim. *Isaias. Der Prophet und Sein Buch.* SBS 30. Stuttgart: Katholische Bibelwerk, 1968.

—*Messianic Expectation in the Old Testament.* Translated by David E. Green. Philadelphia: Fortress, 1980.

Begg, C. "Zedekiah and the Servant." *ETL* 62 (1986): 393–98.

Begrich, J. *Studien zu Deuterojesaja.* BWANT 77. Stuttgart: W. Kohlhammer, 1938.

Behr, J. W. *The Writings of Deutero-Isaiah and the Neo-Babylonian Royal Inscription: A Comparison of the Language and Style.* Arts 3/3. Pretoria: Publications of the University of Pretoria, 1937.

Bentzen, Aage. *Jesaja.* Copenhagen: G. E. C. Gads, 1943.

—*King and Messiah.* Lutterworth Studies in Church and Bible. London: Lutterworth, 1955.

—*Messias-Moses Redivivus-Menschensohn.* London: Lutterworth, 1955.

Berger, K. "Die Königlichen Messiastraditionen des Neuen Testaments." *NTS* 20 (1973–74): 1–44.

—"Zum Problem der Messianität Jesu." *ZThK* 71 (1974): 1–30.

Berges, Ulrich. *Das Buch Jesaja. Komposition und Endgestalt.* Herder Biblische Studien 16. Freiburg: Herder, 1998.

Berlin, Adele. *The Dynamics of Biblical Parallelism.* Bloomington: Indiana University Press, 1992.

Beuken, W. A. M. "Did Israel Need a Messiah?" Pages 3–13 in *Messianism Through History.* Edited by W. Beuken, S. Freyne and A. Weiler. London: SCM Press. Maryknoll, N.Y.: Orbis.

—*Jesaja.* 3 vols. in 5. A Nijkerk: Uitgeverij GF Callenbach, 1989.

—"The Main Theme of Trito-Isaiah." *JSOT* 47 (1990): 67–87.

—"*Mišpat*: The First Servant Song and Its Canonical Context." *VT* 22 (1972): 1–30.

—"Servant and Herald of Good Tidings: Isaiah 61 as an Interpretation of 40–55." Pages 411–42 in Vermeylen, ed., *Le Livre d'Isaïe.*

Bewer, J. A. "The Hellenistic Mystery Religion and the Old Testament." *JBL* 45 (1926): 1–13.

Beyse, Karl Martin. *Serrubbabel und die Königserwartungen der Propheten Haggai und Sacharja.* Stuttgart: Calwer, 1972.

Blank, Sheldon H. *Prophetic Faith in Isaiah.* London: A. & C. Black, 1958.

—"Studies in Deutero-Isaiah." *HUCA* 15 (1940): 1–25.

Blocher, Henri. *The Songs of the Servant.* Downers Grove, Ill.: Intervarsity, 1975.

Blythin, Islwyn. "A Consideration of Difficulties in the Hebrew Text of Isaiah 53:11." *BT* 17 (1966): 27–31.

Bonhoeffer, Dietrich, *Life Together: Prayerbook of the Bible.* Edited by B. Kelly. Translated by Daniel W. Bloesch. Philadelphia: Fortress, 1995.

—*Psalms: The Prayer Book of the Bible.* Minneapolis: Augsburg Fortress, 1974.

Bonnard, P. E. *Le Second Isaïe.* EBib. Paris: Gabalda, 1972.

Borger, Rykle. "Babylonisch-Assyrische Lesestücke." *AnOr* 54 (1979): 329–32.

Box, George H. *The Book of Isaiah: Translated from a Text Revised in Accordance with the Results of Recent Criticism.* London: Sir Isaac Pitman & Sons, 1908.

Boyce, Mary. *A History of Zoroastrianism.* Handbuch der Orientalistik 2. Leiden: Brill, 1982.

Böhl, Franz Marius, Theodore de Liagre. *De "Knecht des Heeren" in Jesaja 53.* Overdruk-Uitgaaf Onze 7. Haarlem: Erven F. Bohn, 1923.

—"Nebukadnezar en Jojachin." Pages 423–29 in *Opera Minora.*

—*Opera Minora: Studies en Bijdragen Op Assyriologisch en Oudtestamentlisch Terrein.* Groningen: J. B. Wolters, 1953.

—"Profetisme en Plaatsvervangend Lijden in Assyrië en Israël." *NedTT* 4 (1949–50): 81–91, 161–76.

—"Propheten und Stellvertrendes Leiden in Assyrien und Israel." Pages 63–80 in *Opera Minora.*

Briggs, Charles. *Messianic Prophecies.* 2d ed. New York: Scribner's Sons, 1893.

Bright, John. *A History of Israel.* Philadelphia: Westminster, 1981.

—*The Kingdom of God.* Nashville: Abingdon, 1953.

Brooke, George J. "4Q Testament of Levi[d] (?) and the Messianic Servant High Priest." Pages 83–100 in *From Jesus to John: Essays on Jesus and New Testament Christology in Honour of Marinus de Jonge.* Edited by M. de Boer. JSNTSup 84. Sheffield: JSOT Press, 1993.

—"The Messiah of Aaron in the Damascus Document." *RevQ* 15 (1991): 215–30.

Brown, Francis, S. R. Driver, and Charles Briggs. *A Hebrew and English Lexicon of the Old Testament*. Oxford: Clarendon, 1980.

Brown, Raymond E. "The Messianism of Qumrân." *CBQ* 19 (1957): 53–82.

Brownlee, William Hugh. "Messianic Motifs of Qumran and the New Testament." *NTS* 3 (1956–57): 12–30.

—"*Mshty* (Is. 52:14 1QIs^a)." *BASOR* 132 (1953): 8–15.

—"Text of Isaiah VI 13 in Light of DSIa." *VT* 1 (1951): 296–98.

Brueggemann, Walter. *Isaiah 1–39*. Westminster Bible Companion. Louisville, Ky.: Westminster John Knox, 1998.

—*Isaiah 40–66*. Westminster Bible Companion. Louisville, Ky.: Westminster John Knox, 1998.

Bruno, Violet. "Zum Rechten Verständnis der Nazarethperikope Lc 4,14–30." *ZNW* 37 (1938): 251–71.

Bruston, Henry. "Le serviteur de l'éternel dans l'avenir." Pages 37–44 in *Vom Alten Testament Karl Marti zum Siebzigsten Geburtstage*. Edited by Karl Budde. Giessen: A. Töpelmann, 1925.

Buber, Martin. *Der Glaube der Propheten*. Zurich: Manesse, 1950.

—*The Prophetic Faith*. New York: Harper & Brothers (Harper Torchbooks/The Cloister Library), 1960.

Buber, Salomon. *Midrash Rabbah: Lamentations*. Vilna, 1899.

Budde, Karl. *Jesaja's Erleben. Eine Gemeinverstandliche Auslegung der Denkschrift des Propheten (Kap 6:1–9:6)*. Gotha: L. Klotz, 1928.

—"The So-Called 'Ebed-Yahweh Songs' in Isaiah." *AJTh* 3 (1899): 499–540.

—"Über die Schranken, die Jesajas Prophetischer Botschaft zu Setzen." *ZAW* 41 (1923): 154–203.

Calvin, Jean. *Commentary on the Book of the Prophet Isaiah*. Edinburgh: T. Constable, 1850.

—*Commentary on the Book of the Prophet Isaiah*. Translated by W. Pringle. 4 vols. Grand Rapids: Eerdmans, 1948.

Cannon, George E. "Isaiah 61, 1–3 as Ebed-Jahweh Poem." *ZAW* 40 (1929): 284–88.

Caquot, André. "Ben Sira et le Messianisme." *Sem* 16 (1966): 43–68.

Carmignac, Jean. "L'infinitif absolu chez Ben Sira et à Qumran." *RevQ* 12, no. 2 (1986): 251–61.

Carr, David. "Reaching for Unity in Isaiah." *JSOT* 57 (1993): 61–80.

Carroll, Robert P. "Inner Tradition Shifts in Meaning in Isaiah 1–11." *ExpTim* 89 (1977/78): 301–4.

—"Second Isaiah and the Failure of Prophecy." *StTh* 32 (1978): 119–31.

—*When Prophecy Failed: Reactions and Responses to Failure in the Old Testament Prophetic Traditions*. London: SCM Press, 1979.

Casciaro, José Mariá, et al. *The Navarre Bible: Saint Luke's Gospel*. Translated by Brian McCarthy. Dublin: Four Courts, 1987.

Casetti, P. "Funktionen der Musik in der Bibel." *FZPhTh* 24 (1977): 366–89.

Caspari, W. *Lieder und Gottessprüche de Rückwanderer (Jes 40–55)*. BZAW 65. Giessen: Töpelmann, 1934.

Cazelles, H. "Les Poèmes du Serviteur." *Recherches de Science Religieuse* 43 (1955): 5–55.

Charlesworth, James H. "Introduction: From Messianology to Christlogy." Pages 3–35 in Charlesworth, ed., *The Messiah*.

304 *Messianism within the Scriptural Scroll of Isaiah*

—, ed. *The Messiah: Developments in Earliest Judaism and Christianity.* Minneapolis: Fortress, 1992.

Cheyne, Thomas K. *The Prophecies of Isaiah: A New Translation with Commentary and Appendices.* 5th edn. 2 vols. London: Kegan, Paul, Trench & Co., 1889.

Childs, Brevard S. *Biblical Theology of the Old and New Testaments.* Philadelphia: Fortress, 1993.

—*Introduction to the Old Testament as Scripture.* Philadelphia: Fortress, 1979.

—*Isaiah.* OTL. Louisville, Ky.: Westminster John Knox, 2001.

—*Isaiah and the Assyrian Crisis.* SBT, 2d Series 3. London: SCM Press, 1967.

—*Myth and Reality in the Old Testament.* SBT 21. Naperville, Ill.: Alec R. Allenson, 1960.

—*Old Testament Theology in a Canonical Context.* Philadelphia: Fortress, 1986.

—"The Sensus Literalis of Scripture: An Ancient and Modern Problem." Pages 80–95 in *Beiträge zur Alttestamentlichen Theologie: Festschrift für Walter Zimmerli.* Edited by H. Donner and R. Smend. Göttingen: Vandenhoeck & Ruprecht, 1976.

Chilton, Bruce. *The Glory of Israel: The Theology and Provenience of the Isaiah Targum.* JSOTSup 23. Sheffield: JSOT Press, 1983.

Christensen, Dwayne L. "The March of Conquest in Isaiah X,27c–34." *VT* 26 (1976): 385–99.

Clements, Ronald E. "Beyond Tradition History." *JSOT* 31 (1985): 95–113.

—"The Immanuel Prophecy of Isa 7:10–17 and Its Messianic Interpretation." Pages 225–40 in *Die Hebräische Bibel, Festschrift for Rolf Rendtorff.* Edited by Erhardt Blum et al. Neukirchen–Vluyn: Neukirchener, 1990.

—*Isaiah 1–39.* The New Century Bible Commentary. Grand Rapids: Eerdmans, 1980b.

—"The Prophecies of Isaiah and the Fall of Jerusalem in 587 B.C." *VT* 30 (1980a): 421–36.

Clifford, Richard J. *Fair Spoken and Persuading.* New York: Paulist, 1984.

—"Second Isaiah." Pages 571–96 in Mays, ed., *Harper's Bible Commentary* (1988).

Clines, David J. A. *I, He, We, and They: A Literary Approach to Isaiah 53.* JSOTSup 1. Sheffield: JSOT Press, 1976.

Cohen, Mark. *The Canonical Lamentations of Ancient Mesopotamia.* Potomac: Capital Decisions, 1988.

Cohn-Sherbok, Dan. *The Jewish Messiah.* Edinburgh: T. & T. Clark, 1997.

Collins, John J. "Apocalypse: The Morphology of a Genre." *Semia* 14 (1979): 59–67.

—*The Apocalyptic Vision of the Book of Daniel.* Ann Arbor: University of Michigan Press, 1977.

—*Introduction to Apocalyptic Literature.* Grand Rapids: Eerdmans, 1984.

 The Scepter and the Star: The Messiahs of the Dead Sea Scrolls and Other Ancient Literature. New York: Doubleday, 1995.

—*The Sibylline Oracles of Egyptian Judaism.* Missoula, Mont.: Society of Biblical Literature for the Pseudepigrapha Group, 1974.

Conrad, Edgar. *Reading the Book of Isaiah.* OBT. Minneapolis: Fortress, 1991.

Cook, Stanely A. *The Cambridge Ancient History.* Cambridge: Cambridge University Press, 1923–39.

—"The Servant of the Lord." *ExpTim* 34 (1922–23): 440–42.

Coppens, Joseph C. L. *Nieuw licht over de Ebed-Jahweh-Liedern.* ALBO 2/15. Gembloux: Duculot, 1950.

—"L'interprétation d'Is, VII, 14, a la lumière des études les plus récentes." Pages 31–45 in *Lex Tua Veritas: Für H. Junker*. Edited by H. Gross and F. Musser. Trier: Paulinus, 1961.

—*Le messianisme et sa relève prophétique*. BETL 38. Gembloux: Duculot, 1974.

—*Le messianisme royal: Ses origines, son développement, son accomplissement*. LD 54. Paris: Cerf, 1968.

Corley, D. H. "Messianic Prophecy in First Isaiah." *AJSL* 39 (1922/23): 220–24.

Crenshaw, James L. *Prophetic Conflict: Its Effect Upon Israelite Religion*. BZAW 124. Berlin: de Gruyter, 1971.

Crook, Margaret B. "Did Amos and Micah Know Isaiah 92–7 and 11:2–9?" *JBL* 73 (1954): 144–51.

—"A Suggested Occasion for Isaiah 9:2–7 and 11:1–9." *JBL* 48 (1949): 213–24.

Cross, Frank Moore. *Canaanite Myth and Hebrew Epic*. Cambridge, Mass.: Harvard University Press, 1973.

Crüsemann, Frank. *Studien zur Formgeschichte von Hymnus und Danklied in Israel*. WMANT 32. Neukirchen–Vluyn: Neukirchener, 1969.

Dahl, N. A. "Messianic Ideas and the Crucifixion of Jesus." Pages 382–403 in Charlesworth, ed., *The Messiah*.

Dahood, Mitchell. "Isaiah 53:8–12 and Massoretic Misconstructions." *Bib* 63 (1982): 566–70.

—"Phoenician Elements in Isaiah 52:13–53:12." Pages 63–73 in *Near Eastern Studies in Honour of W. F. Albright*. Edited by H. Goedicke. Baltimore: The Johns Hopkins University Press, 1971.

—"Textual Problems in Isaiah." *CBQ* 22 (1960): 400–409.

Danker, Frederick W. *Introductory Hebrew Grammar: Hebrew Syntax*. 3d ed. Edinburgh: T. & T. Clark, 1976.

—*Luke*. Proclamation Commentaries. Philadelphia: Fortress, 1976.

Davidson, Andrew B. *Introductory Hebrew Grammar: Hebrew Syntax*. 3d ed.; Edinburgh: T. & T. Clark, 1976.

Davies, Philip R. "God of Cyrus, God of Israel." Pages 207–25 in *Words Remembered, Texts Renewed: Essays in Honour of John F. A. Sawyer*. Edited by Wilfred G. E. Watson. JSOTSup 195. Sheffield: Sheffield Academic Press, 1995.

Davies, William David. "The Jewish Sources of Matthew's Messianism." Pages 494–511 in Charlesworth, ed., *The Messiah*.

—*Paul and Rabbinic Judaism: Some Rabbinic Elements in Pauline Theology*. London: SPCK, 1911.

Davis, John D. "The Child Whose Name is Wonderful." Pages 93–108 in *Biblical and Theological Studies*. Princeton Centenary Volume. New York: Scribner's Sons, 1912.

Day, John. "*Da'at* 'Humiliation' in Is 53:11 in Light of Is 53:3 and Dan 12:4, and the Oldest Known Interpretation of the Suffering Servant." *VT* 30 (1980): 97–103.

Delitzsch, Franz. *Biblical Commentary on the Prophecies of Isaiah*. Translated by James Martin. 3d ed. 2 vols. Edinburgh: T. & T. Clark, 1875.

Dietrich, W. *Jesaja und die Politik*. BEvT 74. Munich: Kaiser, 1976.

Dillmann, August. *Der Prophet Jesaia*. 5th ed. Kurzgefasstes Exegetisches Handbuch zum Alten Testament 6. Leipzig: S. Hirzel, 1890.

Dion, H. M. "Le genre litteraire Sumerien de 'l'hymne à soi-même' et quelques passages du Deutéro-Isaïe." *RB* 74 (1967): 215–34.

Dion, Paul. *Hebrew Poetics.* 2d ed. Mississauga, Ont.: Benben, 1992.

Dix, G. H. "The Influence of Babylonian Ideas on Jewish Messianism." *JTS* 26 (1925): 241–56.

Dobbs-Allsopp, F. W. *Weep, O Daughter of Zion: A Study of the City-Lament Genre in the Hebrew Bible.* Rome: Pontificio Istituto Biblico, 1993.

Dodd, Charles H. *According to Scripture: The Sub-Structure of New Testament Theology.* Digswell Place: James Nisbet & Co., 1961.

Donner, H. *Israel unter den Völkern. Die Stellung der Klassischen Propheten des 8. Jahrhunderts v. Chr. zur Aussenpolitik der Könige von Israel und Juda.* VTSup 11. Leiden: Brill, 1964.

Donner, H., and W. Röllig. *Kanaanäische und Aramäische Inschriften.* Wiesbaden: Otto Harrassowitz, 1962–64.

Donner, Herbert. "Der Feind aus dem Norden. Topographische und Archaologische Erwagungen zu Jes 10:287b–34." *ZDPV* 84 (1968): 46–54.

Driver, Godfrey R. "Isaiah 52:13–53:12: The Servant of the Lord." Pages 90–105 in *In Memoriam Paul Kahle.* Edited by G. Fohrer and M. Black. BZAW 103. Berlin: Töpelmann, 1968.

—"Isaiah i–xxxix: Textual and Linguistic Problems." *JJS* 13 (1968b): 36–57.

—"Isaianic Problems." Pages 43–49 in *Festschrift für Wilhelm Eiler.* Edited by G. Wiessner. Wiesbaden: Otto Harrassowitz, 1967.

—"Linguistic and Textual Problems: Isa. 40–66." *JTS* 36 (1935): 396–406.

—"Once Again Abbreviations." *Textus* 4 (1964): 76–94.

Driver, Samuel R. "Introduction." Translated by James Martin. Pages 1–27 in *F. Delitzsch's Biblical Commentary on the Prophecies of Isaiah,* vol. 1. 4th ed. Edinburgh: T. & T. Clark, 1892.

Driver, Samuel R., and Adolf Neubauer, trans. *The "Suffering Servant" of Isaiah According to the Jewish Interpreters.* Oxford: James Parker & Co., 1877.

Duhm, D. Bernhard. *Das Buch Jesaja.* 1st ed. HKAT 3. Göttingen: Vandenhoeck & Ruprecht, 1892.

—*Das Buch Jesaja Übersetzt und Erklärt.* 4th ed. Göttinger Handkommentar zum Alten Testament. Göttingen: Vandenhoeck & Ruprecht, 1922.

—*Die Theologie der Propheten als Grundlage für die Innere Entwicklungsgeschichte der Israelischen Religion.* Bonn: Adolph Marcus, 1875.

Duling, D. C. "Testament of Solomon: A New Translation and Introduction." *OTP* 1 933–87.

Dunn, J. D. G. "Messianic Ideas and Their Influence on the Jesus of History." Pages 365–81 in Charlesworth, ed., *The Messiah.*

Dupont, Jacques. *Les Béattitudes.* Bruges: Abbaye de Saint-André, 1969.

Dürr, Lorenz. *Ursprung und Ausbau der Israelitischen-Judischen Heilandserwartung: Ein Beitrag zur Theologie des Alten Testamentes.* Berlin: Schwetschke & Sohn, 1925.

Eaton, J. H. *Festal Drama in Deutero-Isaiah.* London: SPCK, 1979.

Edzard, Dietz O. *Die "Zweite Zwischenzeit" Babyloniens.* Wiesbaden: Otto Harrassowitz, 1957.

Eichhorn, Johann G. *Die hebraischen Propheten.* 3 vols. Göttingen: Vandenhoeck & Ruprecht, 1816–19.

Eichrodt, Walther. *Der Heilige in Israel: Jesaja 1–12.* BAT. Stuttgart: Calwer, 1960.

—*Theology of the Old Testament,* vol. 2. Translated by J. A. Baker. London: SCM Press, 1967.

Eisenman, R. H., and M. Wise. *The Dead Sea Scrolls Uncovered: The First Complete Translation and Interpretation of 50 Key Documents Withheld Over 35 Years.* Rockport, Mass.: Element, 1992.

Eissfeldt, Otto. "The Promises of Grace to David in Isaiah 55:1–5." Pages 196–207 in Anderson and Harrelson, eds., *Israel's Prophetic Heritage.*

—*The Old Testament: An Introduction.* New York: Harper & Row, 1976.

Elliger, Karl. *Die Einheit des Tritojesaia Jesaia 56–66.* BWANT 63. Stuttgart: W. Kohlhammer, 1933.

—"Jes. 53:10: Alte Crux—Neuer Vorschlag." *Mitteilungen des Instituts für Orientforschung* 15 (1969): 228–33.

—"Nochmals Textkritisches zu Jes. 53." Pages 137–44 in *Wort, Lied und Gottesspruch: Festschrift für Joseph Ziegler.* Edited by Josef Schreiner. Wurzburg: Echter, 1972.

Ellis, E. Earle. *Eschatology in Luke.* Edited by John Reumann. Biblical Series. Philadelphia: Fortress, 1972.

—*The Gospel of Luke.* The Century Bible. London: Nelson, 1966.

Emerton, John A. "Some Linguistic and Historical Problems in Isaiah VIII.23." *JSS* 14 (1969): 151–75.

—"The Translation and Interpretation of Isaiah VI,13." Pages 85–118 in *Interpreting the Hebrew Bible: Essays in Honour of E. I. J. Rosenthal.* Edited by J. A. Emerton and S. C. Reif. Cambridge: Cambridge University Press, 1982.

Engell, Ivan. "The 'Ebed Yahweh Songs and the Suffering Messiah in 'Deutero-Isaiah.'" *BJRL* 31 (1948): 54–93.

—*Studies in Divine Kingship.* Uppsala: Almqvist & Wiksell, 1943.

—*Studies in Divine Kingship in the Ancient Near East.* 2d ed. Oxford: Blackwell, 1967. First published Uppsala: Almqvist & Wiksell, 1943.

Everson, A. Joseph. "Isaiah 61:1–6 (To Give them a Garland Instead of Ashes)." *Int* 32 (1978): 69–73.

Ewald, G. H. A. von. *Commentary on the Prophets of the Old Testament.* Translated by J. F. Smith. 5 vols. London: Williams & Norgate, 1875–81.

—*The History of Israel.* 3d ed. London: Longmans, Green & Co., 1876–86.

Farley, Fred A. "Jeremiah and the 'Suffering Servant of Jehovah' in Deutero-Isaiah." *ExpTim* 38 (1926–27): 241–325.

Farrar, Frederic W. *History of Interpretation.* Bampton Lectures Series. Grand Rapids: Baker, 1961.

Feldmann, Franz. *Das Buch Isaias Übersetzt und Erklärt. Exegetisches Handbuch zum Alten.* Münster: Aschendorf, 1925.

—*Der Knecht Gottes in Isaias Kap. 40–55.* Freiburg: Herder, 1907.

Festinger, L., H. W. Riecken, and S. Schacter. *When Prophecy Fails: A Social and Psychological Study of a Modern Group That Predicted the Destruction of the World.* Minneapolis: University of Minnesota Press, 1956.

Filson, Floyd. *The Gospel According to St. Matthew.* New York: Harper, 1960.

Fischer, Johann. *Isaias 40–55 und die Perikopen vom Gottesknecht: Eine Kritisch-Exegetische Studie.* Munster: Aschendorff, 1916.

—*Wer ist der Ebed in den Perikopen Js 42,1–7; 49,1–9a; 50,4–9; 52,13–53, 12? : Eine Exegetische Studie.* Munster: Aschendorff, 1922.

Fishbane, Michael A. *Biblical Interpretation in Ancient Israel.* Oxford: Clarendon, 1985.

Fitzmeyer, Joseph A. *The Gospel According to Luke (I–IX).* AB 28. Garden City, N.Y.: Doubleday, 1981.

Fohrer, Georg. *Das Buch Jesaja*. 3 vols. Zurcher Bibelkommentare. Zurich: Zwingli, 1966.

—"Zu Jes 7,14 im Zusammenhang von Jes 7,10–22." *ZAW* 68 (1956): 54–56. Reprinted in pages 167–69 of *Studien zur Alttestamentlichen Prophetie (1949–65)*. BZAW 99. Berlin: A. Töpelmann, 1967.

France, R. T. "The Servant of the Lord in the Teachings of Jesus." *TynBul* 19 (1968): 26–53.

Freedman, David Noel. "Strophe and Meter in Exodus 15." Pages 163–203 in *A Light Unto My Path: Old Testament Studies in Honor of Jacob Myers*. Edited by H. Goedicke and J. J. M. Roberts. Baltimore: The Johns Hopkins University Press, 1974.

Fretheim, Terrence. *The Suffering of God: An Old Testament Perspective*. OBT 14. Philadelphia: Fortress, 1984.

Freud, Sigmund. *Moses and Monotheism*. London: Hogarth and the Institute of Psycho-Analysis, 1939.

Friedländer, M., ed. *The Commentary of Ibn Ezra on Isaiah*, vol. 3. Edited from MSS and Translated, with Notes, Introduction and Indexes. London: The Society of Hebrew Literature by Trübner & Co., 1877.

Froehlich, Karlfried. *Biblical Interpretation in the Early Church*. Sources of Early Christian Thought. Philadelphia: Fortress, 1984.

Froehlich, Karlfried. *Biblical Interpretation in the Early Church*. Sources of Early Christian Thought. Philadelphia: Fortress, 1984.

Frye, Northrop. *The Great Code: The Bible and Literature*. Toronto: Academic Press Canada, 1982.

Fullerton, Kemper. "The Problem of Isaiah, Chapter 10." *AJSL* 34 (1917/18): 170–84.

—"Viewpoints in the Discussion of Isaiah's Hopes for the Future." *JBL* 41 (1922): 1–101.

Gadd, C. J. "The Second Lamentation for Ur." Pages 59–71 in *Hebrew and Semitic Studies Presented to Godfrey Rolles Driver*. Edited by D. W. Thomas and W. D. McHardy. Oxford: Clarendon, 1963.

Gall, August Freiherr von. *Basileia Tou Theou: Eine Religionsgeschichtliche Studie zur Vorkirchlichen Eschatologie*. Heidelberg: C. Winter, 1926.

Gelston, A. "Some Notes on Second Isaiah." *VT* 21 (1971): 517–27.

Gerleman, Gillis. *Studien zur alttestamentlichen Theologie*. Heidelberg: Schneider, 1980.

Gerstenberger, Erhard. *Psalms: Part 1: With an Introduction to Cultic Poetry*. FOTL. Grand Rapids: Eerdmans, 1987.

—"The Woe-Oracles of the Prophets." *JBL* 81 (1962): 249–63.

Gesenius, Wilhelm. *Gesenius' Hebrew Grammar*. Edited by Emil Kautzsch. Translated by A. E. Cowly. 2d Eng. ed. Oxford: Clarendon, 1910.

Giesebrecht, Friedrich. *Der Knecht Jahwes des Deuterojesaia*. Königsberg: Thomas & Oppermann, 1902.

Ginsburg, H. L. "The Arm of YHWH in Isaiah 51–63 and the Text of Isa 53:10–11." *JBL* 77 (1958): 152–56.

—*The Book of Isaiah*. Philadelphia: The Jewish Publication Society of America, 1973.

—"Pekah and Hoshea of Israel (Isa. 8:23)." *ErIsr* 5 (1958): 61–65.

Gipsen, W. H. "Distinctions Between Clean and Unclean." *OtSt* 5 (1948): 190–96.

Goldingay, John. "The Arrangement of Isaiah Xl–Xlv." *VT* 29 (1979): 289–99.

—*Isaiah*. NIBC. Peabody, Mass.: Hendrickson, 2001.

Gordon, Cyrus H. *Ugaritic Textbook*. Rome: Pontifical Biblical Institute, 1965.

Graham, W. C. "Isaiah's Part in the Syro-Ephraimitic Crisis." *AJSL* 50 (1933/34): 201–16.

Gray, George B. *A Critical and Exegetical Commentary on the Book of Isaiah I–XXVII.* 4th reprint. ICC 10a. Edinburgh: T. & T. Clark, 1956.

Gray, John. *The Biblical Doctrine of the Reign of God.* Edinburgh: T. & T. Clark, 1979.

Grelot, Pierre. "Le Messie dans les Apocryphes de l'Ancien Testament, état de la question." Pages 19–50 in *La venue du Messie: Messianisme et eschatologie.* Edited by E. Massaux. RechBib 6. Bruges: Desclée de Brouwer, 1962.

—*Les poèmes du serviteur: De la lecture critique a l'hermeneutique.* LD 103. Paris: Cerf, 1981.

—"Sur Isaïe LXI: La première consécration d'un grand-prêtre." *RB* 97 (1990): 414–31.

Gressmann, Hugo. *Der Messias.* FRLANT 43. Göttingen: Vandenhoeck & Ruprecht, 1929.

—*Der Ursprung der Israelitisch-Judischen Eschatologie.* FRLANT 6. Göttingen: Vandenhoeck & Ruprecht, 1905.

Guillaume, A. "Some Readings in the Dead Sea Scroll of Isaiah." *JBL* 76 (1957): 41–42.

Gunkel, Hermann. "Knecht Jahvehs." In *Die Religion in Geschichte und Gegenwart.* Tübingen: J. C. B. Mohr (Paul Siebeck), 1912.

—"The Prophets as Writers and Poets." Pages 22–73 in *Prophecy in Israel.* Edited by David L. Petersen. Philadelphia: Fortress, 1987.

—*Die Psalmen.* Göttinger Handkommentar zum Alten Testament 4. Göttingen: Vandenhoeck & Ruprecht, 1926.

—*Ein Vorläufer Jesu.* Zurich: Orell Füssli, 1921.

Gwaltney, W. C., Jr. "The Biblical Book of Lamentations in the Context of Near Eastern Lament Literature." Pages 191–211 in *Scripture in Context II: More Essays on the Comparative Method.* Edited by W. W. Hallo, J. C. Moyer, and L. G. Perdue. Winona Lake, Ind.: Eisenbrauns, 1983.

Haag, Ernst. "Die Botschaft vom Gottesknecht: Ein Weg zur Uberwindung der Gewalt." Pages 159–213 in *Gewalt und Gewaltlosigkeit im Alten Testament.* Edited by N. Lohfink. QD 96. Freiburg: Herder, 1983.

Haag, H. *Der Gottesknecht bei Deuterojesaja.* EdF 233. Darmstadt: Wisenschaftliche Buchgesellschaft, 1985.

Habel, Norman C. *The Book of Job: A Commentary.* Edited by Peter R. Ackroyd, James Barr and Bernhard W. Anderson. OTL. Philadelphia: Westminster, 1985.

Haller, M. "Die Kyroslieder Deuterojesaja." Pages 261–77 in Schmidt, ed., *Eucharistérion.*

Hallo, William. *Early Mesopotamian Royal Titles.* New Haven: Yale University Press, 1957.

Hammershaimb, Erling. "Immanuel Sign [Isa 7:10]." *ST* 3 (1951): 124–42.

—*Some Aspects of Old Testament Prophecy from Isaiah to Malachi.* Teologiske Skrifter 4. Copenhagen: Rosenkilde og Bagger, 1966.

Hanson, Paul D. *The Dawn of Apocalyptic.* Rev. ed. Philadelphia: Fortress, 1979.

—*The Diversity of Scripture.* Edited by Walter Brueggemann. OBT 11. Philadelphia: Fortress, 1982.

—*Dynamic Transcendence: The Correlation of Confessional Heritage and Contemporary Experience in a Biblical Model of Divine Activity.* Philadelphia: Fortress, 1978.

—*Isaiah 40–66.* Interpretation. Louisville, Ky.: John Knox, 1995.

—"Messiahs and Messianic Figures in Proto-Apocalypticism." Pages 67–75 in Charlesworth, ed., *The Messiah.*

Harrelson, Walter. "Nonroyal Motifs in the Royal Eschatology." Pages 147–67 in Anderson and Harrelson, eds., *Israel's Prophetic Heritage*.

Harrison, Roland K. *Introduction to the Old Testament*. Grand Rapids: Eerdmans, 1969.

Harvey, Anthony E. *Jesus and the Constraints of History*. Philadelphia: Westminster, 1982.

Hasel, G. F. *The Remnant: The History and Theology of the Remnant Idea from Genesis to Isaiah*. Andrews University Monographs 5. Berrien Springs, Miss.: Andrews University Press, 1972.

Hatav, Galia. *The Semantics of Aspect and Modality: Evidence from English and Biblical Hebrew*. Studies in Language Companion Series 34. Amsterdam: John Benjamins, 1997.

Hayes, John, and Stuart A. Irvine. *Isaiah, the Eighth-Century Prophet*. Nashville: Abingdon, 1987.

Hays, Richard B. *Echoes of Scripture in the Letters of Paul*. New Haven: Yale University Press, 1993.

Hegermann, Harald. *Jesaja 53 in Hexapla, Targum und Peschitta*. Gütersloh: C. Bertelsmann, 1954.

Heller, H. "Acht Christusämter nach Is. 61:1–3." *Wort und Geist* 32 (1938): 43–67.

Hengel, Martin. "Jesus der Messias Israels." Pages 155–76 in *Messiah and Christos: Studies in Jewish Origins of Christianity*. Edited by I. Gruenwald, S. Shaked and G. Stroumsa. J. C. B. Mohr (Paul Siebeck), 1992.

Hengstenberg, E. W. *Christology of the Old Testament and a Commentary on the Messianic Predictions*. Translated by Thomas Arnold. Grand Rapids: Kregel, 1970. First printed 1847.

Herbert, Arthur S. *The Book of the Prophet Isaiah 1–39*. CBC. Cambridge: Cambridge University Press, 1973.

—*The Book of the Prophet Isaiah 40–66*. CBC. Cambridge: Cambridge University Press, 1975.

Herder, J. G. von. *Vom Geist der Ebräischen Poesie*. Leipzig: J. R. Barth, 1825.

Hermisson, H. J. "Der Lohn des Knechts [Isa 42:1–4; 49:1–4; 50:4–9; 52:13–53:12]." Pages 269–87 in *Die Botschaft und die Boten: Festschrift für Hans Walter Wolff zum 70. Geburtstag*. Edited by Jorg Jeremias and Lothar Perlitt. Neukirchen–Vluyn: Neukirchener, 1981.

—"Zukunftserwartung und Gegenwartshritik in der Verkündigung Jesajas." *EvTh* 33 (1973): 54–77.

Herrmann, S. *A History of Israel in Old Testament Times*. Translated by J. S. Bowden. Rev. ed. London: SCM Press, 1981.

—*Die Prophetischen Heilserwartungen im Allen Testament. Ursprung und Gestaltwandel*. BWANT 5. Stuttgart: Kohlhammer, 1965.

Hertzberg, H. P. "Die 'Abtrünnigen' und die 'Vielen.'" Pages 97–108 in *Verbannung und Heimkehr: Beitrage zur Geschichte und Theologie Israels im 6. und 5. Jahrhundert v. Chr.: Wilhelm Rudolph zum 70. Geburtstage*. Edited by Arnulf Kuschke. Tübingen: J. C. B. Mohr, 1961.

Hillers, Delbert. *Lamentations*. Garden City, N.Y.: Doubleday, 1992.

Hoffmann, H. W. *Die Intention der Verkundigung Jesajas*. BZAW 136. Berlin: de Gruyter, 1974.

Hoffmann, Paul. *Studien zur Theologie der Logienquelle*. Münster: Aschendorff, 1971.

Hofius, Otfried. "Zur Septuaginta-Übersetzung von 52:13b." *ZAW* 104 (1992): 107–10.

Hoftijzer, Jacob. "Remarks Concerning the Use of the Particle '*at* in Classical Hebrew." Pages 1–99 in *Oudtestamentlich Werkgezelschap in Nederland.* Leiden: Brill, 1965.

Holladay, William L. *Isaiah: Scroll of a Prophetic Heritage.* Grand Rapids: Eerdmans, 1978.

Hölscher, Gustaf. "Des Buch der Könige, Seine Quellen und Seine Redaktion." Pages 158–213 in Schmidt, ed., *Eucharistérion.*

—*Die Profeten. Untersuchungen zur Religionsgeschichte Israels.* Leipzig: J. C. Hinrichs, 1914.

Homerski, Józef. "Cierpacy Wybawca i Oredownik." *RocTKan* 24 (1977): 75–90.

—"Cierpacy Mesjasz w Startestamentalnych Przepowiedniach Prorockich." *RocTKan* 27 (1980): 27–42.

Hoonacker, Albin van. "L'ébed Jahvé et la composition littéraire des chapitres Xl. ss d'Isaïe." *RB* 18 (1909): 497–528.

Hooke, Samuel H. *Prophets and Priests.* London: T. Murby & Co., 1938.

Hooker, M. D. *Jesus and the Servant.* London: SPCK, 1959.

Horsley, Richard A. *Bandits, Prophets, and Messiahs: Popular Messianic Movements Around the Time of Jesus.* San Francisco: Harper, 1985.

—"Popular Messianic Movements Around the Time of Jesus." *CBQ* 46 (1984): 471–95.

Hrushovski, Benjamin. "Note On the System of Hebrew Versification." Pages 57–75 in *Hebrew Verse.* Edited by T. Carmi. New York: Penguin, 1981.

—"On Free Rhythms in Poetry." Pages 173–90 in *Style in Language.* Edited by T. Sebeok. Cambridge, Mass.: M. I. T. Press, 1960.

Huber, F. *Jahwe, Juda und die anderen Völker beim Propheten Jesaja.* BZAW 137. Berlin: de Gruyter, 1976.

Hugenberger, Gordon P. "The Servant of the Lord in the 'Servant Songs' of Isaiah." Pages 105–40 in Satterthwaite, Hess, and Wenham, eds., *The Lord's Anointed.*

Hultgård, Anders. "The Davidic Messiah and the Saviour Priest." Pages 93–110 in *Ideal Figures in Ancient Judaism: Profiles and Paradigms.* Edited by John J. Collins and George W. E. Nickelsburg. Missoula, Mont.: Scholars Press for the Society for Biblical Literature, 1980.

Hurowitz, Victor. "The Literary Structures in Samsuiluna A." *JCS* 36, no. 2 (1984): 191–205.

Irenaeus. *Ante-Nicene Fathers: Translations of the Writings of the Fathers Down to A.D. 325.* Vol 1, *Against Heresies.* Edited by Alexander Roberts and James Donaldson. Grand Rapids: Eerdmans, 1993.

Irvine, Stuart A. *Isaiah, Ahaz and the Syro-Ephraimitic Crisis.* Edited by David L. Peterson. SBLDS 123. Atlanta: Scholars Press, 1990.

Jacob, Edmond. *Theology of the Old Testament.* Translated by Arthur W. Heathecote and Philip J. Allcock. New York: Harper & Row, 1958.

Jahnow, H. *Das hebräische Leichenlied im Rahmen der Völkerdichtung.* BZAW 36. Giessen: A. Töpelmann, 1923.

Jamieson, Robert, A. R. Fausset, and David Brown. *Commentary On the Whole Bible.* Grand Rapids: Zondervan, 1945.

Janowski, Bernt. "Er trug unsere Sünden: Jesaja 53 und die Dramatik der Stellvertretung." *ZThK* 90 (1993): 1–24.

Jastrow, Marcus. *Dictionary of the Targum, Talmud Babylonian and Yerushalmi, and Midrashic Literature.* 2 vols. New York: Pardes, 1950.

Jellicoe, Sidney. *The Septuagint and Modern Study.* Oxford: Clarendon, 1968.

Jenkins, A. K. "Hezekiah's Fourteenth Year. A New Interpretation of 2 Kings Xviii:13–Xix:37." *VT* 26 (1976): 284–98.

Jenni, Ernst. *Theologisches Handworterbuch zum Alten Testament.* 2 vols. Munich: Chr. Kaiser. Zurich: Theologischer, 1971.

Jensen, Joseph. *Isaiah 1–39.* OTM 8. Wilmington, Del.: Michael Glazier, 1984.

—*The Use of Tôrâ by Isaiah: His Debate with the Wisdom Tradition.* CBQMS 3. Washington, D.C.: The Catholic Biblical Association of America, 1973.

Jeppesen, K. "Call and Frustration: A New Understanding of Isaiah Viii 21–22." *VT* 32 (1982): 145–57.

Jeremias, Joachim. *Abba: Studien zur Neutestamentlichen Theologie und Zeitgeschichte.* Göttingen: Vandenhoeck & Ruprecht, 1966.

Johansson, Nils. *Parakletoi, Vorstellungen von Fürsprechern für die Menschen vor Gott in der Alttestamentlichen Religion, im Spätjudentum und Urchristentum.* Lund: Gleerupska Universitetsbokhandeln, 1940.

Johnson, A. R. "The Rôle of the King in the Jerusalem Cultus." Pages 71–112 in *The Labyrinth: Further Studies in the Relation Between Myth and Ritual in the Ancient World.* Edited by S. H. Hooke. London: SPCK, 1935.

Jones, Douglas. *Isaiah 56–66 and Joel.* London: SCM Press, 1964.

Jones, Gwilym H. "Abraham and Cyrus: Type and Anti-Type." *VT* 22 (1972): 304–19.

Jones, William. "From Gilgamesh to Qohelet." Pages 349–79 in *The Bible in Light of Cuneiform Literature.* Edited by William Hallo et al. Lewiston, N.Y.: Edwin Mellen, 1990.

Jonge, Marinus de. *Jesus, the Servant Messiah.* New Haven: Yale University Press, 1991.

Jonge, Marinus de, and A. S. van der Woude. "11QMelchizedeq and the New Testament." *NTS* 12 (1966): 301–26.

Juel, Donald. *Messianic Exegesis: Christological Interpretation of the Old Testament in Early Christianity.* Philadelphia: Fortress, 1988.

Junker, H. "Ursprung und Grundzüge des Messiasbildes bei Isajas." Pages 181–96 in *Congress Volume: Strasbourg, 1956.* VTSup 4. Leiden: Brill, 1957.

Kaiser, Otto. *Isaiah 1–12: A Commentary.* Translated by J. Bowden. 1st ed. OTL. London: SCM Press, 1972.

—*Isaiah 1–12: A Commentary.* Translated by J. Bowden. 2d ed. OTL. London: SCM Press, 1983.

—*Der königliche Knecht: Eine traditionsgeschichtlich-exegetisch Studie über die Ebed-Jahweh-Lieder bei Deuterojesaja.* FRLANT 52. Göttingen: Vandenhoeck & Ruprecht, 1959.

Kaiser, Walter C. *The Messiah in the Old Testament.* Studies in Old Testament Theology. Grand Rapids: Zondervan, 1995.

—*Toward an Old Testament Theology.* Grand Rapids: Zondervan, 1978.

—"The Unfailing Kindnesses Promised to David: Isaiah 55:3." *JSOT* 45 (1989): 91–98.

Kaufmann, Yehezkel. *The Babylonian Captivity and Deutero-Isaiah.* New York: Union of American Hebrew Congregations, 1970. An abridged translation from his *Toledot ha-Emunah ha-Yisra'elit.* 4 vols. Jerusalem: Bialik Institute and the Devir Co., 1937–56.

—*The Religion of Israel from Its Beginnings to the Babylonian Exile.* London: George, Allen & Unwin, 1961.

Kee, Howard Clark. "Christology in Mark's Gospel." Pages 187–208 in Neusner, Green, and Frerichs, eds., *Judaisms and Their Messiahs.*

—"Testament of the Twelve Patriarchs: A New Translation and Introduction." *OTP* 1:775–828.

Keel, Othmar. *The Song of Songs*. Translated by Frederick J. Gaiser. Continental Commentaries. Minneapolis: Fortress, 1994.

Kellermann, Ulrich. *Messias und Gesetz. Grundlinien einer altestamentlichen Heilserwartung: Eine traditionsgeschichtliche Einführung.* BibS(N) 61. Neukirchen–Vluyn: Neukirchener, 1971.

Kennett, Robert H. *The Composition of the Book of Isaiah in the Light of History and Archaeology*. The Schweich Lectures 1909. London: Oxford University Press, 1910.

—"The Prophecy in Isaiah IX,1–7 (Heb. VIII,23–IX,6)." *JTS* 7 (1906): 321–42.

Kilian, Rudolf. *Die Verheissung Immanuels. Jes 7,14.* SBS 35. Stuttgart: Katholisches Bibelwerk, 1968.

Kissane, Edward J. *The Book of Isaiah. Translated from a Critically Revised Hebrew Text With Commentary*. 2 vols. Dublin: Browne & Nolan, 1960.

Kittel, Rudolf. "Cyrus und Deuterojesaja." *ZAW* 18 (1898): 149–64.

—*Geschichte des Volkes Israel*. Gotha: Friedrich Andreas Perthes, 1909.

Klein, Ralph W. *Israel in Exile: A Theological Interpretation*. OBT 6. Philadelphia: Fortress, 1979.

Kleinknecht, Karl Theodor. *Der leidende Gerechtfertigte: Die alttestamentlich-jüdische Tradition vom "leidenden gerechten" und ihre Rezeption bei Paulus*. WUNT 13. Tübingen: J. C. B. Mohr, 1984.

Knibb, Michael A. "The Interpretation of Damascus Document VII, 9b–VIII, 2a and XIX, 5b–14." *RevQ* 15 (1991–92): 243–51.

Knight, Douglas A., and Gene M. Tucker. *The Hebrew Bible and Its Modern Interpreters*. SBLCP. Philadelphia: Fortress. Chico, Calif.: Scholars Press, 1985.

Knight, George A. F. *Deutero-Isaiah: A Theological Commentary on Isaiah 40–55*. ITC. Grand Rapids: Eerdmans, 1965.

—*The New Israel: A Commentary on the Book of Isaiah 56–66*. Grand Rapids: Eerdmans, 1985.

—*Servant Theology: A Commentary on the Book of Isaiah 40–55*. Grand Rapids: Eerdmans, 1984.

Kobelski, Paul J. *Melchizedek and Malchiresha*. CBQMS 10. Washington, D.C.: The Catholic Biblical Association of America, 1981.

Koch, Klaus. "Messias und Sündenvergebung in Jesaja 53, Targum: Ein Beitrag zu der Praxis der aramäischen Bibelübersetzung." *JSJ* 3 (1972): 117–48.

—*The Prophets*. Translated by M. Kohl. 2 vols. London: SCM Press, 1982.

Koenen, K. "Textkritische Anmerkungen zu schwierigen Stellen im Tritojesajabuch." *Bib* 69 (1988): 564–73.

Koenig, Jean. *L'herméneutique analogique du Judaïsme antique d'après les témoins textuels d'Isaïe*. VTSup 33. Leiden: Brill, 1982.

Koet, B. J. "'Today this scripture has been fulfilled in your ears': Jesus' Explanation of Scripture." *Bijdragen* 47 (1986): 368–94.

Köhler, Ludwig. *Deuterojesaja Stilkritisch Untersucht*. BZAW 37. Giessen: Töpelmann, 1923.

—"Zum Verstandnis von Jes 7,14." *ZAW* 67 (1955): 48–50.

Köhler, Ludwig, and Walter Baumgartner, eds. *Lexicon in Veteris Testamenti Libros*. 2 vols. Leiden: Brill, 1958.

König, E. *Das Buch Jesaja*. Gütersloh: Bertelsmann, 1926.

Koole, Jan L. *Isaiah.* Part 3, *Isaiah 49–55.* HCOT 2. Leuven: Peeters, 1998.

Kraeling, E. G. "The Immanuel Prophecy." *JBL* 50 (1931): 277–97.

Kraetzschmar, Richard. *Das Buch Ezechiel.* Göttingen: Vandenhoeck & Ruprecht, 1900.

Kramer, Samuel Noah. "Lamentation Over the Destruction of Nippur." *ASJ* 13 (1991): 1–26. Reprinted from *ErIsr* 9 (1969): 89–93.

—*Lamentation Over the Destruction of Ur.* AS 12. Chicago: University of Chicago Press, 1940.

—"Sumerian Literature and the Bible." *AnBib* 12 (1959): 185–204.

—*Sumerian Mythology: A Study of Spiritual and Literary Achievement in the Third Millennium B.C.* Rev. ed. Philadelphia: University of Pennsylvania Press, 1972.

—*The Sumerians: Their History, Culture, and Character.* Chicago: University of Chicago Press, 1963.

Kramer, Samuel Noah, and John Maier. *Myths of Enki, the Crafty God.* Oxford: Oxford University Press, 1989.

Kraus, Hans-Joachim. *Die Königsherrschaft Gottes im Alten Testament. Untersuchungen zu den Liedern von Jahwes Thronbesteigung.* BHT 13. Tübingen: J. C. B. Mohr (Paul Siebeck), 1951.

—*Psalms 60–150.* A Continental Commentary. Translated by Hilton C. Oswald; Minneapolis: Fortress Press, 1993.

Kruse, H. "Alma Redemptoris Mater: Eine Auslegung der Immanuel Weissagung Is 7:14." *TTZ* 74 (1965): 15–36.

—"David's Covenant." *VT* 35 (1985): 139–64.

Kuenen, Abraham. *Historisch kritische Einleitung in die Bücher des Alten Testaments hinsichtlich ihrer Entstehung und Sammlung.* Vol. 2, *Die Prophetischen Bucher.* Leipzig: OR Reisland, 1892.

—*The Prophets and Prophecy in Israel: An Historical and Critical Enquiry.* Translated by A. Milroy. London: Longmans, Green & Co., 1877.

Kugel, James L. *The Idea of Biblical Poetry.* New Haven: Yale University Press, 1981.

Kuhl, Curt. *The Prophets of Israel.* Edinburgh: T. & T. Clark, 1960.

Kutsch, Ernst. *Sein Leiden und Tod—Unser Heil.* BibS(N) 52. Neukirchen–Vluyn: Neukirchener, 1967.

Kutscher, Edward Yechezkel. *The Language and Linguistic Background of the Isaiah Scroll (1QIsaᵃ).* Studies on the Texts of the Desert of Judah. Leiden: Brill, 1974.

Kutscher, Raphael. *Oh Angry Sea (a-ab-ba hu-luh-ha): The History of a Sumerian Congregation Lament.* YNER 6. New Haven: Yale University Press, 1975.

Laato, Antti. *"About Zion I Will Not Be Silent": The Book of Isaiah as an Ideological Unity.* ConBOT 44. Almqvist & Wiksell, 1998.

—*Josiah and David Redivivus: The Historical Josiah and the Messianic Expectations of Exilic and Postexilic Times.* Sweden: Almqvist & Wiksell International, 1992.

—*The Servant of YHWH and Cyrus: A Reinterpretation of the Exilic Messianic Programme in Isaiah 40–55.* ConBOT 35. Stockholm: Almqvist & Wiksell, 1992.

—*A Star is Rising: The Historical Development of the Old Testament Royal Ideology and the Rise of the Jewish Messianic Expectation.* University of South Florida International Studies in Formative Christianity and Judaism 5. Atlanta: Scholars Press, 1997.

—*Who is Immanuel? The Rise and the Foundering of Isaiah's Messianic Expectations.* Åbo Akademi Dissertation. Åbo: Åbo Akademi Press, 1988.

Lampe, Geoffrey W. H., and Kenneth J. Woollcombe. *Essays on Typology*. SBT 22. Naperville, Ill.: Allenson, 1957.

LaSor, William Stanford. *Handbook of Biblical Hebrew*. Grand Rapids: Eerdmans, 1978.

Lassalle, S. "Y-a-t-il dans Isaïe un cinquieme chant du serviteur?" *Bullétin Renan* 98 (1963): 3–4.

Lattey, C. "The Emmanuel Prophecy: Isa. 7:14." *CBQ* 8 (1946): 369–76.

Leeuw, V. van der. *De Ebed Jahweh-profetieen*. Assen: Van Gorcum, 1956.

Lescow, Theodor. "Das Geburtsmotiv in den messianischen Weissagungen bei Jesaja und Micha [Isa 7:14; 9:5,11; Mic 5:1–3]." *ZAW* 79 (1967): 172–207.

Levey, Samson H. *The Messiah: An Aramaic Interpretation; the Messianic Exegesis of the Targum*. HUCM 2. Cincinnati: Hebrew Union College/Jewish Institute of Religion, 1974.

Lim, T. H. "11QMelch, Luke 4 and the Dying Messiah." *JJS* 43 (1992): 90–92.

Lind, Millard. "Monotheism, Power, and Justice: A Study in Isaiah 40–55." *CBQ* 46 (1984): 432–46.

Lindblom, Johannes. *Die Ebed Jahwe-Orakel in der neuentdeckten Jesajahandschrift*. Berlin: A. Töpelmann, 1951.

—*Prophecy in Ancient Israel*. Oxford: Blackwell, 1962.

—*A Study on the Immanuel Section in Isaiah, Isa Vii:1–Ix:6*. Scripta Minora Regiae Societatis Humaniorum Litterarum Lundensis 4. Lund: C. W. K. Gleerup, 1957–58.

Lindhagen, C. *The Servant Motif in the Old Testament*. Uppsala: Almqvist & Wiksell, 1950.

Litwak, Kenneth D. "The Use of Quotations from Isaiah 52:13–53:12 in the New Testament." *JETS* 26 (1983): 385–94.

Lods, Adolphe. *Histoire de la littérature hébraïque et juive: Depuis les origines jusqu'à la ruine de l'état juif*. Paris: Payot, 1950.

—*Les Prophètes d'Israël et les débuts du judaïsme*. Paris: A. Michel, 1935.

Lohfink, Norbert. "Der 'Heilige Krieg' und der 'Bann' in der Bibel." *IKZ* 18 (1989): 104–12.

Lovering, Eugene H. Jr., ed. *Society of Biblical Literature Seminar Papers, 1992*. SBLSP 31. Atlanta: Scholars Press, 1992.

Lowth, William. *A Commentary Upon the Prophet Isaiah*. London: W. Taylor & H. Clements, 1714.

Lust, J. "Immanuel Figure: A Charismatic Judge-Leader [Is 7:10–17]." *ETL* 47, no. 3–4 (1971): 464–70.

Luther, Martin. *Lectures on Isaiah 40–66*. Edited by Hilton C. Oswald. Saint Louis, Miss.: Concordia, 1972.

MacDonald, John. " 't in Classical Hebrew: Some New Data on Its Use with the Nominative." *VT* 14 (1964): 264–75.

Manson, William. *Jesus, the Messiah: The Synoptic Tradition of the Revelation of God in Christ—With Special Reference to Form-Criticism*. London: Hodder & Stoughton, 1944.

Marcus, Joel. *The Way of the Lord: Christological Exegesis of the Old Testament in the Gospel of Mark*. Louisville, Ky.: Westminster John Knox, 1992.

Marmorstein, Arthur. "Zur Erklärung von Jes 53." *ZAW* 3 (1926): 260–65.

Marti, Karl. *Das Buch Jesaja*. KHC 18. Tübingen: J. C. B. Mohr (Paul Siebeck), 1900.

Martyr, Justin. "Dialogue with Trypho." Translated by G. Archambault. In *Œuvres Completes*, vol. 20. Paris: Migne, 1994.

Marx, Karl, and Friedrich Engels. *On Religion*. New York: Schocken, 1964.

Mason, Clarence E. *Prophetic Problems with Alternative Solutions*. Chicago: Moody, 1973.

Mauchline, John. *Isaiah 1–39: Introduction and Commentary*. TBC. London: SCM Press, 1962.

Mays, James Luther. ed. *Harper's Bible Commentary*. San Francisco: Harper & Row, 1988.

—, ed. *HarperCollins Bible Commentary*. San Francisco: Harper, 2000.

—"Isaiah's Royal Theology and the Messiah." Pages 39–51 in Seitz, ed., *Reading and Preaching the Book of Isaiah*.

—"The Place of the Torah Psalms in the Psalter." *JBL* 106 (1987): 3–12.

—"The Question of Context in Psalm Interpretation." Pages 14–20 in *Shape and Shaping of the Psalter*. Edited by J. C. McCann. JSOTSup 159. Sheffield: JSOT Press, 1993.

McBride, S. Dean. "Prophetic Vision and Mosaic Constitution." Pages 22–23 in Mays, ed., *Harper's Bible Commentary* (1988).

McFayden, John E. "The New View of the Servant of the Lord." *ExpTim* 34 (1922–23): 294–96.

McKane, W. "The Interpretation of Isaiah VII,14–25." *VT* 17 (1967): 208–19.

McKenzie, John L. *Second Isaiah*. AB 20. Garden City, N.Y.: Doubleday, 1968.

Meade, David G. *Pseudonymity and Canon*. WUNT 39. Tübingen: J. C. B. Mohr (Paul Siebeck), 1986.

Meinhold, J. *Studien zur israelitischen Religionsgeschichte*. Vol. 1, *Der heilige Rest*. Part 1, *Elias Amos Hosea Jesaja*. Bonn: A. Marcus & E. Weber, 1903.

Mendenhall, George E. *The Tenth Generation: The Origins of the Biblical Tradition*. Baltimore: The Johns Hopkins University Press, 1973.

Mettinger, T. N. D. *King and Messiah: The Civil and Sacral Legitimation of the Israelite Kings*. ConBOT 8. Lund: C. W. K. Gleerup, 1976.

Michel, D. "Zur Eigenart Tritojesajas." *ThViat* 10 (1965–66): 213–30.

Milik, J. T. "Milki-sedek et Milki-resa' dans les ancient écrits juifs et chrétiens." *JJS* 23 (1972): 97–99.

Millard, Matthias. *Die Komposition des Psalters: Ein formgeschichtlicher Ansatz*. Tübingen: J. C. B. Mohr, 1994.

Miller, J. M., and Hayes, J. H. *A History of Ancient Israel and Judah*. Philadelphia: Westminster, 1986.

Miller, Patrick D., Jr. "Luke 4:16–21." *Int* 29 (1975): 417–21.

Moody, D. "The Miraculous Conception." *RevExp* 51 (1954): 495–521.

Morgenstern, Julian. "Isaiah 61." *HUCA* 40 (1969): 109–21.

—"The Message of Deutero-Isaiah in Its Sequential Unfolding." *HUCA* 29 (1958): 1–67.

—"The Message of Deutero-Isaiah in Its Sequential Unfolding." *HUCA* 32 (1961): 169pp.

Motyer, J. Alec. *The Prophecy of Isaiah: An Introduction and Commentary*. Downers Grove, Ill.: Intervarsity, 1993.

Mowinckel, Sigmund. *He That Cometh*. Oxford: Blackwell, 1956.

—*Der Knecht Jahwäs*. Ausgegeben als Beiheft 2 zu Norsk Teologisk Tidsskrift. Giessen: A. Töpelmann, 1921.

—"Die Komposition des deuterojesajanischen Buches." *ZAW* 8 (1931): 87–112, 240–60.

—"Die Komposition des Jesajabuches Kap. 1–39." *AcOr* 11 (1933): 267–92.

—"Neuere Forschungen zu Deuterojesaja, Tritojesaja un dem Äbäd-Jahwä-Problem." *AcOr* 16 (1938): 1–40.

—*The Psalms in Israel's Worship.* Translated by D. R. Ap-Thomas. 2 vols. Oxford: Blackwell, 1951.

Muilenburg, James. *The Book of Isaiah.* Pages 381–773 in vol. 5 of *The Interpreter's Bible.* Edited by George Arthur Buttrick. 12 vols. Nashville: Abingdon, 1956.

Müller, Hans Peter. "Uns ist ein Kind geboren. Jes. 9.1–6 in traditionsgeschichtlicher Sicht." *EvTh* 21 (1961): 409–19.

—"Ein Vorschlag zu Jes 53:10f." *ZAW* 81, no. 3 (1969): 377–80.

Neusner, Jacob. *Messiah in Context.* Philadelphia: Fortress, 1984.

—"Mishnah and Messiah." Pages 265–82 in Neusner, Green, and Frerichs, eds., *Judaisms and Their Messiahs.*

Neusner, Jacob. *Messiah in Context.* Philadelphia: Fortress, 1984.

Neusner, Jacob, William Scott Green, and Ernest S. Frerichs, eds. *Judaisms and Their Messiahs at the Turn of the Christian Era.* Cambridge: Cambridge University Press, 1987.

Newman, Louis I. *Jewish Influence on Christian Reform Movements.* New York: Columbia University Press, 1925.

Nickelsburg, George. "Salvation Without or With a Messiah: Developing Beliefs in Writings Ascribed to Enoch." Pages 49–68 in Neusner, Green, and Frerichs, eds., *Judaisms and Their Messiahs.*

Nielsen, Kirsten. *There is Hope for a Tree: The Tree as Metaphor in Isaiah.* JSOTSup 65. Sheffield: JSOT Press, 1989.

Nikiprowetzky, Valentin. *Le troisième Sibylle.* Paris: La Haye, 1970.

Nolland, John. "Sib. Or. III.:265–94: An Early Maccabean Messianic Oracle." *JTS* 30 (1979): 158–66.

North, Christopher Richard. "The Former Things and the New Things in Deutero-Isaiah." Pages 111–26 in *Studies in Old Testament Prophecy: Presented to Professor Theodore H. Robinson by the Society for Old Testament Studies on His Sixty-Fifth Birthday, August 9, 1946.* Edited by H. H. Rowley. Edinburgh: T. & T. Clark, 1950.

—*The Second Isaiah.* Oxford: Oxford University Press, 1964.

—*The Suffering Servant in Deutero-Isaiah: An Historical and Critical Study.* 2d ed. London: Oxford University Press, 1956.

Nyberg, H. S. "Smärtornas Man: En Studie Till Jes. 52:13–53:12." *SEÅ* 7 (1942): 5–82.

O'Connor, Michael. *Hebrew Verse Structure.* 2d ed. Winona Lake, Ind.: Eisenbrauns, 1997.

Oegema, Gerbern S. *The Anointed and His People: Messianic Expectations from Maccabees to Bar Kochba.* JSPSup 27. Sheffield: Sheffield Academic Press, 1998.

Ogden, Graham. "Cyrus Song [Isaiah 44:24–45:13] and Moses: Some Implications for Mission." *South East Asia Journal of Theology* 18, no. 2 (1977): 41–45.

—"Moses and Cyrus: Literary Affinities Between the Priestly Presentation of Moses in Exodus Vi–Vii and the Cyrus Song in Isaiah Xliv 24–Xlv 13." *VT* 27 (1978): 195–203.

Olivier, J. P. *Contra Celsum.* Cambridge: Cambridge University Press, 1953.

—"The Day of Midian and Isaiah 9:3b." *JNSL* 9 (1981): 143–49.

Orelli, C. von. *The Old Testament Prophecy of the Consummation of God's Kingdom, Traced in Its Historical Development.* Translated by J. S. Banks. Edinburgh: T. & T. Clark, 1889.

Oswalt, John. *The Book of Isaiah 1–39.* NICOT. Grand Rapids: Eerdmans, 1986.

—*The Book of Isaiah: Chapters 40–66.* NICOT. Grand Rapids: Eerdmans, 1998.

O'Toole, Robert F. "Does Luke Also Portray Jesus as the Christ in Luke 4,16–30." *Bib* 76 (1995): 498–522.

Ottley, R. R., trans. and ed. *The Book of Isaiah According to the Septuagint (Codex Alexandrinus).* 2d ed. Cambridge: Cambridge University Press, 1909.

Patterson, Richard D. "A Virgin Shall Conceive [Isa 7:14; Treasures from the Text]." *Fundamentalist Journal* 4, no. 11 (Dec 1985): 64.

Paul, Shalom M. "Deutero-Isaiah and Cuneiform Royal Inscriptions." Pages 180–86 in *Essays in Memory of E. A. Speiser.* Edited by W. Hallo. New Haven: American Oriental Society, 1968.

Pauritsch, Karl. *Die neue Gemeinde: Gott sammelt Ausgestossene und Arme. Jesaia 56–66.* AnBib 47. Rome: Pontifical Biblical Institute, 1971.

Payne, David F. "The Servant of the Lord: Language and Interpretation." *EvQ* 42, no. 3 (1971): 131–43.

Payne Smith, R. *Thesaurus Syriacus.* Oxford: Clarendon, 1897.

Peake, Arthur S. *The Problem of Suffering in the Old Testament.* London: R. Bryant, 1904.

—*The Servant of Yahweh: Three Lectures Delivered at King's College, London.* Manchester: Manchester University Press, 1931.

Peckham, Brian. *History and Prophecy: The Development of Late Judean Literary Traditions.* ABRL. New York: Doubleday, 1993.

Pedersen, Johannes. *Israel: Its Life and Culture,* vols. 3–7. London: Oxford University Press, 1940.

Petersen, David L. *Late Israelite Prophecy: Studies in Deutero-Prophetic Literature and in Chronicles.* SBLMS 23. Missoula, Mont.: Scholars Press, 1977.

—*The Roles of Israel's Prophets.* JSOTSup 17. Sheffield: JSOT, 1981.

Pfeiffer, Robert H. *Introduction to the Old Testament.* New York: Harper & Brothers, 1948.

Phillips, Anthony. "The Servant Symbol of Divine Powerlessness." *ExpTim* 90 (1979): 370–74.

Pierce, F. X. "The Problem of the Servant in Is. 40–66." *Ecclesiastical Review* 92 (1935): 83–95.

Ploeg, J. S. van der. *Les chants du serviteur de Jahvé dans la seconde partie du livre d'Isaïe.* Paris: Gabalda, 1936.

Pomykala, Kenneth E. *The Davidic Dynasty Tradition in Early Judaism: Its History and Significance for Messianism.* SBLEJL 7. Atlanta: Scholars Press, 1995.

Porúbčan, Š. "The Word *'OT* in Isaiah 7,14." *CBQ* 22 (1960): 144–59.

Preuss, H. D. *Deuterojesaja. Eine Einführung in seine Botschaft.* BWANT. Stuttgart: Kohlhammer, 1971.

Procksch, Otto. *Jesaia: Übersetzt und erklärt.* KAT 9/1. Leipzig: A. Deichertsche Verlagsbuchhandlung D. Werner Scholl, 1930.

—*Theologie des Alten Testaments.* Gütersloh: Bertlesmann, 1950.

Puech, Emil. "La figure de Melkisedeq et la fin des demps (11QMelk—4Q180–181— 4QViscAmr—4QTestQah—4Q280—286–287)." Pages 515–62 in vol. 2 of *La croyance des Esséniens en la vie future : immortalité, résurrection, vie éternelle? : histoire d'une croyance dans le judaïsme ancien.* Paris: Gabalda, 1993.

—"Fragments d'une apocryphe de Lévi et le personnage eschatologique. 4QTestLévi (c–d) (?) et 4QAJa." Pages 449–501 in *The Madrid Qumran Congress*. Edited by J. Trebolle Barrera and L. Vegas Montaner. Leiden: Brill, 1992.

—"Notes sur le manuscrit de XIQMelkîsêdeq." *RevQ* 12 (1987): 483–513.

Rad, G. von. *The Message of the Prophets*. London: SCM Press, 1968.

—*Old Testament Theology*. Translated by D. M. G. Stalker. London: SCM Press, 1975.

—"The Royal Ritual in Judah." Translated by E. W. Trueman Dicken. Pages 222–31 in *The Problem of the Hexateuch and Other Essays*. London: Oliver & Boyd, 1966. Reprint from *ThL* 72 (1947): 211–16.

Rehm, Martin. *Der königliche Messias im Licht der Immanuel-Weissagungen des Buches Jesajas*. Eichstöter Studien n.s. 1. Kevelaer: Butzon & Bercker, 1968.

Reicke, Bo. "The Knowledge of the Suffering Servant." Pages 186–92 in *Das Ferne und Nahe Wort: Festschrift L. Rost*. Edited by F. Maas. BZAW 105. Berlin: Töpelmann, 1967.

Reiterer, Friedrich V. *Gerechtigkeit als Heil:* צדק *bei Deuterojesaja. Aussage und Vergleich mit der alttestamentlichen Tradition*. Graz: Akadem. Druck- u. Verlagsanst, 1976.

Renard, H. "Le messianisme dans la premiere partie du livre d'Isaïe." *SP* 1 (1959): 398–407.

Rendtorff, Rolf. *Canon and Theology*. Translated by Margaret Kohl. OBT. Minneapolis: Fortress, 1993.

—"Jesaja 6 im Rahmen der Komposition des Jesajabuches." Pages 73–82 in Vermeylen, ed., *Le livre d'Isaïe*.

—"Zur Komposition des Buches Jesaja." *VT* 34 (1984): 295–320.

—*The Old Testament: An Introduction*. Translated by J. Bowden. London: SCM Press, 1985.

Renker, Alwin. *Propheten—das Gewissen Israels*. Freiburg: Herder, 1990.

Ridderbos, Jan. *Isaiah*. Translated by John Vriend. Bible Student's Commentary. Grand Rapids: Zondervan, 1985.

Riesenfeld, Harald. *Jésus transfiguré: L'arrière-plan du récit évangélique de la transfiguration de notre-seigneur*. Acta Seminarii Neotestamentici Upsaliensis 16. Copenhagen: Ejnar Munksgaard, 1947.

Rignell, Lars G. "Isaiah Chapter I." *ST* 11 (1957): 140–58.

—"A Study of Isaiah 9:2–7." *LQ* 7 (1955): 31–35.

Ringgren, Helmer. *The Messiah in the Old Testament*. SBT 18. London: SCM Press, 1961.

Roberts, J. J. M. "The Old Testament's Contribution to Messianic Expectations." Pages 39 51 in Charlesworth, ed., *The Messiah*.

Robinson, H. Wheeler. *Corporate Personality in Ancient Israel*. Facet Books. Biblical Series. Philadelphia: Fortress, 1967.

—*The Cross in the Old Testament*. London: SCM Press, 1955.

—*Inspiration and Revelation in the Old Testament*. Oxford: Clarendon, 1946.

—*Suffering, Human and Divine*. Great Issues of Life Series. New York: Macmillan, 1939.

Robinson, Robert. *Roman Catholic Exegesis Since Divino Afflante Spiritu: Hermeneutical Implications*. SBLDS 111. Atlanta: Scholars Press, 1988.

Robinson, Theodore H. "Notes on the Text and Interpretation of Isaiah 53:3, 11." *ExpTim* 72 (1959): 383.

Rodgers, Margaret. "Luke 4:16–30: A Call for a Jubilee Year." *RTR* 40 (1981): 72–82.

Rogers, Robert William. *Cuneiform Parallels to the Old Testament*. New York: Eaton & Mains, 1912.

Rosenberg, Roy A. "The Slain Messiah in the Old Testament." *ZAW* 99 (1987): 259–61.

Roth, Wolfgang. *Isaiah*. Edited by John H. Hayes. Knox Preaching Guides. Atlanta: John Knox, 1988.

Rothstein, J. Wilhelm. *Die Genealogie des Königs Jojachin und seiner Nachkommen (1 Chron. 3, 17–24) in geschichtlicher Beleuchtung: Eine kritische Studie zur jüdischen Geschichte und Litteratur*. Berlin: Reuther & Reichard, 1902.

Rowley, H. H. *The Biblical Doctrine of Election*. London: Lutterworth, 1950.

——"Hezekiah's Reform and Rebellion." *BJRL* 44 (1961–62): 395–431.

——*The Servant of the Lord and Other Essays on the Old Testament*. London: Lutterworth, 1952.

Rubinstein, A. "Isaiah LII, 14–Mišhpat—and the DSIa Variant." *Bib* 35 (1954): 475–79.

Ruppert, Lothar. "'Mein Knecht, der gerecht, macht die Vielen gerecht und ihre Verschuldungen—er trägt sie' (Jes 53,11): Universales Heil durch das stellvertretende Strafleiden des Gottesknechtes?" *BZ* 40 (1996): 1–17.

Russell, D. S. *The Method & Message of Jewish Apocalyptic*. OTL. Westminster: Philadelphia, 1964.

Sanders, James A. *Canon and Community: A Guide to Canonical Criticism*. Old Testament Series. Philadelphia: Fortress, 1984.

——"From Isaiah 61 to Luke 4." Pages 75–106 in *Christianity, Judaism and Other Greco-Roman Cults*. Edited by J. Neusner. SJLA 12. Leiden: Brill, 1975.

——*From Sacred Story to Sacred Text: Canon as Paradigm*. Philadelphia: Fortress, 1987.

——"Hermeneutics in True and False Prophecy." Pages 20–41 in *Canon and Authority: Essays in Old Testament Religion and Theology*. Edited by G. W. Coats and Burt O. Long. Philadelphia: Fortress, 1977.

Satterthwaite, Philip E., Richard S. Hess, and Gordon J. Wenham, eds. *The Lord's Anointed: Interpretation of Old Testament Messianic Texts*. Carlisle: Paternoster, 1995.

Sawyer, John F. A. *The Fifth Gospel: Isaiah in the History of Christianity*. Cambridge: Cambridge University Press, 1996.

——*Prophecy and the Biblical Prophets*. Rev ed. Oxford Bible Series. Oxford: Oxford University Press, 1993.

Saydon, P. P. "The Meanings and Uses of the Particle *'et*." *VT* 14 (1964): 192–210.

Schäfer, Peter. "Die messianischen Hoffnungen des rabbinischen Judentums zwischen Naherwartung und religiösem Pragmatismus." Pages 95–125 in *Zukunft in der Gegenwart: Wegweisungen in Judentum und Christentum*. Bern: Herbert Lang, 1976.

Scharbert, Josef. *Heilsmittler im Alten Testament und im Alten Orient*. Freiburg: Herder, 1964.

Schelhaas, Jan. *De lijdende knecht des Heeren. Het Ebed-Jahwe-probleem*. Groningen: Wever, 1933.

Schibler, Daniel. "Messianism and Messianic Prophecy in Isaiah 1–12 and 28–33." Pages 87–104 in Satterthwaite, Hess, and Wenham, eds., *The Lord's Anointed*.

Schiffman, Lawrence H. *From Text to Tradition*. Hoboken, N.J.: Ktav, 1991.

Schmidt, H. *Eucharistérion: Studien zur Religion und Literatur des Alten und Neuen Testaments: Hermann Gunkel zum 60. Geburtstage dem 23. Mai*. FRLANT 36. Göttingen: Vandenhoeck & Ruprecht, 1923.

Schmitt, J. "L'oracle d'Is. LXI 1 ss. et sa relecture par Jésus." *RSR* 54 (1980): 97–108.

Schneider, Gerhard. *Das Evangelium des Lukas*. Gütersloh: Gütersloher Verlagshaus Mohn, 1977.

Schoeps, Hans Joachim. *Aus frühchristlicher Zeit, religionsgeschichtliche Untersuchungen*. Tübingen: Mohr, 1950.

Schoors, Antoon. *I Am God Your Saviour*. VTSup 24. Leiden: Brill, 1973.

Schultz, Richard. "The King in the Book of Isaiah." Pages 141–65 in Satterthwaite, Hess, and Wenham, eds., *The Lord's Anointed*.

Schulz, Siegfried. *Q-Die Spruchquelle der Evangelisten*. Zurich: Theologischer Verlag, 1972.

Schürer, Emil. "The Qumran Messiahs and Messianism." Translated by T. A. Burkill. Pages 550–54 in vol. 2 of Vermes and Millar, eds., *The History of the Jewish People in the Age of Jesus Christ*.

Schürmann, Heinz. *Das Lukasevangelium I*. Freiburg: Herder, 1969.

Schwartz, D. R. "On Quirinius, John the Baptist, the Benedictus, Melchisedek, Qumran and Ephesus." *RevQ* 13 (1988): 635–46.

Schwarz, Gunther. "'...sieht er...wird er satt': Eine Emendation [Jes 53:11]." *ZAW* 84 (1972): 356–58.

Schweizer, Eduard. *The Good News According to Matthew*. Translated by David E. Green. Atlanta: John Knox, 1975.

Scott, R. B. Y. *The Book of Isaiah: Introduction and Exegesis, Chapters 1–39*. Pages 151–381 in vol. 5 of *The Interpreter's Bible*. Edited by George Arthur Buttrick. Nashville: Abingdon, 1956.

Scullion, John J. "Approach to the Understanding of Isaiah 7:10–17." *JBL* 87 (1968): 288–300.

Seeligmann, I. L. "Deixai Autō Phōs." *Tarbiz* 27 (1957): 127–41.

—*The Septuagint Version of Isaiah: A Discussion of Its Problems*. Mededelingen en Verhandelingen 9. Leiden: Brill, 1948.

Seitz, Christopher R. "How is the Prophet Isaiah Present in the Latter Half of the Book? The Logic of Chapters 40–66 Within the Book of Isaiah." *JBL* 115 (1996): 219–40.

—*Isaiah 1–39*. Interpretation 31/1. Louisville, Ky.: John Knox, 1993.

—ed., *Reading and Preaching the Book of Isaiah*. Philadelphia: Fortress, 1988.

—*Zion's Final Destiny*. Minneapolis: Fortress, 1991.

Sekine, Seizo. *Die tritojesajanische Sammlung (Jes 56–66) redactiongeschichtlich untersuch*. BZAW 175. Berlin: de Gruyter, 1989.

Sellin, Ernst. *Das Rätsel des deuterojesajanischen Buches*. Leipzig: A. Deichert'sche verlagsbuchhandlung nachf [G. Böhme], 1908.

—*Serubbabel, ein Beitrag zur Geschichte der messianischen Erwartung und der Entstehung des Jedentums*. Leipzig: A. Deichert, 1898.

Selman, Martin J. "Messianic Mysteries." Pages 281–302 in Satterthwaite, Hess, and Wenham, eds., *The Lord's Anointed*.

Seow, Choon-Leong. *A Grammar for Biblical Hebrew*. Rev ed. Nashville: Abingdon, 1995.

Seybold, K. *Das davidische Königtum im Zeugnis der Propheten*. FRLANT 107. Göttingen: Vandenhoeck & Ruprecht, 1972.

Sheppard, Gerald T. "The Anti-Assyrian Redaction and the Canonical Context of Isaiah 1–39." *JBL* 104 (1985): 193–216.

—"Biblical Wisdom Literature at the End of the Modern Age." Pages 369–98 in *Congress Volume, Oslo 1998*. Edited by A Lemaire and M. Sæbø. Leiden: Brill, 2000.

—"The Book of Isaiah as a Human Witness to Revelation Within the Religions of Judaism and Christianity." Pages 274–80 in *SBL Seminar Papers, 1993*. Edited by Eugene H. Lovering, Jr. SBLSP 32. Atlanta: Scholars Press, 1993.

—"The Book of Isaiah as a Human Witness to Revelation Within the Religions of Judaism and Christianity." Pages 274–80 in *SBL Seminar Papers, 1995*. Edited by Eugene H. Lovering, Jr. SBLSP 34. Atlanta: Scholars Press, 1995.

—"The Book of Isaiah: Competing Structures According to a Late Modern Description of Its Shape and Scope." Pages 549–81 in Lovering, ed., *SBL Seminar Papers, 1992*.

—"Canon Criticism." *ABD* 1:861–66.

—"Childs, Brevard." Pages 575–84 in *Historical Handbook of Major Biblical Interpreters*. Edited by Donald McKim. Downers Grove, Ill.: InterVarsity, 1998.

—"Commentary on Isaiah." Pages 489–537 in Mays, ed., *HarperCollins Bible Commentary* (2000).

—*The Future of the Bible: Beyond Liberalism and Literalism*. Toronto: The United Church of Canada, 1990.

—"Isaiah 1–39." Pages 542–70 in Mays, ed., *Harper's Bible Commentary* (1988).

—"Isaiah 40–66." Pages 489–537 in Mays, ed., *HarperCollins Bible Commentary* (2000).

—"Issues in Contemporary Translation: Late Modern Vantages and Lessons from Past Epochs." Pages 257–85 in *On the Way to Nineveh: Studies in Honour of George M. Landes*. Edited by Steven L. Cook and S. C. Winter. Atlanta: ASOR/Scholars Press, 1999.

—"Pre-modern Criticism in the English Protestant Translations of the Psalms During the 17th Century." Pages 274–80 in *SBL Seminar Papers, 1994*. Edited by Eugene H. Lovering, Jr. SBLSP 33. Atlanta: Scholars Press, 1994.

—"The Role of the Canonical Context in the Interpretation of the Solomonic Books." Pages 67–107 in *William Perkins' A Commentary on Galatians (1617), with Introductory Essays*. Edited by G. T. Sheppard. Cleveland, Ohio: Pilgrim, 1989.

—"The Scope of Isaiah as a Book of Jewish and Christian Scriptures." Pages 257–81 in *New Visions of Isaiah*. Edited by R Melugin and M. Sweeney. JSOTSup 214. Sheffield: Sheffield Academic Press, 1996.

—"True and False Prophecy Within Scriptures." Pages 262–84 in Tucker, Petersen, and Wilson, eds., *Canon, Theology, and Old Testament Interpretation*.

—"Two Turbulent Decades of Isaiah Research." *TST* 9, no. 1 (1993): 107–16.

—*Wisdom as a Hermeneutical Construct: A Study in the Sapientializing of the Old Testament*. BZAW 151. Berlin: de Gruyter, 1980.

Simcox, C. E. "The Role of Cyrus in Deutero-Isaiah." *JAOS* 57 (1937): 158–71.

Skinner, J. *Isaiah Chapters I–XXXIX*. The Cambridge Bible for Schools and Colleges. Cambridge: Cambridge University Press, 1896.

—*Isaiah Chapters XL–LXVI*. The Cambridge Bible for Schools and Colleges. Cambridge: Cambridge University Press, 1922.

Slotki, I. W. *Isaiah: Hebrew Text and Hebrew Translation with an Introduction and Commentary*. 4th ed. Soncino Books of the Bible. London: Soncino, 1961.

Smart, James D. *History and Theology in Second Isaiah: A Commentary on Isaiah 35, 40–66*. Philadelphia: Westminster, 1965.

—"A New Approach to the 'Ebed-Yahweh Problem." *ExpTim* 45 (1933–34): 168–72.

Smelik, Klass A. D. "Distortions of Old Testament Prophecy: The Purpose of Isaiah Xxxvi–Xxxvii." *OtSt* 24 (1989): 70–93.

Smith, G. Adam. *The Book of Isaiah*. Rev. ed. 2 vols. The Expositor's Bible. London: Hodder & Stoughton, 1927.

Smith, Morton. "II Isaiah and the Persians." *JAOS* 83 (1963): 415–21.

Smith, P. A. *Rhetoric and Redaction in Trito Isaiah: The Structure, Growth and Authorship of Isaiah 56–66*. VTSup 62. Leiden: Brill, 1995.

Smith, Wilfred Cantwell. *What is Scripture? A Comparative Approach*. Minneapolis: Fortress, 1993.

Snaith, Norman H. *The Distinctive Ideas of the Old Testament*. New York: Schocken, 1973.

Soggin, J. Alberto. "Tod und Auferstehung des leidenden Gottesknechtes: Jes. 53:8–13." *ZAW* 87 (1975): 346–55.

Sommer, Benjamin. *A Prophet Reads Scripture: Allusions in Isaiah 40–66*. Stanford: Stanford University Press, 1998.

—"Scroll of Isaiah as Jewish Scripture, Or, Why Jews Don't Read Books." Pages 225–42 in *SBL Seminar Papers, 1996*. SBLSP 35. Atlanta: Scholars Press, 1996.

Sonne, I. "Isaiah 53:10–12." *JBL* 78 (1959): 335–42.

Spykerboer, Hendrik Carel. *The Structure and Composition of Deutero-Isaiah*. Meppel: Krips Repro BV, 1976.

Staerk, Willy, and Otto Alexander. *Die Ebed Jahwe-Lieder in Jesaja 40ff.: Ein Beitrag zur Deuterojesaja-Kritik*. Leipzig: J. C. Hinrichs, 1913.

Stamm, Johann Jakob. "La prophétie d'Emmanuel." *Revue de Theologie et de Philosophie* 32 (1944): 97–123.

Starcky, Jean. "Les quatres étapes du messianisme à Qumran." *RB* 70 (1963): 481–505.

Steck, Odil Hannes. "Aspekte des Gottesknechts in Jes. 52,13–53:12." *ZAW* 97 (1985): 36–58.

—*Friedenvorstellungen im Alten Jerusalem. Psalmen, Jesaja, Deuterojesaja*. ThSt 111. Zurich: Theologisches Verlag, 1972.

—*Studien zu Tritojesaja*. BZAW. Berlin: de Gruyter, 1991.

—"Tritojesaja im Jesajabuch." Pages 361–406 in Vermeylen, ed., *Le livre d'Isaïe*.

Steinmann, Jean. *Le livre de la consolation d'Israël et les Prophètes du Retour de l'exil*. LD 28. Paris: Cerf, 1960.

Stendahl, Krister. *The School of St. Matthew and Its Use of the Old Testament*. Philadelphia: Fortress, 1968.

Stenning, J. F., ed. *The Targum of Isaiah*. Oxford: Clarendon, 1949.

Stolz, Fritz. "Die Bäumes des Gottesgartens auf dem Libanon." *ZAW* 84 (1972): 141–56.

Stronstad, Roger. *The Charismatic Theology of St. Luke*. Peabody, Mass.: Hendrickson, 1984.

Stuart, D. K. *Studies in Early Hebrew Meter*. HSM 13. Missoula, Mont.: Scholars Press, 1976.

Stuhlmueller, Carroll. "The Theology of Creation in Second Isaiah." *CBQ* 21 (1959): 447–51.

—"Deutero-Isaiah: Major Transitions in the Prophet's Theology and in Contemporary Scholarship." *CBQ* 42 (1980): 1–29.

Stummer, Friedrich. "Einige keilschriftliche Parallelen zu Jes. 40–66." *JBL* 45 (1926): 171–89.

Sweeney, Marvin. *Isaiah 1–39 with an Introduction to Prophetic Literature*. FOTL 16. Grand Rapids: Eerdmans, 1996.

——"On Multiple Settings." Pages 267–73 in Lovering, ed., *SBL Seminar Papers, 1992*.

Swete, Henry Barclay. *An Introduction to the Old Testament in Greek*. Cambridge: Cambridge University Press, 1914.

Syrén, Roger. "Targum Isaiah 52:13–53:12 and Christian Interpretation." *JJS* 40 (1989): 201–12.

Tadmor, Hayim. "The Campaigns of Sargon II of Assur." *JCS* 12 (1958): 22–40, 77–100.

Talmon, Shemaryahu. "The Concept of Mashiah and Messianism in Early Judaism." Pages 79–115 in Charlesworth, ed., *The Messiah*.

——"Typen der Messiaserwartung um die Zeitenwende." Pages 571–88 in Wolff, ed., *Probleme Biblischer Theologie*.

——"Waiting for the Messiah: The Spiritual Universe of the Qumran Covenanters." Pages 111–37 in Neusner, Green, and Frerichs, eds., *Judaisms and Their Messiahs*.

Tate, M. "King and Messiah in Isaiah of Jerusalem." *RevExp* 65, no. 4 (1968): 409–21.

Thomas, D. Winton. "A Consideration of Isaiah LIII in the Light of Recent Textual and Philological Study." Pages 122–25 in *De Mari à Qumrân: Festschrift J. Coppens*. BETL 24. Glembloux: Duculot, 1969.

Thompson, Michael E.W. "Isaiah's Sign of Immauel [Isa 7:10–17]." *ExpTim* 95 (1983): 67–71.

Thurén, J. "Lukas evangeliets Cantica im Krytans Bruk." Pages 175–93 in *Academia et Ecclesia: Studia in Honorem Frederic Cleve*. Åbo: Åbo Akademis Förlag, 1991.

Tigay, Jeffrey H. *The Evolution of Gilgamesh Epic*. Philadelphia: University of Pennsylvania Press, 1982.

Torrey, Charles C. "Isaiah 41." *HTR* 44 (1951): 121–36.

—*Second Isaiah: A New Interpretation*. New York: Charles Scribner's Sons, 1928.

Tournay, Raymond J. "2d Isaiah: [Review]." *RB* 72 (1965): 129–30.

——"Les chants du serviteur dans la seconde partie d'Isaïe." *RB* 59 (1952): 355–84, 481–512.

Tov, Emanuel. *Textual Criticism of the Hebrew Bible*. Minneapolis: Fortress, 1992.

Townsend, John T., ed. and trans. *Midrash Tanhuma (S. Buber Recension)*. Hoboken, N.J.: Ktav, 1989.

Treves, M. "Little Prince Pele-Joez." *VT* 17 (1967): 464–77.

—"Isaiah 53." *VT* 24 (1974): 98–108.

Trobisch, David. *Die Endredaktion des Neuen Testaments: Eine Untersuchung zur Entstehung der christlichen Bibel*. Freiburg, Schweiz: Universitätsverlag. Göttingen: Vandenhoeck & Ruprecht, 1996.

—*Die Entstehung der Paulusbriefsammlung*. NTOA 10. Freiburg, Schweiz: Universitätsverlag. Göttingen: Vandenhoeck & Ruprecht, 1989.

Tucker, Gene M., David L. Petersen, and Robert R. Wilson, eds. *Canon, Theology, and Old Testament Interpretation: Essays in Honor of Brevard S. Childs*. Philadelphia: Fortress, 1988.

Tull Willey, Patricia. *Remember the Former Things: The Recollection of Previous Texts in Second Isaiah*. SBLDS 161. Atlanta: Scholars Press, 1996.

Vanstiphout, Herman L. J. "The Death of an Era: The Great Mortality in Sumerian City Lament." Pages 83–89 in *Death in Mesopotamia*. Copenhagen: Akademisk, 1980.

Vermes, Geza. *Jesus the Jew: A Historian's Reading of the Gospels*. London: William Collins Sons & Co., 1973.

—"The Oxford Forum for Qumran Research Seminar on the Rule of War from Cave 4." *JJS* 43 (1992): 85–90.

Vermes, Geza, and Fergus Millar, eds. *The History of the Jewish People in the Age of Jesus Christ*. 3 vols. in 4. Edinburgh: T. & T. Clark, 1973–87.

Vermeylen, Jacques, ed. *Le livre d'Isaïe: Les oracles et leurs relecteurs. Unité et complexité de l'ouvrage*. Louvain: Leuven University Press, 1989.

—*Du prophète Isaïe à l'apocalyptique, Isaïe I–XXXV*, vol. 1. Ebib. Paris: Librairie Lecoffre, 1977.

Vischer, Wilhelm. *Die Immanuel-Botschaft im Rahmen des königlichen Zionsfestes*. ThSt 45. Zurich: Zollikon, 1955.

Vollmer, Jochen. *Geschichtliche Ruckblicke und Motive in der Prophetie des Amos, Hosea und Jesaja*. BZAW 119. Berlin: de Gruyter, 1971.

—"Zur Sprache von Jesaja 9,1–6." *ZAW* 80 (1968): 343–50.

Volz, P. *Isaiah II*. Leipzig: A. Deichert'sche Verlagsbuchhandlung D. Werner Scholl, 1932.

—"Jesaja 53." Pages 181–90 in *Beitrage zur alttestamentlichen Wissenschaft Karl Budde zum siebzigsten Geburtstag am 13. April 1920*. Edited by Karl Marti. Giessen: A. Töpelmann, 1920.

—*Die vorexilische Jahweprophetie und der Messias: In ihrem Verhältnis dargestellt*. Göttingen: Vandenhoeck & Ruprecht, 1897.

Vriezen, Theodoro. "Essentials of the Theology of Isaiah." Pages 128–46 in Anderson and Harrelson, eds., *Israel's Prophetic Heritage*.

Wade, G. W. *The Book of the Prophet Isaiah*. London: Methuen, 1911.

—*The Book of the Prophet Isaiah: With Introduction and Notes*. 2d ed. Westminster Commentaries. London: Methuen, 1929.

Waldman, Nahum M. "A Biblical Echo of Mesopotamian Royal Rhetoric." Page 449 in *Essays on the Occasion of the Seventieth Anniversary of Dropsie University*. Edited by Abraham Isaac Katsch and Leon Nemoy. Philadelphia: Dropsie University Press, 1979.

Waldow, H. E. von. "Analass Hintergrund der Verkuendigung des Deuterojesaja." Ph.D diss., University of Bonn, 1953.

Waltke, Bruce K., and Michael O'Connor. *An Introduction to Biblical Hebrew Syntax*. Winona Lake, Ind.: Eisenbrauns, 1990.

Waterman, L. "The Martyred Servant Motif of Is. 53." *JBL* 56 (1937): 27–34.

Watson, W. G. E. *Classical Hebrew Poetry: A Guide to Its Techniques*. 2d ed. JSOTSup 26. Sheffield: JSOT Press, 1986.

Watts, John D. W. "The Formation of Isaiah 1: Its Context in Chapters 1–4." Pages 109–19 in *SBL Seminar Papers, 1978*. Edited by Paul Achtemeier. SBLSP 13/14. Missoula, Mont.: Scholars Press, 1978.

—*Isaiah 1–33*. Edited by David Hubbard and Glenn W. Barker. WBC 24. Waco, Tex.: Word, 1985.

—*Isaiah 34–66*. Edited by David Hubbard and Barker W. Glenn. WBC 25. Waco, Tex.: Word, 1987.

Watts, Rikki E. "Consolation or Confrontation: Isaiah 40–55 and the Delay of the New Exodus." *TynBul* 41 (1990): 31–59.

Webb, Barry G. *The Message of Isaiah*. The Bible Speaks Today. Downers Grove, Ill.: InterVarsity, 1997.

Wegner, Paul. *An Examination of Kingship and Messianic Expectation in Isaiah 1–35.* Lewiston, N.Y.: Edwin Mellen, 1992.

—"A Re-Examination of Isaiah IX 1–6." *VT* 42 (1992b): 103–12.

Werblowsky, R. "Messianism: Jewish Messianism." Pages 472–77 in Vol. 9 of *The Encyclopedia of Religion.* Edited by M. Eliade. New York: MacMillan, 1987.

Werner, Wolfgang. *Eschatologische Texte in Jesaja 1–39: Messias, Heiliger Rest, Völker.* FB 46. Würzburg: Echter, 1982.

Westermann, Claus. *Isaiah 40–66.* Translated by David M. G. Stalker. OTL. Philadelphia: Westminster, 1969.

—*Prophetic Oracles of Salvation in the Old Testament.* Translated by Keith Crim. Louisville, Ky.: Westminster John Knox, 1991.

White, J. B. "Universalization of History in Deutero-Isaiah." Page 180 in *Scripture in Context.* Edited by Carl D. Evans. Pittsburgh: Pickwick, 1980.

Whitehouse, Owen C. *Isaiah I–XXXIX.* 2 vols. The Century Bible. London: Thomas Nelson & Sons, 1905.

—*Isaiah: Introduction.* The Century Bible. Edinburgh: T. C. & E. C. Jack, 1912–13.

Whitley, Charles F. "The Language and Exegesis of Isaiah 8,16–23." *ZAW* 90 (1978): 28–43.

Whybray, Norman. *Isaiah 40–66.* The New Century Bible Commentary. Grand Rapids: Eerdmans, 1975.

—*Thanksgiving for a Liberated Prophet: An Interpretation of Isaiah Chapter 53.* JSOTSup 4. Sheffield: JSOT Press, 1978.

Widengren, G. *Sakrales Königtum im Alten Testament und im Judentum.* Stuttgart: Kohlhammer, 1955.

Widyapranawa, S. H. *The Lord is Savior: Faith in National Crisis; A Commentary on the Book of Isaiah 1–39.* ITC. Grand Rapids: Eerdmans, 1990.

Wilcox, Peter, and David Patton-Williams. "The Servant Songs in Deutero Isaiah." *JSOT* 42 (1988): 79–102.

Wildberger, Hans. *Isaiah 1–12: A Commentary.* Translated by Thomas H. Trapp. Continental Commentaries. Minneapolis: Fortress, 1991.

—*Jesaja 1–12.* 3 vols. BKAT 10. Neukirchen-Vluyn: Neukirchener, 1980.

Williams, Ronald. *Hebrew Syntax.* Toronto: University of Toronto Press, 1988.

Williams, Sam K. *Jesus' Death as a Saving Event.* Missoula, Mont.: Scholars Press, 1975.

Williamson, H. G. M. *The Book Called Isaiah: Deutero-Isaiah's Role in Composition and Redaction.* Oxford: Clarendon, 1994.

—"*Da'at* in Isaiah LIII,11." *VT* 28 (1978): 118–22.

—*Variations on a Theme: King, Messiah and Servant in the Book of Isaiah.* The Didsbury Lectures 1997. Carlisle: Paternoster, 1998.

Willis, J. T. *Isaiah.* The Living Word Commentary on the Old Testament. Austin, Tex: Sweet, 1980.

Wilshire, Leland E. "Jerusalem as the 'Servant City' in Isaiah 40–66." Pages 231–55 in *The Bible in the Light of Cuneiform Literature.* Edited by William W. Hallo, B. W. Jones and G. L. Mattingly. Lewiston, N.Y.: Edwin Mellen, 1990.

—"The Servant City: A New Interpretation of the 'Servant of the Lord' in the Servant Songs of Deutero-Isaiah." *JBL* 94 (1975): 356–67.

Wilson, Robert R. *Prophecy and Society in Ancient Israel.* Philadelphia: Fortress, 1984.

Wolff, Hans Walter. ed., *Probleme Biblischer Theologie. Gerhard von Rad zum 70. Geburtstag.* Munich: Chr. Kaiser, 1971.

—*Jesaja 53 im Urchristentum.* Berlin: Evangelische, 1952.

Workman, George Coulson. *The Servant of Jehovah.* New York: Longmans, Green & Co., 1907.

Würthwein, Ernst. "Jes. 7,1–9. Ein Beitrag zu dem Thema: Prophetie und Politik." Pages 47–63 in *Theologie als Glaubenswagnis. Festschrift für Karl Heim zum 80. Geburtstag.* Hamburg: Furche-Verlag, 1954.

Young, Edward J. *The Book of Isaiah: The English Text with Introduction: Exposition, and Notes.* Vol. 3, *Chapters 40 through 66.* NICOT. Grand Rapids: Eerdmans, 1972.

—"The Immanuel Prophecy: Isaiah 7:14–16." *WTJ* 15–16 (1953): 97–124, 23–50.

—"The Interpretation of *yzh* in Isaiah 52:15." *WTJ* 3 (1941): 125–32.

—"Of Whom Speaketh the Prophet [Acts 8:26ff; Isa 42:1–4; 49:1–6; 52:13–53:12]." *WTJ* 11 (May 1949): 135–55.

—"The Origin of the Suffering Servant Idea." *WTJ* 13 (1950): 19–33.

Young, Frances. *Virtuoso Theology: The Bible and Interpretation.* Cleveland, Ohio: Pilgrim, 1993.

Ziegler, Joseph J., ed. *Septuaginta: Vetus Testamentum Graecum.* 2d ed. Academiae Litterarum Göttingensis Editum 14: Isaias. Göttingen: Vandenhoeck & Ruprecht, 1967.

Ziegler, Joseph J., and Joachim Jeremias. *The Servant of God.* Rev. ed. Studies in Theology 20. Naperville, Ill.: Allenson, 1965.

Zimmerli, Walter. *Old Testament Theology in Outline.* Translated by D. E. Green. Edinburgh: T. & T. Clark, 1978.

—"Die Seligpreisungen der Bergpredigt und das Alte Testament." Pages 17–20 in *Donum Gentilicium: New Testament Studies in Honour of David Daube.* Edited by E. Bammel, C. K. Barrett and W. D. Davies. Oxford: Clarendon, 1978.

INDEXES

INDEX OF REFERENCES

INDEX OF AUTHORS